D1473369

STIKEMAN ELLIOTT

The First Fifty Years

Stikeman Elliott
The First Fifty Years

RICHARD W. POUND

McGill-Queen's University Press

Montreal & Kingston · London · Ithaca

© Richard W. Pound 2002
ISBN 0-7735-2411-8

Legal deposit third quarter 2002
Bibliothèque nationale du Québec

Printed in Canada on acid-free paper
Reprinted 2005

McGill-Queen's University Press acknowledges the financial
support of the Government of Canada through the Book
Publishing Industry Development Program (BPIDP) for its
activities. It also acknowledges the support of the Canada
Council for the Arts for its publishing program.

National Library of Canada Cataloguing in Publication

Pound, Richard W.
    Stikeman Elliott: the first fifty years / Richard W. Pound

    Includes bibliographical references and index.
    ISBN 0-7735-2411-8

    1. Stikeman, Elliott (Firm) – History. 2. Law firms –
Canada – History. I. Title.
    KE395.P68 2002   340'.06'071   C2002-901973-7

Produced for McGill-Queen's University Press by
Focus Strategic Communications Incorporated.
This book was typeset in 10/12 Sabon.

Contents

Foreword

Heward Stikeman and Fraser Elliott opened the doors of a small boutique law firm in Montreal on February 1, 1952. Fifty years later, the ampersand has been removed from the name of the firm, but we have gained many colleagues, and we are almost 400 lawyers across Canada and around the world. What remains constant are the essentials.

The first of these is that Stikeman Elliott has always prided itself on the fact that values bind us together and drive the organization. Several years ago, they were articulated and embedded not only into the fabric of the firm, but at a more mundane level, into a lucite paperweight distributed to all members of the firm at the time. These values relate to:

- a passion for excellence and integrity
- challenging our people to stretch their capacity
- welcoming diversity and individual initiative and furtherance of the overall interests of the firm
- treating each other and those we encounter with respect, dignity, and fairness
- a spirit of adventure
- an open, democratic partnership with accountable, accessible leadership

Like any enduring institution, Stikeman Elliott lives in the minds of our people. As illustrated throughout this book, the firm's success has rarely been driven by strategic analysis. Rather, much of the leadership focus has been on a constant renewal of the firm's values. The mark of the firm's success has been that as we struggle with competitive challenges, we continue to re-examine and renew our values. They have served (and hopefully will continue to serve) as a litmus test for most things we do. Ultimately, it is through them that we have helped our people and our clients realize their aspirations.

One values-based issue we have constantly struggled with is the choice between entrepreneurial leadership and managerial competence. Growth has tended to be accompanied by the need for better managerial and administrative leadership in the firm. On the other hand, the firm is firmly rooted in a legacy of leaders who have taken entrepreneurial risks within the organization, making a lasting impression and creating significant opportunities for those who follow. We have worked hard to continue to maintain the balance between those who mould the firm by providing managerial leadership and those (often the same individuals) who break the mould, thereby taking the firm to new levels of opportunity and achievement.

Another values-based challenge has to do with regarding people as assets that require continual development. Strategy can be copied – getting the right people in place and constantly challenging and nurturing them has been critical to the firm's success. As noted in the book, there is also a great tradition in the firm of developing leaders – not just for our own organization and profession, but for business, public service, and the communities we are privileged to be a part of. Historically, this has been an implicit raison d'être of the firm.

The second constant has been the critical importance of relationships – among ourselves and with our clients. There is a tradition of investing in those relationships, to understand how we can work together more effectively and how we can better contribute to our clients' ability to succeed in their endeavours. We know for certain that technology and market structure will continue to change rapidly, often in ways we may not adequately anticipate. In that environment, the strength of our relationships will determine the willingness of our clients (and colleagues) to work together through the changes, for ultimately, our continuing success will not be driven by our ability to spot trends or excel in strategic planning. Far more important is that everyone will have a strong, enthusiastic, and passionate commitment to the firm and to our clients.

Attracting the right kind of people and providing them with the opportunity to realize their potential in the broadest sense has always been our hallmark. Rather than directing, the tradition has been to enable – seeking to attract the most challenging work, providing scope for individual action, and holding everyone accountable for the highest level of performance. This is a more enduring legacy than short-term profitability or the profile of any particular mandate or individual.

Managing in this environment is a unique, somewhat humbling, experience. As with life's natural creative processes, the firm's are orderly but cannot be controlled by anyone. Diversity and chaos are the essence of the firm's sustainability and the source of much of its intellectual capital. Self-organization (much more than active management) is the process that generates new growth and development.

Leaving aside the day-to-day issues that someone needs to decide, it may well be that the most significant challenge in leading a law firm such as ours is to create conditions that free up these natural processes within the organization and align the firm's energy around a shared identity of purpose, values, and vision.

This book attempts to capture that sense of identity and trace its evolution over our first half-century. It is a reflection of the efforts of many to make a difference. We hope the story will be of interest to others and will encourage those who follow to preserve and develop the firm's culture, just as those who have preceded have done.

Edward J. Waitzer
Chairman

Toronto, July 2002

Preface

It was serendipity that brought them together, friendship and mutual respect that led them to practise together, inevitability that set them off on a new course, and a combination of ambition and ability that created a remarkable venture in Canadian legal history. Harry Heward Stikeman and Roy Fraser Elliott founded Stikeman & Elliott in Montreal on February 1, 1952. Later, the name was changed to Stikeman Elliott, and today, fifty years later, the original small boutique firm has grown to some 400 lawyers in nine cities in Canada and around the world. However, the values of Stikeman and Elliott remain as the foundation of one of the most successful law firms in this country, known as such throughout Canada and around the world.

While their talents lay in different areas, it was their complementary personalities and competencies, their mutual trust and respect, and their ability to work together that laid the ground for the "culture" of their firm. Their dedication to each other and their mutual goals permitted them to create an environment that attracted some of the best legal talents in the marketplace and to provide them with a platform from which to conduct their respective careers. Their broad range of interests in the fields of business, law, art, sports, as well as their raw curiosity created a formidable team.

Spirits ran high in Canada following the victory of the Allies in World War II. Canada was enjoying a rapid transformation from an agrarian society to an industrialized one, which many believed was second only to Japan. Montreal was home to approximately one quarter of the major head offices in Canada and to individuals in numerous fields with world reputations including Doctor Wilder Penfield of the Montreal Neurological Hospital and Sam Bronfman, the legendary architect of the world's largest distiller. The square-mile was the site of some of the most elegant homes in the country, and the Mount Royal Club boasted a roster of members unlike any other in Canada. Maurice "the Rocket" Richard was playing for the Montreal Canadiens, and Frank Scott, Canada's extraordinary constitutional lawyer and poet, was challenging Premier Maurice Duplessis's government's

Padlock Act. It was an exciting and dynamic crucible, ideal for the new breed of post-war Canadians.

It is a measure of the generosity of both men that whenever the idea of a chronicle of the firm has been mooted, as it has from time to time, they insisted that more attention be given to the younger generation of lawyers they have attracted to the firm than to themselves as founders. However, the quality of the new generations within the firm is such that they consider it unthinkable not to recognize that their success stems from the absorption of the ethics and pre-eminence of the founders.

The partners of the firm considered the fiftieth anniversary of Stikeman Elliott to be an appropriate occasion to record the details of their joint odyssey. We decided that the firm history should be a serious critical examination of what has been accomplished and how it has been accomplished, rather than a mere promotional exercise. We are conscious that our firm remains a work in progress and that no journey is without occasional misadventure, detour, and tangent. We are equally conscious that those who do not learn from their mistakes are doomed to repeat them, but that we should concentrate on those factors that have led to our achievements.

The single greatest problem in writing this work – apart from recognizing that it is impossible (in a book that is already quite long) to describe every lawyer and staff member – has been how to organize the wealth of material that exists. When the firm was small, it was possible to put together a single story in a generally chronologically arranged narrative. The initial chapter is somewhat more formally written than the balance of the work, but that merely reflects those more formal times. There is also material that relates to Colin Fraser Elliott, which has been included because he had such a profound effect on both his son and Stikeman even though he came from a different era.

Once the firm began to expand and to establish new offices, a purely chronological treatment became impossible. My working method changed to deal separately with the smaller offices and to merge the later story of the expanded and integrated firm into the different practice groups. Thus, the separate Montreal portion ends with the beginning of the 1970s and the Toronto chapter ends at the beginning of the 1980s when a critical mass had been achieved in that office. The foreign offices – those portions of the work that deal with the road warriors, particularly chapter 5 – are given an importance that might seem exaggerated, but they are such a singular feature of a Canadian law firm that they deserve to be recounted in more detail. While the overall story stands on its own, I have nevertheless tried to provide some perspective in the last two chapters as the firm enters into the second half-century of its existence.

In the case of external sources, I have provided references for readers who may wish to look further for more extensive treatment of the subject matter. Many other quotations or extracts come from internal firm records, and I have not provided specific references to these, although I have kept a separate collection of these should members of the firm want to obtain greater detail. Other material has been derived from interviews with members or alumni of the firm or third parties, and my notes of these have also been kept separately. It is impossible to deal with the full professional lives of 400 current and perhaps as many former colleagues with the firm, so I have picked certain stories and transactions that are designed to give the flavour of the experience and the inclusion (or non-inclusion) of any particular lawyer is not meant to suggest a weighting of his or her importance to the sculpture we have created together. The whole is much greater than the sum of its parts. I express my deepest thanks to all those who so willingly shared their experiences and who encouraged the recording of our work in progress together.

The nature of the professional relationships in the legal profession is such that client confidences must be kept that way, which inhibits disclosure of many fascinating details. I have tried to walk the line in such matters and to discuss only matters that are already within the public domain or for which clients have given their consent. Internal matters are less subject to such considerations, but again, I have tried not to disclose certain purely personal information. The interpretations in this work are my own, and the firm has been scrupulous in not imposing any restrictions on the expression of that opinion.

I confess to having had some difficulty deciding how I would deal with my own involvement in the firm. It is meant to be a history of the firm, not an autobiography, but since I have been present in one way or another for more than thirty years, for some 60 per cent of its existence, I do "appear" from time to time in this work. I have decided that rather than forcing someone else to write those portions in which I am one of the actors (and then adding the superlative modifiers) or referring to myself in the third person, I will fall back on the first person singular when appropriate and hope that this occurs only as often as the circumstances, viewed in historical perspective, warrant.

My own connection with the firm came in two tranches. I was recruited in the fall of 1964 by Ray Lawson, a third- or fourth-year student at McGill, to work part-time during my first year at law school. The firm had only recently moved from the Bank of Canada building on Victoria Square into the CIBC building and occupied only half of the twenty-sixth floor. Stanley Hartt, the articling student at the time, was pleased to see me there in this new capacity since it meant that he could off-load the court run. I did some inconsequential memos for various lawyers, demonstrating how little a first-term law student really knows. Jim Robb asked me to find all the intersection accident cases that had ever been reported in connection with some "bumper" case that had come his way, just the sort of open-ended memo that lands on the desks of hapless law students. Somehow, I doubt that the project fulfilled any useful purpose for either of us.

My big chance to meet Heward Stikeman came after I had been there for a month or so. Clearly, my fame had spread, and he knew what a jewel he had landed – a law student with a CA – and the call came to report to his office. I got a pad and a couple of sharp pencils and raced to the inner sanctum to help him solve whatever massive problem he had on his desk. It proved to be a transportation matter. What he needed from me, he said, was to pick up his new licence plates at Latimer Motors, a nearby automobile dealer.

I did not work there the next summer because I had previously agreed to go back to Riddell Stead Graham & Hutchison, the chartered accounting firm with which I had previously worked. In fact, I did not return to the firm for several years thereafter since I was lured away the following year to what is now McCarthy Tétrault but which was then known by the user-friendly name of Chishom, Smith, Davis, Anglin, Laing, Weldon & Courtois. It was the combination of tax reform (derived in the main from the 1966 Carter Commission Report) and the opening of the Toronto office, both of which occurred in 1971, in addition to the opening of a London office, that led to my return. I thought that due to tax reform, we (by then Laing, Weldon, Courtois, Clarkson, Parsons, Gonthier & Tétrault) had a rare opportunity to get into the income tax sphere since everyone was starting in the new regime on an equal footing, even Stikeman Elliott. I tried without success to persuade Jacques Tétrault that this was the case, and I offered to be responsible for building a tax practice, but I would need someone like him for mature judgment since he was the only one with a real tax background. He was not interested and thought it was too complicated and (not without some element of prescience) that the accountants would take over the tax field in the future. There seemed to be no alternative but to look elsewhere.

I was very conscious of the fact that in those days, it was rare indeed for lawyers to change firms, especially at my level (just over three years at the Bar), and that firms were very prickly about other firms raiding their talent. So in early December, I placed a call to Jim Grant, with whom I had played duplicate bridge on Wednesday evenings at the Montreal Amateur Athletic Association, and invited him to lunch at the MAAA, making it clear, to preserve the inter-firm niceties, that it was I who was inviting him and not the reverse. We had the Ionesco-type encounter, which occasionally occurs with Grant, followed by several circuits in the snow around Dominion Square, and it was soon agreed that I would join the firm the following month. I advised Peter Laing and Tétrault that I had decided to seek my fortune elsewhere and arrived at the firm as the new income tax system came on stream. McCarthy Tétrault has been playing catch-up in the tax field ever since.

It has been an enjoyable privilege to have been part of such a remarkable firm for more than thirty years and an additional delight to have had this opportunity to help share its story with its members, staff, alumni, friends, and others. I hope I have been able to convey at least some aspects of the excitement the experience has generated for everyone involved.

Our deepest collective regret is that Heward Stikeman is not among us as this book is published. It has been a profound loss to all of us. Despite the intellectual knowledge that time marches on, nevertheless, having lived with daily evidence of his indefatigable energy and enthusiasm, we simply never contemplated the possibility that on this anniversary, he would be with us in spirit only.

Montreal, July 2002

STIKEMAN ELLIOTT

The First Fifty Years

CHAPTER I

The Early Years

HARRY HEWARD STIKEMAN

Harry Heward Stikeman, son of Harry Frederick Cawthorn Stikeman and Dorothea Horstmann, was born in Montreal on July 8, 1913. This event, little remarked upon outside the immediate Stikeman family, occurred some four years prior to the enactment of a Canadian statute imposing a temporary tax on personal income to help finance Canada's participation in the Great War of 1914–18. Stikeman's father, like so many Canadians, went into military service overseas. During the period of his father's absence, his mother took him to her native home in Philadelphia, where he remained until 1925, when his father joined them after the war to manage the Horstmann business for a few years. His early schooling was at Chestnut Hill Academy in Philadelphia, and upon returning to Montreal, aged twelve, he spent two years at Selwyn House School before going on to Trinity College School (TCS) in Port Hope, Ontario, in 1927. Emerging from TCS with his senior matriculation, he enrolled at McGill University and was graduated in arts in the class of 1935. That same fall, he entered the faculty of law at McGill, graduating in 1938.

Law was not Stikeman's first choice as a career. He had given much thought to architecture and had worked with the Philadelphia firm of Howe & Lescaze, designers of the Philadelphia Saving Fund Society Building, one of the first modern skyscrapers. If for no other reason, the prospective career in architecture was abandoned as Stikeman was driven inexorably to the conclusion that his mathematics were not up to the challenge of designing buildings that had any reasonable prospect of remaining upright. This deficiency proved, in time, to be no barrier to the design and construction of some of the most elaborate business and tax structures ever to be encountered on the Canadian legal scene.

While travelling in England during the summer of 1934, as an undergraduate in arts, he spent his twenty-first birthday at the home of friends of his parents. His hosts were Sir Archibald and Lady Flower, and they entertained Stikeman in their house, named "The Hill," near Stratford-on-Avon. A dinner party was given for the occasion, at which he was placed next to an English lawyer, apparently of some renown. Stikeman described the occasion much later in his life:

At the dinner I was placed next to Lord Reading, making one gaffe after another. In fact I had never heard of him. How he had the patience to continue to be interested in me I will never know, because throughout the dinner, he would mention some interesting facet of his varied career: e.g., that he had been on the Bench. I would say "When were you on the bench?" and he would reply, "When I was Lord Chancellor, and later when I was Chief Justice." Later on he said, "When I was in India ..." and again I enquired, "When?" "Oh, the time that I was Viceroy ..."

Finally, he said, "You really do not know who I am. Meet me at the tennis court tomorrow." So, the next day at 10 o'clock on the tennis court ... Rufus Isaacs sat me down and told me the story of his amazing life. He concluded by saying that Canada appeared to him to be a country with great industrial prospects, particularly if there was to be a war, which we all assumed was near, and the field to get into was law from a corporate and preferably the fiscal side ...

He believed that tax law offered the greatest opportunity within the field of corporate law in a growing economy ...

The Depression years during which Stikeman pursued his education were very difficult for the entire country and had a lasting impact on everyone in his generation. Stikeman's description of the circumstances of the time and the terrible economic situation, coming from someone who had lived through the period, gives a more poignant touch to the statistics, of which many will be generally aware:

The Depression continued to deepen during the summer of 1934. Activity was light, and the real estate business was being affected by a feeling of endless stagnation. The suicide rate among my father's friends began to increase and affected my own generation. Three of my close friends at McGill committed suicide by getting into their father's cars in closed garages and running the engines until they were asphyxiated. There seemed absolutely no chance of any of us getting out of college into a job to earn a living or of renting an apartment or of marrying. Those of us who could afford to, kept on grinding away at higher education in the rather forlorn hope that we might equip ourselves so that if something did ever turn up, we could take advantage of it.

I spoke in public whenever possible and enrolled in public speaking courses in both languages. My self-assurance as a writer in print and as a speaker in public grew and has remained with me to great advantage all my life. One thing soon became crystal clear. If I did practice, I'd steer clear of corporate law and civil law. What was left? Tax law, and Lord Reading's advice loomed large as the objective.

He and a friend from McGill, Bill Hulbig, got together to study for their Bar exams following completion of their law degrees. As he later described it: "The exams were written in Quebec City at the old Ursulines Hall of Laval University. The day was July 8, 1938 – my 25th birthday. To our surprise and relief, Bill and I both passed – with very high rankings in the Province. I have never opened either the Quebec Civil Code or the Code of Civil Procedure since that day! But I became eligible to practice! The question was how to begin." Graduation from the faculty of law and even a call to the Bar provided no guarantee of gainful employment. Stikeman looked in vain for an opening in the profession, calling upon dozens of law firms and businesses in Montreal, to no avail. He concluded that he would either have to start a practice on his own or sell insurance. In fact, he did resort to selling insurance for Aetna Life, with limited success. "I made the rounds of all the law firms, of all the trust companies, of all the banks, the CPR, CNR – and finally ... Aetna Life Insurance Co. took me on as a trainee under its cheerful and brilliant young manager, Gilbert W. Boright."

Even familial connections in the practice of law in Montreal produced no job offers. His cousin, Chilion Heward, a senior partner in the firm of Meredith, Holden, Heward & Holden, one of the oldest law firms in Montreal, having been established in 1817, the same year as one of its most stalwart clients, the Bank of Montreal, could not find him work. "Full of hope, I presented myself to my cousin Chilion Heward, K.C. at Meredith, Holden, Heward & Holden, to be told there was no chance of employment there. The let-down was tremendous. I felt the world had ended before it had begun." Chilion Heward did, however, for the small comfort it provided, concur in the advice that Stikeman had received from Lord Reading. Stikeman also contacted an old friend of his father, Frank Common, Sr, who in turn arranged for his partner, Warwick Chipman, to help him. Chipman introduced Stikeman to one of his own friends, the Honourable J.L. Ralston, then the senior partner of Ralston, Kearney, Duquet & MacKay. Ralston had the advantage of additional connections in Ottawa since he was, at that time, conducting the well-known "Bren Gun Inquiry."[1] He had been minister of National Defence (1926–30) and would be again (1940–44). Ralston knew the Honourable James Lorimer Ilsley, then minister of National Revenue, and he called him, saying that he had a bright young lawyer who wanted to work in Ottawa, who might be an asset to either the Department of Justice or the Department of National Revenue.

I shall never forget the kindness and helpful support of these many very busy men, each of whom in his own way gave my career a push. They were also most supportive after I returned to practice law in Montreal in 1946. I only hope that some of the things I have tried to do for younger men over the years have had as happy results as their efforts for me in 1938.

My interview with Ralston was prophetic. I had never seen a real live lawyer at work on a case before. He was holed up in a suite at the Chateau Laurier Hotel in Ottawa. The room was littered with piles of factums, accounts, books, open brief cases – paper everywhere – two stenos were taking dictation, and J.L. was walking up and down, dictating in his shirt sleeves and braces. Two obsequious juniors were sitting, nodding approval as he spoke.

To me, this was disorder incarnate. He could not really be a great lawyer in a front-page headline case! Ralston greeted me with the greatest courtesy and read the letter F.B.C.[ommon] had given me to show him. "So you want a job in income tax?" "Yes, sir."

With no more ado, he picked up the phone and called C. Fraser Elliott K.C., the then Commissioner of Income Tax and father of my present partner in S & E. The conversation indicated that I should "go through channels" and start by seeing the Minister in charge. Ralston arranged an appointment at once.

That afternoon, I spent two hours meeting with The Hon. J.L. Ilsley, Minister of National Revenue. He was a Maritimer who had practiced law for several years in the town of Kentville, near Halifax, and was most frugal and Spartan of character, and a very great human being. He was much respected by all parties and eventually rose within the government as Minister of Justice and subsequently Minister of Finance. To me at this point, he was an august, Olympian, figure. He began by telling me that he had never earned more than $3,000 a year in his professional life and didn't know how I could want any more as a beginner, although I had not yet asked for anything! After reminiscing on his own hard beginnings in the Maritimes, he referred me to Fraser Elliott to see whether I would be suitable material. As a parting shot, he said that, as he was being pressed to appoint two Liberal lawyers to jobs in Revenue Canada, it might help him politically if he put "some Conservative meat in the sandwich," meaning me. The interview concluded with his calling "the Commissioner," Fraser Elliott, and suggesting that he should see me.

This interview took place some time in July of 1938. By August, I had presented myself at the office of Mr Elliott to be greeted by his formidable, but very charming secretary, Miss Agnes Weatherdon, or "Aggie," as we called her (much later!). Working in the same department was an old friend of my father, a Mr Lewis, who vouched for my character second hand. I managed to hit it off with Aggie and got an appointment with CFE, who at once impressed me and remains in my memory as one of the finest and most charming people I have ever met. He reminded me so much of the late Alan G. Law, with his very direct and gruff approach kept human by his dry wit, that I instinctively knew how to handle him. From that moment on, we became fast friends and mutual supporters.

The confluence of these events brought together two young lawyers, each of whom would in his own way have a profound effect on the Canadian legal system. Elliott had previously been in contact, through Ross Tolmie, with Wilbur Roy Jackett, a Saskatchewan Rhodes scholar and lawyer who had been searching, with the same lack of success as had Heward Stikeman, for legal employ. Conditions in Saskatchewan during the Depression were even more severe than in Montreal, which had a broader base of industry and commerce. Elliott had given some indication to Jackett that a position within the Department of National Revenue might be available. Ilsley's intervention to introduce Stikeman changed that landscape considerably. There were at the time three order-in-council appointments available within the Department of National Revenue. Two were Liberals, and to avoid the appearance of complete political bias, Ilsley was looking for a Conservative to fit between his two Liberal bookends. Ilsley, coming as he did from the Maritimes, also made it clear that he was damned if he was going to waste an order-in-council appointment on someone from Saskatchewan. So,

Stikeman got the National Revenue job, at the princely sum of $3,240 per year, just prior to the outbreak of World War II. Jackett, in turn, was hired by the Department of Justice, but at a somewhat lesser salary, and went on to become deputy minister of Justice, president of the Exchequer Court of Canada, and the first chief justice of the Federal Court of Canada. In the end, both got into the fields that most interested them, and both became extraordinary leaders in those fields. Told first-hand by Stikeman:

In any event, after many trips to Ottawa and another visit to J.L. Ilsley, I was appointed solicitor to the Taxation Division of the Department of National Revenue at a salary of $3,240 per year, $270 monthly. The job was to start February 1, 1939. The two Liberals who were appointed with me were E.S. MacLatchey from Truro, NS and Edouard Belleau, from Ottawa. As well, there were appointed three other persons, not lawyers, who worked with us to form a review committee to bring the backlog of files up to date throughout the Department. These three, who became very good friends of mine, were R. Ferrier Burns, CA, Harry Milburn, CA, and Gordon Code, who had recently been private secretary to Ilsley. The six of us were put in a room together, given a stack of old files by CFE, and told to clean them up. This turned out to be a very valuable experience, since for almost one year, Ted MacLatchey and I were thrown in with older and more experienced men with topflight accounting training and previous tax experience. Only the Depression could have forced such talent out of their professions. The government was luckier to have them than it realized.

They taught us the ropes as well as the tricks used by taxpayers, and gave us a sound grounding in the accounting approach and a respect for facts which we had never got as law undergraduates. This foundation provided me with a facility to work with CAs, to understand them, and to value their assistance as a member of a team on almost every tax problem that I was to have in the Department and later in practice. Harry Milburn went on to become an Assistant Deputy Minister and one of the ablest in the top echelon of the Department.

Meanwhile at the office, I was beginning to get some grasp on tax matters and remember, as one of my first important cases, an involved, lengthy technical legal argument with a retired colonel in Nova Scotia regarding a refund of something under $1.00. As a matter of principle, Ted MacLatchey and I were determined to collect it, and he was equally determined not to pay it. The legal research that went into it was a good post-graduate course in tax law, and we eventually compromised by splitting the amount with him.

Stikeman described some of the elements of his adventures in Ottawa in an interview for an unpublished history of the Department of National Revenue. "The first job I had was to do the *Excess Profits Tax Act*, which came in 1940. It was done as a result of a meeting with Mr Elliott, Mr Lazarus Phillips of Phillips & Vineberg, who is now a senator, and a man called Henry Norman, who is the senior partner of Price Waterhouse. I was the novice lawyer, and after this very pressing meeting at which things were discussed which meant nothing to me, they said, you go ahead and draft the act. It was so bad that it had to be withdrawn from the House of Commons and redrafted 90 days later."[2]

THE WAR YEARS AND COLIN FRASER ELLIOTT

Income taxation by the federal government in Canada had commenced with the passage of the *Special War Revenue Act,* which received royal assent April 8, 1915. Under Part I of the act, administered at that time by the minister of Finance, trust and loan companies carrying on business in Canada were taxed on income received on and after January 1, 1915. In addition, certain insurance companies authorized to transact business in Canada were liable to pay a tax based upon the net premiums received in Canada on and after January 1, 1915. With the passage of the *Income War Tax Act,* which received royal assent on September 20, 1917, the minister of Finance became responsible for the administration and collection of income taxes under three statutes: the *Special War Revenue Act,* 1915; the *Business Profits War Tax Act,* 1916 (assented to May 18, 1916); and the *Income War Tax Act,* 1917. Effective August 9, 1924, the taxation branch of the Department of Finance, responsible for the collection of income taxes, was transferred from the Department of Finance to the control and supervision of the Department of Customs and Excise.

Colin Fraser Elliott[3] had been appointed assistant commissioner of Income Tax from 1929–32 by order-in-council and was named commissioner of Income Tax on July 15, 1932, also by order-in-council, at a salary of $7,000 per year. The department had gone through some major changes just prior to Elliott's appointment. The office of Minister of Customs and Excise was abolished, and the office of Minister of National Revenue was created under the *Department of National Revenue Act.*[4] William Daum Euler, previously minister of Customs and Excise from September 1926, became minister of the new department from March 1927 until August 1930. The position of commissioner of Income Tax, occupied by C.F. Elliott, was later changed to deputy minister of National Revenue for Taxation by amendment to the *Departmental Act,* assented to on July 24, 1943.

Stikeman could not have had a better mentor than C.F. Elliott, nor have arrived at National Revenue at a better time. The opportunities for young lawyers during the war were without precedent. Responsibilities expanded as quickly and pervasively as talent and energy permitted. Under wartime legislation, particularly the *War Measures Act,* a great deal of the business of legislation, ordinarily in the hands of Parliament, was done through orders-in-council. Preparation of these documents gave the lawyers extensive experience in the drafting of comprehensible quasi-legislation. In addition to orders-in-council, Stikeman was involved, as he recounted, in the drafting of the *Excess Profits Tax Act* of 1940 and the first *Canada-United States Income Tax Convention,* which came into force in 1942. This was likely something that should have occurred sooner, given the increasing volume of trade between Canada and the United States, but the previously low rates of income tax kept such an agreement from becoming a priority until the rapid expansion of trade during the war, due in part to the difficulties of trans-Atlantic trade at that time.

For many years, notwithstanding section 5 of the *Department of Justice Act,* which gave responsibility for representation of the Crown in legal proceedings to the Department of Justice, in revenue matters the practice had developed, with the active support of Elliott, of having lawyers attached to the legal branch of the Department of National Revenue represent the Crown in such proceedings. In due course, an internecine war of sorts developed between Elliott and the deputy minister of Justice, Frederick Percy Varcoe, appointed in 1941, as to how such litigation would be conducted. Varcoe and Elliott continued to spar, and Elliott, who was concerned with the practical aspects of making the Department of National Revenue work and of collecting taxes under a legislative system that was relatively primitive and left much to the discretion of officials, was often heard to exclaim, "God save us from civil servants and Varcoe!"

An uneasy truce was reached with the adoption of a modus vivendi that the Department of Justice would have formal responsibility for such litigation, but that, in revenue matters, there would be a lawyer from the Department of National Revenue assigned to each case as well. As a practical solution, this had some utility, since, for the most part, the lawyers at the Department of National Revenue had a much better understanding of tax matters than did the Department of Justice lawyers, who were far less specialized. Stikeman actually appeared with Varcoe in *The King v. Toronto General Trusts Corp.*[5] and was not impressed with his performance. He thought that the situation was unclear from the beginning and that Varcoe had done little to remove that confusion in his presentation to the court.

Stikeman had, therefore, many opportunities to be on his feet arguing revenue cases, principally before the Exchequer Court of Canada, in front of the patrician presidents of that court, initially Alexander K. Maclean, and commencing in 1942, Joseph Thorarrin Thorson, and occasionally, before the Supreme Court of Canada.[6] Some of these cases involved working with or against some of the leading counsel of the day, a heaven-sent opportunity for any young lawyer. He gained enough confidence in the subject matter of tax that he published an article in the *Canadian Bar Review* of 1942, entitled "Carrying on Business in Canada in Dominion Tax Law."[7]

Cases were settled and district offices canvassed for suggested changes in fiscal policy. Many meetings were held with taxpayers themselves to discuss changes the taxpayers thought were necessary both in tax policy and the implementation of such policy. In the result, by the end of the war, Stikeman was well known, both within government and by a broad spectrum of corporate and individual taxpayers. It was extraordinarily wide exposure to the older segments of the Canadian professions and the senior officers of the largest Canadian businesses and industries for someone of his years. This formal exposure was augmented by many appearances to explain fiscal law and policy to professional and business audiences, particularly among the legal and accounting professions as part of refresher courses and lectures on policy pertaining to income tax, excess profits tax, price controls, and similar matters.

The travel engendered by the administrative responsibilities took him from coast to coast, normally by train, but eventually on the new national airline,

Trans Canada Airlines, in twin-engine propeller-driven planes. Stikeman described some of the early experiences on the airline:

The summer of 1939 saw Trans Canada Airlines, as Air Canada was then called, establish its passenger service from coast to coast. The mail route had been opened the year before and by February of 1939, the 8-passenger Lockheed Electras were in service on scheduled runs. The trip took approximately 16 hours from Halifax to Vancouver and approximately 12 hours from Ottawa to the same point. The planes carried one stewardess but were not pressurized and rarely flew above 10,000 ft. For going over the Rockies, oxygen was supplied through masks that one strapped to one's face. Each mask had a bladder, much like a football's rubber interior, attached to a long tube, also of rubber, connected to pipes in the walls of the aircraft. At 10,000 ft., one donned the mask and began to breath through the bladder, which expanded and contacted, thus providing oxygen in the appropriate amounts. The single stewardess was connected to this system by a long rubber tube, and it trailed behind her as she moved up and down the aisle. This hose, however, did not have to be too long since there were only four rows of seats with one passenger on each side of the aisle. The Lockheed Electra used by TCA was the same model as the one in which Amelia Earhart and her navigator were lost over the Pacific a year earlier, 1937.

The war years brought heavy demands for revenue to support the war effort, as well as substantial reductions in the level of exemptions from taxation. This led to a huge increase in the number of taxpayers liable to tax, higher rates, and the introduction of a new concept of deductions of tax at the source of taxable payments. That, in turn, put pressure on the administration for quick processing of refunds and a reduction in the delays in making formal tax assessments.[8] This was an aspect that was later raised as a criticism of the department, when it appeared that only 82 per cent of individual returns and 86 per cent of corporate returns filed between 1941 and 1945 had been assessed. Elliott's response to the criticism was that he would rather stand his ground and say that in due course, the department would assess everybody on the same basis, under the same law, with equal treatment, even though there would be some delay. There were also new pieces of legislation to administer, such as the *Excess Profits Tax Act,* and a broadening of administrative discretionary powers. On August 8, 1940, section 75 (2) of the *Income War Tax Act* had conferred on the minister broad powers to "make any regulations deemed necessary" for the administration of the act as well as the authority to delegate such powers to the commissioner of Income Tax. These powers were formally delegated to the commissioner on the same day by appropriate publication in the *Canada Gazette.*

Fraser and I had a tremendous relationship ... To give an idea of the kind of man he was, I'll give you one example. In England, Fraser had lost the sight in an eye, permanently.[9] When he came back, the doctors told him that he had to have the eye out. So he had it out. Now this is wartime, but he got permission to get some dollars and go south to one of the islands for a two-week rest; and he left me in charge.

While I was in charge, a politically explosive issue came up. A certain aviation company which was building fighter aircraft paid for the rights to a certain patent to build airplanes, about $500,000, to another Canadian company. I had ruled that those rights were a capital gain to the company which received the money for them and a deductible expense to the company that had paid for them. So under the 100 percent excess profits tax, there was no tax on the recipient and no tax on the payor; which is technically, legally correct. While Fraser was away, the Opposition got hold of this, and they thought that it was wrong, and the CCF, the NDP of today, tried to crucify Mackenzie King. The Conservatives got on the bandwagon, and Mackenzie King decided that I was going to be the goat. So he got me up there in front of a three-party parliamentary committee to explain why I had done this dreadful thing.

Well, the day of the hearing was the day that Elliott got back from his trip to have his eye rested. He arrived at the office at nine o'clock, and I said, "Mr Elliott, I've got something to tell you. I'm going to be hung, drawn, and quartered this morning, and it would have been better if you'd stayed home." I told him all about it. "Well," he said, "you're my Deputy. I'm going to go up there, and I'm going to tell them I did it." I said, "Like hell you are." I said, "We're going up there together." "Well," he said, "we're right, the law is right." This is right off. He'd never heard of this thing before. There was never any criticism, never any why did you do it. He just read the document and said, "You're right; let's go." So an hour later, we walk up to the Hill, and we go into the House, and there's everybody sitting around waiting to get these two civil servants. Fraser argued, and he was very brilliant. He argued it from every conceivable point of view, but never told them about the legal position, for two days. He finally got them to accept it as an economical thing, that it was a desirable thing for the country, that we'd acted properly. Then he casually got up, and on the way out, he said, "Well gentlemen, just in case you think that I may be wrong, you may be interested to know that Mr Stikeman here acted on the strength of two Privy Council decisions," and he sort of threw them on the table, and we walked out of the room. And that was it. Now that's the kind of boss to have.

There's one other occasion. I think I should not name names, but a certain senator was suspected of having paid quite a lot of money to have his depreciation tables revised. People used to offer you money all the time. I got offered $25,000 once by a senator from the northern part of Quebec to alter some of his depreciation schedules, and I reported him to the Prime Minister. It was standard form of practice, if we got a bribe, to report it to King. This was quite a big one, and he was a very important guy, and we got the word from the PMO that we were not to prosecute this man. I had the writs, and I was just ready to put him in the "jug." But Fraser called me in, and he says, "I've just received word that we're not going to go ahead," and I said, "What did you do?" He said, "I didn't do much, but I'm going to do something," and he called in his secretary and dictated his resignation and then my resignation, and we both signed. Then he said, "Now we'll go up and see the Prime Minister." The whole story was in the resignation, so there was great consternation at the PMO that two guys would not only quit, but that they would put it in the papers with the names and the amounts and everything else, and why they had quit, and who called us up to tell us to lay off. But King was smart. He was very polite and said that we were doing a great job. He offered us all kinds of things, and then he said, "Of course if you don't want to change your mind, I would like to suggest that the individual pay the tax and then put the amount of the fine into the Party coffers." Well it wasn't said as baldly as that, but words to that effect. So Fraser pulls out his resignation again and sort of reads it to himself. Then he looks around the room, you know, and everybody sort of coughs politely, and he says, "Well, I think that we had better reconsider that." So we prosecuted. But that was the kind of thing that he used to do. He was terrific.

Exercise of discretionary powers increased exposure of the tax administrators to the annoyance of taxpayers when it seemed futile to try and reverse apparently arbitrary decisions. Regardless of the even-handedness with which he exercised the statutory powers of discretion, it was this conscientious application of the law that would eventually lead to the end of Elliott's career in tax administration. It became apparent that many senators had friends and clients to whom Elliott had said "no" too often, despite the fact that the exercise of discretion was legal and had been expressly contemplated by Parliament. He was more than ready, when circumstances required, to take on even the prime minister. A letter had been sent to R.B. Bennett, complaining that National Revenue (i.e., Fraser Elliott) had refused to allow as charitable deductions payments made by the complainant to his in-laws in respect of a house they occupied. The prime minister wrote to Elliott, asking him to look at the matter "closely." Elliott took this as a challenge to his authority, or at least the use of political pressure. He responded by explaining the statutory provision and stating that the minister did not "see fit" to provide for such an allowance. He responded similarly to further questions from the prime minister, and the matter was settled as determined, in the first place, by Elliott. But, as time passed, and as the war began to turn around, and people began to think that it might actually be won, which was by no means apparent for the first two and a half years when every kind of sacrifice was made, they began to resist the crushing rate of taxation and the rather high-handed way in which the departmental officials ran the tax regime. There was a great movement, not only to get rid of Elliott, but also to reform the act because there were thirty or forty instances of ministerial discretion in the statute that gave the minister absolute discretion to do what he wanted, and Elliott and his officials were quite ready to use the discretion.

In 1943, Stikeman was appointed assistant deputy minister, legal, a promotion from mere counsel, thus acquiring line responsibility for administration, supervision, and where circumstances warranted, direction of the tax collecting function throughout the country.

As the war came to a conclusion in 1945, attention turned to conversion of the war effort, to which Canada had made an enormous contribution – far beyond anything that could have been expected from such a small country – into a peacetime economy. The importance of taxation had become even more apparent as the result of the war, which led to consideration of the role of taxation in the post-war economy. A special Committee of the Senate of Canada was convened on the initiative of Senator J.J. Bench of St Catharines and Senator G. Peter Campbell of Toronto, then senior partner of Campbell, Godfrey & Lewtas, under the chairmanship of a former minister of National Revenue, the Honourable William Euler. There was, undoubtedly, also an element of political revenge of a personal nature implicit in the process with respect to C.F. Elliott. Stikeman said it appeared to have been the result of "what many in Canada considered to have been very autocratic and high handed administration during the war years." Stikeman was appointed as counsel to the special committee. The proceedings of the special committee would continue for some two years. "So when the War was over, there was a big political rampage to get rid of Fraser Elliott. I went to practice here in Montreal, and it wasn't very long after that a Senator – Joe Bench of St Catharines – and Bill Euler called me up and said that they wanted to have a committee to investigate the administration of the Tax Department, and to reform the Income Tax law itself; would I be counsel? Well I thought that that was great because I felt that I knew enough about it to ask the right questions." From the conclusions of the senate committee, it does not appear that the witnesses questioned were attacking the integrity of the departmental officials – the real criticism appeared to be the law itself and the processes derived from it. Much of this was due to the astute questioning of Stikeman in the course of dealing with the witnesses. Stikeman had by now worked both sides of the street and was so insistent in getting the exact focus of the criticism from one of the witnesses that Senator Haig, apparently only half jokingly, said to him, "We are keeping close watch on you Mr Stikeman. We think you still have a little touch of the Department about you."[10]

It appeared that the main thrust of the hearings was to establish an independent appeals board to settle disputes. Elliott himself was not particularly in favour of the change. One of his observations was that creation of such a board might mean that "departmental assessors might lightly pass the work on to those charged with finality, or indeed they might be overly generous in their discretion and that the Board be tough."[11] Nor was he much in favour of revising the law to eliminate discretion. "My belief is that more damage will be done by rigidity, affording, thereby, no relief to a taxpayer, no matter how reasonable he may be in his action, as opposed to making it possible for some consideration to be granted under the terms of the law."[12] It appeared to Elliott that the proposed board was meant to supplant the matter of the exercise of discretion. True to his background, Elliott thought the minister should have the final responsibility. He did not think there was any need for a court, whether old or new, to assist in the exercise of ministerial discretion. Nor was he a particular fan of the use of loopholes found by practitioners, especially those that appeared to have been sanctioned by the courts. "The judiciary, in precise pronouncement, have in a broad sense influenced adversely the moral tendency of the public in their approach to, and consideration of, tax contributions on any ability-to-pay basis by stating that one may 'avoid tax but must not evade it.' In effect, this gives judicial approval of the constant shift of the affairs of taxpayers to avoid tax which the law intended them to pay and, but for the shift, required them to pay."

There was never the slightest voice of any concern regarding Elliott's personal integrity, which had been demonstrated so uniformly, just the feeling that through the exercise of power, he had become intransigent and an obstacle to change. Certainly there was not much doubt that once he set his mind against some course of action, not even a team of wild horses could move him. Walter Gordon, a former Liberal minister of Finance, recalled an incident early in his career that illustrated Elliott's courage in the face of pressure from even the most powerful politician of the day – Clarence Decatur ("C.D.") Howe:

In the late forties, Gordon told Robert Bothwell, Howe's biographer, "I went to see Fraser Elliott about a tax ruling adversely affecting one of my clients. Elliott rejected my complaint, and I called on Arnold Heeney to ask if a Cabinet committee – Heeney and some others – couldn't look at it. Elliott was called before them to explain. The ministers were horrified and instructed him to reverse his ruling. Time passed, and Elliott did not make the change. When I saw him, he refused point blank. This time I went to see Howe. I knew how to do it. "C.D.," I said "I think you're losing your grip." He flushed. "Oh?" said Howe, and so it went until C.D. was jumping up and down with rage.[13]

But, rage as the great man might, Elliott did not change the ruling.

Unrelenting and severe as he often was, Elliott was not without a sense of humour. One evening, having been invited to speak at the annual dinner of the Institute of Chartered Accountants of Ontario, Elliott was discussing the mostly thankless job of the taxman and seized the opportunity to poke a bit of gentle fun at the accounting profession.

Incidentally, a recent dream of mine of being forestalled of Heavenly entrance was overcome by the fact that, by remote control, I administered a district, namely the Yukon District, in which I had never been, had never met the taxpayers, and was removed therefrom by many, many thousands of miles. St Peter said "Come in, you are the man we want. We have no trouble in Heaven and, but for a special condition, we certainly do not want you, but the fact is, we are having a hell of a time collecting tolls from the district of Hades, and your remote control methods sound good. The trouble is that the place is full of accountants." I took the job so that we might continue in our related work in our related positions. I woke up greatly refreshed.[14]

In the end, Elliott's integrity was never impeached, but the momentum toward some form of administrative tribunal in tax matters was such that the Tax Appeal Board was established, and many of the circumstances in which the minister, and through him his senior officials, had virtually absolute discretion were scaled back. The final report was received, and at the 1947 session of Parliament, Bill 454 was given first reading. Because it was close to the end of the session, it was held over until the following year. In the meantime, the minister of Finance invited suggestions from the business community, tax associations, and other interested parties. So many suggestions were received that the bill was almost completely revamped and was presented as new Bill 338, which eventually received royal assent on June 30, 1948 and was made effective in 1949. Demonstrating that there had been no whiff of improper conduct, despite a resolute and often unpopular exercise of the statutory discretion provided by the statute, Elliott remained highly enough regarded within government that he was named Canadian Ambassador to Chile on October 17, 1946.

LEGAL WRITING: BEGINNING A TRADITION

While still with the Department of National Revenue during the war, Stikeman had tried some legal writing to attempt to augment his governmental salary. He had managed to get an article – a staid and serious article on how farmers could save taxes and how the depreciation system that then existed worked – published in the *Financial Post*. For this effort, he received a fee of five dollars. He had the cheque framed and hung it in his office for many years, as a testimonial to his first earnings from the pen. Realizing that writing was not too lucrative on a piecework basis, he decided that he would write a tax service to match that then produced by Ross Tolmie, who worked with the legal branch of National Revenue, for the legal and business publisher Commerce Clearing House (CCH), and on which he had also worked and gained some experience. During his first year in the department, Tolmie had dragooned him, as the new boy, into helping with his service, so he had acquired some knowledge of the operation.

The CCH service treated tax law on a subject-by-subject basis. John Forsythe, the secretary to the legal branch of National Revenue and uncle of the young woman who was later to be Stikeman's long-time secretary, Lil Armstrong (later Lil Gilmour), and Stikeman decided to write a service that dealt with each section of the *Income Tax Act* in sequence. This, they felt, would be easier to use for anyone who knew the act and would be quite different from the CCH service, provided it had a good index. An added feature was that it would put all the material relating to each section directly under each section in a physical sense. It could thus be carried about in parts, if need be. They worked at night and early in the morning for nearly a year. By the middle of 1940, they had a manuscript, and Stikeman received permission from C.F. Elliott to attempt to sell it. To Stikeman's great surprise, no one was interested. He went to all the existing publishers in Toronto, including Canada Law Book, Carswell, and Butterworths, but no one cared for a book on income tax.

In the spring of 1941, Stikeman became acquainted with one of the genuine characters in the Canadian publishing industry, Richard "Dick" De Boo, then a salesman for the Butterworths firm of law book publishers. De Boo, the son of a CNR locomotive engineer, was a dashing, immensely handsome, larger-than-life figure, who drove around in a Cadillac convertible, undoubtedly living, if not beyond, at least certainly ahead of, his income. He had been born in Levis, Quebec, and raised in Campbelltown, NB, at the mouth of the Restigouche River, where as a young boy, he started his entrepreneurial career by poaching and selling salmon from the estuary.

While he had little formal education, he had a very able mind and through dint of much reading and exposure to educated people was able to hold his own in the law book publishing business as a salesman, beginning at age eighteen, with Butterworths, the English law book publisher.

Throughout the Depression, he managed to make a good living selling Halsbury's thirty-six-volume *Laws of England* in Alberta and the backwoods of British Columbia. He would take a set with him as he travelled his beat in his car and in addition, several extra volumes, usually 9, 10, and 11, of the two preceding editions. Upon calling on some local lawyer, he would instantly note whether the man had an earlier edition of Halsbury on his book shelf. If he had, De Boo would casually walk over and pick out the volume of which he had an extra copy in his car. He would flick through it, then tear some of the pages out and put them in the wastepaper basket, thus ruining the lawyer's set, which had probably cost him about $1,500. The enraged solicitor would then be told by De Boo that his whole set was worthless anyway since it was superseded by a better edition, which he happened to have for sale. If the man would not buy it, De Boo would replace the one he had desecrated with his own spare volume. This was typical of his modus operandi and the enthusiasm that led to starting his own company with the first publication of *Words and Phrases*.

Stikeman was sitting at his desk when a self-assured and very handsome man of forty, whom he thought looked rather like Clark Gable, came into his office to ask if he knew anyone in the department who might write a tax service for him. Stikeman did not reply, but reached into his filing cabinet and presented Richard De Boo with a manuscript. A deal was struck at so much per page for maintaining the service on a monthly basis. He was also hired to work on the brand new *Canada Tax Cases,* which would require editorial notes. Stikeman later modelled the series on the *All England Law Reports,* and they have developed into a very successful law reporting series. Some time after his engagement by De Boo, it became necessary to rewrite and repaginate the manuscript to fit a proper loose-leaf service. As a result, although the *Canada Tax Cases* were first published in June of 1942, the *Canada Tax Service* came out some time later, in 1943.

The essential difference between the *Canada Tax Service* and others was that it was written by and for lawyers. Lawyers understand that the *Income Tax Act* is a statute and must be interpreted as such. The service was, therefore, set up following the statutory structure of the act, paragraph by paragraph. It included the text of the statute, its legislative history, a description of the purpose of the particular provision, any administrative policies applicable to it, and finally, an explanation of the provision and an analysis of any judgments of the courts bearing upon it. As Stikeman recalled:

While I never made much money out of it, I have had an enormous amount of fun over the years, not only writing, but from the speaking and lecturing which followed from my wide exposure as Editor in Chief and Assistant Deputy Minister at the same time. Above all, I had fun with Dick De Boo, who remained until his death one of my closest and most fascinating friends. His attitude to life, which involved having as much fun as he could all the time while working hard at something he liked, influenced me strongly. His carefree approach to money, his willingness to take what appeared to be chances, but which were really carefully considered innovative steps, also gave me something to emulate. Above all, he was witty, earthy, worldly wise, and very sure of himself!

De Boo eventually broke away from Butterworths and began his own firm of Richard De Boo Publishers Limited, which was eventually acquired by the Carswell Company Limited, which has, in turn, become part of Thomson Professional Publications. The connection of Stikeman and the firm with the *Canada Tax Service* has continued to this day. Of particular significance to the history of the firm was the fact that several years after the inception of the *Canada Tax Service,* De Boo hired George Tamaki as its editor. Tamaki would later join the firm and become one of its most beloved members.

POST-WAR YEARS

Stikeman left government service at the end of 1945 and as of February 1, 1946, became a partner in the firm of Foster, Hannen, Watt & Stikeman in Montreal. The partnership agreement was not long, consisting of only five articles. Article II provided that the agreement could be terminated by any party on thirty-days' notice in writing. Article III provided that Stikeman, the newcomer, not yet thirty-three years old, would have 33 per cent of the profits of the firm, second only to the 34 per cent of the senior partner, George Buchanan ("Bunny") Foster. The remaining 33 per cent was shared between Francis Raymond Hannen and Alister McAdam Watt at 18 per cent and 15 per cent respectively. Stikeman was allowed to draw $800 per month against his share of profits. [15]

It would be interesting to speculate as to what might have happened had Stikeman been accepted into any of the three firms to which he applied before accepting a partnership with Foster, Hannen & Watt. He had first tried Montgomery, MacMichael, Forsyth, Common, Ker & Cate (already slyly referred to as the "factory" in the 1930s, due to their having the huge number of some seventeen lawyers), Meredith, Holden, Heward & Holden, and finally, MacDougall, MacFarlane, Scott & Hugessen, the latter seeming to have decided not to take him on because they expected, apparently with some prescience, that he would stay for only a short while before starting his own firm. Whatever the reason, his choice of Foster, Hannen, Watt & Stikeman turned out to be an ideal platform for Stikeman. The firm had been founded by Bunny Foster in 1940, following a breakaway from a group of much older lawyers in the firm of Hackett, Mulvena, Foster & Hackett and the attraction of Hannen and Watt, both of whom later became judges of the Superior Court of Quebec. The firm was relatively small, and the leverage Stikeman obtained by reason of his unique qualifications and the freedom of action accorded him within it were extraordinary. Another provision of the partnership agreement carved out his activities as editor and author from the obligation to give his whole time and undivided attention to the interests of the partnership and the practice of his profession and gave him the right to keep any fees derived from such activities as personal income.

Stikeman's first couple of years with Foster were taken up with work as counsel to the special committee, that took him to Ottawa on a regular basis, together with the development of an extremely profitable and specialized practice in taxation matters. Stikeman had participated not only in the drafting of the *Excess Profits Tax Act* of 1940, but was also intimately acquainted, as a result of his duties within the department, with the practices and procedures by which it was administered. During the period 1946–48, the Board of Referees, established under that statute, continued to sit, hearing appeals from assessments made under the act. The board's mandate was to review and, where necessary, revise the "standard" profit that had been determined by tax assessors. This was an important determination since profits deemed to be excessive were effectively confiscated. Many of the criteria used to determine the level of "standard" corporate profits, to establish the base from which to calculate "excess" profits for purposes of administration of the act during the war, were widely considered to have resulted in a standard level of profit that was too low. Stikeman himself thought that the criteria had been developed by "conservative and rather ill-informed senior counsel and accountants." Many corporations continued to seek further revision of the standard profits, as negotiated with or determined by the National Revenue officials, by means of appeals to the Board of Referees.

Who better to retain for the purpose than someone with Stikeman's considerable background? Adding to the initial advantages he enjoyed from practice in the field, Stikeman brought what he called "the brashness of youth" and in the result was able to "double and, in some cases, quadruple the standard profit base for very large corporations." The results were huge savings of tax, refunded with interest. The fees were, by the standards of the day, similarly large. Stikeman had an early lesson in how to charge professional fees when a result that he had obtained in a particular case represented a financial windfall for the client, amounting to several hundreds of thousands of dollars, obtained by Stikeman on the basis of a single meeting in Ottawa that took only an hour. With some trepidation, he sent an account, directed to the parent corporation in New York, for $1,000. Immediately upon receipt of the account, the client called Stikeman to say that the amount was completely inappropriate. Considerably chastened, Stikeman asked what the client would suggest as being fair in the circumstances. "Young man," said the client, "you will never do well until you learn to bill what your services are worth. Tear up the account and send me a new one immediately for $10,000." Stikeman was on his way.

Although now no longer within the government, Stikeman was nevertheless retained on a few cases for National Revenue and also began to work the other side of the tax bar, moving with relative ease from the role of gamekeeper to that of poacher. He acted before the Supreme Court of Canada on behalf of the minister in *J.R. Moodie Company Limited v. M.N.R.* [1950]

CTC 61. He was against Wilbur Jackett in *Henry Goldman v. M.N.R.* [1951] CTC 241, where it was settled that an appeal from the Tax Appeal Board to the Exchequer Court of Canada was by way of trial *de novo* and was not an ordinary appeal and later, in the Supreme Court of Canada [1953] CTC 95. He and Bert Bissonette argued *Seven-Up of Montreal Limited v. M.N.R.* [1952] CTC 75 and *Bowman Brothers Limited v. M.N.R.* [1952] CTC 339. Other cases he argued shortly after leaving the Department of National Revenue included *Pan American Trust Company v. M.N.R.* [1949] CTC 229, and *Gairdner Securities Limited v. M.N.R.* [1952] CTC 371. Interestingly enough, in the former case, the client also retained the Hon. J.L. Ralston, who had helped Stikeman get his first job with National Revenue in 1939. Stikeman considered that Ralston was there to cover the "political bases" since he had no palpable knowledge of tax law, and all preparation of the case was left to Stikeman. To the youthful Stikeman, Ralston appeared to spend an inordinate amount of preparation time labouring over minor points in the argument and in dissection of the factual minutiae. In the end, Stikeman was forced to revise his previous low opinion of Ralston's abilities when it proved to be Ralston who isolated and identified the key point in the whole dispute, and their subsequent concentration on that one point proved to be decisive in the eventual outcome of the appeal.

In the *Gairdner Securities* case, the question was whether or not the gain on a sale of shares was capital or income, a classic matter of the intention of the parties. James Gairdner's corporation had a large block of shares in Dominion Malting Company, then controlled by the well-known industrialist E.P. Taylor, and Gairdner was intent on taking it over. Taylor would have none of this and mounted a determined resistance to the effort, to the point that Gairdner finally sold its block of shares to Taylor. The Department of National Revenue had, despite the bitter personal antagonism that marked the negotiations, formed the view that Gairdner had acquired its block of shares with a view to selling it to Taylor at a profit, which would have clothed the transaction with the quality of income. It was vital, therefore, that Taylor not appear to have been on speaking terms with Gairdner and to portray Gairdner as his bitter enemy during the relevant period. As it turned out, however, not only since the time of the transaction, but also for years before it, Gairdner and Taylor had been friends. When Stikeman called Taylor away from his study of the Canadian *Racing Form* into the witness box and asked him the question as to his relations with Gairdner during the takeover contest, Taylor beamed his well-known smile and replied, "... the best of friends, and we never had any differences between us." Beatific smiles spread across the faces of Crown counsel, who coasted home to a win. When the dust had settled, Taylor came up to Stikeman and said, cheerfully, "Well, I guess I blew it for Jim [Gairdner], didn't I?" Stikeman replied, "I guess we both did. You forgot to remember and I forgot to remind you." Machiavellian as it may seem, perhaps, the negotiations had been just as bitter as they had appeared, and Gairdner's gain on the transaction was, on the strength of Taylor's evidence, cut in half by the taxes.

THE LAST CASE IN THE PRIVY COUNCIL

Heward Stikeman has the distinction of having been the last Canadian lawyer to appear before the Privy Council in respect of a case arising from the
Canadian courts. This was *St Catharines Flying Training School Limited
v. M.N.R.* [1953] CTC 362; [1955] CTC 189; PC (leave refused). The point
at issue in the case was whether a flying training school, incorporated as a
limited company with share capital provided by private subscribers, could be
assessed for income tax in respect of profits over and above what it spent in
training allied airmen during the war. The company had a special provision
in its charter prohibiting the declaration of dividends or the distribution of
profits during hostilities or during the period that the company was required
to carry on elementary training under the British Commonwealth Air Training Plan. In 1940, the directors had made a declaration of trust, providing
that the capital should be returned to the donor companies without interest
or increase and that the shares should be held in trust for the St Catharines
Flying Club, a charitable organization, so that it might be the beneficiary
of any surplus of the club.

On the termination of its contract for training airmen, into which it
had entered with the Crown and the Department of National Defence, the
company had retained some $83,000 in excess of its capital, pursuant to an
agreement that the club had with the government. The arrangement provided
that any amounts retained by the company should be held by it in a reserve
account until the termination of the contract on March 31, 1945, when the
funds then in the account should be paid to a flying club approved by the
minister of National Defence, failing which the funds were to revert to the
Crown. The St Catharines Flying Club had not yet been approved by the
minister of National Defence as the surplus recipient, and it was, therefore,
claimed by the tax authorities that the surplus should either be returned to
the ministry or be taxable as income.

On appeal, the Exchequer Court of Canada held that just because the
company made profits, it did not follow that it was not operated for non-
profitable purposes. It also held that no part of the company's income inured
to the benefit of any of its stockholders or members and that it was exempt
from tax under section 4(h) of the *Income War Tax Act*. The appeal was
allowed. The Supreme Court of Canada reversed this finding and decided
that the profits realized were properly taxed as income because the company
was carrying out one of the declared objects for which it was incorporated
under Part I of the *Companies Act* (precursor to the *Canada Business Corporations Act*). It also held that the prohibition against declaring dividends
and distributing profits was not permanently restrictive. The question of the
taxability did not depend upon the intention of the promoters or shareholders
as to the distribution of the profits, but upon a consideration of the terms
of the letters patent, the nature of the business authorized to be carried on
and the business that was actually carried on, which resulted in the earning of income. However, the court also concluded that the profits realized
under that part of the agreement, which provided that the surplus should

be held by the company upon terms that they go to a flying club, in default of which they were to be paid to the Crown, was the same as saying that the respondent held the surplus in trust for the Crown. No statement was made, however, as to whether on the facts the company was charitable or was organized and operated solely for non-profitable purposes.

An appeal was taken to the Privy Council, and Stikeman went with Merton A. Seymour. Bert Bissonnette, who had assisted in the hearing before the Supreme Court of Canada, did not accompany him to England. Because it was the practice of the English Bar that any colonial or Commonwealth counsel who appeared before the Privy Council should have with him a junior from the English Bar, versed in the procedures and practices of the Privy Council and that Bar, Stikeman retained, on the advice of Slaughter & May, a young barrister by the name of Philip Sherbourne, then approximately thirty-two years of age and already a recognized leader at the Revenue Bar, although he had not yet "taken silk" (i.e., become a Q.C.). Sherbourne soon became and remained over the years one of Stikeman's fast friends in many enterprises.[16]

Sherbourne advised him well since the matter was not without difficulty. The Government of Canada had recently abolished all appeals from the Supreme Court of Canada to the Privy Council, except for those arising from "judicial proceedings commenced prior to December 31, 1949." The notice of objection and appeal to the Exchequer Court in the *St Catharines Flying Training School* case had been filed prior to this cut-off date. The question, therefore, was whether the client was precluded from having the right to appeal to the Privy Council. The issue turned upon whether the filing of a notice of objection and an appeal under the *Income War Tax Act* were "judicial proceedings" within the meaning of that term, as it existed in the Canadian legislation that closed off such appeals.

Thus, the question upon which they went to England was not only whether they could argue the substance of the appeal, but whether they would be allowed to appear at all. Sherbourne urged Stikeman to equip himself for this ordeal, and he spent several weeks beforehand in London going over the matter with Sherbourne and preparing himself. Sherbourne then advised him to appear with an old gown. Stikeman had been nominated as a Q.C. only a couple of years earlier and had not yet acquired his "silk," so he had to borrow an older, suitably shabby and torn, gown and to rent a wig that looked tattered, yellowed, and somewhat dirty. Sherbourne said that it would never do to appear in a new wig because it would look as if he were (as indeed he was) a neophyte before the committee.

Merton Seymour and I flew the Atlantic in a Boeing Stratocruiser, one of those great airplanes which had a full bar downstairs and eighteen complete bunks upstairs which were made up while one dined down below. The crossing took 18 hours going eastward and 24 hours going westward. It was, however, done in the utmost comfort. One got on in Montreal at 7 p.m., was seated downstairs for a drink and dinner, and proceeded upstairs after dinner to find a made-up berth waiting for one – full sheets, blankets, and curtains, exactly the same as in a railway sleeping car. One was awakened over Ireland for breakfast in bed after eight hours of sleep. Two hours later, the London landing was announced. In one week, I recall having made four consecutive flights across the ocean – Monday night, Montreal-London, Tuesday night, London-Montreal, Wednesday night, Montreal-London, and Thursday night, London-Montreal. On two occasions, because of headwinds on the westward leg, we put down at Shannon for refuelling, and I was given dinner in the airport dining room. The waiter asked me if I was staying at the hotel, and I hadn't the heart to tell him that I was really living in the air somewhere over the North Atlantic. However, we never missed a beat, and I was able to do two trials at once, one in Montreal and one in London, without too much difficulty.

In any event, on the first flight to London, we were late, and although we arrived the day before the hearing, we missed a large part of the opportunity of meeting with the English counsel and discussing the issues ahead of time and also being able to see how the procedures were actually carried out within the Privy Council office.

Nevertheless, the next morning, they proceeded, complete with grey-striped pants and the old wig and gown, to 11 Downing Street, where the Privy Council sat. They were taken through a rather bare-looking legal library into a large room where there was a podium on which stood a reading lamp and a rack for counsel's papers. Below Stikeman, in the body of the room, some distance removed, was a round table surrounded by chairs. When they opened at 10:30 AM, Stikeman was surprised to see that the chairs were occupied by some elderly gentlemen in business suits; some even were wearing tweed jackets and plus fours. On the table in the middle was a bottle of sherry, and each man had a glass. They were the Judicial Committee of Her Majesty's Privy Council in full session. They paid not the slightest attention to him when he began but, after a while, as he warmed to his theme, one or another bored-looking old man would look up, glance over his shoulder, and in a languid British-accented voice say, "Mr Stikeman, is that *quite* according to the facts? My factum does not appear to substantiate it. Would you please tell me the page and line to which you are referring?" When it was all over, some two hours later, they refused "to hear" them. They did so ostensibly on the grounds that a notice of objection and a notice of appeal were only procedures under the *Income War Tax Act* and not judicial proceedings in the sense contemplated by the new law abolishing appeals.

On the way out, a kindly old gentleman in a tweed suit came up to me and said that I should not be too disappointed at the result because I had made a good argument and Their Lordships had been impressed. Unfortunately, he added, they could not possibly hear the case, or any other appeal from Canada, since, after the passage of the Canadian legislation, they had sold off their Canadian law library! They thus were not in the mood to reopen the Canadian scene or hear any more of our appeals.

He then said, "In case you were not able to recognize me, as I was sitting with my back to you, my name is Simonds." I was immediately awed, since he had been the Lord Chancellor and a very famous judge in revenue law. He finished by inviting me home that night for dinner. I spent a very pleasant evening alone with him, since he did not include Mr Seymour, for reasons which I could never understand, save that he was obviously my client, and one did not mix clients with their counsel and their judges. Viscount Simonds, as had Lord Reading many years before, told me the story of his life and enthused with me over the joys of practising fiscal law in a growing and industrialized nation on the post-war era. It was one of the most pleasant and most memorable evenings in my life ... In any event, we flew home dejected and broke, but with the knowledge that we had done the best for our clients and at least had had the honour, if not the pleasure, of being the last Canadian lawyers to appear before that very impressive and august gathering of judges and men, the Judicial Committee of the Queen's Privy Council.

Oddly enough, on the other side of the case, F.P. Varcoe, the deputy minister of Justice, with whom C.F. Elliott had had such bitter struggles, was so convinced that Stikeman would get his leave to appeal that he had sent only a junior lawyer, Keith Eaton, to represent the Crown, even though Varcoe himself would certainly have argued the appeal had the Privy Council decided to hear it. On the strict legal merits of the case, Varcoe was probably correct. The disappearing court library probably had precisely the effect that Viscount Simonds suggested.

ROY FRASER ELLIOTT

In Ottawa, while working at the Department of National Revenue under C.F. Elliott, Stikeman was invited from time to time to his boss's home. On those occasions, he met with Elliott's son, Roy Fraser Elliott, who was home for the odd weekend during his studies at Queen's University, and a close and lasting friendship developed between them that extended to the idea that, some day, they might be associated with each other in the practice of law.

Roy Fraser Elliott was born on November 25, 1921 in Ottawa, son of Colin Fraser Elliott and Marjorie Sypher. The family had moved to Ottawa, following his father's service overseas in the artillery during World War 1, where C.F. Elliott had accepted a position with the federal government. His primary schooling was at Hopewell Avenue Public School and Glebe Collegiate. He received a commerce degree at Queen's University in Kingston, graduating in 1943, and then attended Osgoode Hall, obtaining his law degree in 1946. He was articled to Henry Borden, senior partner of Borden, Elliott, Kelley, Palmer & Sankey, and was admitted to the Ontario Bar in 1946. He and Stikeman had maintained their contact after Stikeman had returned to Montreal to take up private practice, and in the spring of 1946, shortly after he was called to the Ontario Bar, Elliott went to Montreal to be interviewed by Bunny Foster at the firm Stikeman had already joined. Not only was Foster agreeable to his joining the firm as an associate, subject, of course, to passing the requisite examinations for admission to the Quebec Bar, but also suggested that he might do so forthwith. Elliott had, however, on the advice of his father, decided to attend the Harvard School of Business Administration. Foster was amenable to the delay that would flow from this proposal, so Elliott began his studies with the comfort of the assurance he would have a legal job after obtaining his MBA.

His course at Harvard was completed by the fall of 1947, and he returned to Montreal, where the job with Foster, Hannen, Watt & Stikeman was still available, as soon as he was admitted to the Bar of Quebec. Having never practised law in Ontario following his call there, he was unable to avail himself of the fast-track admission, on the basis of previous practice in another province. Accordingly, he asked to be allowed to write the full Bar exams along with the following year's Quebec graduating class. This petition was granted, and he sat down in the office to begin studying for the next set of Bar examinations, scheduled for July 1948. The exercise had but one objective – passing the Bar examinations – so he engaged a tutor, a former employee of the Canadian Broadcasting Corporation, who supplied him with the Bar examination questions for the previous twenty years. Instead of studying the law as a whole, Elliott simply prepared himself to answer any of the questions previously asked. The gamble paid off. Not only did he pass the exams, but he finished thirteenth overall among that year's candidates. He recalls, with some amusement, that there were two new questions on the 1948 exam for which he had no canned answers. Admission to the Bar in hand, he joined Foster, Hannen, Watt & Stikeman that summer.

By the end of 1948, therefore, the long-planned association in the practice of law had been realized, an objective they had established at the Elliott family home in Ottawa several years earlier and had nurtured throughout Elliott's studies at Osgoode Hall and Harvard. Such was the combined ability, enthusiasm, and ambition of the two that barely two years after joining the firm, Elliott was made a partner of Foster, Hannen, Watt, Stikeman & Elliott in 1950. This was a partnership track that made many of their contemporaries green with envy and will, undoubtedly, cause many of today's associates to sigh as they look at the much more extended period of associateship in today's law firms.

Within the firm, the two young lawyers quickly carved out a remarkably successful practice. The big drawing card at the time was Stikeman's unparalleled knowledge and experience in tax matters, which led to many of the new mandates of the firm. Notwithstanding a personal disinclination for the taxation field, and despite his commerce and business background, much of Elliott's initial time after joining the firm was spent in tax planning matters, as opposed to the resolution of disputes. Elliott did not like court work; he went once, had a bad experience, and irrevocably declared himself to be out of that field. In any event, as far as Elliott was concerned, the strength of the firm was in its tax planning, not the putting out of fires, even though for Stikeman, much of the fun was dealing with things that had already gone wrong. Tax planning, however, often involved a good deal of corporate and business arrangements, entered into for the purpose of minimizing exposure to tax liability, which generated related corporate and business work, to which Elliott was particularly well suited and which he much preferred. Stikeman would develop the tax strategy, setting out the parameters of risks and safe conduct, and Elliott would develop the corporate and business aspects of the implementation of the strategy. Knowledge of accounting and the principles of business organization derived from his academic work provided Elliott with a distinct advantage over most lawyers, especially young lawyers in the field. As Elliott describes it: "I'd had five years of it. You had to have had accounting in the kind of practice in which I was engaged. For that reason, since I knew accountancy, much of the business I generated came to me through chartered accountants who wanted to deal with a lawyer. Chartered accountants are the first, as a rule, to see the businessman's problems, and if they can go to a lawyer to whom they can speak 'in their own language' and be understood, it is obviously a help. The greatest source of my business, to begin with, was chartered accountants." Stikeman's episodic tax clients often remained Elliott clients for ongoing business and corporate advice. It was not long, therefore, before both Stikeman and Elliott were attracting more than their share of new clients to the firm.

Building on Stikeman's example, in the first half of 1948, Elliott began to write and subsequently edited the *Quebec Corporations Manual,* also with De Boo, filling a lacuna regarding published material on the Quebec *Companies Act,* for which there had been no service analogous to that available in respect of the Canadian and Ontario statutes. The *Manual* was published in 1949.

His business and accounting background led Elliott, almost naturally, into the financial and related management of Foster, Hannen, Watt, Stikeman & Elliott. The subject matter was easy for him, and it took almost no time to master the relatively simple business and accounting features of a small law firm. It also became apparent very quickly how much of the business and income of the firm were being generated by the two young lawyers. Within three years, the financial, although not personal, tension created by this anomaly would lead to their decision to leave the firm and establish their own.

The offices in the Aldred Building were not air-conditioned. Few, if any, commercial buildings of the day had such a feature, and heat waves were handled by opening the windows. Marj Cornell remembers an occasion when three of the secretaries were working overtime, waging the usual battles with sheets of carbon paper and manual typewriters, exacerbated by the thick, humid air seeping in through the open windows. The windows had no screens, so there was the added distraction of the shadflies that plagued the city. The secretaries had rolled their nylons to their knees, loosened their clothing, and kicked off their shoes, when the door opened and someone ushered in a handsome male, with the words, "... and this is the general office and secretarial section." Dead silence ensued, except for the shadflies, until they all burst out laughing. The handsome male was a new client. Cornell was tempted to say, "Welcome to the strip joint," but wisdom prevailed.

EVERYONE LEARNS THE HARD WAY

In 1949, Stikeman was the uncomfortable recipient of a lesson that he never forgot. He would describe it later as "a classic example of how one can

get caught out by associating with the wrong type of client and not taking instructions in writing." This was the infamous *United Distillers* case.
The background to the problem had been wartime regulations regarding
the production of alcoholic beverages. Such production had been severely
limited in order to be sure that alcohol was available for munitions. At the
end of the war, the only mature stocks of alcohol available for distillation of
whisky were those that existed prior to the war. The largest of these stocks
were owned by United Distillers of Canada Limited and had been stored in
British Columbia.

A group of us individuals, one of whom was the brother of a director of
United Distillers of Canada Limited, identified a ready and highly profitable
market in the United States for the alcohol. The difficulty for this group was
that the us Office of Price Administration (OPA) had responsibility, *inter alia,*
for enforcing regulations to prevent the sale of alcohol within the United
States at prices higher than a certain percentage over the cost to the seller.
There was, therefore, not much advantage to be gained by selling the Canadian alcohol into the American market directly from Canada. The group
concocted a plan to sell the alcohol through a chain of interposed buyers. In
each case, a special purpose corporation set up in Panama or the West Indies
would purport to acquire ownership of the alcohol, passing it up the chain,
marking up the price each time, until the cost to the final purchaser, the us
entrepreneurs, was far in excess of the cost to United Distillers in Canada.
Having acquired the alcohol at the marked-up cost, the latter cost would be
used for the applicable calculations in the United States. The scheme came
to the attention of the OPA.

Not all of the details of the scheme were known to Stikeman. It appears
that at some stage, the us group considered it desirable to ensure that there
was no interference by officials in Canada. It was alleged (although never
conclusively established) that as part of the substantial exchanges of cash
in the various transactions, a briefcase containing one million dollars was
brought by overnight train from New York to Canada, with the apparent
intention of paying off various government officials, cabinet ministers, and
even, it was suggested, some judges. Legend has it that the briefcase was left
behind the statue of Sir Wilfred Laurier in the lobby of the Château Laurier in
Ottawa and was picked up by a Canadian government official during lunch.
Neither the briefcase nor the money was ever seen, but rumours abounded,
and there was much discussion of the affair.

At various times during the series of transactions, substantial sums had
been deposited in the Royal Bank of Canada in both Ottawa and Toronto in
the names of three of the principal entrepreneurs composing the us group:
H.H. Klein, Ellis Rosenberg, and Murray Haas. Once the OPA probe was set
in motion, the Canadian income tax authorities learned of the matter and
moved to seize all assets of any of the intermediate companies they could
find in Canada, including those of United Distillers of Canada Limited. The
tax authorities took the view that profits had been made on the transactions
and that regardless of whether or not the transactions existed only on paper,
they had nevertheless not been reported in Canada. The tax question was

referred to Stikeman by Mr Justice Locke of the Supreme Court of Canada, who had, prior to his appointment, been a director of United Distillers of Canada. Stikeman was able to prove to the satisfaction of the authorities that Mr Justice Locke was not privy to the transactions in issue.

The Bank of Canada, acting under the authority of the existing Foreign Exchange Control regulations, sequestered all funds then banked in Canada by the US group, which brought their problems to Stikeman as well. Stikeman was thus involved in representing United Distillers of Canada Limited on the tax matter and the US group on the Foreign Exchange Control problem. The tax claim was relatively simple. A settlement was reached with the deputy minister of National Revenue, Charles C. Gavsie, who was a successor to C.F. Elliott,[17] and United Distillers agreed to pay a nominal tax on some of the actual profits realized in Canada from the first sale of alcohol to the company at the bottom of the chain of intermediate firms. The settlement involved paying tax of approximately half a million dollars, measured against potential assessments of several millions of dollars.

The Foreign Exchange Control problem was much more difficult. Stikeman had had no reason to doubt the integrity of his clients. In fact, Rosenberg and Klein had been introduced to him by none other than C.F. Elliott. Whatever their conduct had been in relation to US law, there had been so far as he was aware no breach of Canadian law. Briefed with instructions from Rosenberg, Klein & Haas, unfortunately almost never in writing, Stikeman made many trips to New York, Washington, and to the west coast in attempts to resolve the matter. His mandate from the American clients, as he understood it, was to approach Robert Tarr, then deputy governor of the Bank of Canada and administrator of the Foreign Exchange Control Board, to get his permission to remove the funds from the Canadian bank accounts, provided their release had first been approved by the Department of National Revenue. The legal position was that the funds were not owned by residents of Canada, that they did not have their origin in Canada, and that their ultimate destination was outside Canada. He was able to establish these facts to the satisfaction of both government authorities, and the funds were duly released.

On the other side of the border, the OPA action intensified. In due course, Stikeman's letters to the Foreign Exchange Control Board were seized upon by the OPA as evidence that Stikeman had lent himself to the scheme with the knowledge of the identity of the principals. The OPA, exhibiting the "muscle" so often exercised by American regulatory authorities without regard to other jurisdictions, wanted Stikeman to appear in New York and testify in grand jury proceedings launched by the OPA against Rosenberg, Klein & Haas. They wanted him to provide the OPA with evidence that could then be used against his clients, something to which he obviously could not agree. In particular, and doubtless with good reason, it appeared that any testimony given by him within the United States might not be subject to professional privilege. In addition, it would almost certainly become public knowledge and might be damaging to his clients and possibly expose him to a personal law suit on the part of his clients. On the question of privilege, he consulted

Cravath, Swaine & Moore in New York, whose advice was that no solicitor-client privilege could be claimed by Stikeman while testifying in the United States. Under most grand jury rules in the United States, a witness does not have the right to remain silent and can only refuse to testify on the basis that any such evidence might tend to incriminate him.

Stikeman advised the US Department of Justice that with regret, he could not appear. Not surprisingly, the US Department of Justice assured him that "his privilege would be respected" and strongly urged him to appear. The compromise Stikeman offered was that the US Department of Justice should send a delegation to Canada to question him upon oath, on the basis that he would answer without reserve all questions put to him to the extent that the solicitor-client privilege, fully recognized in Canada, might allow him to answer. His clients were entitled in Canada to the benefit of such privilege, not having waived it.

Stikeman was interviewed in Montreal on March 25, 1950. As part of the arrangement, however, he insisted that the examination be attended by Max Fell, then head of the Special Investigations Division of the Department of National Revenue, C.F. Elliott, who had known the US entrepreneurs personally and had dealt with them officially, W.E. McElhone of the US Internal Revenue Service, and William J. Hulbig. The transcript was some fifty pages in length and provided US officials with all information legally available to them without any breach of the solicitor-client privilege.

In retrospect, the wisdom of choosing this method of co-operation was demonstrated by the fact that one of the Panamanian lawyers, who had received and relied upon assurances similar to those proffered to Stikeman by the US Department of Justice regarding the sanctity of professional privilege, did agree to appear before the grand jury in New York, only to learn in midstream that there was no professional privilege available in respect of instructions received from a corporate client. The evidence thus extracted from the Panamanian lawyer was fatal to his clients, and they were sentenced to five years in prison in the United States.

The importance of knowing one's clients and being certain of instructions has never been lost on Stikeman and the lawyers in his firm.

ECONOMIC IMPERATIVES

The offices of Foster, Hannen, Watt & Stikeman occupied on January 3, 1946 were in the Aldred Building on Place d'Armes in the Owners Suite. Such was the luxury of the premises that there was a working fireplace in Bunny Foster's office. The partners were the named partners on the letterhead. There were initially two juniors, Graham Gould and Robert C. Leggat. William J. Hulbig[18] joined in 1947, followed shortly by John H.E. Colby. Fraser Elliott had arrived in 1948 and Graham Gould left the firm in 1949. Shortly thereafter, Albert L. Bissonnette[19] joined the firm as well.

The firm's total revenue forecast for 1946, the year Stikeman joined the firm, was $76,000. There was a provision for $26,000 of expenses, leaving $50,000 to be divided between the four partners. Their prediction for gross revenue for the second year was $86,000, and for the third year, $92,000. They had not sufficiently appreciated the effect Stikeman would have on their business: his personal income for 1946 was $36,000, for 1947, $56,000 and for 1948, $77,000.[20] When Elliott arrived, the amounts became even greater. Even before his admission to the partnership in 1950, only two years after his call to the Quebec Bar, Elliott was earning more than any of the partners except for Stikeman.

One of the stories that emerged from the Foster firm has to do with a client by the name of Brandram-Henderson Paint Company, a very successful paint company that was being wooed over succession, when the last of the founders was retiring. As the recollection goes, Elliott not only persuaded him to sell the company, generating a fee for the legal services performed, but also negotiated a finder's fee in respect of the sale. He told Bunny Foster that he assumed that the additional fee thus generated would, therefore, make a difference in his remuneration for the year. Foster said it would not. This may well have accelerated the eventual decision to leave.

Once Elliott became a partner in 1950 and began to run the firm, he set about preparing an analysis of how the rewards might better be distributed. His idea was that one-third should accrue to the partner introducing new business, one-third to those who did the work, and the final one-third to the firm in general. Any application of a formula of this nature made it clear that Stikeman and Elliott stood to receive an even larger portion of the firm's annual income. That was not, however, the partnership "deal," and the impending breakup of the firm began to become more apparent.

CHAPTER 2

Setting Out on Their Own

By the early 1950s, Stikeman had developed an impressive number of contacts and an admirable reputation he had achieved as assistant deputy minister of National Revenue, followed by being counsel to the Senate Committee, the identification with the *Canada Tax Service,* and his wide-ranging lecture appearances among the professions while with government. He knew that he would eventually have to form his own base in order to capitalize on these qualities and the growing public awareness of him as a leader in the emerging field. It was equally apparent that he would need a practical partner versed in accounting and the business aspects of law who could complement his own qualifications with a broader range of corporate experience and business judgment. This could be none other than Fraser Elliott.

The fateful step was taken on Sunday night, December 16, 1951, as Elliott observed, his only day off during the week, in the basement of Stikeman's home at 48 Aberdeen Avenue in Westmount. Stikeman's recollection of the seminal moment is as follows: "I was painting a table upon which to put an electric train for my children. R. Fraser Elliott dropped in for a beer as he sometimes did, and we began to discuss the continuing problem of how to deal fairly with the Foster firm. For some reason, which I cannot now recall, I blurted out that I had come to the conclusion that I was going to leave as soon as I could get space – would he like to join me? Without any hesitation, Fraser said the same thought had been in his mind, and he agreed we should leave as soon as we could find space." They wondered, that decision taken, whether some of their colleagues might wish to follow them into the new venture. They picked up the phone and called Bill Hulbig, whom Stikeman had known before he had joined the firm from the legal branch of the Department of National Revenue in Ottawa, and before that, as a friend in both arts and law at McGill, including studying together for the Bar exams at the Stikeman residence in Senneville. They also spoke to Albert Bissonnette. Both agreed to join the new firm.

After a few telephone calls that Sunday night, Fraser and I began to write out in pencil on the unpainted portion of the model railway table our proposed budget ... after we had decided that we could probably afford it, we then estimated our probable take from fees as against outlay and costs, quickly painted the whole thing over, walked up the street to Bunny Foster's house, also on Aberdeen Avenue, and told him that we were going to leave. He did not seem as surprised as we had expected. We told him we could not leave the next morning because we had no office space of our own in which to work, and that there was none of suitable kind then available in Montreal.

We wished we said to put him on notice that we would move out as soon as we could, and in a fashion that would not disturb his practice nor rob him of the clients which we shared, to the extent of their business which was in the competence of Foster and his associates.

It would be more than two months before they were able to move out of the Foster premises since office space was very tight in Montreal after the war. The opportunity to get premises of their own arose from the announcement by the Canadian government that Foreign Exchange Control would end as of February 1, 1952. The practical effect of that announcement was that considerable footage in the Bank of Canada building at the base of Beaver Hall Hill, fronting on Victoria Square, would soon become free. Stikeman lost no time in getting the help of his personal friend James A. Coyne, then chairman of the Bank of Canada in Ottawa, as well as Robert Tarr, for the purpose of obtaining space in the building as soon as the Foreign Exchange Control Board would move out. Both individuals assured Stikeman that the new firm would be a satisfactory tenant and that there would be no difficulty since the new enterprise would not require the whole floor, merely 3,000 square feet of space. Stikeman confirmed his understanding of the arrangement in a letter dated December 21, 1951 to L.P. Saint-Amour, assistant deputy governor of the Bank of Canada, namely that the new firm would take all of the space on the south half of the fifth floor, with the exception of a small portion that they would sublet to the firm of Fairfield & Grant. The rental rate was to be $3.50 per square foot per annum, and the term of the lease was to be five years. They would, as well, buy some filing cabinets, tables, waste paper baskets, hall trees, and an oak secretarial desk and oak straight-backed swivel chair from the Bank of Canada.

A somewhat dramatic change in circumstances was thrust upon them because the resolved purpose of the Bank of Canada was to let the entire floor space, some 10,000 square feet, to a single tenant. Stikeman learned of this only after he and Elliott had separated themselves from Foster and had sent out announcements of the new firm and its quarters, believing the new firm had rented a modest area of the building sufficient for its needs. As luck would further have it, the businessman of the two, Elliott, had left before this news broke and had just, as Stikeman says, "with typical panache," gone off on a world tour, leaving him alone in Montreal to deal with the crisis. The obvious solution, that of finding a subtenant for the excess space, proved to be particularly difficult since the Bank of Canada had an aversion to sharing space with anyone whose activities might be seen as even remotely competitive in the financial field. None of the subtenants proposed by Stikeman and Elliott seemed, for one reason or another, to be satisfactory to the

Bank. Stikeman tracked down Elliott, whose travels had by then taken him to New Delhi, early one morning from the Château Laurier in Ottawa, to say that it looked as if the new firm might be stuck with the entire floor. Some 12,000 miles from the fray, Elliott seemed much more sanguine about the prospect than Stikeman did, an attitude made easier, Stikeman surmised, by Elliott's geographic separation from the problem. Even then, Stikeman knew how much he needed Elliott's business acumen for the new firm. There is a delightful telegram in the firm's files, sent by Stikeman in the midst of the mini-crisis, to Elliott, by then visiting his parents in Canberra, where C.F. Elliott had been appointed Canadian High Commissioner:

Montreal, December 27/51

Roy Fraser Elliott
Care High Commission for Canada to Australia
32 Mugga Way
Canberra

Have Exchange Control space upstairs Moving February First Stop Please do not overstay schedule Stop Letter in Air Please cable where send copy

Stikeman

The spectre of economic disaster was, however, averted when the Bank of Canada finally agreed that the Newfoundland American Insurance Company, a wholly owned subsidiary of American Universal Insurance Company, would be acceptable as a subtenant, and it took all of the extra floor space. Business instincts fully intact following his world tour, Elliott swooped in, obtained the legal business of Newfoundland American, and joined its board of directors. Turning his attention to the south, he also bought an interest in American Universal and joined their board. Stikeman & Elliott kept the insurance company's business even after it was bought out by a larger US insurance company.

Financing of the new firm had an interesting background. Elliott had wanted, two or three years earlier, to get some capital for purposes of investment, having no capital of his own. He knew even then that if he were to earn any serious money, he would have to borrow funds to invest. Shortly after joining Foster, Watt, Hannen & Stikeman in early 1949, Elliott decided to approach the Bank of Montreal, the head office of which was diagonally across Place d'Armes, to obtain a loan in the heady amount of $5,000. Since he already banked there, he arranged a meeting with two of the assistant general managers. One was Mr Corner; the other was Mr Window, a juxtaposition of names not lost on Elliott. A loan of this magnitude, they solemnly advised Elliott, would require that he provide the bank with a personal balance sheet. That would be easy, replied Elliott, but he advised them that although such a balance sheet would show nothing negative, neither would it show anything positive. Corner and Window, being cautious souls, were not prepared to advance such a significant loan in such circumstances.

Annoyed but undaunted, Elliott continued further west along St James Street to the then main branch of the Canadian Bank of Commerce[1] and arranged a meeting with the assistant manager, Reginald Clute, who listened carefully to his proposal. Having heard it, Clute reached into his desk drawer, produced some standard bank promissory notes, and pushed them toward Elliott, saying, "Sign these notes and there will be $5,000 in your account." Thus began a flourishing personal relationship with the Bank of Commerce that culminated with Elliott joining its board and in due course, with the new firm doing legal work for the bank in Montreal and later in Toronto and elsewhere.

When the new firm of Stikeman & Elliott was in the process of being established, the two about-to-be partners went to see the manager of the Bank of Commerce's main branch, George S. Unwin, a personal friend of both. Not only did Unwin immediately agree to finance the new venture, but he also gave them some personal as well as banking advice. First, "Don't worry about repaying the bank. If you worry, your business will suffer and I won't get paid." Second, "Let me know if you get sick ..." Signature cards were provided to the bank on January 26, 1952, with either Stikeman's or Elliott's signature to suffice, and cheques could be written on the new Stikeman & Elliott account commencing the week of January 28. Additional banking documents were sent by Unwin for signature and were completed by January 31. A trust account was opened by the end of February, with the same signing officers. Hulbig was added as a signing authority on December 3, 1952.

Immediately after the movement to a new firm was under way, Stikeman began the process of moving toward getting legal work from the bank and trying to get Elliott on the bank's board of directors. In a letter dated February 1, 1952, Frank H. Brown, a director of the bank from Vancouver, wrote to Stikeman, obviously following up on discussions they had had on the subject.

I had a talk with George Unwin before leaving Montreal but had to change my plans to go to Toronto. However, the General Manager of The Canadian Bank of Commerce was out here at Mr [C.D.] Howe's dinner, and I had a chance to talk to him about the legal picture of the Montreal branch. I said to him that the accent on youth which governs the Bank of Commerce today should also govern in such a matter as legal representation wherever possible.

He expects to be in Montreal fairly soon and will make a point of getting in touch with you.

In my talk with Unwin, I found that there really was no change in the policy which the Bank followed in the '30s of dividing the work out among two or three legal advisors. Matters affecting the *Bank Act* went usually to a firm with a specialized knowledge of this legislation – not many legal firms know much about it – and it is a field for study in itself.

Unwin thought that there might be some chance that Foster would be made a director should Dr Colby retire from the Board. Personally, I think this is highly unlikely because the Bank's interest is in moving forward substantially in Montreal. It will need aggressive as well as influential people. You may rest assured that Mr

Stewart is sympathetic to you [added by hand], but of course in the appointment of directors, he is not the final authority.

The firm has remained grateful to the bank throughout its existence, and the bank also benefited from the loyalty generated by its enlightened treatment of two talented young men. The firm has been a major tenant of two of the bank's major office towers in Montreal and Toronto, moving immediately, as the bank's first outside tenant, into the new office building in Montreal at 1155 Dorchester Boulevard West (now René-Lévesque Boulevard) when it opened in 1962, and in Toronto, first in cramped quarters at 25 King Street West, and later in Commerce Court West, from the moment the firm began its Toronto operations in 1971.[2]

The Bank of Canada Building on Victoria Square was a prestigious location for the new firm, on the edge of the financial and legal district of the city. Within ten years, this centre of business and legal gravity would move away from St James and Notre Dame Streets and Place D'Armes, further from the river, up to Dorchester Boulevard, but in the meantime, it was a perfect location, and the building provided, at no incremental cost to the firm, the additional *gravitas* of an RCMP officer, in full red serge regalia, outside the front entrance during business hours. Being a tenant of the Bank of Canada had its advantages. The Bank of Canada Building, says John Turner, who joined shortly after the firm was established, was a great building. The firm was on the fifth floor and shared premises with the insurance company. The physical arrangement was not much changed from the Foster Hannen set-up, with a general office and a secretarial section.

The students were quartered in the library, one door of which opened into the secretarial section. One of the students, Ron Robertson, a good-looking macho type, was accused by a temporary employee of staring at her suggestively. Robertson was infuriated, not so much for the suggestion that he had stared, but "at *her*!" That was an insult, he said. The complainant was discovered to be partial to the bottle and by noon, as Marj Cornell says, "was pretty well bombed," so her accusation was not considered credible, and her temporary employment soon ceased. Robertson was the student who said, in both awe and admiration, that Fraser Elliott was the only person in the world who could spot a dollar bill on the floor thirty feet away – in the dark. Below them on the fourth floor was Peat Marwick, and above them on the sixth was the Dixon, Claxton, Senecal & Stairs firm, then one of the venerable Montreal law firms but which has completely disappeared. At noon hour, there was generally a bridge game in the "vault" that held all the office file folders but still had room for a single table. Both Elliott and Jim Robb enjoyed the games, and there was often a second game going in the ladies locker room.

IF YOU BUILD IT, THEY WILL COME

It is, of course, one thing to have located premises for a new venture and to have arranged bank financing, but quite another to generate the revenues required to support the endeavour. To have broken away, as young lawyers,

from an established firm to start on their own was, at the very least, precocious, and there were many within the legal establishment who were quite
willing to see the effort fail and many who actively hoped that it would.
Brash young lawyers were not to be encouraged in this form of initiative;
their job was to support the lifestyles of senior lawyers. So, they were justly
nervous when they opened their doors on February 1, 1952. They had built
it, but would "they" come?

Although it is easy to say in retrospect, they need not have worried. The
first of many clients that followed them from Foster Hannen was Furness,
Withy. The new partners had agreed to leave their civil law work with
Foster, so they felt morally free to take on the problems of a tax, corporate,
and administrative nature that were beyond the capability of the old firm
to handle. The first day of business also saw them call upon or telephone
Henry Morgan & Company, Molson Breweries, Standard Oil Company of
California, Harold W. Siebens, the K.C. Irving companies, Eric Harvie of
Western Leaseholds and Western Minerals in Calgary, the Government of
Canada (which produced two briefs to argue cases in the Supreme Court of
Canada), Jules Timmins of Hollinger Gold Mines, and Arthur Schmon of
the Ontario Paper Company. It was a promising beginning.

Relations with the former firm were very cordial in the circumstances,
and Stikeman followed up the commencement of the new firm with a letter
to Bunny Foster, dated February 26, 1952, confirming the ongoing connection with them.

Dear Mr Foster:

This will confirm our earlier discussions relating to the payment by this Firm of a
retainer to you and your associates at least for the first year after our separation. It
is understood that the retainer will be paid in the amount of $500 per month, which
will entitle us to a priority upon your time and knowledge in matters relating to civil
law and insurance, together with the right to discuss our clients' problems with you
at all times. In addition to professional services, we shall also be entitled to access to
your library when necessary.

Would you please confirm this arrangement, which I understand is to last until
April 1953.

Yours faithfully,
(sgd) H. Heward Stikeman

Civility prevailed, and the share of Stikeman and Elliott in the profits of the
Foster firm for the year ended January 31, 1952 were remitted to them on
March 17, 1952: $ 15,077.74 for Stikeman and $5,830.48 for Elliott. Values
after depreciation of the furniture they had acquired were to be worked out
by the auditors, and they would be advised accordingly.

While things obviously change over time, to give some idea of the domi-
nance of Stikeman at the beginning of their relationship, the first partnership agreement between the two new partners, dated January 18, 1952, was
short and very specific.

ARTICLE I. The Parties hereto shall be associated as partners in the practice of the profession of the Law from February 1, 1952, under the firm name and style of STIKEMAN & ELLIOTT.

ARTICLE II. This Agreement may be terminated by either party hereto upon giving Thirty (30) days' notice in writing to the other party hereto.

ARTICLE III. The parties hereto shall share in the first Seventy Thousand Dollars ($70,000.00) of net profits and shall pay debts and liabilities of the partnership in an amount equal thereto in the following proportions:

> Mr Stikeman – Two-thirds (⅔)
> Mr Elliott – One-third (⅓)

ARTICLE IV. The parties hereto shall share in the net profits in excess of the first Seventy Thousand Dollars ($70,000.00) referred to in Article III hereof, and shall pay debts and liabilities of the partnership in excess of Seventy Thousand Dollars ($70,000.00) in the following proportions:

> Mr Stikeman – Five-sixths (⅚)
> Mr Elliott – One-sixth (⅙)

ARTICLE V. The net profits of the partnership shall be divided on December 31 in each year or so soon thereafter as may be convenient. But each partner shall be entitled to draw monthly against his share of profits: Mr Stikeman, Eight Hundred Dollars ($800.00) and Mr Elliott, Five Hundred Dollars ($500.00), unless cash in hand at any time does not reasonably permit such drawings, in which case they shall be proportionately reduced.

IN WITNESS WHEREOF the parties hereto have signed at the place and on the date hereinabove firstly written.

The billings of the new firm for the first year of operations amounted to $243,137.90. After expenses, the net profit was $149,456.84, which was split, giving Stikeman $95,644.08 and Elliott $53,812.76. By the following year, things were somewhat clearer. Billings had increased to $307,619.81. The first three articles of the agreement for that year were the same, except that the initial threshold amount had been raised to $75,000, and Stikeman's monthly draw was increased to $1,000; Elliott's remained at $500. As to the excess of profits over $75,000, Stikeman was to get the next $50,000 and Elliott, the following $25,000. If the profits were to exceed $150,000, then Stikeman was entitled to the entire amount of the excess. Were there to be losses, they would be borne accordingly as well. The net profit for the second year was $189,379.32, of which Stikeman got $135,897.34 and Elliott, $53,481.98.[3]

Small offices lend themselves to micromanagement, and both Stikeman and Elliott were no exceptions to the practice. There is a scrawled memorandum from 1952 from Stikeman to Hulbig:

While on the subject of neatness (i.e., lunch at desk), how about asking the switchboard girl to keep her area tidier –

> i.e., no messages in well
> no material on floor behind table
> keep her coat and shoes in back
> keep knitting out of sight

How long will typewriter be there?

Clients are beginning to notice.   H.

Hulbig's reply was short: "Done." Elliott made a point of mentioning to Marj Cornell, who would become den mother of the firm in later years, that he did not think the red shoes she was wearing were appropriate for a law firm, whereupon she bopped him on his bald spot, then only the size of a quarter. Elliott said he always made sure clients noticed this feature since he felt it indicated maturity when dealing with those who were much older than he was.

2.

Each year and for many years after the new firm began, Elliott continued a practice that he had begun in 1948 – to take three weeks and go across Canada, calling on lawyers in all the cities he visited, often six or seven calls a day, to get to know people. He sometimes went with Stikeman and was never shy about using his connection with his father to gain entry and credibility. He travelled in both Europe and Asia for the same purpose and would invite people from there to his home. Stikeman, for his part, preferred to travel back and forth to Europe, in first class, on the ocean liners that were then a regular feature of Atlantic crossings. Shyness was a concept that was entirely foreign to both. They met hundreds of possible clients and made a disciplined point of staying in touch, creating an enviable network of contacts.

Effective February 1, 1954, Hulbig became a partner. Of the first $165,000 of net profits, Hulbig was entitled to $15,000, and Stikeman and Elliott shared the balance, two-thirds for Stikeman and one-third for Elliott. The same proportions applied to losses. The big change that year was that for net profits in excess of $165,000, Hulbig got 10 per cent, and Stikeman and Elliott each got 45 per cent. Stikeman's draw against anticipated profits was $1,000 per month; Elliott's increased to $800, and Hulbig was to draw $500 per month.

Hulbig, who did not feel that he was particularly suited to the frenetic pace set by Stikeman and Elliott nor that he was imbued with the same level of ambition, withdrew from the partnership to return to Sun Life, giving notice in March 1955, and the two partners went back to a variation on the original arrangement, this time with a sixty-day notice period. Stikeman was to have two-thirds of the first $150,000 of net profits, and Elliott, one-third. Excess profits were to be shared in the same proportions. Elliott's monthly draw shrank to $500. This continued until February 1, 1958, when the arrangement became fifty-fifty for the first $200,000. Stikeman would then get the next $25,000, and Elliott the next $25,000 after that. In Stikeman's words (this was a simple letter between them), "If for any extraordinary reason we earn more than that, we will share again fifty-fifty."

On September 8 of the same year, the partners exchanged a letter dealing with what might happen in the event of the death of either, Elliott writing to Stikeman:

It is my understanding that we have agreed between us, so long as we are the only two partners of Stikeman & Elliott, that in the event of the death of either of us, an audited statement will be taken off as of that date showing the allocation of profit to date on the cash basis in accordance with our Partnership Agreement at the time. Capital Account shall be payable to the deceased partner's estate within one year. The Accounts receivable of the partnership outstanding at the time shall be divided in two by account, and one-half of each Account Receivable, when collected, will be paid to the estate of the deceased partner without deduction of any expenses of the firm whatsoever paid after death. On the other hand, it is my further understanding that the value of unbilled time shall belong to the surviving partner, and the deceased partner shall have no interest in billings made after the date of his death.

If this is in accordance with your understanding, would you please sign the second copy hereof and return it to me.

He did. By the end of the fiscal year ending January 31, 1959, billings had reached almost $460,000, and the profit was in excess of $250,000.

NAMCO AND CAE

From 1946 to 1956, Elliott and Stikeman were attempting to build some future security outside the law firm. In 1949, Stikeman had learned from his friend Grant Glassco, senior partner in Clarkson Gordon & Co., that he and Walter Gordon had formed a company called Canadian Management Limited, which was designed to acquire control of strong operating companies with large liquid surpluses. By means of the then frequently used tactic available under the income tax statute, the surpluses could be extracted by tax-free dividends and used to repay the bank loans obtained to purchase the share control of the target company. In this way, substantial companies could be purchased with their own money at little or no commercial risk.

The two friends considered this investment vehicle to be an ideal solution to their problem since they had no capital and few bankable assets. Together, they interested a group of friends, and in 1949, formed a company called North American Management Corporation, commonly known as Namco. Namco's shareholders, besides Stikeman and Elliott, included Bart Morgan, Léon Simard, Gordon Hutchison, Alex Pierce (the two latter were partners of the chartered accounting firm of Riddell Stead Graham & Hutchison), C.N. Moisan, and Wilfrid Gagnon. Their plan was to do the same thing as Canadian Management had done, and initially they succeeded extremely well. Elliott's description of the technique was as follows:

The procedure was that Namco would buy the shares of a company with a large surplus. Namco would then cause the company which it had acquired to pay all its assets, including its capital, to Namco as a dividend, all of which was non-taxable in the hands of Namco. The original selling shareholders would then incorporate a new company of the same name as the one of the shares of which they had sold, invest the proceeds of the sale of their shares in the new company, and the new company would then buy the assets that had been distributed to Namco at a price somewhat lower than the value of the assets themselves. The resulting profit of Namco nearly always consisted of cash, and if it did not, the assets remaining in Namco which were not cash were disposed of to third parties for cash. The "commission" paid to Namco was considerably less than the original shareholders would have had to pay in tax had they distributed the surplus to themselves, and they ended up with a company with no surplus in it at all. It must be remembered that in those days, capital gains tax was non-existent, so, effectively, no tax was paid by anyone.

Namco continued surplus stripping for about two years. The reputation of Stikeman and Elliott brought owners of companies with large trapped surpluses to them to have their surpluses released. The directors of Namco, who consisted of representatives of the principal shareholders, were charged with the responsibility of investing the profits of Namco in other endeavours. These included such companies as the Hart Shoe Company Limited, Ontario Plumbing and Heating Supply Company Limited, Howarths Limited, a laundry and dry cleaning company in Montreal, and a 50 per cent interest in a newly incorporated company, Canadian Aviation Electronics Limited (CAE), which had commenced a radar and repair overhaul business in a hangar at St Hubert Air Base across the river from Montreal. These investments were all made by 1952.

The CAE investment was suggested by Henry Benson, a partner in the investment dealer firm of Jones Heward & Co., who thought that they should buy control of the fledgling operation. The genesis of CAE was a brilliant engineer, John Bull, who developed the idea of building flight simulators. His breakthrough in the field was the migration from analog technology to digital, an innovation that others in the business, such as Curtiss Wright, had not yet adopted. In the initial phase, the principal clients were governments purchasing simulators for military aircraft. Other companies, such as Link, did only military work, but CAE had begun to move into the field of commercial aviation. Its timing was excellent since business and tourist travel began a period of exponential growth. The company, owned and operated by Kenneth R. Patrick and other investors, was badly in need of a capital infusion. Namco, after realizing on some of its assets, purchased control of CAE, leaving Patrick in the management seat.

Namco hired managers to operate the other companies, and Elliott obtained some sound practical experience in the financing and overseeing of varied enterprises which was to prove particularly valuable in later years. There were, however, some problems on the horizon. By 1956, Elliott, who began as secretary of the company, had become a director of Namco and was thoroughly familiar with its affairs, but he was only a small shareholder.

The manager of the company at the time was James Hayman, a Harvard classmate of Elliott's. It had become apparent, at least to Elliott, that all of the companies that Namco had acquired were in trouble to the point that they and through them Namco, faced bankruptcy. It was particularly frustrating to them because Walter Gordon's Canadian Management was doing extremely well on the same model but with better investment management. In a move that would profoundly affect his later profile in the Canadian business community, Elliott made the rounds of all the Namco shareholders, asking them for a six-month option on 51 per cent of the Namco shares on the basis that if the shareholders were to grant the options, he would personally take the time during the option period to reorganize the company's affairs and change the management. The cost of taking up such options was far beyond his means as well as the combined means of the two partners, so he went to Russell Harrison of the Canadian Bank of Commerce to make arrangements to have the quarter-million or more dollars available when needed. Between themselves, the two law partners agreed that the options would be held 51 per cent by Elliott and 49 per cent by Stikeman. The other Namco shareholders readily agreed with the idea, and, in fact, options were proffered for considerably more than the 51 per cent that Elliott had requested. Elliott then proceeded to sell all of the shares owned by Namco in the various companies with the exception of CAE, into which he invested the extra funds.

Patrick, the CAE president, had launched the company on a diversification program that involved selling consumer products as well as flight simulators. There was a substantial inventory of products like refrigerators, lawn mowers, washing machines, and Dumont television sets. At the same time, the flight simulation production was almost entirely limited to government sales as it was not until much later that CAE was able to obtain contracts from civilian airlines. The flight simulator business made a lot of money each year, and the consumer products business lost almost as much. Patrick proved to be a poor manager of people and was absolutely intractable in the face of any suggestions put to him, primarily by Elliott, about scrapping the consumer products business. Elliott was convinced that CAE could sustain its defence business but only if all the other businesses it carried on were to cease.

One day, Elliott called Patrick to his office and told him that Patrick was not going to work there any more. When Patrick left Elliott's office, he went back to the CAE plant and sold his shares of the company to anyone and everyone who was willing to buy them, at very low prices. This, laughs Elliott, may have been the first time CAE went "public." To get rid of the other goods that had been cluttering the CAE inventory, they rented a large barn on Côte de Liesse, which they painted yellow. Written on its side in ten-foot-high letters was "Bargain Barn." They filled it with the unsold inventory of consumer products and sold this over a period of some six months to all comers. The additional funds realized from the sale of the Namco assets were also reinvested in CAE, and Namco was later wound up, the shareholders getting as part of the distribution their portion of the CAE shares held by Namco.

On the same day that Elliott fired Patrick, he hired, as the CEO, James Tooley, a chartered accountant from Winnipeg who had been a friend for many years. He was a good manager and a tough individual, at the time vice-president of finance of Canadair. Elliott became chairman. Tooley would remain for nine years until Douglas Reekie, at the time running Northwest Industries in Edmonton, replaced him. Reekie stayed at the helm of CAE for seventeen years until his retirement in October 1985. Apart from wanting him to do a superlative job running CAE, Elliott had an essential condition for Reekie: he was not to agree to sit on any other corporate boards. Elliott wanted him to concentrate solely on CAE business. Elliott and Stikeman then bought out the other Namco shareholders, with the exception of Bart Morgan. The next step was to expand the flight simulator market beyond the military requirements of government. This proved extremely difficult. As to the government contracts, when the Conservatives came to power under Diefenbaker in 1957, CAE hoped for an improvement in governmental procurement relations. To their consternation, they found a changed and almost hostile governmental attitude to private industry – quite different from the Liberals with whom they had dealt before.

The Conservative government was filled with inexperienced idealists, of which the best example was Howard Green who became the minister in charge of the department dealing with CAE. Green's theory was that all government contracts, even those already confirmed, should be renegotiated and thrown open on a worldwide basis to the lowest bidder. CAE had just obtained a fairly good contract to make flight simulators for the Royal Canadian Air Force and to its chagrin, was then informed that pursuant to this new policy, Green wished to reopen that contract and call for new tenders. This meant that the Japanese and the British could both, if they chose, undersell CAE because of lower labour costs, although it was generally accepted that they did not make as good a product as did CAE. After a month or so, it became apparent that CAE's retender offers were being more than matched by the Japanese and by Rediffusion in England. CAE discovered the cause of this through their good contacts in the government. Someone was apparently telegraphing the CAE bids to the opposition, a thing unheard of in any normal business or government environment.

Stikeman remembered one winter afternoon driving to Ottawa with Elliott and Tooley to confront Green with this situation, of which he personally seemed to be completely unaware. Although Stikeman was a lifelong Conservative and had eagerly awaited the return of that party to power, he started the interview with Green by saying that he would prefer five minutes with C.D. Howe, his Liberal predecessor, than five years of that Conservative government. This so surprised Green and their feelings were so evidently sincere that the minister was jolted and listened seriously to the allegations of the telegraphed bids and their praise of the quality of CAE's Canadian product even though it was more expensive.

As a result of their representations, Green relented, and CAE got the contract on the understanding that it would make no profit, itself a surprising position for a Conservative government to take. However, the contract served one very vital purpose: it enabled CAE to pay and keep busy the brilliant group of scientists and engineers it had recruited. Had they lost the contract, the technical teams would have been disbanded and gone to the competition. CAE would have been finished, and today's success story would have disappeared. No one realized this more keenly than the three of them at the time. They drove home from Ottawa in Stikeman's old Buick Roadmaster over icy highways late at night, singing enthusiastically, if not tunefully, until they got to the Stikeman family home in Senneville on the west end of the Island of Montreal. There they stopped, lit a roaring fire, and consumed industrial quantities of whiskey into the small hours of the morning. They had been under tremendous tension for nearly six months and felt they could at last see the future clearly. As it turned out, Tooley was able to generate a few surreptitious cents of profit on the contract. The company survived its worst crisis and soon emerged as a world leader in the simulator field.

It was not long before the CAE balance sheet was strong enough to permit a secondary offering to be made of the stock. This was necessary to establish a value not only for succession duty purposes, but also to create a market for future underwriting. They knew that CAE would have to raise substantial amounts of equity capital if the company were to survive for long in the fiercely competitive world markets. Greenshields had always blown hot and cold on the company, but, nevertheless, because of the friendship of Elliott and Stikeman with R.O. Johnson and Lord Hardinge, both senior players in Greenshields, CAE made them the lead underwriters for the secondary issue in 1962. At this crucial time, Elliott, says Stikeman, again went on a trip abroad. To be fair, this occurred after they had arrived at agreement as to the price and the number of shares to be offered, and everything appeared well settled. However, shortly after Elliott left Montreal and two days before the issue was to go on the market, Greenshields telephoned Stikeman to say that they had decided not to go through with their underwriting commitment. At this point, the stock had been distributed across Canada to various dealers ready to be handed out to subscribers, and the marketing mechanics were complete.

Stikeman was aghast. He pointed out that the underwriting agreement had been signed, that everything was in progress, and that to pull the issue now would be disastrous to the public's confidence in the company. It seemed that Greenshields's only problem was that it feared the market was weakening and would, as they put it, "fall out of bed" before they got the underwritten issue off their hands. Stikeman, uncharacteristically, got extremely angry and threatened legal action and everything else he could conjure up for the occasion, wishing that Elliott had been there to jump on them as well. Greenshields finally capitulated, and the issue went forward. This produced the first real "cash" return the two young partners had ever seen. They each received about $766,476.25 cash and a relatively small number of CAE shares – 14,747 at $24.50 per share, to be held for future growth – making the total value each received $1,277,777. In 1962, there was no capital gains tax, so all the money was theirs to keep.[4] They put some of the cash back into more shares of the company and invested the rest in other securities. Stikeman's final total of CAE stock at the time was 20,000. Elliott had become the largest individual shareholder of the company and served as chairman of the board until his retirement from that position on June 10, 1993.

None of the investments that they made over the next thirty years approached the values that they had seen in their CAE stock. This early offering paved the way for a wider listing of the company, which is now traded in considerable daily volume on the Toronto Stock Exchange and pays a respectable dividend. Elliott had the innovative idea that if the share price could be kept low, CAE shares would be more attractive to a wider spectrum of shareholders, so every time the share price got over about $20, he caused the stock to be split; if the value was around $20, the split was two-for-one and if over $25, three-for-one. Since 1956, the stock has been split into 324 shares for each one then held.[5] Elliott's career has been as much involved with the building of CAE as it has been that of the law firm.

ON WITH THE PRACTICE OF LAW

Following eight years of foreign service, first as ambassador to Chile and subsequently as Canadian High Commissioner to Australia, Colin Fraser Elliott retired from the public service and joined the new firm in 1954 as counsel. This added considerable stature to the firm as well as a network that was unrivalled. The senior Elliott was the first to hoist the firm's flag in Ottawa and maintained what the firm now describes as the "original" Ottawa office. The Canadian Bar Association convention was held that year in Ottawa, and the firm used the occasion to invite leading participants to the senior Elliott's cottage at Gleneagles on the Gatineau River, some 15 miles from Ottawa near Kirk's Ferry, for refreshments, cocktails, and a swim on August 30, providing, as the invitation stated, all the required transportation – and towels! The Ottawa office was made available to any of the firm's lawyers who might have business in the nation's capital and was often used in particular by Stikeman on his many forays to the Departments of Finance and National Revenue, and by Jim Robb, who was developing an administrative law practice, which called for many meetings with federal regulators. When Elliott retired, the office fell into disuse and was "temporarily" abandoned.

TAMAKI, TURNER, AND OTHERS

George Takakasu Tamaki was a consummate tax lawyer and a delightful person who had had to overcome many difficulties just in order to become a lawyer. He was a first-generation Canadian, born of Japanese parents on October 25, 1916, in New Westminster, BC. He attended the University of British Columbia, obtaining a BA in economics in 1938. He then enrolled in law at Dalhousie University, where he spent his first year, going to the University of Saskatchewan for the second year and returning to Dalhousie for the final year, graduating near the top of his class in 1941. He served his articles with the Halifax firm of Pearson, Rutledge & Donald until February 1942, when Pearl Harbour had by then brought Japan into the war. Despite being eligible to be called to the Nova Scotia Bar, the chief justice of Nova Scotia, Sir Joseph Chisholm, would have none of it, clearly because of Tamaki's Japanese ancestry. Following a letter of protest from Professor James Gibson of UBC to the Nova Scotia Barristers' Society, Chief Justice Chisholm was urged to reconsider, but he refused to do so until well after the war was over, and Tamaki would be called to the Nova Scotia Bar only in 1946.

There was more. During the war, there was a government program (that followed immediately upon the institution of a similar program in the United States in February 1942) for internment of Japanese Canadians, and his family was sent away from the coast to the interior of British Columbia, where Tamaki joined them for much of 1942 and 1943. Circumstances improved to the point that he was permitted to attend the University of Toronto in the fall of 1943, and he received an LLM the next spring. For the next two years, however, the only work he could get was with Richard De Boo, the legal publisher, but he later got a job with the Saskatchewan CCF government of Tommy Douglas in Regina and was called to the Saskatchewan Bar, also in 1946. De Boo arranged for him to move to Toronto to continue his work in the publishing field. It was during this period that he met Stikeman, who eventually persuaded him to leave De Boo's offices in Toronto and come to Montreal, with premises in the Foster offices, where he was still attached to the publishing company as assistant editor of the *Canada Tax Service*.

The idea of persuading Tamaki to join the new firm was born on the famous evening at Stikeman's train table, but it took a few months for the cautious Tamaki to decide to cut his ties with De Boo. He also had to qualify for the Quebec Bar, which he did in June 1952 and immediately thereafter became part of the firm. By the time he was ready to be admitted to the Quebec Bar, it was clear to everyone that Tamaki, by then thirty-five years of age, was not only a person of absolutely impeccable character, but also an outstanding lawyer, so he was not put through the full process of rigorous examination. He was given only a pro forma oral examination for the purpose, consisting of a single tax question, an implicit recognition of his standing. Tamaki certainly knew far more about the subject matter than did any combination of his "examiners" at the time. He recalled with amusement that when the time came for him to swear the requisite oath, he was asked whether he was to swear on the Bible! He also enjoyed hearing, while sitting one day out in the yard of his cottage on Chateauguay Lake, a fisherman, while pointing at the property, say that it belonged "to a big Chinese lawyer from Montreal."

William Grant joined the firm for a short period of time to do litigation, but soon returned to the more comfortable establishment quarters at what is now Ogilvy Renault.[6]

The next recruit was John Turner, a future prime minister of Canada. His name first appeared on the firm's masthead in 1955.[7] Turner proved to be a gifted lawyer. As the first of many students who became lawyers with the firm, he pleaded some tax cases with Stikeman, mainly before the Income Tax Appeal Board, but occasionally in the Exchequer Court of Canada and the Supreme Court of Canada, a couple of which were particularly noteworthy. One, which is still a leading case, was *The Royal Trust Company v. M.N.R.* [1957] CTC 32, in which the issue was whether membership fees in business clubs could be deducted for tax purposes. The case was heard before the formidable president of the Exchequer Court of Canada, Joseph Thorson. Stikeman let Turner do some of the cross-examination and lead the evidence of the chairman of the client, Conrad Featherstonhaugh Harrington, who, says Turner, was the most magnificent witness he had ever encountered. The club fees at issue were for the St James's Club in Montreal, then located on University Street, where Place Ville Marie now stands. Turner asked him how often he went there. "About two or three times per week." And how is the food? "Quite ordinary," he was told. Did he go there for business? He would not go there otherwise, Harrington assured him. At this point, Thorson intervened. You say the food is not extraordinary? "It is adequate," came the response, "but no better." Had he ever put together a deal over lunch at the club? Harrington thereupon reeled off several deals, including some for Shawinigan Power (one of the companies that later became Hydro-Québec) and Bell Canada, which had amounted to something in excess of a billion dollars, impressive numbers, especially in the 1950s. When he had finished with his questions, Thorson turned to the Department of Justice lawyer, Keith Eaton, and asked him whether he had any further questions or "should they wind this up now?"

Turner had another case involving some Mennonites from Lethbridge, who came dressed in tall black hats to see him. They had been designated as a church and were, accordingly, free of income tax. This status had been challenged by the Department of National Revenue, which had been very aggressive in its pursuit of the matter. Turner asked the clients whether they really were a church and accepted their invitation to come out to Alberta to make his own inspection. He asked why they were coming to see him instead of getting local counsel. They said they could not get anyone in Alberta to represent them as the matter had become viciously political. The leader of the Mennonites then peeled off a large number of thousand dollar bills, saying they were ready to pay the full costs of having good representation. When Turner recounted this to Stikeman, the latter said, "Suddenly, I am very interested in this case." Because of the political factors involved, they were forced to go all the way to the Supreme Court of Canada, which ruled unanimously in their favour. Tamaki had a somewhat similar experience, years later, when visited by three members of the Mennonite community. The elder asked Tamaki what his hourly rate was, and Tamaki, somewhat embarrassed, told him, whereupon the elder took out a wad of cash and put on the table an amount that would pay for an hour's worth of advice. Tamaki remarked, after the fact, that it was amazing how that concentrated the mind.

Turner gradually branched off from tax into other fields and did more and more corporate work for Elliott, with whom he developed a closer relationship than he had with Stikeman. Turner learned how to draft short contracts from Elliott, who was the finest draftsman of short contracts he had ever seen. He remembers one day asking Elliott if one of his two secretaries, Mary Spraklin or Margot Quinn, could do a particular job for him. Elliott said, in typical fashion, "You do it. Her time is far more valuable than yours." Turner agrees. He and Elliott were bachelors in those days, and after office hours, they were often found dining, not always alone, at well-known establishments of the day, such as Mother Martin's, Drury's, and the Maritime Bar at the Ritz Carleton. For a number of years on Fridays, Turner would get a lift from Elliott as far as Kirk's Ferry in the Gatineau, where the senior Elliott had his cottage, and then be met and taken up to visit friends in Manawaki, return from there to Kirk's Ferry on Sundays, and thence to Montreal. Turner's apartment at 1536 Summerhill Avenue, near Guy and Sherbrooke Streets, became the location of the early Christmas parties after they outgrew Elliott's small flat in the Gleneagles Apartments on Côte des Neiges. The parties, he maintains, were always great and not always fully politically correct, although even in the early days, he says, he always arranged for cabs to take the participants home so that no one was driving after all the good food! Later on, the parties became too large to manage in their apartments, so they moved to clubs for the occasions. Turner claims to have introduced Elliott to Betty Anne McNicoll, whom Elliott was later to marry.

While a student in Paris in 1952–53, during one of the many periods of student activism that particularly characterized French university students, especially within the context of relations with the government, Turner was added as a member of the *Comité des Sept,* self-charged to deal with *les autorités* on behalf of the students. He was designated as the representative of the international students. The *Comité* had many negotiations with the government, represented at the time by François Mitterand, then a powerful minister of the Interior. It is a sign of the quality of the briefing afforded to French officials, says Turner, that many years after the event, when Mitterand was president of France and Turner a federal cabinet minister, Mitterand remarked to him that he thought the occasion of their meeting in Canada was not the first time they had encountered each other.

Turner has a wonderful recollection of getting a major client. While at a restaurant in the Communist section of Paris with his *Comité* colleagues, celebrating the gains achieved as a result of their negotiations, Turner noticed a well-known Canadian industrialist, no longer alive, having dinner *à deux* with a gorgeous woman. He draws, expressly, no conclusion, even today, regarding the propriety of the combination, while nevertheless taking due note that the restaurant would have been well off the normal beaten track for major industrialist dining. Turner knew him, and he knew Turner. Turner gave no sign of his recognition, but did make certain that he walked by their table on his way out of the restaurant. Turner said nothing of this to anyone, including his father, who would have been delighted with the gossip, then nor ever after. A few years later, Margot Farrell, the firm's receptionist, rang Turner's office in high excitement to say that the industrialist, whose name was a household word in Canadian business, was in the reception area waiting to see him. The industrialist had a major mandate in respect of which he wanted to retain Turner so that Turner would get the credit for bringing in the business not one of the partners. Turner is convinced that this was a reward for his years of absolute silence, and even when Elliott wondered aloud how on earth the welcome business had come to the firm through Turner, his lips remained sealed.

Over and above the corporate work for Elliott, Turner branched out into litigation in the maritime field and some transportation law, but despite having clients like Cast and Eastern Canada Stevedoring, he was not able to crack the shipping establishment. He did some early criminal cases, but that did not continue because Elliott did not like the reception area filled with clients of that sort. He became Elliott's "hit man" for CAE problems. Maritime work, which eventually flowed to David Angus, who would develop it into a specialty, was generally in the area of cargo and insurance claims, in which he competed primarily with William Tetley and Jean Brisset, and there were a number of other stevedoring clients. He handled a case for John Colford Contracting Company that arose when cracks appeared in the bathtubs installed in the new flagship Hilton Queen Elizabeth Hotel.

In transportation litigation, Turner was once in Winnipeg on a rate case, having been retained by the Canadian Truckers Association. The railways had co-opted, he says, all the good lawyers, such as John L. O'Brien (father of Peter O'Brien), so the truckers were left with a relatively inexperienced young lawyer. He was appearing against one of the icons of Canadian law, Isaac Pitblado, who had been hired by Ian Sinclair of the CPR, and furthermore, Turner was competing with Pitblado in Winnipeg, his home territory. He was again before Thorson, P. of the Exchequer Court of Canada, who said just prior to the beginning of a recess, "Turner, I want to see you in my chambers." Once there, Thorson said, "This is not a good day to be appearing against Mr Pitblado." "Why," asked Turner? "Why?" responded Thorson, "Because it is his ninetieth birthday, and I am certainly not going to rule against Mr Pitblado on his ninetieth birthday." Thorson then went on, "If you were smart, you would rise in court after this recess, congratulate Mr Pitblado on his birthday, and suggest that we all retire to the Manitoba Club to celebrate this auspicious occasion." After the recess, Turner got to his feet to say, "My Lord, on a question of procedure, I want to congratulate Mr Pitblado, an exemplary member of the Bar, on his birthday, and to suggest that we should not be proceeding on this matter on such an occasion, but that we should, instead, adjourn to the Manitoba Club to celebrate this milestone in a more appropriate manner." Thorson replied, "Turner, that is one of the few smart things you have ever said before me. We will adjourn. Lunch will be on counsel, and you will get the account for it, but I will preside." Thorson had also taken the precaution of advising the *Winnipeg Free Press*, which just happened to have a photographer handy, and there was a front-page story proclaiming, "Bench and Bar Honour Isaac Pitblado." Counsel on the case got the bill and paid for Thorson's party.

In addition to being an excellent lawyer, from the time of his arrival in Montreal, Turner became interested in politics. At the municipal level, he was Jean Drapeau's English-speaking organizer in two elections, in which Drapeau lost once to Sarto Fournier in 1957 and won the next in 1961. This experience served only to whet Turner's own appetite to enter partisan politics, which he did shortly thereafter, winning a seat as Member of Parliament from the incumbent Progressive Conservative member, Egan Chambers, in the general election of June 18, 1962, in the riding then known as St Lawrence-St George in downtown Montreal. His campaign manager was John Claxton, son of Brooke Claxton, a former minister of Defence, whose son, Ted, is now a partner of the firm. This election proved to be the beginning of the country's farewell to the Diefenbaker government, which barely retained power, with 116 seats, to one hundred for the Liberals, thirty for the Social Credit, and nineteen for the NDP. Less than a year later, in a new general election held on April 8, 1963, the Liberals won 129 seats, with the Progressive Conservatives getting ninety-five, the Social Credit, twenty-four, and the NDP, seventeen.

The riding was bounded by Guy Street to the west, St Denis Street to the east, Jean Talon to the north, and the St Lawrence River to the south. It was composed roughly of thirds: one-third francophone, one-third anglophone, and one-third allophone. It included Montreal's red-light district. Turner remembers a phone call from a woman by the name of Pamela Ambrose, who ran a couple of houses of ill repute on Stanley or Drummond Street above Sherbrooke Street. She called his office in Ottawa not long after his election to say that the City of Montreal had put a couple of No Parking signs in front of her establishment, and this was having an adverse effect on her business. He explained that he was a federal MP and had no jurisdiction whatsoever in municipal affairs. Ambrose was unmoved by this protestation and told him to call "his friend Jean Drapeau" to get the matter fixed. Turner called Drapeau's executive assistant to explain the situation. The offending signs were gone within an hour. This was, he recalls, his first lesson in politics of not letting jurisdiction interfere with getting a problem solved.

In 1965, having accepted an invitation to join the cabinet of Lester B. Pearson's Liberal government as minister without portfolio, he was required, to avoid any possible conflict of interest, to leave the firm of which he had by then become a nominal partner, with his name as part of the firm's name. Turner had an excellent career in public service, holding many important ministerial positions, including Transport, Consumer and Corporate Affairs (called at the time Registrar General), Justice, and Finance.[8] He ran for the leadership of the Liberal Party in April 1968, but he lost to Pierre Elliott Trudeau, then riding the wave of popularity that would give rise to the description of "Trudeaumania," and who became prime minister on April 20, 1968. When Turner first left politics, resigning as minister of Finance on September 10, 1975 although remaining as a Member of Parliament until 1976 for Ottawa-Carleton for which he had run since 1968, the firm made a concerted effort to get him back, but he would not commit to staying out of politics in the future. (The "call," he was wont to say, might come at any time.) So the effort came to naught, and he joined the McMillan Binch firm in Toronto on February 14, 1976. He did go back to the political arena in the spring of 1984 when Pierre Elliott Trudeau resigned. His political friends called him while he was on vacation in Jamaica and asked, "What are you going to do?" He re-entered the fray, won the leadership convention on June 16, 1984, and became prime minister for a time beginning June 30, 1984, running out of Vancouver Quadra at the urging of John Farris, but at the end of the Trudeau era, the country wanted a change. The Liberals went down to heavy defeat in the general election of September 4, 1984.[9] He retired for good in 1990, going to Miller Thomson in Toronto, where he remains to this day.

Looking back almost fifty years later on his early days at the new firm, Turner reflects that he had never had so much fun in the practice of law as with the small group that had decided to take on the establishment in Montreal. It was a great atmosphere, with everything out in the open. Turner was earmarked by Elliott as someone who could run the firm when Elliott decided to withdraw from daily activity to run Namco, and he was already doing a good deal of the daily administration as well as recruiting. Once he got to that stage, Stikeman told him that since he was doing much of the management of the firm, he should no longer observe the protocol of referring to him as "Mr Stikeman." Turner identified James Robb and recruited J. Hamilton Quain from Ottawa, one of the early lawyers to combine law with a chartered accountant designation, although Quain returned to Ottawa almost as soon as he was called to the Bar to practise with his father's firm. As a member of Grey's Inn, Turner was a member of the Barbados, Jamaica, and Trinidad Bars, and Elliott encouraged him to keep up his membership despite the fact that apart from a small amount of work on some of the Alcan problems with bauxite in Jamaica, the firm had little, if any, work in the Caribbean. It was, however, exotic enough in a small Montreal firm, to have someone who could, if necessary, act in those jurisdictions. In 1960, with the encouragement of both Stikeman and Elliott, he became president of the Quebec Junior Bar Association, something that was hard to do in those days from the political base of a small and out-of-the-box firm.

James A. Robb[10] had been recruited by Bill Hulbig after being prospected by Turner, along with Hamilton Quain, as the first "student" to be hired by the new firm. As a result of Hulbig's efforts, Robb decided not to accept an offer he had received from the Chauvin Martineau Walker firm and joined in 1955, lured at least in part he admits with full candour, by the fact that he was offered much more money than by the other firm. He and Turner were the juniors of the day, and both worked hard at generating the team spirit that helped make the new firm cohesive, playing bridge with the staff at lunch and once the institution of the firm Christmas party was established, making sure that between them, everyone was asked to dance. After serving as the site for some of the early parties, Turner's basement apartment on Summerhill Avenue, furnished in a "passionate purple" that the handsome bachelor of the day evidently regarded as "cool," was later used for the less formal and far more entertaining aftermaths, during which their livers were exposed to considerable risk.

One year, over the Grey Cup weekend, Robb was helping Elliott with a deal that was to close in Ottawa on the day of the game. Apart from his legal responsibilities in relation to the file, Robb's principal and overriding assignment was to ensure that there would be a television set for Elliott's room so that they could watch the game. This occasion occurred early enough, in the mid-1950s, that televisions were not nearly as common as they are now. Try as he might, Robb could not wrest confirmation from the hotel that a set would be available, and despite many efforts to get such assurances, he was forced to report to Elliott on the morning of the game that he had failed to accomplish his mission. Upon hearing this, Elliott immediately picked up the phone to announce that, "This is Mr Elliott, and I want a television set up here, right now." Sure enough, a set was delivered within ten minutes. It transpired that Elliott had arranged the entire performance in advance, including the hotel's refusal to supply a set in response to Robb's pleadings.

Gerald McCarthy[11] was a reserved and cerebral lawyer whose field of practice was corporate law, in which he was a thorough and capable drafts-man. He, like Turner, learned the art of crisp drafting from Elliott. He had articled with the established firm of Martineau Walker and had been a classmate of Quain. No one was ever certain why he agreed to join such a frontier operation as the new firm, but he provided excellent support for the business aspects of tax planning and the business law in which Elliott was active. He worked, in particular, on many of the mandates generated by Elliott from the Canadian Imperial Bank of Commerce.

Thomas McKenna[12] had been at the predecessor firm of Foster Hannen following his call to the Bar in 1947 and then went to the Montreal Stock Exchange until 1956, when he joined the new firm. He stayed for only a year before leaving to become a partner in Stewart Crépeau & McKenna, also a new firm that began to carry on business in Montreal. Elliott thought he was a good lawyer but perhaps too gentle and not forceful enough to generate much business on his own account. Jean Monet,[13] who joined in 1957, had a varied practice, but he eventually became expert in the field of estate and succession planning, in which he became recognized as a creative planner. Monet's connection with the firm was primarily the result of Stikeman's friendship with his father, Fabio Monet, the first chairman of the Income Tax Appeal Board. In Monet's family, apparently most of the males, with the exception of his father, had a tendency to die quite young, often before they reached fifty years. Monet always drove fast cars and lived at the edge of things, like someone who did not expect to be around all that long. To everyone's surprise, including his own, he survived.

Pat Thorsteinsson,[14] a gifted tax practitioner originally from Vancouver, joined the new firm in 1958, and he developed into an excellent tax litigator. Thorsteinsson had been working at Davis & Co. in Vancouver for a few months when John Boland at the legal branch of the Department of National Revenue called him to follow up an application he had sent some months earlier. Thorsteinsson accepted the offer. The legal branch was quite large at the time, with fifteen or twenty lawyers, including Robert Bourassa, later premier of Quebec. These lawyers argued the cases before the Tax Appeal Board and acted as juniors in the Exchequer Court cases for the agents appointed on behalf of the Crown. At the time, these were normally political appointments. He left the legal branch, having been recruited after a couple of years by Arthur Patillo at Blake Cassels & Graydon in Toronto, where he was the first in the firm to do nothing but tax. Stikeman had been up in Ottawa to see John Boland at National Revenue, saying he was looking for litigation help. Boland pointed him toward Thorsteinsson, and in late 1957, Stikeman persuaded him to come to Montreal and write the Bar examinations the following spring. He appeared with Stikeman in *Gorkin v. M.N.R.* [1962] CTC 245 before the Supreme Court of Canada, a succession duties appeal in which a transfer of family company shares was held to have been a gift rather than a transfer for consideration or partial consideration. He assisted Stikeman and Turner in the *Colford* appeal in the Supreme Court of Canada and was with Stikeman and Donald Johnston in the *Hollinger North Shore Exploration* appeal in the same court.

The west remains a powerful magnet for those who have grown up there, even though Thorsteinsson thought that Montreal between 1957 and 1964 was one of the finest and most vibrant cities in North America. But by 1964, Thorsteinsson decided that if he was ever going to go back to Vancouver, it would have to be before his four-year-old daughter began school. As the fates would have it, he had two or three ongoing cases in Vancouver that called for him to visit from time to time, and on a trip there in March 1964, there were three beautiful days in a row. That clinched the matter for him, and by August, he was back in Vancouver. When he told Stikeman that he was going, Stikeman was typically enthusiastic and said that would be great; he could be "their man" in Vancouver. Thorsteinsson had to tell him that this was not going to work and that such an arrangement was not what he had in mind, since he wanted to start his own firm. It was, however, a very amicable separation, and he had several appearances in the Supreme Court of Canada thereafter with Stikeman, including the appeals in *Johnston Testers, George Steer,* and *Dobieco.* They had an amusing contretemps in the *BC Power* appeal in the Supreme Court of Canada when Thorsteinsson appeared on behalf of the Crown and Stikeman appeared on behalf of the taxpayer. In the course of his argument, Stikeman referred to a case, the name of which he could not recall, so he turned to Thorsteinsson, his former junior and now opponent, and said, "Pat, what was the name of that case?" and Thorsteinsson automatically responded with the name in mid-argument.[15]

Stikeman spent his whole life trying to be in more than one place at once, taking on far too many things at the same time. In litigation, he never allowed himself enough time to prepare, which of course was one of the reasons he had gone looking for someone like Thorsteinsson. Thorsteinsson remembers a time when they were up in Ottawa together. The previous case had run over, which meant that they had an extra day to prepare. Stikeman spent it in the library. Thorsteinsson was very impressed with what Stikeman could do with the additional time for preparation. Stikeman was great to work for, especially since there was too much for him to do. Every time he opened a door, he seemed to be assuring a client that he could do everything. In dealing with Thorsteinsson, there was no question of Stikeman keeping anything to himself in terms either of preparation or argument of a case, and there were no restrictions whatsoever on the younger lawyers that would prevent their development. Stikeman needed someone to prepare his cases for him, and the junior lawyers were able to take on as much responsibility as they wanted. In the early days of the firm, they had probably more good tax mandates arising out of Toronto than anywhere else because the firm was from out of town, and it was therefore safe to refer work to it. This model was responsible in part for the design of the niche practice for Thorsteinsson's own firm in Vancouver. They had a close relationship with Arthur Gilmour (who married Stikeman's secretary, Lil Armstrong) of Clarkson Gordon & Co. and his sidekick Phil Nutt. There was, he says, always litigation arising out of Gilmour's schemes because he was forever well past the edge of what National Revenue considered reasonable. In all their efforts, they were backed up by George Tamaki, who was unquestionably the best tax solicitor in the country.

Donald J. Johnston,[16] an individual of great talent, joined the firm in 1961 and soon became one of the leading corporate lawyers in Montreal. His initial connection with the firm was as a student in 1958, when he was paid $80 per month to help see him through the winter. He had arranged for an accelerated study program, with two years of arts at McGill University, followed by three years in law, in the course of which he won the gold medal as the top student in the faculty. Turner and Robb invited him to lunch to persuade him to join the firm. He had something of a dilemma as a result of an archaic rule of the Quebec Bar, which in order to practise law in the Province of Quebec, one had to have a Bachelor of Arts degree and to have studied Latin and philosophy. Not only that, but this had to be accomplished four years prior to a call to the Bar. A Nobel Prize winner in astrophysics, who had taken a law degree thereafter, would not have been able to practise in Quebec because he did not have a BA.

Although this nonsensical rule has since disappeared, it was a hurdle for Johnston. He won a Macdonald Travelling Scholarship to attend the Université de Grenoble for a year, and on his return, he persuaded the redoubtable dean of arts at McGill, C.D. Solin, to credit that year toward his BA and to allow him to do a fourth year of arts while studying the fourth year of law (the precursor to the current Bar admission program) at the Université de Montréal. Even with all these arrangements in place, he still did not have the requisite four years of elapsed time after this late-awarded arts degree, so the firm paid for a private bill before the Quebec Legislature. It was then still a bicameral house, and the bill was introduced in the assembly by Harry Blank and in the Upper Chamber by George Marler. The moment the bill was passed, Turner took Johnston to the bâtonnier to be sworn in as an advocate. He became much admired in the firm, and while the others were important lawyers, Johnston was the one who both Stikeman and Elliott had identified as having the most potential to develop into a real superstar. Thorsteinsson, with whom he did a lot of work, always thought that Johnston was the best all-round lawyer in the group and that he had a remarkable degree of wisdom even though he was only twenty-seven years old.

Johnston learned a great deal from both partners, but particularly from Elliott who taught him the importance of recognizing that clients, not necessarily the lawyers, were the asset of the firm. He remembers the vital lesson of keeping his clients informed. Elliott had given him something to handle on behalf of the Mercantile Bank, a matter that was drifting along waiting for some others to complete their part of the negotiated arrangements. Elliott asked him how things were going, and Johnston reported that he was waiting for the others to act. "But," said Elliott, "does Henry [the Mercantile executive] know that?" It was Elliott's way of reminding Johnston of the importance of making sure the client knew exactly what was going on at every stage and that you were on the job.

Elliott was smart in terms of judging people and events. The firm had always paid somewhat more, although not hugely, for its lawyers from the very start and did not have the ingrained attitude of some of the older firms that "some day, all of this will be yours." On the other hand, Johnston learned the hard way about negotiating for salary with Elliott. When he started as a lawyer, he was to meet with Elliott to discuss his remuneration. Elliott pre-empted the process by asking him how much he wanted. Johnston, not knowing enough about such discussions ("My brother [David] would never have negotiated with Elliott that way," he admits), said "$400 per month." Elliott agreed, and Johnston left the office knowing he had just learned a lesson.

Johnston remembers an occasion when Turner's office door was closed. Turner generally had the policy of keeping his door open all the time except when he had a client with whom he was discussing something, in which case he was not to be disturbed. A call on the firm's single night line, intended for Turner, had somehow been forwarded to Elliott's office, and Elliott was making his way down the hall to Turner's office, where he encountered Johnson, who said, "But Mr Elliott, the door is closed." Johnson says Elliott had a particular Archie Bunker look, which he seemed to have perfected. He gave Johnston "the look" and said, "Well, why don't you open it?" It was not unlike Elliott's style when giving directions. He would go into great detail, but then he would say, "You come to a stop sign." And then he would add, deadpan, "and you stop."

Turner, then in charge of recruiting for the firm, had in the process found Jim Grant, made the initial contacts with François Mercier (of whom more will be said later), and was the person who first recruited Stanley Hartt, having known both Hartt's brother Joel and his father, Morris, who had been a Member of Parliament in the Montreal riding of Cartier from 1947 until his death in 1949. Turner remembers, while seeking support for the nomination in St Lawrence-St George, having lunch in a restaurant on St Antoine Street opposite the old Court House, and there meeting Hartt's uncle, Samuel Gallay, who said that he must know his nephew, Stanley. Turner did not. Well, he was informed, you should if you think you are going to run for office because he is the president of the Liberal Club at McGill University, which was located in the middle of his riding. They met, Turner ran, and he recruited Hartt.

James A. Grant[17] was the last of the original lawyers who practised with the firm in the Bank of Canada building. Don Johnston remembers the office Christmas party in 1961, which was held at the Montreal Badminton & Squash Club. At the time, Grant was a fourth-year student, very quiet and reserved, but when everyone was called upon to say something on the occasion, he gave a very witty review about each of the lawyers in the firm. As for Elliott, Grant observed that he was walking down the hall in the office one day when he encountered Elliott coming the other way, cigar in hand, and he wondered to himself whether Elliott had even the faintest idea who he might be. His worst suspicions were confirmed as they passed, when Elliott said, "Hi, fella."

The business of building the firm continued, with Elliott concentrating on the corporate sector and Stikeman on both tax planning and tax litigation. Both were assiduous in courting the chartered accounting firms as sources of business. The accounting firms had not yet begun their assault on the legal aspects of tax practice that would lead them into full competition with law firms rather than being active mainly in the area of compliance. Much of the firm's early business was directed to it from the accounting sector, to Stikeman because he understood tax, and to Elliott because he could understand the accountants. In addition to the tax planning that was the main element of the tax practice, there was always ongoing negotiation with the taxation authorities on behalf of clients in the effort to settle cases that might otherwise go to court.

Good settlements are often achieved when the other side is concerned that it might be out-lawyered, and this healthy attitude required regular maintenance by taking cases to court when necessary to keep the younger generations of assessors and governmental tax lawyers in the appropriate awe of Stikeman. That does not necessarily require winning all one's appeals but merely demonstrating that any case can, and will, be prepared and presented at a level that will give pause to one's opponents in their contemplation of pushing a case with any weakness as far as the courtroom. It also means being able to prove, to the satisfaction of a court, representations of fact made to the taxation authorities prior to litigation. Stikeman often claimed that tax cases were 90 per cent fact, 5 per cent law, and 5 per cent good counsel work, not to belittle either of the latter portions, but to emphasize the importance of getting the facts straight.

Tax litigation continued. Stikeman and Turner took the question of goodwill before the Exchequer Court of Canada in *Losey v. M.N.R.* [1957] CTC 146, only to be told that the legal principles were quite different from the commercial and accounting concepts and that payments for goodwill might well be taxable as benefits to the transferor. Later the same year, he and Turner lost an argument that timber licences had been acquired for purposes of cutting timber and were accordingly capital assets free of tax on disposition when the court held, in *Gillies Brothers & Co. v. M.N.R.* [1957] CTC 190, that the company had an original intention either to cut timber or to sell the licences at a profit. Stikeman appeared as counsel before the Exchequer Court of Canada in the leading case of *Curran v. M.N.R.* [1957] CTC 384, which established the principle that receipt of an inducement to accept employment was itself remuneration, subject to tax. The case of *Western Leaseholds Ltd. v. M.N.R.* [1959] CTC 531 went all the way to the Supreme Court of Canada. Once the critical finding of fact was made that the various agreements were all contemplated in the letters patent of the company, Stikeman was able to argue (with Robb) that this followed a constant jurisprudence to the effect that all receipts from any of such activities were income. In *Sterling Paper Mills Inc. v. M.N.R.* [1960] CTC 215, Stikeman and Thorsteinsson won an important victory when they successfully argued that more than mere intention eventually to dispose of an asset is required to turn the resulting gain on its disposition into income as opposed to a capital gain.

More or less in the same line of cases, testing the judicial doctrines of intention and secondary intention as the principal indicators of whether gains should be treated as capital or income, Stikeman and Robb were unsuccessful in *Archambault v. M.N.R.* [1962] CTC 176 in persuading the court that a gain resulting from the sale of a property that could not be zoned for development should be capital. Stikeman argued the case of *Bell v. M.N.R.* [1962] CTC 253 by himself, in which he tried to argue that a consulting arrangement following the sale of shares should be regarded as part of the proceeds of the sale of the shares (a non-taxable capital gain) and not as ordinary income. One of the most important Canadian tax cases dealing with the principles of timing of income recognition is *M.N.R. v. John Colford Contracting Co.* [1962] CTC 546, which was argued by Stikeman, Turner, and Thorsteinsson in the Supreme Court of Canada. It stands for the proposition that amounts held back in the progress of construction contracts are not to be recognized as income until there has been acceptance of the work done in the form of an architect's or engineer's certificate.

GETTING READY TO MOVE UPTOWN

In the late 1950s and early 1960s, there was a commercial building boom in Montreal with the construction of several new office buildings, located away from the former financial district of Montreal on St James Street, on Dorchester (now René-Lévesque) Boulevard. These were the early days of the post-Duplessis era in Quebec,[18] which eventually led to the election of the Lesage Liberal government as the old Union Nationale imploded under a suc-cession of interim leaders and the huge Expo '67 project got under way. The initial steps in this direction were taken once the decision was made to cover the CNR tracks that entered Central Station from the tunnel under Mount Royal, bringing thousands of commuters into the city each day. Prior to this construction, the area between Mansfield Street to the west and University

Street to the east was open, and there was a bridge over the excavation that looked like a large quarry right in the middle of the downtown area. At that time, the only building of significance along Dorchester Boulevard was the venerable Sun Life Building, at one time recognized as the largest building in the British Empire, which fronted on Dominion Square, occupying the block between Metcalfe and Mansfield Streets across from what was then the Windsor Hotel on Peel Street.[19]

The first new building, known initially as the CIL Building, acknowledging Canadian Industries Limited as its lead tenant, was 630 Dorchester Boulevard, a thirty-two-storey, extremely well-designed and efficient office tower, on the south side between University Street to the west and Union Street to the east. It was built by Greenespoon, Freedlander & Dunne and Skidmore, Owings & Merril, and construction began in 1959. It opened for tenants in March 1961, more than a year ahead of schedule. The next project was the far more ambitious cruciform building, Place Ville Marie, plus three other smaller buildings in the overall concept. Designed and erected by the eccentric William Zeckendorf, it was located directly over the CNR excavation at the south end of the Mount Royal Tunnel, which had to be covered over for the purpose. Even the venerable St James's Club, then on University Street, gave way to this onslaught of new construction. Place Ville Marie would become the headquarters of the Royal Bank of Canada, which moved up town from its former location at 360 St James Street.

The interbank competition spurred the Canadian Imperial Bank of Commerce to commence its own building at the corner of Peel Street and Dorchester Boulevard. The most important question seemed to be which of the banks would have the taller building. Place Ville Marie responded to the challenge with an avante-garde restaurant on top of its office tower called Altitude 737, the height it reached above ground. The commercially testosterone-driven riposte of the CIBC was to add an observation tower at a new forty-fifth floor level and to open the tower to visitors who could survey the whole of the city from this lofty height. The only significant building that was built close to the old financial district during this period was Place Victoria, constructed during 1963–64 with significant financial involvement of the Vatican interests. Shortly thereafter, the Laurentian Hotel at the southwest corner of Peel and Dorchester was demolished, followed many years later by the demise of the old Queens Hotel below Windsor Station on Peel Street. The bus terminal at Stanley and Dorchester was moved east to its present location at the corner of Berri Street and de Maisonneuve Boulevard to link more closely with the new Metro system, then in its infancy.

During this period, the firm was under some pressure to move. It had a lease in the Bank of Canada building, but the bank needed more space for its own expanding activities, and so did the law firm. The expansion of their own business was one of the fundamental issues that Stikeman and Elliott had to face. When they had started, the firm was deliberately designed as a tax and corporate boutique, and they had originally thought that that was the way it should remain. Their success, however, was such that more and more work, and more varied work, kept coming their way, and there was no practical alternative but to take it on. Elliott says this decision was effectively taken out of their hands even though he remained personally convinced that they could have made more money had they remained a small boutique since the early financial results of the firm had demonstrated this to be a successful model.

The combination of this pressure and the firm's close connection with the CIBC led to the decision to take up space in the bank's new building. The firm was the first of its new tenants, occupying approximately two-thirds of the twenty-sixth floor, in early 1962, even before construction had been fully completed. The move itself was another opportunity for the firm to show its entrepreneurial nature. One set of the bank's regular lawyers of the day was Lafleur & Brown, headed up by Max Bolton. The bank asked them to move into the new building on Dorchester Boulevard, but they declined. Elliott, ever with his ear to the business ground, heard about this and immediately offered to move in on the condition that the firm would get more work from the bank. The arrangements were negotiated in a hotel room at the Windsor Hotel between Elliott and Russell Harrison of the CIBC. Naturally, Elliott included in the negotiations options for further space in the building. The desired business relationship with the bank was strengthened, and the other firm suffered. By 1973, Lafleur, Brown was putting out feelers about a possible merger of the two firms. They met with a brick wall. Indeed, although the firm has over the years considered a number of possible mergers with other firms or the acquisition of other practices, it has become a distinguishing feature of Stikeman Elliott that it has never merged. The organization has grown from within and from occasional strategic lateral hires but not through efforts, which are almost always doomed to failure, of trying to mix the differing cultures of two firms.

CHAPTER 3

Moving Uptown – The 1960s

There were still workmen on the floors when the firm occupied a portion of the twenty-sixth floor of the Canadian Imperial Bank of Commerce Building at 1155 Dorchester Boulevard in 1962. Marj Cornell said to anyone who would listen, "This is a public building, not the well-guarded Bank of Canada. The back stairwells are open to all. Anyone can enter the offices, so watch your wallets and purses." This proved to be prescient when Pat Thorsteinsson's wallet disappeared within an hour of occupying his new office.

By the end of the year prior to the move, the firm's billings had reached more than half a million dollars, and the two partners were sharing profits in excess of two hundred thousand dollars.[1] During the 1963 fiscal year that finished on January 31, 1963,[2] the billings of the firm had reached almost $700,000, and the two partners shared equally in the profit, which exceeded $250,000. A singular feature of the times was that profits of a professional firm could be computed on a cash, rather than an accrual, basis. This would eventually change to some degree with the tax reform that was to be enacted effective January 1, 1972, but in the meantime, accounts receivable did not form part of the profits that were distributed (although this would later change as well), and work in progress was irrelevant to the computation of the income of a professional firm. With only two partners, the income of the firm could be timed and controlled very much as they wished, and they chose to operate in a most conservative fashion. Once they had earned sufficient professional income for their personal needs and the amount they decided to share with the other lawyers through bonuses, billings for the year could be controlled, saving many accounts that may have been ripe for immediate billing until a subsequent fiscal period, so that there was always "money in the bank" available for the following year.

At times there were in excess of two years' worth of accounts that could have been billed but which were saved for a possible figurative rainy day. Often, as the year-end approached, Elliott would ask to see, for his approval, all accounts that lawyers proposed to send to clients. That might take an apparently inordinate time from the normally fast-moving Elliott, with the result that the billing lawyer would often not get the draft accounts back until early in the succeeding year, with Elliott's "suggestion" that a new date be affixed before sending them to the client. Nor was it wholly uncommon for Elliott to find in his drawer in early February, as if by accident, some cheques that had been received, but not deposited, prior to the end of the fiscal year just past. Modern management consultants would be aghast at such planning. Elliott also made arrangements to prepay a number of expenses for the succeeding year, which would be taken into account in the calculation of the profit for the previous year on a cash basis. In some cases, he even prepaid the entire year's salaries to certain lawyers when he was satisfied that they were responsible enough not to blow all the money before the end of the year. Elliott notes that there were some lawyers with whom he dared not take such a risk.

To give some idea of remuneration levels of the day, in 1962, George Tamaki had a salary of $20,000 per year but got a bonus of $22,500.[3] Jim Grant's salary was $4,800, with a bonus of $1,500. The next year, Tamaki's salary remained at the same level, but his bonus was $25,000. Grant's salary was increased to $6,000, and his bonus was again $1,500. These were the highest salaries of Montreal lawyers at the time. I remember working forty hours a week as a second-year law student in 1965 at what was then Chisholm, Smith, Davis, Anglin, Laing, Weldon & Courtois[4] for $100 per month and being scandalized, along with the junior lawyers there, when we learned that Stikeman & Elliott was billing Grant's services to clients at the outrageously high rate of $40 per hour. We thought that this was well beyond the bounds of professional propriety and wondered, darkly, when something would be "done" about it.

New premises, however, and the constant expansion of the firm's business meant that even more lawyers could be engaged. The first of these was David Angus,[5] who was called to the Bar in 1963 after working as a student for a summer in the old quarters at the Bank of Canada, and who came on board as soon as he was qualified. Angus had begun working as a student in second-year law on the same day that Grant had started as a lawyer. Angus knew Elliott from their mutual passion for golf, and his and Stikeman's families knew each other. Although Angus was being recruited by two firms that had marine law practices, Stikeman had told his father that there was a place at the firm, and his father encouraged him to take it. Angus had not been interested in becoming a lawyer following his graduation from Princeton in 1959. He had worked at the Montreal *Gazette* during his summers, wrote well, and was fascinated by journalism. He covered the court beat during the summer following his graduation, working with Leon Levinson on the civil side and Al Palmer on the criminal matters. He loved the experience and accepted a full-time job. In mid-November 1959, Charles S. Peters, the publisher, invited him to his office to say that he had demonstrated such perceptiveness regarding the legal beat that he thought he should go to law school and become a lawyer. Peters assured him that he could continue to work for the *Gazette* during the evenings. This was followed by a lunch with William Meredith, dean of the McGill law faculty, who acknowledged that the Princeton degree should be satisfactory for admission. After discussion with his father, who would have preferred that he come into the family ship-ping business, he decided to enter the faculty.

Angus had a bit of a rocky start with Turner, who was running the of-fice logistics, since Stikeman had forgotten to tell Turner that Angus was acting as campaign manager for Peter Kerrigan, the Conservative candidate in Westmount, the riding adjacent to St Lawrence-St George, in the 1963 general election. Turner was quite put out by his failure to show up on the date that Turner had expected, but the rift was soon smoothed over, and they worked together on a number of cases. Angus was struck by the electric atmosphere in the firm and remembers particularly the meetings in the firm's small library, where the lawyers discussed legal problems of every nature. It was an intellectual beehive, immensely stimulating and challenging. He did the usual work for each of Stikeman and Elliott but soon moved into the maritime field that had been pioneered by Turner, later developing this into a specialty practice that he has headed up since the late-1960s.

In September 1963, the firm recruited Maurice Régnier from Duquet, MacKay & Weldon.[6] Régnier had first encountered members of the firm at National Revenue, arguing cases against Stikeman, Turner, and Thor-steinsson. He remembers a lengthy trial against Stikeman before the Tax Appeal Board on a mundane net worth assessment matter, arguing in the annex of the Old Court House in Montreal on an exceptionally hot day in September. There was no air conditioning, and the presiding member of the board, Maurice Boisvert, could not seem to make heads or tails of the case. Stikeman was frustrated with the effort to penetrate the impenetrable and eventually suggested that the case be adjourned to see if a settlement could be reached. It was. On another occasion, this time in a case against John Turner who had not yet gone into politics, in front of Reginald Fordham during an adjournment, Fordham learned that Turner had had a well-publicized dance with Princess Margaret, who had recently visited Canada. Fordham, mused Régnier, was someone who following his morning prayers each day, prob-ably then stood to sing "Rule Britannia." Upon resumption of the hearing, Fordham began to query Turner on this remarkable terpsichorean achieve-ment. Régnier's recollection is that National Revenue lost its case.

Following his departure from National Revenue in 1960 and very shortly thereafter, from the small firm to which he had first gone, Régnier, as a young lawyer with no job and a wife and three children to support, knocked on Stikeman's door, looking for a job. Stikeman said that unfortunately, there was no place in his firm at the time but said that he would make some calls, which he did immediately. One was to De Wolfe MacKay, whose office was then at the Royal Bank Building at 360 St James Street, whom Régnier visited the same afternoon as Stikeman's call. Jacques Tétrault had just decided to leave Duquet MacKay to go to Macklair, Chisholm, Smith,[7] and MacKay needed a young tax assistant. It was Stikeman's attitude that Régnier remembers most. Here was one of the busiest and most distinguished practitioners in his field, dealing with a young lawyer whom he probably barely remembered. But Stikeman took the time to meet with him, and even though he had no position to offer, he attempted to resolve the situation by trying to find him a place with someone else. It was typical of Stikeman that he understood the difficult situation in which Régnier found himself. Stikeman always put human considerations over professional matters to find a satisfactory solution.

About three years later, Régnier was approached by Jean Monet, who asked him to meet with George Tamaki to discuss the possibility of joining the firm. He jumped at the chance, arriving for work on September 1, 1963. As the tax work of the firm developed, Stikeman's practice of involving the other young, non-tax lawyers in his tax appeals dropped off, and the tax work became concentrated in the hands of Stikeman, Tamaki, and Régnier, especially after Thorsteinsson had announced that he was leaving, with Jean Monet handling most of the estate planning. In matters of tax litigation, Stikeman, although always ready to do his part, was also more than willing to give full rein to those helping him in the preparation of the cases, which allowed them to develop the confidence to fly on their own much sooner than would have occurred in other firms. He was a pleasure to work with, and he was careful never to criticize opinions or professional comportment.

Given the huge volume of work that he attracted, Stikeman would often ask juniors to prepare drafts, memoranda, opinions, and court documents for him and did not quibble over minor wording. Until the late 1970s, the firm had a practice of circulating a copy of all outgoing correspondence, using a pink carbon copy, the daily collection of which was referred to simply as the "pinks." The practice was abandoned as the firm grew bigger and the volume of correspondence became too great to review on a timely basis. Reviewing the "pinks," younger lawyers were regularly astonished, flattered, and terrified to see that many of their memoranda to "Stike" had been transformed, verbatim, into letters to clients or submissions to Revenue Canada, signed by Stikeman himself. This practice certainly served to focus their attention on making certain that they were legally sound, and importantly from the perspective of their professional development, written in a manner that Stikeman, a master craftsman of elegant writing, would approve.

The twenth-sixth-floor premises were guarded, as had been the offices at the Bank of Canada Building, by the firm's Mother Superior, "Mrs" Farrell, who sat right behind the glass door in the firm's reception area. She was always "Mrs" Farrell to the junior lawyers, never "Margot," and among her other responsibilities, she was in charge of the hockey tickets, so she enjoyed an additional position of great influence. The firm was still small enough that the Christmas parties could be held in the Red Room of the Windsor Hotel (before graduating to one of the larger rooms in later years), from which those still standing repaired to Don Johnston's bachelor pad on Pine Avenue. As the organization grew bigger, there became more of a sense of separate practice sections within the firm, and Mrs Farrell was heard to lament, "I've lost all my babies!" Increasing size meant that the firm was also able to maintain an active, if of mixed quality, team in the lawyers' softball league. On the business side, an accountant, Al Boudrias, was engaged to run the general offices, accounting, and personnel functions. It was not long before the space on the twenty-sixth floor became too small for the expanding business and it was necessary to move to the thirty-ninth floor, but even that did not suffice for long, and the thirty-eighth and fortieth floors were soon occupied. At the time of writing, the firm has taken over all the floors from thirty-four to forty-five and has far more space than any occupant except the CIBC.

In the early days in the building, the firm had its acknowledged haunts, one of which was Murray's Restaurant on the fifteenth floor, which was used regularly by the lawyers and staff. But, to everyone's great disappointment, it closed at the end of February 1992. The only legacy from the experience is that the firm hired one of its most popular waitresses, Barbara Popowich, who now works in the communications centre. The other favourite place was the Lantern in the adjacent Windsor Hotel, which, too, has disappeared. One of the lamentable side effects of the firm's increased size is that there are no longer convenient hangouts that the lawyers can use to maintain the camaraderie that comes more naturally to a smaller organization.

RITES OF PASSAGE: TAX LITIGATION WITH STIKEMAN

It appeared for a time that no young lawyer's education in the firm was considered complete unless he had participated in one or more tax cases with Heward Stikeman. Almost all of the young lawyers had this unique experience, including Turner, Robb, Johnston, Grant, and Angus, as would many of those who followed them. Many of the cases were landmark tax decisions since routine tax disputes did not need a Heward Stikeman. Other cases were taken on behalf of friends who had become clients and who wanted the comfort of knowing that Stikeman was personally willing to take their case to court, often knowing that it would be an uphill struggle but wanting the comfort of having the best in the country arguing on their behalf.

Stikeman, Thorsteinsson, and Johnston appeared before the Supreme Court of Canada in *M.N.R. v. Hollinger North Shore Exploration Co.* [1963] CTC 51 and won their argument that an overriding royalty based on the value of ore removed from a mine operated by a subtenant of the company was nevertheless income derived from the operation of a mine even though the taxpayer had not itself operated the mine. With Thorsteinsson, he lost the appeal in *Dobieco Ltd. v. M.N.R.* [1963] CTC 143 when the court held that securities in a dealer's inventory could not be written down to less than the quoted market price, partly because it was almost impossible to demonstrate to the court's satisfaction what the right value should be.

Stikeman and Régnier won *Johnson's Asbestos Corporation v. M.N.R.* [1965] CTC 165 before the relatively new president of the Exchequer Court of Canada and former counterpart of Stikeman while in the public service, Wilbur Jackett. The case dealt with the special characteristics of asbestos and the exploration and development of the particular mineral in the Thetford Mines area at Megantic. Because of the nature of asbestos, which is found in small quantities and in small veins, it was held that exploration could be considered as continuing even after significant amounts had already been found, unlike what might have been the case of a gold mine, for example, where once the vein is located, exploration as such ceases. The additional and highly technical issue was whether the expenses could be deducted from income even in respect of the three years' exemption from tax attaching to the operations of a new mine. The minister had argued that the income might well be exempt, but the expenses nevertheless had to be taken into account during that period. The court disagreed and said that all income and deductions relating to the particular source of income (the mine) were to be disregarded, so the deductions were available in the later years in which they had been claimed. The same two were again successful before Jackett, P. in *M.N.R. v. Firestone Management Limited* [1966] CTC 771, where a gain derived from the sale of shares of a subsidiary company was held to be capital and that there had been no conversion of the shares from capital to inventory when a decision was made to sell them to raise money for the parent company.

With Angus and the newly arrived Peter Cumyn, there was limited success in the appeal of *Furness, Withy & Company Limited v. M.N.R.* [1966] CTC 482. They were unsuccessful in persuading the Supreme Court of Canada that income earned in Canada from general stevedoring activities was income attributable to the operation of ships and should, accordingly, be subject to protection under the Canada-UK Tax Agreement. On the other hand, they fended off the minister's appeal against the finding of the Exchequer Court that such activities in respect of their own vessels did so qualify for treaty protection.[8] Cumyn was with Stikeman in the *Western Electric Company Inc. v. M.N.R.* [1969] CTC 274 when the Supreme Court of Canada characterized payments for know-how as similar in nature to rents and royalties, thus making them subject to withholding tax when paid by a Canadian resident. Not long after this case was decided, George Tamaki was retained by the Department of National Revenue to draft the definitive *Interpretation Bulletin* on the subject (IT-303), which I wrote and he made intelligible.[9]

One of the tax plans that attracted a great deal of professional and public attention in the 1960s was the famous "dividend stripping" scheme that Stikeman developed. Canada has always had a taxation policy that contemplated the double taxation of corporate income. Such income was first taxed in the hands of the corporation when it was earned, and the balance was taxed again when it was distributed to individuals in the form of dividends. Naturally, efforts to avoid the second level of tax were rife within the tax community. In addition, because of the second level of taxation, many corporations, especially those that were privately controlled, were reluctant to prepay any such personal taxes, so they did not declare dividends but simply retained the funds within the corporations and used them as required for the business or often just to earn investment income, which tended to be taxed at lower rates than if earned by individuals. Since there was no additional tax extracted if the funds were retained by the corporations, there was also more money to be invested. Over time, huge pools of corporate assets were built up, and the government enacted legislation designed to encourage taxpayers to pay dividends, which would be taxed at a low rate of only 15 per cent. Even that incentive, however, was not sufficient for sophisticated taxpayers and their advisers.

In the infancy of such schemes, it was all too easy for taxpayers to sell the shares of their companies for tax-free capital gains and for the acquiring companies to reimburse themselves by declaring tax-free intercorporate dividends to themselves. This led to the development of a legislative concept of "designated surplus," essentially the existing surplus of the company, the shares of which had been sold, which could not be distributed in the former tax-free manner to the acquiring corporation. Stikeman then set about designing a complicated technique that would, on a very technical interpretation of the statute, allow even such "designated" surpluses to be transmogrified into capital gains. The scheme, which amounted to very aggressive tax planning, attracted huge attention, and large numbers of taxpayers flocked to Stikeman to have their surpluses "stripped" in this manner. Prior to 1972, capital gains were wholly exempt from tax, and the accumulated income, assuming the scheme worked, could effectively be distributed tax-free.

This result drove the taxation authorities mad, and they attacked it with every resource at their disposal including new legislation and the threat of discretionary assessments that might have resulted in full taxation in excess of 50 per cent rather than the special low rate of 15 per cent under the existing legislation. It would have been too much of a risk for most taxpayers to accept, so Stikeman went to Revenue Canada, where because he was Heward Stikeman, he was able to negotiate an extraordinary settlement on their behalf on the basis of which, notwithstanding their failure to elect to have the 15 per cent rate apply, the clients would still be entitled to that beneficial rate. The clients all ended up no worse off than if they had not taken the gamble. Interestingly enough, the attacks by National Revenue were not against Stikeman's plans but against others that had not been as well considered. The taxpayers under attack all came to Stikeman to see if he could save their bacon. One of Stikeman's clients, Conn Smythe, an obstinate "scrapper" by nature, decided that he would nevertheless, together with his feisty friend, Clarence "Hap" Day, fight the matter rather than settle. It was a mark of Stikeman's complete professional honesty that having developed the avoidance technique and having recommended it as technically defensible, he was personally willing to go through the entire court system, all the way to the Supreme Court of Canada,[10] even with someone else's weak case and to go down professionally unrepentant with his client. I remember discussing the case with him a few years later in the context of another tax avoidance plan, by which time he had become philosophical, saying that a lawyer often becomes better known for his losses than for his wins.

LITIGATION: MOVING TOWARD A FULL-SERVICE FIRM

As the firm's status grew and the Montreal legal community was reluctantly forced to acknowledge that not only was Stikeman & Elliott here to stay, but it was also a force to be reckoned with in both tax and corporate law, the firm did not rest on its laurels. There was an area of practice that the firm had not yet occupied – namely, major litigation. We had a wealth of minor accident- and insurance-related matters that were referred by Canadian Universal Insurance, of which Elliott had become a director, that gave Bissonette and Robb plenty of court work. To be a full-service law firm, however, required that it be able to handle important litigious disputes on behalf of clients or risk losing that business and possibly the clients themselves to other firms that could provide a complete range of legal services. Stikeman and Elliott decided that a concerted effort was required to acquire the necessary capacity in the field. They began to cast about to find an established litigator who could attract and hold clients with serious problems of this nature. The need had been demonstrated in the well-known *Cargill* case, arising out of the collapse of the silos and gallery at the company's Baie Comeau grain facility complex. The firm was involved for a time, and many of the younger lawyers worked on the case (instructed by the Mudge Stern Rose Nixon firm in New York), including Bissonette, Turner, Robb, and Johnston. But the firm eventually withdrew from the record when it became clear that it did not have the senior litigation resources to mount a long, major, and complicated trial.

The search led them, through John Turner's initial suggestion, to François Mercier,[11] in practice at the time with Brais, Campbell, Mercier, Leduc & Pepper, who had just won a major case for *Reader's Digest*. Operating on the basis that one had to give a person the opportunity to say "yes," Elliott called Mercier in mid-July 1963, inviting him to have lunch with him and Stikeman at the Embassy Club in the Windsor Hotel. Mercier knew them at the time only by name and as partners of a sophisticated tax and corporate boutique. The lunch was cordial and constructive. They told him they were looking for a court lawyer to establish a litigation practice, which they did not have. Despite a productive association with his firm at the time, Mercier, then forty years of age, recognized an exciting challenge and agreed, subject to becoming a full partner from day one and having his name on the firm letterhead. They all agreed that Mercier would need help in establishing a litigation section, so he brought with him André Brossard, then working as a junior at Brais Campbell.[12] On January 3, 1964, Mercier and Brossard moved to the twenty-sixth floor of the CIBC Building, the firm name became Stikeman Elliott Tamaki Mercier & Turner, effective February 1, 1964, and the litigation section of the firm was born.

By the following year, the three partners entered into the same form of arrangement in the case of the death of any of them that had existed between Stikeman and Elliott since the 1950s, the proportions in the new arrangement being initially five-twelfths of the accounts receivable for each of Stikeman and Elliott and one-sixth for Mercier. The relationship was successful enough that the next year, the proportions changed to 40.352 per cent for Stikeman and Elliott and 19.35 per cent for Mercier. Because Stikeman and Elliott were committed to the concept of a full-service firm, it was the understanding that Mercier would draw the same as Tamaki (approximately $60,000 per year), and the firm's accounts, still kept on a cash basis, were carefully managed by Elliott to ensure that this result was obtained.

Mercier was a brilliant courtroom lawyer. His demeanour was unfailingly calm and polite. He was unrelentingly honest before the judges, which made them trust what he said, an asset that many court lawyers never possess and the lack of which severely limits their effectiveness before the courts, where the judges quickly learn which lawyers can be trusted and which cannot. He had the ability to break the most complex cases into their essential elements and to focus the full force of his presentation and argument on those portions of the case that were the key to success. Cross-examination was gentle but implacably directed at obtaining the admissions that were crucial to the case. Witnesses were led, inexorably, to making the statements or admissions that Mercier had decided were important to him; the slightest discrepancies in a witness's testimony were quietly seized upon, and the hapless witness was gently confronted with them and left with the impossible task of trying to explain the inconsistencies to a court that was invariably fascinated by the mellifluous and seductive voice and the subtle strategy of one of Montreal's finest barristers. Argument was generally short, crystal clear, and directed to the central point of the matter.

The guidance provided to the younger lawyers was second to none. The opportunity to watch and participate in a case organized and presented by someone like Mercier was a post-graduate course in litigation. Almost all of the senior litigation lawyers in the Montreal office today owe a good part of their success before the courts to the example set by Mercier and reinforced by Brossard, although no one has yet matched the supremely elegant courtroom style of Mercier at the height of his powers. But there are many ways to win cases, and the firm has developed a host of lawyers capable of handling the biggest trials and most complex appeals.

Most of the experience of Mercier and Brossard prior to joining the firm had been in insurance-related matters, acting for or against those with insurance backup. Their practice melded well with the more commercial practice that Robb had begun to build up in addition to the insurance-related work already in-house and the related litigation in the firm's marine section, later to become the admiralty section, which focused on cargo claims and the occasional ship collision. They were the recognized "civilians" among the firm's lawyers, and Mercier always had both the *Civil Code* and the *Code of Civil Procedure* side by side on his desk, which he religiously kept free of all other materials. It did not take them long, however, to see the potential offered by the firm to get into major litigation, outside the routine of insurance claims. They were willing to take on any case, whether mainstream or well off the beaten track.

The year Mercier and Brossard arrived also marked the arrival of one of the most unusual talents the firm was to attract in its first fifty years, in the person of Stanley Hartt.[13] He was hired as a student prior to going to Paris on his McGill-awarded Macdonald Travelling Scholarship. Stikeman's daughter, Ginny, was studying in Paris at the same time and when he visited her, he would often meet with Hartt as well to make sure that he would not be going "anywhere else" when he got back to Montreal. When he returned, he was articling at the same time as Michel Vennat, Stikeman's son, Robert, and Paul Labbé. The firm had a nascent predisposition not to hire the children of its lawyers, so Robert, to Stikeman's personal regret, went elsewhere to practise in Ontario. Labbé went into government service – to the Foreign Investment Review Agency, the Export Development Corporation, and later to the Citibank group of companies.

Hartt's first significant encounter with Elliott occurred in the washroom, while they were both staring fixedly at the wall in front of them. Elliott said, "I hear that you are joining us." Hartt was surprised at this since he was not aware that a formal decision had been made. Elliott confirmed it and said that he was glad to have him aboard. Hartt was delighted and asked how he might find out what he would be earning. Elliott informed him that he was, of course, not joining the firm for the money but for the future. "You will get whatever Angus got," announced Elliott on his way out the door. That princely sum was $4,800 per year. When Hartt led the Bar exams in the spring of 1965, Elliott asked him what sort of tangible reward might be appropriate to celebrate the accomplishment. Hartt screwed up his courage and said that he did not think he could live on less than $5,200 per year. He got the $400 raise. Hartt was the first Jewish lawyer hired in Montreal by a non-Jewish firm, breaking what had previously been an unacknowledged barrier in the Montreal legal community.[14] Stikeman and Elliott had earlier tried to hire Alan Golden, but he had gone to Phillips & Vineberg. At lunch one day, Stikeman advised Hartt, in his inimitable disingenuous manner, that he was hired not in spite of being Jewish, but because of it. Clients had been asking whether the firm would hire any Jewish lawyers and, Stikeman said, "in any event, half of them think I am Jewish." I first encountered Hartt in the fall of 1964, during the fourth-year articling period, which has since been replaced by an even more idiotic Bar admission process. At the time, he was happy to try to off-load the court run on a first-year law student who knew nothing about anything and who would not have known a writ from a title deed if it hit him in the face. It was Hartt's considered view, expressed to anyone within earshot, that an orangutan could be trained to do the court run. For a few weeks, I acquired a new appreciation for the intellectual capacity of the orangutan.

Like most of the junior lawyers, Hartt started with Stikeman, but he eventually gravitated toward Elliott. Elliott would send him memos in which he would ask questions without giving any details or context. Hartt remembers getting such a memo as a student, and in it, Elliott simply asked how a trust paid school taxes. Hartt replied that it was according to the religion of the trustee, which then determined whether taxes would be calculated on the basis of the Catholic, Protestant, or neutral panel, the rates of which differed for each. The next instruction was for Hartt to set up a trust that would own some $30 million in real estate. He created a trust, called Canadian Properties Trust, for properties previously owned by corporations resident in Ontario that had been paying taxes on the neutral panel, which was the highest rate but now were owned by the trust thus created, of which

Stikeman was a trustee and Elliott's six children were the residuary beneficiaries. The underlying gift, then required under Quebec law to create a
valid trust, was $10,000, contributed by Elliott. The property tax savings
from the new arrangement exceeded by many times the costs of the trust.
In developing the mechanics of establishing the trust, Hartt, still a student,
was dealing with the Montreal Trust Company, represented for the purpose
by a very senior establishment lawyer from Toronto – John A. Tory. Hartt's
only non-negotiable demand in the whole arrangement was that the closing
occur on April 26, 1965 because he had to get some time to study for the Bar
exams the following month. This turned out to be serendipitous because that
very day, the Pearson government announced a federal budget that prevented
such arrangements in the future. All the parties were convinced that Hartt
must have had personal knowledge of the budget contents, but the innocent
explanation for the closing date of the arrangement had nothing to do with
the budget – just Hartt's need to study for the Bar examinations. The next
task he had from Elliott was to take three pairs of his trousers to Howarths
for alterations. This crucial assignment was, said Elliott with a smile, "just
so you don't get a swelled head."

Hartt has other stories of Elliott's method of training young lawyers.
Elliott on Legal Pedagogy would not be a heavy tome. One day, Hartt
arrived to find on his desk a thick file for J.J. Newbury Co., which related
to the acquisition of some Woolworth stores. It had obviously come from
Elliott, but there was no transmittal memo attached. Hartt went to Elliott
and asked him what he wanted him to do. "Handle it," said Elliott. Did he
have any instructions, persisted Hartt? "Yes," Elliott advised, "I only want
to hear about it once you have done the work, billed it, and I get a call from
the client to say what a good job you have done." Given such clear instructions, he knew exactly what needed to be done.

With the circulation of copies of firm correspondence and memoranda, a
practice that continued until the late 1970s when it became too cumbersome
to maintain in a growing firm, Hartt was able to see the new file-opening
memoranda that Elliott wrote when new matters had been referred to him
and he had in turn delegated them to other lawyers once the file had been
opened. Shortly after he had brought in some business from Steinberg's, the
supermarket chain, Hartt began to notice that few, if any, of these matters
were being sent his way, so he went to Elliott to ask why this was happening. "Because, my boy," he was informed, "you are going to get your own
clients."

Hartt's practice, as was he, was very eclectic. He drifted into labour law
as a result of walking into Elliott's office one day while Elliott was on the
phone discussing CAE matters. The company had plants in several locations
and was having the usual problems with organized labour. Hartt whispered
to Elliott, asking who was on the phone. Elliott covered the mouthpiece and
said, "Jack Spector." Hartt whispered back, "Jack Spector is a Commie."
Elliott then asked him who could handle CAE's labour problems. Hartt immediately pointed to himself, and that was his beginning as a labour lawyer.
He soon became an acknowledged leader in the field. In his early years, he

also did much of the "dog" litigation that François Mercier brought in and would be sent regularly to court to argue cases in which an overall success rate of 45 per cent was regarded as a major triumph. He remembers winning a case on behalf of a client who had run into another vehicle from the rear. Hartt's theory, which worked on this occasion but is not one that has attracted subsequent judicial following, was that a driver was entitled to the expectation that the vehicle in front of him would not stop suddenly due to an accident!

Once, arguing a case on behalf of Montreal Tramways in which there had been a minor collision between a bus and a taxi as the bus was turning into what was then the Place d'Armes terminus, he had what he thought was a clear winner. The bus had been turning into the terminus in a normal manner. A taxi parked there had begun to edge forward as the bus was turning, and the mishap occurred. In the days before no-fault insurance, both sides claimed the other was in the wrong. Fortunately for Hartt, there was an independent witness, a computer expert, who was seated on the bus at the point of impact. The witness gave cogent and uncontradicted evidence as to what had happened: the taxi had edged forward as the bus was making its turn, and it (the taxi) had caused the accident, which would not have occurred but for the forward movement of the taxi. While Hartt was on his feet summing up the evidence and making his argument, the judge told him to sit down, saying that in his thirty years on the bench, he had never heard a case argued on behalf of the Montreal Tramways authorities in which they did not have a carefully prepared witness willing to swear that the accident was someone else's fault. The judge gave judgment forthwith in favour of the plaintiff taxi driver.

Eventually, Hartt became a mediator in labour matters, mainly in order to get out of the protracted negotiations that kept him out of the office for days or weeks on end. His corporate practice was, he confesses, rather dilettantish, but possessing one of the widest-ranging minds of all the lawyers in the firm, he was entirely capable of dealing with any sort of legal problem. One year, he filed more prospectuses for public issues of mutual funds than all other Canadian lawyers combined. Hartt, a bundle of barely controlled energy, was a "pacer"; he could not sit down to work. He paced around his office, around his overloaded desk (which had no useful remaining working surface), and while on the phone, which had a long and inextricably tangled cord, he paced while dictating at high speed; he paced in the corridors while reading complicated documents, often doing several laps of the thirty-ninth floor in the course of reading a long document.

Hartt was a colourful character. Over the years, he experimented with a variety of Afro hairstyles, to which his wiry hair seemed to have a particular affinity. His office was cluttered, as was his personal life, which was always chaotic. He was a complete slave – he insists he was merely devoted – to his children and would often – he swears it was only once – leave meetings and closings to take them to events such as their hockey practice. But he was highly entertaining and an extremely productive lawyer who was always involved in high-profile mandates and who generated fierce loyalty from clients. We had a good but difficult client for many years by the name of David Pik. Hartt was chronically late in returning his calls, but one day, by some miracle, Pik got through and announced himself, with considerable irritation, in heavily accented English, as "Pik, Pik, Pik," to which Hartt replied "Oink, oink, oink" and hung up.

In 1985, Hartt was invited by Prime Minister Brian Mulroney to become deputy minister of Finance. Hartt's ability to accumulate debt made him, in the collective view of his partners, admirably suited to the task of doing so on a national basis. The temptation was irresistible to Hartt, who had come from a political background and who had been tempted on several occasions to run for political office. Fortunately, the firm had talked him out of the earlier initiatives not only for its own benefit, not wanting to lose an outstanding lawyer, but also because with his endlessly precarious financial situation, Hartt simply could not afford to do so. When the opportunity came to have arguably the top job in Canada's public service, the firm did not stand in his way. Hartt remembers going to speak with Stikeman to get his advice about the offer, but he was concerned that he simply could not manage it financially. Stikeman asked him, rhetorically, if a Catholic boy were asked to become the Pope, would he go to the village priest to ask permission? "If you want to do it, do it, and we'll figure out the finances later." Several partners chipped in to help him put his affairs in order. He went to Ottawa for three years, and when his term was completed on May 1, 1988, the firm welcomed him back as a partner. We enjoyed, as much as did he, seeing his familiar signature on the banknotes issued by the Bank of Canada.

Unfortunately, the heady taste of Ottawa led to his accepting, on January 31, 1989, another offer from Mulroney, this time to become his chief of staff. This was something that Hartt wanted far more than his partners did, and when he left for the second time, it was by no means certain that he would have the same level of welcome had he wanted to return. As it turned out, when he left Mulroney's office in September 1990, he did come back to the firm, but soon he was recruited by a headhunter to become the successor to Robert Campeau, the Ottawa real estate tycoon whose corporate and real estate empire was in incipient collapse. Campeau himself had been fired in August 1990, and at the invitation of the Campeau Corporation board of directors, Hartt became its chief executive officer in November. As a public, if not personal, debt expert, Hartt, with his additional experience in commercial law, was the perfect choice for the project. One of the assets in the empire was the well-known Bloomingdales department store in New York, and Hartt used to relish the opportunity presented when girlfriends in New York would ask him (if he could contain himself from confessing it in advance) what he did for a living, and he could say, "Well, I own Bloomingdales!" He now heads up the Salomon Brothers Canadian operations in Toronto and continues to add to an entertaining repertoire of war stories.

EXODUS

By far the most dramatic event faced by the new firm was the departure, in early 1967, of Gerry McCarthy, Jean Monet, and Don Johnston, who went on to start their own firm of McCarthy, Monet & Johnston. It came as a complete surprise to everyone when they told Elliott, just prior to Christmas in 1966, despite the fact that it seemed to have been planned over a period of some months.

By 1965, Johnston had been thinking of getting married and was, at the same time, supporting his mother, who was ill and dying of cancer. He invited Elliott out to lunch at the Hillside Tennis Club to explain the situation and to say that he needed more money. Elliott agreed to an increased salary and began to pay the new amount immediately, but when Johnston's 1965 Christmas bonus came along, it was much smaller than in the past and significantly less than he had expected, which rather soured him on the way the firm was being run. In this mood, he detected some unhappiness in Gerry McCarthy and invited him out to dinner at Hong Kong House, where he brought up the idea of setting up their own firm. There is no doubt that it was a big gamble because, although they did fine legal work that the well-served clients recognized and appreciated, virtually all Stikeman & Elliott's business was generated by the two founding partners, and the other lawyers primarily did the work. If they left, it would be with almost no certainty that clients would follow them but with complete certainty that Stikeman and Elliott would put on a full-court press to retain their clients. (Elliott maintains that he and Stikeman were successful in that effort.) But Johnston and McCarthy decided to go forward and approached Jean Monet and Peter Blaikie, who was then a first-year lawyer. They went to Russell Harrison at the Canadian Imperial Bank of Commerce to borrow $25,000, located premises in the IBM Building in the Place Ville Marie complex, then announced the intention to leave. Roy Heenan joined them the following year from Holden Hutchinson, and the firm eventually became known as Heenan Blaikie.

One surprise for most of the lawyers was that Jim Grant, despite being a close friend of Johnston's, was not invited to join the departing lawyers. Grant knew about the impending departures in advance, and it was somewhat painful to him that he was not included among the group. Johnston told him that Blaikie was cheaper and that they could not afford Grant. He was too young to be a partner and too expensive to be an associate. They may also, Grant wondered, have thought that he was not good enough for them. Johnston tried to console Grant by saying that Grant would look back twenty years later and say that not including him was the greatest favour they could have done him. Interestingly enough, Grant would become the unwitting chief beneficiary of the exodus after only five years of practice.

Looking back, it is somewhat easier to understand now than it was at the time. From the beginning, the firm had operated on the basis that there would be only two partners: Stikeman and Elliott. When lawyers were recruited, they were invited to come and work hard but told in advance that they would never become partners, even though they would be well paid. When Grant was hired, Stikeman recited all this and said that he would fully understand were Grant to leave the firm at some time in the future. Despite having their names on the firm letterhead, even the other nominal partners were not legal partners. They shared in the firm profits on the basis of an annual "bonus" determined by Elliott, who controlled the amount of income of the firm.

McCarthy was clearly bothered by this limitation. He was intellectually superb and was one of the best legal minds in the firm, with a background of Jesuit training and a very Cartesian disposition. It was the principle of non-partnership that seemed to be the most important factor, not the money, since money was of little importance to him and he lived very frugally. McCarthy says the reasons for his decision are for his own memoir, and he simply says that he, as well as the others, had decided that they would do better else-where. Monet was something of a mystery and was a natural iconoclast. He did not share work with ease and kept close track of everything he brought in, but he was no more comfortable with the concept of partnership and sharing than he would have been with the existing arrangements in the firm. His association with McCarthy and Johnston did not last long, and he has gone through several other partnerships since leaving that firm. Johnston's motivation was somewhat different. As the designated heir apparent, he was a regular participant in the promotional dinners that Elliott hosted at home. Despite this privileged position, it was not as easy then as it later became to work with Elliott, who was dominating, controlling, and hard-edged. It is almost certain that Johnston felt that Elliott took too much of the "oxygen" and that Johnston did not believe he could achieve a full development of his own personality and skills within such a relationship. Valerie Higgins, who joined the firm in 1959 and had been Pat Thorsteinsson's secretary until he returned to Vancouver in 1964, became Johnston's secretary and followed the new group to their new firm. She thinks that the group had seen the success of Stikeman and Elliott and thought that they could gain the same amount if they were to start on their own.[15] Blaikie was just starting and was the junior that the others needed. He was, at the time, very much an unknown quantity, and there was no sense of loss when he left. The only irony was that the firm had vacillated in its choice of juniors the previous year, with the result that Michael Flavell, the McGill gold medallist in law the year prior to Blaikie, grew tired of waiting and left to join the Chisholm Smith firm, now McCarthy Tétrault.

Elliott, in particular, did not want Johnston to leave and did his best to persuade him not to do so, but to no avail. Johnston thinks the shock of the departure was very good for Elliott, who had made a great deal of money on his CAE investment, was on the board of the CIBC, and was generally content with things. John Turner remembers having said to Elliott, when he left in 1965 to devote his full time to politics, that Elliott needed to spend more time nurturing the younger lawyers since no one was spending enough time with them for that purpose. This departure focused Elliott's energy on getting back to business, and although their personal relationship was testy for a while, it was later sorted out. January 1967 was spent mainly in the process of handing over the files on which they had been working, and they started business on February 1, 1967 with premises, staff, letterhead, and their own receptionist. Elliott returned "full throttle" to getting business, and there was nobody, in Johnston's view, who could come close to Elliott in developing a business plan and directing a law firm composed of very talented people. The exodus simply confirmed that predisposition.

The only immediate action by the senior partners had been to advise Robb that his name would go on the firm letterhead immediately, replacing Turner, whose name had been removed when he left in 1965. The young lawyers – Grant, Angus, Brossard, and Hartt – met to discuss the situation. The entire middle of a small firm had just been eviscerated, and they were very much concerned with their own futures. They had, it seemed to them, three options: to leave and start their own firm; to talk with McCarthy, Monet, and Johnston about joining them; or to speak with Elliott and see what he might have in mind. They first went to speak with Angus's father, Mel, at his home, to see what advice, as a savvy and experienced businessman, he might have for them. Angus's *père* opined that they should probably stay, in maritime terms, with the big ship. He knew both Stikeman and Elliott and advised the group that they should not negotiate with them and should not ask for raises or bonuses, but rather, they should just buckle down to work and they would be well treated.

They followed that advice and worked almost around the clock for the next year. During this time, their thoughts turned to the matter of partnership, and perhaps naively, they thought that they might now have some leverage with which to deal with Elliott, something almost unthinkable in the past. Again, they called on Mel Angus for counsel, and he told them that partnership was not an entitlement but more like admission to a club, which was a decision made by existing members on prospective members. It would be fine to raise the issue, he said, but they should not lose sight of this fundamental. This led to a lunch at the Beaver Club in the Queen Elizabeth Hotel with Elliott, attended by Grant, Brossard, Angus, and Hartt. Grant was the designated spokesman. Their pitch to Elliott was that they would stay and that they were not asking to be made partners, but they thought that the "no partners" rule should disappear since in their view, it had been one of the principal causes of the exodus. More importantly at the time, the young lawyers did not want anyone senior to them to be hired without their approval. They were willing to continue working two shifts per day to fill the gap and said they would fill the void with replacements who would come from behind them. Elliott agreed and to his credit, honoured the arrangement. The remaining lawyers, with their teams of secretaries, worked like dogs many late nights for at least two full years while casting about for likely recruits. Filling the gap meant that there was a fairly large number of lawyers, by relative standards, of approximately the same age.

Although the defection had come as a shock to the entire firm, the remaining lawyers regrouped and filled the gap so quickly and effectively that life continued with no apparent interruption of service to the firm's clients. Grant took over the CIBC work that McCarthy had done, and Hartt dealt with the Mercantile Bank of Canada. This was all done in addition to the already existing and heavy workloads. The only noticeable effect was that on major corporate transactions, the Stikeman lawyer was almost certain to be the youngest at the table. The deals got done.

Experience was acquired in the trenches, without the comfort of being able to learn at the feet of a senior partner. And a lean, mean group of corporate lawyers was now in the forefront of deals, often to the consternation of their more senior counterparts from other firms, who now had to respond to the speed and standards of a new generation. The fifteen-year-old Montreal firm had always been seen as precocious by its rivals, but this was a whole new ball game. It was a gamble that paid off handsomely and was a tribute to the entrepreneurial spirit of Stikeman and Elliott. As young lawyers, they had themselves set out on their own, and they were willing to risk their own futures on such a gamble. Grant himself moved into the position of heir apparent and was groomed, in particular by Elliott, to become the head of the commercial practice. The response to the exodus also enshrined a principle that has become a hallmark of the firm – that initiative and talent are given the earliest recognition and that there is never any limit to upward mobility within the firm.

When Elliott decided that he would now concentrate on Grant for the future, he told him that he needed to learn some accounting beyond the barely rudimentary course provided in law school. So Grant duly enrolled in an evening course at Sir George Williams University in intermediate accounting. The experience was an eye-opener for him since he saw a different student base from that of the privileged day students at McGill; they were largely mature students, already in the work force, struggling to make better careers for themselves while carrying the burden of day jobs and families, all at much lower salary levels than he enjoyed. He dutifully attended the lectures and completed the assignments. When the time came for the course examination in the spring, he was of the view that it was not necessary; he had done the work and understood accounting better. His wife, Nancy, insisted that he take the examination. Under her uxorious pressure (wives are far more practical in these matters than their husbands are) he did, and he passed. A couple of months later, while playing golf with Elliott on a Saturday afternoon, Elliott asked him out of the blue if he remembered his advice to take an accounting course. Grant replied that he did and that he had enrolled in the course. Elliott asked him whether he had taken the examination. Yes. Had he passed the examination? Yes. Grant occasionally wonders what might have happened had he answered "no" to any of the questions. Elliott had a big influence on him as a young lawyer. Grant was raw, and Elliott made him much tougher and was a major factor in making him a "serious" person. It was clear to most of the lawyers that this was a significant influence. Grant even wrote and tried to sound very much like Elliott, and he developed a facility of getting to the crux of a problem with the least amount of wasted time, even at the occasional risk of seeming to be unnecessarily abrupt.

Grant, like almost every lawyer in the firm, had his ups and downs with Elliott, and he had encountered some difficulties with him. After three or four years working at the firm, he noticed that his bonus at Christmas was smaller than the year before, so he went to Elliott, nervously – as one did in respect of almost any matter but especially in matters of money in which Elliott's word was law – and said that he had noticed that he had got a smaller bonus and asked whether there was some kind of a message in that. Elliott said to him, yes; he and Heward had decided that Grant had a problem. So Grant asked, even more nervously, "What is the problem?" Elliott said he didn't know but that, "Heward and I think you have a problem." Grant went home and agonized over this for some time, wondering even whether he should think of changing firms, but finally decided he would just put his nose to the grindstone and continue to work hard for the next year. The next year at Christmas, he got a big bonus and went to Elliott to thank him. Elliott said to him, "You know that problem you had? Well, you don't have it any more."

FILLING THE GAP

Michael Richards[16] was a classmate of Stanley Hartt and joined the firm in 1967. Richards had been a notary at the Pratt Stevenson firm in Montreal but thought that notarial practice was too narrow to provide a satisfying career, so he decided that he would convert to becoming a lawyer. In addition to approaching the firm, he interviewed at Lafleur Brown with Ken Brown, at Martineau Walker with Peter Mackell, and at Howard Cate[17] with Thomas Montgomery and Yves Fortier. Richards met with Elliott who asked him why he was changing professions, and Elliott was the only one who asked him what he thought was the most important question! Elliott then asked, "What are you making?" Richards replied that he was earning between $5,200 and $5,700. "Come here. We'll pay you $8,000," announced Elliott. Richards accepted, wrote the Bar exams, and started effective July 1, 1967.

A week later, he was invited to play golf with friends at Kanawaki Golf Club on the Mohawk Reservation, but he was a bit worried about doing so this early in his new career with the firm. He checked to see where Elliott played: Royal Montreal. Tamaki played at Beaconsfield. The coast was clear, so off he went. On the first hole, he hit his ball left of the green, and while looking for it, he found another ball, which he put in his pocket. After putting out and walking to the next tee, he saw someone in the same area in which he had found the ball. It was Elliott, playing as a guest of one of his friends. He had driven his ball there from another tee. Richards confessed to Elliott that he had the ball and showed him where it had been. "Young man, never pick up a ball on the golf course," he was admonished, "even if it is your own." Continuing to create a "favourable" impression on the senior partner, not long thereafter, Richards hit a home run at a firm softball game, and the ball dented Elliott's Cadillac Eldorado, which was parked beyond the playing field.

The year of the exodus (1967) was a good time to have come to the firm. That year, Harold P. ("Sonny") Gordon[18] arrived, fresh from two years in

Ottawa, and Peter Cumyn came from the Department of Justice. Gordon had been contacted by Stanley Hartt, who said they were looking for young talent and asked if he would be prepared to meet with Fraser Elliott. As special assistant to Maurice Sauvé, whose wife, Jeanne, later became Governor General of Canada, Gordon was earning, at the time, $12,000 per year, and while he had never thought very seriously about using his legal training, he recognized that this might be a great opportunity, so he agreed to meet. Looking back, he reflects that had he not made the move at that time, he probably would never have practised law. But here was a chance to play in the big leagues as, he says, "the Number Two Jew" in the firm. The only other offer on the horizon was a job under Michael Pitfield in the Privy Council Office, so he decided to come and started at the beginning of May 1967, just as Expo '67 was putting Montreal on the international map.

It was easy for Gordon to see how the firm had started and how it had become so successful so quickly. Stikeman and Elliott were both great self-promoters, if somewhat different in style. Elliott had made sure that he joined all the right clubs, that he had a large fancy car and a big house, and that as he lived big, he became big. He was, to Gordon, supremely self-confident. Stikeman, on the other hand, while equally confident, had a more understated, country-gentry manner. The combination covered the whole spectrum. Gordon himself was not short of self-confidence, and to say that he was gregarious is a masterpiece of understatement. The latter quality almost led him back into politics since Pierre Elliott Trudeau was just beginning his challenge for the Liberal leadership and his election team was opening an office in Ottawa. Gordon was one of the first to become involved in this Ottawa office, and he had the choice of going into politics on a full-time basis, a very exciting prospect as the possibilities of a charismatic new leader opened up. It was clear that he would not be able to combine the political activity at that level with his responsibilities at the firm, but for a few months, he had the excitement of travelling across the country to organize meetings for Trudeau, who won the Liberal leadership convention on April 6, 1968 and was sworn in as prime minister on April 20 of the same year.

His indoctrination at the firm was well short of overwhelming. If zero was a base, he recalls his experience as not much above that. It may have been the preoccupation with filling the workload gap or the general sink-or-swim nature of the firm, but the period passed soon enough, and Gordon proved to be one of the swimmers. He would become one of the most important lawyers in the corporate and commercial practice, which was gradually replacing tax as the driving force of the firm. One of his first major assignments came from George Tamaki, who had, says Gordon, a particular capacity to be helpful, to make you feel like a full partner on any job from the start and to make you look good. Seeing Tamaki in action was a privilege. Gordon says that the Department of National Revenue treated Tamaki with a respect that bordered upon awe. In one case, National Revenue wanted to value some privately held shares at their market value, but this would have bankrupted the estate. So Tamaki and Gordon went to meet with the department and talked the officials into an offer that could be managed by the estate. Tamaki said quietly to Gordon, "Don't smile." The chit-chat went on for a while after the offer had been put forward, and then, just before leaving, with the unbelievable offer still on the table, Tamaki said that he would do his best to "talk the client into it." Gordon's knowledge of the Ottawa political scene was helpful in the effort to negotiate the settlement for clients on the dividend strips, where he helped to direct the memoranda and submissions to the right places. Knowledge of the Ottawa environment also helped him assist in the subsequent recruitment of Michel Vennat.

The job conferred on him by Tamaki was the sale and leaseback of the grain elevator at Port Cartier, Quebec in a transaction on behalf of Louis Dreyfus, a client of the firm. He found himself, as did all of the firm's commercial lawyers, across the table from far more senior counsel, in this case, John Nolan from the O'Brien firm, who soon after that would be appointed to the Quebec bench.[19] The opening of the elevator was the occasion of a huge party at Port Cartier, which Gordon attended with Stanley Hartt, and which was presided over by Jean Louis-Dreyfus, who had come over from France for the ceremony. They flew to Sept-Îles and then had a special train to Gagnon, Quebec, for a tour of the iron mine. This was an integral part of the whole Port Cartier project since to be economical, the port had to handle both grain and ore carriers. After the formal dinner, Hartt and Gordon were counselled by the locals to pay a visit to the Port Cartier BBQ, which was part barbecue establishment and part strip joint, offering breasts and thighs, according to species and taste, in different sections of the premises. The local experts assured them (correctly, it appears) that they would have a good time there. Gordon was quick to follow up on the Dreyfus contacts and made a point of visiting Europe to maintain contact with the family, especially with Theo Joseph Dreyfus. Over the years, the initial experience with Louis-Dreyfus led Gordon to eventual work for several of the other large grain companies, including Cargill, Garnac, and Range Grain, part of the André group. He recalls with great pleasure the occasion that he was able to go to Europe and work on an André deal for two weeks, holiday for two weeks, and work for another two weeks, all on the same ticket paid for by the client.

Other early transactions in which he found himself across the table from senior counsel included Edper Investments' acquisition of Great West Saddlery; on this occasion, he was opposite Trevor Eyton from the Tory firm in Toronto and the legendary Philip Vineberg in Montreal. An exciting deal that occurred early in his practice – his first "home run" – was the acquisition of Aquilla Computer Services for our client John O'Brien (son of the well-known lawyer, John L. O'Brien, and brother of Montreal partner Peter O'Brien). The price for the acquisition was to be paid in shares, which were valued at forty cents each when the agreement was negotiated. The notice of the relevant shareholders' meeting had been properly mailed, but a postal strike delayed the meeting. In the meantime, the price of the shares had gone through the roof, climbing to the $25 range. The challenge was to close the deal without letting the selling shareholders off the hook, which they managed, despite the squeals and prevarications of the other side.

Peter Cumyn,[20] who was recruited from the Department of Justice in Ottawa, also in 1967, was one of the most flexible and creative thinkers in the firm. He developed a specialty in international taxation, particularly following his period in London, England between September 1969 and January 1972, when he opened the firm's office there. Cumyn developed many of the most sophisticated tax plans, and once he had worked out the intricacies in his mind and was satisfied with their legal basis, he was absolutely without fear in recommending them to clients. None was successfully attacked by the tax authorities. It was always a challenge to follow his logic because, like so many wizards, he could skip the details of many of the intervening considerations without foundering on the apparent gaps in the process. When working with him, it was always important to make him explain every step since many tax plans are rather similar to the methods used in the old dancing schools in which the dance steps were painted on the floor, and as long as you followed each footprint, you could dance. If you strayed from the pattern, however, you would certainly trip and fall. Like many of the tax lawyers, he relied very heavily on George Tamaki, who was thorough and patient, willing to undertake a careful review of anything one of the tax lawyers wrote. The role of educated second-guessing was one for which Tamaki was particularly suited and one that Stikeman himself could not fill. It was always a matter of amazement to the younger lawyers to see how much meat Tamaki could get into his normally short opinions. They had to be studied with the utmost care; each word seemed to weigh a literary ton.

The big challenge for the firm was to keep Cumyn from getting bored. He is one of those people who has enormous energy and the facility of having a hundred ideas a day of which some were more practical (and practicable) than others. One idea he had, almost as soon as he returned from London, was to establish within the tax section a personal tax planning division specializing in estate planning, will drafting, estates administration, and general related advice. The idea never caught on, other than to undertake a review of clients' wills in order to be sure that the provisions were compatible with the new *Income Tax Act* that had come into force on January 1, 1972. An idea that *did* catch on was the tax section's weekly lunches for the entire group, something that was quite common among the London firms. He also seized on the idea that the firm should publish books on the Canadian taxation system for non-residents. He persuaded the firm to hire a young German lawyer, Sylvilin Frisch from Munich, for a couple of summers, and between them, they produced and published in 1975 a tax guide for German businessmen, *Ein Fuerher Durch Das Kanadischen Steuergetz.* This was followed in 1980 with the English-language equivalent, *A Non-Resident's Guide to Canadian Taxation,* published by the ubiquitous De Boo in 1980. Then in 1985, working with Pierre Archambault, Monique Mercier, and Lucie Lamarre, he also produced a French-language version, entitled simply *Canada,* which was published by Les Editions Francis Lefebvre in Paris. He almost left the firm in 1973 to work for R. Jack Adams, a brilliant and eccentric entrepreneur, but at the last moment, he decided against it. Fortunately, the complex international tax field provided good fare for his intellect, and he practised with enthusiasm for several years before finally deciding to go off at the beginning of 1993 to try the investment field, combined with international tax planning, as a principal in the Ermitage Group, moving back and forth between London and Montreal.

Another of the class of 1967, joining at the same time as Cumyn, was Bruce Verchere, who was working at the time with the Department of Justice in Ottawa in the tax litigation section. He stayed with the firm as a tax lawyer until 1973, when he was invited to leave. The direct cause of this was a badly misjudged effort on his part to oust Stikeman from the firm, so badly misjudged, in fact, that he attempted to induce Elliott to participate in the effort. He had the temerity to invite Elliott to lunch at the Ritz Carleton to propose that he and Elliott should be the partners of the firm and that Stikeman should be removed. Elliott recounted this to Stikeman, and they fired him the same day.[21]

Michel Vennat[22] was first contacted as a student who had never heard of the firm, by Jim Robb. Although enrolled at the Université de Montréal, he spent his second year of law at the Université Laval, where his classmates included Brian Mulroney, Michael Meighen, Peter White, Michel Cogger, Lucien Bouchard, and Pierre DeBané. The faculty members at Laval were mostly practitioners, and there were few full-time academics. He scored 100 per cent in each of the three examinations in his first term. He went back to the Université de Montréal for his third year, where one of his classmates was Bernard Landry. He worked at the office during the summer of 1963 before going to Oxford for his Rhodes Scholarship. John Turner, himself a Rhodes Scholar, was still practising, as was Bert Bissonnette, who had been at Dieppe with Vennat's father,[23] and the only other student was Stanley Hartt. Vennat was in Oxford from the fall of 1963 until June 1965, when he went to Ottawa, having written the foreign service examinations while in England, to work at External Affairs for a couple of years. His first boss in the foreign service was Geoffrey Pearson, son of Lester B. Pearson, and Vennat was involved in United Nations development work, spending a session at the United Nations in New York that fall. While still working in government, he wrote the Bar exams in 1966. He met and worked for Mitchell Sharp, then minister of Finance, for two and a half years from the spring of 1968 until the fall of 1970. Pierre Elliott Trudeau asked him to work in his office, and he was faced with a decision of whether to stay in politics or start a career. Vennat had kept in touch with the office, and at one stage, Fraser Elliott had invited him to lunch in Ottawa to say that Vennat was getting a bit old and perhaps a bit pricey, Elliott's inimitable way of suggesting that he might become too expensive for a law firm to hire, given his lack of legal experience. He knew Harold Gordon from student politics and from being on the circuit in Ottawa, as well as Peter Cumyn from his year at Laval and from the Department of Justice in Ottawa. Vennat eventually decided that he would leave politics and work as a full-time lawyer, starting at the firm on October 1, 1970. He became part of the corporate and commercial section, the first francophone in that section. He knew the firm as a business firm, and he was himself interested in business.

In 1969, the firm had moved to what the lawyers used to refer to as "T4 partners." These partners had a fixed salary, which was a deductible expense to the partnership, and a variable bonus as a share in the profits of the firm. Tamaki and Grant did not participate as "partners" since Elliott remained willing to pay them their full year's salary in advance. Toward the end of each year, Elliott would walk the halls and throw a small envelope into each lawyer's office containing a hand-written note, indicating the "partner's" salary for the next year and the bonus for the current year. The numbers were not there for discussion. They were set. One year, Maurice Régnier concluded that he had not been properly compensated, and the matter of additional remuneration came before a partners meeting. Elliott looked around and asked if there were a seconder for such a proposal. There was none.

This manner of dealing with remuneration continued until the early 1970s and was accelerated by the changes to the income tax rules applicable to partnerships. It was also the result of a change in Elliott's attitude regarding the admission of new partners. He finally came to realize the implications of the fact that he and Stikeman, under the existing arrangements, were the only two responsible for the debts of the partnership and thought it wiser, in the long run, to spread the risks. In addition, he and Grant correctly understood that a small group could still run the partnership even if there were many partners. The current concept of "points" resulted from Robb's conclusion that it was humiliating for partners to have situations such as Régnier had encountered. He thought there should be a system whereby they could agree in advance how the profits should be shared so that everyone would know. He suggested the use of points rather than a percentage, which would constantly have to be adjusted, usually downwards, as new partners were admitted. Points would allow the relative positions to be known, and the number of points did not have to be reduced each time a new partner was admitted.

FULL SERVICE AND INCREMENTAL VALUE

Notwithstanding his desire to have a full-service firm, Elliott never seemed to attach the same importance to the litigation lawyers as he did to those in the commercial and tax sections. In the late 1960s, after the younger group had stepped into the breach caused by the exodus, Elliott called in Grant, Angus, and Hartt to say that he had decided to pay them more than Brossard. How much? they asked. They were told, $250. It was, said Elliott, to make a point. They refused, saying that when they had met with Mel Angus, they had agreed that it was one for all and all for one. Elliott told them that they did not get it. His view was that one could buy litigators for a dime a dozen. But if that was what they wanted, that was fine with him. They would all get the same as they had got the previous year. The next year, Elliott called them in again and proposed a greater increase. This time, they capitulated. Brossard took this differentiation as a slight against French

Canadians since most of the litigators were francophone; there developed
a myth, which lingered for many years, that Elliott treated anglophone
lawyers better than he treated francophone ones. In fact, the motivation
had nothing to do with language but, rather, reflected Elliott's view of the
relative value of the different areas of practice and their contribution to the
economic fortunes of the firm. There would be continual fallout from this
perception, culminating in the spring of 1993.

Brossard was active in the Bar and eventually became bâtonnier of the
Province of Quebec, where he supervised the change of the archaic rule
that prohibited the names of persons no longer in practice from appearing
on the letterhead of a law firm. This was an important step for the firm
since it was in the process of trying to institutionalize the Stikeman Elliott
name as a "brand" in Quebec and Canadian law and had to face the fact
that neither of the founding partners would practise forever. The lawyers
nevertheless wanted the name to remain as the banner under which the firm
would continue into the future. It was an important consideration for the
firm and one of the reasons – in addition to general support, as would be
the case years later when Claudette Picard ran for similar election – why it
encouraged Brossard to pursue his efforts to become bâtonnier. Not long
after his term in office, Brossard, undoubtedly still smarting to some degree
from the firm's apparent view of litigation lawyers and the fact that François
Mercier showed no signs of willingness to pass over leadership of the litigation section, resigned from the firm to go to Desjardins, Ducharme before
accepting an appointment to the Quebec Court of Appeal, where he has
become a very conscientious and capable judge.[24]

GETTING READY FOR THE 1970S

By the end of the 1960s, the billings of the firm, even on Elliott's highly
conservative view of an appropriate cash-basis reckoning, had reached more
than a million and a half dollars, and the two original partners were sharing
residual profits of more than $525,000.[25] More importantly, however, there
was a foothold established in Europe, described in chapter 5, and a growing
understanding that the next challenge for the firm was to take advantage
of the increasing flow of legal business from both Montreal and elsewhere
in the direction of Toronto, which was rapidly replacing Montreal as the
traditional business centre of Canada. Business from Europe was avoiding
Montreal as the nationalist movement gained momentum and uncertainty
about the future of Quebec within Canada increased. It was time to adjust
the firm's sights to yet another market.

CHAPTER 4

Stikeman Elliott in Toronto

The flight of business from Montreal to Toronto, amid growing concerns about the political stability of Quebec and the focus of inbound business from abroad in the Toronto area, were viewed with despair by the Montreal legal community. There could be a great deal of bluster about the number of head offices of major corporations that remained in Quebec, but more and more, this amounted to whistling past the graveyard. It did not take a rocket scientist to see that while the statutory head office of the Bank of Montreal was still the beautiful domed building on Place d'Armes, its new building in Toronto was the real sign of where the business was being generated. The same became true of the Royal Bank of Canada. The Royal Trust Company of Montreal was eclipsed by Royal Trustco. The Sun Life Assurance Company of Canada would abandon Montreal as its head office. And so it went.

While the other Montreal law firms fretted, Stikeman and Elliott acted. They would open in Toronto and direct the fleeing business to their own firm, not just refer it to other law firms, which were all too ready to absorb the manna from the Quebec heaven and to forget as soon as decently possible whence it had come. Of course, the Toronto beneficiaries might send their Quebec work in return, which usually meant little more than translating prospectuses for what was then the Quebec Securities Commission and handling local filings, but it was nothing of interest and was certainly not the kind of work that excited any of the firm's lawyers. In those days, accounting records were not sophisticated enough to enable firms to determine the amount and value of business referred to various Toronto firms. Once the Toronto firm was established, the firm was astounded at how much business it was able to direct to it and at how much had been lost to other firms. It was like turning a pyramid on its end so that the source of diffuse business to the other firms was now reversed. The many sources of outbound business in the Montreal firm now had a single channel to one Toronto firm in which the partners could now both quantify and participate in the profits. Not surprisingly, the Toronto firm was profitable from the very beginning.

But before this could happen, there were the usual problems of provincial qualification that plagued any effort to build a national practice, and that would remain until the rule was successfully challenged by McCarthy & McCarthy in Alberta in 1989.[1] Often cloaked in self-serving wrappings that proclaimed the rules to be in the public interest, but which were often little more than an effort to retain territorial cartels, the law societies of each province sought to prevent lawyers from other jurisdictions from practising on their turf. The Law Society of Upper Canada, charged with the sacred trust of preventing contamination of the local practice by "unqualified" outsiders, would have no truck with a Quebec firm purporting to practise Ontario law. It would be necessary, therefore, to create an entirely separate firm, consisting solely of lawyers entitled to practise law in Ontario. Fortunately, both Stikeman and Elliott had calls to the Ontario Bar, which meant that their names could appear on an Ontario firm letterhead, an important factor since even with less than twenty years of practice under the shorthand banner of "Stikeman, Elliott," there was national and international goodwill attached to the name that could be of assistance, even in Toronto. That was a good start, but they needed more than simply their own names to attract attention in a city that was far from welcoming toward any upstarts from Lower Canada. As Stikeman described the genesis:

It was apparent by late 1970 that an office outside of Montreal could be managed competently. It was also apparent that by having an office in London, we were putting pressure on ourselves to open in Toronto since the European and British investment communities were avoiding Quebec because of its apparent political instability. Our European clients told us that if we wished to keep the business they sent us through London, we must be able to service it in Toronto. We got the message, and Fraser and I began to undertake the Toronto venture by ourselves as we had already done in the case of the investment in London. We personally assumed the bank loan, personally rented space, and then asked our other partners if they "wanted in." This was because, as in the case of the London office, we could not get a consensus from our partners, but we two realized that we had to move outward from Montreal to safeguard the future of the firm.

In 1970, John Robarts announced his retirement after ten years as Premier of Ontario. Fraser and I visited him one day at his offices at Queen's Park and invited him to join us in our newest venture (Toronto!), which was not yet then announced. He agreed at once, principally, I thought, because by joining a small group from Montreal and not a large Ontario Law firm, all of which were wooing him assiduously, he would not antagonize anyone in Toronto.

There were many consultations regarding the possibility of starting up a new firm. One of the most important was with Kenneth Jarvis, secretary of the Law Society of Upper Canada, the principal guardian of the Ontario gate. Jarvis proved to be reasonably sanguine about the prospect and generally helpful in the effort; indeed, he was barely short of telling them that all they had to do was to rent some space and put out their sign.

Stikeman had also approached Donald Bowman,[2] then director of tax litigation with the federal Department of Justice, whom he had known from his tax litigation forays against the Crown, and for whom he had the highest professional and personal regard. The first discussions between them were in the fall of 1970. Later, Stikeman took Bowman and his wife, Marjorie, to the old Rideau Club in Ottawa (prior to the fire that destroyed it in 1979) for dinner to pursue the matter somewhat further. Bowman recalls that his wife, who had memories of the Depression, was quite hesitant about the prospect of him leaving the security of a good government job in which Bowman had already demonstrated his capabilities and had a healthy, assured pension at the end of the road, and taking up the challenge of starting a new firm in Toronto. So nothing came of the evening. Not long afterwards, Bowman came down with the mumps and was laid up at home, strategically packaged in ice, with a phone installed by the bed from which he was unable to move. Stikeman called again and asked him if he had reconsidered coming with him to start the new firm in Toronto, the name of which would, incidentally, be Stikeman, Elliott, Robarts & Bowman. Bowman figures he was too weak to say no. Stikeman was, perhaps, a bit ahead of the curve on the firm name since Robarts had not yet agreed to having his name included in the letterhead, but the strategy served the twofold purpose of associating Bowman – who was not from Toronto and was not well known outside the tax community – with a highly recognized personality and also of not having to go back at some later time to say that a new name had gone ahead of Bowman's. In addition, Bowman would take over the day-to-day administration of the new firm since neither Stikeman nor Elliott would be there on a full-time basis, and Robarts had no interest in running the firm.

Stikeman and Elliott met with Jarvis on December 8, 1970 and were sufficiently encouraged that in his follow-up letter dated December 11, Stikeman felt able to confirm the substance of their discussion:

Fraser and I have acted upon your suggestion and have found space in Toronto. It is in the present Canadian Imperial Bank of Commerce Building from which we will be able to move into the Commerce Court when it is completed without a change of address. We have also consolidated our partnership agreements with the senior of our two future partners: a senior Ottawa civil servant and an active member of the Law Society. He has now given notice to his Deputy Minister of his intention to leave and is looking for a home in Toronto.

As a matter of good order, I would like your confirmation that we have correctly understood what you told us, namely, that Fraser Elliott and Heward Stikeman may form a partnership to practice law in the Province of Ontario under the name of Stikeman & Elliott and may associate with it either as partners or as employees other members in good standing of the Law Society of Upper Canada. We will have premises in the City of Toronto and will install in those premises from the outset at least two and perhaps three lawyers who are members of the Law Society. We ourselves will visit the premises from time to time at a frequency determined by the need for our services by our Ontario clientele.

We will keep books and records entirely separate from those of any other firm with which we may be connected, clearly showing the revenues and disbursements of the Ontario partnership. From time to time, we may retain Stikeman, Elliott, Tamaki, Mercier & Robb or any other law firm as required by our professional needs and will pay such fees as may be proper which will be shown as disbursements on the books of the Toronto partnership.

In short, we will be in all respects a partnership of lawyers in Ontario, affiliated with no one else, engaged primarily in the practice of tax law and related problems.

...

I may say that we have come to this decision after some thought and in order to give better service to our clients in Toronto. As you know, we both spend a considerable amount of time in Ontario on business having to do with Federal and Ontario taxation and other matters, and we are happy to be able to finally establish ourselves in a permanent *pied à terre* with an operating legal firm in your Province in order to render our professional activities there more effective and continuous.

If I have in any way misstated your understanding of the situation, please let me know; otherwise we are proceeding with enthusiasm toward the goal of an early opening.

Jarvis replied to Stikeman following the Christmas holidays, on January 13, 1971.

I have your letter of the 11th of December, 1970 and confirm that my recollection of our conversation is exactly the same as your own.

It was a pleasure to see you again, and I wish you and Fraser good fortune with your new development, not only in this new year but in the times to come.

Elliott then reported to John Robarts, still Premier of Ontario, on January 15.

Since our brief telephone conversation early in December, which, of course, has remained entirely confidential, a few things have begun to firm up.

Heward and I have both seen Mr Jarvis (the Secretary) and Art Martin (the Treasurer) of The Law Society, and there do not appear to be any problems.

Through the good offices of Neil MacKinnon, who is enthusiastically supporting our endeavours, we will be able to have space in the present Bank of Commerce building, pending completion of Commerce Court, at which time we will move in there.

Our timing for opening, while flexible, would appear to be the end of June or middle of July, with the possibility of an announcement sometime before then.

During the early Fall, under the auspices of Richard De Boo, a symposium will be held on The White Paper legislation,[3] at which some two hundred specially invited guests from across Canada will attend. At this time, the office should become thoroughly known.

The lead man in the office to date will be Don Bowman from the Department of Justice in Ottawa, who is presently Director, Tax Litigation Section. There may be another young man, named Lindsay, who is presently writing the legislation for Mr Benson's White Paper on Taxation. The projected name so far will be Stikeman, Elliott & Bowman, subject to an expression of interest on your part. Heward and/or I expect to spend a considerable amount of time there.

At your convenience, after the convention, we might have a conversation.

On February 18, 1971, Elliott sent a memorandum concerning "our Toronto office, which it now appears will be accelerated," to all the nominal
partners of the firm, asking them to identify any problems that might have to
be solved in order to "get the operation off and running." Since the initiative
had been driven almost entirely by Stikeman and Elliott, many of the other
partners had not given much thought to the practical issues involved in the
start-up of a new, but closely associated, firm. London had been simply a
branch office of the Montreal firm. Toronto, however, would be a separate
law firm, subject to the rules of a different law society, in which those
Montreal partners who were not also members of the Law Society of Upper
Canada (of which there were none at the time other than Stikeman and Elliott) would not be allowed to be partners, even though they might well be
affected by the financial risks of the new venture. Several of the Montreal
partners (actual and de facto) had questions to be addressed.

Grant, by then playing an increasing role in the management of the Montreal office, raised a series of administrative issues that would have to be
dealt with such as accounting and billing systems and engagement of lawyers
and personnel. He also wanted to address the matter of the requirements of
each of the two provincial legislative systems governing the practice of law
since up to that time, it appeared to him that everyone had just been specu-
lating as to what could or could not be done since this type of arrangement
had never been tried before. Discussions had begun about the possibility of
creating a management company to handle the financing and administrative
function, the form of arrangement of the new partnership, and the formal
relationship that would be necessary between the two partnerships. Grant
was concerned that from the outset, they should establish the principle
that the only reason for the separate Ontario partnership was the Ontario
qualification requirement of the Law Society of Upper Canada and that all
financial relationships and controls should be set up as if they were dealing
with only one partnership.

André Brossard was concerned as to how the new firm would be financed
and how it would tie in with Montreal, especially once the initial start-up
period came to an end. He, too, was inclined to the view that a management company might be the best way to manage the financing, and that it
might also provide a way of equalizing earnings between the two firms. He
thought there should be some way to indicate the association of the two
firms. Maurice Régnier had questions about the integration of office systems
and the financing of the firm. As a tax lawyer, his concerns were somewhat
more technical than the general financing matters addressed by others: were
a management company to be formed, what would be the maximum "reasonable" fee that could be charged for its services, and what steps could be
taken to ensure that interest on any borrowed money used for the purpose
of acquiring shares of the company would be deductible in computing the
income of the persons putting up the money. He wondered as well about the
cross-promotion of the two firms.

David Angus was also concerned about the nature of the new partnership and its relationship, especially to the ten Montreal partners, and he

wanted to know what written agreements would be put in place to reflect the understandings. The two sets of Bar regulations would have to be carefully studied to be certain what could or could not be done. Thus far, there had been far too many "maybes" for his comfort. How could the Montreal partners benefit if the Toronto office succeeded, and how could they lose were it to go belly up? Several individuals, he said, without identifying them, felt that, "Toronto is in theory a super idea, especially with Robarts, but that in practice, they will not benefit materially and will even possibly lose if the power base, from a partner and revenue point of view, shifts from Montreal to Toronto." Whatever validity there might be to such a view, he thought the question should be aired at the outset and the situation be clearly spelled out so that everyone would know where they stood. He had the usual administrative questions and was very much in favour of a management company to be owned by the ten Montreal partners.

Stanley Hartt thought the most serious problem was the funding of the Toronto operation while preserving the tax deductibility of the amounts underwritten by the Montreal partners. He wanted to maintain control of the Toronto operation and keep its financial position essentially "flat" so that the benefits of a successful operation would accrue to the Montreal partners who were assuming the financial risks. He, too, thought the idea of a management company, of which the partners would be the shareholders, was a good idea. He was already worried about the severability of the Toronto firm and had noted that those who were partners of both firms could help to "flat out" the Toronto earnings. He thought the firm should consider having a couple of young lawyers attached to and be articled to Robarts rather than rushing off to hire new lawyers in Toronto before it had become self-supporting.

ॐ

Both Stikeman and Elliott were fully aware of the importance of the association of John Robarts with the firm. Robarts hailed from London, Ontario, and he had had his own firm there, which was quite naturally anxious to have him back. The question for Robarts was where his principal connection would be. Elliott had been following the matter with careful attention and sent a memo outlining his concerns to Stikeman on March 8, 1971.

On March 4th, John Robarts called me, I having placed a call to him. He indicated that he was going away to have a rest and will be back on the 18th. I told him that I would call him on the 19th because I think we should get together either in London, Toronto, or here [Montreal] shortly thereafter.

Our telephone conversation lasted for about one half hour, during the course of which he said he had thought that it would be better for him to be counsel in our firm and keep his name in his London firm. I told him that in principle, I did not like this because it raised very difficult problems of division of clientele. For example, I asked him *à propos* of his proposed trip to London [England], which I described and which he seemed to like, whether, when we got a large number of clients as a result of that trip, they should be considered clients of our firm in Toronto of which he would be counsel or of his firm in London. He was unable to answer and immediately realized the difficulty. I then urged him to reconsider plans which would make him counsel to his firm in London and have his name in our firm in Toronto. I indicated that it would be possible to have a fairly close liaison in some respects with his firm in London since his throw-off business from the tax business in the initial stages might well be done by some of his London partners if they were competent, i.e., company work and general common law work. He is to give this some thought and is beginning to realize that the mechanics do have some relationship to making clear the division of labour and the proper allocation of clients.

He then said that one of his fears was that if he came into our firm in name, he would not spend enough time at it to justify it, and that he really wanted to live in London. I told him that we discussed this before in Toronto and that we were quite agreeable to that since we did not expect him to do day-to-day work but merely to act as a guided missile with perhaps a little bit more knowledge and know-how, which he would acquire by his own efforts, than most nominal counsel of large firms. I pointed out to him that nominal counsel of large firms were generally regarded by the public and the Bar as people who had gone on the shelf and ceased to be operating. We did not want to give that impression of him, and I suspected that he did not want to either since we did not want the public to think we were getting him merely to have a name but that we were getting him because he would contribute something in terms of expertise, judgment, and counsel work in the true sense. All of this he agreed with, and I think his attitude changed materially during the course of our conversation.

It is most important that you and I go to see him or get him down here, which he is willing to do as soon as he returns. Hence, no matter what, we must phone him on the 19th, and I suggest that I do. I would think it would be a good idea to get him down here so that he can see the kind of establishment we have and then for me and/or you to go with him to London to see the kind of establishment they have there. He has not changed his mind in principle but is having difficulty in sorting himself out.

I also said I thought his re-entry problems would be serious. He said on the contrary; they are a welcome relief, and he is itching to get going. We should discuss the relationships in the various alternatives at our meeting on the 16th – hence this memorandum. Please speak to me before the 16th if you get a chance as I have certain other information of some import to convey to you that I do not wish to put in this memorandum.

The same day, Stikeman's memorandum crossed Elliott's in the internal mail. In it, Stikeman expressed concern about the extent to which the firm could draw attention to the existence of the London office, which was proving to be problematic. He was also anxious to meet with Robarts.

I spoke with Kenneth Jarvis by telephone, and we cannot put Peter's [Cumyn] name on the letterhead or the name of any person who is not a member of the Law Society of Upper Canada. This would preclude a crossreference to this firm or to the fact that we had a London representative. We have to get somebody who is a member of the Law Society of Upper Canada in the London office so that we can show the

London office. We might, however, be able to say "London Office" and give the address, but I would not do it at this stage. I put in a call to John Robarts but could not get him in his office, and am giving you this memorandum in case I should not have reached him by the time you get back. I would like to make an appointment to go and see him in Toronto and spend a couple of hours going over the details with him such as how we are going to start, when and how he is going to be covered by those of us who will be going to Toronto, and a detailed review of the plans for Europe in the spring and the White Paper proposal conference which now perhaps will take place in early summer.

As the decision date grew closer, Elliott advised Stikeman on March 29.

I spoke to Robarts this morning, and he agrees that we should proceed. He wants to put an announcement in the Toronto and London papers that he is rejoining his own firm and subsequently, 6 or 8 weeks from now, join our firm. I am going to meet him Thursday to have breakfast and look at space, and if you think we should have a joint announcement or some plan other than his, you might let me know after lunch today. I will be back around 2:30 and leave at 4:00. Bowman should get permission for the announcement. I spoke to John Turner on Friday, and he is not against the announcement but left it entirely to his Deputy.

HANGING OUT THE SHINGLE

The announcement of the Toronto firm was sent out in April 1971, and the name of John Robarts drew instant recognition to the new players. There was mixed admiration and envy from the Bay Street firms. The Montreal legal community was stunned. My reaction was perhaps typical, located at the time as a third-year associate at what is now McCarthy Tétrault. I said to myself, "God, that is *so* smart." It was one of the factors that influenced my decision the same year to leave that firm and return to Stikeman Elliott, where I had soldiered during my first year of law, before being lured away.

The Toronto firm's initial quarters were – continuing the long-standing relationship with the bank and as indicated to Jarvis in the communications with the Law Society of Upper Canada – in the Bank of Commerce Building at 25 King Street West, its long-time head office. They were small and cramped, even for the fledgling firm. Neither Stikeman nor Elliott was in Toronto on a full-time basis, and Robarts had not been brought on board for the purposes of grinding out routine legal work, besides which he did not appear in person until some time after the firm opened for business. The initial cast of full-time lawyers was Bowman, Fred Von Veh,[4] and shortly thereafter, Thomas Baldwin.[5] Fred Von Veh had come from Matthews, Dinsdale & Clark and did labour work. Baldwin, who had done junior mining financings at Wooley Hames, became the lawyer responsible for Citibank work and a few mutual funds. A month or so after the firm commenced operations, Richard Sankey, who had some lineal connection with the English law lord, Viscount Sankey, was hired from Campbell, Godfrey & Lewtas and became the designated head of the commercial practice. Sankey was very bright and talented though he did not always stay on each job to see matters through to their conclusion and was often elsewhere at crucial moments when he was nominally in charge of transactions. This eventually became a problem with the increasing workload assumed by the small corporate group, and Sankey left the firm a few years later. The collateral benefit for the younger lawyers was that they became expert in the field much sooner as a result of Sankey not being on the job at all times.

They were all so nervous that Bowman felt they lived on Maalox. His own first new client, who wanted several companies incorporated, had the work done and then promptly stiffed him for the bill. Stikeman and Tamaki steered a number of files to Toronto, and one of Bowman's first clients was Shell, with which he maintained a relationship for the entire time he was with the firm. John Robarts was a director of Reed Stenhouse, the large insurance broker for which Bowman did a great deal of work over the years. His work also included the field of captive insurance companies, which had become one of the major tax planning strategies for many large businesses, especially national and multinational organizations. The key to such plans was threefold: (1) to ensure that the premiums paid to these captives were, as a matter of insurance law, actually premiums for insurance, the concept of which involved the sharing of a risk, and as such, were properly deductible in computing income for tax purposes; (2) to avoid having the captives regarded as either mere agents of the companies or residents of Canada (in which case the tax savings would disappear); and (3) to be certain that risks were covered through adequate reinsurance.

Bowman, as the partner in charge of the office, immediately set about trying to fill the roster to get the firm to at least a minimum critical mass so that it could handle the flow of work ready to be referred to it from the Montreal office. The first students were Osgoode Hall classmates Jamie Davis[6] and John Dingle.[7] Davis had gone to Europe after his graduation from law, but he was successfully recruited by Dingle upon his return. The two enjoy the claim of being the first articling students to have been hired back by the firm as lawyers. While Davis and Dingle were completing their articles, Wayne Shaw[8] was discovered while doing a master's of laws degree at the University of Toronto, and he was hired by Bowman, initially to do tax work. Shaw had originally qualified in Alberta and had worked for about six months for the Calgary firm of Howard, Mackie before coming back east. The premises were so small that when Shaw came on board, his office was in the firm's library. He began, as anticipated, by doing tax work with Bowman, but by late 1974, he had gravitated toward a commercial practice as that portion of the firm's work grew in importance.

By August 1971, Stikeman was able to provide an update to the Montreal partners regarding clients represented by the Toronto firm. Many of these clients engaged the Toronto firm as counsel to assist on special matters, and others engaged the firm directly. Bowman was a good drawing card for counsel work since in addition to his tax expertise, he had a very sound general knowledge of the law and was able to give advice on, and appear in, non-tax matters with confidence. By the summer of 1971, Bowman was counsel for Affiliated Realty Corporation, David Dennis, Abbott Laboratories Ltd., Advocate Mines Ltd., Crucible Steel of Canada Ltd., Gibson Bros., Duncan Morris, Loblaw Groceterias, and Weldwood Canada Ltd. The firm itself had been retained by several clients, including Ceebee Services Ltd., Rita Edwards, Richard Schleissner, Dunlea Global Livestock Ltd., Shell Oil Canada Ltd., Permaflex Industries, Elaine and Brian Magee, Spencer Clark, Queen-Yonge Investments Ltd., Leonard Wolinsky, Loram, Iroquois Salt, J.R. Timmins & Co., and Planned Investments Corp. Much of this work was specifically directed from Montreal to the Toronto firm to help it get started, and but for the existence of the Toronto firm, it might very well have stayed with the Montreal office or been lost to other Toronto firms.

Effective February 1, 1972, it was agreed that Sankey, Von Veh, and Baldwin would become partners of the Toronto firm, joining Robarts and Bowman as resident partners. In Montreal, Bruce Verchere was the only new partner that year, but his tenure would be short. The partnership agreements had a formula built into them to deal with the separate incomes of the Montreal and Toronto firms, which effectively aggregated the profits of the firms and applied an appropriate factor to the units held by the partners of both firms. The complex mathematics, which had been developed by Elliott with the assistance of James Wilson, a partner of Peat, Marwick, Mitchell, are not worth the effort to reproduce in this work.

By early 1972, the idea of creating a management company had matured. S&E Management Ltd. was incorporated as a federal company and as of March 1, 1972, it acquired all the physical assets of the two partnerships, including all the leasehold improvements, at their book value (on January 31, 1972, the most recent fiscal year-end of the partnerships). The partnerships thereafter paid S&E Management for the rent and the salaries of all personnel, other than lawyers, and all the expenses of administration that were necessary for the partnerships to carry on their business. The fee paid to the company for these services was fixed at 10 per cent of the various costs incurred by the company. It was agreed, in a very egalitarian decision driven by the senior partners, that each partner of the two firms would own an equal number of shares in S&E Management Ltd. and that new partners, upon admission, would buy the same number of shares as those held by the existing partners, at their then book value.

The use of management companies became the rage for most of the professions – including legal, medical, and dental – since the technique had, in addition to separating the administration of the business from the practice of the profession, the potential to allow some of what might otherwise have been professional income (i.e., the fee based on expenses paid by the management company) to be split among the professionals and their spouses or children. The firm did not follow some of the more aggressive strategies used by others, which allowed each of their partners to incorporate personal holding companies, the shares of which might be held by family members, and then to form a partnership of the holding companies to provide the administrative services, the fees for which would be divided among the companies and flowed to other family members as salary or dividends. We insisted that the partners of the firm hold their shares in S&E Management directly. Those of us in the tax section of the firm used to speculate, wryly, that we were rather like the cobbler's children, with no shoes of our own, and that had we advised clients to act as conservatively as we ourselves were doing, we might well have been sued for professional negligence.

Ground had been broken for the new Commerce Court complex in June 1969. The skeletal steel tower was completed by April 1971, and the building was officially opened in June 1973. We moved in, taking half of the fifty-second floor of Commerce Court West, quarters that seemed palatial at the time. There have been several subsequent moves to different floors, with expanded premises on each occasion – first to the forty-ninth, then in July 1983, to the fourteenth and part of the fifteenth, later extended to include all of the fifteenth. In July 1986, we got the thirteenth floor; in August 1991, we moved to occupy the fifty-third, fifty-fourth, fifty-fifth, and fifty-seventh; in August 1994, we took on half the fifty-second; in September 1997, half of the fifty-first was ours; and in January 2002, our premises included the remaining half of the fifty-second floor. Back in 1981, while we were on the forty-ninth floor, it was by no means clear that the firm would stay at Commerce Court West since it appeared that there was no more space available to deal with our expanded needs. We explored the possibility of relocating to the Sun Life Building or to the Toronto-Dominion complex. In the end, we got some of the Edper and Falconbridge premises in Commerce Court West, and the prospect of relocating diminished, which given the firm's relationship with the CIBC, was undoubtedly the best possible outcome.

James Arnett[9] was recruited from Davies Ward & Beck in 1973, primarily because it was already recognized that Sankey would not have a long-term future with the firm, and it would be necessary to have someone who could manage the commercial practice. Arnett had seen the announcement of the new firm and had been impressed that it had been able to attract Robarts, a huge name in Ontario. Bowman, whom Arnett had known slightly while Arnett was at the Department of Justice, ran into him one day in the elevator, since the Davies Ward premises were on the forty-seventh floor, and they renewed their acquaintance that had been dormant for seven or eight years. They kept in touch, and Bowman told him that the firm was hoping to develop its commercial and corporate practice. Even though at the time it was not common to change firms, especially as a partner, Arnett was intrigued by the possibility and said he might be interested. He heard nothing for a while until one morning, while sitting in his office, the phone rang and the receptionist said, "There's a Mr Stikeman waiting to see you." Stikeman had been in to see David Ward on a professional matter, and as he was on his way out of the offices, he simply decided, in a typical Stikeman manner, to call on Arnett. Arnett was terrified that Bob Davies, his hard-driving and intensely competitive senior partner, might discover this and divine the purpose of the call.

Stikeman was whisked into his office and the door was closed. While praying that Davies would not stick his head in the door, Arnett tried to figure out how to get Stikeman out without being seen by anyone in authority. Nothing happened on that occasion, but the discussions continued, and Arnett accepted the firm's offer on November 1, 1973, becoming a partner in the firm at the beginning of 1974. The firm was so swamped with work that the question of whether Arnett would bring clients with him was not a factor in his recruitment. There was a good deal of work from the London office, including the eventual acquisition of Loblaw's Tamblyn Drugs chain by Boots the Chemist. Shortly after Arnett arrived, the Foreign Investment Review Agency was set up, and the firm moved quickly into that field of activity.

As only the eighth practising lawyer, since Robarts was not considered to be in full-time practice, Arnett added depth to the thin corporate group of Sankey and Baldwin and provided a calming influence. His real job was to help build the corporate and commercial capacity of the firm. He talked Wayne Shaw, then working mainly for Bowman in tax, into becoming a corporate lawyer. Jamie Davis was at the Bar admission course when he arrived and was hired back upon completing the examinations. It was, recalls Arnett, a strange little firm, but one that was not without its charm. There was a great feeling of informal collegiality, which as the firm grew, gradually gave way to the more formal communication by memoranda. There was the fun of being a small firm, but one that got big firm mandates from Montreal and the London office as international business overflew Montreal in favour of Toronto. As the roster expanded by the end of the 1970s, the firm started to have a local platform that enabled it to attract major talent on its own, which in turn accelerated the growth and development of even more talent.

Brian Rose[10] joined the Toronto firm as a student in 1974, along with Jane Avery. Because he was then married to Stikeman's daughter, Elizabeth, Rose had never considered applying to the firm. In fact, his first formal contact with the firm was as a client at the London office, then manned by Peter Cumyn, while he was working at Space Research for the notorious Gerald Bull, who was later murdered in connection with some of his international dealings. Stanley Hartt from the Montreal office took up the initiative of recruiting him and had Rose call on Don Bowman, who hired him forthwith as a student. Even as a student, Rose had some major transactions on which he acted as if he were a lawyer. Sankey sent him off to work on the Fednav acquisition of the Hudson's Bay fleet operating in and around James Bay. In one of life's coincidences, one of the directors was Richard Hunter, the brother-in-law of Virginia Guy, Stikeman's former wife. He also found himself opposite two of the leading lawyers in Toronto, John Tory and David Ward, in the acquisition financed by Citibank of the Nanisivik Mine on Baffin Island, in which Metallgesellschaft was involved.

The corporate section was inundated with work, much of which was derived from Montreal, and it became necessary to seek lateral hires to expand the firm's base of associates. Among the efforts made to encourage applications, an advertisement was placed in the *Ontario Reports,* seeking senior associate-level corporate lawyers. In the spring of 1975, Marvin Yontef[11] was a third-year associate at Blake Cassels & Graydon, wallowing in the slough of despond habitually occupied by young salaried lawyers, preoccupied with how much he was overworked and underpaid. He spotted the firm's advertisement in the *Ontario Reports* and sent in a resumé, solely for the purpose, he swears, of confirming the degree to which he was underpaid. Despite the urgency suggested by the advertisement, the firm was not very responsive, so about a month later, he called Dick Sankey to ask if he had received the resumé. Sankey, picking up the fumbled ball on about the thirtieth bounce, responded that he had indeed been meaning to get back to him, and how about coming up that very afternoon? A bizarre interview followed, during which the trio of Sankey, Bowman, and Arnett left Yontef with such a positive impression that he left without even finding out how much he would be paid. He was certain that there was no way that he would ever work there.

Two weeks later, Sonny Gordon called him at Blake Cassels and asked for a meeting. Gordon, operating as always in full "sales" mode, turned on the charm. If Central Casting had been asked to identify the perfect example of the Montreal office's dreams for a corporate lawyer in the Toronto firm, said Gordon, Yontef was it. And so forth. This bait led Yontef, rising like a trout to the fly, to try to convince Gordon that he could not possibly be wrong. They parted with Gordon saying, "You really must meet Stanley Hartt." A week or so later, Yontef met Elliott, and within an hour, he had decided that he would take the job. Elliott also concluded that, "You really must meet Stanley Hartt."

Yontef was a very significant addition to the firm, especially in the area of corporate finance. He started work in September 1975, ostensibly to help Tom Baldwin with the Citibank work, and he joined at the same time as the new real estate lawyer, Sam Wakim.[12] Within weeks, Richard Pyne[13] joined from the federal Department of Justice in Ottawa. Brian Rose had just finished his articles, and he was going back to the Bar admissions course. Most people inside and outside of the office, then as much as today, assumed that Rose was much more senior than he, in fact, was, and they wondered how the firm could possibly get along without him.

Shortly after Yontef and Wakim joined the firm, Jim Grant suggested that they fly down to Montreal to meet some of the Montreal partners. Sitting beside Wakim on the plane, Yontef noticed that he had his briefcase, which he thought was a bit strange since they were going to Montreal just for dinner, to return the same evening. Wakim replied to Yontef's query that he thought he might learn the *Condominium Act* on the way down. Five minutes into the flight, Wakim duly pulled out a copy of the act and started to read it. Ten minutes into the flight, he put it back into his briefcase, announcing that he was surprised that the statute was far less complicated than he had been led to believe it was. Dinner at Les Halles was great. Yontef saw Gordon again and met Jim Grant, Mike Richards, Mortimer Freiheit, and others. A wonderful evening was made less so only by the absence of the person whom he was really supposed to meet. Stanley Hartt failed to show. Yontef took the opportunity to announce his conclusion that Stanley Hartt did not really exist; he was just a Stikeman Elliott fiction. Almost a year later, Hartt finally appeared at his office door, introducing himself by announcing that he had heard that Yontef thought he did not exist.

The growth of the firm's practice, as Yontef recalls, was largely due to the Montreal office dragging its clients, kicking and screaming, into the Toronto office, to be introduced to their new lawyers. Sometimes it worked. More often, as one of the firm's competitors once observed, we had an amazing ability to attract work but little flair for holding on to it. The situation was, to be sure, somewhat unusual since the quality and volume of work directed to this small firm was far beyond the level that would have occurred in the normal course of starting a small firm. As it was, they simply did not have the time or the luxury of growing in the usual organic manner of recruiting and training their own stock of students although they did this as well as looking elsewhere for talent and ambition. Richard Clark[14] was hired in 1975 from Torys, where he had articled, and he began working at the firm on March 1, 1976.

Rod Barrett[15] arrived in the Toronto office as a student in May 1975. He was recruited by Jim Arnett, who was acquainted with family friends, and by Jamie Davis. He avers modestly that Stikeman Elliott was the only firm that would have him. He was just after Brian Rose, who occupied enough of the office that Barrett thought he might be a senior partner. During his articling period, he did quite a lot of real estate work and continued in this field even when Sam Wakim came on board shortly thereafter despite the fact that Wakim was meant to be the real estate guru. Michael Bonner,[16] who appeared a short time later, had also been engaged, notwithstanding his background as a tax litigator in the federal Department of Justice, to do real estate. Following his call to the Bar, Barrett joined the corporate section and worked for most of his first year with Yontef, who had arrived about the time he began his articling process, doing general corporate work, drafting agreements, and buying and selling companies. Toward the end of his first year, he had two introductions to clients that would shape his eventual practice.

One was to Peter McNamara of the Mercantile Bank of Canada, arranged by Wayne Shaw, on a deal in which Shaw wanted some help. The firm had had a long connection with the Mercantile Bank of Canada through Stikeman, who was a long-time director.[17] Citibank had acquired its interest, approximately 25 per cent, in the Mercantile from a Dutch bank. This caused a big crisis in the early 1960s when the chairman of Citibank, Stillman Rockefeller, had been reported as having been condescending toward the Canadian minister of Finance, Walter Gordon, and its ownership level was frozen by the Canadian government. Faced with this, Citibank evolved its position into having a wholly owned "near bank" in the form of Citibank Limited, which was incorporated by the Toronto office, represented by Tom Baldwin, later changing its name to Citibank Canada Inc. Its activities at the time amounted, in essence, to the selling of commercial paper. Mercantile, in its own right, did a considerable volume of construction loans, many of which were handled by Jamie Davis. In the late 1970s, Citibank, which did not know Olympia & York, refused to participate in the financial arrangements for the funding of the Shell Oil Building in Calgary. Later, of course,

Citibank joined with many of the other banks that ended up with significant amounts of Olympia & York debt. The second introduction, arranged by Tom Baldwin, was to Citibank itself, which began with financing the acquisition of A & A Records from NBC. Even today, a huge portion of Barrett's work can be traced back to these initial contacts. Many of the people involved have moved to other clients, but the network was established and has been a constant source of work over many years. In the early years, Citibank accounted for a disproportionate percentage of the Toronto firm's business.

LOVER'S LOUNGE

In the first few years of the Toronto's firm's existence, many of its serious non-legal decisions and the development of policy were made in the Lover's Lounge Bar, which grew to be a virtual branch office in which Sankey presided. No fool he, he would regularly drag the managing partner, Bowman, to this lair and spend much of the evening telling the managing partner how terrific he (Bowman) was. Apart from capacity constraints, recalls Yontef, the hardest thing about having a drink with them was listening to Sankey convince Bowman that John Robinette, Bud Estey, and other extraordinary counsel of that era were distant second-raters compared to Bowman.

It was from this auspicious location that Sankey, in a burst of enthusiasm, prompted no doubt by the surroundings, grandly hired Lorraine Gilroy, a bartender in the Lover's Lounge, as the first administrative person in Toronto. Her accounting skills may well have been equal to the task of totalling bar bills but fell well short of what was required for the office manger of a law firm. One of the highlights of her brief stewardship, and the stimulus to bring this uncertain venture to an abrupt end, was that she left the firm's books of account on the subway one evening when she had taken them with her, she said, to do some work at home. It was from Lover's Lounge that practically the entire office watched Paul Henderson score his famous goal in the Canada-USSR hockey series in 1972. The establishment has since been demolished, and there is no plaque to commemorate its importance in the evolution of the firm. *Sic transit gloria mundi.* Another odd haunt frequented by members of the Toronto office was the Mercury Restaurant, a greasy spoon on Bay Street just south of Wellington, which had a motley collection of waiters. It was torn down in the late 1970s to make way for the BCE/Canada Trust complex.

ELLIOTT TAKES OVER TORONTO

The principal growth of the Toronto office began when Elliott moved to Toronto in order to take over management of the firm in that city. The firm was, despite some excellent mandates and the presence of several good lawyers, still very much a bit player in the Toronto market. It had by then become all too clear that the Montreal market would not keep pace with Toronto. Toronto was, however, a market that worked very much on the basis of a well-ordered old boys' establishment and was not welcoming of any perceived interlopers, especially from Montreal. Elliott had excellent business credentials, derived in part from the enormous success of CAE, of which he was chairman, and from his position as a member of the board of the Canadian Imperial Bank of Commerce, so he could not be disregarded. But the legal landscape of the day was still very much one dominated by the local establishment, and the major clients, including the banks, were comfortably divided among them. Mounting any campaign to move into the top ranks of the establishment required careful preparation, and Elliott planned his entry with typical calculation. Arnett remembers Elliott coming into his office in mid-1976 to ask what he thought about the possibility of his coming to Toronto. Arnett said he thought it would be fantastic since the firm, despite the *gravitas* brought by Robarts, did not have much commercial heft in the Toronto community.

The avowedly separatist government of the Parti Québécois had been elected in November 1976, and business confidence in Quebec was extremely low. Elliott had remained in Montreal long enough to vote in the Quebec elections, but he moved formally to Toronto before the end of the year. It is typical of his approach to life that it did not take him long to come to the view, albeit with some element of doublethink, that not only was Toronto the place to be, but that it had always been the place to be. His arrival brought greater stability to the operations of the office and relieved Bowman from many of the duties that were distracting him from his real forte, which was tax planning and litigation. There had been some problems that Elliott had identified in the makeup of the office, including people he himself had originally hired, and Elliott set himself the task of solving them, which involved replacing certain partners who had not made the adjustment from a small practice to one that had aspirations of becoming a first-tier Toronto firm.

Prior to Elliott's arrival, although the venture had been financially successful in the sense that there were profits generated within the Toronto firm, it was safe to say that it had not been a complete organizational success. Most of the work had been provided by the Montreal office, and the firm had not cracked the Toronto legal market in its own right. The expansion under Elliott's leadership would prove to be remarkable. In new surroundings and with a new mission that engaged his full attention, Elliott asserted himself in leading the change of focus from a boutique operation into a firm that would challenge all the major Toronto firms.

It took Elliott no time at all to become immersed in the Toronto community. He had, and maintains, an abiding interest in art, and he had accumulated an extensive personal collection of outstanding Canadian and international art, much of which he has on display in both the Montreal and Toronto offices. He soon became the president of the Art Gallery of Ontario and later chairman of the Canadian Cultural Property Export Review Board. He served on the board of the Canadian Opera Company, the Toronto Symphony Orchestra, and the Toronto General Hospital. Elliott has quietly become a major benefactor to a wide variety of causes and will undoubtedly be uncomfortable to be recognized for his extraordinary generosity. His foundation, the Fraser Elliott Foundation, has made many important contributions to charities and public organizations such as the Agnes Etherington Art Centre at Queen's University in Kingston. At the Toronto General & Western Hospital Foundation, where he was a board member and chairman, he endowed two chairs: one in vascular surgery and another in transplantation research. His donation of one million dollars to the Toronto Symphony Orchestra in 1998 was the largest amount ever received by the TSO from a single donor. In 2001, in addition to an earlier donation of $4 million, he made a $6-million donation to establish a new emergency service at the Toronto General Hospital. The old Toronto establishment has undergone a radical transformation, and Elliott has been a significant factor in its transmogrification.

Apart from the new focus on growing the business and strength of the firm, there is the usual collection of anecdotes involving Elliott that are the stuff of legend. When Bowman would order a martini "not very dry," Elliott would point out dryly, "that's not how you drink them." The overall appearance of the office, the decor of which someone once described as early American bus terminal, enjoyed an immediate turn for the better when Elliott arrived. Tom Baldwin, the "office manager," had organized the frugal purchase of some Marimekko fabric and had it put on a stretcher; this became the central work of art in the main boardroom. Elliott quietly approached Baldwin to ask if he could buy this boardroom "art" for his own fabulous collection and promised that he would try to replace the fabric with something suitable. The Lawren Harris Group of Seven painting became the centrepiece for many years.

Lunch with Elliott was a special event. He always started with a double martini, toward the end of which he would have shrimp cocktail, spearing each shrimp from a dizzying height. This would be followed by a slab of very rare roast beef, washed down with another martini. All this took place every single day at the same table at the Imperial Room of the Royal York Hotel, after which he would return to work in the afternoon. I remember an occasion in Montreal when Dan Colson and I were doing some work for the British Rail Pension Fund and wanted to impress the crusty fund manager with an appearance by a senior partner. We arranged a dinner at the Ritz Carleton Hotel in Montreal, at which Elliott would preside and favour the British client with some of his more trenchant observations on the economy or business world. The waiter asked Elliott if he would have his "usual" Steak Charles. The Brit ordered well-done lamb. The Steak Charles proved to be a filet mignon, sliced horizontally, which was if not raw then barely warm. It put the guest quite off his feed to see Elliott devouring what appeared to him to be raw meat.

LITIGATION STRENGTH

Whatever may be said of the firm's commercial presence in the early days, it was not even on the radar screen of litigation firms in Toronto. Bowman made the occasional foray into the civil courts to deal with some of the work directed to the firm, but this was at best a sideline to his main concentration in tax. No student with a serious interest in litigation would consider looking at Stikeman, Elliott. This was to change partly as a result of a decision in 1977 to try to get into the field of counsel work by first attracting a senior counsel and partly from serendipity. Edgar Sexton, now a judge on the Federal Court of Appeal but then a fashionable counsel at McKinnon McTaggart, was known to be looking around, and Fred Von Veh suggested him as a possible candidate. Some of the lawyers met with him and were favourably impressed, but they decided they needed to check further before moving forward. So Bowman called John Sopinka at Fasken & Calvin, with whom he had roomed for a time at university, to see what he thought of Sexton as a potential senior counsel for the firm. There may have been some miscommunication involved in the process since it later appeared that Sexton had thought he had reached some form of agreement in principle with Elliott.

To Bowman's considerable surprise, Sopinka replied that if they were serious about looking for senior counsel, what about himself? The patriarch counsel then at the Fasken firm was the venerable Walter Williston, and there were several heirs apparent, with a good deal of infighting among them. Sopinka had apparently been thinking of leaving and of inviting Sid Lederman,[18] who had been at Faskens for a time but was then teaching at the Osgoode Hall law school, to come back and join him in practice. The two of them had collaborated in the writing of an excellent book, *The Law of Evidence in Civil Cases*.[19] Bowman immediately put him in touch with Elliott, and an arrangement was made. Sopinka was one of the first Toronto counsel of reputation to change firms, and it gave us instant standing in the litigation field. Sopinka wanted to bring Sid Lederman with him as part of a package deal. Interestingly enough, the package deal was made over the strenuous objections of Von Veh, who considered Osgoode Hall to be a hotbed of radicalism and thought Lederman, as an academic at the institution, must therefore be some sort of pinko who would not be suitable for the firm.

Counsel do much of their work out of the office, and as a result, Sopinka was not physically present as much as many of the lawyers. He was not even on the scene the day he and Lederman officially started. Catherine Bruce, a student at the time, needed some help, and Lederman, who had been out of practice for several years at that stage, was immediately thrown into the middle of some complex procedural matters. One of Sopinka's early clients was John Pope, someone who at the very least would be described as eccentric, but who, fortunately for the firm, was ready to litigate his causes at the drop of a hat, one of which is described in chapter 10. He arrived at the office one day looking for Sopinka, having been told he had an appointment with him, but Sopinka was off somewhere involved in a trial. To attract attention, Pope had stuck a retainer cheque to his forehead. Bowman, who had adapted with admirable speed to the exigencies of private, as opposed to government, practice, moved in quickly to announce that he could relieve Pope of this heavy burden.

With Sopinka as a senior and much respected counsel and Lederman with his distinguished academic credentials in place, the firm was positioned to attract promising associates and students interested in a litigation career including Robert Reuter[20] in July 1978 and John Judge[21] in November of the same year. Students included Kathryn Chalmers, Peter Howard, Donald Houston, and David Brown. Jan Weir[22] joined the firm about the same time. Attracting Sopinka was a coup that paved the way for instant credibility within the Toronto litigation scene and served notice that the firm was no longer just a niche operation in the corporate and tax fields. Senior counsel in Toronto enjoyed far more prestige than almost anywhere in Canada, and the duo of Sopinka and Lederman, already linked through their publication, added a great deal to the cachet of the firm. They, but particularly Sopinka, set about attracting the headline cases needed in the field as a magnet to further and better cases. These headline cases had the desired effect, and each day there would be a stack of telephone messages for Sopinka from would-be clients, which he would pass out among the juniors with instructions to call back and determine whether the potential cases were worthy of attention.

Elliott's arrival in Toronto was probably difficult for Bowman. He had been hired to be the managing partner of the Toronto firm and to have his name on the firm letterhead, so he was no doubt somewhat apprehensive about the advent of the big hitter from Montreal. His role would be made more ambiguous when the chairman of the firm was in the same place as the managing partner of the major non-Montreal office. In time, the management devolved into sectional practices, with Bowman as the head of tax, Arnett as leader of the corporate section, Sopinka in litigation, and Von Veh in labour. Elliott became the main policy-maker, and the others dealt with the departmental problems. There were certainly some tensions, particularly with Sopinka, who had a robust and healthy ego and sharp elbows and who fought hard to preserve the autonomy of the litigation section and his own place in the firm.

MORE FROM MONTREAL

It was not long before others from Montreal followed Elliott's example of moving to Toronto. George Tamaki, Robert Couzin, and David Finkelstein[23] were all very much upset by the political developments in Quebec and wrote the Ontario Bar exams as soon as they were able to make the time available to study for them. They all moved to Toronto. Couzin was the first, arriving in late 1977, providing an important additional platform for tax planning and occasional forays into tax litigation. George Tamaki, who had already experienced during the war what can happen to innocent individuals at the hands of governments, wrote the Ontario Bar exams in 1978 and also moved to Toronto in 1979. Finkelstein got a call to the Ontario Bar in 1978 and moved at the same time as Tamaki. This provided the office with a major capacity, with the related bench-strength to handle any tax matters that could be developed in Toronto. Jimmy Wyatt, a Texan by origin, wrote the exams and moved in 1984 to supplement the corporate section.

The arrival of Tamaki and Finkelstein in 1979 was another important turning point for the Toronto firm. Tamaki was so remarkable that whenever you spoke with him, says Yontef, you came away vowing that you would try to be more like him. He was a wonderful lawyer and the most gentle person. There was an occasion when one of the tax partners had made a mistake on an oil and gas merger transaction, having assumed that foreign exploration expenses would be treated in the same manner, for tax purposes, as domestic exploration expenses. To everyone's horror, we learned of the mistake well after the merger had been completed and into the following fiscal year. Undaunted, Tamaki personally took on the task of going to Ottawa, speaking to every senior civil servant who would make time for him – in short, all of them – explaining that we had made a terrible mistake and leaving the distinct impression that it was he who had made it. The Toronto partners were convinced that the only reason a legislative amendment was introduced to fix the problem was to acknowledge all of Tamaki's years of good work. He would never get upset about anything that was happening in the firm. His universal response was that the firm had been too good to him for him to be complaining about anything. Finkelstein, for his part, was a careful and low-key practitioner who earned the respect and loyalty of any client for whom he worked and was a major addition to the tax capacity of the firm. Both were almost the complete opposite of the lightning-fast and edgy Couzin.

HOW MUCH IS TOO MUCH?

Several lawyers in the Montreal firm, including Maurice Régnier, Mike Richards, Morty Freiheit, Peter Cumyn, Martin Scheim, Calin Rovinescu, Robert Raizenne, and I, made a point of qualifying for the Ontario Bar but did not leave Montreal. The reason for this was partly to have a fallback position in case something precipitous were to happen in Quebec and partly to help the firm organize the shared remuneration between the two legally separate firms. We had always treated ourselves as part of a single firm, notwithstanding the separate legal entities, and effectively pooled the profits of both for distribution among the partners of both. The technique was to have what were designated as "bridging" partners who were in both firms and who could, depending on the respective fortunes in any particular year, draw their share of the profits from either or both of the firms.

We were always a bit worried, both in Montreal and Toronto, that the Law Society of Upper Canada might want to stop the apparent flood of Stikeman, Elliott lawyers from descending on Toronto. Had they wished to, the society could have done this relatively easily. For civil lawyers who had not had the benefit of the joint civil and common law program offered by McGill University beginning in the fall of 1968, the process of admission to the Ontario Bar, after a minimum of three years' practice in another Canadian jurisdiction, was to apply and then to write comprehensive common law examinations in order to demonstrate adequate knowledge of common law principles. If successful at that stage, the next step was to write examinations on the statute law of Ontario to demonstrate that the applicant was sufficiently knowledgeable on the Ontario law in respect of which he or she would be giving advice. The final hurdle was an oral examination, a viva for those having an English university tradition, in front of three benchers of the Law Society. It was at this stage that if the examiners had it in their minds to fail you, they could ask questions that no one could answer, so it was no mere pro forma guest appearance to see if they liked the cut of your suit.

I was one of the last of the first wave of the firm's lawyers to apply for admission to the Ontario Bar, in 1980. I had no intention of leaving Quebec although I liked the idea of a safety net just in case even though my CA designation, with its national transferability, was already probably more than sufficient. So I was happy to wait until Couzin, Finkelstein, Régnier, Cumyn, and Tamaki from our tax section had all finished before I tried my luck. Besides, we needed to make sure that we could satisfy our clients' needs while other members of the section were studying. By the time my turn arrived, however, there had been several Stikeman, Elliott lawyers passing through the eye of that particular needle, so when I submitted my application, I used my home address, and since there was no requirement to do so, I did not disclose the name of the firm in which I had been in "private practice" for the requisite minimum period. The common law examinations and statute examinations were not difficult for someone who had been in practice for twelve years and possessed a reasonable memory. I wrote the common law examinations under the watchful eye of Professor John Durnford[24] in his office at the McGill University faculty of law. The statute examinations, which were written in Toronto, were more detailed but certainly not an overwhelming problem. It was the oral examination that would be the key. I appeared at the hour summoned, and to my horror, three benchers, fully gowned for the occasion, solemnly entered the room. They reviewed my file and remarked that they had noticed that I had obtained a BCL from McGill University in 1967. I had. I had been called to the Quebec Bar in 1968? I had. I had the designation of chartered accountant? I had. I had been in continuous private practice since my call to the Quebec Bar in 1968? I had. Was I in practice as a sole practitioner or within a firm? With a firm. Which firm? It was, I replied with some foreboding, with a firm called Stikeman, Elliott. "Oh, no!" exclaimed the presiding bencher. "Not another one!" Then the questions began, with the examiners making it clear that they could reduce me to dust if they chose to do so.

ჳა

James Riley[25] came to the firm in 1977 as a student through the connection between Stikeman and Dick De Boo, who was Riley's stepfather. Riley had worked for Stikeman for a couple of summers, fixing up and caring for his sailboat, the *Xanadu III,* which had to be specially rigged for passage through the Rideau Canal system. This meant that its mast had to be capable of being lowered; otherwise, it could touch some of the electrical wires and electrocute anyone on board who was touching anything metal. The manoeuvrability of the mast was achieved as a result of a specially machined pin that was removed when the mast was to be lowered to the foredeck. Stikeman, despite his many sporting and other activities, was not particularly well coordinated and one day dropped the pin overboard in the Kingston harbour. Since it was specially made, there was no replacement, so the pin had to be found. Riley tied Stikeman's Swiss army knife to a string and dropped it overboard at the spot where Stikeman had been standing, the theory being that it would come to rest in the general neighbourhood of the pin. He put on a mask and went over the side into some twenty feet of water. This did not give him much time at the bottom, but on the second effort, he found it and emerged triumphant. Stikeman commended him on a "masterly" stroke. Later, Riley looked up Stikeman's usage of the term in a dictionary, believing that "masterful" stroke was the correct expression, only to find that even in the excitement of narrowly avoiding a disaster, Stikeman had in fact been entirely grammatically correct. Only Stikeman, he thought, would have used precisely the correct word in the circumstances. The waters of the Kingston harbour were so polluted that the string attached to the knife disintegrated, and Riley had to go over the side once again to recover the knife. He said his skin itched and tingled for about a week.

Riley also recalls another incident involving Stikeman at one of the Thursday afternoon races at the Royal St Lawrence Yacht Club in Dorval. They had to negotiate a narrow channel in Lac St Louis to get to the course, and the steering mechanism on the boat broke when a pin sheared. There was a big blow coming, and they could easily have been run aground. Stikeman was completely unflustered and asked him to fetch the backup steering tiller. Riley did not have the faintest idea what this was. Stikeman said it looked like a big pipe, and it was stored below deck. Riley remembered seeing a large pipe that he had almost thrown away during the cleaning process of the boat and brought it to Stikeman, who put it in place, and the situation was resolved. Riley says that Stikeman was at his best when things were going badly; he seemed to almost live for moments of that nature. He had the curious knack of being able to think quickly in such situations, to see clearly the solution to the problem, and to not be paralyzed into inaction. He inspired confidence, had no wasted motion, and was gentle throughout any emergency with those whose help was needed. It was this same quality that was so important in the race around the Isle of Wight, described in chapter 5, when it was Stikeman who was able to keep the boat on course through a heavy storm, while many others turned back or were in distress.

Riley was very fond of his stepfather, who he said was a most remarkable man. When selling law books for Butterworths during the Depression, he was so good that even then, he sold enough to be able to take the summers off. He remembers De Boo describing the evening he had with Stikeman shortly after the two first met. They went out for a huge dinner at the Château Laurier in Ottawa after Stikeman had shown him the draft of what was to become the *Canada Tax Service,* a seminal work in a new and expanding field, and De Boo had agreed to publish it. De Boo spent the last of his money at the dinner and had to borrow cab fare from Stikeman to get home. He lived for the moment and was always prepared to take huge entrepreneurial risks, as he did when he started Richard De Boo Publishing Limited, with which the firm has had an unbroken connection since it was founded. It was also typical of De Boo when he had enlisted well under age during World War I to become a stretcher-bearer, serving overseas in France at the age of fourteen or fifteen. De Boo, a constant smoker during his lifetime, died of lung cancer in 1970.

Riley, perhaps because of the relationship between his stepfather and Stikeman, never thought of applying elsewhere for a job when he finished law school, where he had thought, he says, now shaking his head in disbelief, that he wanted to be a tax lawyer. As it happened, after he had been hired, he was the gold medallist at the University of Toronto in his graduating year. He remembers calling Yontef to tell him and that Yontef seemed quite pleased with the result. It seemed to have come as something of a surprise, but it certainly reinforced the decision, taken to some degree at the time on spec, to hire him. Riley responded well to the challenges of practice. When a partner at the huge New York law firm of White & Case, during a Texaco transaction, turned to Yontef during the closing dinner and whispered that the firm had been terrific and that Riley was the best young associate that he had ever seen, Yontef did not have the heart to tell his host that Riley had only been articling for five or six months.

Ron Durand's[26] entry into the firm as a student in July 1978 almost foundered on the shoal of internal politics. Durand made the "mistake" of writing to Yontef, as someone who had also been to Harvard, asking if he could summer with the firm and work in tax. Yontef went down the hall with the excellent resumé, expecting to receive full credit from Don Bowman for his recruiting skills, seeking only confirmation that Durand could work for Bowman for the summer. Bowman proved to be unimpressed, wondering why the application to work in tax had not come directly to him. The most Bowman would agree to do was try him once. Some exaggeration of the truth occurs from time to time in the recruiting process. Yontef told Durand all was clear. Fortunately, Robert Couzin had moved to Toronto before Durand started, and he recognized his abilities and championed his return to the firm after the Bar admission course. William Innes[27] was recruited by Bowman to help him with tax cases, and he became well regarded as a capable and careful litigator while with the firm. Together with Bowman and Couzin, he rounded out the firm's capacity before the courts.

Preliminary difficulties notwithstanding, it was clear by the late 1970s that something was working. The firm was pressing on the recruiting side. We were not dropping the ball as often, and every now and again, we benefited from some blind luck. Kathryn Chalmers[28] applied for an articling job, and everyone was excited that we were to "be in the running." Chalmers, based on her resumé alone, was a sure bet to be hired. Those on the students hiring committee naturally took full personal credit for her having had the good sense to apply and for her having been sufficiently taken with the opportunity to work in litigation to join. As to her recruitment, Chalmers recalls that it occurred in the days when law firms were allowed to send letters to students, and she presumed she got one from Stikeman Elliott because she won the tax prize. She previously had an apartment on campus, and the landlady was not very efficient in forwarding her mail to her new address, so she was about to phone Davies Ward & Beck to accept an offer from them when the letter from Stikeman Elliott arrived after a delay of some six weeks. She phoned the firm, mainly to apologize for the delay in answering, but John Dingle, to whom she spoke, asked her to come in that afternoon and perhaps they could meet.

She jumped on the GO train from Hamilton, enjoyed the interview, and agreed to join the firm. She was one of six articling students to arrive that year, and of all of them, only she and Bruce Pollack are still with the firm. Dingle asked if she could start in litigation, which was not something she had considered especially since in the early days, the reputation of the litigation department in Toronto was that it was simply a collection agency for debts sent to it by Montreal. Bob Reuter had just joined the firm that May, and Ernie Rovet was still there. Sopinka was off on a major criminal trial involving the Hamilton dredging scandal, having hired Jan Weir to work with him on that, and they were working together with François Mercier and Jim Woods in Montreal. Sid Lederman was doing his thing, and between them, they constituted the entire litigation department. The same committee also took credit for the Blake Cassels anti-nepotism policy that brought Oxford graduate and Olympic-class rider Peter Howard[29] to the firm. An investment banker who was introduced to Yontef once said that he had heard Yontef's name but "had not lived the legend." Howard, in contrast, already lived his legend and was an instant hit with the growing "in" crowd.

As the 1970s came to an end, the Toronto firm was on the legal map, occupying if not the first tier, then very much the top of the second. While we had no lock on any of the major banks and corporate giants, we had moved into the position of being on everyone's list as second choice when conflicts or other opportunities beckoned. We had moved from being a curiosity and a collection of arrivistes to a recognized player in the Toronto market. We had thirty lawyers in-house and the necessary infrastructure. In Churchillian terms, although it was not the end nor even the beginning of the end, it was definitely the end of the beginning.

CHAPTER 5

The Road Warriors

Looking back with the familiarity of more than thirty years of foreign offices, it may be easy to forget what an unusual feature it was at the outset for a small Canadian law firm to venture into international waters. Even of the firms today, the size of which would have been unthinkable at the time, very few have dared to take the step of putting themselves on the line other than in Canada. We have, in our country, a tradition of internal exploration of a vast and largely empty land but almost none of external exploration. It was a risky business to leave the relative comfort of Canadian shores to recross the Atlantic, which had been the path for much of the current population, later to cross the broader and deeper Pacific Ocean, and still later, to step into the huge and powerful US market. It took vision, courage, and the willingness to risk funds and reputation that such initiatives implied, as well as a generosity of spirit toward future generations of lawyers in the firm who would benefit from the generational subsidy assumed by the original partners. This is a chapter that tries to give some of the flavour of what the outposts were like and how our *légion étrangère* – road warriors – fared far from Canada and almost always, without the backup they would have enjoyed had they stayed at home.

LONDON

Notwithstanding the body blow delivered by the 1967 exodus to a small firm barely fifteen years old with about the same number of lawyers, Stikeman had decided by 1968 that the firm should be in London, then already the acknowledged financial centre of Europe. He had many contacts there and was his usual optimistic and energetic self, convincing Elliott that it would be a good idea. Elliott did not initially subscribe wholeheartedly to the idea, but Stikeman swept all before him, and it was agreed. If there was an operating rule of thumb in those days, it was "Whatever Heward wants, Heward gets." All they knew for certain was that Stikeman, who was a gold mine of business, would be able to make happen whatever needed to happen. The question was who should go, not an easy matter to solve given the small number of lawyers in the firm. In 1969, they settled on Peter Cumyn, who had joined the firm's tax practice from the federal Department of Justice two years earlier. As Cumyn recalls the occasion, he encountered Stikeman in the corridor one morning and noticing that he seemed preoccupied, asked him what was on his mind. Stikeman replied that he had been trying to persuade Elliott to open an office in London, but there was no one whom they could send. Cumyn said, "I'll go." Stikeman seemed surprised at first, then excited, and said he would speak to him after lunch. Having jumped down the well, Cumyn quickly called his wife, Madeleine, to see how she felt about it – just in case – and got the all clear. The decision was made the same afternoon.

Permission to practise in London, even though the firm would not be practising English law, had to be obtained from the Home Office upon advice of the Law Society, a process that routinely took as long as three months. Applicants had to write a letter, signed by the senior partner of the firm, to the Home Office, with a copy to the Law Society, setting forth the purposes of the proposed London office, the names and descriptions of the persons in charge, a description of Canadian clients having international operations, a history of the firm, a description of its activities and size, a description of the activities of its partners, an indication of where the London office would be located, the present assets of the firm, its London banking arrangements, and all topped off with professional and financial references in London. It was a tedious but unavoidable process, and permission was granted in due course.

Cumyn made a preliminary trip to London in May 1969 to see what possibilities for business might exist and to determine what premises might be available. The preliminary contacts had been diffusely encouraging, but there were no major promises of work from English sources, many of whom had few Canadian legal problems, and the Canadian companies in London had a tendency to refer their own problems back to their Canadian head offices. The most promising (although unconfirmed) sources of business appeared to be the merchant banks. By the end of July, it was determined that Cumyn would relocate to London as of September 1 and that a permanent office would be established by the end of October. Cumyn circulated a memorandum throughout the firm, asking all lawyers to provide contacts and names of those who should be notified of the existence of the London office. Space had not been confirmed by the end of August before he left, but temporary accommodation was to be provided by the CIBC at 2 Lombard Street, London, EC 2, and Cumyn had located quarters for himself in fashionable South Kensington.

Not even lip service was paid to the idea of a business plan. When the time came to open up shop, Cumyn was for all intents and purposes given a box of calling cards and sent off on his own to drum up whatever business he could find. [1] The extent of the planning was to guess what it might cost, not what profit was expected. If it would cost, say, $100,000 per year to keep Stikeman happy, the firm would spend that amount. There is no doubt, for example, that had Stikeman decided that he wanted an additional $100,000 from the profits of the firm, everyone would have been more than willing to agree. Apart from his own salary, Cumyn estimated that the budget for the first year might amount to some $40,000–$45,000, but senior management thought it would be considerably higher, probably in the range of 50 per cent more. During his exploratory trip in May, he had been concerned that he did not have enough of an idea regarding the source of sufficient business to be sure of success, but he considered it crucial to be able to intercept a considerable part of the Canadian tax business referred by British accounting firms to their Canadian partners or associates. It was vaguely reminiscent of the old western movies in which the young lieutenant is assigned some impossibly dangerous mission, which he is certain not to survive, and as he salutes and turns bravely to leave, the commanding officer says, "Oh, and Lieutenant ..." "Yes, sir?" responds the brave, but doomed, young man. "Good luck," says the commanding officer, returning to his papers.

After arriving in England, Cumyn located small two-office premises of no particular character at Compter House, 4/6 Wood Street, in the "City." At a reception and dinner at the Savoy Hotel on October 16, 1969, which was attended by Stikeman, Elliott, Mercier, Robb, and Angus from Montreal, the firm's presence was announced, and the London office became a reality.[2] Stikeman had been a friend of Hans Frank of Fried Frank in New York, and the two of them had always hoped their firms could do something together, but their underlings never managed to make it work even though, for a time, we effectively shared London office space with them. The offices remained at Compter House until 1976, when we moved to Leith House at 47/57 Gresham Street, also in the City.

Prices in London had not yet begun their astronomical increase, but the costs of opening in London at the time were roughly equivalent to the profits of two full partners at a time when there were less than a half a dozen partners in the firm. It was a significant investment and gives an indication of what an aggressive initiative it represented for a firm that was not yet fully established in its home market. Cumyn was, fortunately, full of energy and not afraid of making cold calls, at which he soon became expert, making sure that the major firms, banks, and investment dealers were aware that there was a Canadian law firm on the ground in London. The establishment of the office was more daring than most people appreciated. At this time, even most of the big American firms were not represented in London, giving us a head start of more than two years when we had the field virtually to ourselves.

Stikeman had, several years earlier, been co-founder of a group of lawyers and accountants under the ambitious description of Multinational Fiscal Associates, which was composed of leading international tax practitioners from around the world, to whom they referred among themselves as the "Mufia." The principal British figure in the group was his long-time friend Hobart Moore, a well-known chartered accountant and senior partner of Moore Stephens; Moore was very helpful in the early days, making introductions and including Cumyn in many conferences and social occasions. Other members included: John Hemingway of Freshfields; Sidney Pine of New York, a co-founder of the group with Stikeman; Thomas Baer of Zurich; Kendall

Munro of Sullivan & Cromwell in New York; John McLean of Deacons in Hong Kong; and William Quasha from the Philippines. There was always some suspicion among the more cynical of the Montreal tax lawyers that Stikeman had formed this particular organization so that the expenses of getting together would be deductible for tax purposes because the Canadian legislation, and perhaps others, had changed to restrict deductibility of convention expenses where the convention did not take place within the obvious geographical limitations of the organization. This legislation had the practical effect, for example, of preventing the Canadian Bar Association from holding its (winter) meetings in Barbados. There was never any suggestion that the organization was not a good source of business for the firm, although the business was derived almost exclusively through the personal involvement of Stikeman. Moore was an excellent contact, and the relationship was carefully nurtured.

The work in London was confined to the practice of Canadian law since it was considered unhelpful to be poaching on the territory of the English firms, which would clearly not be too interested in giving work to their competitors. Cumyn's specialty was tax, in which he could provide state-of-the-art advice for British firms and their clients, and he established good contacts with the professional firms and merchant bankers who might be thinking of tax-driven financial products or financing projects. His biggest commercial deal in the early days was to coordinate, with English solicitors, the takeover of a small public shipping company by Stikeman's Montreal-based client Fednav, which was owned by the Pathy family. Burnett Steamship & Navigation Co. owned two ships that had been chartered by Fednav. In the aftermath of a market change, its shareholders became disenchanted with their investment, and Fednav was able to buy the shares at a bargain basement price.

By the early 1970s, a feeling developed within the Montreal and Toronto offices that there was potential for more commercial work to be garnered through the London presence. One of the rationales for having opened in Toronto was the flow of work to that city from European investors. This led to the conclusion that the next impetus in the London office should be aimed at corporate work rather than continuing to be essentially tax-driven and doing only some corporate work. Harold (Sonny) Gordon was identified as the new London representative, and he arrived in October 1971 to begin a transition period that would end with Cumyn's return to Montreal in January 1972, a period during which Gordon claims never to have eaten so much smoked salmon in his life.

Gordon was just as gregarious as Cumyn but with a style of his own. As a long-time and dedicated bachelor, he enjoyed a combined social and business life that was unparalleled in the firm's history. When he arrived in London, Gordon considered himself to be very green and inexperienced, and he regards the experience as an incredible finishing school. He had an uncanny and affable ability to work any room and could be counted upon to meet anyone at any time. Everyone at a reception he attended would invariably remember him. Indeed, the recognition factor attached to our

London representatives has been remarkable from the very beginning of the venture. In Gordon's case, members of the firm used to joke about his ability to get to know people by applying the well-known joke about appearing on the Vatican balcony with the Pope and having the assembled Roman crowd wonder aloud who was up there with Sonny. Gordon regards his four years in London as the most formative of his life, especially in the matter of how to relate to people for the purpose of doing business with them. The range of business continued to expand during Gordon's stewardship and was helped by his familiarity with the provisions of the *Foreign Investment Review Act,* although he left to return to Montreal in September 1974 before the new system was fully under way.

Gordon got involved in an anti-dumping case on behalf of some thirty UK mills in the north counties, which were charged with dumping double-knit goods (who would now admit to ever having worn them?) into Canada. He remembers another case in which he had been retained by Bill Hutchison of International Computers Ltd. on a contract consultation that required lengthy drafting, never one of Gordon's great loves in the law. Months after he had finished the assignment, he got a call from Hutchison, saying that he was coming to London and that he absolutely needed Gordon to attend. Gordon showed up at the appointed time and place to find a room filled with thirty people, twenty on one side and ten or so on the other, all with the air of thoughtful concern of persons with major digestive tract problems. "Thank God you're here. This is what your client has failed to do," he was told, and they reeled off a lengthy list of defaults. "Now," they said, "what are you going to do about that?" Gordon thought for a moment and then said that he was immediately going to send a telegram with the following message: "Fuck you. Strong letter to follow." This was a big hit with all those present and completely broke the glacial atmosphere that had settled over the meeting, enough so that at the dinner the same evening, he was presented with a plaque to commemorate the event. Evidently, the "strong letter" was not strong enough since in the end, his client did not perform.

Gordon's stewardship of the office raised the profile of the firm, especially within the Canadian expatriate community, but that community did not have the inroads required to get into the big accounting and law firms that controlled the type of work for which we were looking. While this activity was significant in raising the profile of the firm in London, the promotional activity was essentially lost on the professional firms.

The *Foreign Investment Review Act* (FIRA) proved to be a mixed blessing, and from the perspective of making Canada an attractive place for non-residents to invest, it was a disaster. The legislation, enacted in 1973 and coming into effect as of April 9, 1974, was one of Canada's periodic reactions to concerns that too great a portion of Canadian businesses was in the hands of foreigners and that steps had to be taken to restrict such ownership. There was a complicated application process involved for acquisitions and the commencement of any substantial new business. Although the principal target of the legislation was the United States, its provisions nevertheless applied to acquisitions by other foreigners as well. The administrative attitude was predominately negative. On the other hand, for clients who were willing to take on the challenge of working through the bureaucratic mess, it proved to be a great source of business for the firm, and Gordon's thorough understanding of the legislation and an unparalleled knowledge of its administration was one of our greatest business-attracting assets.

Gordon conducted seminars on FIRA for the benefit of several organizations and was sufficiently expert that even after he had returned to Montreal, he was asked back by the Canadian High Commission in London to participate in a conference hosted by the High Commission in October 1974, to which the Foreign Investment Review Agency itself sent representatives. This was an effort to defuse some of the profoundly negative reaction to the legislation. About seventy of the major investments banks attended the conference for an entire day, and this impetus was the real basis for the development of working relationships with them. The conference was followed up with lunches and private seminars for the banks such as Warburgs as well as certain clients, and although the banks got all their advice for free, they did reciprocate by referring work to the firm. Gordon was also instrumental in the preparation of a brief submitted by the Canadian Bar Association to the government, requesting changes to the legislation to make it more workable. The firm handled a remarkable portion of the inbound investment into Canada from Europe during the heyday of FIRA, including Boots, GKN, Chloride, Rentokil, British American Tobacco, the British Rail Pension Fund, GEC, Taylor Woodrow, and British Airways. FIRA seminars were also given in Germany after Cumyn identified the interest of German investors in Canadian real estate. Stikeman went over for the purpose, and the seminars led to the representation of RWI in Canada, for which we have done a great deal of work over the years. When Stikeman came to London or Europe for meetings of this nature, he was, says Gordon, like a one-man wrecking crew, meeting everyone in London who mattered, but he always made certain that Gordon was included in the meetings set up with the English firms such as Freshfields and Linklaters.

In the early 1970s, there was considerable concern about the Soviet Union and its possible designs on more of Western Europe. There had been many complications of a legal nature arising out of the two previous European wars, and attention began to focus on what might be the best structures in the event of further difficulties. We had been involved in many complicated plans to deal with the legal ownership of assets when hostile powers occupied a country, and Stikeman had been a close advisor of Thomas Bata, whose family enterprise had been confiscated by the Soviet Union and its puppet government in Czechoslovakia after World War II. This concern persisted until well into the 1980s and gave rise to many complex plans designed to provide legal protection that could be invoked against the occupying powers, whether actual or anticipated, in domestic and international courts. For the most part, they involved complicated schemes to transfer effective ownership of assets and companies from the nationals in the occupied territories to other entities that could prosecute claims in foreign jurisdictions and international courts.

One clear problem was that of sovereign risk, whereby the jurisdiction of incorporation could be affected by an occupying power. A solution that seemed to have considerable appeal in later years was to form a Canadian company (where the sovereign risk was not European despite the fact that the company was owned by Europeans) that would not be resident in Canada for tax purposes and that would operate its businesses through offshore branches. The key was to have a Canadian company that could advance claims against an occupying power, but that would not be subject to Canadian taxes in the meantime. There were a number of technical legal hoops through which one had to jump, but the legal form preserved the ability for clients to protect their investments should confiscation occur. There was a mechanism that could be used in New Brunswick through companies incorporated by special acts put through the legislature as private bills. Some New Brunswick MPPs eventually balked at this, apparently under the impression that someone was up to no good although the "no good" could never be identified. In the latter part of the 1980s, it was discovered that a dozen or so such companies had been incorporated in Prince Edward Island but had never been owned by Canadian residents (and were not considered for tax purposes as "Canadian" companies), which the owners were prepared to sell, naturally, for large amounts. Marc Lalonde,[3] by then a member of the firm, was dispatched to speak with Premier Joe Ghiz to assure him that there would be no embarrassment to the PEI government, but that our clients simply wanted to do offshore business. We managed to get a tax ruling that the entities would not be taxable on the basis that the mind and management of the companies would be outside of Canada. One such plan was Transatlantic Trust, put together by Gordon and Richard Hay, with Freshfields as English counsel and Osler Hoskin in Toronto. While the lead lawyer from Oslers was Alan Beatty, the whole arrangement almost foundered when Bertha Wilson, not yet appointed to the Supreme Court of Canada, expressed in one of her memoranda the view that she did not think it would work. The objection was overridden.

Next to go to London, in October 1974, was Daniel Colson, again from the Montreal office via Loyola College and the Université Laval in Quebec City, where he was a friend of Conrad Black, a connection that would prove significant for the London office. Colson had originally been hired as a lawyer in the Montreal office by Gordon, who was not prepared to be impressed by someone who had gone to Loyola and Laval and who had not had particularly impressive marks until he got to law school. After two and a half hours in his office, Colson had completely charmed Gordon, so when he was contemplating his return to Montreal, Gordon suggested to Elliott that Colson be his replacement in London. They overlapped for three months. Danny and Suzanne Colson became indefatigable ambassadors of the firm in London, constantly entertaining clients and wooing prospective ones. No opportunity to attend and participate in conferences was too unimportant for the new Stikeman Elliott standard-bearer.

Colson was, in his youth, quite uneducated in the inimitable ways of the British and had many occasions to experience the highly developed English condescension reserved for presumptuous colonials who might find themselves in the mother country. He was once assigned the task by Suzanne of returning from work with a brie cheese for a dinner party they were hosting at their apartment that evening. In execution of this important mandate, he presented himself in the Cheese Hall at Harrod's, where he was met by the person in charge, duly attired in a morning coat and striped trousers. "Good afternoon, sir," said this worthy, in the plummiest accent imaginable. "And how may I be of service?" "I need a cheese," said Colson. "Very good, sir. And what kind of cheese did you have in mind?" "A brie," announced Colson, in pursuance of the uxorious instructions. "Very good, sir," was the reply. "Shall we repair to the brie section." Arriving there, they settled on the size required, and the Harrod's major-domo began to search among the industrial quantities of brie for a cheese of the appropriate ripeness. He asked, "When is the cheese to be served, sir?" Colson said it was for the same evening. "Very good, sir," came the response that put him in his proper colonial place. "And at what time this evening will it be served?"

The Colsons made the acquaintance of a local policeman, who adopted the habit of dropping by for a drink, and he did so often enough that he was christened the Sheriff of Belgravia. One evening, when they were due to attend the theatre with Fraser Elliott, who was in town, Colson arrived home to find the Sheriff ensconced, already on his third mahogany-coloured scotch whiskey and chatting incessantly, delaying their departure. The punctuality problem was solved when the Sheriff offered to drive them to the theatre. They arrived in the back of a police car, with the lights flashing and siren blaring, to the distinct non-amusement of Elliott. They were, however, as Colson points out, on time for the performance.

Colson's approach to the development of the firm's business was much more closely aligned with Cumyn's original objectives of finding and developing good contacts with the London professional firms who had clients with Canadian interests and to set the tone both as to the reason why the office had been established and the nature of the practice we sought. Colson changed the focus of the approach away from the Canadian expatriate community. If we were there to stay, then both the firm and its client base needed to become institutionalized, recognized as fixtures in the London business and legal communities, and strengthened by addition to the roster, which grew during Colson's time to some seven lawyers.

He became a regular attendee at summer garden parties at Ascot, Cowes, and Buckingham Palace. He turned the nature of the firm's practice toward the nascent privatization tendencies, Eurobond loans, and cross-border transactions, the latter including not only Canadian transactions as such, but also work on behalf of Canadian companies in other European countries. He set out to meet every British investment banker and lawyer in London who might have had any connection with Canada or Canadian clients, identifying them as the sources of business for a Canadian law firm that was in place for the long term. By the second year that he was in London, the firm's operations broke even and thereafter grew significantly. FIRA grew into a profitable niche practice area, but it remained overall a profoundly negative influence in respect of the perception of Canada by the international business community. Many of the large potential transactions on which we were consulted did not proceed due to fear of regulatory rejection. The whole scheme was very much an international black mark for Canada, and it took some time for the politicians to recognize this fact and to dismantle FIRA, as an agency to screen (with a predilection to deny) investment, and to institute Investment Canada as an agency with a mandate to promote external investment, which finally occurred in 1985.

Next in line for managing the London office was Brian Rose, the first to go to a foreign posting from the Toronto office, arriving there in August 1978. He had been sitting in his office in Toronto one day when Elliott came in to say that "we" had decided that it would be in the best interests of the firm that Rose go to London. This did not sound to him like a subject that Elliott had come to debate, so off he went. It took little time for him to add his personal recognition factor to that of the firm in general, particularly at Samuel Montagu, where a separate chair had to be found for him after he broke one of their collection of Chippendales. He is an enormous man, some six feet six and well over 300 pounds, the exact weight remaining a variable but always secret number depending on his current level of dedication to his diet. Rose had the same philosophy and approach to business as Colson, which was to establish a level of recognition for the firm and to expand the financially related client base.

Reflecting on almost five years in London, Rose prepared a lengthy memorandum to Jim Grant, managing partner of the Montreal office, concerning the status of the London office, the business of the firm, and the position of non-resident partners. Much of it is too detailed to go into here, but certain portions help to give the flavour of what it was like to be in the field, cut off from the daily support available at home, where you can walk down the hall to get assistance when something is beyond your personal experience. Compare that to working in a small office, the existence of which is barely known by the obvious sources of work.

We found upon arrival in the UK the firm was well known as Danny and his predecessors had done an excellent job of making initial contacts. Much of what we did was directed at following up those contacts as opposed to attempting to develop new ones, again because of limited resources in London.

In summary, our major method of marketing was to continue to keep a high profile in London directed at the "right" people and to try to develop personal associations with those people. Personal relationships could be critical, particularly in the very mobile merchant banking and investment banking communities, and those contacts developed other contacts or they moved within firms. It must be understood for some firms, particularly merchant and investment bankers, personal contact and performance counted for much more than the firm. They want someone they know who they know will perform and in whom they have confidence. They don't care whether that person is an individual practitioner or a member of a large firm. This necessity to maintain contact cannot be overemphasized and does create difficulties ...

Harry Heward Stikeman.

Roy Fraser Elliott.

George T. Tamaki.

John N. Turner.

Stanley H. Hartt.

Harold P. Gordon.

John Sopinka.

"Justices" David Brown, John Judge, Patrick O'Kelly in the Supreme Court of Canada under the watchful eye of Justice John Sopinka.

Richard De Boo.

Donald G.H. Bowman.

Robert Couzin, James Grant, John Stransman.

Helen Xenos, François Mercier, Hélène Latour.

Fraser Elliott and Heward Stikeman.

Heward Stikeman, Chief Pilot, "StikeAir."

Heward Stikeman, 1991 Christmas Party.

James Grant and Edward Waitzer, second and third chairmen of the firm.

Peter O'Brien, Gérald Tremblay, Senator Maurice Riel.

David Angus, Marvin Yontef, Fraser Elliott.

Milton Hess, Michael Richards, James Robb.

Even with some of these challenges, the marketing efforts of the firm were successful despite the fact that Canada presented a rather unfavourable investment climate during the FIRA years. We did increasing amounts of work for virtually all of the UK merchant bankers and were known to the director of each such bank who was responsible for the Canadian market. Within the London legal firms, there was a practice that each lawyer was free to refer work when other counsel were needed rather than doing so on a firm-wide basis, so it meant trying to get to know as many lawyers as possible, not an easy challenge with a small staff on the ground. Continuity was the real problem. There had been some criticism of the turnover when partners left to return home or go to some other office, some of which was abated when Colson returned, but it was almost as important to build the one-on-one relationships as it was to be known generally as a good firm. At the very least, he thought, the senior lawyers should stay in place as long as possible; changes of junior lawyers were not as serious.

By the time Rose presented these thoughts, other offices had been opened, but the network of foreign offices was relatively small. As time passed, one of the principal challenges was generating the necessary support for the foreign offices from busy practitioners in the Canadian offices. We have never operated with excess capacity and have always been known as a firm where all the lawyers work hard and where we do not generally hire ahead of our anticipated needs. As a result, our road warriors have been faced with the additional challenge of attracting attention to their needs and regularly encountered the "out-of-sight, out-of-mind" syndrome. Rose had the further concern that there was insufficient follow-up with clients referred to the Canadian offices because the Canadian lawyers were so busy with their own work that, especially in Toronto, the new clients were not receiving enough attention, and much of the relationship building had to be done from the Montreal office. We did great work for the clients, he concluded, but we fell short on personal cultivation of them.

Strangers in strange lands need more than just business cards and a hearty handshake to make a lasting impression, and many law firms developed the practice of producing regular bulletins or short summaries of developments that could be of interest to clients and potential clients. For a firm that had such a distinguished record of producing the *Canada Tax Service, Doing Business in Canada,* and the various corporate law manuals, it took us a surprisingly long time to get to the point of having some handouts that our foreign office lawyers could leave behind. Our publication on FIRA was a major success, and although it was a one-time-only effort, we milked it very well, and that put us on the map in the field. The success of the publication led Rose to comment on the need for other such initiatives:

In the time that I was in London, we did not have a sufficiently good understanding with our offices in Canada to permit maximum utilization of the marketing techniques described above. In addition to the "stroking" difficulty, we do not as a firm produce memoranda on developments of law, such as those produced by Blakes [Blake Cassels] or by the American firms, for dissemination to clients. It would be extremely helpful to the London office to continually receive updates on major changes in law, which could be sent to clients and then followed up with clients. In my view, the only way to effect that is to have someone in each of the offices who is responsible for liaising with the London office (and perhaps it should be on a section-by-section basis) and have the offices in Canada as aware of their responsibility for this as they are for the work they are doing for Matthew Bender [the firm's publication, *Doing Business in Canada*] and the *Tax Service*. It may be that this is simply impractical in terms of the amount of work involved, and this should be considered further.

Colson returned to London in December 1983, bringing with him Brian Hansen from the Hong Kong office. His return preceded by a few months the arrival in London of Yvon Martineau, a corporate lawyer from Montreal of considerable intelligence and high energy, who was being sent there in the hope that he might be able to expand his horizons from a decidedly provincial base. It was an experiment that enjoyed limited success, and he returned to Montreal in 1986 but would depart a few years later. The return of Colson was far more newsworthy than the arrival of Martineau, but both were marked by receptions in early April 1984, organized by Rose as the outgoing London partner and designated hitter for the fledgling New York office.

By the time Colson and Hansen arrived in London, the office was located in Leith House, immediately next door to Linklaters, where it remained for several years before moving across the Thames to the Cottons Centre at the south end of London Bridge in 1988. Apart from the obvious value of adding Hansen to the London team, his presence in London also meant that he switched over from part-time, which had been the arrangement in Hong Kong, to full-time practice with the firm. Not long thereafter, we became the first reputable firm to move south of the river, where we took space next to the Canadian Imperial Bank of Commerce, a worldwide habit the firm appears to have adopted. Colson and Hansen spent about two months sounding out clients to determine whether a move across the river would be detrimental in any way to our practice, but they said they did not care where we worked. They did not come to visit us, and all they were concerned about was that we would come to them and were close enough to do that. The move, in summary, made absolutely no difference to the quality or the quantity of the practice.

The development of the Eurobond market was important for the growth of the firm, both in profile and in billings. A number of factors contributed to the success that was enjoyed in London, including the presence of investment bankers specializing in Eurodollar loans, which were very much in vogue as the petrodollars multiplied with the massive increases in oil prices and these funds had to be re-deployed in some manner within the world economy. This activity had to be managed in tandem with the ongoing activities of the Canadian Foreign Investment Review Agency, which screened all significant foreign investment in Canada. The firm handled a huge proportion of the inbound investment and was able to act on many of the Eurodollar loans that originated in London. This was a valuable source of referred work, initially in Montreal and later in Toronto, as the shift away from Montreal as the traditional business centre in Canada accelerated in the mid-1970s and the Toronto office became increasingly active.

The five-year period in London from 1983 to 1988 was a remarkable time in the expansion of the London office. Up to then, the practice had been extremely good, but there had been a relative scarcity of very large transactions between London and Canada or in the European market from Canada. This expansion had less to do with Colson and Hansen than with the fortunate turn in markets during the time they were there. The first major breakthrough in the London office came in the Eurobond market about three months after their arrival in 1983. This was a boom time in European capital markets, and that, combined with English law firms grossly underpaying their associates, resulted in the investment banks hiring large numbers of securities associates from the large UK firms, which then were severely stretched for legal talent. Before this, the London office had never handled a Eurobond transaction, all such work having been undertaken by the English law firms as underwriters' counsel.

Hansen received a phone call one afternoon from Charles Fisher at Orion Royal Bank to say that they had been appointed as manager for a Eurobond offering by a British Columbia telephone company and asked if we could do the transaction for them. Hansen stated, with fingers crossed, that the firm had a great deal of experience in this area, and the next morning, he was on a plane to British Columbia. This was a novel experience for the firm. Hansen remembers spending hours on the phone with David Finkelstein in the Toronto office, trying to absorb the intricacies of the *Income Tax Act* with regard to such issues as exemptions from Canadian withholding taxes on interest payments by the borrowers. He finally became comfortable that we could provide the requisite tax opinion, and once the template had been mastered, issues became quite simple after that. But the most important thing we achieved, probably unbeknownst to the managers, was to put all the documentation, except for the underwriting agreement and the manager's agreement, under the laws of British Columbia. From that time on, Colson and Hansen feverishly marketed all the investment banks in London with the theory that all the latest deals in the Eurobond market were being done under Canadian law and that it was much cheaper than to do it under English law. The economic argument worked extremely well. They then managed to convince the merchant banks that there was no sense in having an English law firm and a Canadian law firm working on the same transaction. They also managed to get them to put the underwriting or manager's agreement and the subunderwriting agreements under the equivalent Canadian law as well. This could have been an ongoing breakthrough had the firm been in a position to devote more resources to the London and Eurobond practices. Had the use of Canadian law for such an international practice become universally accepted, it might have pre-empted the later shift to the use of English or US law that developed when the English and American firms turned their attention and their superior financial and manpower resources to the Eurobond markets. Although it would have required a massive commitment, which may well have been beyond our means, the inability to maintain the initial momentum toward the use of Canadian law for all such transactions may be counted as a missed opportunity.

There were four or five heady years in London in the mid-1980s. Stikeman, Elliott was ranked as high as fourth among international law firms as underwriters' counsel on Eurobond offerings, and the London lawyers travelled all around the world doing these transactions. In two of these years, they did almost one hundred deals in the European market. Orion Bank was the first to handle a Eurobond offering by a Canadian issuer and denominated in Canadian dollars. One of the biggest in the early days was a $300-million issue by the Montreal Urban Community. They were very remunerative in those days, and before they eventually became routine, the fees amounted to in excess of £10,000 on every transaction, and deals such as the US/Canadian/New Zealand dollar currency swap transactions for Goldman Sachs, which were popular for a period of twelve months, generated upwards of £20,000 a transaction. This was at a time when the Royal Bank of Canada, the Bank of Montreal, the Bank of Nova Scotia, and Royal Trust, both in Canada and through their subsidiaries in Australia and New Zealand, were undertaking transactions in the market. It is a testament to the firm that it has retained dominance in that market, firstly through Jamie Davis and then through Marianne Sussex. While the level of work and fees have reduced, the Eurobond practice – which includes normal bond offerings, medium-term notes, NIFs (note issuance facilities), RUFFs (revolving underwriting financing facilities), and other variations – remains an important part of the practice of the office. In those days, Hansen had a Reuters screen in the office, which tracked the transactions as they occurred, and we were often on to the investment banks asking for the mandate before the London traders, especially those not connected with the offering manager's bank, had even realized that the transaction was occurring. We acted on Eurobond transactions for Orion Bank, Hambros, CIBC, Commerzbank, Bank of Nova Scotia, UBS, CSFB, Toronto-Dominion Bank, Deutsche Bank, Morgan Grenfell Ltd. and others, as well as for Samuel Montagu, Rothschilds, and Hill Samuel in securities and pension transactions.[4] It could almost be said that we had the market cornered.

The second major development in the London office was the privatization of the large United Kingdom government-owned corporations. Margaret Thatcher had come to power in 1979, and within a few years, she had embarked on a major program of privatization. These divestments had begun in earnest by 1982 and included British Airways, British Airports Authority, Jaguar, British Steel, British Telecom, and the electricity industry. Many of these transactions were actually done as public offerings into Canada. This was well before the days the multi-jurisdictional disclosure regulations came into effect with the Canadian securities commissions, so a public offering into Canada involved many serious legal issues. Colson, in his inimitable fashion, maximized the firm's participation in these transactions. They went on for months, with meetings of ten, twelve, or fourteen hours a day, and every single day, there was someone from Stikeman Elliott sitting at the table. Even when the companies realized that public offerings into Canada were unnecessary and that private placements to institutions were sufficient, the London office still managed to carve a substantial amount out of this work. A review of the large number of Canadian private placements done on the back of international offerings would demonstrate that the firm had an extraordinarily large percentage of the offerings either acting for the underwriters, for the UK government, or for the issuing corporation. Probably no one other than Colson could have built up the practice in this area in this manner, even though he was not a securities lawyer. Each time we acted on a transaction, Colson added it to a list appended to a six-page promotional letter he sent to government agencies or issuers as a demonstration that they should choose Stikeman Elliott. Jim Grant was horrified by the self-promotional tone of the document, but Colson continued sending it (it is much easier for a young lawyer to ask for forgiveness than for permission), and we did far more work of this nature than any other Canadian and most US firms, in addition to the growing volume of Eurobond work that was a staple of the office.

The third major development in the office was the fact that Colson got retained by his former classmate, Conrad Black, to handle his negotiations with respect to the acquisition of the *Daily Telegraph*. This became the focus of Colson's professional life and why, not surprisingly, he ultimately decided to leave the firm. Like Frank Sixt, he got an offer he could not refuse, in his case, to become vice-chairman of Hollinger and CEO of the *Daily Telegraph* in 1992. It is a testament to Colson's loyalty to the firm that Hollinger and the *Daily Telegraph* still provide an enormous amount of work for the London office and have kept people like Bill Scott, Phil Henderson, and Jeffrey Keey heavily involved.

Colson had started acting for Conrad Black through the Hollinger Group in 1984, and this soon became a major portion of his professional activity. In 1985–86, Hollinger achieved the takeover of the Telegraph Group, a similar takeover in 1987 of the *Spectator* magazine, the *Jerusalem Post* in 1988 in Israel, and in 1991–92, Colson, along with Bill Scott, became involved in the high-profile acquisition of the insolvent Fairfax newspaper empire in Australia. This is described in detail in the book *Corporate Cannibals,*[5] but suffice it to say that it was the most acrimonious takeover in Australian history, a country well known for having more than its share of acrimony. Hollinger's local partner was Kerry Packer, the mountainous and eccentric Australian media magnate, who was effectively forced out of the bid by the government because of his position as owner of one of the major television networks in Australia. The deal was brokered by Malcolm Turnbull, a former Rhodes Scholar and barrister-turned-investment banker, who was well known for his defence of Peter Wright in the *Spycatcher*[6] case and his leadership of the anti-monarchist movement in Australia. Colson's relationship with Turnbull could best be described as "tumultuous." Packer had thought the Fairfax bid would fail when he withdrew. After the new venture (despite expectations) succeeded in acquiring Fairfax, Packer spent the next five years trying to get rid of Hollinger and eventually succeeded, although Hollinger made $450 million on its original investment. Colson became a director of Hollinger in 1985 and after the acquisition, a director of the Telegraph Group. He remained in both positions until he went to Hollinger on a full-time basis in 1992. He reflects that by 1985, he was practically masquerading as a lawyer since he was working almost exclusively for Hollinger.

Colson made some sixty-seven round trips between London and Sydney during this period, spending a total number of hours equivalent to four months in the air, and despite all this, he never enjoyed travelling and was distinctly nervous about flying. At the beginning of one particular flight, the person beside him noticed his obvious discomfort and asked if he were nervous. Colson admitted that he was and that he did not enjoy flying. The other passenger remarked that he, too, had once been a nervous flyer, but that he realized that "if his time had come, his time had come," and with this comforting thought of destiny, his nervousness had disappeared. Colson listened to this and replied, "Yeah, but what if the guy in row 17's time has come?" The seatmate grew strangely quiet for the duration of the flight.

Colson had an amusing experience while working on the acquisition of the *Jerusalem Post* for Hollinger in 1988. He was in and out of Jerusalem several times and experienced the exceptionally heavy security that surrounded all flights into and out of Israel. Usually he had no difficulties, but after a few trips, he must have fit within some suspicious profile because he was taken aside and questioned at length about the purpose and frequency of his trips. His passport was given particular scrutiny. The officer decided that the matter of Colson had to be dealt with by a higher authority, who was duly summoned and who went through what seemed to be the same endless questions. The senior officer asked him to account for the reason why he was in Israel, to which Colson said he had come to buy the *Jerusalem Post*. The officer asked, "Why? They don't sell it in London?"

Not all of the work in the office was of this globe-trotting nature. We had started to develop the five-year immigration trust practice (which allowed immigrants to shield their incomes from Canadian taxes for a limited period), and this generated a very large amount of tax work for the office. With respect to the tax work, Elinore Richardson in Montreal and Scott Wilkie in Toronto were invaluable in their advice, and we could not have undertaken the significant degree of European capital markets work without their assistance. In addition to the high-profile work described, there was the constant development of acquisitions from England and Europe into Canada and the normal run of securities work in Europe that involved the Canadian jurisdictions. There were some amazing characters who came through the office as clients and became great friends of both Colson and Hansen – one, in particular. We undertook a series of major acquisitions of UK private companies for an Indian client, whose real name is not necessary for these purposes, who went by the favoured description of "Spitty" for reasons that will soon become obvious. Spitty always wore a dark suit with a plain white shirt, which was disastrous because he constantly chewed beetlenut. The consequences of this were that his white shirt invariably acquired a distinctly pink tinge. Spitty was an extremely astute businessman and a very generous person and every year provided the two lawyers with champagne and the largest round of Stilton cheese they had ever seen. Hansen remembers the first year they received this cheese and left it in the kitchen. It took about three weeks to deduce why the area smelled like something had died.

London was a tremendous place to practise during the late 1980s, and the firm was lucky enough to be there at a time when, while costly, it was not exorbitantly expensive. We were also there at a time when virtually all the investment banks in Canada were being acquired by the clearing-house banks, and we were actively involved directly and indirectly in those transactions. As one of the principal securities counsel at the time for the banks in the Eurobond market, the Canadian banks in particular, Hansen remembers with amusement some of the more disastrous planning decisions at this time. The Canadian banks seemed to have distinct problems deciding whether to retain or dispose of their London subsidiaries, and when they acquired Canadian investment banks, they did not know what to do with their staff and excess space in London. Those readers willing to dig a little deeper will discover some wonderful stories about the demise of Orion Royal Bank, the opening of Number 1 London Wall, and the non-utilization of the brand new trading floor developed by CIBC at the time of its acquisition of Wood Gundy Securities. Clearly the staff at Wood Gundy did not share the views of Stikeman, Elliott as to working south of the Thames! They certainly did not appear to subscribe to the theory of "if you build it, they will come."

Jamie Davis from the Toronto office spent the years between 1987 and 1993 in London. He was able to take on the Eurobond practice, arriving three or four months before Hansen's departure to open the firm's new office in Vancouver. At the time, the firm was regarded in London as having a monopoly on the market, and Hansen was extremely well known. By bringing Davis out and giving him time to settle in, the transition was absolutely smooth, and no investment bank seemed even aware that a change in personnel had occurred. While Hansen notes that it may be extremely dampening to his ego, there was nevertheless a certain pride that the hand-off was so seamless and Davis was an extremely capable commercial lawyer who took immediately to the practice. After Davis's return to the Toronto office in 1993, Marianne Sussex, the longest-serving Canadian lawyer in the London office, performed sterling work, acting as the "general" adviser around the office and taking on responsibility for the extremely successful and important Eurobond practice. Having decided to retire in early 2002, she will be sadly missed in the London office, and it is in many ways a tribute to the firm that we managed to keep Marianne happy for almost twenty years.

Richard Hay[7] was recruited by Colson in 1987, the same year that Davis arrived, and the most unusual feature of this was that he was hired directly by the London office, without passing through Toronto, which regarded itself as the notional keeper of the gate on all the firm's common law lawyers. He was to assist Hansen with the five-year immigration trust work, an important tax planning arrangement that was of inestimable value for high net worth individuals entering Canada. The practice started to develop very quickly, with a tremendous amount of work in the transnational trust area under the transnational trusts legislation in New Brunswick, which was the fad in those days. We became the only Canadian firm in Canada to be regarded as expert in this area. Hay acquired the practice from Hansen over a period of time and is now known as one of the world's experts in the area of international trust and tax planning. His practice takes him all over the world, and he is probably as well known internationally as any lawyer in the firm.

The news that Colson was leaving to join Hollinger meant that the firm had to find someone to replace him in London. Calin Rovinescu from the Montreal office was recruited for the purpose and would spend three years there before returning to Montreal to become the managing partner of that office. It was already clear that he would have a significant future with the firm, and in addition to the several months he had spent in Japan on a government-sponsored program, the international exposure would be helpful to him as part of the seasoning process. London created an exciting and unique opportunity for Rovinescu, who had until then enjoyed an interesting and diverse practice in broad-based commercial transactions, film production and financing, securities law, and mergers and acquisitions. He was thirty-seven years old and had been appointed head of the Montreal office's corporate and commercial group several years earlier. Despite the many interesting things with which he was dealing, he nevertheless sought change and a new challenge that moving to London provided.

Although the firm was well established in London, the combined effect of Conrad Black's presence in the London business community and Colson's well-known and highly publicized involvement with his affairs combined to make Colson a somewhat larger-than-life figure and a very tough act to follow. At the time of Colson's departure, Hollinger represented a disproportionate share of that office's business, mostly from a string of acquisitions coordinated by Colson, which had drawn to a close shortly before Rovinescu's arrival. It had also been decided that Jamie Davis, the office's next most senior lawyer and a very experienced capital markets specialist, would return to Canada at the same time that Colson was leaving, providing Rovinescu with virtually a clean slate. The time was ripe for reinvention – to put a new face on the London office. The firm felt it could no longer justify an increasingly expensive presence based primarily on the personal contacts and friendships of the senior partner. Nor could the office thrive through the competitive 1990s by being nothing but a representative port of call for UK companies investing in Canada. Following the 1991 Gulf War, the economy was far from buoyant, and Canada itself was not the flavour of the month for foreign investors.

In addition, the UK privatizations such as British Airways, British Gas, and Britoil were finished, taking away much of the bread-and-butter work for the Canadian firms, which handled one or another of the three sides to the Canadian tranches of these global equity offerings – government, issuer, or underwriters. Many of these firms, which had arrived on the scene primarily for the privatization work, had forged significant new contacts in the City, formerly the near-exclusive domain of Stikeman Elliott, creating a much more competitive environment for a small Canadian legal market. Firms included Blakes, Oslers, McCarthys, Ogilvy Renault, Torys, and Faskens. The firm's franchise seemed to be significantly larger and stronger than the potential market for pure Canadian legal services, but we had to find a way to preserve that and capitalize on our mature market presence. After some discussion with Colson and Davis, as well as with Bill Scott, Marianne Sussex, Richard Hay, Marc Barbeau, and Daphne Mackenzie, and later with Michele Buchignani, Rovinescu felt that the firm had enough talent to transform the office into a boutique international transaction operation. The lawyers in that office had the ability to work with the very best advisors in the world on matters ranging from takeover bids to capital markets transactions, from securitizations to complex mergers and acquisitions, from privatization advisory work to private capital planning for clients. Regardless of the applicable jurisdiction, they were able to call on staffing resources from the Canadian offices or from local UK law firms where UK law was involved.

While not abandoning our expertise in Canadian law, this seemed to be a natural evolution as Canadian companies were becoming global investors. Central and Eastern Europe were opening up to entrepreneurial activity, and Canadians generally were spreading their wings in areas such as telecommunications, high tech, and biotech. Rovinescu believed that the firm could become the transaction "quarterback" for larger international deals instead of simply remaining as a member of specialty teams, to be called in only when there was a Canadian issue.

The new strategy took shape quickly. Canadian corporate clients were indeed starting to become more active internationally, and coincidentally, many were clients with whom Rovinescu had had a special relationship for several years. BioChem Pharma, then Canada's leading homegrown biotechnology company, embarked on a complex acquisition of Serono Diagnostics of Switzerland, with operations in several European countries. Negotiations were conducted over several weeks in Geneva, Rome, Bologna, and Milan. In addition to the Swiss and Italian operations, due diligence was undertaken by our team in Germany, France, and the UK. A dozen or so local law firms were engaged to assist us, but we called the plays. This acquisition was extremely strategic for BioChem at the time since it had to establish a sufficient revenue base from its commercial products to enable it to complete the research required for its leading AIDS drug, which ultimately defined the company and provided a very lucrative royalty structure. The "deal quarterback" strategy solidified and was met with increasing success as other large Canadian companies, such as Stone Consolidated and Western Star Trucks, embarked on large acquisition strategies either in the UK or Continental Europe. The team's expertise in negotiating, performing the due diligence, and closing transactions led them to becoming experts on waste disposal in Scotland, food processing in the Midlands, and military simulators in Essex. In addition, the principals in the London office, Bill Scott in particular, would also work closely with the Budapest office to provide the corporate finance component to the privatization work.

CAE, one of the world's leading electronics and flight stimulator companies, recognized that after the most recent recession, it could not rely solely
on the commercial aviation market. Following the Gulf War, when demand
for air travel dried up, so did the demand for commercial flight simulators.
CAE had to get back into the defence business, and the most successful defence companies had European operations. In consequence, CAE embarked
on an aggressive international operation, including a strategic acquisition of
a defence contractor, and subsequently bid and won a major defence contract
from the UK government for military work. In addition to the opportunity to
quarterback a fairly large UK acquisition, this transaction provided the firm
with an opening into the emerging public-private partnership (PPP) business,
which was becoming a global trend, as governments (led in some measure by
the UK) recognized that they could more efficiently execute large, complex
projects through partnerships with the private sector. In large measure, the
CAE public-private partnership was later used as the stepping stone for the
firm to build a local English law capability.

Telesystem International Wireless Corporation (TIWC), a company controlled by the flamboyant Quebec entrepreneur Charles Sirois, was aggres-
sively taking on the international wireless world, with ambitious acquisition
projects in China, India, and Eastern and Central Europe. Rovinescu and his
wife, Elaine, first met TIWC's CEO, Bruno Ducharme, in prenatal classes some
ten years earlier. Rovinescu did the course; Elaine did the work. Ducharme
enthusiastically supported the international transaction initiative and retained the firm to manage the acquisition of numerous businesses, ranging
from a mobile paging business in the Netherlands to a broadband licence
acquisition in the UK to some of the first global system for mobile (GSM)
communications projects in Central European countries such as Poland,
the Czech Republic, and Romania. This work was a strategic springboard
for the London office to develop expertise in European joint ventures since
inevitably, each of these projects had a local partner. As well, it helped in
building our base with the players in the new economy, particularly those
institutions that were interested in financing Eastern and Central Europe
such as some of the major investment banks based in London, including
Rothschilds, Hambros, Schroeders, and the European Bank for Reconstruction and Development (EBRD).

The early days of structuring the GSM bid transactions in the Central
European countries was an experience for which law school did not prepare
the lawyers. Michele Buchignani, who arrived in London in 1994 and is now
with CIBC World Markets in New York as a merchant banker, led one of the
bid teams in Poland. In addition to having the dubious fortune of spending
the better parts of November and December in Poland, the country's least
attractive time of the year, she quickly realized that everyone she was dealing
with operated on the assumption that the phone lines were bugged. Every
conversation became an intricate challenge of using code names for each
and every person involved in the transaction, for each and every step in the
transaction, and for each and every government official. The assumption was
that you could not even order room service without someone listening in.

Keeping the deal on track was as much a problem of managing the logistics of hiring local assistants who could speak Polish, installing and operating fax machines in hotel rooms, and arranging for secure venues for meetings with potential consortium partners as it was about understanding the Polish telecommunication laws and maintaining a firm grip on the US Foreign Corrupt Practices legislation that applied not just to US corporations, but also to their subsidiaries and many other organizations that might find themselves subject to US law.

The firm has a well-established connection with the prestigious Canada Club, London's oldest speakers club, which meets several times a year in a black-tie environment, attracting some of the world's best-known speakers.[8] This provided the firm with the unique opportunity to spend time with political, business, and academic leaders and be at the leading edge of current thinking. We always managed to either host a luncheon for, or at least have some quiet time with, the speaker. The firm has always enjoyed a unique relationship with the Canadian High Commission in London as a result of our thirty-year commitment to the city and the personalities of Colson, Rose, and others. During Rovinescu's three years in London, there were three different High Commissioners – Fred Eaton, Royce Frith, and Roy McLaren. He served with the High Commissioners on the boards of various arts and educational institutions, including the Institute for Canadian Studies in the United Kingdom and the Shakespeare Globe Theatre.

As Rovinescu returned to Montreal in 1996 to take up his new duties, he was replaced by Kip Cobbett[9], a latecomer to the firm via Heenan Blaikie and Astral-Bellevue Films. He would also remain for three years before returning to Montreal, where he, like Rovinescu, became the managing partner. Philip Henderson,[10] from the Toronto office, was dispatched to London at the same time, and together, he and Cobbett were a formidable team. One of their principal mandates was to engage English solicitors so that the London office could provide advice on English law in addition to the Canadian law which we had practised since our arrival in 1969. Without this, it was becoming increasingly difficult to provide the full service that the firm considered necessary for the extended transactions it was now handling. There was no intention to practise English law on a full scale. However, given the concerns that had existed from the outset about disturbing the English firms and possibly losing referrals had they regarded the firm as a full-fledged "competitor," once the preferred choice of English solicitor, in the person of Jeffrey Keey, had been identified, Cobbett and Henderson made the rounds of all the major London law firms to assure the senior partners that Stikeman Elliott was not really invading on their preserve. They were relieved to find that this was not a problem and somewhat bemused to learn that most of the firms already thought we had such a capacity. The firm established a separate multinational partnership to ensure that we did not impinge on any UK Law Society rules.

Twenty-seven years after the opening of the London office, a reception was organized to mark the departure of Rovinescu and to introduce the new senior Canadian lawyers. Stikeman was on hand for the occasion to say a few words to the invited guests.

I promise not to speak for more than five minutes – but – lawyers are like water taps. Once you turn them on, they run until you turn them off.

There are only two reasons why I am speaking at all.

First, to express pride and some wonderment at the job my partners, associates, and staff have done to make this office so happy and successful.

Second, to thank all of you clients and friends for having helped us to do it.

When I first saw London as an impecunious student living in a Brunswick Square B & B at ten shillings a day, I little imagined that 62 years later, I would stand here representing a Canadian law firm that had already been in London for 27 of those years.

Of all the many offices that we have opened around the world, London was our first great adventure and remains one closest to my heart. Perhaps I should add, with Philippe Ewart in the room, our latest hostage to fortune, Budapest, runs a close second.

Over the years, so much talent and hard work have gone into the practice here that it is not possible to credit any one person.

Nevertheless, I must mention Peter Cumyn, who at a tender age in 1969, took on London for us, cold-turkey. By virtue of his iron constitution, a forgiving liver, and a remarkably agile mind, he put us on the map in three years.

Our first reception was a huge exercise in bravado. We hired a large room in the Savoy, engaged an announcer with a stentorian voice, and invited everyone we knew or hoped to know in London. As each arriving name reverberated through the room, Fraser Elliott and I said a silent prayer of thanks and finally put our worry beads away.

Each succeeding managing partner has built upon this base. Calin [Rovinescu] leaves a rich field for Kip Cobbett to plough in his turn.

But nothing would have happened without you, our friends and clients, your loyalty, your friendship, your uplifting confidence.

This evening is, therefore, much more than a *frater ave atque vale* to Calin Rovinescu and Kip Cobbett. It is, as they say in Quebec, *un grand remerciement à vous tous*.

Before I go, I want everyone to be witness to an important commitment I am asking of Kip as a stipulation of his coming here: that he accept the next invitation from Air Canada for a Stikeman Elliott crew to once again enter the Air Canada Cup and to let me continue to be part of it. As you know, this is the premier sailing race around the Isle of Wight.

Thank you all for coming.

The Air Canada Cup, awarded for a sailing race around the Isle of Wight, was an event to which the firm was devoted, and it was no idle expression of interest to which Stikeman had given voice. We were fortunate in having an excellent skipper in Scott Morgan from the Montreal office, along with intrepid sailors from Montreal, Toronto, and London, but none could match the enthusiasm of Stikeman himself, who participated in all three years during which the event was held. That same year, the crew had a disastrous experience.

We had recruited crew for the Air Canada races by circulating memoranda in the various offices. Morgan was principally responsible for organizing in

Montreal, and Peter Hamilton helped with the Toronto contingent. One day, Morgan called him to say that Stikeman had expressed an interest in sailing with us. He asked what Hamilton thought. Recalling that the race in the previous year had been very rough, Hamilton said he thought it was probably not a great idea, thinking that he did not really want to be responsible for losing the firm's founding partner. Morgan also agreed that it was not a terrific idea but then put it to Hamilton, do you want to tell him! Both agreed that neither really wanted to be the one to tell Stikeman he could not come, and so he did come and he did very well.

Stikeman played his customary role as navigator. This was his first year with his new global positioning system (GPS), a satellite navigation system, which was new and mysterious technology to the rest of the crew. At the beginning of the race, Stikeman and David Skinner were able to work some magic with this system because it enabled them to deduce the strength of the tidal current based on the difference between their speed through the water and the speed over land. Later in the race, they had an old-fashioned communications breakdown and spent about forty-five minutes sailing in the wrong direction, mostly because the crew were all trying to fix something wrong with the sails and not paying any attention to the navigator.

Hamilton had taken the train with Stikeman from London to Portsmouth before one of the races. In the course of that train ride, Stikeman described something that had happened to him while flying over the northern United States. He was with a friend in a small two-seater aircraft when weather began to close in. Thinking in the circumstances that it would be a good idea to find a place to land, he asked his friend to look for nearby airports. His friend located an airport and the frequency of its control tower. When Stikeman called to request landing instructions, a loud and powerful signal informed him that he had reached the Strategic Air Command, that his aircraft was entering restricted air space, and that he should depart the area immediately. Not really liking the look of the weather, Stikeman decided to land anyway. He turned away from the airport for a brief distance, descended to low altitude, and proceeded to land without instructions. On the ground, he was immediately surrounded by a number of jeeps and heavily armed military police, all of whom must have suspected that he was a potential Russian spy or saboteur. He was then approached by a person, whom he described as having many stars on his shoulder, who inquired whether he was declaring an emergency. When Stikeman stated that he was not, the general responded that it would be a very good idea if he did declare an emergency. He took the hint. The upshot of the story was that Stikeman was flying a Cessna aircraft on which many of the more senior officers at the airbase had first learned to fly, either in flight training or as a spotter aircraft in Vietnam. They all fawned over the aircraft, and Stikeman became the centre of attention.

In the second of the races, before the start, they had been manoeuvring in very rough water. Morgan had the helm of the boat, with Hamilton helping. They were on port tack, which meant that they did not have the right-of-way. Two boats were approaching them on reciprocal courses, both on starboard tack, one to windward and one to leeward. Morgan asked Hamilton whether he thought it was safe to pass between them. He told him that it was, but he was wrong. As they passed between the two, the boat to windward of them was heeled over further by gusts, and their boat came more upright as they sailed into its wind shadow. As a result, the tips of the masts touched and locked together. The Stikeman Elliott boat was proceeding in one direction at six or eight knots (which is quite fast for a sailboat), and the other boat was proceeding in the opposite direction at the same speed. The other boat was pulled around behind them, so that its course was now perpendicular to theirs; at the same time, it was heeled well over on its side. The Stikeman Elliott boat continued on its way, its mast bending backwards. The top of the mask then snapped off and hung down. An instant later, the rest of the mask was sheared, and the whole thing fell backwards into the boat, more or less where Hamilton was sitting. He recalls looking at the mast above him, which was ready to fall, and wondering whether he should go over the side. He concluded that that was not a very good idea since the water was cold and he likely would not float given the amount of gear he was wearing. Fortunately, the mast appeared to miss everyone. As they looked around and counted heads, however, they were missing one person – the boss. Then, to the relief of all, Stikeman stuck his head up through the wreckage, having gone below to look for bolt cutters in the event they had to cut the mast loose.

Cobbett secured the invitation for the third event in 1997, and we duly appeared. That year, Samantha Horn from Toronto was delighted to be able to attend because Hamilton had to back out at the last minute. She avers that the crew definitely got the short end of the stick since she had no racing experience and very little sailing experience. Again, Morgan was the captain and Stikeman the navigator. On the train from London to Portsmouth for the race, Stikeman was busy fine-tuning his GPS system. As a result of the previous year's debacle, when our boat had been dismasted at the start, the other participants were giving Morgan some friendly grief by asking him to stay away from them at the start line. The crew (Peter Cullen, Karen McCarthy, Lynn Maxwell, David Skinner, Horn, Morgan, and Stikeman) took the boat out on Friday to practise. They sailed all day, running through drills of taking the sails up and down, coming about, and tacking.

The sixteen-hour race started for the still jetlagged crew on Saturday morning in May from Portsmouth at 11:00 AM. It started out sunny, but it was very cold. By the long leg of the journey out to the marker to the east of the Isle of Wight, the crew was in seventh or eighth place out of sixteen boats. On the turnaround at the marker, Morgan made an excellent tactical move, and they were suddenly in fourth or fifth place. By this time, the seas were getting quite rough. The winds were in the twenty-five-knot range, and the seas were up to fifteen feet at times. Around the south of the Isle of Wight, you are actually in the English Channel, which, says Horn, is as close to the Atlantic Ocean as she ever wanted to get. By this time, it was the middle of the night and pitch black, so the captain decided it was time to make sure that everyone was all "clipped on" to the boat. The boat was tossing and turning so much that Stikeman was being thrown around in the cabin. They made up nicknames for everyone, and Stikeman was "Iron Stomach Stike." Even with her seasickness medication, Horn could not stay in the cabin for more than a few minutes.

The Stikeman Elliott crew finished the race in third place. This was all the more exciting because with the octogenarian Stikeman, we had the eldest crew member in the race and the only one with three women on board. In addition, some of the other boats were exclusively crewed with racing sailors. After returning to shore and having a much-needed shower and some sleep, we went to brunch at Cowes and received our third place award. We found out that the seas had been so rough that almost half the racers had turned back. We also learned that at numerous times during our race, even Morgan had thought we should turn back. However, the victory was sweet, and the previous year's embarrassment was eradicated. This race will go down in history also because the 1997 event was the last one held. On the way back to the train in the cab, Stikeman tried to recruit Horn to practise in tax since it was so much fun!

In order to commemorate the race, Horn wanted to chart the course on a map she bought in Cowes, but Stikeman went one better; he actually ordered the chart for her and mapped the chart himself, which now hangs in her Toronto office, along with a professional photo taken by one of the photographers of all of them on the boat during the race. He also sent each of the crew a copy of his video about the race.

Prior to his move to London in 1996, Henderson had a well-developed practice in finance, securities law, and mergers and acquisitions, but he was particularly well known as one of Canada's leading derivatives lawyers, along with Margaret Grottenthaler, Mike Carman, Bill Scott, and others, a group that was often retained by the International Swaps and Derivatives Association on Canadian matters. While in London, he co-authored the leading text *The Law of Financial Derivatives in Canada* (Carswell, 1999) with Grottenthaler, to whom he had transferred most of his Canadian derivatives practice upon his departure for London. When Henderson was asked to transfer to the London office, his wife, Kim Alletson, also a partner in the Toronto office, was on an extended maternity leave with their third child. Henderson and Alletson accepted the London offer, and Alletson decided to use their time in London as an opportunity to be at home with their three sons and to do her LLM in international finance at the London School of Economics. Alletson, a former Olympic figure skater for Canada, also took up marathon running while in England. They made their home in Sevenoaks, Kent, where many City law firm partners and bankers also lived, and Alletson coordinated the constant entertaining of clients and prospective clients of the firm between Sevenoaks and London.

Cobbett and Henderson both maintained a close relationship with Colson while in London and like Colson, were regular attendees at Ascot and various royal events. During his first few weeks in London, Henderson attended a reception and engaged in conversation with a senior partner from one of the Magic Circle law firms. In his fine Oxbridge accent, this particular gentleman asked Henderson where he was from originally. Henderson replied Toronto, innocently pronouncing his birthplace as "Toronno," the way most locals say it. He was quickly rebuked. Being helpful, the English lawyer (who can remain nameless) said, "You're not from Tirana, Philip; you're from Toronto," accentuating the second "t" in Toronto. "Tirana is the capital of Albania." That was the first of many lessons Henderson had in London, and he now pronounces the name of his hometown carefully and properly.

Bill Scott, who was based in the London office until July 1997 when he moved to Singapore, provided the continuity for Cobbett and Henderson in the early days together. Colson, now at the *Daily Telegraph,* turned to Scott regularly for assistance on many of Hollinger's transactions outside North America. In fairly short order, the new team in London managed to attract significant mandates for the office. The UK privatization work of the 1980s was now largely a memory, but further integration and liberalization in the European Union resulted in a new spate of privatizations of major European companies. In late 1996, Henderson was engaged by the underwriters as Canadian counsel on the privatization and global offering of shares of France Telecom by the French government. A full public offering was made in Canada using a Canadian prospectus under the then evolving draft National Policy No. 53 (NP 53) governing international offering procedures. Given the relative unimportance of Canadian capital markets in a global offering, however, underwriters of these European privatizations often vacillated on whether to bother with a retail public offering in Canada or simply to proceed with institutional private placements into Canada. While the London office was successful in landing subsequent mandates on the global public offering by Alstom using the draft NP 53 procedures and was instrumental in the Sydney office being retained on the global public offering by Telstra using the draft NP 53 procedures, the bonanza of the 1980s was not to return as the other European privatizations (including a subsequent France Telecom offering) tended to proceed by way of private placement.

In early 1997, Rovinescu's earlier work for CAE, in connection with its bid under the UK private finance initiative for the construction and operation of a medium-support helicopter and aircrew training facility, paid dividends when CAE was named preferred bidder. Cobbett led this team, and the firm gained major credibility with a host of UK professionals as a result of this predominantly domestic transaction. In the early days for Cobbett and Henderson, the ongoing Hollinger work, the France Telecom privatization, and the CAE mandate kept the office humming in addition to the usual Eurobond, capital markets, cross-border mergers and acquisitions, and tax advisory work going through the office.

With the closure of the Budapest office in mid-1998, the mandate of the London office expanded to cover all of Europe. Given the limited resources available in the London office, participating in a meaningful way in transactions in Central and Eastern Europe was unrealistic, so Cobbett and Henderson decided that more limited ambitions were appropriate and that their goal would be to continue to represent Canadian clients doing transactions in the region. In the most significant work arising out of this new strategy, Henderson was retained by TrizecHahn Corporation and its Hungarian joint venture, TriGranit, in connection with several project finance mandates in Hungary, the most important being the $US110-million project financing of TriGranit's construction and development of the West End Center in downtown Budapest – a massive retail/entertainment complex built at the famous Western railway station designed by Gustav Eiffel. The Budapest office had previously done work for TrizecHahn in Hungary and other countries in the region and had developed strong local relationships. Henderson, in addition, was able to get the Hungarian project finance mandates from TrizecHahn's head office in Toronto and its representatives in London.

Henderson's derivatives and structured finance background paid unexpected dividends in another area. Richard Hay's practice was exposing him to problems facing the private client divisions of major global banks with respect to their Latin American private client portfolios. Henderson and Hay collaborated on developing a number of unique structures to address changing Latin American tax rules, and Hay was successful in introducing these structures to his private bank clients. Hay's private capital practice in London ballooned in this area and continues to be a very significant contributor to the work of the London office. As a result of these initiatives, the firm hired Heather Tibbo, a trusts specialist from Jersey, and tax associate Robert Reymond moved from the Montreal office to support Hay's practice.

In 1997 and 1998, two major Canadian law firms, Oslers and Torys, closed their London offices. Both firms had focused on capital markets work, after the successful UK privatization work of the 1980s, to the exclusion of other practice areas, and they ultimately concluded that they could not be profitable in London on that basis alone. Cobbett and Henderson routinely take credit for their retreat from London. In March 1998, the firm moved its offices back across the river to the City, taking relatively posh premises in Regis House at 45 King William Street at the north end of London Bridge. Although operating for ten years from Cottons Centre on the south bank of the River Thames had not hampered our progress or tarnished our reputation, there was nevertheless some relief within the London office that we were back in the City.

Notwithstanding the many directions in which the practice in London was developing, the firm maintained its keen commitment to the Canadian business and financial communities in London. Hay became chairman of the Canada Club, and he handed on the responsibilities of honourary secretary to his successor, Jonathan Worsley, a Canadian resident in London. Cobbett and, after him, Henderson served on the board of directors of the Institute for Canadian Studies in the United Kingdom, and Henderson served on the board of directors of the Canada-United Kingdom Chamber of Commerce. While few meaningful legal matters came directly from the Canadian community in London, the firm's high profile and participation in the Canadian community in London continues to be indirectly responsible for many important mandates.

Upon Cobbett's return to Montreal in 1999, Henderson took control of the London office. With the possible exception of Colson's two stints as managing partner in London, Henderson's appointment represented the first time the firm achieved both succession and continuity in the London office. Henderson was now the only Canadian corporate partner in the ten-lawyer London office and set about to build on what he and Cobbett had achieved together. Like Cobbett, Henderson believed that the continued financial success of the office depended upon a number of factors and practice areas. The combination of the traditional Canadian business law advisory function with a strong Eurobond and capital markets practice, a leading international tax practice primarily representing the private client operations of the global banks, a boutique international transactions practice representing principally Canadian clients, a structured finance practice representing many of the Canadian banks in London, and a limited English law capability supporting these various practice areas was a formidable recipe for success, unmatched by any other Canadian law firm in London.

Henderson's approach was to continue to find and develop good contacts within the London professional firms and the commercial and investment banks that had clients with Canadian interests, but he was determined to focus more heavily than before on outbound work from Canada for Canadian clients. There continued to be an unfavourable investment climate in the UK and Europe vis-à-vis Canada, and the key to continued success in the London office was flexibility and the development of niche practice areas. Henderson was known as a well-rounded corporate finance and mergers and acquisitions lawyer and had the ability to change very quickly the focus of the day-to-day practice of the London office. While in many ways Henderson carried on with the vision of his predecessors in London, he focused more heavily on capturing outbound work from Canada. Henderson and Keey made regular trips back to Canada to sell the capabilities of the London office to Canadian clients.

Henderson was convinced that our ability to compete head-to-head with major global law firms for international transactions in the UK and Europe was significantly constrained by the perception that the firm offered legal services fundamentally from a Canadian law platform, so his strategy was to target Canadian clients doing transactions in the UK and Europe who were not hampered by this perception. During this period, the London office acted for numerous large Canadian corporations on mergers and acquisitions transactions (CAE, CanWest, BioChem Pharma, BCE Emergis, Hollinger), major Canadian pension funds in connection with UK and European investments, Export Development Corporation (now Export Development Canada) on UK and Irish-based financings, and Canadian banks in London on structured finance activities.

Since 1999, the Organisation for Economic Co-operation and Development (OECD), the world organization that includes most of the developed countries, has demanded sweeping changes in the design and transparency of the world's offshore financial centres. The OECD seeks exchanges of tax information and threatens sanctions directed against offshore centres that refuse to comply with their demands. The Financial Action Task Force, a G7 chartered agency housed in the OECD offices in Paris, has mounted a campaign with complementary objectives to combat money laundering. The firm is one of the principal professional actors in this battle between onshore and offshore, and in 2000, the London office began acting as counsel to the Government of the Bahamas in their negotiations with the OECD, the Financial Action Task Force, and in respect of a tax information exchange agreement with the US government. In September 2000, Hay accompanied the Bahamas prime minister, minister of Finance, and the governor of the Central Bank to meet Donald Johnston, Secretary-General of OECD and other OECD officials running the Harmful Tax Competition project. The atmosphere in the meeting was electric given the high stakes for both sides because after the Cayman Islands and Bermuda made "advance commitments" in the spring of 2000, the Bahamas became the principal offshore centre in the Caribbean that has not struck agreement with OECD. When the formal meeting started, amid great tension, Johnston discovered that the counsel introduced to OECD as representing the government in a meeting at OECD offices in Paris came from his old firm. He clearly enjoyed the moment and relaxed. The significance of the reaction was not lost on the Bahamas delegation.

The "anniversary" team in the London office is headed by Shawna Miller, one of the firm's most committed road warriors. Her foreign office experience began when she was part of the small group consisting of herself, Robert Hayhurst, Leslie Mack, and some support staff, which was parachuted into Budapest in the fall of 1992 to help Jean Philippe Ewart get started. On the few occasions that allowed for vacation travel, she visited London and became an instant Londonophile. After the Budapest adventure, she spent some time in the Hong Kong office, and because there was no opening in London when that assignment finished, she left the partnership in April 2000 to join the debt capital markets team at CIBC World Markets in London. A year and a half later, Ed Waitzer, by then chairman of the firm, approached her to ask if she would be willing to return to manage the London office, an opportunity she seized, effective September 2001, and she has continued to capitalize on the groundwork laid by Henderson with the Canadian banks in the structured finance area. The response in the London legal and client communities to the appointment of the first woman managing partner of our London office has been warm and welcoming. The only trouble that she has faced on occasion in the new position is from the serving staff of some of the more posh venues where she has either attended or hosted client functions over the course of the past few months. The staff seems unable to believe that a woman could actually be the one responsible for the ordering of the wine or the paying of the bill, leaving her a bit red-faced at times. The upside to this predicament is that the clients find it quite amusing.

Since her arrival, there has been a whirlwind of client meetings, receptions, dinners, and luncheons, starting with the tremendously successful reception that the firm hosted at the Imperial War Museum in October. A group of partners from the Montreal and Toronto offices went to London in order to attend this event, at which over 350 clients listened to short speeches from Waitzer and Miller and enjoyed viewing the various exhibits at the museum. A few of the firm members were concerned about holding the reception at this venue so soon after the events of September 11, but it turned out to be a fascinating location for those in attendance. Some were enjoying themselves so much that they did not want to leave. In fact, at the end of the evening, the hosts had to literally haul three very intoxicated clients out of a mini-submarine display, each of whom were clutching their own personal bottles of champagne at the time and trying to convince them that they still had enough time to attempt to board and fly the spitfire that was suspended from the ceiling! The only disappointment about the evening, expressed by one client, was that he thought the parting gift (which was handed out in very elegant burgundy felt bags) was a small bottle of good ol' Canadian whiskey, only to discover upon tasting it that it was, in fact, a small bottle of good ol' Canadian maple syrup!

The current complement in the office consists of three partners – Miller, Hay, and Keey – and six associates – Erin Needra, Robert Reymond, Dan Thomson, Louis Morisset, Liza Zucconi, Heather Tibbo, and Marianne Sussex, who left at the end of February but has been so important to the office that for purposes of this work, she deserves special mention on the fiftieth anniversary as a member of the team and was, indeed, in place at the time. Geneviève Roy elected not to return from maternity leave, and Tom Vowinckel from the Toronto office has been working part-time from London in the tax planning area. As was the case in the past, the focus of the corporate/commercial side of the firm's practice in London tends to be predicated on the type of work that the then current managing partner brings to the table. In Miller's case, her background is in structured corporate finance, including securitization, banking, CLOs/CBOs (collateralized loan obligations/collateralized bond obligations), and derivatives. As a result, in addition to maintaining the established relationships with UK law firms on the Canadian mergers and acquisition and securities front, the team is working together successfully to attract such additional business to the London office. Generally speaking, the London financial market is start-ing to show signs of recovery from the last quarter of 2001, although most anticipate that for the short term, IPOs will still be few and far between. There is, however, considerable activity in mergers and acquisitions, both private and public. Given the tremendous success of the introduction of the Euro in January 2002, there is also talk (and some political pressure) to hold an early vote on the UK joining the Euro community, which would be a significant stimulus to business.

The London office continues to be an important source of referral work for the other offices of the firm. What is changing, however, is that the other offices of the firm are now becoming an increasingly important source of referral work for the London office – a model followed by many US law firms with offices in London.

HONG KONG

There were, as usual in the late 1970s, two distinct forces that led the firm to open an office in Hong Kong – business and enthusiasm. The business impetus came from Russell Harrison, then chairman and CEO of the CIBC, who suggested the idea to Elliott. The bank had commenced a relationship with Li Ka-shing, a very prominent Hong Kong businessman, which had already proved to be tremendously beneficial to the bank. Even though Li had not yet commenced to do any Canadian business, this was becoming a possibility of which Harrison thought Elliott should be aware and further, that the firm should meet Li and try to establish some connection with him. In the end, it would be the assessment by Elliott that there were good business opportunities available through the CIBC connection that tipped the scale in favour of going to Hong Kong.

The enthusiasm quotient came from Stikeman, who was his customary irrepressible and boundlessly optimistic self. Stikeman's involvement with the Multinational Fiscal Associates (MFA) also proved to be very helpful in moving along the firm's Hong Kong initiative. There was, despite the prospect of bank-led business through Li, a good deal of vacillation about the idea during the latter part of the 1970s, but momentum began to grow as the London outpost matured, and the natural connection between London and Hong Kong dating back to the days of the Empire also impressed itself upon the firm's consciousness. Beachheads had already been established in the colony by other non-Hong Kong law firms, primarily from the UK and US, so we would not face the additional hurdle of breaking new philosophical ground.

There was a partners meeting in Montreal on May 23, 1979 to consider the idea of opening in Hong Kong. Stikeman had obviously been talking about the possibility with Wayne Quasha of the Philippines, a senior lawyer in Manila and colleague from the MFA, and he had apparently held out the prospect of some joint venture. However, there were differing views as to the nature of the possible relationship, and Stikeman found an elegant way of bringing the idea to an end. There had been discussions with Danny Colson, then in London, and they had clearly whetted his appetite for Hong Kong, enough so that he was involved in talks with the Quasha interests about the nature of a joint venture relationship that might be pursued. Colson was not at all enthusiastic about the joint venture and did not think that an association with Quasha's firm would benefit our firm. Nor did he feel that they were particularly interested in the practice of law but rather in expanding the personal family interests in that part of the world in addition to the Philippines and Bangkok, where they were already active. Colson proposed that we open either by ourselves or in some loose association with a New York firm since he was aware that Stikeman had also been discussing Hong Kong with friends at the prominent New York law firm of Sullivan & Cromwell. Prior to the meeting, Elliott had concluded that, "If we do it, we should do it alone initially." He had also concluded that Colson "wants to do it." The discussion was inconclusive, other than determining that Stikeman and Elliott should make a *visite des lieux* together later in the year.

In November 1979, they set forth for the purpose, arriving the evening of November 13. From rough and spartan quarters in a suite at the Mandarin Hotel, they proceeded to meet some of the leading lawyers, bankers, and other officials in the colony, some known to them already and others by way of introductions from other acquaintances. It was a genuine tour de force and definitely not anyone's B-list, including several directors of Jardine Matheson & Co., the chief justice of Hong Kong, the Canadian High Commissioner, partners in other law firms in Hong Kong (including Eddie Rubin, the Phillips & Vineberg partner), the managing director of Inchroy Credit Corporation Limited, the Far East area manager of the CIBC (Holger Kluge), the Bank of Bermuda, the financial secretary of the colonial government, and of course, someone who would play a large part in the overall growth of the firm, Li Ka-shing. All seemed relaxed about the prospect of another Canadian law firm entering the area. Formally, the only issue was the signing of the customary declaration that the foreign firm would not practise local law. The biggest problem foreseen by all was the availability of good office space in a desirable location given the acute shortage in the areas regarded as suitable if a firm was to have the proper standing and attract quality business. By the end of their second day in Hong Kong, Stikeman and Elliott had several people scouring the market for suitable space, which meant it should be in one of the buildings connected with others for easy communication during the rainy season.

It is interesting to note the instant attraction between the firm and Li Ka-shing. Stikeman's lengthy memo, dictated following their return, describes Li as follows:

He is involved in real estate and manufacturing and has recently purchased the Hilton Hotel – has other interests in hotels and offices throughout Victoria, Kowloon, and the New Territories. Mr Li was recently elected a member of the International Advisory Council for the Bank of Commerce, of which he is extremely proud. One of his companies, Cheung Kong (Holdings) Limited and the CIBC, have a joint venture in Hong Kong and is considered to be the most profitable finance company in the Colony. Mr Li is certainly one of Hong Kong's most successful and prominent businessmen ... Mr Li was kindness itself and invited us to luncheon in his office dining room in the penthouse of the China Building for November 16th and was one of the guests of honour at a dinner given for us by Holger Kluge at the Hong Kong Rotary Club on November 15th, of which more anon. Suffice it to say that Mr Li, perhaps because of his association with the CIBC but also perhaps because of his natural interest in the entrepreneurial spirit which Stikeman & Elliott is exhibiting and his friendship for Mr Holger Kluge, has proved and will continue to prove, I am sure, our most important contact in the Colony and the most prestigious entrée that we could have anywhere in the business and financial community of Hong Kong. He is a man respected and admired by all factions. He is straight, conservative, and represents all that is best in the Chinese element in Hong Kong, which, out of 4½ million people, comprise all but about 50 thousand of the inhabitants.

The real estate issue was one that had to be dealt with quickly if something acceptable came on the market. Decisions had to be made almost instantaneously if a suitable space were located or it would be taken up by other bidders. Neither Stikeman nor Elliott told the many explorers for real estate that they had still to gain a consensus with their partners in Montreal regarding opening an office in Hong Kong; Stikeman was diplomatically careful to include this matter in a memorandum he circulated to the Montreal partners. It was, of course, largely a courtesy since if Stikeman and Elliott had decided (as the memo clearly indicated to be the case) that the firm should be in Hong Kong, we would be in Hong Kong. But it was a nice gesture for the other partners to be able to solemnly approve what had already been decided, and there was, in fact, a good deal of general enthusiasm for the venture.

Stikeman's concluding assessment of the Hong Kong visit was as follows:

All in all, my reaction is that although Hong Kong does fluctuate in an economic sense over periods of time, it has steadily been increasing as a centre of financial, commercial, investment, and speculative activity of all kinds. This activity is not confined to investment or speculation in the Colony itself but, to the contrary, embraces all of Southeast Asia, the People's Republic of China increasingly, and interestingly enough, for the first time, North America and Canada in a very large way. It would seem therefore that the throw-off of business for the Canadian offices from a presence in Hong Kong could be materially greater than that which has occurred from London, with the additional bonus that we would be on the spot to take advantage of Chinese development. The theme repeatedly heard in conversations with Chinese businessmen is the fact that they believe oil to be present in the immediate vicinity of Hong Kong and along the Chinese coast, as well, of course, as that already discovered in Mainland China. This will mean that the Chinese, now anxious to exploit and further explore for oil through off-shore drilling rigs and other facilities, are looking to Hong Kong as being the staging ground for the entire operation. If this happens, and apparently it is beginning to happen as Mr Li said there is a project for 36 off-shore drilling rigs to be established up the South China Sea coast of China, then the need for sophisticated legal and tax expertise in the oil industry will be enormous. This will generate in turn need for legal and tax expertise on the financial side, the contractual side, and the international law side. From all of these events, we, if here, would benefit immediately and to my mind enormously. When I say "enormously," I do not mean perhaps in the immediate financial sense, although that would undoubtedly follow, but in the development of a recognized world-wide expertise as international tax lawyers and people competent to render services of this kind to clients on the spot.

It was borne in upon us by Mr Li and others that the field is very competitive and that business moves very fast and that we would lose face if we had to refer problems to head office. The man on the spot must be able to make many of the decisions. However, from the problems that we had expressed to us, it seems that these decisions would not be difficult and will be akin to those now being made every day in London.

Elliott also made a separate trip to Hong Kong and established a personal relationship with Li, who in the custom of honouring guests, made a car and chauffeur available to him during his visits. They went out on the harbour in Li's large boat and then used a speedboat that was on-board. Most of Li's guests were nervous about getting in the speedboat with him because he drove it very fast, but Elliott had no such concerns, and the two became friends as well as associates. On this and other occasions, Li would even drive out to the airport with him when Elliott was on his way out of Hong Kong. Elliott also used the trip to Hong Kong as a springboard to visit Beijing, the arrangements for which were made by Li. There, over many Chinese dinners, he discussed firm and bank business, and as well connections on behalf of the Toronto General Hospital, of which he was a board member. He visited several Chinese hospitals to see how they practised medicine and made arrangements for five Chinese interns to attend the Toronto hospital. Later, he made similar arrangements for Chinese lawyers to come to Canada to learn how law was practised in the West. After so many Chinese dinners, Elliott decided that he should reciprocate with a Western meal in Beijing at a restaurant operated by a chef from one of the leading Parisian restaurants – either Maxim's or La Tour d'Argent. This was a great success, marred only by the fact that one of the guests of the CIBC ordered a chocolate mousse for dessert that took some forty-five minutes to prepare while everyone else waited.

So, after the customary nanosecond of collective sober reflection on the wisdom of the conclusion already reached by Stikeman and Elliott, it was resolved to pursue the opening of a Hong Kong office. As noted, well before their visit to Hong Kong, Stikeman and Elliott had already explored the matter of moving to Hong Kong with Danny Colson, then in London. With his characteristic effusiveness, Stikeman had already assumed that the deal was done. When discussing some people they had met, including Peter Willoughby, whose wife was a partner in a British solicitors firm, Stikeman blithely recorded that, "She told us that her other partner in Hong Kong in Simmons & Simmons is one Bill Knight, recently from London, who is a personal friend of Danny and Suzanne Colson in London and who would welcome his addition to the colony's social life."

Colson arrived in Hong Kong in October 1980 with Suzanne and their six-month-old son, Charles, and it took them some four months to find accommodation. In the meantime, they lived at the Hilton Hotel in Queen's Road, Central, which was owned by Li Ka-shing. The hotel had avocado-coloured walls with orange trim and a rusty swimming pool, and it has since been demolished to make way for Li's flagship office headquarters. Prices were astronomical in Hong Kong, and even with the generous budget provided by the firm and Colson's salary, there was no possibility of buying an apartment. Finally, in January, he wrote to Bob Hart, advising him that he had been lucky and had found an apartment that cost only $100,000. Hart replied that he had not realized he would be buying a place in Hong Kong, and Colson was forced to advise him that the amount, in US dollars, was the rent for a single year.

Moving in to the new premises in the China Building brought some early lessons to Colson about doing business in the area. The building was owned by Li Ka-shing, and when the furniture was all moved in and organized to Colson's satisfaction, he found that he could not get any local employees until after the premises had been inspected and pronounced propitious by an acknowledged feng shui practitioner. This resulted, predictably, in having to move all the furniture in order to obtain the necessary blessing, following which the locals would be prepared to work there. The impact of feng shui in the Hong Kong office cannot be discounted. Colson and Hansen had little understanding of it, regarding it as nothing more than superstition. However, when the Lau Brothers built their building opposite the China Building, which allegedly took the good feng shui away from the building, strange events started to happen. We had parents of staff in the office die, and people became mysteriously sick. The most unusual example of feng shui occurred when Andes Lin joined us from McCarthy Tétrault. Lin was in his own way extremely Chinese and advised Hansen one day that his office had been classified by a feng shui expert as having extremely bad luck. He asked whether he could renovate his office slightly, and Hansen told him he had absolutely no objection, provided he could not see it from the outside and it did not cost anything. Lin advised Hansen that many of his problems could be remedied if a large brass plate were put under his door, but the feng shui man had advised that the door could not be cut off at the bottom to accommodate the plate. Hansen told Lin that there was no way he was going to cut a brand new carpet to insert the plate because our rug expert had advised that if this was done, the carpet would gradually fray right across the office. Accordingly, we witnessed the amazing sight for about four hours of three Chinese workmen hammering down the carpet within a three foot square area outlined with white chalk in order to depress the carpet the half inch necessary to install the brass plate.

Colson hired Eileen Wong as his secretary. Eileen had a mind of her own and was not willing to let just anyone interrupt her boss with calls she regarded as frivolous. In preparation for Chinese New Year, Eileen came into Colson's office one day, bringing with her a box, which she put on his desk. It contained a pair of red shoes. Eileen challenged him, "You like?" Colson allowed as how they looked nice. "Good," she replied. "You give me for New Year." The Colsons had, however, already planned ahead for the Chinese New Year, and he told her that Suzanne had already bought her a present for the occasion. Eileen was unmoved, "You tell wife, keep present and give me shoes." On the same day, Suzanne called asking to speak with Colson. Eileen informed her that he was in a meeting. Suzanne asked how long he would be. Maybe one hour, she was informed. An hour later, she called back to be informed that he was still in the meeting. She called back an hour later, and Eileen retorted, "You again?" She was only allowed to speak with him once Eileen decided the time was appropriate.

Their office equipment was supplied by a man whom Colson christened Rolex Wong because he was able to produce knock-offs of all major name brands within twenty-four hours of orders being placed, all of which he transported in his own knock-off Louis Vuitton bag. The stationery supplier was a slight man, who invariably came to the office wearing a singlet underwear shirt. After about a year, he approached Colson and asked if he could speak with him. It turned out that he had two daughters, both attending the very exclusive Bishop Strachan girls' school in Toronto, and he wanted to set up some sort of trust to make sure that their needs were properly assured. Colson was stunned to discover that the man had more than $US1.5 million available for the purpose, and this was in 1981. Hong Kong was indeed a land of great opportunity.

There were many adventures that could only have occurred in Hong Kong. One of the main attractions was a floating gin palace in Aberdeen Harbour, a huge boat the owners of which took the admirable precaution of ensuring that it never left its berth. Another was a small, very rustic restaurant that Colson described to his visitors and guests as the Lama Hilton (in contrast to the real Hilton). Located on Lama Island across the harbour, it could be reached only by junks hired for the purpose or contributed by clients including, for this occasion, Rothschilds Bank. Upon arrival at a rickety dock, you had to climb up through a hatch to reach the restaurant. The food, mainly fish, was generally delightful, but a warning well worth bearing in mind was never, never, to look in the kitchen. David Angus feasted there with Colson one evening, which was followed by three days in hospital with food poisoning.

On another occasion, Colson and Suzanne decided to go to Manila for a few days. There were, as he said, "dozens" of forms to be filled out to get into the Philippines, and he completed Suzanne's for her since she was busy coping with Charles, their young son. Under occupation, he jokingly put "topless dancer," and when they arrived in Manila, she and the baby were pulled aside by the immigration officials who, as is the case with such authorities throughout the world, have had all traces of a sense of humour removed at birth. They insisted on knowing where she proposed to ply her trade. History does not record the subsequent matrimonial discussion, but it is perhaps safe to conclude that it was mostly a one-way conversation.

Two years after the decision-making trip in 1979, Stikeman was back in Hong Kong, with Ladi Pathy of Fednav, on a trip that was combined with the christening of two bulk coal carriers built at the Hyundai yards in Ulsan, Korea for Fednav and bare-boat chartered for ten years to Navios Shipping, one of the United States Steel shipping companies. He, of course, inspected the office and was characteristically pleased with what he saw.

The office is extremely attractive, comprised of three rooms in a very good building, the quality of which space is as good as or better than that of Commerce Court, Toronto. We have an extremely attractive and able receptionist by the name of Eileen, a Chinese girl who worked for some years with Phillips, Vineberg, which fact was not known to Danny Colson as he hired her through an agency.[11] It appears, however, that Phillips, Vineberg are doing nothing in Hong Kong, and the rumours that they have sent more men out to join Eddie Rubin are false. Eddie is almost totally taken up with his own personal commercial ventures and does very little other than look after some of the Royal Bank work.

On the other hand, our office is a hive of activity. We are at the moment acting for Hongkong Land, and indirectly Jardine Matheson, in the construction of the new hotel venture in Vancouver. We are also acting for Li Ka-shing in his real estate ventures in Canada and elsewhere. Since Li Ka-shing has been attempting to take over Jardine Matheson, and since Jardine and Hongkong Land purchased each other's shares as a mutual protection against this attack, it sometimes becomes delicate when Jardine, Hongkong Land, and/or Li Ka-shing learn that we are acting in different deals. However, these are the plum clients of the Hong Kong real estate community at this time, and we have them – much to the envy of the American and English law firms who have been trying to land them. In addition, we now have the exclusive business of COSCO, China Ocean Shipping Corporation. This is a corporation which owns the largest mercantile fleet in the world, and we have already received quite a lot of business from it. Again, it has been sought by two of the big American law firms for over a year without success, those firms being Shearman & Sterling and Coudert Bros. It would be much appreciated by Danny if some of the Maritime law group of this firm could visit him in Hong Kong from time to time to meet the clients and to lend depth and credibility to his attempts to deal with the matters on the ground.

There were signs of a turning away from Canada by the Hong Kong community. Jardine Matheson had absolutely no confidence in Canada as a place to invest and was seriously concerned with its exposure, through Hongkong Land, in the Vancouver hotel project, which would also affect the business they directed to the firm in Canada. The feeling in Hong Kong was that the Trudeau government was wildly socialist, the FIRA program was being strengthened, and that the feeling of nationalization was permeating the entire economy. Stikeman and the Canadian trade attaché did their best to allay the fears, but they did not believe they enjoyed much success. Fortunately, Hongkong Land seemed to be of an opposite view.

This warning given, the next day Stikeman and Colson enjoyed a lunch with Li Ka-shing and engaged him in a discussion of his appreciation of the Canadian investment scene. He was, with one serious caveat, generally favourably inclined, especially as a place for people from crowded areas, because we had a small population, such a large land mass, and so many natural resources that we would in time see on our scale the same kind of development that made Hong Kong rich. This was, he warned, provided that the Canadian government did not pursue its socialist course since that would make Canada the England of North America in ten years were it not to be reversed. Stikeman tried to reassure him on the point. He said that even within the civil service, there was a growing change of attitude, people having realized that they had been too theoretical and had bitten off more than they could chew. They were also coming to the conclusion that the political repercussions of failed socialism might well be worse than those of failed capitalism. While he knew to some degree that this was whistling in the dark, it was borne out by some of the events of the previous two weeks[12] and was echoed by the diplomatic staff in Hong Kong.

Li knew the firm was acting for COSCO and encouraged us to have a greater maritime law presence in Hong Kong. Li himself had significant shipping and offshore drilling interests. He also indicated that although Hongkong Land was active in Vancouver, he was thinking about expanding his own real estate interests into the east, particularly around Toronto, which he regarded as the most desirable place for real estate investment for the next twenty years in Canada, notwithstanding the boom in Calgary, Edmonton, and Vancouver. Li went out of his way to compliment Colson and to propose a toast to the firm. More face was accorded to Colson when Li accepted an invitation to a cocktail party hosted by the Colsons at their home. This was quite a coup for Colson because Li refused literally hundreds of similar invitations per week. Li almost single-handedly put Stikeman Elliott on the Hong Kong map. Hong Kong, says Colson, is all about "face" and connections. To be publicly identified as Li's lawyers was hugely important, and the firm could not have had a better calling card. Li got along very well with Ladi Pathy and was very much intrigued by the story of his run at Abitibi and the fact that the asset values of Canadian Pacific Railways were probably worth four times the share price. As Stikeman noted, "his eyes lit up. Who knows?"

Stikeman's report continued with a description of the people they met, many of whom were existing clients or who had referred work to the firm, and the high regard in which the firm and Danny and Suzanne Colson were held. By then, Eddie Rubin had left Phillips, Vineberg, and the prospect of getting work from Coudert Bros., with whom Phillips, Vineberg had shared space in a relationship that was never too happy, looked very promising. Always upbeat and generous with his praise, Stikeman reported, "Everywhere I go, I hear only the best comments about Danny and our firm and astonishment at the inroads we have made into the top-quality business in the Colony in our short one-year presence. Danny and Suzanne can be given all the credit for this. They have entertained on the average five nights a week, Danny entertaining at lunch almost five days a week throughout the year. They do it well, and they know everybody, and they are accepted by all age groups as the coming couple socially and professionally. We are extremely lucky." Near the end of his memo, there was a short observation, following a meeting with various people attending the ship christening in Ulsan, which gave the oracle watchers a hint of yet another possible direction for the firm.

Among these people, however, was the husband of one of the two ladies who christened one of the ships, a Mr Dune, the senior partner of the old New York law firm of Cadwalader, Wickersham & Taft. Mr Dune was going down to Hong Kong to consider whether or not his firm should open in that city, and I gave him Danny's card with whom he will discuss the matter. What interested me in my conversations with Mr Dune was that he felt that we, or some Canadian law firm, should definitely open a branch in New York. He stated that law firms of many other countries – Pinheiro Neto of Brazil, the big English solicitors firms we know in

London, Japanese firms, Argentinian firms, Mexican firms, etc. – all open branches in New York, and they have proved to be of inestimable value to the New York Bar who has access to the laws of these various countries and to assistance in dealing with problems of their clients in relation to them without going to the countries themselves. I indicated that we had always felt that the one-hour plane trip made it unnecessary, but he was very definitely of the view that that was not enough and that personal presence on the spot would be of value not only to the New York Bar, but to any Canadian lawyer who went down there.

The firm always had its eye on the much-promised land of China and the possibility that as its relations with the rest of the world expanded, so would trade and so would the need for lawyers with experience in international business and taxation. In that respect, we were far from alone in our aspirations and probably no less naive in our expectations than almost every business and every professional firm hoping to make inroads into China. Everyone, including our firm, seriously underestimated the difficulties involved and the length of time, plus the investment of financial and human resources that would be required to make even the tiniest inroads. Our hope was to manage the China relationship from Hong Kong with trips to China as required or as could be arranged. If the firm needed introductions in Hong Kong before it could be successful, the situation in Beijing was even more difficult. One could disappear into the bureaucracy and never be seen or heard from again (figuratively speaking), and no business would ever come from the effort. The description of one of the early trips made by Jacques Courtois after he left his former firm to join us gives some sense of how complicated any relationship would be and how long it would probably take to develop any meaningful business.

One initiative that seemed likely to attract attention from the Chinese was the willingness of the firm to receive Chinese lawyers for training in Canada for a period of at least a year. The Chinese had come to recognize that their concepts of law and contract were quite different from the standards that applied throughout most of the commercially developed world. Whatever their view of the relative merits of the respective legal systems, they knew that they had to become more capable of dealing with the Western legal concepts and that they needed their own Chinese lawyers to be able to advise them. With the Chinese, it was one thing to have confidence in foreign lawyers they could trust but quite another to have their own on whom they believed they could rely completely. So the offer we made to take on several of their lawyers was well received. This offer went back to the fall of 1981 when Courtois had made a preliminary suggestion in this direction. It was followed by an invitation, through the Canada-China Trade Council, to visit Beijing the next spring, formally extended by the legal affairs department of the China Council for the Promotion of International Trade (CCPIT).

Arriving in Beijing on March 29, Courtois was met and provided with a full agenda, beginning the following morning. He had a business talk with the CCPIT legal department and several of its lawyers. In the afternoon, he gave a lecture on the Canadian legal system, FIRA, and the taxation of foreign trading operations in Canada. In the evening, he was guest of honour at a dinner hosted by Ren Jianxin, the vice-chairman of CCPIT and head of its legal department. Jianxin took the occasion to express gratitude for our offer to train lawyers in Canada and held out the hope that this would be only the beginning of an association with the firm that could expand and be beneficial to both parties. This was undoubtedly not the first time this speech had been given. On March 31, Courtois met with China International Economic Consultants, Inc., a branch of China International Trust and Investment Corp. The consulting group was formed to provide legal consulting services for domestic and foreign investments and to draft or revise articles of association of companies or contracts and agreements on investments. It also advised on the financial, accounting, banking, and taxation issues related to Chinese-foreign ventures, foreign wholly owned enterprises, or other co-operative projects in China. Over and above this, it served as legal and accounting consultants to clients on an annual retainer basis. Courtois then visited the law faculty of Peking University, prior to dinner with the Canadian ambassador, Michel Gauvin, who offered his assistance.

The next day brought a meeting with the director of the foreign tax policy office in the general taxation bureau of the Ministry of Finance, where he was told that China proposed to invite foreign tax experts to Beijing to help them with the drafting of tax legislation and that he would visit foreign countries to learn about tax legislation. Courtois said we would be happy to help and to receive any delegation they might send. He also met with an official of China International Machinery and Equipment Import and Export Corp. Everywhere he went, Courtois left a copy of the firm's entry in Martindale-Hubbell. He was, despite the warm welcome, quite realistic about the likelihood that the firm would benefit in the short run from significant work emanating from China. It was more likely that we could be of use to Canadian firms that might be panting to get into China.

Although I believe that we might obtain a number of Chinese organizations as clients, it seems to me that they do not yet fully understand the role of the Western law firm and the fact that they have to pay substantial fees for advice. Up to now, the Chinese have been spoiled by foreigners providing assistance free in the hope of doing worthwhile business in the future. If we maintain good contacts in China, however, it should be helpful to us to get business from Canadian firms interested in doing business there.

Our offer to train Chinese lawyers here, originally made to CCPIT, was known to all those I called upon and was received with genuine gratitude. The Chinese have asked me to confirm the offer in writing, and I hope to be able to do that in a near future, after consultation with some of you.

I believe we should maintain our contacts with the Chinese, and we might discuss that with Dan Colson, who could probably call on the people I have seen at regular intervals.

We did follow up on the promise and have had at various times Chinese lawyers and even judges in our offices, principally in Montreal, to see how law is practised in North America and to learn about the Western concepts of drafting documents. Perhaps even more importantly, they learned how contractual and other rights are enforced through an independent and impartial court system, where the courts are not simply tools of the administrative or executive branch of government. We have also had scores of Chinese delegations though the offices on their many fact-finding missions and have always endeavoured to provide as much assistance as possible to them as they try to come to terms with a business and legal environment that is as foreign to them as China is to us. Whether in the long run this will prove to be a worthwhile effort and investment of our time remains to be seen. The Chinese are not known for quick action, and taking the time to make a decision that they consider to be in their best interests is not something we understand in the West. If the Chinese err on the side of ready, aim, aim, aim, aim, our tendency would seem to them to be ready, fire, aim. The Chinese have finally achieved membership in the World Trade Organization, which will require certain changes in their commercial comportment. So, as Stikeman said in his memorandum about Hong Kong, "Who knows?"

We worked with Alcan Asia in their China matters and more generally in Asia, including their Thai transaction with Reynolds Aluminium. The COSCO work was principally maritime, and the client was serviced mainly by Angus and Prager out of Montreal. We acted in connection with a major loan made by a consortium of Canadian banks (US banks were not welcome) to help finance a duck farm that produced more than a million ducks per year for export. Part of the due diligence on the loan required a visit to the premises, an operation that had led to the development of a community of some 40,000 people. According to Colson, you could smell the overpowering stench from five miles away. Colson says that many of the promises the firm obtained from prospective clients in Hong Kong never produced any business and that a great deal of the business ended up coming from sources that were the least expected. As an example, we acted in connection with a Vancouver hotel project for Hongkong Land, controlled by Jardine, a business "enemy" of Li Ka-shing, and we had to be sure that Li understood that this was not in any way a defection from him.

By early 1981, Colson was pleading with the senior management of the firm for more help in Hong Kong so that there would be two full-time lawyers on hand. In the meantime, he had hired on a part-time basis Brian Hansen,[13] a New Zealand lawyer who was also qualified in Canada. Hansen had arrived in Hong Kong a few months after Colson and went almost immediately to see if there might be some part-time work available. This was relatively easy for Hansen to arrange because he was in charge of the timetable at the University of Hong Kong, where he had been engaged as a professor of law. Despite being delighted to have some backup in place, even if only part-time, Colson was convinced that the second full-time lawyer should have tax expertise and urged that the reinforcement arrive by September of that year.

Hansen is an unabashed admirer of Colson, and this is almost certainly why he was willing to follow him to London in 1983. Hansen had resigned his position in Stikeman Elliott and was ready to take up a position with Chapman Tripp in New Zealand, but Colson convinced him that it made more sense to spend a few years in the centre of civilization rather than on the southern tip, so he and his wife, Jen, agreed to go.

Danny Colson is, in simple terms, one of the best lawyers I have ever had the pleasure to work with. He is not in any sense a specialist in any area (leaving aside newspapers, where, of course, he is eminently qualified by now), but he has two absolutely remarkable skills which are instrumental to his success in the international offices. The first (and perhaps the most important) is his amazing ability to remember the name of almost every single person he has met in his life. I remember phone numbers and faces if I am lucky. Danny can walk into a room of a hundred people, he will know ninety of that hundred within the space of an hour and be their best friend, and he will come across four or five people he has not seen for five years and remember instinctively their name and something bad they did during the period he knew them, which forms the basis for an initial joke. There is no one in the firm who is better remembered by people he has met than Danny except perhaps for Brian Rose. Secondly, over the years, I was initially nervous with Danny talking to clients on what I considered to be relatively complicated matters that he had not analysed in great detail. I soon changed my mind. I have never met anyone who has the ability to talk generally about complicated situations where he is not a specialist and yet to talk in a manner that relays all the material aspects of the matter to the client and never make a mistake or mislead the client in what he is saying. This is perhaps the essential talent required of those in small international offices, and Danny is absolutely incredible at this.

By mid-1983, Colson was getting ready to leave Hong Kong to return to London at the end of the year and said that he nevertheless thought that it was in the best interests of the firm, and particularly for the Hong Kong office, that he maintain his contacts as much as possible. To that end, he proposed to return every six months or as required since virtually none of the firm's clients were "institutionalized" as they were in Canada but were personal, and the continuity was particularly important. He was also willing to assume a certain degree of responsibility for overseeing the Hong Kong office during the next few years or until such time as it had a resident partner. He agreed, but for different reasons, with the staffing of the London office proposed by Brian Rose.

The early years in Hong Kong were solid and quite relaxed. These were the days when you could take a junk out in Hong Kong Harbour and swim in clean water – a practice no longer recommended nor even possible – and where there was very heavy corporate entertaining. This was a practice in which Stikeman Elliott indulged very infrequently and of which we were often keen beneficiaries. There are some wonderful stories out of Hong Kong. Hansen remembers the occasion when he and Colson walked into the wrong reception by mistake and left half an hour later after Colson had, of course, introduced himself to everyone in the room. On leaving, Colson received a very large piece of electronic equipment as a gift. They later discovered that they had walked into the Toyota reception, with which they had absolutely nothing to do, but people obviously thought they deserved a memento of the occasion when they left. There was also the time when Colson had to fire his Filipino amah when he discovered that she was a local prostitute in Hong Kong. Someone rang up and in response to Danny's request to leave a message, told him to tell his maid that she could contact the caller at three o'clock in room 306 at the Mandarin Hotel. Everyone in the office seemed far more amused than the Colsons.

Hansen's wife, Jen, has her favourite story of Hong Kong. At a time when she was fed up with the long hours that Hansen was working, he had gone to work in a rush in the morning after having about four hours sleep and had felt slightly uncomfortable in his shoes. The discomfort was not, however, annoying enough to bother investigating. He worked throughout the morning, went to lunch and got back about 2:00 PM. He was sitting at his desk and his secretary, Teresa Wong, was standing in front of him, when he suddenly became aware of something in his shoe. He unlaced and took it off to take out what he thought was a stone, only to find a cockroach, which he swears was no shorter than three inches, emerge from under his foot, jump out of the shoe, and rocket across the floor to join the other two hundred thousand cockroaches in the wall in China Building. Teresa may never have recovered from the shock.

There was always a constant flow of work in the early years in Hong Kong. These were the days when we started, with the assistance of Elinore Richardson, to develop the offshore tax-based immigration practice that was such a boon for the firm in subsequent years. This was the time when wealthy individuals were beginning to emigrate from Hong Kong to Canada, and very quickly, they became aware of the opportunities provided by "five-year trusts." This would not have been possible without Richardson's assistance in analysing provisions to which people in Canada had not paid much attention to date. In the early days, this practice was conducted in a relatively unsophisticated manner, but when Frank Sixt and subsequently Paul Setlakwe arrived on Hansen's departure, the practice was elevated to a new level of sophistication.

Christian Salbaing was transferred from London, where he had worked since 1981, to the Hong Kong office in 1983, and having the same difficulties as Colson had experienced in finding suitable quarters, he lived with them for the first couple of months. When Colson and Hansen left Hong Kong in the fall of that year, the office was staffed by Chris Salbaing, who now is with Hutchison Telecom in charge of Italy, Spain, and France. He is a very bright lawyer who gets along with everyone tremendously well and is great fun to be around. He was joined by Frank Sixt and some time thereafter, by Ralph Lutes[14] from the Toronto office. Sixt, in particular, but with the assistance of Lutes and Ching-wo Ng, brought the practice to another level. Sixt was a tremendous lawyer and completely dominated the tax practice in Hong Kong, developing the most sophisticated structures for Hong Kong taxpayers moving to Canada. He also built on the substantial relationship that Colson and Hansen had developed with the Li family, particularly with Canning Fok and Victor Li, and was instrumental in two extremely large transactions that the Li family and their corporate group undertook in Canada. These included the successful tendering for the Expo Lands site in Vancouver, the subsequent development of that site, and the acquisition (initially of a 50 per cent interest and thereafter, 95 per cent) of Husky Oil and Gas, the balance held by the CIBC. The agreements surrounding these transactions were absolutely mind-boggling. Hansen became involved in the transactions after they had been completed and said it took him about two months working with Sixt to understand the shareholders agreements dealing in particular with the Expo Lands and the tax planning behind the structures, a compliment to Sixt's creativity. The only sad thing for the firm about Sixt's success in Hong Kong is that it was too great since after a brief period with the firm in Vancouver, he went to join the Li family business, where he is now group finance director of Hutchison Whampoa, the world's most profitable company in 2001.

Ching-wo Ng[15] was recruited from Edmonton, where he had practised for several years, and joined the firm in Hong Kong as of May 1, 1986. He spoke both Mandarin and Cantonese and was someone who could handle matters for us in Hong Kong, Taiwan, and mainland China. Over and above a brilliant legal mind, Ng had a remarkable stamina and capacity to work apparently endlessly and often had to be reminded to eat meals while toiling away at his desk. By August of the same year, the office was ready to begin generating a quarterly newsletter entitled *China Brief* on new developments in the People's Republic of China, and the initial issue was circulated that month to some 190 key China contacts in Canada and elsewhere. It was a targeted publication to decision makers of potential Canadian corporate clients in the manufacturing and services industries (especially high tech, transportation, mining, forestry, telecommunications, power generation, and agriculture), who might be likely to send work or to have a specific interest in China. It included sections dealing with general news, new laws and regulations, banking and finance, taxation, Canada-China initiatives, and business opportunities. Our principal lack in Hong Kong at this stage, with Sixt about to leave to go to Vancouver, was again someone with tax expertise, a situation confirmed repeatedly by both Hansen (from London) and Salbaing.

Sixt left the Hong Kong office to relocate in Vancouver at the beginning of 1990, and his replacement, Paul Setlakwe, arrived from Montreal on September 1, 1989 to get acquainted with the local practice and clients. At the firm partners' meeting in the fall of 1988, Paul Setlakwe had been approached by Brian Rose, who suggested that he should think about going to Hong Kong. Having thought about it, he was disposed to do so and negotiated the customary one-on-one deal with Sonny Gordon, who was generally responsible for the foreign offices. Setlakwe is convinced that one of the reasons for the success of the foreign offices was that the firm and those it sent to staff them were prepared to operate under often difficult conditions on a shoestring budget, such as was the case when Sixt and his wife had stayed for their first two months at Salbaing's apartment. Setlakwe remained in Hong Kong from 1989 until 1992, carrying on from where Sixt had left off, bringing the much-needed tax capacity to the office, which he managed as well following Lutes's return to Canada.

This was not a comfortable economic time in Asia, and Paul Setlakwe, Ng, and Eric Kong, who arrived shortly after Setlakwe (and who left the firm in 1997 to go back to Vancouver with a former client) did remarkably well to sustain the office at the level they did. Again, Setlakwe did it too successfully and so impressed the Ho family with his work that after returning to Montreal and working there for several years, he received an offer from the Ho family that he could not resist. Fortunately for the firm, Setlakwe still remains in the Montreal office. It was a great testament to him that a large number of the clients with whom he had dealt, including Hongkong and Shanghai Bank Trustees, still preferred to deal with Setlakwe directly in Montreal even after Hansen returned to the Hong Kong office.

Dominic Tsun[16] from the Toronto office had arrived in the latter part of 1988 and was still there when Setlakwe arrived. Eric Kong, a member of the BC Bar, was recruited from Hong Kong and was due to arrive in the summer of 1990 after a six-month posting in the Vancouver office to get to know the firm. The ramping up of staff had necessitated the move in April 1989 to expanded quarters, fortunately in the same building. Despite increasing competition from other Canadian firms, which had finally woken up to the business potential of Hong Kong, we continued to consolidate our position in that market as the pre-eminent Canadian firm, offering the highest quality and most complete range of services, albeit at some expense. The increase and expansion of business inevitably led to the need for more support staff, both paralegal and administrative, for better and more sophisticated equipment and systems, and a resulting need to keep an eye on the costs of carrying on business. Lutes came back to Vancouver in August 1990 and a couple of years later, moved on to Canadian Imperial Bank of Commerce in Singapore, where we continued to deal with him. Upon returning to Canada, he practised as a general counsel for a technology company out of Whistler, BC, before rejoining the firm at the beginning of 2002.

Following the disastrous miscalculations on both sides of the political spectrum that led to the Tiananmen Square events on June 4, 1989, record numbers of Chinese sought Canadian refuge for themselves and whatever assets they may have been able to get out. Even though the firm steered away from an immigration practice, the surge of business that resulted from the collapse of confidence in the future of Hong Kong was unprecedented. Hong Kong Chinese, in particular, developed an appetite for Canadian real estate, both residential and commercial, a large portion of which was focused on the Vancouver area. The effect was significant enough that market values were driven to ever-increasing levels to the consternation of local buyers and the delight of sellers. This investment was often combined with the taking up of Canadian residence, which provided the firm with many new opportunities for pre-residence tax planning on behalf of high net worth individuals. This proved to be a natural fit with the program of the federal government for immigration-linked investment. Many of the financial institutions developed "packages" for products of this nature, and the firm worked with many of their clients as well. The pre-immigration practice became a staple of the Hong Kong office, but it led to even more interesting work, which was the international quarterbacking of the tax and family structures for multinational families as they sought both stability and the ability to transfer wealth from one generation to another and in different countries.

At roughly the same time, we discerned the opportunity for additional business generated in Taiwan and established a representative office in Taipei. The concomitant challenge was to be able to provide such services from a base in Hong Kong, where the office was already under some strain just trying to deal with Hong Kong business. Ng and Tsun each spent about a week per month in Taiwan during 1990. With the departure of Tsun to Vancouver early the following year, Ng was forced to cover the still exciting Taiwan on his own during 1991. This was tough sledding for Ng, who did not want to move to Taiwan and was, therefore, in the position of trying to develop a practice in two separate countries at the same time. He was also working his contacts in Thailand and was trying to develop China business in conjunction with his Japanese and Taiwan contacts.

There was very little significant investment into Canada by major Hong Kong-based groups during 1990, although we had some work on smaller investments and there was follow-up work on earlier major investments. China work was slow as what may have initially appeared to be a bonanza of opportunity got a serious reality check due to the difficulties of doing business in China. Some of the US firms, which had arrived in Hong Kong with the China carpet bags in hand, began to reassess the situation and closed their offices. We still got work from Alcan in relation to its own investment in China, and our real estate conveyancing work derived from Hong Kong continued apace when a new project adjacent to the Expo site in Vancouver was put on the market by Grand Adex in December 1990.

By mid-1990, the potential of Singapore, a centre that Stikeman had discussed with Li Ka-shing eleven or twelve years earlier, had been identified, and visits were made from Hong Kong to meet with accounting and law firms, financial institutions, and the Canadian High Commission. As was the case with the initial trips made by Stikeman and Elliott in the early days of the firm, such visits produced new work. The Royal Bank of Canada, the CIBC, and the Canadian High Commission all referred mandates to the firm, as did the well-known investment bank Hill Samuel. Canada was working with the Government of Singapore Investment Corporation with respect to proposed investments in Canada. No decision was made at that time to open a separate office in Singapore since foreign law firms had had a mixed experience. Several, such as the huge English firm of Freshfields, had closed their offices, while others, such as Coudert Bros., had scaled back considerably. Part of the reason for this was that certain cross-border loans that had previously been governed by US law now came under Singapore law. On the other hand, another of the large English firms, Linklaters, was expected to open an office shortly.

An ongoing issue was the relationship of the firm with local Hong Kong lawyers so that work could be done in the Hong Kong market. We had provided the usual undertaking when we opened the office that we would not do "local" work that was the reserved legal territory of members of the Hong Kong Bar. Other firms had developed so-called international partnerships with a resident Hong Kong partner and the Canadian partners operating from Hong Kong, among them McMillan Binch, Bull, Houser, and Byers Casgrain. This would not be resolved until 1995. Our initial discussions with Canadian institutions active in Hong Kong and with local clients elicited very promising responses, so we continued our review of the potential throughout 1992. In the interim, beginning in 1991, Joanna Shum and her husband, Kelvin, managed a parallel firm (Shum & Company) doing local work, with which we were associated. In making this decision, we were motivated heavily by promises of substantial local residential real estate projects, which were not available to Stikeman Elliott as a foreign firm, but which were highly profitable.

We managed to retain Shum, who had left Johnson Stokes & Master and was living in Australia, one of the most competent real estate lawyers in Hong Kong. Shum established the base for the real estate practice, and for a period of two and a half to three years, it operated in an extremely profitable manner. This local Hong Kong practice was run in conjunction with a Canadian real estate practice organized by Eric Kong, which consisted largely of selling Vancouver and Toronto condominiums to Asian investors. It was a highly profitable but risky practice even when run on a careful and conservative basis, as we learned from being sued on a couple of occasions. It is a practice from which we exited very quickly when the Asian economic crisis began to hit in 1997, and it is no longer part of our practice in the Hong Kong office. The local rules required that there be separate entrances for each of the firms, but the association was nevertheless very close. By the end of November 1993, Hansen was ready to initiate the formal request of the Home Office to allow us to practise local law in Hong Kong, and he reported to the firm executive committee at the end of January 1994 that the local laws were expected to change, thus allowing the consolidated firms of Stikeman Elliott and Shum & Company to operate under a single name. The final step was taken at the end of the firm's fiscal year on January 31, 1995.

With the return of Lutes from Hong Kong to the Vancouver office in August 1990, followed by the repatriation of Tsun in March 1991, the firm's executive committee decided that Brian Hansen should return to Hong Kong from Vancouver. Although this was perceived as a good initiative, it meant that there would now be two relatively senior partners in place. By mid-1992, Hansen was back, and despite some slowdown due to the fact that Canada was not particularly well regarded by Asia investors, prospects still remained good. The other Canadian firms were rather defensive in the face of the firm's aggressive presence in Hong Kong, and everyone was quite sanguine about the future.

Eugene Kwan, then in the Vancouver office, was instrumental in getting extra work from Henderson Land Developments, and the firm's relationship with Sun Hung Kai Properties and New World remained sound despite their limited interest in Canada at the time. We acted on a substantial mandate from TVBI, owned by Sir Run Run Shaw, and got extensive work from the Stanley Ho Group. More significantly from the international operations perspective, we began to get more corporate work that was regional in basis and not governed by Canadian law, including clients in Vietnam.

By mid-1992, it appeared that the other Canadian firms were beginning to lose heart and were reconsidering their positions in Hong Kong, including McCarthy Tétrault, Goodman Freeman Vineberg, Lawson & Tory, and Fraser & Beatty. Some were pulling back their partners in the area, and others were in danger of losing key personnel to us. The opportunities seemed, therefore, to be opening up once again. Thought was given to attempting to get an article in the local media in English and Chinese describing the changing Canadian legal environment. In the second half of 1992, we did, in fact, engage the services of Andes Lin of McCarthy Tétrault, who was highly regarded in the area for his offshore tax work, for his extensive contacts in Hong Kong and Taipei, and for his knowledge of both Cantonese and Mandarin, all of which filled a major gap in our previous ability to provide full service from the Hong Kong base. Lin left the firm in 1995, and his shoes were filled by Clifford Ng from the Vancouver office.

At the same time as the real estate practice was developing, the firm started to do a large amount of major China work. We acted for clients such as Singapore Power, Cheung Kong, CEF, CIBC, Onex Corporation, Bank of Montreal, Royal Bank of Canada, and others in their infrastructure, trade, and banking activities on the mainland. Ching-wo Ng was invaluable in this area, in which his careful legal work and fluent command of Mandarin made him a favourite among westerners investing in China. Two of the best relationships forged by the firm during this period were with Northern Telecom and Atomic Energy of Canada (AECL).

The firm did not do any work for Northern Telecom in Asia until one day, the company's vice-president, legal, rang up Hansen to say that its general counsel, Clive Allen, was in town and wanted to chat about Asia to fill in half an hour. Could Hansen help him? Hansen replied affirmatively without any real hope, although Shawna Miller from London had told him that we should chase after work from Northern Telecom. This had been tried, but without success. Allen came in, and they had a pleasant conversation. Three weeks after that, the firm started to get a tremendous amount of work from Northern Telecom in China and in the Philippines and, in fact, ended up doing the joint venture banking work for all Northern Telecom's financing joint ventures in China. Hansen has absolutely no doubt that the reason we got the work had less to do with our expertise than the fact that Clive Allen noticed that we were one of the first companies in Hong Kong actually to buy and use Northern Telecom's telephones. That relationship with Northern Telecom on the corporate side (we had always done some tax work for the company in

Canada) has now been developed by Marvin Yontef to the stage where they are an extremely important client of the firm.

The other relationship with AECL was one of the highlights for Ng and Hansen. Hansen was given the opportunity to talk to AECL by Michel Vennat and subsequently was retained to act for the organization on the negotiation and the building of the Quinshan nuclear plant in China. This was an absolutely remarkable occasion, which involved the staff of AECL being followed around in planes by mysterious people – who may have been suspected to be members of the People's Liberation Army – who were trying to keep the head of AECL and their general counsel apart, and weeks of work in Beijing where one saw nothing but the inside of a hotel. Operating with ten people against a negotiating team of over a hundred is not something Hansen would like to go through again, but it was a memorable experience. Again, that relationship forged in Hong Kong had led to the firm getting work from AECL in both Montreal and Toronto and more recently, in Australia, where we acted for AECL on its bid for the Lucas Heights nuclear research reactor in Sydney.

The situation in Hong Kong was greatly affected by several factors in the late 1990s. One was the return of Hong Kong from Britain to China in 1997, an event that triggered huge uncertainties as to the future of the former colony and significant exodus of capital in the direction of other areas considered more secure by the Chinese and other business communities. Those refuges included Canada, and the firm had considerable business from Chinese who moved some assets and themselves to Canada. Hundreds, if not thousands, of Hong Kong Chinese invested heavily in Canada, much of this in western Canada, and took steps to become Canadian citizens so they would have Canadian passports (in addition to any other) in case they had to leave when the People's Republic of China assumed control of the colony. Preparations of this nature were delicate in the extreme, and the greatest precautions were taken to keep any such activities as confidential as possible. Meetings were often arranged in hotel rooms so that there would be no evidence of a Canadian lawyer attending at the client's office or alternatively, no possibility of the client being seen visiting the offices of Canadian lawyers. This was as long as it was broad since in the end, the falling Canadian dollar had a negative impact on continued investment in Canada, which persisted for several years.

The separation from Britain was accomplished relatively smoothly despite enormous levels of suspicion between the British and the Chinese and a well-expressed resentment by Britain of the ejection from its former position.[17] Another factor was the economic downturn in Asia generally, which affected business and particularly, the formerly booming real estate market. The firm had developed, with local involvement of Shum & Company, a considerable conveyancing practice, which had to be drastically trimmed in 1998, the year after the return of Hong Kong to Chinese rule. Thereafter, the focus was directed at developing work in the People's Republic of China using Hong Kong as the base for ancillary operations and the ongoing servicing of Canadian-related work.

When Hansen went down to Sydney to open up the firm's office at the beginning of 1997, Hong Kong was left in the capable hands of Eric Kong. Unfortunately, only three or four months later, Kong decided that he was leaving the firm, which left us in an extremely difficult position in Hong Kong. The person who stood up to take the responsibility of looking after the office was Eugene Kwan.

At a time when no one else was prepared to take the risk, Kwan left Vancouver and travelled to Hong Kong to do his best in the radically altered circumstances. This included finishing the job of trimming the staff and trying to put the office back on a reasonable economic footing. This was a most difficult environment in which to operate, and Kwan and Clifford Ng did a creditable job in restoring some measured order to the operations. It is, however, very difficult to run an office of even four or five lawyers when there is simply no work available. What there was, Kwan and Ng got, but there was not a great deal of it around. Kwan left the firm to join Hutchison Telecom in 2000.

To further complicate matters in 1998, being too dependent on real estate, we got caught in the Asian crisis with too large an office and staff. It was not that the occurrence of the crisis was unanticipated, but its speed and severity were quite unexpected. Real estate crashed, and investment in China came to a virtual halt. As a consequence, we lost substantial amounts of money in Hong Kong and had to trim the lawyers and staff from more than thirty down to nine or less. The effects of the Asian crisis were a solid dose of reality for those who thought themselves so capable while running through the profitable times. It was also a good reminder that as a smallish firm in world terms, no matter how successful domestically and aggressive in its international operations, it is extremely difficult to sit out a major economic downturn in the same manner that the large UK and US law firms are able to do. Those jurisdictions always have a constant flow of business from home into different parts of the world. When times turn bad, Canadian companies basically stop investing overseas completely, with the rare exception of companies such as Northern Telecom. At the time of the Asian crisis, Royal Bank of Canada and Bank of Montreal, for example, basically left China altogether, the CIBC essentially closed its Singapore operations, and most of the Canadian banks reduced their operations substantially. The firm lost much of its client base almost overnight.

At the nadir of the Hong Kong practice, the firm was reduced to four lawyers, but it has now built back to nine and has returned to a profitable basis, focusing on the local and cross-border corporate, M&A, securities, tax, and financial services sectors. As Ng, who took over management of the office at the dawn of the new millennium, says, we do the work that the big international firms will not do and that the local firms cannot. The major international clients do most of their transactions under US or UK law now, and Canadian law is seldom a factor in the huge deals, with the result that firms such as Herbert Smith have grown to more than a hundred lawyers in Hong Kong, while our numbers have stayed more or less constant, and we occupy a specialized planning and servicing niche. The team consists of lawyers trained in Canada, the United States, and the UK and has a strong base of local corporate clients, financial institutions, and Canadian and US corporations active in the region. In the roller-coaster market of Hong Kong, the firm is once again recognized as the dominant Canadian firm in town and is developing a strong reputation for sophisticated local work.

The relationship with the Li family continues, and the firm was honoured by them with a dinner in 2001 to celebrate the twentieth anniversary of practice in Hong Kong in the seventieth-floor boardroom of the group's headquarters on the site of the former Hilton Hotel. Our cocktail reception to commemorate the event was attended by both Li Ka-shing and his son, Victor, along with the senior directors and officers of the group and other leaders in the business and legal community in Hong Kong.

NEW YORK

At the general partners meeting of the firm in 1983, Sonny Gordon and Marvin Yontef were asked to investigate the feasibility of a New York office. They did a budget on the back of a napkin, which was far more investigation than had been done to date, and they presented it to the meeting. Since this was at the height of the firm's phase of opening offices, there was general agreement that we should proceed. Everyone thought that the plan should be to have Rose leave London and use his many contacts to open doors for work, and that he should be supported on the technical side by Jim Riley, then still an associate.

Opening offices was not expensive at first since it was viewed as simply moving existing lawyers and topping up that expense with some rent and operating funds. Gordon found some space in the Seagram Building and decorated it in his inimitable style. He was given a similar job in the Montreal office – to bring the fortieth floor boardroom suite up to the standards that would enable clients to appreciate why their bills were so high. He used to boast that he had been given an unlimited budget for the purpose and that he had exceeded it. Arrangements had to be made with the New York Bar over what could go on the letterhead, and it was eventually agreed that the name could be used provided that the firm was indicated as not having been admitted in New York, and the resident lawyers were to be described as legal consultants. It was, however, possible to show the addresses of our other offices including Montreal, Toronto, Ottawa, London, and Hong Kong.

A brownstone apartment in Manhattan was located for Rose at 62nd and Park Avenue, which had the advantage of being not only a "steal" at $US5,000 per month, but also of having been Warren Beatty's New York apartment. Rose's dinner parties were highly rated. One of the firm's New York legal contacts was heard to exclaim, "You guys must really be coining it in Canada!" There was one incident that might have marred the New York stay. Rose's wife was hassled by a would-be mugger at the front door of the apartment building. She was trying to get into the apartment, had rung the bell, and was trying to get the door opened, when Rose appeared at the door. It was a mugger's nightmare. Suddenly, there was a six-foot-six,

300-plus-pound angry husband of his intended victim. Not only was he going to come away empty-handed from his venture, but also, if he did not get out of there quickly, he would be going directly to a hospital – or worse.

Rose returned to Toronto in 1985, which was probably a shame since it was considered, by Colson in particular, to have been a mistake not to continue to capitalize on the recognition – institutional and personal – that he brought to the firm. Rose had gone to New York on the understanding that it would require a five-year commitment to establish the office and build a client base. This was supported not only by his personal experience in London, but also by that of other foreign law firms, and it was shared by visiting lawyers such as Stanley Hartt and Marc Lalonde. It takes time to convert the personal relationships with individuals into an identification with the firm. Rose was concerned that the personal contacts had to be transferred before he left rather than through him and then to Waitzer, a concern arising from the transition that had occurred in London when both he and Salbaing left and there was an unsuccessful transfer of some of the clients.

Jim Riley came in the fall of 1983 but stayed only a year, thinking he had made a bad financial deal with Grant. One of the main problems with any of the foreign offices was the matter of compensation and the differential in expenses that the lawyer assigned to a foreign office would inevitably incur. Rents and housing in London, New York, and Hong Kong were far more expensive than in Canada, and there was always a series of ad hoc negotiations to try to reach the right "number" for each of the lawyers. Added to this was the difficulty in tax planning for partners who ceased to be resident in Canada. The New York office wanted to be sure that Riley's *Bank Act* expertise remained available to them in New York after he left and urged that he be freed up enough to travel to New York as required.

Elizabeth Skelton[18] followed from the Montreal office. Ed Waitzer came at the same time and stayed for almost three years, from late 1985 until 1988. He and John Stransman had been working together on policy work for the Ontario Securities Commission, and Waitzer had been retained as outside counsel for hearings that had led the commission to deregulate brokerage commission rates at the Toronto Stock Exchange in 1982. They were both counsel for the commission on hearings that led to the relaxation of entry barriers, both for foreign investment firms and for banks seeking entry into the domestic securities industry. This background made it logical to consider a stint in New York. The ground had already been broken by Rose and Riley, so his task was considerably simpler. With entry barriers dropped, most of the major banks and "money centre" banks were looking at opportunities in Canada. Given his experience at the Toronto Stock Exchange as a lawyer handling mergers and acquisitions and corporate finance transactions, many of which were cross-border, and as counsel to the Ontario Securities Commission on the rules allowing entry, it was easy to gain an audience and often mandates. In many ways, New York was a refreshing experience, precisely because it was so much less of a "club" than Canada. Anyone with good ideas and energy was welcomed, and there was more than enough activity to keep everyone busy.

Waitzer, too, experienced the difficulties in the foreign offices of staffing large transactions from small operational bases. There was a succession of refinancings handled for Domtar and Massey-Ferguson (now Varity Corporation). At one stage, he arranged for a young associate to come to New York to audit meetings on a Varity restructuring that was underway. His instructions to the associate were to sit at one end of the boardroom table and call him if there were any issues that required his immediate attention. If not, he was to call Waitzer at the end of the day for a briefing, an occasion to which the associate looked forward, having developed an infatuation for the childrens' nanny. The associate did his job, and things progressed smoothly, so smoothly in fact that after several weeks, Waitzer got a call from Jean Fraser of Osler Hoskin & Harcourt, one of the other Canadian counsels on the deal. She told him that she had finally realized that the chap sitting at the end of the table was not Waitzer himself.

The work of assisting assorted investment banks establish their Canadian operations often raised questions of conflict of interest. Waitzer had testy discussions with the head of Canadian business for what was then Salomon Brothers, which had until then historically enjoyed the premier franchise of the US firms in Canada. He made it clear that he could not countenance us working for his firm and at the same time, for Drexel Burnham Lambert. Waitzer finally had to explain that he was a director of the Canadian subsidiaries of both firms, and practicality overcame testosterone. The office became successful because of the convergence of a number of circumstances. Firstly, the relaxation of entry barriers into the Canadian financial services sector made Canada an interesting market for the major investment banks and money centre banks. As important was the advent of hostile takeover bids in the mid-1980s, which challenged managerial incumbency and broke down long-time client relationships (whether with law firms or bankers) in favour of more transaction-focused relationships. Hence it was that the firm could act for virtually every investment bank contemporaneously. A final, related factor was the interest of Canadian firms to raise capital and acquire assets in the deeper, broader market to the south. This led to new cross-border transactional structures and regulatory frameworks, many of which were developed with our vital involvement.

Ken Ottenbreit[19] began his career at Stikeman as an articling student in the Toronto office in July 1983. On his first day of work, he left the office at 5:00 PM, changed into his baseball uniform, and went to play that evening for his team in the Toronto Senior Men's League. The game was rained out, so he decided to return to the office to pick up some reading, expecting that no one would be around. Around 8:30 PM, he walked by Milton Hess's office and heard someone call out, "Hello. Come back here." Hess introduced himself and asked Ottenbreit whether he was a corporate student. Hess then sat Ottenbreit, still in his baseball uniform, in his office and offered him some jelly beans, while unloading real estate files that had accumulated during his vacation.

Within the first few weeks in the corporate department, he was "Domed" by Yontef and added to the Stikeman Elliott team that was representing the syndicate of four Canadian banks on the various financial restructurings relating to Dome Petroleum. Upon completion of his corporate rotation, he moved to the litigation section and was immediately drafted for the team working with John Sopinka on the representation of Susan Nelles before the Grange Commission. Though many students worked on this file, Ottenbreit had the good fortune of working on the Nelles file at the time when the nurses began testifying and when Sopinka was arguing before the Trial Court and Court of Appeal in connection with whether Justice Grange could "name names" in his commission report. While working on the *Nelles* case, Ottenbreit was given another project by Sopinka, which was to prepare a libel claim by Prime Minister Lynden Pindling of the Bahamas, who had retained Sopinka as Canadian counsel and sued NBC for libel in connection with various reports the network had aired about the alleged drug trade in the Bahamas. The challenge was to serve libel notices on Canadian television stations, satellite companies, and cable channels that had picked up the NBC broadcast. Ottenbreit prepared a memorandum on libel rules under Canadian law, which was ultimately reviewed by F. Lee Bailey (because of the different libel standards under Canadian and US law), who was US counsel for Pindling on the same matter and who was coordinating legal strategy with Sopinka.

Ottenbreit, who had become a regular squash partner of Sopinka, remembers another call he got at 9:00 AM requesting that he immediately go to Sopinka's office with his squash equipment and his driver's licence. Ottenbreit drove Sopinka, in Sopinka's car, to Hamilton, where Sopinka was to argue an appeal. Ottenbreit remembers being told to drive, and that Sopinka told him not to speak to him while he prepared for the case in the passenger's seat. Ottenbreit had grown up in Saskatchewan and had not driven a car during his time at law school, and certainly not in and around Toronto and Hamilton, yet he managed to drive Sopinka to Hamilton safely through some of the heaviest traffic in the country. He watched Sopinka argue the appeal, had lunch, and then they played a squash game before Sopinka dropped him off at the Oakville train station for his return to Toronto.

When Ottenbreit rejoined the corporate department in 1985, he continued to work extensively on the Dome Petroleum file with Michael Allen. He also worked with John Stransman on a series of public offerings for companies such as Amca International, Co-Steel, and Scintrex, as well as on private M&A matters with Richard Clark, including acquisitions for Wickes Companies and Saatchi & Saatchi. In November 1987, he began working with Allen and Stransman on the financial restructuring of Turbo Resources and during a three-month period from November 1987 to January 1988, spent virtually all of his time in Calgary working at the head offices of Turbo. Unbeknownst to him, this provided the genesis of an assignment to New York that began innocently enough. With a summons to Allen's office, he was asked whether he would be willing to move to New York for "four months" while the firm looked for a permanent replacement for Ed Waitzer, who had left that office in November. It was not the first time he had thought about one of the foreign offices, having previously discussed with Colson the possibility of going to London during the latter part of 1987. This time, he agreed to go to the New York office on the express condition that he return to Toronto at the agreed date of June 30, 1988.

The twenty-nine-year-old Ottenbreit moved temporarily to the New York office in February 1988 and immediately began working with Elizabeth Skelton on a range of banking and other projects. In July 1988, he agreed to extend his four months by one year, and thus began a series of informal one-year extensions that ultimately became a permanent position in the New York office. During his first stint, he continued his work on the Dome Petroleum file and attended the closing of the purchase by Amoco Canada of Dome Petroleum in Calgary in August 1988. He also started to develop a broker-dealer and underwriters' practice with Ed Waitzer, representing US underwriters on Canada-US offerings, including a series of financings representing Kidder Peabody and Salomon Brothers on US underwritings for Domtar Inc., and to develop a practice representing "international dealers" and "international advisers" registered with the Ontario Securities Commission. Handling the regulatory matters for these large US clients has become an important service business of the New York office, has created a useful profile for the firm, and has generated numerous referrals from dealers, advisers, and the US law firms that represent them.

When the Canadian securities administrators and the Securities and Exchange Commission (SEC) of the US adopted the multi-jurisdictional disclosure system (MJDS) to create a reciprocal prospectus filing system for Canadian and US issuers, Ottenbreit worked on a number of the first MJDS offerings, representing US underwriters, and on many other cross-border offerings for companies such as Dynacare, Sun Media, Open Text, Hummingbird Communications, QUNO Inc., Ivaco, Golden Star Resources, Mobile Data Systems, Crown Packaging Corporation, CanWest Media, and others. In the first years in the New York office, Ottenbreit also developed a close working relationship with John Leopold of the Montreal office based on that already developed between Skelton and Leopold. Ottenbreit worked on a number of private M&A transactions with Leopold in 1988 and 1989, and this formed a close working team that would develop into a significant marketing initiative and personal friendship over the years.

As Ottenbreit's tenure and status in the New York office became more permanent during 1989, Skelton and he developed a comprehensive marketing strategy for the New York office.

The purpose of this memorandum is to provide a framework for our marketing/business development efforts in New York. While the time spent on marketing during any particular day (or week) ranges from 0–100%, a rough estimate is that on annual basis, between 30–35% of our time is spent on marketing. The marketing strategy of SENY has evolved (and will continue to evolve) since the opening of the office, and now that contacts have been established with a wide range of people and organizations, we believe we can benefit from a "stated" marketing strategy, which, in part, focuses on a select group of contacts.

It is important to identify what we are trying to market in New York: We are a major Canadian (national) firm with an established international presence and practice and with a reputation for "excellence" in our practice areas and our delivery of services. We are known as a "business-oriented" firm with a significant emphasis on transaction work.

Our major marketing goal in New York is to obtain legal (Canadian and international) work for the firm (all offices) in the areas of greatest cross-border activity, i.e. corporate (M&A, securities), tax, banking, and trade. This is to be accomplished in two ways: 1) by developing and maintaining a "presence" in the business and legal community such that Stikeman Elliott is generally known in New York; and 2) by establishing relationships with the organizations and individuals who are most likely to be in a position to give or refer business to us.

There are two interrelated levels of marketing relevant to our efforts in New York. *Level One* is "name recognition, awareness, and presence" in the New York business and legal community. This level is attained when a person recognizes that Stikeman Elliott is a major Canadian law firm with an office in New York. *Level Two* is the development of an "ongoing" relationship with a regular contact.

In their memorandum, Skelton and Ottenbreit also discussed the more-or-less inverse relationship between the time spent on business development and the stand-alone results of the New York office. They noted the importance of establishing the firm's overall approach and philosophy with respect to the financial targets for the New York office and the value attributed to the referral of work to other offices. During the same period, Ottenbreit developed a networked, computerized database for contacts, clients, and friends of the firm, which became a major marketing tool.

As the firm continued to wrestle with the concept and role of foreign offices, the two New York lawyers contributed their thoughts to the firm's constitution committee in the spring of 1991.

"With complementary areas such as Ottawa, New York, London, and Hong Kong, continued vitality should depend less on office profitability on a regional basis and entirely on contribution towards achieving central objectives. With increasing globalization of our business, greater attention must be paid to the commitment of our resources to, and the staffing of, these offices."

We are in full agreement with this statement. Whether or not a foreign office can be an independent profit center depends on its size. We also believe that a focus on "profits" in a foreign office will undoubtedly and unproductively distort the priorities and objectives of a foreign office. Also, whether or not a foreign office is profitable or contributes is also a question of philosophy.

It is our view that if lawyers in a small foreign office are to spend their time usefully, a significant percentage of their time should be spent on business development. In our view, a primary objective of the business development efforts of a foreign office should be to increase the level of business for the firm *as a whole* over the long term.

As mentioned earlier, we feel there is a growing potential for business from foreign clients, and although there is a tendency to pay little attention to the foreign offices while business is good domestically or indeed while the foreign office itself is perceived to be doing well, our foreign offices should be viewed as long term commitment, and we should attempt to arrive at a consensus with respect to the objectives for these offices, which will form the basis for deciding on the staffing of these offices.

It is an article of faith in a two-person office, especially an office with one partner from each of Toronto and Montreal, that we cannot function without a very high level of support from partners in the home offices. At the moment, we are highly dependent on the significant efforts of a few partners from these offices. If our mission statement continues to include the reference to "international," we would suggest that it is the individual responsibility of each partner to have a basic understanding of the objectives of the foreign offices, and that the latter should be established, stated, and communicated.

One strategy that was developed was a plan to build better relationships with US law firms by participating in the activities of the American Bar Association (ABA). Ottenbreit and Skelton wrote a memorandum to the management committee on March 6, 1990 regarding the ABA and stated that:

The purpose of this memorandum is to provide a general outline for suggested participation by SE lawyers (from all offices) in the activities of the sections and committees of the ABA. In our marketing memorandum, we recommended that SE lawyers participate in the activities of groups such as the ABA for business development reasons as its activities provide an opportunity to meet partners of US law firms. Membership in the ABA and participation in its activities is an excellent way to develop contacts with partners of law firms in major American cities. The key practice areas are corporate (M&A, securities), banking, trade, and tax. Many of the committees and subcommittees are working committees which offer an opportunity not only to develop contacts, but also to improve and demonstrate expertise.

In order to begin participating in the ABA, it was decided that Leopold and Martin Scheim from the Montreal office and one representative from the New York office would go to the annual ABA meeting in August 1989 in Honolulu, Hawaii. Initially, Skelton planned to attend the meeting, but she was unable to do so, so Ottenbreit went. Before he left, Skelton and Leopold informed him that there was a ten-kilometre road race through the Diamond Head volcano crater in Honolulu as part of the ABA meeting, and that if he was going to Hawaii, he had better win that race or his career at Stikeman Elliott would suffer. Ottenbreit had been a track and cross-country runner in high school and college, so he easily won the ten-kilometre race, noting in fairness that no one under the age of forty-five went to Hawaii to represent his or her firm at the ABA meeting. In retrospect, his only regret, although it might well have been an inspired career move, was that he narrowly missed defeating Leopold, who was completing the five-kilometre portion of the event. For several years afterwards, Ottenbreit was always remembered by the ABA members as the young ringer from Stikeman Elliott who won the ten-kilometre run in Hawaii.

Ottenbreit was involved in a number of writing projects to increase the profile of the firm in New York and the US market. He and Ted Claxton, then assigned to the London office, and a US lawyer from the London office of Skadden Arps wrote an *International Financial Law Review* article in 1989, entitled: "MJDS – A Practitioner's View." In 1991, he, Jamie Davis, then in the London office, and Derek Woods in Toronto wrote the Canadian chapter for the *IFLR* supplement on International M&A, a guide to the regulation of mergers and acquisitions worldwide. Ottenbreit wrote an article on Canadian private placements that appeared in a special 1993 edition of the University of Pennsylvania *Journal of International Business Law,* entitled: "Exemptions for Institutional Investors on Concepts of Non-Public Offerings: A Comparative Study – Annual Project of the Committee on International Banking, Securities and Financial Transactions of the International Law and Practice Section of the New York State Bar Association (NYSBA)." In addition, Ottenbreit and Skelton spoke at many conferences, gave presentations, and generally did whatever they could to market the firm. Ottenbreit also became an active member of the New York State Bar Association – Federal Regulation of Securities Committee – and was the draftsperson of the committee's comment letter to the SEC on proposed amendments to the MJDS. He worked as well on other SEC comment letters relating to international securities regulation. He and John Mercury, a student who worked in the New York office during the summer of 1994, worked on a chapter on the MJDS for a treatise entitled "US Securities Law for International Financial Transactions and Capital Markets."

Another targeted area was business development in other US cities. A very successful example was a trip that Ottenbreit, Brian Rose, Pierre Raymond, and John Leopold made to San Francisco-Palo Alto. During the trip, they had meetings with twenty-one different US law firms, four investment dealers, and one bank, arranged for the most part through contacts they had developed from New York.

The office expanded beyond two lawyers during 1993, and the staffing was ranged between three and four lawyers from 1993 to 1996. Simon Romano was sent to New York in 1993, in his case to be "parked" for a year with the financial benefits of partnership, without yet having been admitted to the partnership. Since 1996, the staffing has been between five and nine lawyers. Initially, lawyers were always transferred from Toronto or Montreal on a rotation basis. Skelton developed a strong cross-border banking practice and worked with virtually all of the major US law firms on cross-border loans for companies such as Seagram's and St Lawrence Cement, and her banking clients included Bankers Trust, Chase Manhattan Bank, Westpac Banking Corporation, Union Bank of Switzerland, Transamerica, Bank of America, Barclays Bank, Goldman Sachs, Chemical Bank, and Banque Paribas.

During the years before Sonny Gordon joined Hasbro but while he was on the Hasbro board, he would come to New York for monthly board meetings and would set aside time for Ottenbreit to schedule marketing meetings. As a result, he and Gordon had many meetings together, which provided important marketing training, augmented by working closely with Brian

Rose. He also developed a close relationship with Calin Rovinescu, which began when Rovinescu pinch-hit for Skelton during a six-week stint in the New York office during the summer of 1989 while Skelton went to Australia to investigate the prospects of opening an office there. The relationship with Rovinescu continued through the years, including the time that Rovinescu was the managing partner of the London office and then on the executive committee, with oversight responsibility for foreign offices.

When Ottenbreit first moved to New York, he assumed he would have to give up many of his sports pursuits, particularly hockey, but he was able to continue playing. Several years ago, a story about the first night he played hockey in Manhattan appeared in the Regina *Leader-Post*, written by Dale Eisler, who now works as assistant deputy minister to Paul Martin in Ottawa.

New York – It's a long way from the Murray Balfour Arena in south Regina to the Sky Rink in a tenderloin area of Manhattan known as Hell's Kitchen. In fact, it's probably the most unlikely place you would expect to find two guys from Saskatchewan playing late-night commercial men's hockey.

But then, this is New York, where the unlikely is the ordinary.

To find the Sky Rink, you head about four blocks west of Madison Square Garden along 33rd Street into what was once the garment district of Manhattan. It's on the edge of an area of the city, where you're advised not to wander alone at night.

There are no signs directing people to the Sky Rink, and you certainly won't notice it if you walk past. The reason is simple: this hockey rink is on the top floor of a 16-storey office building.

But what really sets this rink apart is the view. From the ice, you look up through windows to see the skyline of a city where the lights from landmarks like the Empire State Building and Rockefeller Center glow in the distance.

Waiting to jump over the boards is Ken Ottenbreit of Regina, a partner with the law firm of Stikeman Elliott, who came to New York six years ago. In the dressing room, still pulling on his equipment, is Howie Lind, also from Regina, who arrived in New York eight years ago to start his own business after getting an MBA at Harvard University in Cambridge, Mass.

Both Ottenbreit and Lind, who got their undergraduate degrees from the University of Regina, play on a team called The Stranglers.

"They call us the wheat boys because we're from Saskatchewan," says Lind as he rushes to get into his equipment before the game starts. Usually, the wheat boys play on the same line for the Stranglers, with Lind at centre and Ottenbreit on leftwing.

"I don't think Ken was here a day before I got him on the team," says Lind, who lives on Long Island and arrived two years before Ottenbreit's law firm sent him down from Toronto. "I'll never forget the first time I came out to play. As you know, this district has a few, how would you say, ladies of the evening on the streets. I remember I got out of the car and this lady asked me if I'd like a date. I said no thanks, but, hey this New York sure is a friendly place."

John Walker[20] had been a summer student in the New York office in July 1992, and upon his call to the Ontario Bar, he worked extensively with

Ottenbreit in 1994 on a major report for the Canadian federal government – director, corporate review branch (Ministry of Industry, Science, and Technology Canada) – entitled "Learning from the Delaware Experience: A Comparison of the Canada Business Corporations Act and the Delaware General Corporation Law," which was one of the reports that has led to the recent amendments to the *Canada Business Corporations Act*. A summary of the report was a feature article in the February 1998 volume of the *Canadian Business Law Journal*. He and Walker also wrote and presented a paper at the 1994 Joint Business Valuation Conference in San Diego of the Canadian Institute of Chartered Business Valuators and the American Society of Appraisers, entitled "Canadian Business Valuators look South of the Border: An International Perspective and Canadian Law Update." This collaborative work and the time he spent in New York as a student developed a relationship that would ultimately lead to Walker moving to the New York office in 1997, where he worked until August 2001 before moving on.

One of the favourite client events in New York is the annual Canadian Society of New York Hockey dinner, at which hockey greats are honoured. Past recipients of the annual award included Gordie Howe, Bobby Hull, Maurice Richard, Jean Béliveau, Guy Lafleur, Ken Dryden, Denis Potvin, Bryan Trottier, and Mario Lemieux. During one of those evenings in the early 1990s, Scotty Bowman, who was then with the Pittsburgh Penguins, brought the Stanley Cup to the Waldorf Astoria Hotel to the annual dinner at which more than 800 people were in attendance. The Stanley Cup was placed on the lower dais of the head table. After the dinner was over, Ottenbreit and a few clients decided that instead of having their picture taken standing beside the Stanley Cup, like everyone else was doing, the only way to get a picture with the Stanley Cup was the proper way, with the cup hoisted over his head in victory celebration. Ottenbreit decided that since there was no rope keeping him away from the Stanley Cup, there was nothing that could stop him from grabbing it and putting it over his head with enough time to get a picture taken, fully expecting that he would be thrown out by someone from Scotty Bowman's entourage. He took the calculated risk that they would not be too rough on a guy in a suit at the Waldorf Astoria.

It was duly arranged that William Rosenberg,[21] who was there from the Montreal office, would get on the upper dais to take the picture as soon as Ottenbreit grabbed the Stanley Cup. At an opportune moment, Ottenbreit grabbed the cup, hoisted it over his head, turned around, and prepared for the photograph. As Ottenbreit turned around, all he saw was the back of Rosenberg's head. Rosenberg was busy talking to, and getting an autograph from, Guy Lafleur. When Scotty Bowman saw what Ottenbreit was doing to the cup, he began yelling at somebody beside him, who was about twice Ottenbreit's size, to go and tell that guy to put the cup down. Meanwhile, there was no way Ottenbreit was going to put the cup down until Rosenberg took the picture, so he was yelling at Rosenberg to get his attention. After Ottenbreit's quick and very intense negotiation with Bowman's "heavy," Rosenberg finally turned around and took the picture. Ottenbreit has had the photo in his office from that day and continues to remind Rosenberg of the importance that photo had in the continuation of Rosenberg's career.

Ottenbreit became very active in the Canadian Club of New York, serving as president from 1994 to 1997, and during that time, when trying to create a charitable activity for the club, he founded the Terry Fox Run for Cancer Research in New York City, which he has organized ever since. The run first took place in Riverside Park on Manhattan's west side in 1994 and then moved to Central Park, where it has been held since 1998. A number of celebrities – including Ambassador Ken Taylor; Paul Shaffer; Colin Campbell; Kevin Lowe; Karen Percy-Lowe; Natasha Henstridge; Betty Fox; Darrell Fox; Stephane Quintall; Wayne Gretzky; New York City Park's Commissioner Henry Stern; president of the Achilles Track Club, Dick Traum; president of the New York Road Runner's Club, Alan Steinfeld; and others – have participated or helped to support the run since its inception in New York. Ottenbreit has received special recognition from Betty Fox, Terry's mother, for his efforts.

Skelton decided to leave the firm at the end of 1996 to move to Boston, where her husband was professionally active, but she has nevertheless maintained a close relationship with the office. The only sour note in the entire New York experience was the arrival of Robert Couzin after the Paris office had been abandoned. He thought that he had come to be the managing partner, but Ottenbreit had not been informed of this, nor apparently had any decision been made to that effect within the partnership. To deal with this conundrum, it was proposed to have joint managing partners in New York, but when this came to naught, Couzin decided to leave the firm and went to Ernst & Young in 1997.

Ottenbreit worked with Rovinescu and Stransman in 1997 to develop a comprehensive business plan for the New York office. Its goals were to enhance the reputation of Stikeman Elliott in the New York and US markets as a major Canadian and international law firm known for excellence and high-quality legal services and to make a positive financial contribution to the firm both through providing legal services in New York and through developing significant business opportunities throughout the US and elsewhere. At that stage, the cross-border securities (MJDS, public offerings, private placements, broker-dealer regulation) and mergers and acquisitions practices were more developed than the cross-border banking practice, which was identified as particularly important because a number of clients were now providing one-stop shopping to their own clients with simultaneous bank loans and underwritings. The corporate tax practice needed strengthening, both on its own account and as an integral part of the securities, banking, and mergers and acquisitions practices.

During the discussions leading to development of the new business plan, it was decided that Ottenbreit should look for opportunities to hire lawyers locally for the New York office. The rotation system was too expensive and was not meeting the needs either of the New York office or of the office sending the associate. As a result, a number of local hires have joined the New York office in recent years. Alix d'Anglejan-Chatillon, who had worked in the Montreal office in the late 1980s and then moved to Paris to work with Salans Hertzfeld Heilbronn, was the first, in 1997. Though d'Anglejan's initial term was to be only one or two years, it developed into a more permanent position in New York, and upon her return to Montreal, she became a partner effective January 1, 2001. Isabelle Laflèche joined the New York office in 1999 after spending five years as in-house counsel at Nesbitt Burns in Toronto and Montreal. Isabelle has been an excellent addition and has developed a strong cross-border practice, representing us broker-dealers on a variety of matters. Ralph Hipsher also joined the New York office in 1999. He has worked primarily on Canadian private place-ments and dealer registration matters and is developing a practice similar to that of Marianne Sussex in the London. Marie-Josée Henri was a student in the Montreal office and worked with a Montreal-based litigation firm before moving to New York in 2000, where she has worked primarily on M&A mandates.

François Gaudet had a very productive two-year run in the New York office, and he, like Ottenbreit and Skelton, had a real zest for life in Man-hattan. Though he worked hard, he took full advantage of New York City and what it had to offer. Michel Gélinas, a lateral hire from Ogilvy Renault in Montreal, moved to the New York office shortly after he joined the firm in Montreal. Gélinas arrived during a very busy and difficult time in 1997 and 1998, and for sheer hard work, commitment, and loyalty to the firm, it would be difficult to surpass the contribution that he made to the New York office during his two years there.

Similar to the Eurodollar financing practice in London, the New York office developed an international private placement business, where us and international issuers and underwriters routinely sold on a Canadian private placement basis international offerings to Canadian institutional purchasers. This has been an important business for the New York office and the firm. Apart from providing some steady revenue for the office, it was tremendous from a marketing perspective since the firm had the op-portunity to work regularly with us securities dealers and us law firms. In 1998, the *IFLR* published an international equity offering league table in which Stikeman Elliott was listed as the top Canadian law firm in in-ternational equity deals with fifty-three offerings (the nearest Canadian competitor had twenty-five), and of these, more than thirty were handled by the New York office. In 2001, the *IFLR* published the international equity league table again, and this time, Stikeman Elliott finished tenth overall in the worldwide rankings (the only Canadian law firm listed in the top twenty). In a much slower market, Stikeman Elliott had sixteen offerings that qualified for the league table, and thirteen of these were handled by the New York office.

No story about the New York office would be complete without mention-ing Louise Siudy, who joined Stikeman Elliott in 1989 and who has been an excellent and loyal employee in the New York office. Dawn France-Somersel has been a secretary in New York for more than five years and recently became the local person responsible for computer technology.

Building relationships, marketing the firm, and generating new clients and referrals has been the primary purpose of the New York office. While it is no longer possible to track sources of work, the following list is representative of the corporate clients that the New York has developed for the firm: Attwoods PLC, Hillenbrand Industries, BarterTrust.com, Bain Capital, Grubb & Ellis Company, Pyropower Corporation, Tandem Computers, Insituform Technologies Inc., Great Lakes Chemical Corporation, Graham-Field Health Products, IMED Corporation, Corporate Express, EOS Partners, Acerero Del Norte, Pfizer Inc., Kroll Associates, Cisco Systems, Sun Microsystems, International Technology, Reltec Inc., Nextera Inc., Chase Capital Partners, Hockey Hall of Fame, Precise Technology, and Viag AG.

In June 1999, upon returning from a meeting, Ottenbreit found an urgent message from Jim Grant, who was then still chairman of the firm. Urgent messages from the chairman are seldom good news, so he was not certain whether it meant that some very serious work needed to be done at once or whether he should start updating his curriculum vitae. As it turned out, Grant needed someone to take his place at the annual Slevin Matches, a three-way friendly golf competition between Stikeman Elliott, Ballard Spahr, and Clifford Chance. The 1999 matches were to be held in the Philadelphia area, and Grant, knowing that Ottenbreit was a golfer, called to insist he take his place. Even though they had just had their first child in late April 1999, Ottenbreit was very happy to announce to his wife that, at the chairman's request, his firm responsibility demanded that he spend three days golfing at Pine Valley and Merion, two of the best golf courses in the world, with a team consisting of David Angus, Mike Richards, and David McCarthy. Foreign service is, indeed, a dark and lonely job.

During 2000, Ottenbreit and Louis Samson, together with a team from the Toronto office including Daphne MacKenzie and John Lorito, worked on the acquisition by an affiliate of The Carlyle Group, the large Washington, DC-based fund of two affiliated Canadian public companies – Tritech Precision Inc. and Trimin Enterprises Inc. – which also had a controlling interest in another Canadian public company, Haley Industries Inc. The two also represented CIBC as US underwriters on a $US600-million high-yield bridge loan and their offering for CanWest Media. The Montreal offices also represented The Carlyle Group in the private acquisition of an international company with significant Canadian-based assets. The financial results were well ahead of budget, and the referral work to other offices was significant as both had been during the previous year.

As the firm's fiftieth anniversary approached, Ottenbreit wrote the following to the executive committee in November 2001:

It would not be possible to write this report without discussing the horrible tragedy of September 11th. While none of our employees or their immediate families were direct victims of the attack, we all experienced the shock of the events, and many of us knew some of the victims and their families. Also, many of our clients, contacts, and friends have been permanently or temporarily displaced by the attack. We have offered to assist clients and friends of the firm in any way that we can, and to that end, we have three people from Lehman Brothers (principal investments group) working temporarily from our offices, and we expect they will be with us until at least December 1st.

For your information, we took advantage of the firm-wide Employee Assistance Program and provided a voluntary trauma counselling session in our office on September 20th, and all lawyers and staff participated.

Work came to a complete standstill on September 11th, and virtually nothing from a business perspective got done for about two weeks. Since then, as people have re-located and attempted to resume "normal" life activities, business has resumed, and fortunately and surprisingly, we have been busy with a range of projects since late September.

In late November, Ottenbreit was one of a dozen people contacted to lead the New York Committee of the "Canada Loves New York" weekend (November 30 to December 2), which was being organized by Senator Jerry Grafstein and others in Toronto, Montreal, Ottawa, and Vancouver. This was entirely a voluntary effort, and Ottenbreit soon became the principal organizer for the December 1 rally at the Roseland Ballroom and on the sur-rounding streets. He drafted every available person – lawyers and staff – to work on the rally, and the New York office became the temporary headquar-ters for the organizational effort. He spent several days working around the clock organizing the event, which was attended by more than 20,000 people. Capacity at the Roseland was only 4,000, so he and a team of more than 150 volunteers had to organize an indoor event and an outdoor event – a street party with Jumbotron – and deal with crowd control, security, secret service, public relations, press briefings, police, and emergency medical services, as well as arranging for ushers, water, hats, posters, pins, flags, set-up, dressing room, cleanup, and everything else inherent in such an event. Though almost everything went wrong or worked differently from what had been planned, the rally was an overwhelming success. He worked closely throughout the day with Gabor Apor, the event producer, Senator Grafstein, the secret ser-vice, and the advance teams for the prime minister, the mayor and the New York police and fire departments. After the rally, Ottenbreit was personally thanked by Prime Minister Jean Chrétien for his efforts.

BUDAPEST

The firm's initiative in Budapest proved to be the only occasion on which it entered a market that had not already been established as a developed or relatively sophisticated place in which to practise law. Central and Eastern Europe had been under the domination of the Soviet Union since the end of World War II, and it was only following the demolition of the Berlin Wall in 1989 and the subsequent sudden collapse and disintegration of the Soviet Union in 1992 that there was any prospect of Western legal influence in those countries. The field was brand new and wide open as, with practically no pause, these countries passed from the worst excesses of Communism to those of capitalism. It would be no exaggeration to say that Central and Eastern Europe became, almost overnight, the new Wild West of the world. The firm became part of the critical early years in that region and was extremely active in many of the transitions from state-owned enterprise to privatization.

It was typical of Stikeman Elliott that the opportunity was seized to establish a presence in those countries. Most of the legal and business structures in Central and Eastern Europe were in a vestigial state of development due to the crushing presence of the former Soviet regime. All of the countries had an enormous challenge in adapting to the needs of private sector financing and methods of doing business. And they all needed outside funds, but there was virtually no understanding of the exigencies of obtaining international financial support nor of the contractual and structural demands of conversion from wholly state-run enterprises to private sector-based arrangements. The concepts of contractual commitment and accountability were completely foreign to these countries. Privatization of state-run businesses and utilities had to be accomplished on impossibly short schedules as the impecunious central governments had no hope of maintaining essential public services.

Marc Lalonde was a member of the consultative committee for the Czech and Slovak governments in the early 1990s and was most interested in having the firm look at Eastern Europe as a place to do business. He kept pressure on the firm's executive committee until it was finally agreed that Calin Rovinescu would go with him on a mission to Budapest, Prague, and Bratislava, followed by a visit to London to meet with the European Bank for Reconstruction and Development. Lalonde was treated as if he were royalty, and while he did not represent himself as such, neither did he take Herculean steps to dispel the impression that he was still a federal minister. A banquet was organized for him, and they came away with the feeling that the firm could get anything that was available and that we wanted. A myth developed that Eastern Europe was filled with low-hanging fruit. It was later to appear that the fruits were not perennial and that far from being low-hanging, a step ladder was required to get at them.

Hungary was tentatively identified by the firm's executive committee, on the urging of the mission, as the country with the most potential in this field, having suffered the least in its suspended animation under the tender care of the Soviet Union. On March 5, 1992, the firm announced that it was opening a representative Budapest office at Petofi ter 2, in close collaboration with two Hungarian lawyers, Laszlo Réti and Gyorgy Antall. This was followed by several typical memoranda written by Stikeman between March and July, outlining the reasons for a Stikeman Elliott presence in the area. In July, Grant advised the executive committee that the firm had entered into an association with a Budapest firm and that it was about to conclude a similar agreement with another firm in Prague. Since this was demonstrably short of a real presence of the firm, the executive committee decided that if we were to become involved at this level, we would need one of "our own" to be in place in Eastern Europe. An ad hoc committee of Stikeman, Lalonde, Erik Richer La Fleche, and Jim Robb was established to consider the possibilities in Eastern Europe. The original thought was that there might be one associate in each of Prague and Budapest. A modest budget was established for the purpose of sending an associate for a year.

That it would take an unusual individual to head up such an effort in a part of the world where neither English nor French was the operating language, where legal traditions as we know them did not exist, and where those on the ground would be operating without lifelines or at best, tenuous lifelines, went almost without saying. Jean Philippe Ewart from the Montreal office, who had just finished a long and complicated mandate restructuring the financially troubled Mont-Tremblant enterprise and had nothing in particular on his plate at the time, was dispatched to Eastern Europe on October 1, 1992 to see what might be the prospects on the ground and report in January on whether we should open an office. The executive committee decided that we needed a young go-getter, someone who would be aggressive in getting business and someone who would go through a wall if need be to get to a cocktail party whether or not he was on the guest list. Ewart was sent off with virtually nothing.

When Ewart arrived in Prague, Lalonde was playing tennis with Ambassador Paul Fraser at the official residence. He spent three days in Prague and Budapest with Lalonde. There was to be a three-month study of the conditions, which were made somewhat more complicated by the formal separation of the Czech and Slovak republics, effective December 31, 1992. When Ewart came back, he met with Grant and Gordon, who said, "OK, we'll do it if you will do it, and we will not do it if you will not do it." Ewart said, all right, he would go back to Europe and see what it would be like, and then he would come back and decide what to do. In fact, he never had a chance to return because once he got there, the business started, and he was off and running. He lived in a hotel with no phone and out of his suitcase for weeks on end.

The initial experiences were both exciting and rewarding. The first mandate in Prague was for Northern Telecom Switzerland, which was doing a financing in Uzbekistan. The firm's first association in Prague was with Jiri Balastik, a former deputy minister of Justice following the revolution, whom Ewart had met with Lalonde. But the rest of the office in Prague was not very aggressive, and Balastik himself left after a few months to go to Allen and Overy, so a certain coolness developed between them as a result. Thereafter, Ewart started to go to Budapest, first working with the European Bank for Reconstruction and Development, doing due diligence work on a financing for Matáv, the largest project in Europe undertaken to date by the bank. One of the issues on the Matáv deal was that two of the thirteen exchanges for the telephone system were located in buildings restored to the Roman Catholic Church, and the whole civil law issue of immovable-by-destination came into play. Bob Bryant of the Toronto office was on holiday in Europe, and when Ewart called to get help, Bryant was dispatched to Budapest. He slept on a couch in the television room in Ewart's small apartment while the deal was done. Ewart went back and forth by car or train for meetings in Prague and Budapest. He met the eventual Hungarian partners, Réti and Antall, who operated in premises consisting of a single room in the Jewish ghetto of Budapest and one telephone line. The phone had to be disconnected in order to hook up to the fax. The EBRD mandate had been obtained by Bruno Arnould in Montreal through a submission for the project, and the fact that he had got it gave Ewart an important job and helped build the relationship with Réti and Antall. Antall was well connected since his father, József Antall, had been the first post-war democratically elected prime minister of Hungary, and he died in office in late 1993. Réti also had numerous contacts at high levels of the government. Their firm was being pursued by firms from the US and elsewhere, but they came with us out of friendship.

Ewart's progress report was delivered in January, but he said he needed some more time prior to making a formal recommendation. In March 1993, he reported that he was inclined to believe that Budapest was the place to be, but he needed still more time to be sure. By the following month, after returning to Eastern Europe, he was able to report on the mandates that had been developed, and although he had not had enough time to prepare a business plan and budget, he thought the firm should definitely open an office in the area. In mid-July 1993, after a review of Ewart's comprehensive report, the executive committee resolved to open an office in Budapest on a scaled-down basis. By the middle of October, we had four lawyers in place – Ewart, Robert Hayhurst, Leslie Mack, and Shawna Miller – along with five staff, including D.C. Thompson. The first permanent members of the SWAT team to assist Ewart were Hayhurst, Miller, and Mack. Upon Miller's arrival, Ewart told her that she and Hayhurst (whom she had never met) would be sharing accommodation since according to Ewart, good "modern" flats were like gold in Budapest in those days. What Ewart did not tell her was that it was a one bedroom apartment, and because Hayhurst had arrived two days earlier, he had already taken the bedroom. For three months, Miller slept on the couch in the living room. The office, which was open twenty-four hours a day, seven days a week, had three computers, two printers, a fax machine, and six telephone lines. By the following May, the office in Budapest had grown from its original complement of four (Ewart, Réti, Antall, and a secretary) to thirty-one, with eight Hungarian lawyers and six Canadian expatriates, and they were ready to move to new offices. Ewart reported that they were now competing with the top US firms, such as Skaden Arps and White & Case, principally for privatization mandates for the state-owned businesses. At the time, we were also using our experience in this area to seek similar mandates in India and China. As perhaps a portent of things to come, Ewart had not had enough time to report fully on administrative matters. He was, however, pleased with the support received from the London office and the additional lawyers seconded to Budapest, including Hayhurst, Bob Bryant, Gina Papageorgiou, Mack, Miller, Melissa Taylor, David Skinner, Marc Barbeau, Bill Scott, and Daphne MacKenzie.

An excellent relationship soon blossomed with the group of Hungarian lawyers, who practised under the firm name and style of Réti & Antall. The firm shared premises with them, first in a very crowded set of offices at Kertesz utca ("utca" is "street" in Hungarian) 40, and later, after a five-month search, at Andrássy ut 100. Ewart reported, with considerable relief, that the move was an emergence from the ghetto – from a building in which the paint was peeling off the walls, which showed the bullet holes from World War II and the 1956 revolution, and in which the somewhat deranged seventy-year-old widow next door would begin yelling at her deceased husband in the middle of the day. After the Communists came to power in Hungary following World War II, most of the large "bourgeois" apartments were subdivided into small cubbyholes so that deserving members of the proletariat could be given their own modest apartments. The apartment inhabited by the widow was the vestige of one of the formerly grand apartments, the other portion being the offices that we shared. She apparently believed that her husband was captive in part of the former home to which she no longer had access. Many of her extremely loud ravings included (we were advised) choice obscenities directed at the lawyers who had "imprisoned" her husband, a constant source of embarrassment and amusement for our Hungarian colleagues. An additional feature of the Kertesz premises was an almost continual musical accompaniment to the daily work. The daytime portion resulted from the renowned Ferenc Listz musical academy that was kitty-corner to the offices, and there was a constant strain of classical music from a variety of instruments generated by students hard at work honing their skills. The evening portion was provided from the inner courtyard, which was a gathering place for the many gypsies inhabiting the building, and where they practised at all hours of the day. The building was not air-conditioned, and the windows had to be kept open during the summer months, so the music was always audible and ever-present.

The Hungarian lawyers were essential to our ability to operate effectively with the local authorities, and we were helpful to them in demonstrating the level of professionalism and drafting that international legal and financial standards demanded. They were bright and ambitious, learning quickly to respond to the rigours of practice and the usual impossibly unrealistic demands of domestic and foreign clients for instant service, a far cry from the level and pace to which they had been subjected under the former Communist system. The friendships that developed were deep and genuine as the small teams literally invented a modern legal practice in the area.

On June 29, 1994, the socialists (the former Communists) came back into power. Ewart thought it would be several months before the impact of this could be evaluated. Marc Lalonde visited Budapest in early September 1994, and with his customary energy and his facility in dealing with senior leaders, he managed to squeeze in a dozen meetings in the course of two and a half days, including with the secretary of state for Industry and Commerce, the under secretary of state for Transport and Communications, the High Commissioner for privatization, the chief executive officer of Credit Suisse First Boston in Hungary, the chairman of the National Bank of Hungary, the chief executive officer of Magyar Hitel Bank Rt. (the largest commercial bank in Hungary), the chairman of InterEuropa Bank who became the head of the banking privatization program in Hungary, the chairman of the Hungarian Foreign Trade Bank, the chief executive officer of Citibank Hungary, and the minister of Finance. Other visitors to Budapest included myself, Rovinescu,

Scott, Richards, Chalmers, and Bob Hart, the latter to oversee the accounting system set up by Margaret Jackson of the London office.

It was a daunting challenge for the young lawyers in particularly difficult circumstances, but Ewart was a person of enormous energy and boundless enthusiasm and enjoyed a remarkable early success, getting impressive mandates to privatize several public utilities and institutions. Among them were the Hungarian banking industry, in which we acted as advisors to Credit Suisse First Boston; the Hungarian Foreign Trade Bank, working for J.P. Morgan; the Budapest Bank Ltd., acting for Salomon Brothers International Ltd.; and the huge privatization of Magyar Villamos Muvek (MVM) Rt., the Hungarian electricity utility, which was by far the largest privatization in the region to date, a mandate that was obtained by Antall, who was able to rely on the legal muscle that Stikeman Elliott could add to the equation. In the process, they developed unusual lifestyles. They often started work only at noon, but worked until well after midnight, with highly irregular work, sleep, and feeding habits. Meetings could be called at any time by Ewart, including weekends, but he was often so busy or preoccupied that he would fail to show up at meetings he had called, and the others would wonder what they were supposed to do since only Ewart had what everyone thought and hoped was the full picture in his mind.

Bill Scott's first visit to Budapest was in the winter of 1992, shortly after the office had been established. Ewart had invited him down to help out on an ICC arbitration in which we were representing a Hungarian bank against a New York property developer in connection with a failed hotel-office development project on the Danube. Ewart had his two Siberian huskies with him from Canada, usually to be found sleeping under his desk during the day. One of the dogs created a huge commotion when it got away from the secretary who had taken it out for its afternoon constitutional. Ewart immediately mobilized everyone in the office, the local radio stations, the local taxi companies, and the city police to be on the lookout for the dog. A war room was set up with a large map of Budapest, and as reports of sightings filtered in, the dog's journey across the city was marked with stick pins. After a frantic night of searching, the dog appeared to have circled the city at least two times and was last seen in a large park on the other side of the Danube. At that point, Ewart, who had been contemplating chartering a helicopter to conduct an aerial search of the city, sped off to the park in his Jeep Cherokee (with Quebec licence plates) and succeeded in bringing the dog home. As Scott told him at the time, if he ever lost a child, he would definitely want Ewart to be in charge of the search. Apart from the screaming lady in the apartment next door, his favourite memory of that time was when Sid Lederman came over to help advise on the arbitration, and given the shortage of space, he was forced to compose his statement of defence while perched on a metal folding chair and using the windowsill as his desk.

By mid-1994, the office relocated, together with Réti & Antall, to a much more prestigious address on Andrássy Boulevard, Budapest's main thoroughfare, which was close to Heroes' Square. Scott spent the better part of six months in Budapest working on the privatization of the Hungarian electricity industry. This involved the auction by way of trade sales of some six electricity supply and distribution companies, seven power generation companies, and a minority stake in MVM Rt. itself, the national grid company, although this was ultimately not sold. The privatization process, at least in terms of the time available to accomplish what needed to be done, could best be described in the words of Thomas Hobbes as "nasty, brutish, and short." The government insisted upon completing the sales by Christmas, and a process that ought to have taken two years was squashed into the space of six months, to which additional pressure was added by the fact that offers were received only in November. This was unquestionably, Scott says even years after the event, the most difficult transaction on which he had ever worked.

The transaction was complex, both in terms of the legal and regulatory framework, much of which was invented and drafted by the lawyers as they progressed through the deal. Moreover, the political machinations that went on, particularly among many of the officers of the electricity holding company (MVM) who may have feared that they would be out of a job once the privatization was completed and therefore resisted the process, complicated matters. It was particularly difficult to obtain information required as part of the due diligence process. The infighting led to interminable meetings in smoke-filled rooms at the privatization agency (APV) in which our clients, who for the most part did not speak English, would communicate through translators. These meetings often deteriorated into lengthy disputes between the translators and our own Hungarian lawyers as to what had been said and to whom. Finally, when some consensus was reached, the information would be transmitted to the various data rooms, which were located in the offices of the companies and therefore spread throughout the country, and to the lawyers who were preparing the final documentation.

The Budapest office during this period became a veritable crucible in which lawyers from the Toronto, Montreal, Ottawa, Calgary, Vancouver, London, and Paris offices all lived and worked very closely together along with the Hungarian lawyers and staff of Réti & Antall. At one time, we had approximately twenty-five Canadians together with about a dozen Hungarians working on the electricity project. We were scattered in various self-contained offices throughout three floors of Andrássy as well as the attic and basement of the building. Dinner was usually Chinese food in the boardroom late at night. Since most of the Canadians had nowhere else to go but their hotel rooms, it was a monastic existence. To exacerbate matters, Ewart ordered cots (actually lawn chairs with thin mattresses) to be laid out in the basement "war room." Many of the lawyers would work eighteen to twenty hours a day and then catch a few hours of sleep in the basement on these cots before going back at it again. When heading down for some rest, they would leave stickers on the pillar in the secretarial centre to let whomever was on duty know when they wished to be wakened. Lest there be any suggestion that only the lawyers worked hard, the Canadian secretaries, headed by Louise Guérin, worked incredibly long and tense hours under the constant pressure of the lawyers.

Alain Massicotte, looking back on the Budapest experience, came away with the overall impression that they had all been serving in the foreign legion. They were a motley group of Canadians, Hungarians, Czechs, Romanians, and Bulgarians, together with injections of lawyers from all the Canadian offices, who might never have had the occasion to work closely with each other but for the Budapest adventure. The shared experience, under the most trying conditions, especially during the electricity privatization, led to the development of relationships within and outside the firm that continue to this day. Many of them may never look a bowl of goulash in the eye again nor relish the ubiquitous taste of paprika, which flavours practically everything in Hungary including some ice creams. Despite the rigorous working schedules, the younger lawyers nevertheless managed to keep track of the hottest night clubs in Budapest to relax after long working days. Travelling from country to country, they often lost track of the values of the various currencies and probably paid far too much for many of their taxi rides, never knowing whether 500 or 5,000 forints was a reasonable price.

They remember trying, in what often seemed like a dialogue of the deaf, to negotiate the long-term power purchase agreements required by the purchasers of the electricity supply and generation companies. The current operators, habituated to the Soviet concept of five-year plans, wanted no truck with the longer contracts, and they had to be dragged, kicking and screaming, into the new economic reality through day-and-night negotiations. In order to make even vestigial progress, we had to produce Hungarian versions of the English documents, without which it would have been impossible even to begin to negotiate. These negotiations took their toll. When our team arrived early one morning at the utility offices, they were informed that the executive in charge had been taken by ambulance to the hospital, suffering from nervous exhaustion. Massicotte and Lawrence Wilde returned to the office to report on the development to Ewart and to discuss the effect of the possible delays in the project that might result. In the process, the phone rang and Ewart answered. When he hung up, he discovered that Massicotte and Wilde had both fallen asleep in their chairs, so he ordered them back to the hotel to get some rest. In the process of walking back to the hotel, delighted with the prospect of a brief period of relief, the cellular phone rang. It was Ewart. They were to return to the office immediately to deal with an urgent matter.

The privatization of the electricity industry in Hungary was one of the great accomplishments in Central Europe of those times. Not only was it the largest transaction of the day, but it was achieved in a remarkably short time, inventing much of the legal infrastructure necessary to support an industry that was reorganized to meet external requirements with which it had no previous experience. Both sides of the transaction learned as they went along, ending up with a radically changed legal and economic structure affecting the entire country.

In preparation for the solicitation of bids, complex tender documentation had to be prepared for circulation to potential bidders, describing the assets that were on offer in sufficient detail that the bidders would know what they might acquire and be in a position to make the best bids possible. Since they would be the basis on which the eventual transaction would be consummated, they had to be prepared with the degree of sophistication that would satisfy international purchasers contemplating a billion-dollar investment. There were a number of occasions on which vast amounts of documents had to be produced for distribution to potential bidders. During the final push, the Budapest lawyers had to produce approximately one hundred customized agreements over the course of a weekend. These were delivered to the APV (much to their surprise) ten minutes prior to the deadline. At the end of one of these crisis weekends earlier in the year, Heward and Mary Stikeman showed up, fresh as daisies, and proceeded to tour the office and videotape the inmates, most of whom by that time looked like cast members from *The Dirty Dozen*.[22] Much to Scott's surprise, the privatization came together in the end despite the fact that several of the companies did not sell on the first attempt and netted the Hungarian government $US1.3 billion, far more than was anticipated. Subsequently, some of the companies that had not been sold were retendered and eventually acquired by foreign investors, resulting in additional proceeds in excess of $US200 million. The privatization would also enable further billions of dollars of direct investment in coming years as the new owners poured in funds to revamp their newly acquired assets and to build new power generating assets in Hungary.

On October 16, 1995, Bill Scott circulated a memorandum to all staff and lawyers of Réti & Antall and Stikeman Elliott Budapest regarding the Hungarian electricity privatization mandate.

The Duke of Wellington is reported to have said about the Battle of Waterloo that it was a "damn close run thing." I now know the feeling.

Over the last week and, in particular, Thursday evening, our two firms were presented with a challenge which I am convinced no other law office in Hungary could have handled. In less than 24, we produced final versions (in English and Hungarian) of 13 Shareholders' Agreements (in several variations), 7 Call Agreements (in 2 variations) and a Share Exchange Agreement, and (in English) a Model Share Purchase Agreement for Supply Companies, a Model Share Purchase Agreement for power companies (2 versions), a Share Purchase Agreement and Shareholders' Agreement for MVM Rt., and various model legal opinions. What is more, we actually got MVM to sign the Call and Shareholder Agreements! This was in addition to earlier completing our 500+ page due diligence reports DDR and providing 24 hour-turnaround comments on the 250+ pages of the general section of Schroders' information memorandum.

We succeeded in pulling these tasks off only through the tremendous commitment and effort of all individuals involved in the process, in particular the members of the secretarial staff. On behalf of Stikeman Elliott (and personally), I want to thank each and every one of you for your help and assistance, which was well above and beyond the call of duty.

I have likened this electricity privatization process to an expedition walking across Antarctica (some 3,000 miles from coast to coast). We have now made it to the South Pole but have 1,500 more miles to go. It is clear that careful thought needs to be given to documentation logistics in preparation for the closing, and we plan to commence work on this immediately. We have got this far only through concentrated teamwork. We will continue to depend upon your support to accomplish this project. We must continue to work together to get to the end of this project (and, like Amundson's successful expedition to the South Pole rather than the ill-fated expedition of my namesake, Captain Scott, get everyone back to home base safe and sound). Thank you again very much for all your help.

A memorandum addressed to the Budapest office the same day from Calin Rovinescu, then managing the London office, said: "Congratulations to you and the rest of the team on getting the MVM document out. To say this was an outstanding achievement would be the understatement of the year, if not the millennium. Your client does not know how lucky it is. We are all very proud."

They had their share of amusement. One morning in the hotel, a young lawyer was having breakfast in the hotel dining room. A very attractive young lady, obviously a regular patron of the hotel whom they had all seen on many occasions, sat down at the table next to him and struck up a conversation, asking him what he did. He announced that he was a business lawyer. What a coincidence, she said, because she, too, was in business. The lawyer, returning the expression of polite interest, asked what business she was in. "Sex," she announced, to the accompaniment of general laughter from all his colleagues who had witnessed the brief courtship. One of the lawyers and his wife, who had located an apartment of marginal comfort in Budapest, decided that they would take a brief vacation and left the key with a local they trusted to keep an eye on the place. Upon their return, they learned from their neighbours that in their absence, the apartment had been used as the scene for a pornographic film. Understandably outraged over this violation of their privacy, they fretted over what to do. Could they sue, but whom? Seize the copies of the film, but where and from whom? In the end, they threw out the bed and bought a new one. And held onto their keys.

Despite the enormous amount of work required to complete the privatization of Hungary's electricity industry, the firm also found the time to carry out numerous other significant mandates. On July 15, 1994, the firm managed the closing of the first privatization of a bank in Hungary, the Magyar Külkereskedelmi Bank Rt., in which the strategic investors were the Bayerishe Landesbank, Girozentrale, and the European Bank for Reconstruction and Development. They also handled the acquisition, on behalf of a French group, of the state-owned aluminium foundry of Hungary, a division of Hungalu Rt., in September of the same year. Following the closing of the first bank privatization, the Hungarian government retained the firm to act on the privatization of Országos Takarékpénztár és Kereskeldmi Bank Rt., Hungary's largest bank. The strategic investor on that occasion was a group led by George Soros of the United States, but the negotiations ended in October without an agreement, a fact that made the front page of newspapers both in Hungary and the surrounding regions.

The firm also acted on behalf of Alliance Communications in connection with an acquisition of a 25 per cent share interest in a television station in Hungary, a mandate obtained through the efforts of Sonny Gordon. The firm also acted as co-counsel with Heenan Blaikie in Toronto, working with George Burger, who concentrated on the sale of the programming aspects of the transaction as well as background arrangements with Andrew Sarlos, who was a co-venturer with Alliance. The efforts of Gordon and Lalonde led to them being retained to act as lead counsel to the lending syndicate on the construction of the new terminal of the Budapest International Airport, although that mandate was eventually lost when EBRD was brought into the financing arrangements and implemented its own mandatory process for tendering for counsel. A competing international law firm, which fielded a full team fresh from completing a similar financing in another developing country, eventually won the mandate.

Northern Telecom Europe Limited retained the firm in late August 1994 to the assist with the establishment of their operations in Slovakia. KPMG Peat Marwick, acting as financial advisors to the Hungarian government, engaged the Budapest office as its legal subcontractor in setting up housing co-operatives and condominium associations in Hungary for residential dwellings, which were to be occupied by approximately 10,000 tenants. The initial phase of the mandate was to recommend the best legal structure for such a project, although the full involvement we sought did not pan out. Peter O'Brien and William Rosenberg in the Montreal office were essential supporters, providing the background documentation and information. Meanwhile, privatization of the electricity industry was moving ahead, with the firm working on initial recommendations in connection with the new legal and regulatory framework.

By June 1995, we had completed work on the first privatization of the written press in Hungary, acting for the strategic investor Hebdo Mag International. This was the first privatization under the new socialist government, elected the previous year, and it attracted major attention in the media, including some fifty separate articles in newspapers and many television interviews in which the firm was prominently featured. Not unexpectedly, the whole matter was extremely political, with repeated interventions by the the Prime Minister's Office and direct negotiations with the minister of Privatization. The firm was retained by the Export Development Corporation to deal with performance guarantees on the construction of a desulphurization plant for the Hungarian Oil and Gas Corporation, probably the result of a visit in May by Hansen, Rovinescu, and Ewart to the Export Development Corporation in Ottawa to meet with the general counsel of the corporation and other colleagues. Our work as exclusive legal advisor with respect to the privatization of the Hungarian electricity industry continued. In May the same year, we were retained by Bombardier Inc. in connection with an acquisition in Hungary, performing a due diligence review of the target company with a ten-person Bombardier team. This was the first mandate Bombardier had granted to the firm in several years.

In the general area of Central and Eastern Europe, we did work at the request of the president of the Bulgarian Foreign Investment Agency and acted for Glidden Trading Ltd. on multi-jurisdiction licensing distribution arrangements with the national Centre for Parasitic and Contagious Diseases in Sofia, Bulgaria. In Romania, we acted on multi-jurisdiction bill of exchange matters for Leumi-Hitel Bank, and together with the London office, we examined a possible target on behalf of Alcan Aluminium. Shawna Miller completed a project financing arrangement in Uzbekistan on behalf of Northern Telecom Europe. As a result of inroads made by James Arnett with the World Bank in relation to a legislative reform project in Azerbaijan and a visit by David Skinner for several days in Baku, Rowland Harrison visited Baku in October 1995 to negotiate the terms of reference of a mandate to establish the oil and gas legislation in the Republic of Azerbaijan.

The firm bid on many projects, and there were countless visits and business promotion exercises, including those by Rowland Harrison (in February with respect to a bid in Sofia), Marc Lalonde, myself, Marvin Yontef, Kathyrn Chalmers, Michael Richards, Calin Rovinescu, Bill Scott, and several others. Stikeman Elliott sponsored the 1995 International Mathematics Olympiads at the request of Northern Telecom Canada, with special sponsorship for the Hungarian team at the closing dinner, which was attended by Brian Rose and Rob Hyndman of the Toronto office. The firm gave seminars in conjunction with Dalhousie University's Business School and various Canadian corporations in May 1995. It was the main sponsor of the Euro Congress Seminar in September 1995, which dealt with privatization in Hungary and at which the main speakers included the minister of Finance, the minister of Privatization, the Hungarian director of the European Bank for Reconstruction and Development, and Ewart. Ewart was a speaker at the International Tax Planning Association conference in Budapest in March 1996, and several of the lawyers were participants in seminars on privatization, electricity, and oil and gas matters in Romania, Bulgaria, Portugal, and London. The firm acted as counsel to Enron (well before the notorious debacle) regarding the privatization of the Hungarian gas distribution and supply utility and acted in the privatization of several media interests as well as the Lauda Group. The team got the mandates by getting close to the governments and by showing initiative and hard work.

The firm's presence on the ground in Central and Eastern Europe added additional impetus to the desire to obtain international mandates, both there and elsewhere. Many considered that work being done in that region would be the precursor to similar privatization mandates in India and China, so there developed an extremely competitive atmosphere among all the foreign firms for such projects. Working in these areas, while exciting and challenging, was fraught with difficulty. International legal consulting involved advising and assisting on legal matters in a foreign jurisdiction, where the lawyers were not necessarily advising Canadian clients or on Canadian law despite the fact that our advice was based primarily upon our Canadian expertise. The principal users of such services were multilateral development agencies or foreign governments or agencies financed by them. There are quite often formal competitive bidding procedures in order to obtain the work. For a firm with global aspirations, this type of practice was strategically important. It provided new markets during periods of stagnation in Canada and enabled us to export legal services in addition to building on local experience and skills. Where mandates were successfully carried out, it enabled the firm to demonstrate an expertise in those markets that would be attractive to current and potential Canadian clients and the possible opportunity to act internationally on behalf of multinational corporations. Moreover, the foreign-acquired expertise led to domestic mandates in the electricity industries in Alberta, Quebec, and Ontario.

Based on the early experiences, it was fairly clear that the firm was able to compete in emerging markets with almost anyone, including firms much larger than itself. This was not always the case in developed markets, where it was more difficult to compete with some of the most prominent US and UK firms. The business was, however, extremely competitive, and some of the law firms with whom we were quite close in their home markets occasionally behaved in a very difficult and even unprofessional manner in the emerging markets. We had occasions when firms with which we worked quite closely in the UK tried to dislodge us from mandates we had already obtained. Investment banks are extremely important players in the emerging markets, and a special effort had to be undertaken to get them to consider us as legal advisors in those markets. One way in which a small firm could increase its chances of success was in joint venturing with other consultants to contracting entities, including legal and accounting firms. That would provide increased possibilities for securing mandates and, of course, a reduction in the cost of preparing bids. Even unsuccessful bids nevertheless generated "friends" for future occasions. Venturing with other law firms was regarded as helpful when we needed their expertise, either technical or local, or their strategic assistance, as in the case of politically well-connected local firms. Being a relatively small firm in this field, there was some benefit to be derived from sectoral concentration such as power, mining, oil, and gas. Another factor of importance in getting such mandates was to be sure that all members of the firm were aware of the interest in such matters and remained vigilant as to the possibilities for new opportunities.

In Budapest, by mid-1996, the firm had been retained by ING Bank Rt. in connection with its offer for certain assets of Dunabank Rt.; by Fonderies et Ateliers du Bélier, a French investor, with respect to its phase two acquisition of the foundry operations of the state-owned Hungarian aluminum industry, a division of Hungalu Rt.; and as general counsel to Crédit Lyonnais Hungary for their activities in Hungary, including full review and redrafting of all standard loan documentation of the bank. The US law firm Dechart Price & Rhoads engaged us to deal with the export of equipment to Russia. The firm became general counsel to Société Générale de Financement of Paris in relation to its new presence in Hungary through a subsidiary corporation. Work on the electricity privatization continued, including the launch of new tenders for five of the power companies not picked up on the original offering in 1995, the sale of hydroelectric assets and other restructuring within the Hungarian electricity industry, the preparation of long-term power purchase agreements and supply agreements, and regulatory work for the Hungarian Energy office. In the case of the new privatization tenders, the Budapest lawyers handled the sale of Tisza Power Company Limited to AES Summit, a UK subsidiary of the American AES Corporation. We were retained by MVM Rt. for the sale of shares of Mátrai Erömü Rt. to RWE Energie AG and Energie Versorgung Schwaben EG. We also acted on the sale of Budapest Power Company Limited to a consortium formed by IVO of Finland and Tomen Corporation of Japan. Similar work continued through the first quarter of 1997 and into the second quarter, but by that time, the volume of business had begun to slacken.

There was a major shift in the market in Hungary – from one of large privatizations in which we had a strong presence and in which we had concentrated our principal efforts and time, to the post-privatization phase in which securities issues and project financing were far more in focus. We had not broken into the IPO market at all nor the project financing field except for some work in the power sector, where Massicotte and Hayhurst worked on the first independent power project in Hungary. This segment of the market was proving to be an increasingly difficult hurdle to overcome as the volume of such transactions grew and the application of UK or US law to the financing documentation, encouraged by the huge English and American law firms, became the norm. In addition, as the market grew more domestic, there were significant constraints on fee structures, which other firms dealt with by reducing the number of expatriates in Hungary. It was clear that we would have to restructure the expatriate profile by reducing the number of short-term rotations, modifying the scale of the seniority of the lawyers on site, and balancing lateral hires possessing local language skills, who were generally less costly than domestic-based firm expatriates, against the concerns of the firm regarding overall competence and quality. As these developments had begun to occur, Ewart and the others focused on exploring markets in other countries such as Ukraine, Poland, Croatia, and Romania, each of which had its own dynamics and made the process reasonably costly not only in terms of expenditure but also in the loss of billable activities.[23] It was in the first quarter of 1997 that the first operating deficit occurred. The firm's accounting system proved to be inadequate despite regular visits by Bob Hart and Richard Taylor. The situation was complicated by the fact that many of the expenses were handled either out of the Montreal or Toronto office, so that there was often an *ex post facto* discovery of many late expenses that were allocated to the Budapest office.

By mid-October 1997, Ewart had prepared a comprehensive review regarding the financial position of the firm in Central and Eastern Europe, the measures taken to address the recent operating deficit, and recommendations for a strategy to be considered. He thought that operations in Prague had not been successful and that the office should be scaled back or closed. Within Hungary, the market had changed, and the firm's position had not evolved, having acted principally on the sale side of transactions when privatization occurred and this on behalf of a relatively narrow base of clients. Although we had acted on most of the major transactions between 1994 and 1996, the competition had been enlarging its client and contact base with larger numbers of smaller transactions. Having acted on the sale side of many of these mandates, there was no repeat business to be derived, and in many cases, we were effectively eliminated by reason of conflicts of interest, within the industry. Such a narrow base of mandates had not fostered a diversified level of contacts with investment banks and other financial intermediaries, a situation that Ewart thought would take considerable time to remedy. In addition, the agreement with Réti & Antall meant that the firm did not profit from any fees generated by the local attorneys. Activities in Ukraine would require a long-term commitment, and despite considerable efforts, billable work was only just starting to emerge. The situation in Bulgaria was considered as marginal, although neighbouring Romania was in a situation more or less analogous to Hungary in 1992–93, with a major and accelerated program of privatizations just beginning. For cost reduction, we had sublet part of the premises and had cut back on the number of lawyers and staff. Both Ewart and Kathleen Ward, the senior-level partners in place, were planning to return to Canada within the next few months. It was also clear that the accounting information flow needed to be improved to ensure that monthly assessments could be made of the entire financial situation.

By the end of October, however, it was clear that the firm's executive committee considered the bloom to be off the rose; it did not want to build a Central European firm due to the lack of resources necessary to do so as well as the lack of an international client base justifying such an ambitious program. There was very small likelihood of any significant referral business into Canada to be derived from Central and Eastern Europe. The executive committee tended toward development of a niche corporate finance group in the form of a SWAT team operating from a Canadian base, which would develop a business plan to identify interesting privatizations, mergers and acquisitions, and banking opportunities, but which would generally exclude commercial work, basic contract work, and dispute resolution as this work could be done by the team on the ground. It decided that operations at that time should focus on Hungary and Romania, in accordance with Ewart's recommendations, but that the commitments to offices in Prague, Sofia, and Kiev should be terminated. It wanted the arrangement with Réti & Antall to be one in which they would bill the firm for significantly lower rates than they would otherwise charge, which would enable the referrals to them from the firm to generate, in effect, a "royalty" income. The executive committee concurred with the recommendation that Ward and Ewart should return to Canada, preferably by the end of the year and no later than February 28, 1998. These decisions were confirmed by the partnership board in November, and by early December, Ewart had taken the steps necessary to reduce the size of the Budapest operation to one of approximately six Canadian lawyers, to close the other offices, and to have Massicotte become the managing principal in Budapest as at March 1, 1998 for an initial period of eighteen months, reporting to the managing principal in the London office.

What we had not fully understood at the height of the privatization frenzy was that once these mandates were completed, there was virtually no flow of work emanating from these countries in the direction of Canada, with the result that continued success depended on a continuous flow of mandates that could be generated and performed in those countries. This had led Ewart to continued expansion, and as he charged ahead, he became very much like US General George S. Patton, miles ahead of the logistical support, including funds, that he needed from headquarters to sustain his troops in the field. We used to discover, after the fact, that we now had representative offices in all sorts of places that we had not contemplated and could not support, such as Sofia, Bucharest, and Kiev. Marc Lalonde, along with Raymond Barre, Zbigniew Brezinski, and others, was on an advisory board that provided assistance to the president of Ukraine. This was all Ewart needed, and we opened an office in Kiev, staffed by Christina Macew, who was formerly advisor to the government, and she became Stikeman Elliott in Kiev. Ewart opened offices by simply printing new letterhead on the computer. Because there were not enough lawyers in place to attract the major financing work, they needed to specialize in the privatization aspect of the emerging economy and its transition from state-owned to private enterprise. In order to get even that work, Ewart was convinced that they needed a regional network of offices and contacts. In his typical fashion, he did not wait for the partnership to confirm each of the offices he opened. At that time, under the terms of the partnership agreements, it required a full vote of the partnership in order to open a new office. As the expenses – which we had not controlled to the extent necessary – began to mount and were not matched by related revenues, it became clear that we could not sensibly sustain operations on such a scale, and we reached the inescapable conclusion that it was no longer viable to remain there. So the Budapest office was, with considerable regret, closed in mid-1998.

Ewart, who had enjoyed the experience and thrill of being his own man and being supremely entrepreneurial in the process, found that he no longer enjoyed the practice of law by itself in Montreal, so he decided to leave the firm and take up development work on his own account. Another casualty of the firm resulting from the choice to close the operations in Budapest and to manage Central European work from London was the decision of Robert Hayhurst, who had completely fallen in love with Central Europe, to remain there and to operate on his own from Budapest. Hayhurst had been one of the genuine rocks on which our practice there had been built, and he was fully at home in the environment. One of the risks that a firm like Stikeman Elliott must accept is that many of the most talented lawyers needed to staff such foreign offices may well become charmed by the new countries and not wish to return to the rigours of mainstream legal practice in Canada, even to a large and exciting firm that is in the forefront of legal developments in major transactions. Hayhurst's firm, Hayhurst Berlad Robinson, now has twenty-five lawyers from Canada, the United States, the United Kingdom, Hungary, Romania, Bulgaria, and Australia. It has been involved in many of the high-profile transactions in recent years, including the acquisition by MOL Rt., the Hungarian national oil and gas company, and of Slovnaft, a.s., the Slovak national refining company. Hayhurst has maintained and expanded the former Stikeman Elliott offices in Budapest, Bucharest, and Sofia, and his firm acts on mandates throughout the region, including Slovakia, Poland, and Croatia, making Hayhurst Berlad Robinson the only truly regional law firm in that part of the world. The Bucharest office has grown to ten lawyers due in part to the belated Romanian commitment to privatize and attract more foreign direct investment, as Ewart had foreseen in 1997. Hayhurst attributes his firm's success to the values embodied in Stikeman Elliott: hard work, a commitment to excellence and client service, and a desire to "go where no lawyer has gone before." He considers, in this sense, that the spirit of Stikeman Elliott has survived and continues to flourish in Central and Eastern Europe, both figuratively and literally, the latter under an association agreement between the firms. For their part, Réti and Antall established a new Hungarian law firm affiliated with PricewaterhouseCoopers, and they probably now enjoy the position of having one of the largest firms between the Danube and the Urals.

WASHINGTON

The firm made its second foray into the United States with the opening of an office in Washington, DC in the fall of 1993. Jim Arnett from the Toronto office was dispatched as our ambassador, with the very ambitious mandate of trying to establish a viable presence to pursue our interests in international trade matters, regulatory issues, international corporate and financial transactions and related advice, Latin-American business, and in cross-border advice generally. There were two essential objectives. One was to get mandates through the presence of international financial institutions, such as the World Bank and the Inter-American Development Bank. The big US and London firms, especially Linklaters, were getting interesting international work through connections with these agencies, and we wanted to pursue our objective of being perceived as a Canadian law firm doing international work. The other principal objective was to get more cross-border work, doing counsel work in the US for Canadian clients and to attract Canadian work from US clients.

It was a tough assignment in a tough town, one that proved to be an eventual disappointment, especially in attracting Canadian work from US clients. Arnett went into Washington totally cold and was very surprised by the complete lack of name recognition: no one in Washington had even heard of Stikeman Elliott. As a Harvard alumnus, Arnett was able to join the National Press Club, and the firm held an opening reception there, attracting a large turnout – which was built around Allan Gotlieb (who had joined the firm as a consultant after leaving the foreign service) and Marc Lalonde – attended as well by some of the other partners, including Jim Grant from Montreal and Elizabeth Skelton, then in New York. There were short speeches by the three main attractions, and Arnett got some idea of the extraordinary reputation Gotlieb enjoyed in Washington when he introduced him. As Gotlieb was moving to the lectern to begin his remarks, the entire audience stood up and applauded.

Arnett found a house for rent in the Cleveland Park area in the District of Columbia and was the next door neighbour of Bill Ince, a Washington lawyer and Princeton classmate of David Angus and Eric Molson. The key was to try to find an angle to make oneself known since in Washington, Canada was not considered very interesting. People, he says, were vaguely bemused when he introduced himself in Washington as a Canadian. It was not unlike the spoof in the famous 1950s McGill University musical, *My Fur Lady,* in which the character playing the part of the president of the United States kept confusing Canada with Ghana. "No, no!" the Canadian prime minister would have to keep insisting. "Not Ghana, Canada!" Canada is a country that Americans, other than those involved in border trade, comprehend dimly, if at all. One has only to mention the name to see Americans' eyes glaze over and the attention begin to wander. In Washington, which is consumed with the issue of political power, domestic and foreign, Canada simply does not matter. In times of crisis, it can generally be counted upon, virtually automatically, to support the US position, and until there is a crisis, it can be and is safely ignored.

Canadian clients wanting to be active in the US had no compunction in going directly to US lawyers for their advice or to lobbyists who specialized in the intricate workings of the US political system. Indeed, they were cheerfully directed to do so by their own Canadian counsel, who were probably giving them the right advice in so doing and who had, in any event, no appetite for directing them to another ambitious Canadian firm. Outward-bound work into Canada was not as realistic as we had hoped, primarily because Washington is not a business city. We had also hoped that the regulatory practices of the Ottawa office might integrate more closely with the United States, but once we got on the ground, we found that these areas tended to be more local than federal and that a small office in the national capital had little chance of making a dent in the huge apparatus represented in Washington, which was teeming with representatives of the thousands of special interest groups much more capable of dealing with politicians and especially with the House of Representatives, the concerns of which are highly local, specific, and short term since members stand for election every two years.

Arnett laboured mightily to promote the firm's interests generally and to advertise the presence of the firm on Capitol Hill. As just one example, I was in Washington in May 1995 to speak at the Canadian Ambassador's Lecture Series on the forthcoming Atlanta Olympic Games, and Arnett, who made the best of every occasion when one of the firm's lawyers was in town, arranged a dinner party at his home and invited several of the firm's Washington contacts to continue the promotional efforts. He helped to develop our relationships with the international agencies located in Washington, and he is still working on a mandate in Chad, obtained from the World Bank, dealing with the largest infrastructure project in Africa, which we definitely would not have got without a presence in Washington and Arnett's relentless pursuit of business directed by the organization. We obtained a fair amount of business from the International Development Bank, including mandates in Guyana and Belize, but the Latin-American agenda was not, at the time, a major concern in Washington, especially since the NAFTA arrangements were in their infancy and the US orientation was far more self-interested in the US-Mexico perspective than an overall concept of how all three countries might work together. Canadian clients having interests in Mexico and other Latin-American countries were also specific rather than general, and they did not require US intervention to be successful. In retrospect, it might have been more productive to have explored the prospect of opening directly in Mexico more thoroughly than we did at the time, but we did not have the resources that would permit such an initiative, especially since the Stikeman Elliott catechism was that we send our own people to the places where we opened rather than "buying" representation by merging with people we did not know and whose personal and business cultures might be significantly different from our own. Interestingly enough, the existence of the Montreal office was of more interest in Washington since it was unique in having major capacity to perform services in French, and we did not face the same competition as we did with the unilingual English-speaking firms, particularly for projects in French-speaking Africa.

The objective of providing cross-border advice on commercial matters generally from a Washington base also turned out to be far less productive than we had hoped. Whatever its many qualities as a source of business might be, Washington is a government not a business capital. The concerns that drive and fascinate Washington are not essentially business. They are first and foremost domestic political issues; secondly, international political issues; and only distantly, a consideration of how those issues may be affected by business considerations. The Washington scene was not one that had a particularly high regard for the business community as such. Its principal impact was through the pressure groups and lobbyists who advocated for specific benefits through a highly effective and well-developed network of contacts. Businesses with particular interests had their own lawyers, especially in the large US firms, and they had their own specialists in foreign law, often just as capable (and sometimes more capable) as the local Latin-American law firms. Even Linklaters staffed their Washington office with just an associate and ran the show from its New York office, which would probably have been a more sensible course for us as well.

Our experience demonstrated that the best source of business in cross-border activities was directly from the US law firms, which was better developed from our activities and personal contacts in organizations such as the American Bar Association and International Bar Association. Increasingly, the Canadian businesses that had significant US activities used their own US lawyers, and our interests were better served by maintaining as much contact as possible with our clients as they moved south and by working directly with those firms.

One of the collateral benefits derived from the foreign offices was the many experiences of the lawyers involved, which could never be duplicated had they stayed at home in Toronto or Montreal. Arnett had one such experience, related to the Million Man March, which was organized in Washington by Louis Farrakhan, leader of the Nation of Islam, to demonstrate that Afro-American males should show some form of solidarity. It was a huge event, and the authorities were very nervous about the potential for it to turn ugly. People were warned not to go into the city. Arnett and Rowland Harrison had, however, arranged a meeting with a Dutch lawyer for the preparation of a joint bid for an oil deal in the Caspian Sea and could not reschedule it. The city was dead. Out of nothing more than curiosity, they decided to go and see the march and walked down to the mall for the purpose. Arnett says they were the only white faces in a space of almost a mile, and they felt very conspicuous in their blue suits and white shirts. The atmosphere was great and quite low-key, and they had been there for about twenty minutes, when someone pointed them out and shouted, "Three suits!" They wondered, all of a sudden, whether they had made a big, and possibly fatal, mistake in coming. Someone approached them and said, "What do you think?" The three lawyers said they thought it was great. "Thanks for coming," was the rejoinder. It turned out to be a great and unique experience. Arnett even parted with a few dollars to purchase a T-shirt to celebrate his "participation."

By the end of 1995, it was clear that the Washington foothold was likely to remain marginal as an effective source of business and that we could not, without some kind of association with a major us firm, make significant inroads into the legal practice in that environment. An association of that nature appeared to us to be of limited value and just as likely to drive our clients into the hands of other firms as redound to our own benefit. Even our association with Allan Gotlieb, the former Canadian ambassador to Washington, proved to be insufficient to break through the barriers to achieve a demonstrable and effective presence in that city. So we withdrew, somewhat sadder, but certainly more aware of the vicissitudes of the centre of the universe. The firm's executive committee met on January 24, 1996 and agreed that Grant and Arnett should meet to settle on the appropriate course of action, which was that Arnett should return to Toronto in the spring. It was agreed that we would keep the Washington office on the firm letterhead for a couple of years and that Arnett and especially Gotlieb would continue to service it through regular trips to Washington. Gotlieb would retain his association with the firm and spend a week per month in Washington.

Arnett returned to Toronto in June 1996, but was soon recruited out of the blue by Eric Molson, his former neighbour in Toronto, to become first an outside director and seven months later, president of Molsons, a position he agreed to take on for two or three years while the company restored its focus on the core activity of brewing. Arnett accomplished it, including the hiring of his successor, in just over three years. He retired in June 2000, the same day that Molson announced the decision to sell control of the Montreal Canadiens hockey team, the Molson board thanking Arnett for his "exceptional contribution" to Molson's long history.

PARIS

The firm would never have been in Paris but for the presence of Robert Couzin and his desire to try something different from the high-level tax practice that he maintained, first in Montreal and later in Toronto. This venture was also launched in 1993. Compliance with French requirements meant that the firm had to operate as a separate entity in France as a Société Juridique Internationale, and we acquired a French associate, Jean-Baptiste Guillot, to help Robert, an acknowledged francophile, who almost immediately upon his arrival was converted into an instant boulevardier, complete with beret and scarf. His objective was to represent the firm in France and on the continent generally, with a view to promoting the Canadian and other foreign offices, seeking mandates from European and Canadian clients, to be carried out in those offices in conjunction with Paris or otherwise as circumstances dictated. Liaison with London and Budapest would, we hoped, be sufficient to create a pan-European network, with on-the-spot tax expertise to cement the ties. He was also equipped to provide Canadian and (to a limited extent) French legal advice to Canadian clients active in Europe.

Of all the firm's foreign ventures, the most doubt of eventual success was attached to the opening in Paris. The city of light is a wonderful capital and a delight to visit, but from a business perspective, it is little more than a regional centre. French businesses were not at the expansionary stage that they were to reach during the late 1990s, and French investment in North America, to the extent that it existed, was directed mainly at the United States, not at Canada. Paris was just not the international financial capital that London was. But Couzin was an asset of inestimable value to the firm, and we were willing to take the financial risk in order to give him a chance to succeed. Even though we held our collective noses and took the plunge, we were very concerned that it would never be viable. On the other hand, if anyone could do it, Couzin was the one best suited to the purpose.

French bureaucracy was a particular hassle for a small office. One illustration came from the office lease, which contained an express provision as to the date it ended, and both the firm and the landlord were in full agreement on all possible points of contention. All this notwithstanding, it was obligatory to engage the services of a bailiff to serve the landlord with a formal notice of all that had been agreed between the contracting parties.

There was not nearly the volume of work to be derived from France that had been hoped for or expected. It proved very difficult to generate interest in matters Canadian. French-based multinationals had at the time relatively little interest in their Canadian subsidiaries, and they had a generally passive approach to tax planning and even, Couzin suspected, to commerce as a whole. He published articles and worked on a proposed seminar with a tax boutique in Paris, Bureau Francis Lefebvre, on a recent amendment to the protocol of the Canada-France Income Tax Convention, but the idea collapsed from lack of interest on the part of the French business community. Useful exposure was generated through participation on the tax committee of the Business and Industry Advisory Group (BIAC) of the OECD and membership on a BIAC group of experts advising on a proposed Multilateral Agreement on Investments, where Couzin's tax expertise was very helpful. The work was intellectually stimulating and gave exposure to representatives of national business organizations as well as in-house legal, tax, or business development advisors although the volume of actual business developed through these contacts remained minimal.

In the end, the venture was unsuccessful. The office was closed in October 1996, and Couzin returned to North America at the end of the year, with the intention of joining the New York office, but following the misunderstanding as to who would be the managing partner of that office, he left the firm in 1997 to join the international accounting firm of Ernst & Young, where he now practices. It was a big loss to the firm, as he is a lawyer of great ability and acknowledged brilliance. Jim Grant, reflecting as chairman emeritus of the firm, says that Couzin was one of the few lawyers in the firm who was so smart that he could make those with whom he worked feel smart as well.

SINGAPORE

Hong Kong is the traditional international business centre of Asia, but over the past two or three decades, Singapore has also developed into an important centre in its own right, with particular importance in Southeast Asia. We reached the conclusion in early 1996 that Singapore provided a natural enhancement of our activities in Asia since other major centres – such as Tokyo, Beijing, and Seoul – were effectively closed to foreigners, with one or two grandfathered exceptions, mainly American firms. It was too time-consuming for the Hong Kong partners to try to manage that part of the world from Hong Kong, so we opened a small office in Singapore in that year, thinking that there would be a substantial amount of investment from Southeast Asia into Canada and vice versa.

We found Franca Ciambella, available after she had represented the Osler, Renault joint venture that had preceded us in Singapore. She was without doubt the best-known Canadian professional in Singapore, and she managed to secure some extremely valuable work from Alcan in Japan, from Malaysia, and several other good files. We never managed, however, to really secure a major role on a large transaction. At its heyday, we had five lawyers in the Singapore office. Bill Scott and John Paterson had come from the Toronto office, Scott by way of the London office. In addition to Ciambella, the firm hired two lawyers locally: Timothy Goh, a New Zealand-trained lawyer hired in Singapore; and Geneviève Roy, until recently (when she became a full-time mother) in the London office. Susan Hutton, from the Ottawa office, was there for a period while her husband had a diplomatic posting in the area. Scott was involved in order to try to gain access to the banking and securitization market in the region, with John Paterson to provide assistance. We could not have had worse timing since shortly after Scott arrived, the economies throughout Southeast Asia started to slide. Even someone with his demonstrated expertise in working in a small office in

London over the previous years could do nothing to bring sizable pieces of work into the office.

The Singapore office was small, located on the thirteenth floor of a 1960s vintage office building located in the old financial centre of town. From his office, Scott could look through the perennially unwashed windows across the straits to the nearby islands of the Indonesian archipelago. The heat and humidity were insufferable, particularly as the air conditioning would go off at 6:00 PM sharp and the temperature in the office would rise by approximately twenty degrees Fahrenheit. Shorts and T-shirts were then the prescribed attire. We were also constantly barraged by the sound of jackhammers as nearby buildings were being torn down for redevelopment. The work was varied and often included road trips to countries such as Vietnam, Thailand, Malaysia, and Indonesia. Much of the work involved inward investment by Canadian companies, usually steered in our direction with assistance from the Canadian High Commissions and embassies in the region. We also worked for the Canadian banks (for example, Ralph Lutes was the general counsel at CIBC's Singapore branch) and a variety of other clients.

While Southeast Asia was an exciting place to be, the economic meltdown in Asia and the fall of Suharto in Indonesia in 1997–98 had a severe impact on the financings Scott had gone out to Singapore to work on, all of which were cancelled. He remembers large numbers of ethnic Chinese (including some Canadians we knew) having to leave Jakarta suddenly as a result of racial violence. At that time, the luxury hotels of Singapore were full of refugees dressed in Gucci shoes and Armani suits for several weeks. From September to Christmas 1997, they had to endure the "haze," the visible smoke from forest fires in Borneo and Sumatra that covered much of the region and blocked out the sun for almost three months. The same year, Scott participated in the Terry Fox Run – through the jungle. The Singapore version of the run is sponsored by numerous local corporations and the national television broadcaster and attracts approximately 10,000 participants. Apparently, they raise more money for cancer research in that one race than in any other Terry Fox Run in the world. The event has been so completely co-opted by the Singaporeans that if you were to ask where Terry Fox was from, Scott suspects that 99 per cent of the participants would not know he was a Canadian.

Singapore was never a huge success, but it did provide a foothold for some of our international work in countries such as Vietnam, where we were engaged to help bring its statutory and regulatory structures up to international standards. When we finally got down to analysing whether our whole foreign office concept was the best way of delivering relevant legal services to our clients and prospects, we reached the inevitable conclusion that having only a small operation in Singapore was not the right solution. Either we had to commit to a major investment, or we had to close. The office was reduced to Ciambella and the local hires by June 30, 1998 and effectively closed down in February 1999.

SYDNEY

The most recent foreign initiative of the firm has been to have an office in Sydney. We are represented by Brian Hansen, one of our venerable road warriors, who has managed our Asian practice for many years. He located a very experienced Australian partner in Roy Randall,[24] and they engaged in a practice involving primarily international transactions with admittedly limited Australian implications. The firm has excellent offices in Cheffley Square and a wide range of local and international contacts, but Australian firms have no particular interest in sharing work with Canadians unless their clients insist. Nor are they particularly enthusiastic about a competitor for the same international mandates they are seeking for their own accounts. It was hoped that there would be significant cross-fertilization between Sydney, Singapore, and Hong Kong, but with the Asian economic meltdown during the late 1990s, this simply did not develop although the Sydney and Hong Kong offices have worked together on a substantial number of files. Randall himself elected to reduce the level of his association with the firm during 2001 and to become a consultant rather than a full partner.

The Sydney office does not undertake any serious local Australian law work, although Hansen, through his China experience, was retained to represent Atomic Energy of Canada Limited on its bid for the Lucas Heights Nuclear Reactor. The office will never match the Canadian offices in terms of profitability – it is too small and has no leverage. However, it performs two valuable roles. Firstly, as the only Canadian legal presence in Australia, it obtains for the Canadian offices virtually all major Canadian legal work emanating out of Australia. This includes securities work (Telstra, Paper Link, One Steel, Mayne Nickless), some very substantial merger and acquisition work (Orica and Westfield), and financing and investment banking issues (Macquarie Bank and Brambles). Secondly, Hansen has extremely close links with the Li Family and acts as effective general counsel for most of the companies in the group in their acquisitions in Australia and on occasion, elsewhere in the world. During his time in Sydney, Cheung Kong Infrastructure Holdings Limited and Hongkong Electric Holdings Limited have become the largest electricity distributors in Australia. In addition, CKIH is the largest shareholder in Envestra Limited, Hongkong Electric has become the largest shareholder in a new 1,500-MW power plant in Thailand, and there have been bids on other very substantial infrastructure tenders. Stikeman, Elliott has acted on all these and maintains its very close links with one of the firm's principal clients.

INTERNATIONAL ADVISORY SERVICES

There were many opportunities to provide services to international clients on an ad hoc basis, in respect of which it was not worthwhile for the firm to establish a permanent physical presence. A special SWAT team of lawyers from the Montreal office coalesced, as a variation on the road warriors theme, to seek and perform such mandates. The team had a core nucleus composed of Erik Richer La Fleche,[25] Martin Scheim,[26] and Alain Massi-cotte. They were reinforced as required by many others, including Jean Carrier,[27] Viateur Chénard,[28] Christine Desaulniers,[29] Sterling Dietze,[30] Sydney Isaacs,[31] and Greg Kane. Building on many of the experiences developed in the Canadian offices and the established foreign offices, as well as some expertise they created as a result of their own efforts or invented as they went along, they set out to conquer new fields. In their endeavours, they had the additional advantage of the presence and reputation of Marc Lalonde, with his particular ability to open doors and to contribute in a meaningful way to the accomplishment of international mandates. The team completed assignments in over thirty countries and had some remarkable experiences on every continent except Antarctica. Knowledge gained abroad also enabled them to innovate in Canada.

Asia

As a result of a chance encounter on Montreal's Peel Street in 1994 with Qays Zu'bi, an English solicitor practising in Bahrain, Erik Richer La Fleche learned that the Government of Bahrain was about to launch a call for tenders to retain counsel in its partial privatization of the Bahraini electricity sector and the development of a privately owned 349-MW power plant and associated 30 million imperial gallons per day (MIGD) water desalinization facility, to be developed on a build, own, and operate (BOO) basis by British Gas. The competitors were huge international law firms such as Clifford Chance and Norton Rose, all with offices and experience in that region. After getting the firm's name onto the short list, La Fleche approached Bob Hart, the office manager, to provide the means to go to Bahrain with Martin Scheim to make their pitch for the $US300-million project. He had gone to Hart because he had very cordial relations with him and knew that Hart, unlike some of the partners, cautious about spending their own money, would listen to his business case arguments in favour of the trip. This, he admits, was more difficult than usual since he had none. The firm had little regional or sectoral experience, and its chances appeared slim. Hart knew all this, but probably bemused by the whole thing, relented, and La Fleche got the funds. They went to score their first international win. Once the work was obtained, they faced an aspect of possible tension by sending Martin Scheim, one of the Jewish lawyers from Montreal, and Christine Desaulniers, a woman, to Bahrain to work on the project. Although they may have been apprehensive at the outset, there were no problems, and both ended up being well liked by the client and others involved in the project.

The work in Bahrain led to a number of power reform mandates in Asia, most notably in the Indian states of Andhra Pradesh, Madhya Pradesh, Gujarat, Kerala, and Rajasthan. In the latter case, they also advised the Rajasthan State Electricity Board on the preparation of tender documentation, bid evaluation, and negotiation of project agreements for the Barsingar coal mine and power plant complex. In 1998, they were engaged by the electricity board of the state of Tamil Nadu, India to negotiate with the developers of six different projects. This involved work on all deal aspects, including the drafting of project agreements and the review of each project's limited recourse financing.

On his first trip to India, La Fleche arrived at Chennai, the capital of Tamil Nadu, after twenty-four hours in the air, but he only had time to go to the hotel for a shave and shower before setting off to meet with the client. When he finally arrived at the client's offices, he was taken to a room where there were about forty Indian civil servants – the client's negotiating team – and on the other side of the table sat five Indian gentlemen from the sponsors of one of the projects and ten foreign individuals, the sponsors' lawyers, and representatives from the Bank of America and HSBC. At that stage, the sponsors had been negotiating for some nine years! La Fleche had no instructions from the client and had never spoken to them. Nor did the senior members of the client's delegation want to break to confer. Immediately after being introduced, La Fleche was summoned imperiously by the banks' American counsel to deliver his comments on a number of draft agreements that had been tabled three months earlier but which La Fleche had not seen.

Not knowing what to do, he asked the developer's lawyers and bankers to explain, in everyday language and using the blackboard in the room, the issues they were trying to address in their draft agreements. The response was about thirty minutes of righteous indignation, after which La Fleche smiled and asked his side if anyone understood the position of the sponsors and their bankers and generally, the risks associated with a project of that size, namely a $US1.3-billion power plant. The ensuing agitation and cacophony indicated clearly to the other side that they were not getting through to the client and that they had better start from the beginning even though it was nine years later. By the end of the day, La Fleche was pronounced by the principals on both sides, excluding, of course, the lawyers and bankers, to be a "wise" man, a distinction he felt he had not earned but nevertheless bore with as much modesty as he could summon. During the course of the mandate, three of the six projects reached financial closure and are now commissioned, a considerable achievement in light of the enormous difficulties in the Indian power sector during the 1990s. Their reputation in India led to mandates in Maharashtra and Uttar Pradesh, where they represented Indian private power developers and more recently, to Egypt, where La Fleche is assisting the government to develop a 230-MW thermal and solar hybrid power plant on a BOO basis.

They were engaged by Dessau International (Canada) to advise on joint venture agreements with the People's Republic of China and in Thailand. Beginning in 1996, Lalonde has assisted the highest spheres of the Vietnamese government in a CIDA-funded policy assistance project. His involvement has included advice to the prime minister's Research Committee (a mini-PMO), legislative and social affairs advice to a committee of the National Assembly, and assistance on WTO matters. A second phase of the project now provides advice in connection with information technology as well as grassroots democracy and its implementation. Rowland Harrison advised the government of Vietnam in connection with regulatory responsibilities in the oil and gas industry.

Oceania

In the Solomon Islands, the team won a mandate in 1999 from the Asian Development Bank (ADB) to privatize a diverse batch of state-owned enterprises, including coconut groves, and to provide some regulatory advice. The sale of the first privatization candidate, the national telecommunications company, had barely been satisfactorily concluded when everything was dramatically interrupted. Just as the team was finally getting used to its bungalow, with swimming pool, the inhabitants of Guadalcanal, one of the constituent islands of the country, decided to rebel and invade the capital, Honiara. Although the Australian navy quickly restored order, the same could not be said about the shaken confidence of foreign investors, and the ADB suspended the project *sine die*. This was a bittersweet moment for Alain Massicotte. Although he would have to say goodbye to some of the best snorkelling and diving grounds in the world, he would no longer have to worry about his wardrobe while he was at work since the housemaid, despite strict instructions to the contrary, insisted on putting his suits and silk ties in the washing machine.

Africa

The team obtained interesting work in Africa. In Morocco, La Fleche and Massicotte advised on the preparation and drafting of an electricity code for the country, which led to a further assignment to prepare national legislation dealing with the difficult problem of concessions. In Botswana, they used the experience the firm had gained with the two phases of the privatization of Air Canada to help International Finance Corporation (IFC) privatize Air Botswana, a well-run, profitable airline. This assignment was important because it proved to be the first time that a Canadian law firm would handle a substantive mandate for IFC, the private sector arm of the World Bank, which had until then been the private preserve of a handful of New York and London firms. Equally important, the mandate enabled La Fleche, as part of his personal due diligence, to experience first-hand the luxury of Botswana's rich safari heritage.

Chad proved to be a source of important work and some extraordinary personal experiences for the lawyers involved. In 1996, the firm won a competitive bid to represent Chad in what is the largest-ever infrastructure project in Africa and one of the largest in the world – the 1,200-kilometre Chad-Cameroon oil pipeline, sponsored by a consortium headed by Exxon. The idea to bid for the $US3.7-billion project had come from Jim Arnett in the Washington office, but both the Calgary and Toronto offices turned him down. Undaunted, Arnett came to La Fleche with only ten days to go before the deadline, and they put together the winning bid. The mandate required the winner to assist Chad in the negotiation of all agreements for the pipeline, upstream oilfields, and downstream off-take facilities, as well as the preparation or review of several pieces of legislation, including a law designed to ensure that most of Chad's take from the project – estimated at $US2 billion in royalties, dividends, and taxes over the first twenty-five years – would be invested directly by the state to improve the life of its citizens. The law also provided for international monitoring of Chad's contractual undertakings, a world's first.

Upon winning the bid, La Fleche and Massicotte proceeded to N'Djamena, Chad's dusty frontier-like capital, which had just awoken from a lengthy civil war to begin negotiations on the contract between the firm and Chad. However, on their arrival, they learned that for reasons beyond anyone's control, no one could meet with them for a week. There were no flights out, and there was nothing to do but stay at their indifferent hotel, close to the pool, and twiddle their thumbs. That was how La Fleche passed his fortieth birthday. They had a celebratory dinner in one of the few restaurants outside the hotel but could not stay late because the protocol for everyone who was non-suicidal was that when the French légionnaires left the restaurant, all sane inhabitants of the capital took the opportunity to follow their truck. This made passage through the various warlord checkpoints easier and served as a deterrent to robbers.

Later on that same trip, both La Fleche and Massicotte were attacked, with the intent to rob, in the middle of the day on the busiest street of the capital. They had been walking on Charles De Gaulle Boulevard (all the former French colonies had one) and were approached by five men, two of whom tried to engage them in conversation ("Are you French?" "No, Canadian." "Ah, I have a sister who lives in Canada." And so forth), while the other three followed. Those behind tried to grab Massicotte's wallet, which he had been careful not to leave in his back pocket, and all five of them began to beat the two Canadians, trying to get their wallets and watches. They were fighting the robbers off and calling for help when they finally heard a police whistle and a policeman came to the middle of the street. He asked the obvious question whether anything was wrong but did not approach them any closer. It was clear that he was not ready to intervene. Just then, a car driven by an Indian, accompanied by his wife and child, stopped. He did not get out of the car but opened the back door, and the two lawyers literally dove headfirst into the car and escaped.

Another day, acting out of sheer boredom, they decided to ask their driver to take them into the Sahara. After an hour, both asked the driver to stop for a bio-break. The car stopped, and they went into the desert, about fifty metres from the road, to do their best to help solve the local drought problem. Upon their return to the car, having carefully shepherded a crucial piece of knowledge until after the fact, the driver warned them never to do that again because the area along that route had not been de-mined.

Cultural differences often lead to misunderstandings and negative results, but on occasion, it can work the other way. Massicotte was by himself in Yaoundé, Cameroon, in the early stages of negotiations between Chad and the petroleum consortium, dealing with the minority interest that would accrue to Chad. The corporate law statute of the day dated from the French colonial period and contained no provisions that would adequately protect minority shareholders. He was consulting regularly with La Fleche and apart from the advantage that flowed from the time zone differences, was able to get regular support from him. The working conditions were very difficult, including the fierce heat and lack of general comforts, and they were complicated by the fact that the clients were almost completely ignorant of many of the business and legal issues involved in such a huge project. This led to them having a dozen representatives or more at each meeting, mainly to get on-the-job training, not unlike the situation he and La Fleche had encountered earlier in India.

Massicotte was in the process of trying to negotiate with the consortium to obtain certain protective clauses in favour of his clients, and the consortium was decidedly cool to these. He finally invoked the modern concept known as the "oppression remedy," which is quite common in more recent corporate statutes. Whether there were translation problems or simply because the clients had no idea what this meant, following the meeting, the Chad delegation all shook his hand warmly and said that he was the first white man they had ever heard tell other white men that they were oppressing blacks!

They eventually got what they wanted. After more than five years of continuous and sustained involvement and numerous two-week-long negotiating sessions on three continents, including Houston and Atlanta during the summer and Yaoundé in the rainy season, the mandate finally reached financial closure during the summer of 2001 under the leadership of Martin Scheim, who spent the better part of those five years working on the pipeline.

In the Ivory Coast, Massicotte helped with the development of an agency designed to promote investment in the electricity sector of this emerging economy. In Rwanda, led by Lalonde, we advised the government in connection with construction procurement matters arising from a World Bank finance project. During 1997 and 1998, Jean Carrier and Viateur Chénard assisted Guinea in connection with the study and harmonization of its legislation and regulations pertaining to the mining industry, the environment, and foreign investments in order to promote and attract more foreign investments in these sectors. Although La Fleche was the team leader for this World Bank mandate, his earlier experience with that country, and particularly its rubbish-strewn and vulture-infested capital, convinced him that he should be particularly generous to younger lawyers and allow them to expand their personal horizons by experiencing first-hand that country's delights. Massicotte had much the same view, having narrowly escaped robbery and serious injury on his last day in the country. He was in the car arranged to take him to the airport and was taking video footage of the main mosque when someone grabbed the video camera, the strap of which was around his neck. A struggle ensued, and punches were exchanged. The situation was resolved only by the driver speeding up despite the risk posed to Massicotte's neck had the robber been able to hold onto the camera. Luckily, he was not injured. Chénard became similarly enlightened shortly after his second trip, and Carrier was left ably to carry on with the file. Carrier's fortitude was rewarded. In 1998, he earned enough points on Air France to become one of its ten best Canadian customers and was feted accordingly by a grateful airline at the Montreal Ritz Carleton.

La Fleche had first visited Guinea in 1987 at the request of the World Bank, not long after the fall of Sékou Touré, one of Africa's most destructive, albeit charismatic, despots, who had ruled since independence. After disembarking and manoeuvring around the wreckage of a Soviet-built Il-lyushin that had crashed some time previously next to the smallish airport terminal, La Fleche stopped to survey the mayhem at the customs and passport inspection area. At that stage, he was accosted by a sympathetic police lieutenant who offered to simplify his life by putting himself and his police car at La Fleche's disposal for the duration of his stay. After a little quiet bargaining, the Canadian agreed and escorted by his new-found friend, walked out of the airport without addressing such minor details as customs and immigration. Conakry, the capital, was a mess with thousands of refugees squatting in roofless buildings. There was little electrical power, no television, and practically no phones. The lieutenant's assistance was invaluable in securing the numerous appointments required to give the trip any semblance of a business purpose. Each night, La Fleche would give him envelopes containing his credentials and requests for meetings. By mid-morning the next day, they would meet again to draw up La Fleche's schedule based on answers from the various ministries and state-owned enterprises. After ten days of proceeding in this romantic fashion, La Fleche came to the realization that the country would offer little immediate opportunity and returned to Canada. To his surprise, the trip did bear fruit, albeit ten years later, when the firm was invited by Guinea to bid on the job handled by Carrier and Chénard.

Europe

In Bosnia and Herzegovina, Massicotte helped prepare a national law dealing with concessions, and elsewhere in the Balkans, La Fleche and Massicotte are providing assistance on a major restructuring of the region's electricity sector and the eventual creation of a regional transmission network extending from Slovenia and Albania in the west all the way to Moldova and Romania in the east. Robert Couzin provided advice to the International Monetary Fund with respect to revision of the Estonian tax code.

America

In the Americas, beginning in 1997, the team provided advice to the governments of six Central American countries with respect to the regional interconnection of electricity transmission facilities and the preparation of independent electricity pilot projects. The team also assisted the government of Bolivia in 1995 with the privatization of state-owned mines. The call for tenders for the first mine to be privatized was an unmitigated failure as not a single tender was received. This might have had something to do with the fierce resistance put up by the miners and their unions to the privatization plans. In addition to pitched battles with police in the streets of La Paz, the unions' tactics included intimidating due diligence teams at the entrance of the mine; they would warn them that they would have no difficulty descending underground, but their return to the surface could not be guaranteed. Predictably, no due diligence was carried by prospective bidders below ground.

WMC Limited of Australia, the world's third-largest nickel producer, engaged the firm from 1994 to 1998, after a worldwide competitive bid, to provide advice in connection with the development of a $US700-million greenfield nickel and cobalt mine in Cuba, to be financed on a limited recourse basis. WMC was a client of Bill Braithwaite in Toronto, and when he heard of the opportunity, he suggested to La Fleche that he contact WMC in Melbourne and Toronto to see whether the firm could join the bidding process. A team was struck, written submissions were made, and after some nail-biting, we were declared the winner.

La Fleche travelled to Cuba more than forty times and spent, in the aggregate, over a year in Havana, mostly on the executive floor of Hotel Nacional de Cuba. During the course of the adventure, he entertained virtually every Cuban minister, including a small dinner for twelve with Fidel Castro. He had more than his share of midnight classical piano recitals given through clouds of cigar smoke by proteges of Marco Portal, Cuba's then minister of Basic Industries. He received numerous letters from Cuban-American organizations insisting that he desist from further involvement in Cuba, and after adoption of the US Helms-Burton legislation, he received similarly helpful letters from the Canadian government, advising him of the penalties under Canadian law for succumbing to US pressure and ceasing to do business with Cuba. More than a dozen of the firm's people, including secretaries, flew to Cuba to work on the file, often stopping in Cancun on the way down for a quick lunch and dip in the sea. The file had a number of firsts for Cuba: it was the largest foreign direct investment (FDI) project, a special tax regime, redrafted by La Fleche, special GAAP (generally accepted accounting principles), and special mining concessions. In fact, almost everything about the entire transaction was special. At one stage, in 1996, his wife, Carolina, a former Stikeman Elliott associate, arrived in Cuba on the executive jet with the chief executive officer of WMC. Upon her arrival, Cuban protocol girls passed flowers and other tokens on her. There was considerable consternation when the various ministers assembled at the airport learned that she was the wife of the dreaded WMC lawyer and not of the CEO, but Carolina, who is half Venezuelan and spoke fluent Spanish, carried off the whole affair, and the flowers, with great aplomb. We helped acquire and dispose of a number of Quebec mining properties for the same client.

Following a recommendation from WMC, Unilever engaged La Fleche from 1996 to 1998 to help with the arrangements for a manufacturing joint venture in Cuba. Since 2000, La Fleche and Josée Gravel have been advising GMAT

Inc. in the construction of a railway in the Mexican state of Guanajuanto. The project had been drifting for six years until that state's former governor, Vincente Fox, an ardent supporter of the project, became the first non-PRI president of Mexico in over seventy-one years. Earlier, in 1987, La Fleche was working in Mexico for Jorge Larrea, one of the wealthiest men in the country, one of whose mining companies had a problem with the Canadian engineering firm SNC-Lavalin. He had been there for two weeks trying to help find a solution to the problem, and one day, just following the massive earthquake, Larrea summoned him to a meeting and sent his car and driver for the purpose. They were late for the meeting due to the traffic in Mexico City, which was its usual impenetrable mass of intransigent vehicles. The driver, not short of initiative if not detailed knowledge of the motor vehicle code, decided that for the last two kilometres, he would drive on the sidewalk, scattering pedestrians and street vendors in the process of not displeasing his boss.

Among the projects completed was one in Guyana, where Barnett and Johnson provided a report to the government on law reform, particularly relating to the law of secured transactions and the consolidation of commercial laws. Johnson also led an orientation mission to Belize to analyse the existing land tenure system in preparation for an agricultural rehabilitation loan by the International Development Bank.

Canada

The team also obtained work at home in Canada. There was some interesting walk-on business that came their way, not the least of which was *fonorola* Inc. The commencement of our relationship was unusual. In 1987, a young man by the name of Nelson Lifshitz landed at the reception of the Montreal office and asked to meet with Jacques Courtois, of whom he had read in the papers as a prominent lawyer and president of the Montreal Canadiens. Under his arm, he had a business plan for an alternate long distance telecommunications company to compete with Bell Canada in the US-Canada transborder market. Courtois agreed to meet with him and after fifteen minutes, called La Fleche to have him take a look at the matter. There was some initial shock that anyone would want to take on Bell Canada, which La Fleche, probably not unlike most people, believed had a monopoly that was all but de jure in the field. In fact, there was no longer such a monopoly provided one could work through and around a series of decisions issued by the CRTC. La Fleche quietly proceeded to work for free for about eighteen months to see if the concept could be refined. Lifshitz and La Fleche eventually located a small capital venture boutique, Boyd, Peeters & Molson (BPM), that was willing to work on the financing.

When BPM had entered the picture, they wanted the file transferred to Ogilvy Renault, with whom they had a relationship. Lifshitz objected and insisted that La Fleche remain in place. The only lawyer BPM knew at the firm was Sonny Gordon, so they said he would have to be involved. That was not a problem since La Fleche worked regularly with him. BPM had an unusual relationship with Rothschilds in London. They seemed able to get funding on the strength of their word, and paperwork could always wait. By the end of 1988, *fonorola* was incorporated with a paid-up capital of $10,000, a supplier credit of $5 million from Northern Telecom (now Nortel), a Bell Canada affiliate at the time, and a $5-million Rothschilds revolving subordinated note facility cobbled together by La Fleche with the sometimes bewildering tax advice of Elinore Richardson. After a difficult gestation period, including the creation of a joint venture with Canadian National Railway to build and operate a fibre-optic telecommunications network along CN's rights-of-way in Canada and the United States, the company went public in 1993 in an issue valued at $30 million. Five years later, it was taken over by Sprint Canada for more than $1.8 billion. The takeover was contested, and as a result, the offering price ended up higher than would otherwise have been the case.[32] Gordon and La Fleche were members of the board at the time of the takeover.

Mitsui Corporation of Japan used the firm in connection with its joint venture to manufacture helicopters north of Montreal, as did Jefferson Smurfit Corporation when it concluded a paper making joint venture with Tembec in Quebec. We helped Johnson & Johnson Inc. to reorganize certain of its manufacturing operations in Canada and lberma of Germany to acquire its North American distribution network. Kobe Steel, Ltd. and Marubeni Corporation participated in the Alouette joint venture to build and operate a 215,000-ton aluminum plant in Quebec. This turned out to be a six-party joint venture to build a smelter in Sept-Îsles, a mandate obtained by Jim Robb through his many Japanese contacts. Project "Alouette" was a very complicated arrangement, and our client's financing was the largest US-dollar limited recourse loan ever governed by Quebec law. The banking syndicate, composed exclusively of Japanese and US banks, had wanted to follow accepted practice and have the loan governed by New York law. La Fleche convinced them otherwise. The importance and complexity of the project came home to La Fleche only when he visited Freshfields (which had represented part of the banking syndicate) in Paris in 1994 to find the project featured prominently in their capital project brochures as a prime example of their ability to push the envelope in such arrangements.

The Great Lakes Hydro Income Fund was a mandate that arose following the Great Ice Storm of 1998. Nexfor Inc. had been approached by Hydro-Québec immediately after the storm to see whether it might be prepared to joint venture with it to build a high voltage transmission line over Nexfor property in the Outaouais region, linking Hydro-Québec with Hydro Ontario. The ostensible purpose was to strengthen the transmission system after the ice storm. Nexfor organized a "beauty contest," and despite some reluctance on Nexfor's part, the firm, thanks to Marc Laurin and Pierrette Sinclair, was invited to participate and explain how we would structure the proposed venture. While preparing for the presentation, La Fleche learned that Nexfor had three generating facilities of some 248 MW on the Lievre River, interconnected with each other as well as with Hydro-Québec's grid, and remarkably, it owned rather than leased most of the water rights used to produce electricity. Even more remarkably, it owned high voltage transmission lines over the Ottawa River linking its network with that of Hydro Ontario.

In La Fleche's view, Nexfor, with a little house cleaning, could sell power to Ontario and the lucrative Northeastern US market without the necessity of having to go through Hydro-Québec, something it would have refused to do in any event. Moreover, Quebec had adopted new legislation *(la loi sur la régie de l'énergie)* that appeared to clarify the rights of private electricity systems. At the beauty contest, held in February 1998 at Masson, Quebec, accompanied by Pierrette Sinclair and Viateur Chénard, La Fleche barely addressed the joint venture in his low-tech "transparency" presentation – the other firms had used higher-tech PowerPoint – but instead suggested that Nexfor spin off its power system and do an IPO. The system was carried in its books of account at about $26 million, and the replacement cost of 248 MW was about $350 million. The idea for the presentation had come in large part from a mandate in Laos the previous year for the ADB, when La Fleche had spent six months trying to find the best way to develop the not inconsiderable hydro power resources of that country and to transmit power from Laos to Thailand, Vietnam, and China. La Fleche was the project leader and was fortunate to be assisted by several extraordinary individuals from Hydro-Québec, all much senior to him in age and experience, all helping to educate him on the intricacies of power generation and transmission.

Notwithstanding the obvious merits – to La Fleche at least – in unbundling Nexfor's power assets, his presentation was deemed unresponsive to the joint venture proposal, and the firm did not win the beauty contest. Upon hearing the news, a rather dispirited La Fleche departed for India to work on the Tamil Nadu mandate. On his return in April, he was greeted with a call from Nexfor, saying that it was looking to do a spinoff and that although he knew nothing, he had shown imagination and enthusiasm, and the company wanted him to lead a team from the firm. The start was rocky. The file was complex, and La Fleche could only assure Nexfor, and especially Brascan, its very demanding shareholder, that the file would progress in a careful and deliberate manner. Moreover, Quebec's tightly knit electricity Bar did not agree with his interpretation of the new legislation and was not afraid to so advise Nexfor and Brascan at every opportunity. They argued that despite what was said or not said in the legislation, the law did not conform with Hydro-Québec's wishes and therefore, Quebec government policy. The difficulties were overcome after about four months, the necessary momentum was generated, and the first of two public issues was closed in October 1999. Robert Hogan devised a novel tax structure that was possible only with the use of two trusts governed by Quebec law, the use of which increased the proceeds paid to Nexfor by more than $15 million. The structure has been replicated across Canada many times since then. Nexfor raised in excess of $265 million, and we had more than forty lawyers working on the file. Michèle Baillargeon[33] and Roger Forget[34] were monopolized for more than a year and ended up generating the most title work of any file handled by the Montreal office.

Work continues on all fronts – at home and abroad – to attract and complete mandates in all of the foreign offices by and for the road warriors, who have contributed so much to the vitality and reputation of the firm "brand." They have been typical of the combination of drive, talent, and ambition that has brought the firm to the forefront of legal practice and have provided a flavour to Stikeman Elliott that cannot be matched by any other Canadian law firm.

CHAPTER 6

Vancouver

Given the firm's national and global ambition, the success of the Hong Kong office, and the flow of people and investment from Hong Kong to Canada in the mid to late 1980s, particularly into Vancouver, a Vancouver office became more and more of a requirement. Just as the Toronto office had been opened some fifteen years earlier, in part to capture the investment flow from London and support the new London office, it seemed logical to have a Vancouver office to capture the investment flow from Hong Kong and provide similar backup to the new Hong Kong office. In the mid-1980s, Frank Sixt, Ralph Lutes, and Ching-wo Ng were running the Hong Kong operation, and in November 1987, they submitted a memorandum to the executive committee stating that from their perspective, a presence in Vancouver was essential not only to capture this influx of business into Vancouver, but also to strategically expand the Stikeman Elliott network.

With this strong recommendation in hand, the executive committee considered the merits of committing significant resources, both financial and professional, to establishing a Vancouver office. While it is likely that a decision to move forward with the opening of the Vancouver office would have been made by the executive committee in the usual course, given the logical and strategic bases articulated by Messrs Sixt, Lutes, and Ng, the truth is that the Vancouver office was established largely through circumstance, luck, and a healthy measure of Heward Stikeman's spontaneity. In fact, the Vancouver office came into existence by virtue of Li Ka-shing, along with several of his business colleagues, winning the international tender for the development of the Expo Lands in Vancouver, now known as Concord Pacific Place. The Expo Lands project was a massive real estate development play that was put together by Frank Sixt in Hong Kong. It is one of the largest transactions the firm has done for the Li family, and the Stikeman Elliott team assembled to negotiate and close this deal was drawn from Hong Kong (Sixt, Lutes) and Toronto (Wayne Shaw, Milton Hess, John Dow, Ron Durand). In short, the project entailed acquiring and then undertaking the complete transformation of a highly industrialized (and partially contaminated) 250-acre site located in the heart of downtown Vancouver, within the old Yaletown District, into a comprehensive and highly integrated planned residential neighbourhood for upwards of 15,000 people. It was in 1988, during the long hours of preparing the Li family response to the British Columbia government's request for proposals that Stikeman, in one of his spontaneous bursts of enthusiasm, told Li that if his bid to acquire the Expo Lands was successful, Stikeman Elliott would open an office in Vancouver. The Li family won, and Stikeman made good on his promise.

One problem with opening a Vancouver office was that British Columbia's legislative framework together with the BC Law Society rules discouraged (some would say prohibited) interprovincial law firms. These laws and rules were challenged in 1984 by a proposed merger of the Toronto firm of McCarthy & McCarthy and the Vancouver firm of Shrum Liddle & Hebenton. When the McCarthy/Shrum merger was announced, the Law Society of British Columbia set up the McKinnon Committee to consider the issue and solicit the views of the profession. In May 1985, the British Columbia benchers debated and rejected a motion that endorsed the formation of interprovincial law firms, and that December, the British Columbia government amended the BC *Barristers and Solicitors Act* to prohibit interjurisdictional partnerships in which not all of the partners of the merging firms were members of the British Columbia Bar.

Into the regulatory and political fray entered Heward Stikeman. He got on top of the situation with his usual enthusiasm. Fuelled by his promise to Li Ka-shing to open an office in Vancouver and by his belief that these protectionist laws and rules were simply illogical, he energized the firm's effort to press ahead against the tide to establish a Vancouver office. After discussions with Heward and others within the firm, Ching-wo Ng wrote to British Columbia Premier Bill Vander Zalm in December 1987, outlining the benefits to British Columbia of opening its doors to national and international firms, including Stikeman Elliott. Ng had met with the premier during a state visit to Hong Kong earlier in 1987. In his letter, Ng stated that two of the firm's senior partners, Heward Stikeman and Marc Lalonde, would welcome the opportunity to discuss in more detail the firm's interest in opening an office in Vancouver.

In January 1988, Stikeman and Marc Lalonde met with Vander Zalm to discuss the merits of interprovincial firms and the possibility of Stikeman Elliott opening an office in Vancouver. Following that meeting, at Vander Zalm's suggestion, Stikeman returned in March to meet with the British Columbia Attorney General Brian Smith. He reported that he had found Smith receptive to multi-jurisdictional firms within British Columbia. Apparently, Smith indicated to Stikeman that although he was originally opposed to the idea, he had concluded that events had overtaken the prohibiting British Columbia legislation such that the safeguards built into the legislation were no longer necessary and that to continue such a restrictive approach to professional associations would be anti-competitive and leave British Columbia somewhat isolated.

In the course of his follow-up letter to Smith dated March 29, 1988, Stikeman provided him with some interesting insights into the firm, explaining that

Stikeman Elliott was one of the few actual working examples of a Canadian multi-jurisdictional and multinational law firm, and that whatever concerns Smith might have had could be alleviated based on the firm's experience. He also wanted to demonstrate the benefits to the province were the firm to open a BC office. He described the birth of the firm in Montreal in 1952 and its orientation toward an international clientele, and in order to service such clientele, the need to expand out of Quebec – to London, Toronto, and later, to Hong Kong. Because of the strong synergistic results from London and Hong Kong, the firm attracted clients from Asia, Western Canada, and the United States.

Accordingly, we now realize that it is in the interest of our clients and the wish of many of them that we open somewhere in Western Canada, preferably British Columbia, although Alberta should not be ruled out. I personally believe that Vancouver is the logical place for us to open and that we would attract a great deal of business to the Province, which we would share not only with other law firms in BC, but the whole financial community.

On this particular point, as I think I told you, our experience has been that wherever we have opened a branch office, we have developed business locally from which that branch office has grown. We have also generated a lot of what we call "throw off" business, which we pass on to other law firms. The business which we generate, however, is not only legal but new investment and commercial activity. We have become a welcome addition to the various economic communities in which we now practise. I might mention, however, that in some of these jurisdictions, our reception at the beginning was not warm since the local bars were not happy at the thought that we might come onto their turf and extract business for the benefit of our eastern offices. Soon, however, the local bars everywhere we practise became our most ardent supporters! I am sure that the same will turn out to be true in BC.

When I am sitting in our Hong Kong office seeking to advise Asian clients where to invest or commence business operations in Canada, I am more inclined to send them to a jurisdiction in which we have an office than otherwise. It is my earnest hope that I will soon be in a position to direct such business to BC.

As an illustration of our growing connection with the West Coast, you might be interested to know that we have, over the past few years, already generated business with BC and Alberta law firms, which have resulted in many hundreds of thousands of dollars of fees being paid to them. Our Pacific Rim interest is not limited to Hong Kong but currently embraces the People's Republic of China, Manila, Bangkok, and Tokyo. We anticipate that with a West Coast base, this business can be greatly enlarged for the benefit of everyone.

He then went on to discuss the position taken by the Western provinces with respect to multi-jurisdictional firms and tried to suggest that BC would suffer only were it to remain out of the mainstream of what was likely to be the outcome of the challenge in Alberta to its own protectionist rules.

As you are aware, the decision of the Supreme Court in what is known as "the Black case" will probably be rendered fairly soon. Should this decision go against the efforts of the Alberta Bar and permit multi-jurisdictional law firms in Alberta, and should your present legislation remain on the books, there could be a natural disposition on the part of many multi-jurisdictional firms to open in Alberta rather than BC. I would regard this as unfortunate in our particular case since I believe that BC is the logical venue for the kind of activity we wish to develop. However, as a matter of practicality, it would be possible to do much the same thing from an Alberta branch. Nevertheless, because of my long association with BC, my many professional friendships in Vancouver, and also my admiration for your government's attitude to free enterprise and to Pacific Rim development, I would much prefer to have an opportunity of opening a branch of Stikeman, Elliott in BC. I believe we can do more for your province and for our clients from such a branch than we can from an office anywhere else.

• • •

In a word, my partners believe that the public interest of BC and the BC Bar is best helped by letting us serve our clients' interests in BC and not somewhere else.

I do not think you should concern yourself about the difficulties of regulating lawyers who come into the province and are properly called there. There are many examples of how this can be done very effectively. I need only mention the method used in Ontario and those provisions, which I understand the BC Law Society has already drafted in case they should be required in future.

He closed by noting that he had been able to find twenty Ontario or Quebec law firms with at least two offices within Canada and elsewhere and more than forty US and twenty UK firms with such multi-jurisdictional connections. He noted that if they could get suitable changes to the legislation, the province and the firm would have a most exciting future together and looked forward to the firm being solid "legal" citizens of BC in every respect. The letter represents Stikeman at his best – audacious, confident, and bold – the ultimate firm salesman. Upon reading his letter, the only question one might feel compelled to ask is how British Columbia had managed to survive so long without a Stikeman Elliott office!

In September 1988, the British Columbia Supreme Court's decision on the constitutional challenge to the December 1985 amendments to the BC *Barristers and Solicitors Act* (known as the *Martin* case) held that the legislation was contrary to the Canadian *Bill of Rights* and was null and void. This result was similar to the earlier *Black* case in Alberta covering more or less the same issue. On September 9, Stikeman wrote to Premier Vander Zalm and Attorney General Brian Smith, advising each of them that Stikeman Elliott intended to open a small office in Vancouver, staffed by lawyers admitted to the British Columbia Bar, in the immediate future.

It was clear that one way or the other, the British Columbia regulatory maze was now not going to be a serious impediment to opening a Vancouver office. At the joint partnership meeting of May 7, 1988, the executive committee was given the authority to pursue the opening of such an office. Stikeman wrote to George Magnus of the Li Group on May 12, one day after the Expo Land purchase closing, to confirm that the firm would be opening a Vancouver office, as he had promised to Li earlier in 1988.

Originally, the firm intended to open the Vancouver office with Daniel McIntyre, a British Columbia lawyer then practising in Hong Kong. The discussions with McIntyre were explorative, and after a short period of time, the firm decided to pursue other possibilities. Ultimately, Brian Hansen, by then having Canadian, Hong Kong, and London experience, moved from London to Vancouver in July 1988 to open the Vancouver office once the British Columbia regulations permitted. Prior to Hansen's relocation to Vancouver, he had in fact already resigned his position as a partner in Stikeman Elliott, with immediate plans to move to Australia to join Freehill Hollingdale & Page. Although Hansen's resignation was in hand, Elliott called him in London and asked him to attend what would have been his last partners' meeting in Toronto that spring. Hansen left for Toronto, while his wife, Jen, stayed in London to deal with the move. When Hansen arrived at the partners' meeting, he was met by Stikeman, who insisted in his normal fashion that Hansen was going to Vancouver, not Sydney. When Hansen responded that he was going "further west than that," to Sydney, Stikeman said that if he wanted to live by the water, then he should at least do it with people he knew. Thus persuaded, he rang Jen from Toronto and told her that she had five minutes to make up her mind where they were going – Sydney or Vancouver. As the story goes, she responded within the deadline by stating that "she would do anything to stop her boys from growing up as Australian males." And so, the Hansens were Vancouver-bound. There is a certain irony in this as the Hansens ended up in Sydney after all – to open the firm's new office there in the mid 1990s.

When Hansen arrived in Vancouver in July 1988, the firm had no office, no employees, but one very, very large real estate mandate to contend with along with scores of Vancouver-based clients who had heard that Stikeman Elliott was coming to Vancouver. Interestingly, many of these clients had historical connections with the firm in either Toronto or Montreal since our lawyers in those offices had introduced these clients to Vancouver-based lawyers. With the firm's plans to open an office in Vancouver, many of these clients expressed loyalty to the firm by indicating their intentions to shift their legal work to our Vancouver lawyers once the office was opened.

Initially, Hansen operated out of the offices of Concord Pacific Developments Ltd., which was the Canadian operating entity of the Li family established specifically to advance the development of the Expo Lands. Stanley Kwok, the well-known Vancouver architect with strong connections to Hong Kong, was appointed by Li Ka-shing to oversee all aspects of the project. He was joined by Jon Markoulis and W.Y. Fung, both of whom had been involved in other Li family businesses in the United States and Hong Kong. At this time, the British Columbia Law Society rules that made it impossible for national law firms to open in British Columbia still remained in effect. The firm took the view and calculated risk that these rules were unconstitutional as a restriction on the ability to trade. The executive committee of the firm was well aware of the *Black* case in Alberta, which had been lost in the lower courts but was on its way to the Supreme Court of Canada. The firm decided not to launch its own challenge against the British Columbia Law

Society in part because the challenge involving McCarthy Tétrault was well advanced, and the costs of any such litigation could, therefore, be avoided. Several years later, the Supreme Court of Canada decided that such Law Society rules and the related provincial legislation were unconstitutional, and these restrictive measures were struck down.

During this interregnum, the Vancouver office operated without any problem although the spectre of official action by the Law Society always loomed in the background. The Law Society, instead, attempted to exert an impact on our Vancouver operations by refusing to allow Hansen to write the Law Society transfer exams, which was the most expeditious means by which Hansen could become a member of the British Columbia Bar. Somewhere in his possession, Hansen still has a letter from the British Columbia Law Society that says, more or less, that he was less qualified to write the transfer exams than a lawyer in Newfoundland who does one will and one incorporation per year. In pursuance of this absurd position, Hansen was required to undertake a full year of articles and was formally articled to John Paton, who is mentioned below as among the first six lawyers to constitute the Vancouver office. The official opening of the office, located on one-half of the sixth floor of 1090 West Pender Street, one floor below the Concord Pacific offices, was on October 3, 1988.

The first hire in Vancouver was Nicholas Paczkowski, who was then a vice-president with the British Columbia Enterprise Corporation (BCEC), the Crown corporation charged with the responsibility of selling the Expo Lands. In fact, Paczkowski had been front and centre, along with Kevin Murphy and Bruce Woolley, as part of the province's team negotiating the Expo Lands sale. In the years that ensued, it was not uncommon for Paczkowski to be seen to discretely step back from important negotiations among the Province of British Columbia, the City of Vancouver, and Concord Pacific, which involved documentation or commitments that he had negotiated on behalf of the province in his capacity as vice-president of BCEC. Following Paczkowski's hire, a group of Vancouver lawyers was hired, headed up by Eugene Kwan,[1] who has since left the firm to work in the Li family enterprise of Hutchison Telecommunications. Included in this group was John Paton,[2] who had worked with Kwan for many years at a small local firm called Macdonald, Kwan & Lewis. Maureen St Cyr also joined us with Kwan and Paton, but she did not stay with the firm for very long. Kwan added to the office what he is well known for throughout the firm: his endless contacts in Vancouver and his never-ending positive attitude to life. Paton was, and remains, one of the crucial elements in the Vancouver office, particularly during the formative years. Of particular value is his ability to practise at a consistently high level across a very broad spectrum of areas, notably in the commercial, real estate, and banking field. His services were invaluable in the early years prior to assuming a much more senior role in the banking and commercial practice in the office.

In September 1988, before the Vancouver office officially opened, Hansen met with Ross MacDonald,[3] who was then practising real estate and securities law with Clark, Wilson, a local Vancouver law firm. Earlier that summer, during the negotiations and closing of the Expo Lands transaction, MacDonald met with Bruce Woolley (who was then general counsel to BCEC, and who would later practise with our Vancouver office for the better part of ten years), and the subject of Stikeman Elliott arose in the course of general conversation. Woolley was very impressed with the firm's representatives during the Expo Lands deal, particularly with Wayne Shaw of the Toronto office. At Woolley's suggestion, MacDonald wrote to Hansen to enquire about opportunities to work on the Expo project. Hansen was persuaded, and MacDonald signed on as the sixth lawyer in the Vancouver office. He remains primarily responsible for the Concord Pacific Place project.

After the initial six lawyers, a series of hires followed that proved to be extremely important in the development of the office. David Gillanders[4] moved to Stikeman's from Lawson Lundell, where he was one of the senior real estate practitioners in Vancouver, with a very strong practice involving commercial leasing and developing shopping centres. Shortly after that, Jonathan Drance,[5] also from Lawson Lundell, joined the firm as a partner. Drance had not been with the firm for very long when he began to be retained on substantial work from underwriting firms like RBC Dominion Securities. He is an excellent securities and M&A practitioner, and with his far-ranging intellect, he can practise in many other commercial areas of the law. Outside his mainstream legal practice, Drance has an extremely detailed knowledge of, and interest in, US politics, and for the unwary person who held loosely formulated views on politics, a typically brief debate with Drance on matters political was a highlight of the Friday evening drinks in the boardroom.

In addition to Gillanders and Drance, a number of outstanding younger lawyers were hired by the Vancouver office, which by early 1989, had attracted the attention and mystique of the local Bar. Many resumés, most from top-notch candidates in Vancouver and beyond, were received each week, all expressing an interest in becoming part of this start-up operation that was fast developing a reputation for attracting sophisticated and high-profile mandates. During the early part of 1989, the firm hired Richard Fyfe, who is now a senior solicitor with the Ministry of the Attorney General, and Dallas Brodie, who is now producing the Rafe Mair radio talk show for CKNW. At the same time, it hired Deborah Fahy, who later became a partner of the firm and is now associated with the Vancouver office as a consultant when her real job of being a mother of five children permits the time. Alan Pinkney, an associate who also was admitted as a partner and who moved from Vancouver to Calgary, has since left the firm to work in business. Greg Plater, now a partner in the Calgary office, joined the Vancouver office after he completed his articles with McCarthy Tétrault. Shortly after that, Richard Jackson,[6] who is now a partner in the firm, was hired. Jackson has assumed day-to-day responsibility, along with MacDonald, as lead counsel to the CPGI group of companies and the Concord Pacific Place project. David Farrell[7] articled in the Vancouver office, spent some time in Budapest, returned to Vancouver, and then spent over a year in our London office. He again returned to the Vancouver office and is now working with a venture capital firm based in Vancouver. The list of outstanding early hires goes on and on.

Michael Allen and David Weekes transferred out to Vancouver from the Toronto office. Allen arrived in Vancouver in January 1989 and remained for ten years before departing to join Russell & DuMoulin (now Fasken Martineau DuMoulin) for two and a half years, but in October 2001, he rejoined the firm. He handled the expansion and modernization of the Celgar Pulp mill in Castlegar, BC, where the firm acted for Stone Consolidated on the financing aspects as well as the joint venture and environmental issues inherent in the transactions. He became expert in a series of financings for Methanex and coordinated the legal aspects of the opening of ARCO's operations in British Columbia. Allen is the kind of lawyer who attracts big deals, and the deals follow him. While at Faskens, he managed the largest-ever private financing in Canada, acting for the Toronto-Dominion-led syndicate, which loaned Telus $7.7 billion to buy ClearNet, a file that followed him upon his return to the firm. He also did the financing of the Julietta gold mine in Russia for Bema Gold, which won international recognition as a result of the difficulties of closing a private financing in Russia. Weekes is a partner with the firm, and his travels have taken him from Toronto to Vancouver, back to Toronto, and now to Calgary.

In 1995, Tookie Angus and Hein Poulus[8] joined the Vancouver office as partners. Angus and Poulus were partners with Smith Lyons in Vancouver and were looking for a change. Angus is perhaps the best-known mining lawyer in Vancouver and among the top mining lawyers in Canada. His robust personality added a dimension to the Vancouver office, and his penchant for fine wines and good restaurants set the high-water mark on partners' expense allowances. Angus left the firm in early 2001. Poulus came across to the Vancouver office as its first litigation counsel, and he has since built a very credible litigation group. Poulus's background is typically unconventional, not unlike many others at the firm. Having worked with John McAlpine for many years, he took a hiatus from law to assume duties as the general manager for the Denver Broncos. In fact, he has the distinction of signing John Elway to his first NFL contract.

In the very early days of the Vancouver office, a number of excellent students were hired, some of whom have "grown up" through the ranks and are now partners with the firm, having completed a professional life cycle. Most of the hiring for the Vancouver office was initially done by Hansen and MacDonald, both of whom will frankly admit to a less than scientific approach to recruiting and hiring. What they looked for were recruits who were smart enough to achieve excellent marks from a "good" law school and to develop an interesting life away from school, were likeable enough during the interview, and most importantly, were prepared to work very hard and jump headfirst into the deep water. They also had to be seen very subjectively by both Hansen and MacDonald as individuals who would fit into what was evolving into a very eclectic but harmonious group of personalities. Notable among these student hires are Clifford Ng[9] and John Anderson,[10] both of whom are now partners in the firm, with Ng heading up the Hong Kong office. Ng was the very first student hired by the Vancouver office. He approached Hansen during the Christmas break in his first year at Dalhousie and came into the office for an interview. He easily passed the Hansen/MacDonald "test" and was hired pretty well on the spot. Anderson came to our attention via his best friend, Mike Stuart, who articled with the firm in 1990. Anderson had already accepted summer articles with McCarthy Tétrault, who permitted him to withdraw to allow him to begin with the firm in May 1989.

The original focus of the work in the Vancouver office was the Expo Land development, which spawned a tremendous amount of work not only there, but also for the Hong Kong office. When Frank Sixt arrived in Vancouver from Hong Kong, soon to be followed by Ralph Lutes, the Vancouver office developed highly sophisticated corporate and tax structures to facilitate off-shore marketing of the development throughout Southeast Asia and to maximize cash flow from the retail sales from the development. This structure now serves as a model used by many large-scale Canadian real estate developers who are looking to market their developments outside of Canada.

Important as it was, the Expo Lands project was not the only work in the office. It is testament to the scope of talent within the Vancouver group that even in 1988, when the office was in its infancy and was scrambling to have telephones installed, carpet laid, and office doors hung, the offices in Montreal, Toronto, New York, and London continued to refer very substantial amounts of work. It was these early mandates from other offices within the firm that established the foundation for what is clearly a very successful and vibrant business. In addition, the Vancouver office independently attracted many extremely significant mandates, which constituted very high-profile work with the community.

Perhaps the best-known of these mandates involved Terry Peabody and Western Star Trucks. Peabody needed a Vancouver law firm to represent him in the acquisition of the company, which was then the largest independent truck manufacturer in Canada. Peabody distributed the Canadian trucks in Australia, and his distributorship was suffering because Western Star Trucks was going broke. Peabody asked a professional acquaintance in Vancouver for a reference, and he was directed to Hansen. Drance and Hansen ended up acting for Peabody to acquire Western Star Trucks in a bailout, which involved loans from the provincial government and accommodations by company employees and management. In the past couple of years, Peabody sold the business, after an initial partial IPO, to Daimler Benz's truck division at a handsome profit. That work over a period of five to eight years kept several people in the office busy on a constant basis.

In addition, Drance, Allen, MacDonald, and Gillanders continued to bring in interesting work, including virtually all of the major investment dealers, Tree Island Industries, Cadillac Fairview, the Bentall Group, and a wide variety of other commercial clients. The Vancouver office never suffered for lack of work, and the principal lawyers within it have never taken for granted the benefits that flow from the credibility and goodwill generated by the Stikeman Elliott name.

The wonderful thing about the Vancouver office was the spirit that was maintained there during its early years. Everyone worked hard and played hard, and there are many offbeat and hilarious stories involving the zany collection of personalities that have come and gone over the years. There is no question that Vancouver is a family town, and for those who joined the Vancouver office from other places, like Sixt and Hansen, it was an adjustment. They would watch as the "Vancouver people" would pack up by six o'clock to go play baseball or basketball or soccer with their kids. It made it even worse for the newcomers when their wives started pressing them to conform to this most wonderful and civilized way of life.

Despite the importance of spending time with family and friends away from the office, the Vancouver lawyers never ceased to work hard and to relax among themselves as part of maintaining the spirit of the office and releasing the stress of an active practice. On the last Thursday of every month, the Vancouver office had associate dinners that might well have rivalled the mischief in Montreal in its best years. For many within the firm, the hallmark of a great lawyer's social aptitude was attendance without the need for arm-twisting or the sense that attendance was an obligation. In Vancouver, especially in the first three or four years, the attendance for the associate dinners was almost always 100 per cent and sometimes more if visiting lawyers from other offices were in town. Frankly, the dinners got out of hand more often than not, and at one stage, the options available for dinner venues got quite limited. Not to be denied, the organizers of the ensuing associate dinners simply booked the restaurant using the good name of McCarthy Tétrault. Predictably, in the wee, small hours, the remnants of the group would be asked to leave the restaurant for making too much noise or for formulating (in pen on the fine table linens) an estate plan involving the Cleaver Family and the Brady Bunch. We took delight in knowing at least that with these escapades, our good firm name would not be subject to negative comment.

As if the associate dinners were not enough, every Friday at around 6:00 PM, the nucleus of the office would congregate to play shuffleboard, a game that they claim they played poorly but very seriously in the early days. The only problem with this was that the largest and the very best shuffleboard tables in Vancouver were at a renowned strip joint about 400 yards up the road, which tended to exclude the female lawyers in the office. Nevertheless, Fridays involved playing shuffleboard and drinking a couple of glasses of beer. There was a recurring pattern involving a senior member of the firm, who would join in with the group but would never play shuffleboard. Instead, he would grab a chair and a beer and ogle the local strippers for far too long. No one ever summoned up the courage to make a joke about it to his wife.

In the early days, we also instituted a system of moving associates from one office to another across the country. Toronto, Montreal, and Vancouver all rented two-bedroom apartments, and for a period of two to three years, associates from the different offices would go and work for a period of six months in another city. This was an invaluable experience both for the associates who had the good fortune to make the trip and for the offices where they went to work. Vancouver, in particular, was a beneficiary of this practice because it got a series of outstanding Toronto and Montreal associates who fitted in to the relaxed social atmosphere of the Vancouver office, but who also provided Vancouver with some of the hard black letter expertise that they had developed in the bigger offices.

Perhaps the most exciting time in the Vancouver office in the early years, apart from the time when one of the female partners from another office was accused of sexual harassment by a junior Vancouver associate, was the consequences of the acquisition of Tree Island Industries by a large US steelmaking operation. The acquisition was an extremely successful public takeover bid, referred to the office by Ed Waitzer. Tree Island Industries operated under its new owners for two or three years with great success. Hansen received a call at 7:30 one morning to go out to the Tree Island headquarters in Richmond, BC, where he found fifty-five RCMP and Competition Bureau officers, who had raided the offices on evidence of very substantial price-fixing and bid-rigging. It became apparent that there was, in fact, some substance to the accusations, and we were instructed by the US operation to interview all the executives to get to the truth. We brought Peter Howard out from Toronto, who grilled the senior executives one after the other in our office and managed to get one or two of them to break down and tell the truth. Three Island and some other companies pleaded guilty and were fined. At the request of the Competition Bureau, Hansen was installed as independent director of Tree Island Industries while the investigation was being carried out by the bureau. The culmination to this story was that Hansen had to fire the general manager of Tree Island Industries, who then turned around and sued Tree Island Industries, Stikeman Elliott, and Hansen for fraud, negligence, breach of contract, and everything else you can imagine. We actually had to go through a full trial on this matter where, after years of waiting, we received complete vindication.

Over the years, there have been times when the Vancouver office was simply the most exciting and challenging place to work. To be candid, there have also been times when the Vancouver office has stumbled a bit on account of rapid growth, unanticipated departures, and shifts in the local economy. Starting in 1999, the office has undergone a strategic rebuilding and as a group, is now stronger than ever, both economically and intellectually. This interim period may well have been the result of the initial euphoria that comes from starting a new operation that is wildly successful, more successful than even Heward Stikeman, its biggest supporter, could have imagined. Everybody in the office knew and respected each other. They got on well, and if they did not like something, they told the people running the office about it, and the matters were discussed and resolved without delay. When the office got bigger and a little less personalized, it became more formal, and its character started to change. The normal politics that operate in a big office began to surface. Happily, the situation in the Vancouver office has now come full circle, with everyone there driving together to make it even more successful than it was in the early years.

CHAPTER 7

Ottawa

By 1973, Stikeman was suggesting the possibility of opening (or reopening, as we shall see) the Ottawa office, but no decision had been made to go forward. Although Stikeman was in Ottawa on a regular basis – as was Jim Robb to a lesser extent together with the tax lawyers, who met with appeals officers and Justice officials or who were negotiating with the Department of National Revenue, Taxation to obtain advance income tax rulings and the occasional legislative change – there was not enough regular work to justify setting up full-time offices in the city. It would be almost eight years before there was sufficient momentum and the identification of a lawyer able to take on the challenge of Ottawa. Even so, when it opened on November 2, 1981, the decision was not unanimous and was the subject of considerable debate within the partnership.

The impetus for opening an Ottawa office came from a group of senior partners based in Montreal. The fact that Stikeman had once worked in Ottawa, that Elliott was raised there, and that his father had maintained an office there until his retirement meant that they were supportive, albeit largely for sentimental reasons. The real push for having an Ottawa office came from people such as Jim Robb, Stanley Hartt, and Sonny Gordon, whose practices and political activities brought them to Ottawa on a regular basis. While these practices were corporate and commercial in nature, they recognized the value of the regulatory authorizations that were required in connection with certain of the major corporate transactions before they could proceed. The decade of the 1970s was characterized by a remarkable degree of regulation in many key industrial sectors such as energy, transportation, and communications as well as in furtherance of social and political goals with legislation such as the *Foreign Investment Review Act*.

Robb lobbied for a considerable period for an office in Ottawa and gradually wore down the resistance of many skeptical partners. As has often been the case within the firm, proposals go forward because someone takes the initiative, makes a specific proposal, or pushes the right buttons in order to get whatever approvals might be required. With this in mind, Robb set out to make a specific proposal that would include personnel to staff the office.

It was clear to him that no one (certainly neither himself, Hartt, nor Gordon) wanted to relocate to Ottawa. In 1976, he had met Greg Kane,[1] who was the general counsel of the Consumers' Association of Canada, and Robb was a member of an advisory board for the CAC's Regulated Industries Program. In those days, Robb would say, only half jokingly, that he encouraged the CAC to propose regulatory initiatives in order to generate work for himself to act on behalf of his clients opposing those initiatives. The important point was the value of having an office and practice groups, the focus of which would be the intricacies of government thinking, regulatory attitudes, and action in order to assist clients in their efforts to obtain licences, approvals, and other authorizations.

In the fall of 1980, Kane was practising as a sole practitioner in Ottawa. Over a series of lunches and dinners, Robb discussed the idea of an association with him, and eventually, they worked together to set out a plan for an Ottawa office that would focus on federal regulatory mandates. Robb discussed this plan with partners in the Montreal office and used Kane as an example of the sort of person who could be brought into the firm to open and run the Ottawa office. It was evident to Robb from his discussions with other partners that Ottawa was not going to be an easy sell. Fundamentally, many of the group were not persuaded that regulatory mandates would be a sufficient source of work to justify an office, and others took the less charitable view that it was not the type of work that the firm should be doing. All of this was exacerbated by the fact that if an Ottawa office were to be opened as Robb proposed, then it would be the first time the firm had opened an office without someone from either of the Montreal or Toronto offices being relocated. To many in the firm, the negatives outweighed the positives in the analysis.

One quality that Robb shared with Stikeman was an unabiding sense of optimism that anything and everything would work. To move things along, he persuaded partners to meet with Greg Kane in a series of one-on-one sessions, during which Kane extolled the virtues of a regulatory practice and tried to persuade them that the firm should open an office in Ottawa and that he should be the person to do it. Elliott's input was to tell Robb that he should get the Montreal partners on side first and if successful, to do the same in Toronto. The highlight of Kane's meetings with the Montreal partners was the one with Jim Grant. Kane was not feeling well on that day, but he kept the appointment because he was told that Grant was a key person and the gatekeeper to Elliott. What Kane did not know at the time but found out shortly after was that he was in the early stages of an attack of appendicitis. His meeting with Grant was at four o'clock in the afternoon. The visitors' chairs in Grant's office looked due west, and the sun was at eye level. It was also during the period when many of the Montreal lawyers smoked cigars after lunch. Kane was feeling miserable, with the sun directly in his eyes. Grant was quite enjoying blowing billows of cigar smoke and in his inimitable way, would occasionally grunt a question. Given Kane's great discomfort, he would grunt a response. After a few grunts back and forth, Grant pushed the speed dial button and said, "Fraser, Kane seems OK. You should see him." To this day, Kane considers he owes his entry into Stikeman Elliott to appendicitis because if he had not been suffering as much as he was, he probably would have talked his way out of the job.

Kane did see Elliott after being separated from his troublesome appendix. The discussion went well, and Elliott helped to organize meetings with other partners in Toronto. The discussions continued up to the time of the partners' meeting, in which the formal decision was to be made on whether to open an office in Ottawa and who would staff it. Elliott phoned Kane after the full partners' meeting and said, "We're go if you're go." Kane asked him if this meant that he was hired to open an office? Elliott replied, "Yes." Kane asked him if he would get a letter? Elliott replied, "No." The silence was broken when Elliott continued that Bob Hart would be in touch to take care of the logistics. When Kane started to thank him for the opportunity to open the office in Ottawa, Elliott cut him short and said, "My father opened the Ottawa office after he retired from government. You will be reopening the office."

THE NEW OTTAWA OFFICE

The firm was very conservative in the planning of the Ottawa office. In August 1981, a lease was signed to acquire approximately 1,900 square feet on the tenth floor in the newly constructed Royal Bank Centre on Sparks Street. As promised by Elliott, Bob Hart came to Ottawa on a regular basis during the period of acquiring the space and constructing the leasehold improvements. Kane always thought it was because Hart liked him and took a personal interest in the start-up of the reopening of the Ottawa office. It was discovered some time later that Hart's daughter was living in Ottawa at the time.

At a certain point, the frequency of Hart's visits diminished, but he would telephone on a regular basis to see how things were going. Kane remembers one call when Hart asked whether he had made arrangements for parking. Kane said he had not, but as a result of the call, he quickly arranged with the building management to secure a reserved parking spot. Kane figured he had really "arrived" when he saw his name assigned to a parking spot beside Tony Gabriel, who had been a star with the Ottawa Rough Riders of the Canadian Football League and was then a stockbroker working in the building. About a month later, Kane received a phone call from Hart, who explained that he had just received the monthly statement from the Ottawa office including invoices to be paid. Hart asked for an explanation of the parking invoice. Kane told him it was an invoice for the parking spot that Hart had said he should obtain. There was a slight pause and then an expostulation that grew louder with each breath: "We don't pay for Stikeman's parking. (louder) We don't pay for Elliott's parking. (louder) And we sure as hell are not going to pay for Kane's parking!"

The second person to be hired for the Ottawa office was Marke Raines, in August 1982. Originally from British Columbia, Raines was working at the MacDonald Royal Commission. Being the second person in the office, he quickly became adept at dealing with a wide variety of matters, including acting as junior initially to Stikeman and later to Stuart McCormack in acting for the renowned photographer Yousef Karsh when the Public Archives of Canada acquired Karsh's lifetime collection of photographs and negatives. In 1988, Raines transferred to the Toronto office to gain experience in corporate matters. The Toronto experience was such that he decided to take a step sideways and studied for and received his LLM at Cambridge. He is presently a partner at Shearman and Sterling, based in their London office.

In the fall of 1983, Glenn Cranker and Edward Aust encouraged Kane to meet with Donald Kubesh, who was at that time a senior litigation lawyer in the federal Department of Justice.[2] Aust had been a classmate of Kubesh at McGill, and Glenn had met him in tribunal proceedings with respect to international trade. The expansion of the Ottawa office capability to include international trade was a natural, and Cranker's clinching recommendation was that Kubesh's deep and mellifluous voice would automatically win him half of the cases in which he appeared. He added that Kubesh often won the other half through his aggressive and determined approach to the proceedings.

The discussions with Kubesh culminated in his joining the office early in 1984. He quickly established a strong practice, primarily in the international trade sector. In one particularly fascinating file, Kubesh and Kane worked together advising Wardair, the Canadian charter airline founded by the legendary Max Ward, with respect to innovative approaches to inflight services. Wardair eventually put in place a duty-free purchase program called "RSVP," which permitted Wardair passengers at the time they bought a ticket to an international destination to pre-order duty-free items, which were delivered to them at their seats during the flight. The duty-free advantage and avoidance of regulations was ensured by permitting the customers to "reserve" a product, which they had the option of rejecting when the items were delivered to them at their seats during the flight. The great advantage to Wardair was that it could target the duty-free items that were stored onboard, an important practical issue given space and weight limitations.

Working with Wardair on the duty-free issues, Kane and Kubesh also provided advice that eventually led to a very significant victory over the Liquor Control Board of Ontario. The advice given was that the LCBO was improperly charging Wardair its customary and significant markup on liquor that the company stored in bonded warehouses in Ontario before loading on aircraft for consumption by passengers while in flight, whether domestic or international. Kane and Kubesh confirmed advice provided to Wardair by a commodity tax expert that Wardair was not subject to the licensing structure imposed on it and the accompanying markups and gallon fees because the liquor was consumed in the air and not in the province. In a remarkable meeting with counsel for the LCBO, Kane was informed that the board agreed that Wardair had found a loophole and that the LCBO would not require any payment as long as the airline did not publicize the situation.

This fragile arrangement held until 1990, when Canadian Airlines International acquired Wardair. Canadian quickly discovered the fact that

Wardair was not making these payments and informed the LCBO that the company would follow suit. Canadian also raised the possibility of a claim for refunds, which the LCBO calculated as involving $25 to $30 million spanning some 15 years. Kane met again with LCBO officials, who then took the position that there was no agreement, or if there was one, that it was a mistake. The LCBO also informed Kane that Canadian would have to obtain a licence under the *Liquor Licence Act* in order to gain access to bonded warehouses. In the course of these manoeuvrings, Wardair initiated an action against the LCBO, which Canadian continued. In a trial before the Ontario Court General Division, Kane acted as a witness relative to his discussions with officials in the LCBO. Mr Justice Saunders had "little difficulty finding that there was an agreement" between Wardair and the LCBO, stipulating that Wardair would not be required to pay any markups after December 31, 1983, and that the agreement was not to be disclosed to the other airlines. Kane described his appearance as a witness in the trial as one of the most harrowing experiences in his life.

Kubesh has developed his practice in the trade area, evolving from basic litigation into international trade matters, where any litigation was done in the context of the trade tribunal. He has developed an expertise in quota matters and has acquired the nickname of "cheesehead" given his expertise in that particular field. He has also been involved in a number of federal court battles relating to illegal dairy imports into Canada.

One of the reasons put forward by those who opposed the idea of an Ottawa office was the fact that no other Montreal- or Toronto-based firm had such an office. In late 1980 and early 1981, when the idea was being considered, the only law firms in Ottawa were local. Some of them, such as Scott & Aylen, were into their third generation of family members. Although members of the Ottawa Bar were not openly hostile to the idea of outside firms opening an office, their attitude was definitely frosty. They had a comfortable if regional existence and saw no reason to encourage encroachment on their territory. The fact that no other major law firm based outside of the city had an office in Ottawa was not considered an obstacle by the proponents of the initiative. They turned it to advantage by arguing that it was very much in the entrepreneurial spirit of the firm's move in opening London, Toronto, and elsewhere when others had not. Another feature of resistance to the idea of an Ottawa office was the virtual absence of any clients resident in Ottawa. The focus for business and potential clients was federal regulatory matters. The companies affected were almost without exception based in other parts of Canada or outside the country. The naysayers within the firm were openly skeptical of the ability to attract work from clients in a distant city.

An early example of the potential for referrals from other offices occurred when Kane received a mandate from General Dynamics, through François Mercier in the Montreal office, relating to liquefied natural gas (LNG) tankers. Dome Petroleum at the time proposed to ship LNG to Japan, but the major profits from the arrangement were in the transportation of the product, and the Japanese had negotiated contractual terms that included their right to build the ships and provide the transportation component for the project. The firm intervened in hotly contested proceedings to persuade the National Energy Board that the ships were, in effect, extensions of the pipeline. The mandate grew to involve Stikeman himself, who wanted to try to make this a Canadian shipping project assisted by General Dynamic's expertise in constructing the mammoth LNG tankers, and he worked very closely with the Canadian Shipbuilding Association for the development of a "newco," possibly to be located in Bermuda, with Peter Cumyn working on the technical tax questions inherent in any such arrangement. Kane well remembers being in Stikeman's office where Stikeman used the blackboard mounted on his wall to impress senior counsel from Jenner and Block, US counsel for General Dynamics, by designing and diagramming the whole scheme to make it a Canadian shipping project with offshore tax advantages to all participants.

STIKEMAN AND ELLIOTT

At the time of reopening the Ottawa office, Elliott was the chairman of the Canadian Cultural Property Export Review Board. As a result, he went to Ottawa on a regular basis. Because of that and because of his personal interest in the reopening of the office, he was a frequent visitor. He was very supportive to the point of being protective, and it was evident that he was proud of his connection with Ottawa and that his father had been a senior and highly respected public servant. When Elliott went to Ottawa in conjunction with his work on the Cultural Property Review Board, he frequently made time to take Kane to lunch, usually at the Rideau Club, where he and Stikeman had been members since the 1950s and in which both had maintained non-resident memberships. Elliott would spend most of his time greeting friends and acquaintances and thoroughly enjoying the recognition he properly received.

Stikeman was also a tremendous supporter of the Ottawa office, possibly partly because his tax practice took him to Ottawa from time to time. On one of Stikeman's first visits to the Ottawa office, he wanted to see a particular volume of the *Canada Tax Cases,* of which he was editor-in-chief. Kane explained to him that we did not have anyone practising tax in the Ottawa office and therefore did not have *Canada Tax Cases* or any other tax materials there. Stikeman looked at him and said, without any sense of prolonging the discussion, "You will the next time I come." They did, and still do. He would also pass through Ottawa when he and Mary were travelling to her hometown of Perth and to their cottage on the Big Rideau southwest of Ottawa. The office boardrooms were often used as changing rooms by the two of them when they had social occasions in Ottawa that called for dressing up or dressing down, so everyone had to be careful to understand whether there was a meeting or a quick change in progress when Stikeman was occupying a boardroom.

Everyone who knew him remembers that Stikeman loved to learn from others and to talk with anyone he did not know. On one occasion when he was in Ottawa, the office was having a barbecue at Kane's residence. Stikeman came along and immediately struck up a conversation with the husband of one of the secretaries. Stikeman asked him what he did, and he replied that he worked for CSIS. Not satisfied with being told that the initials stood for the Canadian Security Intelligence Service, he pressed and asked the man to explain exactly what he did. His response, probably the standard one he gave in casual social situations to deflect further discussion, was that if he told Stikeman exactly what he did, he would then have to kill him. Stikeman chuckled and said, "Well, at least I'll die knowing more than I do right now! So go ahead and tell me exactly what you do!" The husband proceeded to do so, and even his wife said that she learned things that night that she had never known before in all their years of marriage.

KEEP IT OR CLOSE IT DOWN?

When he became chairman of the firm, Jim Grant brought a new style of management with regard to the Ottawa office. In contrast with Elliott's attitude of leaving it alone unless there was a problem, Grant actively sought to review the office and its place within the firm. In conversations with Kane in the spring of 1986, Grant had initiated a review, and in a provocative approach to the issue, he asked Kane to report on whether the office should stand pat, expand (and if so, to what extent), or be shut down. The last option hit everyone in the Ottawa office like a thunderbolt, which Grant no doubt intended.

In response, Kane recommended incremental expansion as opposed to maintaining the status quo or rapid expansion. He added that closing the office should be out of the question. He explained that incremental expansion would mean the addition of a certain number of lawyers per year relative to established and new regulatory practice groups. He also recommended expansion into the area of intellectual property as a natural extension of the existing Ottawa office practices and to coordinate with corporate and commercial practices in other offices.

This cautious and small "c" conservative approach was driven by a paranoia on the part of everyone in the office concerning certain constituencies in the partnership that held implacably to the view that an office in Ottawa was not necessary and would ultimately fail. To hold their own within the partnership, the lawyers in Ottawa strove to establish and maintain a positive and successful financial position. To this end, Kane indicated that the approach adopted in the Ottawa office was that expansion should as a general rule be justified by existing and imminent workloads. The executive committee accepted the recommendations and for the moment, left the office to its own devices. This approach has been described by Stikeman as the firm's propensity to "throw people into the deep end of the pool." Whenever he would say that, he would pause and then add with a chuckle, "fortunately we usually find people who can swim," a quotation once picked up by *Maclean's* magazine.

The diversification of the Ottawa office continued when intellectual property was identified as an important area for expansion. The opportunity to move into this area was brought to the firm when Stuart McCormack approached Kane in the fall of 1986. McCormack had an established practice specializing in intellectual property, with extensive experience in trademark, copyright, and licensing matters as well as intellectual property and litigation.[3] He had practised with an Ottawa boutique and spent three years in Japan from 1982 to 1985 as an in-house counsel with Sony Corporation. He had the distinction of being the first foreign professional to work in Sony's head office. His duties included the responsibility for counterfeit matters and licensing negotiations throughout the world.

In the course of deciding whether he should join the firm, McCormack went to Montreal, ostensibly for a hockey game (there were no Ottawa Senators at the time), and Kane suggested he meet with Sonny Gordon. Any thought that the firm might be a sweatshop soon dissolved. At 6:30 PM, Gordon was unable to find any other lawyers to meet with McCormack, except Jim Grant, the managing partner. Grant shook his hand and said, "My daughter is downstairs waiting for me in the car. I'm fifteen minutes late. Sonny tells me you want to work with us. Tell me, what do you bring to the party?" McCormack replied that he brought "a winning personality," which did not seem to be all that amusing to Grant. McCormack was, however, impressed with any firm that could bring together such diverse individuals as Grant and Gordon. That clinched it, and he started with the firm in March 1987, quickly establishing the intellectual law capability in support of corporate transactions being conducted throughout the firm.[4]

In a small office, lawyers tend to do a bit of everything, and the Ottawa office was no exception. While Kane's principal interest and expertise was in the telecommunications and broadcasting areas before the Canadian Radio-television and Telecommunications Commission, opportunities arose to act in energy regulatory files, particularly with respect to proceedings before the National Energy Board. By 1987, it was clear that the volume of work in the regulated energy and telecommunications sectors was such that one or the other had to be dropped or that extra resources had to be brought on to maintain the practices. Rowland Harrison, at the time a professor at the University of Ottawa, approached Kane to inquire about an opportunity to work with the firm during a sabbatical he was proposing to take in 1987. Because Harrison had considerable expertise in the energy sector, it was a perfect fit that was perfectly timed. Among other things, he had been the founding executive director of the Canadian Institute of Resources Law in Calgary. In addition, he had worked in the federal government Canada Oil and Gas Lands Administration. Harrison joined the office in the summer of 1987. The first year went well enough that he asked for and was granted an extension to his sabbatical for the 1988–89 academic year. In the summer of 1989, he advised the university that he would remain with the firm to continue an ever-growing energy law practice. In 1992, Harrison returned to Calgary with his family to assist the firm in opening its office there. He remained with the firm until September 1997, when he accepted an appointment as a member of the National Energy Board.

TIME FOR ANOTHER REVIEW

Spring seemed to provide the appropriate environment to trigger reviews. Just as the 1986 review started in the spring, so did a second one in 1988. As it turned out, the skeptics were right about the potential for failure for outside firms in Ottawa, but this applied to other firms that followed and fortunately not to Stikeman Elliott. But follow they did. The mass invasion of outside firms to Ottawa really took hold following the election of a Conservative government in September 1984. In June 1986, Kane had reported to Grant that "There are now more than 14 firms based outside of Ottawa which have opened an Ottawa office." But for some outside firms, the move to Ottawa was ill advised and based on little more than a personal connection or contact with the new Conservative government. The rise and fall of some firms was quite remarkable.

In a February 8, 1988 memo to the executive committee, Kane provided capsule comments on the Ottawa offices of a number of other firms and reported that the following firms had opened and closed (or were about to close) Ottawa offices: Weir & Foulds; Goodman & Carr; Smith Lyons Torrance Mayer; Byers Casgrain; Burnett, Duckworth & Palmer; Phillips & Vineberg; Bennett Jones; and Lavery, O'Brien.[5] Grant sent the memo back to Kane with a marginal note saying: "You left out Stikeman, Elliott. I would like a report on Stikeman, Elliott as if you were reporting to Oslers." Kane replied that Grant's request had "provided us with an interesting challenge to try and see ourselves as others do." He said that it perhaps would look like this:

Stikeman, Elliott was one of the first outside law firms to establish an Ottawa office. They have grown steadily since opening in November 1981 with one lawyer. The office recently moved to expanded quarters, and they now have five lawyers (with one junior lawyer at present in Toronto, apparently on a temporary assignment). The office has concentrated on administrative law and last year hired an intellectual property law specialist. They do not have a "local" Ottawa practice. We understand they have rejected the idea of growth through merger and will continue to expand through the hiring of individual lawyers possessing a particular expertise related to administrative law.

Kane reminded Grant that he had taken the view from the very beginning that the model for the Ottawa office should be that of American firms opening an office in Washington and concentrating on federal regulatory activity. He repeated his 1981 view that Stikeman Elliott would be at the forefront of a trend whereby major law firms from across Canada would open Ottawa offices. Finally, he reiterated a point from an earlier memorandum that the firm should expect a shake-out in Ottawa just as there had been with Washington offices of American firms.

In a memorandum sent to Grant in April 1988, Kane confirmed matters that had been discussed at an earlier review meeting in Montreal. Kane documented the recommendation made in June 1986 and the steps already described to carry out the incremental expansion option. He then said that the Ottawa partners wanted to see the office continue with a measured expansion, building upon the established strengths and the introduction of new practice areas that provided a fit not only with the Ottawa office but with the firm in general. To this end, Kane recommended the development of a capability in the competition law area stating: "This is a rapidly expanding area of practice and one which complements the commercial practices in Montreal and Toronto. We have made a recommendation concerning a specific individual, and that discussion is at a meaningful, albeit preliminary, stage." The person referred to in fact did not work out, and the initiative to develop a competition law practice within the Ottawa office did not materialize until January 1993, when Lawson Hunter joined the firm from Fraser & Beatty.

In the meantime, T. Bradbrooke Smith, Q.C. was hired from the Department of Justice in October 1988. Smith had a distinguished career with the Department of Justice, and at the time of joining Stikeman Elliott, he was chief general counsel, having previously been assistant deputy Attorney General for Civil Litigation. During his time with Justice, he had argued the federal government position on many of the leading constitutional cases in a number of courts including frequent appearances before the Supreme Court of Canada. Smith represented the federal government on the reference to the Supreme Court of Canada testing the constitutional validity of the goods and services tax, reported at [1992] S.C.R. 445, in which he was successful. He has also been intimately involved on behalf of the federal government, dealing with pension surplus litigation, including unemployment insurance surpluses, and provides ongoing advice on such matters. On a pro bono basis, he chairs meetings on the Hague Conference on Private International Law, dealing with the adoption of the Convention on Recognition and Enforcement of Judgments, which Canada has adopted.

One of his major accomplishments was negotiating the settlement of the debts of the International Tin Council, a spectacular £900-million collapse that occurred in 1985 and was one of the world's largest-ever commercial defaults. It was described in *The Tin Men: A Chronicle of Crisis*, by Ralph Kestenbaum.[6] Smith, as chairman of a working group established by the International Tin Council, was instrumental first in disengaging the parties, producers, and creditors from a series of potentially ruinous international lawsuits, and then moving endless discussions toward a settlement of almost two hundred million pounds in the form of *ex gratia* payments of a portion of the claims of the creditors. It was a difficult and fractious process that involved an endless series of trips back and forth to London and several sets of lost luggage over a period of more than four years, eventually leaving no one happy but thereby reflected a good settlement. As described in *The Tin Men*:

T. Bradbrooke Smith was a Queen's Counsel, an Assistant Deputy Attorney-General at the Department of Justice, who reached the post of Chief General Counsel and subsequently joined the Canadian law firm of Stikeman Elliott in Ottawa. He was also a gentleman farmer who had the good fortune to be married to a lady who did all the ungentlemanly things about the farm when he was off on his tin travels. The farm, 60 kilometers from Ottawa at Burritts Rapids, had the usual cows and horses, plus a designer donkey who was mainly for posing for photographs, two dogs, and several cats. Smith was similar to Ridley and the Kestenbaum and Metcalfe duo in that he, too, was persistent and persuasive. He combined city manners with a North American expansiveness, and without him there would probably not have been a settlement in our time.[7]

In October 1989, the Ottawa office held a reception to welcome both Smith and Allan Gotlieb, who had joined the firm in the Toronto office but had spent much of his public service career in Ottawa and most recently in Washington as one of Canada's mot successful ambassadors to the United States. In a November 1989 memo to Grant from Kane, the reception was described as "a very successful event attended by approximately 300 people from the political, government, diplomatic, and business communities in Ottawa." In the memo, Kane noted that "financially and otherwise, the Ottawa office is having an excellent year" and pointed to the fact that the net revenue was the best yet achieved on either a per-point or per-lawyer basis. With the naysayers clearly in mind, he added "the financial results are not an aberration but rather a continuation of the growth pattern which has been evident for the past few years." He also observed that there was a solid base of practice emanating from the Ottawa office, giving rise to a steady flow of business resulting in consistent billings as opposed to the peaks and valleys it had experienced in the early stages. Kane went on to say that there had been an impressive growth in the practices of all of the lawyers, both in the number of files being handled and the geographical distribution of the clients. He used this point to return to a theme that had been identified from the beginning of considering opening an Ottawa office, saying: "I note this fact to reinforce the point, which we can't make often enough, that 99 per cent of the clients in the Ottawa office come from locations outside of Ottawa. As a result, lawyers in all of the Stikeman, Elliott offices can be of assistance to the Ottawa office by keeping in mind the capability and expertise we can bring to a new client matter."

In the early days of the Ottawa office, Elliott had advised Kane that marketing the Ottawa office and business development generally should be directed as much at other offices within the firm as to potential clients. Elliott's advice as always was eminently sound. It took time for the other of-fices to realize fully the capability that existed in Ottawa. Increasingly, over time, the office was involved to provide the regulatory capability in merger and acquisition activity. This was eventually developed into the strategic practice of deploying a team of lawyers from various offices to provide full and seamless service to clients, exemplified by the Air Canada mandate in the Onex hostile takeover bid battle in 1999. The Stikeman Elliott advantage was described in a *Financial Post* article published on August 7, 2001 about Toronto-based firms opening offices in Montreal:

Onex was represented in its 1999 takeover attempt by Davies Ward & Beck, while Air Canada used Stikeman Elliott, in both cases, longtime corporate counsel.

Stikemans won. Davies morphed.

Within a year, Davies, whose long-stated position was that it was a one-city, high-end transactional firm, had become Davies Ward Phillips & Vineberg – a firm with a substantial Montreal profile.

"Davies is smart like you wouldn't believe; however, there is very little question among the people who watch these things that on that takeover, Davies just got outmanoeuvred like crazy by Stikeman Elliott," a lawyer familiar with the Toronto market said recently. "What Stikes did was mount a masterful coordination of the Toronto-Montreal-Ottawa-Calgary offices of the firm.

"They pulled every possible lever and really showed how a law firm with offices in Toronto, Montreal, Ottawa can work."

PRECURSOR TO THE CALGARY OFFICE

On February 26, 1991, a group of the Ottawa office lawyers gathered in the main boardroom to watch the televised budget speech being delivered by then minister of Finance, Michael Wilson. The Internet was not then as ubiquitous as it is today, so a courier had been dispatched to get printed copies of the budget speech, which arrived shortly after the minister had started his delivery, and the lawyers scrambled to find the appropriate place in order to follow along in the written text. Throughout the speech, lawyers were coming and going, and there was the usual banter and uncomplimentary comments about increases in taxes.

In the midst of some banter, Harrison yelled over the conversation, "Did you hear that?" No one had. Harrison went on to explain that Michael Wilson had just said that the government would be moving the National Energy Board from Ottawa to Calgary. Everyone around the table read furiously, trying to find the reference in the written text. It couldn't be found. This brought on a chorus of expletives and comments about a lame attempt at a joke. But Harrison stuck to his guns and insisted he heard Michael Wilson say in unequivocal terms that the NEB would be moved to Calgary. Both Kane and Harrison agreed to get on the phone and try to confirm since everyone agreed that it was nowhere to be found in the written text. The initial calls were to no avail, but after about an hour, it was confirmed. It must have been a last-minute addition.

At this stage in the development of the Ottawa office, the energy law practice was one of the four pillars. The other three were telecommunications, trade, and intellectual property. After a period of formal and informal meetings, it was decided that two things would be done. First, the lawyers responsible for particular energy clients would contact their clients and assure them that we would be in a position to act on their behalf even with the board's move to Calgary. The lawyers did not anticipate resistance from clients. After all, lawyers in Calgary had maintained strong energy regulatory practices even when the board was located in Ottawa. However, deep down, the lawyers were very uneasy with this argument. The obvious reason why Calgary had strong energy regulatory practices was the fact that most of the companies affected were based in Calgary.

This led to the second thrust, and that was to recommend renewed discussion within the firm about the possibility of opening a Calgary office. The Ottawa office input, based upon the pending move of the National Energy Board, presented an urgency to the issue, which was not previously present, when the firm would have had to be in the vanguard of the constitutional challenge against the Law Society's protectionist rules. Kane wrote to Grant two days later to tell him of the government's announcement of the NEB's move and to provide the Ottawa office perspective. In his memo, he provided a brief description of the state of the energy practice in the Ottawa office and assured him that the lawyers had been in contact with existing clients (principally ANR Pipeline Company, Coastal Corporation, Texaco, and Pacific Gas & Electric). Kane informed Grant that most observers felt that the board move to Calgary would be done quickly and possibly completed as early as September 1991 (which it was, effective September 1). He went on to say: "All of this leads to the obvious inquiry about the status of opening a Stikeman, Elliott Calgary office. While the energy client base described above would not justify the opening of an office in and of itself, this development might well put a different inflection on the current thinking. Simply stated, for the firm to maintain the energy practice, which has been developed to date, a presence in Calgary will probably be required."

The possibility of opening a Calgary office was mentioned in all of the Ottawa office memoranda to Grant and the executive committee from that time forward. In the spring of 1992, the executive finally made a decision to open in Calgary, and Harrison made plans to move from Ottawa to Calgary in August 1992. While the move of one partner has virtually no consequence in offices the size of Montreal and Toronto, the loss of one in an office with only four, has great significance. The strength and stability of the Ottawa office was tested, and it was with obvious relief that Kane reported to the executive committee at the end of 1992 that the office would meet its original budget.

CONTINUING TO MOVE FORWARD COMPETITIVELY

From the outset, the focus for the Ottawa office was regulatory, administrative, and public law. When the firm was thinking of opening the office, partners visited law firms in Washington that were based in other cities such as New York, Chicago, and Los Angeles. The advice received consistently from those firms was to focus the Ottawa practice on federal regulatory and legislative matters. This formula worked very well. Over the years, the office developed strong national practices relating to broadcasting and telecommunications (Kane), international trade (Kubesh and Randall Hofley), intellectual property (McCormack and Mirko Bibic), and competition law (Hunter, Hutton, Bibic, and Hofley). Discussions over many years culminated in a decision in 2001 to develop a corporate capability to service the significant and continually expanding high-tech sector in Ottawa. Mark Burton[8] rejoined the firm in 2001 and moved from Toronto to develop this practice area.

It is interesting to note, looking back, that the events of 1992 occurred in a year when Ottawa was suffering from a recession. In his reports to the executive, Kane made a point of emphasizing that "Ottawa is no longer recession-proof and is clearly feeling the effects of the current recession." In October, he reported:

The Ottawa office of Stikeman, Elliott stands in marked contrast to what I see elsewhere in Ottawa. Each one of us is cautiously optimistic with respect to our respective practices. As noted above, the sum total of our optimism is that we will meet budget, but we are hopeful that the long-awaited turnaround will take place next year. Given the results we will achieve this year, that should lead to even better results next year.

The current state of affairs in other firms in Ottawa also provides an opportunity with respect to possible expansion. We are keeping a close eye on the possibility of a lateral transfer with respect to an individual who has an established and compatible practice. We are dealing from strength, and I believe that there are some interesting prospects to be considered.

This teasing conclusion to the memo was code for the fact that Kane had approached Lawson Hunter[9] to see whether he would be interested in discussing a move to Stikeman Elliott. That fall, Kane had called Hunter to see if he would be interested in a game of squash. Given their conflicting schedules, the game did not take place until early December. To this day, Kane insists that he let Hunter win in order to put him in a good frame of mind for the pitch to follow. Hunter is equally adamant that he won the match fair and square. In any event, Kane quickly moved the post-game conversation to asking Hunter if he would be interested in joining the firm and replicate his practice of being based in Ottawa while maintaining an office and spending time in Toronto. In a planned hand-off, Marvin Yontef was brought in as the closer. This was an obvious strategy because Yontef and Hunter had attended Harvard together while pursuing studies for their LLM degrees. Everything moved quickly, and Lawson joined the firm effective January 1, 1993. The addition of Hunter filled an important gap in competition law. His tenure as director of investigation and research, *Combines Investigation Act*,[10] carried him into private practice among an elite and limited group of specialists in this area. His practice was a perfect complement to the mergers and acquisitions corporate practice throughout the firm, which was about to expand significantly during the decade of the 1990s.

One of the conditions that Hunter established for joining the firm was the hiring of Susan Hutton, a first-year lawyer with him at Fraser & Beatty. Hutton had a strong undergraduate background in economics as well as varied public and private sector experience with respect to international trade and competition. She quickly developed a competition law practice, which was interrupted in 1996 and 1997 when she moved with her husband, Ian Burney, a Canadian foreign service officer, to Vietnam. Taking advantage of her move, she worked in both the Hong Kong and Singapore offices of the firm during her time overseas. Upon her return, she picked up where she left off and joined the partnership in Ottawa in 2001.[11]

Early in 1995, Hunter had discussions with Randall Hofley, then practising in the Ottawa office of Gowling, Strathy & Henderson in the area of public law litigation, focusing on international trade and government regulation of business generally. He joined the Ottawa office in April 1995 and became a partner in 1998.[12]

Mirko Bibic was the first person in the Ottawa office to "hit for the cycle," moving from articling student in 1992–93 to associate and then partner in 2000.[13] His practice has evolved in the intellectual property and transport sectors, and he has acted for a number of prominent companies including Air Canada and the Hockey Hall of Fame. As a third-year lawyer, on behalf of Philippine Airlines, Inc., he negotiated a code share relationship with Canadian Airlines International in Hawaii, and he was involved, again on behalf of Philippine Airlines, in the negotiation of the bilateral air treaty between Canada and the Republic of the Philippines. He argued and won a case before the Federal Court Trial Division, on behalf of Cheung Kong, in *Cheung Kong v. Living Realty Ltd*. [1999] 4 CPR 71, which established a new principle of trademark law concerning confusion between translated marks (English versus Chinese characters) and the relevant "target market" for the purposes of the trademark confusion analysis. As a significant case, it was covered in the *Globe and Mail,* with emphasis on the impact it would have on Chinese business owners in Canada and their trademark rights. He acted for Cobra Golf and Taylor Made in policing the sale of knock-off and counterfeit golf clubs, which included attending a product seizure with the RCMP.

Bibic was the Ottawa point man in the Onex hostile takeover bid battle for Air Canada, which included the review of the proposed transaction by the Competition Bureau (headed by Lawson Hunter), negotiation of the undertakings related to competition with the same bureau, commitments related to transportation with Transport Canada, the Federal Court challenge of the government's section 47 order under the *Canada Transportation Act,* coordination with the other offices of the firm, and as Bibic says, "absolutely everything else one could imagine."

CORPORATE INITIATIVE

From the beginning, taking advantage of Kane's background, the activities of the office had been centred primarily on regulatory and administrative law. Notwithstanding the primary focus, the office had accepted some additional work including some relatively low grade corporate and commercial work, minor amounts of real estate transactions, some employment law, and more importantly, a growing amount of intellectual property law matters, many of which, until the arrival of Stuart McCormack, had to be shared with specialty boutiques due to lack of experience in such matters. Little attention had, however, been paid to the commercial law opportunities that developed in and around Ottawa. Most considered Ottawa to be nothing more than a government town that could not support a meaningful corporate practice, especially for a firm that had developed a taste for major transactional work. But more and more, the Ottawa area was coming on stream as a place where significant businesses were locating, and the firm had done little to capture more than the occasional scrap of such work.

The dominant firm in the Ottawa area was the Gowling Strathy & Henderson firm. Gordon Henderson had been a close friend of Stikeman, dating back to his time with National Revenue during the war, and he had become a leading figure in the Ontario Bar and a much respected advocate for a wide range of clients and causes. There were also a few other, smaller firms of no particular stature, but the changing trend, triggered by the opening of our office, was for Toronto firms to establish branch offices in Ottawa either as outposts for visiting lawyers, merging with the smaller local firms, or annexing specific practice groups of the local firms. By 1986, there were fourteen such firms headquartered outside of Ottawa. These firms, which competed with us, did not purport to restrict their practices to regulatory work.

Firms such as Lang Michener had been particularly aggressive in their recruitment from within the local Bar. Even the venerable Gowlings firm was not immune to such raids, and several of their senior and junior partners were lured away by the incoming carpetbaggers. Consistent with our policy, we had never sought to merge but preferred to grow our own firm rather than to take on the cultural problems of others through amalgamation. It did mean, however, that we now found ourselves competing on a much broader basis with local and outside firms for federal regulatory work from Canadian and, mainly, American clients and for general retainers from Ottawa-based clients such as Crown agencies, national organizations, and high-tech companies as this industry gravitated to the Ottawa Silicon Valley. The plan, as originally developed, had proceeded as envisaged, but consideration had to be given to the next phase of evolution.

Kane thought that the competition from entering firms would accelerate and spur on response by the locals. The alternatives for the firm, he thought, would be threefold. The first alternative involved maintaining the status quo, growing slowly, and restricting our practice, to the extent possible, to regulatory law. The latter would enable us to assimilate new lawyers, but it would necessarily result in lost opportunities in related fields, such as intellectual property, and leave us with a serious competitive disadvantage with respect to full-service competitors. The second possibility was to plan for moderate growth of two to four lawyers per year in regulatory work, combined with staged expansion into other practice areas, with additional lawyers as required. There were obvious advantages to this, but against it were the facts that the present workload of the firm was not such that additional lawyers were then required, and there would be problems in integrating and supervising work in areas in which we did not then have expertise. The third alternative that had at least to be considered was an aggressive expansion, *à la* Lang Michener, of hiring groups or individual lawyers from local firms and moving directly to a full-service operation.

There was certainly a pool of "restive talent" available, and access to it would provide increased flexibility in serving existing clients and attracting new ones. The downside was the time and effort to recruit, integrate, and manage, plus there was no guarantee that incoming lawyers would bring or attract a sufficient volume of work to support the level of required staffing.

Kane had inclined to the view that the second option of moderate growth was the best and had taken immediate steps to add intellectual property as a practice group centred in the Ottawa office. The trademark and copyright boutiques were not only profitable, but they also were national and international in scope. Such a new practice group would be self-supporting and self-supervising and would bring new expertise and strength not only to the Ottawa office, but also to the firm as a whole. Such an initiative would be timely in view of the then current dynamics of the Ottawa legal community and the fact that the office was facing the immediate need to move to larger premises.

In June 1986, Kane noted for the benefit of the firm's executive committee that the approaches being adopted by other outside firms concerning their Ottawa offices varied from establishing an Ottawa outpost for visiting lawyers, to merging with local firms, to annexing practice groups from local firms. He also observed that most of the Ottawa offices of outside firms that competed with us did not restrict their practices to regulatory work. In this respect, a number of the firms were establishing their Ottawa offices with a full-service practice approach. Kane predicted that the influx of law firms into Ottawa could continue, both through mergers and through the absorption of individuals and practice groups from local Ottawa firms. In this respect, he also predicted a more aggressive approach to establishing full-service practices beyond strictly federal regulatory law. This prediction proved to be accurate, and many of the Ottawa offices of outside firms that competed with us transferred corporate lawyers from their Toronto and Montreal offices to establish practices in Ottawa, targeting the burgeoning high-tech sector. In spite of recommendations from the Ottawa office, the firm adopted a "wait and see" attitude and an uncharacteristically cautious approach to exploring such a market.

There was, no doubt, some opportunity lost as a result of this, particularly as the commercial sector in and around Ottawa, much of which was in the high-tech area, came on stream in the late 1980s and throughout the 1990s. There were several major corporate transactions that were in effect "Ottawa deals" but that were handled by the Toronto or Montreal offices. These included the Alcatel purchase of Newbridge and the Cisco purchase of Skystone, managed respectively by Simon Romano and Richard Clark. The Alcatel acquisition was one of the top ten high-tech deals ever concluded and certainly the biggest in Canada. The firm was retained by Alcatel France when Newbridge Networks, controlled by Terrence Matthews, was acquired by it, making Matthews the largest Alcatel shareholder. Newbridge had become very big in Canada, and that spawned a number of companies known generally as the Newbridge affiliates. Matthews had a manner that seemed very brusque because he was so fast, but the acquisition, despite many difficulties and leaks of information, was the deal of a lifetime for any lawyer.

Calin Rovenescu's last big transaction before he left to go to Air Canada was the acquisition by BCE of the CTV Network, which involved the Montreal, Toronto, and Ottawa offices working very closely together. The firm had become involved in the deal before it was public, and one of the challenges for Kane was to confidentially get approval of both a trustee and a trust agreement by the CRTC since a public company was involved. The form of arrangement was for the trustee to operate the company and hold the shares during the period of review of the takeover by the acquirer. If the takeover were to be approved, then the matter would go public, and if the takeover bid were to be successful, then "prior" approval had to be sought on a formal basis from the CRTC. Some twelve months after the initial approach, BCE's acquisition of CTV was approved by the CRTC.[14] With an acquisition cost of $2.3 billion, it was the largest acquisition in the history of Canadian broadcasting.

Major transactions of this nature were coming through Ottawa and to the attention of the corporate section of the firm. Because the firm did not have people on the ground, it might do the work on the acquisition but then be unable to benefit from the follow-up legal work since the deal-flow came from Ottawa but was being served out of the Toronto and Montreal offices. The firm was not regarded as part of the Ottawa business community, and despite its national prominence, it had very little recognition factor within the local business community other than at the very highest levels. Increasingly, however, the firm was acting on mandates for companies in Ottawa or for multinationals acquiring high-tech start-ups in Ottawa. In time, it became clear to everyone that there was a significant market opportunity in Ottawa that the firm was missing. Early in 2001, a decision was made to find a lawyer at the partner level to join the Ottawa office and establish an information technology corporate practice.

Some time after the search began, a perfect match was found. Mark Burton had practised in the Toronto office for some seven years before leaving in 1998 to become the president and ultimately chief executive officer of Digital Processing Systems Inc., a Toronto Stock Exchange-listed manufacturer of innovative computer hardware and software products used throughout the world in the broadcast and post-production industries. Burton was in the midst of re-evaluating his career as a result of a competitor having purchased the company at the end of 2000. The opportunity to return to the practice of law in the Ottawa office to establish a corporate capability geared to the high-tech sector provided a natural fit with his previous legal and corporate career, and he rejoined the firm as a partner in April 2001.

THE NEW CHIEF

In the fall of 1999, the Right Honourable Antonio Lamer, then chief justice of Canada, decided to retire from the Supreme Court of Canada. In the course of speaking with family and friends about his future plans, he spent time with Michel Vennat, a close friend and at that time a senior partner in the Montreal office. Vennat explored the possibility of Lamer joining the firm following his retirement from the bench. He and Ed Waitzer had lunch with Lamer in Ottawa, where the security guards attached to the chief justice ensured, conspicuously, that there would be privacy in the restaurant. Following this, he indicated to Vennat that he might consider such an arrangement, Vennat brought the matter to the executive committee, and in short order, an arrangement was finalized whereby Lamer joined the firm in February 2000 in the Ottawa office.

Not long after Lamer had arrived, I phoned the Ottawa office and asked the receptionist to put me through to "the chief." I had wanted to speak with him in connection with a judgment in which he had participated since I was doing some research for a book involving the person whose case had been argued, and he had been part of a 3–2 majority of the Supreme Court of Canada that had declared her eligible for parole, using the *Charter of Rights and Freedoms*. Not being used to such a request, the receptionist put the call through to Kane, the managing partner of the office. Surprised when Kane came on the phone, but not deterred, I laughed, "Not you, you impostor. Put me through to the real chief!"

ASSOCIATES

The Ottawa office has been strengthened by the participation of a number of associate lawyers. At the time of writing, the following associates are based in Ottawa (year of joining and practice area are in parentheses): Tamra Alexander (1996, international trade and competition), Kim Alexander-Cook (1998, competition), Jonathan Blakey (1998, telecommunications), Nicole Brousseau (1995, trademarks), Jeff Brown (1995, competition), Eugene Derenyi (2000, patents), Nick McHaffie (1998, litigation), and Justine Whitehead (1997, international trade). In 2002, Vicky Eatrides (intellectual property), Roula Eatrides (corporate), and Catherine McKenna (competition, international trade) will join the office following their call to the Bar. Jamie Bocking, who joined the firm in 2000 for intellectual property and competition law, left in the summer of 2001 to do prosecution work for the federal government, but he continued to coach the summer softball league, Stikeouts, through to the end of a winning second season.[15]

STUDENTS

From its second year of operation, the Ottawa office has always had articling students, and as a result, a large number of students have passed through the firm in this capacity. It is an unfortunate fact of life in a small office that not all students can be hired back. Over the years, a remarkable variety of people have been employed as students. One memorable story is told about a student, who in the second portion of her articles was assigned the task of monitoring a regulatory hearing in a different agency from that where she had spent the first half of her articling experience. After the first day, she reported back to Kane that nothing of any particular importance had been raised relative to our client's interest. Immediately after getting this report, Kane received a telephone call from the chair of the board panel asking if Ms X was indeed from Stikeman Elliott and whether he knew that she was attending the hearing. When Kane replied yes to both questions, the panel member informed him that the student was sitting in a prominent place in the front row of the counsel tables, and during the hearing, she was disrupting the proceeding by humming and appearing quite distracted. The student was quickly reassigned to another project.

STAFF

It is axiomatic that lawyers cannot practise effectively unless they have a good staff. The Ottawa office has had the good fortune of attracting extremely capable and dedicated people, too numerous to name. While none has survived the full twenty years that the office has been open, there are records of sixteen and thirteen years respectively. As with the students, there have been some characters. One secretary used to disappear at lunchtime. A minor emergency arose during one of the disappearances, and it was crucial to find her. The receptionist was adamant that the secretary had not passed by to leave the office. After a quick search, she was found sound asleep under her desk, complete with a pillow and blanket! One person who was instrumental in building the administrative support for the office was the office manager, Judy Klein. When she died on February 26, 1993, it had, as might be expected in a small office working environment, a profound effect on everyone.

But it is the dedication of the support staff that stands out. In addition to a willingness to stay late or come in on a weekend, there are special anecdotes that make the point. A few years ago, a secretary was watching the 11:00 PM local news and saw an item about a virus that was predicted to infect computer systems the next day. She immediately drove into the office and went around to each computer to do a backup of all files. Despite finishing in the early hours, she was back in the office on time to further assist in protecting the operating system.

STAMP OF APPROVAL

In October 1998, Kane sent a brief cover note to Stikeman and Elliott, enclosing the most recent report to the executive committee on the Ottawa office. They had both been important to the office, but it had been a while since they had direct contact. Their replies, while short, reflected their fondness and support for the office. Stikeman's memo read: "I have to ... congratulate you on a truly remarkable performance. For so many years, Ottawa has been rather an orphan in the storm and regarded more as a messenger than a free standing business generator, which you have now turned it into."

Elliott replied: "Over the years, you have done an outstanding job in Ottawa. I remember well when it first started. The whole effort has more than met my expectations. Congratulations."

CONCLUSION

From the beginning, the Ottawa office has been fundamentally different from others in the firm, but it has always been a contributor, and in a number of years on a per-lawyer basis, it has been among the most profitable of the firm's offices. The early predictions about the trends in the Ottawa market proved to be remarkably accurate, and the only genuine lost opportunity by the firm was a delay in responding to the expanding local corporate market. While an office geared toward federal regulatory matters may sound to securities lawyers, dull and uninspiring, the range of files, the clients, and the matters dealt with have proven to be remarkably varied and exciting. The office, on its own and through referrals from other offices, has attracted a large number of the leading corporations in Canada and around the world. To paraphrase Stikeman, the originally orphaned office has ridden out the storm and is now a full-fledged member of the family, recognized as a free-standing business generator.

CHAPTER 8

Calgary

The firm's vision statement contemplated a national law firm, and many of the partners wanted to be the first such firm in Canada. In the 1970s, Grant was dispatched to meet with the law societies of Alberta and British Columbia, where he was told in no uncertain terms that he should go home. No member of either law society would be allowed to partner with anyone who was not also a member in good standing of that law society, and there was no possibility that such a rule would change. The idea was put on the shelf as unfeasible, little knowing that these would fall into the category of "famous last words," not unlike the prophetic statement of Yale economics professor Irving Fisher, who announced on October 17, 1929, a week before the market crashed, "Stocks have reached what looks like a permanently high plateau."

Notwithstanding this cold shower, Stikeman, with his typical optimism, applied for admission to the Law Society of Alberta on July 28, 1981, enclosing the usual documentation. Certificates of character were provided by François Mercier of the Quebec Bar and Donald Bowman of the Law Society of Upper Canada, both of whom certified that his character was beyond reproach and that his reputation was outstanding. His application recorded that he was admitted to the Ontario Bar in 1956, but the official certificate from the Law Society, signed by Kenneth Jarvis, provided that his call was in 1954. He was advised on September 1, 1981 that the Professional Examination Board in Law had approved his application as a member of the Law Society of Alberta.

Marvin Yontef had been exposed to the Calgary market through his immersion in the Dome Petroleum saga. Beginning in 1982, a Stikeman Elliott banking team, led by Yontef, was retained by Canadian Imperial Bank of Commerce, Toronto-Dominion Bank, Bank of Montreal, and Royal Bank of Canada (the so-called Four Banks) to document financing provided by those banks to Dome Energy to facilitate Dome's acquisition of 50 per cent of the shares of Hudson's Bay Oil and Gas. In addition to Yontef, the Stikeman Elliott team included Wayne Shaw, Bill Braithwaite, Mike Allen, Kathleen Ward, Ken Ottenbreit, Sean Dunphy, as well as many others.

Dome's financial difficulties led to a series of negotiations and consideration of various options for Dome's lenders, including the Four Banks, which resulted in considerable legal work for the Stikeman Elliott team. Many of the critical issues facing Dome's lenders involved oil and gas law and other questions governed by Alberta law, and we had retained Macleod Dixon as our agents in Alberta to assist us with these. The Citibank Syndicate, Dome's other principal lenders, had also engaged Macleod Dixon for those purposes. There was significant animosity between the Four Banks and the Citibank Syndicate, and it soon became clear that Macleod Dixon could not continue to serve as agents for both groups of lenders. Given the need to change Alberta agents, Wayne Shaw contacted his classmate Neil Wittmann (now Mr Justice Wittmann of the Alberta Court of Appeal) to see whether Wittman's firm, Code Hunter, might be free to assist with Alberta matters relating to the Four Banks' loans to Dome. Code Hunter was available, and Barry Emes[1] and Glenn Cameron[2] headed up a Codes team to work with the Stikeman Elliott Four Banks team on the Dome matter. The results were excellent, and we continued to refer other work to Codes thereafter.

Through the rest of the 1980s and into the early 1990s, there was increasing work on other Stikeman Elliott projects by Emes, Cameron, and others at Code Hunter with various Stikeman Elliott personnel, including members of Yontef's Four Banks team: Stransman, Rovinescu, Chalmers, Alison Youngman, and others. This work included continued work on Four Banks/Dome matters and additional work in respect of Turbo Resources, Pacific Gas and Electric Company, and other Stikeman Elliott clients.

The disinclination to start a fight with the Alberta Law Society continued through the late 1980s despite the increased activity of the firm in Alberta until the McCarthy firm (which was followed by Blake Cassels) simply moved into Calgary and started to practise right in the face, so to speak, of the Alberta Law Society, and it fought the matter through the courts to ultimate success.[3] Even when we had seen that, whether or not the Law Society concurred, it could be done, there was still no consensus that we should take the step of opening an office in Calgary although Grant, as chairman of the firm, had meetings with a number of Calgary firms including Code Hunter (where he met with Emes) to get a better sense of the situation and its possibilities.

The National Energy Board's move to Calgary was the principal catalyst for the decision to open the Calgary office of Stikeman Elliott. Rowland Harrison was a partner in the Ottawa office, and his practice was largely energy regulation matters before the NEB, so when that move was announced, it made sense for Harrison to relocate there as well. This led to discussions among Grant, Emes, and Cameron about the possibility of Emes and Cameron joining Stikeman Elliott and assisting in starting the Calgary office. At the time, it was thought that Michael Allen, a Four Banks team member from the Toronto office, would join Emes and Cameron, but events overtook that plan, and Allen ended up in Vancouver. It was then agreed that Emes, Cameron, and Harrison would establish the Calgary operation.

The partners felt that Marvin Yontef, then as now a person whose opinion mattered, was ambivalent (at best) about further domestic offices. When Yontef joined the discussions in Toronto regarding the opening of the Calgary office, the group (Grant, Finkelstein, Stransman, Emes, Cameron, Harrison, and others) tensed up, knowing Yontef's views on the proposed initiative. Yontef asked how the discussions were going. Emes replied that while the first hour had been heavy sledding, it looked as if we had the name worked out. The collective intake of breath sucked most of the papers off the table.

In furtherance of that plan, Harrison moved to Calgary in the summer of 1992. The decision had been made to lease space for the Calgary office in the East Tower of Bankers Hall, but the leasehold improvements in the new premises would not be completed until December of that year. Stikeman Elliott, together with a Code Hunter team headed by Cameron, had been working on the restructuring of Pacific Gas and Electric Company's Canadian natural gas supply arrangements. Harrison was providing PG&E advice on Canadian energy regulation, and it had established an office in Calgary for its restructuring team. The company loaned us space in those premises that Harrison used until mid-October 1992, when he was able to move into temporary accommodations in Bankers Hall. The Calgary office of Stikeman Elliott opened on the fifteenth floor of Bankers Hall East on December 1, 1992 with a legal staff of four: Emes, Cameron, and Harrison as local partners, together with one associate, Ron Deyholos.

Emes and Cameron were not involved in obtaining space or fitting it up for the opening of the Calgary office; they were still engaged in full-time practice at Code Hunter. Emes and Cameron were under the illusion that the firm was replete with old pros at setting up these kinds of offices and assumed that they would walk in on opening day, and there would be a fully equipped, up-and-running "McStikeman"-style law office. Never assume anything! The day that the Calgary office opened, there were bare floors in the entire common area. Concrete was everywhere, carpets nowhere. There were sawhorses all over and no obvious place in which to practise law. Emes had a closing the following day and left instructions that he was not to be disturbed. When he surfaced, his new secretary indicated that one aggressive fellow had managed to get by the front desk (not surprisingly because there was no door) and got as far as Emes's office door before she interrupted the intruder and explained that he was far too busy to be bothered. The man indicated that he simply wanted to make sure we were set up to function, and if not, we could come upstairs and use a boardroom at Trizec. The intruder was Kevin Benson, then chairman and CEO of Trizec.

The opening cocktail reception for the Calgary office was held at the Westin Hotel on January 28, 1993. That was a good place to have such receptions in January because of the access to the hotel through Calgary's "Plus 15" system, which allowed people to move from building to building without having to go outside into the cold. Heward Stikeman, Fraser Elliott, and their wives attended, as did James Grant, Sonny Gordon, and others. Newly elected Premier Ralph Klein, a former mayor of Calgary, was in attendance, with many other prominent people in the Calgary business community. Stikeman made the following comments on the occasion:

I would like to thank all of you for being here today, but my particular thanks go to those who live in this magnificent city. I would like to add to my thanks a word of caution. In case you think you are welcoming some high binding eastern lawyers, you are mistaken. Stikeman, Elliott's attachment to Calgary and the west has a long history. I first visited the city when I was a fledgling tax collector working as Assistant Deputy Minister of National Revenue in Ottawa in 1941. Times were very different then. There was no skyline, there was no Red Water, there was no Leduc, there was no National Energy Program, but there was the Turner Valley – the pride of Cowtown. I shall never forget on my drive in from the airport, a lady taxi driver, equipped with cowboy boots, jeans, and a Stetson hat, tossed some papers over the back seat of the cab onto my lap and said, "Take a look at these. $5 a share for the best gamble in the world." They were certificates of some unknown drilling company in the Turner Valley.

   After I left government services, my connections with Calgary became stronger, perhaps because I was working on the right side of the street in private practice. Some of my proudest professional memories are working for Eric Harvie and fighting the Western Leasehold's interests through to the Supreme Court of Canada and later being in at the start of the Glenbow Foundation. I was also privileged to work for Mr Nickle and many others of the oil fraternity, the last having been my great friend, Harold Siebens, and now his son, Bill. I have also lectured at the University of Calgary and have participated in many seminars and refresher courses in this City over the years. It is, therefore, with a great sense of pride, satisfaction, and happiness that I see our relationship formalized by the opening of our office, which we are celebrating today. I know that our coming here will produce business for all and that we will learn by being more permanently entrenched in Western Canada to be better, more tolerant, and innovative Canadians.

   Thank you very much.

LIFE IN THE FAST LANE

The Calgary office's objective was to expand the firm's practice into the energy and other sectors of the Alberta economy. There were some existing relationships in the Calgary market to build on – Husky Oil, which was controlled by the Li family, Texaco Canada, and others – and the firm was widely known in the city for its work on Dome, Turbo, and other high-profile mandates and for the tax planning work that Stikeman and others had done. But for the most part, this was a greenfield project.

   The first firm event attended by Emes and Cameron was the fortieth anniversary party at the Ritz Carleton in Montreal, where Stikeman spoke to the gathering about the reasons for the firm's success: hard work and a commitment to the highest quality of legal services. With Stikeman's words in mind, Emes and Cameron set out to establish the firm in the fiercely competitive Calgary market. The Calgary office was extremely busy from the start. Emes was working full-time with Trizec, which was undertaking a flurry of financings and refinancings, together with asset dispositions in response to a deteriorating national and international environment for real estate companies. Emes had referred Trizec to Stikeman Elliott over its problems with its majority-owned subsidiary, Bramalea, and Stransman did his usual wonderful job. This work would lead to the firm's involvement in Trizec's arrangement proceedings with its creditors and other stakeholders. Those proceedings were orchestrated by Stransman, Dunphy, and many others in the Toronto and other offices. In addition to Trizec, Emes maintained what for most others would have been a busy practice, as well as an eclectic selection of firm-related matters.

Cameron had his hands full with the restructuring of the Alberta/California natural gas market and its effect on our client Pacific Gas and Electric Company, along with many additional active matters. Emes, Cameron, and Harrison began to hire associates and recruit lateral partners. However, the opening of the Calgary office had coincided with an upturn in the oil and gas business and legal activity in Calgary, making recruitment of lawyers difficult. The problem with finding new lawyers was exacerbated by the fact that the existing lawyers in the Calgary office were so busy trying to respond to the demands of clients that even had there been a ready supply of lawyers, they did not have a moment to spare to engage in such prospecting. It was a classic case of being too busy to do anything to help themselves.

During this period, Fred Erickson[4] was lured away from Code Hunter. He joined Stikeman Elliott as an associate in March 1993 and became a partner two years later. Erickson had been working with Cameron on the Pacific Gas and Electric Company gas contract restructuring and continued to do so at Stikeman Elliott. Subsequently, he has become an expert in all aspects of the petroleum liquids business in Canada as advisor to BP Canada and other participants in that sector.

A month later, Duane Gillis[5] came over from Macleod Dixon as an associate. Gillis helped ease the workload and participated in establishing a mergers and acquisitions and securities practice in the office. After a few years with the firm, he was attracted by the opportunities to work in the firm's international offices and became a member of the Budapest office from the fall of 1995 until the spring of 1997, when he returned to Calgary. While in Budapest, he participated in the privatization of Hungary's electricity business and established contacts with Ireland's Electricity Supply Board International. After his return to Alberta, Gillis represented ESBI when it bid for and won the position of transmission administrator, one of the key roles in the deregulation of Alberta's electricity business.

The volume of work in the Calgary office continued to be far more than the lawyers on the ground could handle. In November 1993, Cameron, Erickson, Harrison, and others closed the giant Pacific Gas and Electric restructuring project, a matter that had been referred by John Stransman from the Toronto office. This project was an early illustration on how the firm's resources could be delivered to the Calgary market through the new local office. Chalmers, Grotenthaler, and others worked on litigation matters, Harrison provided Canadian regulatory advice, Cameron and Erickson tackled the many commercial elements of the complicated restructuring, Scott Wilkie provided tax advice, and Glenn Cranker handled GST matters.

Over two hundred producers and other commercial and governmental authorities in the United States and Canada participated in the restructuring. It was the largest commercial closing that had ever occurred in Canada, and thousands of documents were required to give effect to the complicated series of transactions. A floor in the Dome Tower was leased as a closing centre to accommodate the logistics required to complete the restructuring. The number of documents being copied was so enormous and the number of people involved was so great that the building managers threatened to lock everyone out of the closing centre, concerned that the combined weight of documents and people could cause the floor to collapse. The documents were eventually arranged by the perimeter walls and around support columns so that closing activities could continue.

Cameron called for the help of Mike Rumball and several associates from the Toronto office to assist with the Pacific Gas and Electric closing. When the Toronto contingent arrived in Calgary, one of them reported in by phone from the airport, saying that since it was already 4:00 PM, they would check into their hotel rooms and come over first thing the next morning. Cameron replied that if they did not mind, could they wander on over to the office directly before checking in at the hotel. The visiting lawyers came over, went straight to work, and did not see their hotel rooms until two and a half days later. As a result of many around-the-clock weeks of work that were required to complete the massive closing, Cameron's deal nickname, awarded by the Toronto contingent, became the "Energizer Bunny."

As indicated, Yontef was something of a contrarian about having a Calgary office at all. Following the closing of the massive Pacific Gas and Electric restructuring, one of the senior in-house counsel of the client was chatting with Emes, who introduced Yontef to the client. The client was effusive in saying to Yontef, "Thank you for opening your Calgary office. Your lawyers have been very helpful to us. You must have had a lot to say about the opening of the office." Before Yontef could answer, Emes jumped in with a quip: "Yes, Marvin did have a lot to say about it," he said, "but we managed to get the office open anyway." A friendly lecture from Yontef to Emes followed.

There was some sensitivity within the firm about hiring too many people from Code Hunter, but Emes nevertheless managed to convince the partnership to permit him to bring James Bruvall[6] over as an associate in December 1993 despite some internal controversy. When James Grant, the then chairman, came out to Calgary for his next visit, Emes introduced him to Bruvall. Grant paused for a moment, nodded knowingly, and said with his characteristic disarming candour, "Oh, yes, you are the one we didn't want." Bruvall was caught off guard, but he survived the encounter and became a partner of the firm in 1996. His versatility helped alleviate the workload in the early years. Emes introduced one of Bruvall's clients, PrimeWest Energy, to Amoco Canada in 1996, resulting in Amoco's sale of a quarter of a billion dollars worth of oil and gas properties to PrimeWest.

Bruvall, working with Tom Vowinckel on tax matters, designed a royalty trust structure for the deal. Bruvall's creativity in this area has resulted in his becoming an expert in these kinds of structures. Bruvall's practical manner and affinity for financial matters led to his being appointed to the firm's finance committee in 1997.

From the start, the Calgary office benefited from the great knowledge and support of the other Stikeman Elliott offices. As an example, a team from the firm consisting of Yontef, Gordon, Shaw, and others combined with Harrison and Erickson in the Calgary office in representing Husky Oil when it and the Province of Saskatchewan bought out the interests of the federal government and the Province of Alberta in the $2-billion Lloydminster heavy oil upgrader.

On another occasion, Emes was in Toronto working when he had a late night call from Erickson and Bruvall who indicated that one of our bank clients had phoned us to do a complicated prepaid heavy oil swap and had advised Erickson and Bruvall (or so they had heard) that it was similar to a "boat" loan. Emes, Erickson, and Bruvall discussed the concepts the transaction must include but could not see how this tied in with any water-going vessel. After about forty-five minutes, it finally struck the group that "boat" must have been "gold." They got on the phone to the Toronto office corporate lawyers and within two hours, had numerous "gold loan" precedents that were extremely useful in proceeding with the transaction, which ultimately made the front page of the *Financial Post*.

In 1994, Emes was retained by Amoco to make a hostile takeover bid for Home Oil. He was assisted by, among others, Sandra Redmond, who was a partner in the Calgary office from 1993 to 1997 and by Stransman and several others in the Toronto office. Although Amoco was ultimately not the successful bidder, the transaction was an illustration to the oil patch of the M&A capability of the Calgary office. During the bid, a number of *Competition Act* issues arose in respect of the Amoco natural gas liquids system, which required the expertise of Lawson Hunter from the Ottawa office, working with David Holgate,[7] then with the Fraser Milner firm, who did the liquids regulatory work for Amoco. This involvement ultimately led to Holgate joining the Calgary office as a partner in January 1997. Although Holgate was presented as a quiet, mild-mannered sort of person, appearances were deceiving. His hobbies include martial arts (blackbelt!) and guitar playing. In addition, he turned out to love a good celebration. Holgate permanently shed his quiet image when he woke up at 5:00 AM in the restroom of a restaurant where a firm event had been held. Of course by this time, all of the other Stikeman Elliott personnel and the staff of the restaurant had left, locking the place up on their way out. Holgate had to force his way out of the restaurant, being lucky to avoid a charge of "breaking and leaving."

Greg Plater[8] transferred to the Calgary office from Vancouver in August 1996, with a stop along the way at the Husky Oil legal department, where he was seconded for a couple of months. Plater assisted Emes with his busy real estate practice, and in addition, he headed up legal recruitment efforts. His enthusiasm for the firm and his friendly manner have contributed to significant improvement in hiring of quality legal personnel for the Calgary office. His admission to the Law Society of Alberta was noteworthy. The concept of individual Bar call ceremonies is unique in this day and age to Alberta. In a manner akin to a remarriage ceremony, both Plater and his Crown prosecutor wife, Lori, were called to the Alberta Bar at the same time in a joint application. Of course, the application was made (successfully) by the ubiquitous Emes.

Stuart Olley[9] joined the office from Code Hunter in January 1997 as an associate. This move was accelerated during his first interview lunch with Emes at an out-of-the-way Italian restaurant. They were squirrelled away in what they thought was a private room, when they looked up to see twelve partners and associates from Olley's then employer, standing in the doorway. Code Hunter had chosen the restaurant for the firm's Christmas lunch. The humour of the situation was not lost on a colleague of Olley's at Codes. He phoned Emes later in the day to comment on Olley's misfortune at being caught in the act of a job interview with Emes. "God does not like Stuart Olley," the caller laughed.

David Weekes,[10] a leading tax practitioner, joined the Calgary office from Toronto in August 1997. He started in the Toronto office in 1984, moved to Vancouver for five years from 1989 to 1994 (he was made a partner in 1990), and then returned to the Toronto office for three years before leaving for Calgary.

Emes had known Kemm Yates[11] since 1973 – they had articled at the same time and had kept in touch. Yates was a very well-respected energy regulatory lawyer with Fraser Milner, where he had worked with David Holgate. After a year and a half courtship, Kemm joined Stikeman Elliott in the Calgary office as a partner in February 1998. The timing of Yates's arrival had been planned to coincide with the completion of a hearing before the NEB, in which Yates was participating as counsel to Alliance Pipeline Canada. Alliance had applied to the NEB for permission to build the Canadian part of the mammoth Alliance Pipeline, which was to deliver natural gas from Fort St John, British Columbia to Chicago. Alliance's application was being vigorously contested by NOVA Pipelines and TransCanada PipeLines, which correctly saw the Alliance Pipeline as a major intrusion into their monopoly service territory. The hearing was supposed to start in November 1997 and be completed just before Christmas that year. In fact, preliminary motions were not finished until the end of 1997. As a result, the hearing did not start until January 1998 and did not finish until the end of May that year. Yates was ready to jump to the Calgary office, but the hearing had just begun, and making a move at that time would have been awkward for the client.

Yates's change of firms was further complicated by the fact that Cameron was acting for the syndicate of lenders providing $US2.6 billion in financing for the project. In view of the potential conflict, we agreed to wall Yates off from Cameron's financing team. So, for his first six months with Stikeman Elliott, Yates was parked behind locked doors in a distant corner of the office away from the rest of the firm with his own office equipment and supplies.

Frequently, the only time Yates's path would cross those of the others in the firm would be as he arrived early in the morning to start his long day just as Cameron's finance team were stumbling out the door after a late night.

Chris Nixon[12] joined Stikeman Elliott Calgary in February of 2001. He is one of the best known M&A and securities lawyers in Calgary, and he was lead counsel in many of the high-profile transactions in Calgary during the 1990s. Nixon's considerable M&A experience has been an important addition to the Calgary office. His courtship was lengthy. Emes and Cameron commenced discussions with him in 1994 when he was with Burnett Duckworth & Palmer, but nothing resulted from those initial contacts. Nixon then joined Osler Hoskin & Harcourt in September 1995, and Emes resumed the conversations with him after that move. This second round of discussions extended over a two-year period and resulted in Nixon joining the firm. As Ed Waitzer noted in introducing Nixon at his first partners meeting, "This courtship lasted longer than the courtship of my wife; either of them, for that matter."

The most recent partner in the Calgary office, Leland Corbett,[13] articled with the firm and practised with us for two years before taking an inside counsel position with an oil and gas company. After that company was taken over, Corbett returned and became a partner at the start of 2002. Other talented associates and students joined the Calgary office during the period described above. On several occasions when SOSS came out from the Calgary office, the firm responded by loaning personnel to get the office through particularly busy periods. John Patterson, Maurice Swan, and Dean Kraus all spent some time as temporary members of the Calgary office during this period.

THE KID FROM PINCHER CREEK

Harrison would remain with the Calgary office until 1999, when he accepted an appointment to the National Energy Board. Harrison had been managing partner of the Calgary office from when it opened in 1993 until 1995. Emes became managing partner of the office at that time until Cameron took over the position in 2001. In addition, Emes was elected to the partnership board in September 1997. He has been the cornerstone of the Calgary office, providing leadership in practice matters, business development, recruitment, and office management. No history of the Calgary office would be complete without some description of his unique personality and its impact on life in the office.

Everyone in the Calgary office has become familiar with Pincher Creek, the small town in southern Alberta where Emes grew up.[14] There has been an endless stream of Pincher Creek anecdotes, some of which go back to the days prior to establishment of the Calgary office. Regardless of the occasion, Emes has a Pincher Creek story. When Stikeman Elliott retained Code Hunter regarding Alberta law matters on the Four Banks/Dome Energy loan, Emes and Cameron were summoned to Toronto to participate in meetings with Marvin's Stikeman Elliott bank team, the Four Banks, Dome, and other parties. On the occasion of Emes and Cameron's first visit to Stikeman's Toronto office (then on the thirteenth, fourteenth, and fifteenth floors of Commerce Court West), Emes and Cameron were overwhelmed with the tastefully done premises, including Elliott's stunning Group of Seven art collection that was hung everywhere. On their arrival, the receptionist had advised Emes and Cameron that they were to be in the London Room. After touring through the offices to find that boardroom (and admiring more art along the way), Emes and Cameron found that the London Room was being used. Returning to the receptionist for further directions, they were sent to the Hong Kong Room, which was also being used, and then to the New York Room, which again was occupied. After about half an hour of touring around to every boardroom in the Toronto office, they were finally directed to the Ottawa Room, which turned out to be available. They began to unpack their materials, still in awe of Stikeman Elliott's magnificent premises in the midst of the towers of power of the Canadian legal establishment. As they were getting settled, Emes was in need of the men's room. He announced to Cameron with, for him, uncharacteristic formality, "Glenn, please excuse me for a moment. If anyone is looking for me, I will be in the Pincher Creek Room."

Emes's signature drink is Diet Coke. In the original offices in the East Tower of Bankers Hall, the receptionist would arrive at 6:45 AM. Her first assignment each morning was to pour a glass of Diet Coke for Emes, so that it would be warm – he does not like it cold – and waiting for him when he arrived shortly after 7:00 AM.

Music is another distinguishing characteristic. Emes has eclectic tastes and an encyclopedic knowledge of music. His favourite, however, is country and western, which he has an unfortunate tendency to sing while walking around the office. Any prospective lateral hire or articling student is well advised to be prepared to discuss and defend his or her taste in music. Emes will often ask the candidate in his usual disarming fashion, "If I were to get into your car after this interview, what CD would be playing?" Successful candidates would reply, something from Steve Earle or a selection from the *O Brother Where Art Thou?* soundtrack. While Emes used to stress that there were "no bad answers," anything by Lionel Ritchie or other elevator music performers came very close.

In the old offices, there were three boardrooms, side by side. Emes never liked working in his office, an affliction suffered by Cameron as well. Instead, Emes would have a file spread out in each of the boardrooms and run back and forth between them, depending on the matter to which he was attending. This frenetic activity prompted one visitor to comment that Emes practised law like a dentist: he had a patient (his file) in each of his three chairs, running back and forth as the freezing wore off.

Most of the firm-wide partners meetings are conducted by conference call, which Emes has made into parties for the Calgary partners. There are always lots of nacho chips, popcorn, cookies, and, of course, Diet Coke. During the meetings, Emes is the master of the mute button on the Calgary conference phone. As a result, his partners never know whether or not his frequently irreverent comments have just been made to the whole partnership. During one such conference call, before the meeting got started, there was an informal, very politically correct, discussion about the firm's harassment policy being conducted by the Toronto partners. During a pause, Emes leaned into the speakerphone with a question for those on the other end of the line: "Pardon me for interrupting," he said. "It's the Calgary office. We've been listening to the discussion, and we are wondering something out here. When you say harass, is that one word or two?" Emes laughed at the look of horror on the Calgary partners' faces as he announced, to their relief, that the mute button was on for that comment.

In some respects, the Calgary office is more formal than would be expected for the Wild West. In fact, it was not until the fall of 2001 that a business casual dress code was adopted. Even after the dress code changed, many of the partners and some of the associates continue to prefer to wear dark suits and white shirts. Except, that is, during Stampede Week. For ten days in July, everyone in the Calgary office (like the rest of the city) wear nothing but cowboy shirts and jeans. And not just any cowboy shirts: those shirts are tastefully monogrammed with the official Stikeman Elliott logo. And to complete the outfit, there are distinctive western belt buckles that Emes had specially designed for the Calgary office. The buckles have become collectors' items. Emes bestows them only on members of the Calgary office and certain select friends and supporters of the office. Those that acquired their buckles in the early days note with some pride that there is a comma between Stikeman and Elliott, an early name for the firm.

So attired, the entire office takes off to a cowboy bar at noon on Parade Day to participate in the barely controlled mayhem that is the Calgary Stampede. These events are legendary affairs. The last partiers typically do not leave until one or two o'clock the following morning, but only after settling a bar bill that has accumulated over the past fourteen hours of partying. Did they really drink all those shooters? Sometimes guests from the other offices who have spent time in the Calgary office are invited to the post-parade party – Lewis Smith and Aaron Atcheson joined the fun in 2000, and Lana Finney came along in 2001. All guests are sworn to secrecy as a condition of attending.

THE PLATFORM FOR THE FUTURE

In February of 2001, the Calgary office moved from the East Tower to the forty-third and forty-fourth floors in the West Tower of Bankers Hall, where the view of the Canadian Rockies is panoramic. The premises design committee of Yates, Plater, and Olley wanted to avoid the scenario of moving in among power tools and sawhorses, which had happened when the office opened in 1992. Notwithstanding an unexpectedly short time frame to complete the renovations, the departure of the office administrator in the midst of the fit up, and a few other unexpected setbacks, the move was successfully accomplished on time, with movers literally clipping the heels of carpenters and carpet layers as the moving dollies rolled in.

On May 7, 2001, there was a reception to celebrate the opening of the new offices. Over 350 prominent members of the Calgary business community attended. The entire partners board, as well as Rose, Stransman, Kane, and other partners, joined the Calgary office in hosting the reception. The following day, the partners board met in Calgary. In nine years, the Calgary office has grown from four to over thirty legal personnel. This growth has occurred in typical Stikeman Elliott fashion – through a combination of lateral hires and internal development rather than by merger.

The objective of the Calgary office has been to expand the firm's practice into the energy and other sectors of the Alberta economy. In the short time it has been operating, the Calgary office has been very successful in building a first-tier practice in a highly competitive market. It represents national and international participants in the energy and other business sectors, financial institutions, and other parties in complex, high-profile transactions that are frequently far larger than those usually undertaken by offices of similar size. It has achieved this goal by employing the work ethic and dedication to the practice exemplified by Heward Stikeman and by utilizing the full resources of the firm to the benefit of our clients in this market.

Throughout the history of the firm, Alberta has been a place of unique opportunity for the business community. The outlook is for this climate of opportunity to continue into the future. The Calgary office plans to grow from its solid base to play an even greater role in that future.

CHAPTER 9

Taking Care of Business

MONTREAL IN THE 1970S

As the 1970s began, the firm was growing in size and importance, but it was not big enough to attract much attention outside its immediate clients, other than for the continually growing reputations of Stikeman and Elliott as major innovators and emerging powers on the business and legal scenes. Elliott was a corporate player, and Stikeman had maintained the glow of his reputation as the leader of a tax Bar that was increasingly important. They were recognized as having attracted a number of highly talented and ambitious lawyers, and the initial expeditionary expansion of a small office into the financial capital of Europe had been followed up by the attack on the legal and business establishment of Toronto with the double coup of capturing Robarts and Bowman. All that remained was the germination of the seeds thus planted, the unleashing of their creative talents, and in due course, some strategic pruning of lawyers who were perfect for their time but unlikely to grow into full flowers as the firm developed into a national and global enterprise. But more of that later.

Stikeman had brought in, among many others, the Siebens family, initially for tax planning matters, and this business generated considerable corporate work connected with the reorganizations of the privately held family companies, as well as Eric Harvie, also from Western Canada. In the east, he represented K.C. Irving for tax planning matters and the reorganization of the complex family interests. Jerry Fryml's Montreal Fast Print organization and the Thomas Karas interests – developed from his invention of Caristrap, a unique nylon device used to hang meat carcasses instead of the traditional steel hooks – were regular clients of the firm and were also brought in by Stikeman. Fednav, probably Stikeman's favourite and of which he was a director, was a faithful client that provided ongoing corporate work as the company expanded its fleet (and it would become even more active during the 1980s) in addition to international tax planning coordinated by Peter Cumyn. The Bata family interests were complex and interesting, and they included efforts to recover the family business in

Central Europe, which had been confiscated by the Communist regime. The firm arranged the reorganization of Laurentian Bank, formerly the Montreal City & District Savings Bank, assisted Chevron with its Canadian operations and structuring, and acted for Lloyd's for whom Stikeman, its Canadian guru, got legislation enacted to allow Lloyd's syndicates to act on non-marine risks situated in Canada.

Robb was involved in the complicated matters arising out of the Canadian Javelin refinery financing and the resultant actions directed against its principal, the high-flying John C. Doyle, who decided that for many reasons, Panama might be more comfortable than Canada. We began a long association with the "maverick" investment dealer Richard G.D. Lafferty, which included many successful investments and as many lawsuits over a period of thirty years. Altamira Financial was a regular client in the investment field, and the firm assisted with the birth of Intertape Polymer, founded by Mel Yull, formerly with Domtar. At Domtar, Yull had been in charge of development for Eastern Coated Papers and thought the company should get into plastics and polymers, but when it did not, he left and carried on the idea on his own. Richards acted for St Laurent Steel, owned by George Thomas, and later for Nova Steel, headed by one of Thomas's former employees, Brian Jones. Nova Steel has become a listed company in the United States.

In the early 1970s, Hartt had a client who had the ambitious idea of buying Investors Overseas Syndicate (IOS), formerly headed by the notorious Bernard Cornfeld, out of bankruptcy, but had to fire the client when it was discovered that he was stealing the firm's letterhead for the purpose of using it for forging an opinion he needed for a prospectus. Robb was involved in three different sales of Champlain Industries Ltd. and four changes of ownership of Klöckner Stadler Hurter. Robb had an interesting client called King Chan, who owned the Rodeo Bar and Grill on St Laurent above La Gauchetière, which became known as the "Lodeo." Chan was charged with paying his topless dancers less than the minimum wage, and when asked whether he had a defence, he replied that he had: he didn't know that they were eighteen!

We represented a character by the name of J. Bob Carter, a very crude, extremely smart person with only a Grade 7 education, who organized several large transactions in the Western Canadian oil patch. One of them involved a takeover bid, in which the issue arose of whether he had already decided to take over the target company, having obtained 10 per cent of the shares. He was being questioned by a series of Wall Street lawyers about his real intention. The questioning, which deteriorated very quickly, proceeded along the following lines: "So you bought x shares?" "Yes." "You are telling us that when you bought these shares, you had no intention of acquiring control of the company?" "Well," he replied, "it is sort of like being in a bar. You meet a girl and buy her a drink. You can't decide whether you want to fuck her, so you buy her another drink, and so forth. Well, it was sort of like that with the shares." He had a cowboy hat and boots, both of which he wore when appearing in front of Mr Justice Gomery of the Quebec Superior Court. At one stage, he actually turned to the judge and said, "My Lord, can you tell me when I'm getting close to contempt?"

The Hunter Douglas group was owned by the Sonenberg family, who had escaped from Germany – leaving its steel business to the tender mercies of the National Socialist government – to start an aluminum siding business in Holland. Hartt took Hunter Douglas first public and later private. When going public, the company insisted on simultaneous closings in Canada and in London so that the securities would be listed in both jurisdictions. Every night, a huge telex had to be prepared and sent to Harold Gordon, then in charge of the London office, in order to be able to work each day from the same set of documents. Hartt also handled the sale of the Cartier Sugar refinery interests by the Steinberg family. He and Martin Scheim acted on a disposition by Consumers Distributing in which there was an acrimonious dispute that led to arbitration on the value of every single item in the retailer's inventory. That was eventually settled only after months of wrangling. On a sale by Conroy of three snowmobile companies, there was a reverse earnout (the price was set at the likely highest amount possible and would be reduced if subsequent earnings did not meet certain negotiated targets), and the seller later sued, claiming that the new management was responsible for failing to meet the targets, a claim that was successfully resolved in favour of the client purchaser. On the Newberry file, a client referred to him by Elliott, Hartt handled the transaction by which Newberry acquired three chains of stores.

Hartt was on the Canadian board of directors of Lombard Odier, the offices of which were in the Air Liquide building, then at 1155 Sherbrooke Street West in Montreal. Lombard Odier had an Italian client who needed to have a special trust created to hold his investments. Hartt told Guy Masson, who was working with him on the matter, that he would be a bit late for the scheduled meeting but that Masson should start without him. Hartt was well over an hour late, not an unusual occurrence, but he arrived laughing, enough so that the Canadian president of Lombard Odier looked at him and asked what had happened. Hartt said he had been on the elevator with an American couple, who had been looking at the signs on the elevator that indicated the floors occupied by Air Liquide. Sounding out the name, the husband had declared to his wife, in a knowledgeable manner, that it must be a Canadian regional carrier.

The corporate and tax clients and those using the growing litigation strength in Montreal were well served. The young team of commercial lawyers had their hands full of the work generated by the two founding partners, and as they developed, they attracted their own clients. This accelerated the need for new lawyers, and a period of phenomenal growth began, to be followed in less than a decade by even more astonishing growth in Toronto and the expansion to other markets in Canada and abroad. In the 1970s, however, the Montreal office was by far the most dominant, both in its own right and in the work that it was able to direct to the new Toronto office. Montreal also recognized the need to increase its capability in French as francophone Quebec began to increase its importance in the business community as a result of the waning influence of the Church and the development of a new breed of ambitious entrepreneurs. It was clear that major changes were working their way through the community in Quebec. The English-speaking establishment would no longer enjoy its previous unchallenged status nor be immune to profound social changes already becoming apparent, which would see the election of a separatist government in the latter half of the decade.

Functional bilingualism was a welcome evolution for most of the anglophone legal community and, arguably, one that was long overdue. North America seems to be the last bastion of a view, held to be fashionable, that it is a major personal accomplishment to speak one language moderately well. Those in the litigation field already required much more than mere familiarity since almost all of the work before the courts was conducted in French and most of the litigators were, in fact, francophone. In the commercial practice, the firm needed to reinforce Michel Vennat and to provide a profile that would enable the firm to present itself not only as user-friendly to the emerging francophone business community, but also fully capable of servicing all its needs. This led to the arrivals of several lawyers, including Jean-Pierre Ouellet,[1] Martin Claude Lepage,[2] and Yvon Martineau.

Jean-Pierre Ouellet's first involvement with the firm began in the spring of 1970, when it consisted of about seventeen lawyers, including Peter Cumyn in London. Ouellet had come to the Bar via Collège St Paul and the Université de Montréal and to the firm as a result of the charm and blandishments of Bruce Verchere, a good mentor from whom he learned a lot about the practice of law. Ouellet left the firm immediately after his call to the Bar in 1971 for two years of study at Oxford on a Rhodes Scholarship, where he earned a BCL in jurisprudence. After graduation in June 1973, he travelled in Europe and South Africa during the summer and returned to Canada in October, following which he worked for Quebec Premier Robert Bourassa until August 1976. His classmates at the firm were Peter O'Brien,[3] Brian Schneiderman, Réal Forest, and Edouard Belliard. The latter was a hairdresser who had decided to become a lawyer, and Ouellet remembers how one evening, he was describing that he worked for this important business law firm in downtown Montreal, only to have the lady next to him announce that her hairdresser worked there! Forest left to attend the London School of Economics for a year and then went to the Sorbonne for a doctorate on the origins of administrative law. Upon completion of that degree, Forest returned to Quebec City, where he worked in the Department of Justice until 1985, when the Liberals came back to power. At that point, he returned to the firm.

Wage and price controls were announced in the fall of 1975, and Ouellet dabbled in that practice for a while. As a junior, like all others, he did some early litigation. He worked with Gérald Tremblay on an important trial that involved three or four weeks of preparation. Tremblay, already a rising star in litigation, got in the cab with him on the way to the courthouse and received his only briefing from Ouellet on this important case during the five-minute ride. When they got into court, Tremblay's adversary asked for a delay, which took for some reason five or ten minutes to explain. Tremblay rose to his feet and said to the court that he was bitterly disappointed at this request for a delay, grandly announcing that "for once, I was ready."

After this brief flurry in litigation, Ouellet moved into the corporate field and financing transactions, the bulk of which were initially private placements. One of his first transactions was a Eurodollar issue by Canadian National, then still a Crown corporation. In fact, everyone in the lending syndicate considered the transaction to be the equivalent of a sovereign credit, but CN thought the credit was being advanced on its own merits. Ouellet remembers the company agonizing over its description of itself for the purposes of the issuing document, as if the company itself really mattered to the purchasers of its debt instruments. The security was listed on the Luxembourg exchange, which is virtually unregulated, and CN went to market twice a year for such issues. Ouellet also represented the Montreal radio station CKAC in its business affairs for several years.

Claude Lepage joined the firm in 1971 following his MBA at the University of Western Ontario and became part of the corporate section, where he developed a specialty in financing, including an interest in developing standard documents that could be used to produce contracts on a far more efficient basis than starting from scratch on each occasion. He soon had a complete set of documents that could be used with ease for a broad range of financing transactions, and he stored them in computerized formats, which greatly simplified putting security for loans in place. He was the first technical guru in the firm and was, with Stikeman, the original impetus for the firm to adopt the computer as the next technical breakthrough in the practice of law.

Yvon Martineau was a lawyer who also had an MBA, and he concentrated almost exclusively on the francophone business community. He was a person of high energy and had the potential to develop into one of the firm's leading corporate lawyers, with a loyal following of clients. But he was never entirely comfortable practising in a firm that he considered to be too anglophone, and so, he left in 1993.

THE COMPUTER AGE

When he joined the firm, Lepage had already been exposed to the power of computers at the MBA program at Western and had learned the two computer languages then in general use: Basic and Fortran. In addition, his wife, Louise, had taken courses at the Université Laval prior to coming with him to London, Ontario, and she was already familiar with the programming language PL1. The firm was the first in Montreal to have its accounting data processed by computer. Bob Hart was very proud of this because we were issued weekly computer printouts of our time and disbursements, which were compiled by an outside firm at Place Victoria, Aquila BST, one of our clients.[4] The computers of the day were big, heavy machines, costing millions of dollars; the advent of the personal computer was still almost ten years in the future.

The next attempt to practise mechanization occurred when Bob Hart purchased an IBM Selectric typewriter, coupled with a magnetic card reader, which was operated by Shirley Delage on the thirty-ninth floor. Before that, the major technological breakthrough had been the purchase of electric typewriters, which made the act of typing less onerous than the previous clunky manual keyboards, which had changed very little over the previous fifty years. Unfortunately, the magnetic card concept was cumbersome technology and not a great success. Then came the era of the Canadian-made AES dedicated word processor, and Lepage was the first to push this technology in the firm despite great reservations by the firm's management – Bob Hart, in particular – due to the significant cost of the machines (in those days, an AES Plus with word processor, complete with online printer, cost upwards of $10,000), and they were reluctant to spread this hardware in the firm. To circumvent the reluctance, Lepage adopted the stratagem of arranging with the distributor for the installation, on a three-month trial basis, of three AES Plus word processors, to be used, at least in the sense of generating documentation that required typing power, by three of the busiest lawyers in the firm – namely, himself, Sonny Gordon, and Yvon Martineau. He knew that if Martineau and Gordon became "hooked" on this typing power, they would never be able to part with the machines and would force Bob Hart to buy them once the three-month trial period was over. He knew as well that once the three lawyers in the firm had the technology, it would not be long before everyone else would want to have it – which is exactly what happened.

The first AES Plus machine was installed in 1979 at the desk of Lepage's secretary, Louise Ortmann, and her typing power increased exponentially. During the next five years, everyone in the firm eventually got an AES machine; some of the heavy users were getting AES Pluses, while the others got smaller models. At the same time, the typing pool was equipped with five or six powerful AES machines with floppy disk readers, which could be interchanged between other firms and other offices of Stikeman Elliott as the technology began spreading very quickly. By 1984 or 1985, a new technology became available, which competed with AES for a share of the dedicated word processing market. The name of that company was NBI, but there were also others in the field – such as Xerox, IBM, and Wang – that were coming out with their own dedicated word processing systems. This new technology did not rely on floppy disks but instead, on a central server to which all the substations were connected. This was perceived as the new future. Essentially, the substations were dummies rather than stand-alone computers, the advantage of which was that documents could be interchanged very quickly between various workstations. The big downside was that the whole system could grind to a halt in the event of a crash of the central server.

At the very strong, persistent push of the Toronto office, Stikeman Elliott adopted the NBI technology in 1985, and that system was installed in both the Montreal and Toronto offices. The old AES machines were sold at nominal prices to whomever might want a slightly used word processing machine. Louise Ortmann bought her own machine. In 1982, Lynn Hanley, the former secretary of Pierre Archambault, came to work for Lepage as a paralegal, and in order to get her an AES word processor, he had to pay for it out of his own pocket, and it was not until 1986 that the firm (namely Bob Hart) agreed to pay him back. When Lynn Hanley left the firm in 1986, her sister, Mary Ann, came to work for him and is still with the firm.

In the mid-1980s, personal computers had become the rage, spearheaded by Apple, and when the Mackintosh hit the market, it revolutionized the user/computer interface with its WIM system (windows/icons/mouse interface). The first in the firm to buy Mackintosh computers were Stikeman and Lepage. In those days, the fastest model was a Mackintosh Plus equipped with a small hard disk and a heavy and bulky desk laser printer. The whole thing had a price tag of about $10,000. Lepage knew the firm would never purchase this kind of equipment for him, so both Stikeman and he bought their own machines, hoping that by demonstrating their huge increase in productivity, they could convince Hart to approve a reimbursement. Not until 1988 did Lepage finally convince Hart and Grant to reimburse his out-of-pocket expenses of roughly $20,000 for his machine, the machine of Mary Ann Hanley, and the laser printer shared between them. The only other desktop computer he can remember at the time was an IBM XT personal computer, which sat on the desk of Elinore Richardson, functioning as a paperweight.

Toward the end of 1985, Lepage began to think about the possibility of developing a new kind of software, not for the processing of raw data, accounting, mathematical calculations, or even regular word processing, but instead, to generate various forms and other largely repetitive documents that lawyers create on a daily basis. His banking practice was particularly suited to this kind of application, and after testing various products available on the market, he and his wife decided to develop their own software, which was custom-made to their own needs. However, it was based on the same principles used by other document assembly software – namely, the creation of a template sprinkled with text and variables, supported by a user-friendly interface between the machine and the lawyer, thus enabling the development of a large bank of templates stored in a fully integrated bank of models from which could be generated, at the touch of a few keys and mouse clicks, complex forms and legal documents in either French or English with unprecedented feed-in quality.

They called this system "autoText," and they worked days and nights and weekends to develop it on the Apple Mackintosh. The system began producing the first hypothecs, loan agreements, and trust deeds at the beginning of 1987. From then on, the system was perfected, amplified in the database, and complemented with hundreds of precedents designed to be used easily by a trained paralegal, thereby substantially reducing the time and cost of producing complex documents, which were formerly the sole prerogative of the experienced, practising lawyer. Now, for a fraction of the previous cost, a well-trained and supervised paralegal could generate most of the documentation needed to close a multi-million-dollar banking transaction. Having demonstrated the power of the system, at the beginning of 1989, the firm approved the creation of the Montreal banking group, which consisted initially of Lepage, Jill Hugessen,[5] François Ouimet,[6] Donald Francoeur,[7] and Mary Ann Hanley.

The firm then equipped everybody in the group with brand-new Apple Mackintosh SE-30 computers, the best available at the time, with a local area network (LAN) linked to a server and to desktop laser printers. This was the first time that the autoText document assembly system became extensively used. Lepage spent a great deal of time developing new templates in both French and English for the use of this small group of high-tech lawyers. In 1990, a great debate ensued as to whether or not the firm was going to switch to WordPerfect and the MS DOS/IBM operating system. At the time, IBM was teetering on the brink of bankruptcy, and WordPerfect was the dominant word processing software in the world. Despite Lepage's objections in favour of the Apple Mackintosh user-friendly interface, the firm decided to hire Solange Crevier as its information technology supervisor and to go ahead with WordPerfect – firm-wide – on IBM computers, running under the MS DOS operating software.

One of the drawbacks of the Apple Mackintosh system was that it was not fully compatible with the IBM system, which had wider acceptance in North America. The firm did not want to invest heavily in technology supported by companies that did not have a good solid track record, as had been the case with the disastrous experience of NBI. As far as the banking group was concerned, this meant that its days with the Mackintosh were numbered, and the Lepages immediately began writing the software to convert the whole system to WordPerfect. By 1992, Microsoft had introduced the new Windows system, namely, Windows 5.1, and it took Lepage and his wife about a year and a half to rewrite the entire software and all its templates on WordPerfect 5.1 and 5.2. Toward the end of 1992, the firm switched again, from WordPerfect to Microsoft Word, and for the third time in ten years, considerably discouraged, they set out to rewrite the templates and the software to support Microsoft Word and the Microsoft Windows operating system.

To complicate the situation even further, in 1993, the Quebec government enacted the new *Civil Code,* and the part of the former *Civil Code* that underwent the greatest changes and upheaval was in the area of security interests, which meant another year and a half of brainstorming, revamping, refreshing, and updating all the templates, taking into account the new legislation, each of which had to be done in both French and English so that any of the output documents could be produced in either language with exactly the same legal effect and substance.[8] Finally, with the advent of Windows 95 and Microsoft Word version 7, the autoText document assembly system stabilized, and no substantial changes in software or legal substance have been required since the end of 1995. AutoText is now licensed to the firm on a non-exclusive contract for a period of ten years ending in 2010. There are about twenty-five lawyers currently using the system, and the job of keeping its legal content up to date, at least until 2004, remains Lepage's responsibility. Despite a few battles of internal persuasion here and there, the firm was always well ahead of any of its Montreal competition in its willingness to experiment with new technology thanks in large part to Stikeman, himself a tinkerer par excellence, who was always sympathetic and supportive of our various forays.

The impact of technology on the practice of law within the past fifty years has been unprecedented. When the firm was founded, output was generated on mechanical typewriters, and little changed from a half-century earlier. Copies were made by an elaborate system of carbon paper and several sheets of thin paper, all of which had to be fed manually into the apparatus in the hope that they would stay aligned and that the keystrokes would be firm enough to produce a legible copy. Errors had to be corrected manually on each of the copies. Where documents had to be reproduced in bulk, there were several brands of copiers, such as Gestetner, but most of them involved messy, smelly fluids. The electric typewriter was seen as a virtual miracle, and SnoPaque, which allowed mistakes to be typed over (other than on carbon copies, where any mistake was particularly apparent), relieved much of the angst of the unlucky typist. The telegram was the principal means of long distance written communication, eventually supplanted by the telex, which could be operated from within business premises. The fax was unheard of until the firm was well-established, and e-mail was but a distant gleam in the eye of a few academics. No lawyer in practice in the 1950s could ever have imagined the volume of work that would be routinely produced by today's generation of lawyers.

MAURICE RIEL

Senator Maurice Riel,[9] appointed to the Senate in 1973 by Pierre Elliott Trudeau, arrived at Stikeman Elliott in 1975 after practising law for thirty years. He had been invited by Elliott, with whom he had worked when they were co-treasurers of the Liberal Party of Canada. Elliott first heard of Riel's possible interest in joining the firm from Michel Vennat, who was then working as Trudeau's assistant and who knew both men from their work in Liberal politics. In addition to spending approximately three months per year in Ottawa to fulfill his Senate duties, Riel was the head of his own law firm, often travelling extensively to Europe on business. He also spent roughly three months per year attending board meetings. Trying to balance all of his activities as the head of a small firm – whether business, legal, or political – proved to be an impossible task. His commitments far exceeded his available time, and he decided that something had to go. Knowing this, Vennat approached Elliott and urged him to talk Riel into joining the firm. Elliott decided that Riel could come in as a partner while continuing to attend to his Senate duties and many meetings.

Riel's arrival provided an entree into the French business community that was unparalleled for the firm, especially with his large European client base. His clients were major French businesses that were only just beginning to give consideration to the opportunities in North America, and they were rethinking their perception of Canada as *"quelques arpents de neige"*[10] as they turned their attention to the huge markets that existed on this continent. To assist Riel with his legal work, Elliott surrounded him with the necessary support, headed by Michel Vennat, who was specifically designated to look after Riel's clients. Much of Vennat's work thereafter came from the clients that Riel brought with him, including Alcatel, BNP, Dumez, Air Liquide, and the Société Lyonnaise des Eaux. Vennat considered himself very much like Elliott and was influenced by him to have a combination of legal practice and outside business interests, interests that ultimately led him to become the chairman of Westburne Inc., one of Riel's former clients.

Vennat was also instrumental in attracting Marc Lalonde, who was thinking of retiring from politics at the end of the Trudeau government years in the early 1980s. Elliott had dinner with Lalonde to see if agreement in principle could be reached, and when the former finance minister showed interest, Grant and Vennat worked out the details. What appears to have attracted him to the firm was its national and international character. Vennat convinced him that it was the best type of firm for him, and he seemed open to this as the best platform to be in Montreal on the national scene. He became a very well-known and respected international arbitrator, and, of course, once the Liberals came back into power, his connections were particularly valuable. There was an uncomfortable interim period when he first returned to private practice during the early years of the Conservative government, but that has long since been overcome.

One could pick, almost at random, years in which fine young lawyers came to the firm. For example, 1979 was a great harvest year, and several rising stars were recruited who would become leaders within the firm. One was Calin Rovinescu,[11] who would become the managing partner in Montreal prior to his departure to Air Canada in March 2000. That was the same year that Frank Sixt,[12] Pierre Raymond,[13] Guy Masson,[14] Guy Sarault, Isabel Pappe, and Daniel Rochefort arrived. Rovinescu had done quite well in the faculty, finishing in the top five or six, but Sixt finished at the top of the class every year by a considerable margin. Sixt had had a band that played on Crescent Street on Thursday, Friday, and Saturday nights and did his law studies on top of this. Grant remembers that when Rovinescu was interviewed as a student, he had given the impression that he had come first in his class, but when the firm discovered that it was, in fact, Sixt who had come first and confronted Rovinescu with this fact, he explained that nobody in the class considered Sixt for such purposes because he was so much better than all the others; they just counted the rest of the students, and Rovinescu was at the top of this group.

Sixt and Rovinescu were hired as summer students in early 1978.[15] Rovinescu had never worked in a law firm; in fact, his only business experience was selling belts on the street at the corner of McGill College Avenue and Ste Catherine Street. On the day he was supposed to begin, he was to meet Claudette Picard, but she was not there. The receptionist showed him around and at 8:00 AM, left him in the students' room with Sixt and Marc Cassavant. Shortly thereafter, a young, attractive blond woman named Susan Shorteno came in and asked for a student to help with a matter. Rovinescu followed her, expecting to meet her boss, only to find out that she was a lawyer, and she started giving him the details, which he desperately scribbled down on a notepad. His assignment was to find a stamp collection thought to be part of some estate, but which could not be located. He spent a couple of days in an apartment in the Benny Farm area at the west end of NDG going through garbage bags, trying without success to find the elusive, and perhaps ephemeral, collection. Two days later, going from the ridiculous to the sublime, he was working with Jimmy Wyatt[16] on a $250-million debenture facility for the Montreal Urban Community, with sophisticated London counsel on the other side.

Rovinescu's work was in the corporate and commercial area, initially doing private commercial transactions, but he got into the film financing area very early on and from that, into securities work, financing, and then to the investment banking community. On the financing side of his practice, Rovinescu did work for the Mercantile Bank of Canada, then a Schedule A bank, which was very aggressive and successful in the mid-market, being able to move faster than the larger banks. Mercantile, in which Citibank had a major stake (the maximum allowed under Canadian banking legislation), was left a bit exposed when Citibank decided it wanted a larger share of the gravy available from Canadian transactions and incorporated its own Schedule B bank. Mercantile got into trouble as a result of the fallout from the bankruptcies of the Western-based Commercial Credit Bank and North-land Bank of Canada and was eventually forced to merge with the National Bank of Canada. When the emergency struck, to stay alive, Mercantile had to get a line of credit from the Bank of Canada within forty-eight hours. It was Stanley Hartt's first day on the job as deputy minister of Finance, and Rovinescu and others from the firm had a meeting with Michael Wilson, the minister of Finance, and Hartt to see who might be willing to buy Mercantile. National Bank was identified. Rovinescu ended up negotiating with Yves Pratte, the former judge on the Supreme Court of Canada, then counsel at McCarthy Tétrault, a lawyer with far more experience – almost a complete career – than he had. It was a difficult negotiation with the imperious Pratte, who was demanding, bullying, and threatening by turn. To show his importance, Pratte demanded that there be meetings over Christmas, thinking that this would discomfit Rovinescu, who, being Jewish, was quite sanguine about the prospect.

Even though he was only twenty-seven or twenty-eight years old, Rovinescu was allowed by Grant to handle such major transactions as preferred share financings. On one of these transactions, on the other side was Ogilvy Renault, represented by a senior partner, Raymond Crevier, and Michel Goudrault. Goudreault had previously worked for the firm and coincidentally, had been part of the team that hired him. Although outweighed by years of seniority, Rovinescu was the senior on our side of the transaction, and he soon came to realize that it did not require seniority to be able to assert himself. By the time he was thirty-one, Rovinescu had already worked on the Stone Consolidated file and the first phase of the Air Canada privatization. He got a call, out of the blue, from John MacBain, whom he did not know but who had been recommended by Monique Mercier, a one-time tax lawyer with the firm. MacBain wanted to acquire a company for some $10 million. He remembers MacBain in particular because he was the first client he had ever had who was younger than him. MacBain had no money at all, but he had a ten-day option to acquire the shares of the target company and was convinced, correctly, that he could find the money.

Younger lawyers continued to come on stream and to take on work that was handled in other firms by much more senior people. Rovinescu and Sixt in Montreal worked together on film financings, with Rovinescu doing the corporate and securities aspects and Sixt, the tax structuring. Raymond moved into the commercial area and would later specialize in securities work. From this entrepreneurial base, they went on to innovative financing structures for large companies to the point that they met with one of the corporate giants in Quebec – Laurent Beaudoin of Bombardier – to propose a tax-driven structure for research and development. The practice involved an expanding mix of small enterprises and huge mega-deals for companies having extensive infrastructures to support them. Introductions to the investment banking community increased, with John Bennett at McLeod, Young, Weir & Co., Brian Drummond, Bernard Tellier, and John Bridgeman at Richardson Greenshields, and others. As transfers of personnel occurred within the investment community, their networks expanded.

John Leopold[17] had done a BA in French-Canadian studies at McGill before attending law school at the Université de Montréal. The firm did not have a great reputation with the students of that faculty, where rumours abounded of it being an anglophone sweatshop with a bad atmosphere. It was not even on Leopold's list of possible firms when he began to think about where he might go. His father, who knew Sonny Gordon, pushed him to the point of an interview. He met with Peter O'Brien and Nina Cherney, completely unprepared for a serious interview, but within five minutes, a connection had been established, and following the customary second interview, he was hired as a student. His experience at the faculty at the Université de Montréal reinforced his intention to stay both within the firm and in Quebec because he enjoyed being in a melting pot of people, talent, and cultures. An initial interest in labour law (he had written an article on picketing while in law school) persisted for a while, and he spent his first summer working for Stanley Hartt, but over time, he did more work with Sonny Gordon in the *Foreign Investment Review Act* sphere. He remembers many limousine trips to Ottawa for the purpose of negotiating the undertakings required to get approval for transactions from the Foreign Investment Review Agency. (One of the agency review agents was Thomas Downer, who acquired the predictable nickname of "Thumbs Downer.") Leopold then went on to a more general corporate law exposure, from which he graduated to his present specialty of mergers and acquisitions. The Montreal students of that year – Marc Cassavant, Bruno Desjardins, Leopold, Line Ouellet, and Elizabeth Skelton[18] – were a close-knit group, a feeling that Leopold believes has spread throughout the firm. All became lawyers with the firm, although Leopold is the only one who remains to this day.

MOTION PICTURES

Put in its proper perspective, the film business can be seen as marking the start of a securities practice within the firm. Until its immersion in the film business, there had been only one lawyer who could vaguely be described as a securities lawyer – Jimmy Wyatt, who had come to Montreal from Texas. He was generally regarded as one of the best draftsmen in the firm and stayed in Montreal until January 31, 1984, when he left to go to the Toronto office, where he remained for exactly ten years to the day. Apart from that, the firm had acted from time to time on the odd bond issue and on conventional bank loans, but it was not well known and was seldom, if ever, consulted by the major investment dealers on their public issues. The firm that is now Ogilvy Renault had a lock on such business. When the firm was small, this helped avoid financial strain when there were market slumps since it meant that there were not several securities lawyers sitting around with nothing to do. However, since each public financing of a film involved either a prospectus or an offering memorandum, the firm soon became quite familiar with the securities markets and developed relationships with the investment dealers, which led to more orthodox public issues in which it had not been regarded as a player prior to this time. It is a practice area in which high volume leads to expertise, especially in the understanding of the requirements of the regulators of the industry.

Stanley Hartt was the first in the office to become involved in the business side of the film industry. Up until then, the only lawyer in Montreal who had been active in the film business was Don Johnston, who had represented Paul Almond in some early productions. Hartt was in at the beginning of the film tax shelter business in the late 1970s, working with J. Ian Collins, a middleman, trying to put together deals for film producers. Collins later rented space with the firm to carry on such activities on a full-time basis. Between them, Hartt and Collins invented the distinction between ownership of the "celluloid" and the exploitation rights of the films, which produced very attractive tax savings for investors even if the films were not commercial successes. The great majority of such films were flops, but the tax savings to investors were considerable. A typical marketing approach to investors was that they could pay for their investment from the tax savings, an irresistible challenge: "Would you rather pay us and have a chance of a profit, or pay taxes to the government?"

Motion pictures became a very active area for the firm in the 1970s. Although residents of Montreal, Toronto, and Vancouver are now quite used to seeing film crews on their streets, it was not until the 1970s that there were any major efforts made to attract the film business to Canada. The key to the Canadian industry boom, in addition to co-production treaties negotiated between Canada and several other countries (excluding the United States), was a combination of production financing available through the Canadian Film Development Corporation (CFDC) and attractive capital cost allowances that produced tax write-offs for investors in the risky business. There were many false starts in the tax area since the persons in the Department of

Finance who were drafting the tax incentive legislation did not understand the film business – not that anyone did, but at least the others were not faced with drafting legislation. In addition, several of the key personnel in Finance were morally certain in their own minds that the whole business was a rip-off. Alan Short, one of the policy gurus in Finance, even said on one occasion when I was up in Ottawa trying to get some changes to the legislation that would make some practical sense for the industry, "I don't know why we are trying to encourage Canadian films. I don't even like them!" It was very difficult to get changes to the legislation that would make it workable for the film industry. The bureaucratic mindset was that the industry should change the way it operated to conform with how the government thought it should work, which led to several years of dialogue between the deaf.

As the interest began to grow, a number of Canadian producers emerged – among them, Denis Héroux, Robert Lantos, Nicolas Clermont, Robin Spry, David Patterson, Neil Léger, Ron Cullen, Steven Roth, John Kemeny, James Shavik (*I Lost the Grounder in the Sun*), Robert Cooper, Ronald Cohen (*Middle Age Crazy,* starring Bruce Dern and Ann-Margret and *Running,* starring Michael Douglas), David Kronenberg, and Pieter Kroonenberg. Some of them made very good movies in time, although others might well have justified Alan Short's reservations about Canadian films. The Seven Arts group of Claude Frénette, Claude Léger (who had a big success with his film *Agaguk*), and Michael Benahim of New York were good clients and made several films with Canadian financing. Some of the films included *Agency* (Robert Mitchum), *Your Ticket Is No Longer Valid* (Richard Harris), *Atlantic City* (Burt Lancaster), and *Meatballs* (Bill Murray), which may still be the highest grossing of all the Canadian films. We represented Ivan Reitman (*Heavy Metal*) and the underwriters in the production of *Prom Night.*

One of the first lessons learned was the entrepreneurial nature of the film business, where a script and a couple of agreements could – with much luck, lots of bafflegab, and enormous chutzpah – be turned into a multi-million-dollar project. The firm also learned that in the film business, a contract is never a contract unless it happens to suit the person obligated under it to perform in accordance with its terms. The ground was always shifting, the characters were often unreliable, and the producers never seemed to have had a cent to their names. It made the Wild West look like a garden party. Generating the funds to get the projects into production led to the development of a securities practice for the firm since each project had to be marketed to the public, which demonstrated, time and again, that P.T. "There's a sucker born every minute" Barnam was right. From the perspective of lawyers, who drafted the prospectuses and had to opine on the underlying contractual structure of the deals that were being marketed, there was a good deal of nail-biting because although the clients and their associates were always sincere about their affairs, they did not have the same respect for the sanctity of the contract that lawyers develop. The movie moguls always believed, with the optimism needed to create something out of nothing, that whatever had to be done, would get done, but in the meantime, they needed the money to start production. Nothing – whether contract, law suit, or threatened suit – would get in the way.

In fact, constant exposure of the movie moguls to lawyers in the process of raising public funds was probably good for them since they were forced to develop some discipline, however rudimentary, especially as the film projects became more substantial and the demands of the investors to receive some return on their investment became somewhat more sophisticated. One of the essential features that marked the increasing skepticism of the investors was a requirement for the producers to arrange for provision of completion bonds so that the contracted films would actually be completed. All too many of the early efforts had failed when the producers either underestimated the costs or ran over budget during the filming stages, and the films died before they were born. From the firm's perspective, it helped the younger lawyers understand the nature of a completely entrepreneurial business and to concentrate on using their own skills to make it possible for their clients to achieve their business objectives. Nor did this stop with legal and business advice. On one film, Don Shebib's *Heartaches*, the talented Frank Sixt, drawing on personal experience with his band that he organized while attending law school at the Université de Montréal, wrote the lyrics for the theme song of the film while working on the legal aspects of the deal.

We provided tax advice for a number of well-known actors, including Donald Sutherland, as well as for non-resident actors anxious not to pay any more Canadian taxes on their income than was absolutely necessary. Many of the firm's lawyers were involved during the heyday of film financing, including Hartt, myself, Scheim, Rovinescu, Michael Prupas, and several others. Beginning in May 1978, we had a consulting arrangement with Joseph Beaubien, who had been general counsel with the Canadian Film Development Corporation for about eight years, to share space in the office and to help advise film producers in relation to their financial dealings with the CFDC and the compliance with certain of the co-production agreements. Beaubien was never formally a member of the firm, and the relationship lasted for less than a year because he decided that he wanted to become more entrepreneurial and become involved as an independent producer in the production and financing of films.

Most of the film work then devolved on Michael Prupas, who concentrated almost exclusively in this work, and he continued with the firm until it began to conclude that this, especially acting for the producers, was no longer an area to which it wanted to devote as much attention as in the past. Prupas decided to leave the firm in June 1980 to join Heenan Blaikie, which had become much more involved in the field and eventually opened offices in Los Angeles, Toronto, and Vancouver in order to follow the work that grew out of the field. On May 31, 1998, Prupas also left that firm, where he had become one of its highest billing lawyers, to begin activities as an independent producer.

In time, the banks got into the film business as well, principally for the purpose of lending production funds against prenegotiated distribution contracts for the films, backed up by completion guarantees for the productions, a niche later occupied by Etienne Massicotte.[19] The banks, understandably, had little interest in the producers themselves, with the inordinate risks attached to lending them money without security. It was the distribution agreements that were the key to any film. The returns to the investors in films were derived primarily from the tax deductions and carefully structured but generally unimpressive shares of distribution revenues. Had the tax incentives not existed, it is safe to say that few, if any, of the productions would ever have seen the light of day. Over the years, the firm's practice gradually shifted from acting for the producers, who never had any money, to acting for the actual financiers of the productions. From the perspective of the firm's self-interest, the risk of acting for impecunious producers was quite high since if they did not get the financing they needed for their projects, they were seldom, if ever, in a position to pay for the legal services performed on their behalf. Our bank, the CIBC, was no exception, and its activities in this area were headed up by Peter Papadopolous.

As 1979 was about to begin, Stikeman Elliott in Toronto also became entertainment lawyers. All of the sparkle and finesse that got the firm into the business in the first place was to be found in Montreal. With Gordon and Hartt carousing (for the most part, in legal terms) on the streets of Montreal, it was not surprising that they would attract an entertainment following. This was melded with what the Toronto lawyers thought was the steely-eyed Toronto financial acumen, where the firm acted for issuers, underwriters, and seemingly, practically everyone in sight. In the course of acting for the underwriter, the firm succeeded in obtaining a tremendous discretionary exemption at the Ontario Securities Commission for 1980's *Prom Night,* starring Jamie Lee Curtis and Leslie Neilson. Apart from the fact that several of the lawyers made a successful investment in this film, since it was more or less *de rigueur* that we "show the flag" by investing in the projects ourselves, the tax incentive securities exemption that the firm obtained was ultimately written into the regulations and still stands. An additional benefit that flowed from this genre of work and what turned out to be the best result of our being close to the movie business was that a young professor at Osgoode Hall called to ask if he could work for the firm for the summer.

Probably no summer student ever had as much fun as did Bill Braithwaite[20] working with Yontef in the summer of 1979. They were acting for what was then Pitfield, MacKay, Ross, which was financing the movie *Melanie.* It starred Burton Cummings, Glynnis O'Connor, and in a minor role, Don Johnson, later of *Miami Vice* fame. By that time, the firm was doing a full-blown prospectus and needed to get into the due diligence. When asked who the firm's copyright person was, after a brief panic, upon hearing that Braithwaite had once taught an introductory course in copyright law, he was immediately so designated. Most of the work was done by day, and as often as not, the star-struck lawyers would go down in the afternoon to watch the "rushes." At the end of the summer, they had the fun of attending the closing cast party. It was a hectic summer, and when Braithwaite went back to teaching, the firm had sown a seed for later harvesting. When he decided to leave teaching several years later, his choice of a law firm may well have been determined in the summer of 1979. The movie flopped.

Other films included *Curtains* (with Samantha Egger), *The Incubus* (with John Cassavetes, in which the firm had to exercise the remedies provided for in the financing contracts, in this case, the seizure of an unfinished film), *Bear Island* (starring Donald Sutherland, done for Selkirk Communications with which Joe Beaubien was involved), and *Ticket to Heaven* (with Nick Mancuso). In many respects, between the Montreal and Toronto offices, we practically invented the film financing business that has become one of the hallmarks of Canada, as American producers were drawn north by the production talent and lower Canadian dollar plus the incentives available for those investors willing to take a flyer on a film yet to be produced.

QUEBEC STOCK SAVINGS PLAN

The Quebec Stock Savings Plan (QSSP) concept was introduced by Jacques Parizeau when he was the very able Quebec minister of Finance. The provisions gave income tax deductions to Quebec taxpayers who subscribed for shares of Quebec companies that made initial public offerings. The QSSP scheme was instrumental in bringing on stream the entrepreneurial talents of small- and medium-sized Quebec businessmen who in the past had had a tendency to develop their enterprises to the point that they could sell them for one or two million dollars and then retire. As the horizons of Quebec businessmen expanded and they were able to obtain public financing for the creation of larger businesses that they could continue to control and manage, a new class of entrepreneur sprang up, arguably the most creative in the country, and "Quebec Inc." was born. The QSSP concept was an extremely successful tool that lasted for a number of years. Many of these companies, such as UAB and BioChem, became clients of the firm and added to our experience in the securities markets.

Throughout the 1980s, many of the corporate and tax lawyers in the firm gained enormous experience in the securities work that the QSSP generated. This work heralded the end of the domination of the Quebec securities practice by Ogilvy Renault, which had left all the other law firms fighting for whatever scraps may have fallen off its table. The QSSP provided an enormous boom, especially since they were not really regulated in the early days, and the brokers developed an active aftermarket in shares, which had originally been conceived as longer term investments. In 1982, the Le Château chain of clothing stores went public under the QSSP program. Its controlling shareholder did not want to give up control even though he wanted the financial benefits of a public issue, so the firm developed the concept of subordinated voting shares, used for the first time in relation to a QSSP. There were major problems with the Department of Revenue getting the idea approved (it was new, and governments tend to eschew newness), but it became commonplace enough that the rules were later changed to allow it, subject, however, to a lower tax benefit. Because the QSSP rules were changed every year, it was a good time for lawyers. This initiative, along with the film business, was the start of the firm's securities practice, which is now headed in the Montreal office by Pierre Raymond and Jean-Marc Huot. [21]

TORONTO, THE SLEEPING GIANT, COMES ON STREAM

The last half of the 1970s consolidated the process by which Toronto became Canada's New York and Montreal, its Boston. The Toronto office gained an increasing share of the country's commercial work, and the signs became increasingly evident that not only was the decision to establish in Toronto an inspired strategy, but also that it would not be long before Toronto would become the principal engine that could drive the firm into the next century. The firm incorporated several companies that evolved into Canadian banks, including Security Pacific, Mellon, Citibank, and Bankers Trust. It became expert in the fishing business when Fishery Products bought their groundfish division from Jannock; the principals of Fishery Products called it not a business but an "adventure." It acted for Foodcorp, which brought Harvey's and Swiss Chalet under the Cara umbrella. While walking through the Swiss Chalet kitchen up to the "head office," the CFO warned Yontef in his (the CFO's) wonderful Irish brogue not to slip on the "grease of production." Wayne Shaw became an expert in aircraft financing. Jamie Davis did a multitude of construction and real estate financings. The tax group was increasingly involved in the structuring of major transactions.

Citibank's activity continued, including its acquisition of the Hamilton Group. The anti-inflation legislation was enacted at the end of 1975, and there were two years of active work in that area prior to its repeal. The same year, a mandate that would last for many years – Old Port Cove, in which Brian B.R. Magee, a long-time friend of Stikeman, was one of the driving forces – came on stream and was headed up by Rose. Rod Barrett started to do more of the Citibank work and branched off into work on venture capital financings. Another client group that has been valuable to the firm, handled principally by Wayne Shaw of the Toronto office, was the Jackson Group. Unlike the Li Group, the Jackson Group was more of a series of companies in which Donald K. Jackson had been involved, all of which have had legal services provided to them by the firm. Shaw's relationship with Jackson went back to the time of his practice in Calgary at Howard, Mackie. This expanded at the new firm to acting for the Tricil Group, a joint venture company established by Trimac Limited of Calgary and Montreal-based CIL Inc., beginning in 1977, a relationship that lasted until 1989 when Tricil Waste Management Services Ltd. was sold to Laidlaw. Tricil was a perfect client for the Toronto office. It was growing rapidly through acquisitions of solid and liquid waste companies in Ontario, Quebec, and the northwestern United States. Tricil also had waste management and energy recovery expertise to sell to cities and municipalities. In both those latter areas, Tricil needed extensive legal input. While its finances were attended to primarily by its shareholders, the firm assisted in all other aspects of its operations. In the early years, not only did Shaw spend a considerable portion of his practice with Tricil, others assisted with the extensive advice provided to this valuable client, including Sankey, Arnett, Von Veh, Barrett, Rose, Kathleen Ward, and Alison Youngman.

After Tricil was purchased by Laidlaw, the firm lost a valuable client. Although efforts were made to secure continuing work from Laidlaw, it had both an in-house counsel group and an established outside counsel. The firm did, however, continue to act for Laidlaw on a major mandate in Montreal relating to the Mercier Lagoon litigation, now handled by Richard Rusk, a mandate that started in the mid-1970s and is still continuing. Later on, when Jackson became president and CEO of Laidlaw in August 1989, the firm did assist Laidlaw with its European initiatives during the early 1990s, including acquisitions in Italy, Norway, and an aborted acquisition in France.

A defining transaction for the Toronto office was an Arctic shipbuilding joint venture on behalf of Federal Commerce and Navigation, the corporate name of which would later be changed to Fednav. As a result of Stikeman's friendship with the Pathys, *père et fils,* the Montreal office had long done ship acquisitions for the family enterprise, but the company had not been active in public transactions. In the late 1970s, the Government of Canada adopted a program to encourage the building of thick-hulled, Arctic-capable bulk carrier ships, which would carry metal ore from Nanisivik in the Arctic to smelters in more temperately located environments. Each of Fednav, Canada Steamship Lines (its CEO, Paul Martin, is now the minister of Finance), and Upper Lakes Shipping were to take a turn at a joint venture, to which the government provided financial support to facilitate the construction of the ships. The *MV Arctic* was the first ship to be launched, a project on which Yontef and Wyatt worked together. The transaction was new, complex, and required a complete series of financial checkpoints. By the time the first advance was due to be processed, Yontef had set up procedures for subsearches that would apply through the life of the building of the ship.

The ship was being built at Port Weller Dry Docks in St Catharines, so the checklist included a visit to the office of the registrar of shipping to determine whether there were any intervening liens. Because under the *Canada Shipping Act,* process (a legal action) in respect of a ship may be commenced by affixing notice to the mast, the checklist called for an inspection of the mast. Just before the first advance, Yontef sent a student over to St Catharines to do the appropriate searches and report. At this stage, the "ship" was nothing more than a number painted on the ground with a circle around it – in this case, it was Hull No. 69 – and adjacent to this marking were the first deliveries of raw materials allocated to it. The student duly arrived and asked where he might find the *MV Arctic,* Hull No. 69. The workmen, seeing this boy wonder in a suit and tie, directed him to the pile of raw materials and painted notation on the ground. Following at a bit of a distance, the workmen saw the disappointed look on the student's face as he climbed over the raw materials, looking for a mast. One of the workers decided that it was time for some sport. He approached the student and suggested that perhaps the student had misheard him because, pointing to a barge at the dock, he identified it as the *MV Arctic.* Much relieved, the student climbed all over the barge for the better part of an hour, and figuring that he must have seen a mast and having found nothing attached to anything he had seen, he left, waving goodbye, not quite understanding why the workmen broke out in gales of laughter. The student was no more than ten minutes out of St Catharines when Yontef got a call from one of the bankers, highly amused, who suggested that the next time, we might send somebody who knew the difference between a ship that had not been started and a barge.

There were several major transactions that were evidence of the new momentum although the regular work for clients such as Citibank and Bankers Trust continued. One was the CIBC tender offer loan to Brascan, which had decided to take a run at the retail giant Woolworth's. Blake Cassels, who was the CIBC's usual counsel in Toronto, acted for Brascan, which meant that CIBC had to go somewhere else to document an unprecedented $700-million loan for Brascan, the proceeds of which were to be used to acquire Woolworth's. Don Fullerton of the CIBC brought his key executive, Tony Melman, down to Elliott's office to ask if the firm could do it. Elliott pulled Yontef into his office to ask if he knew anything about banking. Within hours, the adventure began, and Yontef found himself documenting what might well have been the largest loan in Canadian history by a single bank. The lawyers were very excited because the cutting and pasting (word processing was still in the future) was going well, and they had managed to find a precedent from which they could work. Mike Ross at Shearman & Sterling was the US counsel, and because US margin rules might apply, the simpler and more non-technical the security, the better. This file had almost everything. Among the celebrities they dealt with was Marty Lipton, famous even then, who was representing Lehman Brothers and who was negotiating the loan covenants. Yontef still encounters lawyers in New York who boast of being "juniors" on that file, which he was running as a fifth year associate with occasional help from a student. Yontef had warned Jim Riley that were he to be asked, he should never admit to being a student ("Just say you have been with us for some time now.") The perspectives of a new firm and a mainstream New York firm were brought home to Yontef, who believing the closing of the loan was a momentous occasion, asked Ross if he had ever done anything like this before, to which Ross replied that on average, he did two or three a week. The firm, on the other hand, did not see anything quite like this for almost another five years.

The amalgamation of Texaco Canada (the company that owned the retail gas stations and had public minority shareholders) with the wholly owned subsidiary, Texaco Exploration, the upstream company, was another high point. Texaco Inc. had called George Tamaki, and the file made its way to Wyatt in Montreal (then by far the best commercial draftsman in Montreal, but nonetheless, still an associate). Wyatt called Yontef, a fifth-year associate, and he and Riley, still a student, did the Toronto end. This was a cause for many trips to New York, with Yontef and Wyatt being the senior lawyers and Jim Riley, invariably out of money, being the beast of burden. The firm represented Texaco Inc. and Texaco Exploration while Campbell, Godfrey represented Texaco Canada. Torys represented Wood Gundy, the Canadian financial advisor, and McCarthys represented Morgan, Stanley, the US advisor. White & Case were representing Texaco Canada in the United States.

The firm's team was composed of the youngest people on the transaction by something in the order of ten years. When matters got down to due diligence, Yontef remembers telling Riley to "head out there and find something that nobody else found." This occurred about the time that the West Pembina oil field had been discovered. Riley, all innocence and curiosity, befriended one of the exploration people and asked why, when they had had one successful well, did they then drill some twenty adjacent dry holes right after that? The exploration fellow, no doubt charmed by Riley, said that they thought they had found a major oil field and were basically drilling dry holes at shallower depths so that they could buy more land in the immediate neighbourhood. Armed with this knowledge, the firm was immediately able to upstage all of the other high-priced help in the deal. This was also the file that for several years set the standard and methodology for extravagant behaviour. When the lawyers were in New York, the partner at White & Case could with no apparent effort provide food, drink, theatre tickets, limousines, and what have you on a moment's notice. Naive as they were, they did not realize that he was getting all this from the printer, who would do cartwheels for all the important lawyers that were sitting around. It also explains why lawyers in New York never complain about printer's bills. In fact, it is a point of honour that a serious New York law firm never bills less than the printer, which often results in astronomical accounts for legal services.

A year later, after Conrad Black did his deal with Bud McDougall's widow, acquiring the estate's interest in Argus Corporation, the holding company for a series of companies, including Massey-Ferguson, Dominion Stores, and others, the press uniformly drew the conclusion that Black had, in some way, outsmarted the widow. Her Palm Beach lawyer decided that new Canadian counsel were needed and called Elliott. Elliott asked Yontef if he knew anything about wills and estates, who said that he had once worked on an estate administration during his articling period. He thereby earned a field promotion and became the firm's estates "expert." Yontef often smiled to think that someone like him was the Canadian "estates lawyer" for the several years that this file lasted, dealing with the estate of the then acknowledged former head of the Canadian establishment. He remembers turning to the estate's Palm Beach lawyer, Marshall Criser, asking him what kind of swimming pool could possibly cost $60,000 and who in the family could possibly be that fond of swimming. He was advised, condescendingly, that it was a swimming pool for horses.

Yontef also recalls that the value of the estate was but a fraction of the several hundreds of millions of dollars grandly estimated by the press and that it might be a source of considerable embarrassment were the real figure to become public. After burning some midnight oil in the library, they exhumed an ancient line of cases that stood for the proposition that only parties with an interest in the estate were entitled to know its value. With careful and confidential negotiations handled by people who really did not know anything about such matters, they managed to convince the Surrogate Court Registrar that unless someone could demonstrate that they had "an interest in the estate" (other than merely prurient), the information should not be made public. To this day, the value of the McDougall estate has remained a secret. Interestingly, several years later, someone else attempted the same strategy and publicly asserted the same argument before the Surrogate Court. It was rejected out of hand.

In mid-1981, just weeks after the Hong Kong office opened, the Toronto office received a fax from Daniel Colson in Hong Kong that Li Ka-shing was attempting to purchase the Harbour Castle Hilton Hotel in Toronto. It was either luck or good timing that the Toronto office received a windfall of the largest piece of Canadian work emanating from Hong Kong because had the firm opened six or eight weeks later, it probably would not have got this work, and it would likely have gone to Phillips & Vineberg, which had an operation in Hong Kong. It is quite possible that the entire connection with the Li family over the past twenty-odd years, with all the benefits it has brought to both sides of the relationship, might never have flourished. People often talk about the benefits of marketing but often forget the benefits from being aggressive and being in the right place at the right time. Sometimes luck favours the brave. Wayne Shaw took on the task of advising on the purchase transaction, which marked the beginning of an extended relationship with the Li Group in Canada. The vendor of the hotel was Campeau Corporation, led by the notorious Robert Campeau. Copthorne Holdings Ltd. was incorporated as the purchasing vehicle and subsequently became one of the key Canadian holding companies for the Li family. The client acquisition team included not only Li Ka-shing himself, but George Magnus, William Shurniak, and Canning Fok. The firm's acquisition team included Elliott, Bowman, Shaw, and Hess, each of whom also acted as directors and/or officers of Copthorne, Barrett and Dow. The deal nearly fell apart because Campeau wanted all the paintings that were on the wall of his office, and on the closing date, he showed up with a car and took them all away. That almost wrecked the deal, but the paintings were recovered.

Once acquired, one of the major problems with the operation of the hotel was dealing with Hilton under the inherited hotel management contract. The firm assisted Godfrey Jacobs and Jon Markolis, the key Copthorne officers dealing with the hotel, leading in due course to the termination of the Hilton relationship and a new management contract with Westin. The cancellation of the Hilton management contract was part of a number of shuffles that saw the Toronto Westin on Richmond Street become the Toronto Hilton and the Harbour Castle Hilton become the Harbour Castle Westin – moves that confused Torontonians and Toronto visitors for years. Unfortunately, Copthorne also had problems with Westin's management, which ultimately led to Westin purchasing the hotel from Copthorne in December 1989. Like so much of the Harbour Castle 1980s history, the sale was concluded only after having to overcome several difficult issues. In August 1989, after lengthy negotiations, Copthorne and Westin agreed to the purchase and sale of the hotel, including a price. While the definitive documents were being drafted,

Westin unilaterally introduced a contractual provision that purported to operate so much in its favour that it effectively terminated the transaction. Extended negotiations took place in September and October 1989 in Seattle at the head office of Westin as well as in Vancouver, Toronto, and Hong Kong. Hess and Shaw led the firm's team, with George Magnus, Victor Li, and Jon Markolis negotiating on behalf of Copthorne. By mid-October, a commercial basis for finalizing the sale seemed to disappear. Sid Lederman joined the team to advise on possible litigation solutions. Extensive court documents were prepared and were ready to be filed to launch a specific performance claim against Westin. The parties continued, on a without prejudice basis, to negotiate a commercial resolution to the impasse, and Li Ka-shing himself then intervened. On December 12, 1989, a definitive purchase and sale agreement was signed between Copthorne and Westin and Oaki Corporation, Westin's controlling shareholder. On December 28, 1989, the transaction was closed.

The catalyst that provided significant impetus to the public securities markets practice of the Toronto firm was the appointment of Henry Knowles as chairman of the Ontario Securities Commission in 1980. At that time, the public markets practice was dominated by a few firms such as Blakes, Torys, Oslers and McCarthys. Henry Knowles's "gift" to the firm was that reliance on old precedents, traditional firms, and chumminess with staff was demonstrated not to achieve any better a result for a client in a contested environment than the determined efforts of someone relatively unknown such as, for example, Stikeman Elliott or Davies Ward & Beck. Almost overnight, the firm achieved a disproportionate amount of success at the Ontario Securities Commission and in the process, became a credible alternative and in some cases, the preferred choice.

It began with Fednav taking a position in, and making a takeover bid for, Abitibi Price. This was followed, in short order, by Olympia & York making a competing bid. Then, in turn, Fednav bought a material block of the stock in a private transaction from the Caisse de Dépot in Montreal. Olympia & York, not surprisingly, went ballistic and complained to the Ontario Securities Commission. The next thing Yontef knew, the firm was invited up to the OSC for an "informal chat." Unsuspecting, Yontef appeared at the OSC and found himself in the middle of a what appeared to him to be a star chamber proceeding, with Gar Emerson of Davies Ward & Beck leading the prosecutorial charge, getting a decent assist from staff and off-stage words of wisdom from a young vice-president at the Toronto Stock Exchange by the name of Ed Waitzer, who was not supporting the firm's position in the matter.

There was no one in the Toronto office to help, so Yontef contacted Phil Anisman at the Osgoode Hall law school and asked if he would work with him on the matter. The essence of what was supposed to have been a mere discussion but which turned out to be a much more serious affair – namely, a hearing – was the assertion that Fednav's purchase was not the "kind of thing" the legislation permitted. The firm defended on the basis that the statute was unclear and should have made a more express prohibition than simply to suggest that people guess what might, or might not, be a good idea. The upshot of the hearing was an adjournment, called by the commissioners, to decide Fednav's "punishment." As Yontef and Anisman were scratching their heads trying to figure out what had happened, a settlement offer was floated. If Fednav were to agree not to do "it" again, it could go on its way. All in all, this was a pretty good result, and in the end, Fednav ended up tendering its stock for a substantial profit in response to an increased Olympia & York bid.

Every other week brought a new challenge in the form of proposed changes to banking legislation and more often, hearings at the OSC over regulatory issues. At the time, the Ontario statute had a number of discretionary features in it, which are no longer part of the law. For example, the OSC was entitled to determine that the market price of a security in the trading days preceding a particular transaction did not reflect its true market price. Thus, when Noranda announced that it would try to buy MacMillan Bloedel and that it would sell British Columbia Forest Products, it was a virtual certainty that there would be a hearing over what was the true market price of BCFP following the announcement and the proposed new acquisition of BCFP by a third party. The need to react quickly was essential and typical of the pressures that surrounded such a practice on this transaction. Yontef received a call, late at night, from a Vancouver lawyer, met the client at a Toronto hotel in the morning, and immediately went to participate in a two-day hearing.

Yontef had been doing some work for the federal government's Securities Market Study Group and had seen Ed Waitzer's name as a person copied on some of the materials and papers, but he had never met him. During the course of the Fednav hearings, he approached Waitzer, saying that he was pleased to finally match a face with the name. He suggested that once the proceedings were behind them, they might have lunch to exchange war stories. As Yontef opened the morning paper on the March 1981 day that they were finally going to have lunch, a lead story was that Waitzer had resigned from the Toronto Stock Exchange. Over lunch, he seized the opportunity to suggest that if Waitzer was thinking of law practice, he was anxious to make him an offer he could not refuse. After several weeks of scientific recruiting, as Yontef describes it, of "me begging and pleading while Waitzer expressed all the reasons he didn't see himself as a lawyer," they finally agreed on a "let's get to know each other" consulting arrangement. Waitzer said he was determined to pursue "wealth generation" and philanthropic activities and had no confidence in his legal skills. He hoped for an arrangement as a tenant with a major law firm. There was some demand for his services because of his role at the TSE in developing takeover and related securities regulation, but only two firms were ready to consider his proposed arrangement: ours and Davies Ward & Beck. Of the two, he felt most comfortable with ours, in which he could build on the Montreal franchise and the booming Toronto transactional market.[22]

Upon his arrival, Waitzer was almost immediately involved in two contested takeover bids. One was Genstar's bid for Canada Permanent, a matter referred to the firm through John Sopinka when Genstar became disenchanted with Blake Cassels. First City Financial, then controlled by Sam Belzberg, made a bid to acquire Canada Permanent Trust Company. Genstar, then advised by Blake Cassels, was persuaded to take an option on 5 per cent of Canada Permanent's stock and to make an unconditional bid for the rest. Much to Genstar's surprise and consternation, First City got to 51 per cent in a private transaction and brought an action to nullify the option. Genstar, recognizing the desperate nature of its predicament – it was unconditionally bidding for 49 per cent – decided to change counsel and came to our firm, largely because Sopinka had given a fairly adventurous assessment of our chances to defend the validity of the option.

Yontef, Sopinka, and Waitzer all had important roles in the process. The tactics can best be described as blitzkrieg. They pressed Osler Hoskin, which was acting for First City, to step down as counsel because of a conflict, and they succeeded. Sopinka brought an action against everyone in sight, alleging every imaginable conspiracy, every fraud that had ever been devised, and every manipulative act that may have been conceived against First City Financial, its directors and officers, and anyone else remotely connected with the matter. In advance of the hearing on the option, Sopinka made what Yontef thought was the ultimate spurious offer of settlement, which was generally along the lines that the client would not take up the option if the other side agreed not to vote its shares. Miraculously, Sopinka convinced the judge that the other side was rejecting, out of hand, a perfectly reasonably settlement offer. No doubt, Lorne Morphy, First City Financial's new counsel, was talking to himself all the way back to the office because Sopinka had succeeded in having the option upheld. During the hearings before the OSC, Sopinka was in the process of discussing a "section 11 investigation," and when he was passed a note advising him that it was a violation of the *Securities Act* even to acknowledge the existence of such an investigation, he proceeded in mid-sentence to identify it as "the investigation to which he could make no reference." Matters went downhill from that moment in front of the OSC to the point that the chairman made arrangements for the issuance of a warrant for the general counsel of the firm's client, having concluded when the latter left the hearing room that he was about to leave the country. In fact, he was merely on his way back to our offices to seek advice about the wild and wonderful ways of the OSC.

It did not come as a surprise that by the Saturday evening following the bid, Genstar had agreed to buy the First City position at a small profit. Late in the evening, Waitzer settled the outstanding matters with counsel for First City Financial and was asked by the opposing counsel to prepare a memorandum of settlement. He agreed, hung up the phone, realized that he had not the faintest idea of how to do so, and set out in the corridor looking for help. He came upon Riley in a boardroom, stocking up on his pizza food group, and Riley got the job done, reminding Waitzer for months thereafter of the favour he had thus bestowed. The announcement was made on Monday morning. This was all the local arbitrageurs needed to hear before complaining to the OSC. Henry Knowles needed little provocation to commence the better part of a year's worth of hearings.

The second major transaction for Waitzer was the complex bid for Drum-mond-McCall, an offer that had been made on instructions from Jeffrey Marshall through the Montreal office, which, although ultimately success-ful, was a poor acquisition, and Marshall spent the better part of a decade trying to salvage the situation before finally turning it over to the bank. The bid was memorable for the hearings conducted entirely in French before the Quebec Securities Commission despite the fact that everyone involved was more fluent in English. Also, this was Waitzer's first exposure in his professional career to allegations that the firm's client had Jewish lineage when it appeared that he was going to succeed in acquiring control of an old Montreal family business.

By this stage, the Toronto office was really stretched thin; Waitzer was just coming aboard and by his own desire, was not ready for a full-time commitment, and Phil Anisman had a day job at the law school. Yontef asked Jim Riley if there were any more like him in his class. Riley identi-fied John Stransman[23] and mentioned that from what he had heard on the associate lawyers' grapevine, Stransman, then at McMillan Binch, had not been getting the kind of work he wanted to have. Yontef had met Strans-man a year or two earlier when he was working on a transaction for a doctor/entrepreneur at Hospital for Sick Children. It was not exactly a cold call, but he knew Stransman was not expecting that someone he did not know well would invite him for coffee out of the blue. At that meeting, Yontef suggested that if Stransman wanted to do more contested securities work, Stikeman Elliott was the place to be. With a seeming hatful of files like Genstar, Yontef could easily tell him what he would be working on for the next several months. Stransman mentioned that by coincidence, he was going on holidays to think about what he wanted to do next and that this was a timely inquiry. Several weeks later, he joined the firm. That was the best legacy of the Genstar deal.

John Stransman had not joined as a fully known commodity, so among the first ways to test him was to have him and Riley work with Yontef on the due diligence phase of a Texaco transaction. The trio went down to White Plains with Torys, the other law firm, and as he was leaving to return to Toronto, Yontef told Stransman and Riley to finish up the due diligence, and he gave the usual instruction not to come up empty-handed. Several times, the firm had asked the question about the line item in the regulations, which was applicable to the offer document, entitled "prior valuations." The Texaco officials, with the most sincere of expressions, had repeatedly given assurances that there was no such thing; there were none. A day later, Yontef got a call from Stransman and Riley, still in White Plains, who were barely able to contain themselves. They were reading to him from a file in the Treasury Department, labelled "prior valuations," and they were beside themselves with joy that they had (again, in Riley's case) found the needle in the haystack. Toward the end of the file, Yontef remembers reading a draft document prepared by Riley and Stransman and noticing a typographical error. In a reprise of the never-ending refrain that the firm is paid to get it done right, not just to get it done, he remembers his artful screaming when he asked how many smart guys like them did it take to get a simple document right.

When Yontef was in law school, he had bought twenty-five shares of Dome Petroleum at $14 a share. Several months later, he sold the stock at $60 a share and bought himself a new car. (You could buy a car for that amount in those days.) For the next twelve years, he watched Dome Petroleum become the Canadian Microsoft of the 1970s and the darling of Canada's oil patch. With nationalistic fervour at its height and Canadian ownership of oil and gas reserves the prevailing theme of the moment, Dome Petroleum proclaimed itself the chosen instrument of the Canadian government.

In 1981, Tony Melman of CIBC called Yontef, telling him to pack his bags because they were going to Chicago. A couple of hours later, he called again, telling him they were going to Calgary. Several times that afternoon, the destination flip-flopped. That evening, Riley and Yontef flew to Calgary with a couple of loan agreement precedents in hand to finance a deal for Dome Petroleum. It started easily enough. CIBC, the Royal Bank of Canada, the Bank of Montreal, and the Toronto-Dominion Bank were going to lend Dome Petroleum $US1.5 billion to buy 22 per cent of Conoco. The real object of Dome's affections was Conoco's controlling interest in Hudson's Bay Oil & Gas, and the plan was in essence to swap the 22 per cent of Conoco's stock for the HBOG interest. When they got to Calgary and met in the Bennett Jones (Dome's counsel) offices, it was organized pandemonium. One group of boardrooms was filled with Dome people, Bennett Jones, and Mayer, Brown people working on the tender offer documents. Mac Jones, the senior partner of Bennett Jones and a director of Dome, ushered the new arrivals into a boardroom and invited them to get started. The client's US counsel was Mark Kessel of Shearman & Sterling, and the three of them were trying to keep a boardroom full of bankers at bay while they worked through the terms of the loan agreement. The bankers left at around 1:00 AM Calgary time, with instructions that they proposed to be back at 8:00 or 9:00 in the morning and wanted to see a draft of the loan agreement upon their arrival.

As the night wore on, taken up mainly with the hand-scribbling of covenants, Yontef noticed that Riley had disappeared, but with the intensity of the work and the coffee-assisted adrenalin flow, this did not interrupt their progress. By around 5:00 in the morning, it became impossible to work because of a terrible noise coming from under the table. Yontef investigated, and there was Riley snoring loudly, fast asleep obviously for some time. They took a break long enough to revive Riley, drag him over to Mac Jones's office, and put him to sleep on the couch. Riley had been exhausted from a few all-nighters on an Asamera transaction just before this one had started, but his fellow lawyers spared no mercy in spreading the word that when the going got tough, Riley got caught up on his sleep.

The signing of the Dome Petroleum credit agreement with the four banks was a milestone. At the time, it was by far the largest non-sovereign loan transaction in Canadian history. Several of the banks in the syndicate had committed so large a percentage of their capital to this and prior loans to

Dome that any uncertainty as to Dome's credit-worthiness was an alarming thought. As the lawyers were sitting around caught up with the excitement of the moment after the signing, one of the in-house legal people came rushing in with "changes" to the credit agreement. The lawyers retorted in unison that it was too late because the deal had already been signed and announced. The in-house lawyer was insistent that this had to be changed and as the lawyers probed, they found that although the security of the Conoco shares had been accurately described, there were many errors in the schedule that described some $500 million worth of security on oil and gas properties. Yontef remembers turning to Mark Kessel, saying that with all these mistakes, they may as well have stopped many hours ago and signed one of the early drafts. In the end, there was no harm done, and the Dome Petroleum "deal" became yet another defining moment for the Toronto office and the firm generally.

Dome Petroleum succeeded in getting 22 per cent of Conoco and swapping it for the majority interest in HBOG. The next challenge was how to finance the acquisition of the balance because Dome's acquisition vehicle had all the debt, while its subsidiary, with minority public shareholders, had all the cash flow. Citibank put together a syndicate that lent Dome Petroleum $US1.9 billion to acquire the minority, with the Canadian bank syndicate adding a further $US200 million to solve the problem. To secure these loans, the Citibank syndicate took oil and gas security on all of HBOG's properties. The Canadian bank syndicate took security on virtually everything else.

Kathleen Ward, then a brand-new lawyer with the firm, was labelled by the Dome pranksters as Stikeman Elliott's "Designated Worrier." Although this was more flattering than the label attached to Yontef, the "Evil Penguin," they needed someone on the deal who would keep faithfully working ahead on a rapidly evolving transaction. As a first-year lawyer, she found herself in the exciting position, wrestling with a "springing charge," a mortgage that created itself in the future in the event of a default. She had to translate such legal brainwaves – or paroxysms – into enforceable security documents. Two weeks after one of the closings, Ward was notified that one of the Bennett Jones partners representing Dome had decided that upon reflection, he wanted to withdraw his legal opinion on the springing charge. Yontef replied that this was no problem, but he pointed out that under the loan agreement, were the borrower to question, deny, or attack the security given to the lenders, it was considered a default, and the borrower could simply pay back the loan. Upon yet further reflection and to the great relief of the Designated Worrier, the lawyer allowed his opinion to stand. Rather more importantly perhaps, in the long run, it was never tested.

In 1982, in one of the most complex closings ever, Richard Clark, Kathleen Ward, and Yontef, along with several others, were in Calgary, Michael Allen[24] and others were in New York, and there were people in Ottawa filing papers and orchestrating the transfer of billions of dollars. As if two bank syndicates financing Dome Petroleum – taking out the Bank of Nova Scotia, the large minority shareholder, the Hudson's Bay Company, and other minority shareholders – were not enough, another contemporaneous

Partners meeting, 1977. Seated left to right: François Mercier, Fraser Elliott, Heward Stikeman, George Tamaki, David Angus. First row standing left to right: James Robb, Peter Cumyn, Michael Richards, Michel Vennat, Thomas Baldwin, Fred Von Veh, Sam Wakim, Donald Bowman. Back row left to right: Marvin Yontef, John Dingle, Ernest Rovet, Stanley Hartt, Senator Maurice Riel, Mortimer Freiheit, André Brossard, James Arnett, Jamie Davis, Harold Gordon, Wayne Shaw, Richard Sankey, Daniel Colson, Robert Hart.

Lawson Hunter and Sidney Lederman.

Flower Power: 1990 Stikeman Elliott team in Défi Corporatif Candarel fundraising run for cancer research: Front, William Rosenberg. Standing, left to right: Erik Richer La Fleche, Calin Rovinescu, John Leopold, Michael Richards. The team in this year, as in many others, won the prize for the best-dressed team and has raised a significant portion of the funds raised in the annual event.

Ron Durand, Stuart Cobbett, Mortimer Freiheit.

Claire Fisher, Sandra Walker, Donna Sukman, Fraser Elliott, Donna Shepherd,
Donna Barrett, Mary Brock.

William Scott, Brenda Hebert, Roy Fraser Elliott, Richard Pound.

Suzanne Côté, Louis P. Bélanger, Gérald Tremblay.

Calin Rovinescu's retirement, 2000. Front row, left to right: Mortimer Freiheit, Yves Martineau, Louis-P. Bélanger, Anik Trudel, Calin Rovinescu, Suzanne Côté, William Rosenberg, Jim Grant. Back row, left to right: Jean-Pierre Belhumeur, Martin Scheim, Frédéric Harvey, Stephen Raicek, Marc Lalonde.

Calin Rovinescu's retirement, 2000. Front row, left to right: Erik Richer La Fleche, Christine Desaulniers, Jean Fontaine, Marc-André Coulombe, Benjamin Greenberg, David Angus, John Leopold, Michael Richards. Back row, left to right: Ted Claxton, Marc Laurin, Rovinescu, Eric Mongeau, Jean Lamothe, Kip Cobbett. Back centre: Etienne Massicotte.

Heward Stikeman's 60th anniversary and Fraser Elliott's 50th at the Quebec Bar, 1998. Seated left to right: James Robb, Fraser Elliott, Heward Stikeman, François Mercier, Maurice Riel. Standing left to right: Richard Pound, Robert Hart, Marc Lalonde, Calin Rovinescu, David Angus, Brian Rose, James Grant, Michel Décary, Michel Vennat, Peter O'Brien, Mortimer Freiheit, Michael Richards, Maurice Régnier, Peter Cumyn.

Jean McLeod (Toronto General
Manager), Rod Barrett,
Chantelle Courtney.

Adrian Lang, David Finkelstein.

Stuart Cobbett, Lyse Charette,
Guy Masson.

Allan Gotlieb.

transaction and source of financing was that Dome was selling a portion of its oil and gas properties to a partnership of TransCanada PipeLines and Maligne Resources, a subsidiary of Dow Chemical, with financing, again, from Canadian banks. Virtually unnoticed was the fact that Clark had not done much of this type of work before and that Kathleen Ward had not yet completed her first year as a lawyer.

A large percentage of the Toronto practice was banking and banking finance transactions. Another vital and growing portion was the securities side. As Tony Melman of CIBC had said on the plane ride home with Yontef following the Dome closing, "deal junkies" like the two of them did not often get repeat deals with the same parties, but he nevertheless predicted that CIBC and the firm would be working together on Dome for quite a while because in his view, there was no way that Dome would be able to repay the loan. In the coming months, not only would this prove to be true, but the template for how the firm would deal with the rest of its practice also became apparent. Riley would take on the banking aspects, which would include everything from incorporating the new Schedule B banks to project financings and loan transactions. Stransman would take on the securities practice. Mike Allen, who had recently joined the firm from Borden Elliot, and Ward would stick with Yontef on the Dome Petroleum odyssey.

Although energy prices were high, no conceivable price level could service Dome Petroleum's staggering debt. It had ceased to be an oil and gas play and by any measure, had become an interest rate play that was threatening to sink even the Canadian banks. This led, not surprisingly, to weeks of negotiation between Dome, its largest shareholder, Dome Mines, the four banks, and the Government of Canada in search of a solution. Each of the banks called urgently for their own separate counsel, and the Government of Canada – represented by Marc Lalonde, then minister of Finance, the deputy minister, Marshall (Mickey) Cohen, and Ed Clark – engaged Osler Hoskin, where Purdy Crawford and Brian Levitt worked on the matter. The negotiations often bordered on the surreal. They were carried out by the chairmen of the banks, who may have had great experience in having things done for them but had not negotiated anything by themselves for years. The TD Bank chairman arrived at CIBC's top floor and admired the surroundings he had never seen before. CIBC's chairman reminded the TD Bank's chairman that the latter had once been his paper boy, set out his position on the telephone, and then hung up. The Bank of Montreal's chairman called back to express his position. These were exchanges of edicts, not negotiations. Mickey Cohen looked down to the end of the table where Yontef sat and observed pointedly that it was great to be negotiating with his former student. No posturing was too low or unfair.

Eventually, an agreement in principle (the AIP) was concluded. It was one of the most bizarre documents in Canadian legal and financial history; it provided modest government financial support ($500 million), a temporary guarantee from Petro-Canada (then owned by the federal government), and a great deal of moral suasion. At this stage, the banks decided that they needed counsel to "implement the AIP," and the firm was selected for the purpose. Only the Toronto-Dominion Bank's representative had a perfectly relevant question in the circumstances – namely, whether Yontef thought the firm had the capacity and wherewithal for the job. Unhesitatingly, but with a very fluttery stomach, Yontef assured him that it did.

Once the AIP was signed, the banks then had to "sell the deal" since great concern had developed within the international financial community about the level of Canadian bank exposure to Dome. The Bank of Montreal, Toronto-Dominion Bank, and the Royal Bank took Yontef to New York and then to London to explain the transaction. CIBC stayed back to keep the home waters calm. In what would prove to be the pattern for years to come, the people that were sent to "sell the deal" had not read the AIP and certainly had no concept of what security they might have had for their existing loans. The message in New York began with, "We all have to stick together on this; it would be a disaster if it came apart," and was followed by questions. As each question was posed either about the AIP or about the banks' positions on their individual loans, the bank emissaries turned to Yontef as counsel for him to reply. In London, they fared no better. It was somewhat less hostile because many of the European banks believed that notwithstanding the legal form and content of the AIP, it was nevertheless effectively a Canadian government credit. One of the least charitable remarks came from Crédit Lyonnais, which observed that the only thing about which the Canadian banks had managed to convince them was that they knew how to choose lawyers. Many thousands of dollars of expense account spending behind them, including a Concorde trip to London, Yontef got a note a few days after his return from one of the British banks, asking him to send across nineteen pounds sterling. On the only free night during the hectic trip, the team had gone to a play, and the UK banker thought it "appropriate" that they pay for this entertainment out of their own pockets.

Early on in the debt restructuring exercise, Brian Levitt and Yontef met with a group at the Citibank Institutional Recovery Unit – almost as good a euphemism as the Special Loans Division. Included in the group were Peter Fitts, the reigning czar of restructurings, his Shearman & Sterling lawyer, Bob McKinnon, and the two Citibank vice-presidents who had booked their loan in the first place. As they walked into this otherwise tastefully decorated boardroom, Brian Levitt turned to Yontef and said this was really quite a surprise because he had expected the walls, ceiling, and floor to be covered in white tile, with no furniture, and with a large drain in the centre. Jerry Finneran, one of the loan makers, said to Yontef that they should make a deal today. "People like us," he said, "work by the deal. Workout people work by the hour." Yontef was not entirely sure what he meant, but it sounded good to him. Fitts and MacKinnon railed on in a very professional manner, saying that they knew everything there was to know about these things, having done the Mexico restructuring, the Chrysler restructuring, and the International Harvester restructuring. Yontef replied that no one cared much about those transactions because sovereign debt restructurings were pretty simple stuff, and that this was larger than all the previous commercial ones put together.

As the last of the loan agreements for the four banks was negotiated – the one that permitted the swap of Conoco stock for Hudson's Bay Oil & Gas stock and permitted taking security on any asset that was not nailed down – the banks' lawyers tried to address a last-minute queasy feeling. What if there were an asset they should have secured that either they did not know about or was too difficult to secure, which was not part of the four-bank security package? Since all such concerns seem to arise at 3:00 in the morning, Yontef remembers scribbling a clause – section 4.06 – which in essence prohibited the sale of any asset without the consent of the four banks. He showed it to George Watson, the chief financial officer of Dome at the time, who read it and said he felt there was something wrong with it but that he could not put his finger on why it seemed so terrible. They made some modest adjustments, such as permitting the production and sale of oil and gas in the ordinary course to produce cash flow, and the clause made its way into the ultimate loan agreement.

Yontef wishes he could say it was professional prescience, but this clause, derived solely from lawyers' paranoia, turned out to be among the best assets the four banks had. Not surprisingly, there were many assets that were not secured, partially secured, or that simply had not been considered. Every time Dome Petroleum wanted or needed to sell an asset – which was frequent in the first year or two – it had to request the consent of the banks. The price of the consent was invariably that the proceeds of sale must be applied to pay down a Canadian bank position. So effective was this clause that Harry Roberts, then the treasurer at Dome and now the chief financial officer at Petro-Canada, once said that he had been pleased to have spoken with his counterpart at one of the pipeline companies. What pleased him was that the covenant pattern in the pipeline indenture was tougher than the one with which he had to live. However, he added, nothing known to mankind compared to the impact of one diabolical clause, number 4.06, in his own loan agreement.

With the dollars involved, the number of financial institutions involved, and the number of advisors involved, the task was monumental to say the least. The overall debt restructuring agreement had twenty-three execution pages, which included thirty-four Dome companies and sixty-three financial institutions. The debt restructuring agreement documented the various credit and security arrangements of the various Dome companies, rescheduled the payment amounts of the various credit faculties, and provided various common overriding terms for all credit facilities, including rescheduled interest rates, additional covenants, updated remedies, etc. During the agreed standstill period, the various lenders undertook not to demand or accelerate their loans or related security. The closing of the transaction was originally (and optimistically) set at October 5, 1984, but it eventually occurred on February 5, 1985 in one of the large ballrooms of the Royal York Hotel, and it was certainly the largest closing any of the Canadian lawyers had ever seen. Throughout the entire transaction, whether in Calgary, Toronto, New York, or elsewhere, the firm was a key player in this mammoth undertaking. With the completion of the Dome transaction, if the firm had not previously been a front-line player in Toronto, it assuredly was now.

Just before the crisis that led to the negotiation and settlement of the AIP, Dome Petroleum had sold some foreign properties, located mainly in Indonesia, which netted Dome about $240 million. As part of the AIP, the banks agreed not to scoop the so-called Indonesian proceeds, showing good faith and providing added liquidity as part of the deal by which the Canadian government would provide its backstop. Not long into the "implementation" of the AIP stage, Yontef asked one of the bank representatives what would have prompted the banks to leave this on the table. When the answer came back that this was a good question, he suggested that it made every sense for them to try to get it back. He raised the matter with Brian Levitt, as Dome's representative, who replied that he did not know why, but he remembered that no one had claimed them, which led to him asking that they be left on the table to help secure the Canadian government's commitment. Levitt added that if the banks had said no, they could have had the assets. Yontef persuaded Levitt that the four banks should take the money, and if there were ever a firefight over why, the government would have a moral commitment from the banks to get it back. It did not look like the government would have to put up any money anyway, so why penalize the Canadian banks in the process? The disbelief of the Canadian banks when the firm got the money back some fifteen to eighteen months after the AIP was exceeded only by a comment that Peter Fitts had made a few months earlier. In a fit of frustration with the Canadian banks, he said that he was sick and tired of hearing about his ironclad security and the weak position of the Canadian banks when the Canadian banks had whisked $1.5 billion off the table from under his nose in the first year.

Dome was a high-water mark in another sense. The problems were so enormous and the potential consequences of any default so grave that there would be meetings with perhaps thirty people sitting around a Stikeman Elliott boardroom table at which the nature of a problem would be articulated. All of the Dome and bank representatives would become stunned into inactivity, so catatonic in the face of certain disaster, that lawyers, especially a brash thirty-six-year-old like Yontef, could assert with apparent complete confidence that the answer was simple and would state what should be done. One of the cartoonists at Dome did a sketch that summarized the situation exceptionally well. In it, there were four dreadful looking monsters feeding on Dome Petroleum logos. Each of the monsters had the name of one of the Canadian banks. Strings were attached to each of the monsters, indicating that the monsters were marionettes, and operating the marionettes were devious little people labelled "the banks' lawyers."

One aspect of the Dome transaction not to be overlooked is the fact that this mandate was the beginning of a long-term relationship with two exceptional Calgary lawyers: Barry Emes and Glenn Cameron. Albertan Wayne Shaw became involved in the Dome matters when bankruptcy or receivership loomed as a distinct possibility for the company. As an Alberta native, Shaw was asked and suggested that the firm should retain Code Hunter, including

Bill Code and two of Shaw's Alberta classmates, Neil Wittman and Patrick Peacock. Code Hunter did a full review of the law and options under various Dome insolvency scenarios. As Dome moved from a traditional insolvency situation to one of contractual debt restructuring, the role of Code, Wittman, and Peacock decreased, and two of their corporate partners, Emes and Cameron, became an integral part of the Dome team. The close relationship that developed during the Dome days led to other interesting mandates with Emes and Cameron as well as others in their firm. When the firm decided it was time to open an office in Calgary in September 1992, it was quite simple to begin with the two of them.

When Great Britain decided to privatize a number of its industries in the early to mid-1980s, the British Telecom offering established a template that proved irresistible for Canadian investment banks. The unusual feature of the British Telecom arrangement was that it was sold using "partly paid" shares. The market, especially retail investors, loved the leverage because the expectation was that having paid, for example, 50 or 60 per cent down, they would never have to pay the balance owing because that would be satisfied with the profits from the increase in the market value of the stock rise in the intervening period. Shortly after this immensely successful global offering, Texaco, disgruntled with the National Energy Program in Canada, decided to sell some of its stock in Texaco Canada.

As work on this offering proceeded, the investment bankers concluded that its size could be increased significantly if the company could devise a way to sell "partly paid" shares. The Canadian legal issue was self-evident because contemporary corporate statutes did not permit the issuance of "partly paid" shares. The firm's challenge was to find a way for the client to accomplish its objective, which was resolved because from a market perspective, the same economic result as partly paid shares could be achieved as long as shares were not being issued from treasury. In this case, the fact that Texaco was selling previously issued Texaco Canada shares meant that fully paid shares were being sold on an instalment basis. The result was the largest equity offering in Canada up to that time – some $484 million.

It was not, however, without its difficult moments. As the investment bankers set out to sell the stock to the investing public, it was left to the lawyers to mop up the details. First of all, what could these securities be called? "Partly paid shares" did not work because they were expressly prohibited in the corporate statute, and "legal for life" rules invariably included the expression "fully paid common shares."[25] To this day, the agreed-upon name of "instalment receipts" remains the description of such securities. Second, how could payment of the second instalment be secured? The firm concluded that the stock could be sold to the underwriters, who in turn would give a security interest in the stock for the second instalment. The instalment receipt would give a holder the right to the stock itself only if the balance were to be paid. The lingering question was what would happen were there to be a "deficiency," and the firm had concluded that it would be all but impossible to go after some unsuspecting aftermarket purchaser for the deficiency. Fortunately, Texaco decided it would take the risk of the deficiency on the "dangle," as they called it. Interestingly, instalment receipts flourished without incident, the risk of a deficiency remained real, and, indeed, a selling stockholder in Canadian Fracmaster many years later had to decide whether he could pursue holders of instalment receipts for a deficiency.

Another problem with instalment receipts has never been tested. The opinions given on these transactions were that the "shares" were "legal for life," which begged the question of whether the "shares" were the same as the "instalment receipts." On the eve of closing the Texaco transaction, a solicitor with the federal Department of Insurance called with an innocent enough question: how did the firm and Torys (acting for the underwriters) conclude that this was "legal for life?" A strategy session was convened at the offices of Campbell Godfrey (Texaco Canada's counsel) to rehearse what could be said to this Ottawa solicitor, whose question might well bring the whole plan to ruin. Everyone agreed that it was important not to show any nervousness or anxiety. They would reassure her that they had thought this through, that the three firms were prepared to put their good reputations behind the opinion, and so forth. They led off the conference call by expressing some degree of surprise with her call and that they hoped they could persuade her in short order about any lingering concern. They were not ten seconds into the call when Gord Coleman of Torys interrupted. He could not have been yelling louder if he had cupped his hands and screamed into the telephone's microphone. How dare this woman question their judgment? This was the largest underwriting in Canadian history, and who did she think she was asking questions about it? This was an issue of national and international importance, and how in the world did she think she was qualified to comment on it? So began a ten-minute barrage while the rest of them, whom she could not see since she was in Ottawa, shrank into their chairs and tried to find a spot under the table. After a seeming eternity of this verbal onslaught, she responded by saying that she really had not looked at it very carefully and was willing to follow their judgment. It was an odd testimonial to why subtlety and politeness might well have been the wrong approach.

Asamera was a wonderful client for the firm, exceeded only by the quality of its chief executive officer, Bob Welty. During 1984, the firm was acting for Asamera and working to the conclusion of a public offering of its stock. With four or five days to go before closing, Jim Wyatt came into Yontef's office to ask how it was that Asamera had qualified under the "legal for life" test for Quebec pension funds. "That's easy," Yontef replied, "our Montreal office tells me so." They proceeded to call the young lawyer in the Montreal office and asked the question that Wyatt had asked. "No problem," he replied, "Asamera's shares are listed on an exchange recognized by the Quebec Securities Commission, namely, the Toronto Stock Exchange." Wyatt then asked when the Quebec Securities Commission had recognized the Toronto Stock Exchange. The young lawyer replied that everybody recognized the Toronto Stock Exchange because it was a famous exchange. Disaster loomed when Wyatt said that he did not think so because "recognition" meant a formal declaration such as, for example, what the Quebec Securities Commission had done for the Montreal Stock Exchange. With only four or five days to go, the firm was faced with its commitment to give an opinion, which was obviously incorrect, at closing.

Several of the lawyers discussing this nightmare had various opinions, of which the prevailing one was how quickly the firm's insurer should be called. Remembering one of the famous Lenny Bruce lines – "Even if they have pictures, deny it" – Yontef asked if he could have a few minutes. He called Bob Welty, asking if he had ever thought about listing on the Montreal Stock Exchange. Welty responded by saying candidly that he never had. Yontef invited him to think about doing so now because with the new offering, he would have, for example, shareholders in Quebec. Welty asked if there was any downside. Yontef told him that there would be some French translation issues, but that this was all part of becoming more of a world-class company. When should we do this, Welty wondered. It was ventured that it might be a good idea to do it before closing. Welty, who was probably not fooled at all, asked what was involved and agreed to call a board meeting, especially when we said the firm would get the papers filled in for signature, and in view of the shortness of time, we would depart from firm policy and disburse the listing fee instead of waiting for them to remit it to Montreal.

A series of calls followed. Yontef called Bob Hart and told him to prepare the extravagantly large cheque payable to the Montreal Stock Exchange for listing fees. As Hart was reaching a horrified crescendo that would assuredly end with a refusal, he was given the choice of disbursing the listing fee or permitting Stikeman Elliott to face a $25-million lawsuit. Ever gracious when over a barrel, Hart agreed to disburse the money. The Montreal lawyer was instructed to get the company listed in the couple of days remaining. His reluctance to use up a favour was overtaken by his desire to avoid so limiting a career move. The stock was listed the day before closing, and giving the opinion was a walk in the park. The same year, André Roy[26] recalls a plan of arrangement for Asamera that required a team of twenty corporate and tax lawyers working non-stop for fifty-two hours at Plow & Waters, the printers, to complete and translate a management proxy circular for a special meeting of shareholders to approve the plan of arrangement.

Many trials and tribulations later, Gulf, then controlled by Olympia & York, made an unsolicited and by any measure hostile takeover bid for Asamera. If the client was not completely dead in the water faced with the bid, it was certainly comatose. All of the wit, wisdom, and guile of Goldman Sachs, Dominion Securities, and Stikeman Elliott could come up with nothing compelling to offer by way of defence. As one observer of the corporate scene had noted, often the most successful takeover strategy is to pay the highest price, and this was obviously the bidder's strategy in this case. There was even some thought given to doing a leveraged recapitalization, which was derided by the investment bankers, who said it was a great theory but there was not a chance in the world they could pull it off. While Tom Vowinckel worked with the company's financial people in an adjoining office to come up with the ultimate paid-up capital calculation – this took about a week – Yontef met with Welty.

His argument to Welty was that it was clear that Gulf would prevail, and the only question was price. If they could get more than had been offered, they would look like heroes generally and do a good job for the shareholders. Why not call Mickey Cohen (now with O&Y and representing Gulf) and tell him to raise the price, or else the company would do a leveraged recapitalization? Welty reiterated that according to the investment bankers, this was not possible, to which Yontef replied that both of them knew that, but Cohen did not. Several days later, Welty met with Cohen and told him that unless the price were raised, a leveraged recapitalization would be announced. After some to-and-fro, with Cohen arguing this would be the worst thing Asamera could possibly do, he raised the price by $2.50 per share and Asamera capitulated. So was born the "phantom recap defence."

Not long afterwards, Donna Kaufman[27] of the Montreal office became chair of the Selkirk Communications Independent Committee following an announcement that Southam had agreed to sell its large block in Selkirk to Maclean Hunter. Although, at this stage, John Stransman and Yontef were generally not working together on the same files since Stransman was rapidly becoming established as one of the leading lawyers in the field on his own account, Kaufman called on both of them to help. They worked with the independent directors trying to fashion a defence or to work out a method to secure a higher bid, but this became more problematic with each passing day. Maclean Hunter, after all, had bid a pretty fair price. There was, however, a peculiarity that began to assume critical importance.

Some years earlier, the CRTC had become worried about media cross-ownership. In this case, Southam, a newspaper publisher, was not in a legal position to control Selkirk Communications, a television station and cable TV operator. Some inventive person, on Selkirk's behalf, had worked up a share structure whereby the participating shares became non-voting and were classified as Class A shares, of which Southam was the largest holder. There were a small number of Class B shares, less than a dozen, of which one share was issued to every director. For legal control purposes, Selkirk was therefore controlled by its board, although there was little doubt who "controlled" Selkirk for all practical purposes. When Maclean Hunter made its offer, it assumed – as would be logical – that the Class B shares would follow control of the Class A shares and that Maclean Hunter's "independent director" nominees would succeed to the Class B shares. So it was that the financial advisor, Wood Gundy, was looking for a higher bid even though the largest holder of the Class A shares was locked up.

As the final weekend that the bid would be open approached, there were one or two potential bidders with modest interest, but it was clear that no one was prepared to go up against Maclean Hunter. This was the point at which Yontef and Stransman decided that they would auction off the Class B shares owned by the independent directors. In essence, they concluded that there would be no other bid without a significant incentive, and indeed, it would have to be an extraordinary incentive to go up against someone who had locked up the largest shareholder of class A shares. They suggested that Wood Gundy contact all possible bidders and tell them that if they would bid materially more than Maclean Hunter, the directors would deliver up the Class B voting shares to them. Maclean Hunter was told the same thing.

To say that Maclean Hunter went ballistic understates the measure of their reaction. Their counsel called Yontef and Stransman, saying that this was blatantly illegal, would never withstand a court challenge, and reached for other arguments that ultimately cast doubt on their parentage. The two of them blandly invited the appropriate challenge since, they asserted, the bid festivities would be over by the end of the weekend when any remedial activity would become highly academic. They also made the point that there was no restriction on Maclean Hunter raising its bid since they would happily give them the Class B shares if theirs was the highest. By noon on the Sunday preceding the Monday when the bid expired, the incentive had not worked sufficiently to raise another bid from a third party. However, Maclean Hunter was persuaded to bid against itself and raised the price by $3.50 per share. With apparent great reluctance, they surrendered.

The firm had succeeded with what became described as the "Killer B" defence and happily gave the credit to Wood Gundy, handing out hockey sweaters in black and gold with a bee on the front and giving Ed King, the chief executive officer of Wood Gundy, the jersey with the "C" for captain. Maclean Hunter picked up on the subtleties. Its counsel called Yontef afterwards to say it was the best defence he had ever seen. They had had a gun filled only with blanks, but they had won the day. One of the independent directors, Nat Starr, personally delivered a cheque for the firm's fees, saying that there was no point trusting the mail or giving "the new owners" an opportunity to depreciate what he felt was rightfully theirs.

In the autumn of 1984, several members of the firm went to an International Bar Association convention in Singapore, where the Stikeman Elliott representatives were invited to a dinner hosted by Freehill, Hollingdale & Page of Sydney, Australia. They had heard about this upstart Canadian firm with global aspirations and were interested to learn as much as they could about its plans to conquer the world. Being too embarrassed to admit that the firm was in essence making it up as it went along and being overwhelmed in the process by its own success, they did their best to be modest and charming. About a year later, Roy Randall, then of Freehills and subsequently a partner in our Sydney office, called to ask for assistance on a file in which they were working.

Closed-end "country funds" were the current rage in US capital markets, and with Randall's guidance, some clients in Sydney had launched the First Australia Fund. They were now planning to launch the First Australia Prime Income Fund in the United States, which was to be a closed-end fund that would capitalize on the fact that Australian interest rates were substantially higher than those prevailing in North America. Remembering the firm from the Singapore evening, Randall called from New York, where he was working on the US fund, to ask if they could do a clone in Canada. He neglected to mention that the underwriters had checked this before he had called and had been assured that there was no way that this could be done in Canada. Notwithstanding this omission, Yontef listened to Randall and told him that if British Telecom could do an international offering in which Canada played a minor role, there was no real difference with a closed-end fund. Of course, he assured him, such a thing could be done in Canada!

Bill Braithwaite and Yontef started working on this "international of-fering" for the clients in Sydney. For the time being, Prudential Bache, the underwriters, were not represented. They worked their way carefully through the regulatory concerns, the largest of which was whether this would be a "mutual fund" that would require Canadian investment advisors and a Canadian custodian of the securities. They forged ahead, relying on the technical distinction that this was a "closed-end fund" and that because it was an international offering, minor provincial considerations, such as custodianship of securities, could be overcome. They had been spending quite a lot of time on this when at a drafting meeting, they asked the lo-cal Prudential Bache principal how large an offering they were planning. Frankly, they said, no one had any idea, but a total offering of $10 or $15 million did not seem unreasonable. The two lawyers almost fainted since they had been treating this as the "Rolls Royce" of offerings and had not realized that they were working on such a small flyer.

About a week before the prospectus was to be filed, Prudential Bache hired counsel, and they were informed that Jim Baillie, former chairman of the Ontario Securities Commission, would take a turn at reading the document for this modest offering to the markets. The day before the fil-ing, Baillie called to say that he had read the document carefully and that in his opinion, which was by no means insubstantial, there was no way the Ontario Securities Commission would let this proceed. In his view, the OSC would view this closed-end fund in the same manner as it would a mutual fund and that there were many reasons why it did not qualify. He added that although Torys had given the matter careful thought, they felt so strongly about it that they had come within a hair of resigning from the file altogether. [28] As a good faith gesture, they would permit their name to stand, notwithstanding these overwhelming reservations and in the certainty that it would fail. Not thirty seconds later, the client called in a panic. All we could reply was that the OSC could refuse to qualify any offering for any reason whatsoever, applying its "blue sky" mandate, and there was never a guarantee of acceptance when one filed a prospectus. One thing was, how-ever, certain, and that was that they would never know if they did not try. With this shaky assurance, the client finalized the timetable and for good measure, ignored Jim Baillie's second warning, which was in essence that getting this prospectus cleared across Canada in three and a half weeks was so adventurous as not to warrant serious comment.

The prospectus was filed the following day, and Braithwaite got a call from the prospectus solicitor at the OSC, saying how delighted he was to be working opposite Braithwaite since he remembered with great affection studying under him at the law school. Not missing a beat, Braithwaite men-tioned that he too would enjoy this opportunity, but that he had a special concern with the filing. It did not take long to explain that notwithstanding the compelling merits of the offering, it was as likely to die on the vine because of the time constraints as it might for any other reasons. The former student took the bit between his teeth and within days, the prospectus was cleared in Ontario with only minor deficiencies. A few days after that, with the young man's help, Braithwaite had squeezed comments from each of the other nine provincial securities commissions. The most difficult of the deficiencies was met with the response that there was no merit to the concern because such reputable people were behind this offering. They not only took the offering through regulatory hurdles without a hitch, but succeeded in doing so comfortably within the "impossible" deadline. The best, however, was yet to come.

There were several memorable aspects of the offering. First, the estimate of $10 to $15 million proved to have been a bit light since the offering ultimately sold $225 million worth of shares in this new entity. Second, the offering was clearly international but not nearly as much as had been expected; approximately 90 per cent of it was sold in Canada, with the rest scattered in Europe, seemingly as an accommodation to the characterization that it was an international offering. Third, although Braithwaite had worked on many files by that stage, he had never really done a closing all by himself. As Yontef left for a vacation, Braithwaite orchestrated a closing that took place contemporaneously in three or four countries around the globe – the First Australia Prime Income Investment Company Limited was incorporated in the Cook Islands – and this was an auspicious precursor to his many achievements in the years to come. Lastly, until the management company that advised the fund was sold at the end of 2000, the fund had reached well over $1 billion in size and was an important client of the firm throughout the period.

੩੩

Although the Texaco acquisition of Getty turned out to be a recurring source for work at the firm, it had started out as a single mandate. Texaco had won a battle for Getty Oil in the United States. Because of the application of the *Foreign Investment Review Act* and *Investment Canada Act,* there would be a serious issue of securing the necessary regulatory approvals in Canada. When Texaco called, Gordon from Montreal and Yontef in Toronto were asked if as a first step, they would brief Getty's lawyer, James Farley, who has since gone on to judicial reknown.[29] They met with Farley and on a preliminary basis, were quite surprised to learn that Getty had paid $5,000 for a lobbyist to get them an appointment with the minister of Energy or his deputy minister. Instead, the Getty representatives had met with, and were very disappointed by, Herb Gray, who was quite removed from the energy portfolio. Farley had concluded that they were really sunk because they had no feeling for how the new Conservative government would react. As luck would have it, Yontef was going to the bar mitzvah for the son of one of his friends, and being the "hotshot" working on the massive Dome Petroleum refinancing project and thereby a minor flavour of the month, he got seated beside another guest, Sinclair Stevens, one of the Tory cabinet members. About two-thirds of the way through the dinner, Yontef turned to Stevens and said something to the effect that this was not for tonight but that one of these days, we would be calling on him for some insights on how to deal with the Texaco/Getty issues. Stevens was the Industry minister and technically responsible for the *Foreign Investment Review Act*. Not giving it a second thought, Stevens said that he had to go to the bathroom anyway, so how about Yontef joining him, and they could get started that evening.

The Texaco/Getty acquisition led, unfortunately, to Texaco making a chapter 11 bankruptcy filing in the United States and to it being put under siege by predators, the last of which was the renowned corporate raider Carl Icahn. Pressure was mounting for Texaco to provide value for creditors, and this in turn led to consideration of the sale of Texaco Canada. The Stikeman Elliott team was at that stage Robert Couzin on tax matters, Gordon for government relations – that sounded better than "dealing with Investment Canada" – and Yontef for work on the corporate side. Early in the proceedings, Yontef was invited to a "strategy summit" in White Plains, New York. What Yontef remembers most about the meeting was his feeling of being a kid in a candy shop. Apart from the senior brass at Texaco and their battery of investment bankers, he was on the same side as Joe Flom, who was there in person as the US corporate counsel for Texaco, as well as David Boies, their litigation strategist, whose photo had recently graced the cover of the Sunday *New York Times Magazine* with the caption "The Litigator Everybody Wants." So interesting was the discussion that at one point, Joe Flom, with no briefcase, pad of paper, or any other visible bit of support, turned to Yontef and asked if he could borrow a piece of paper and perhaps a pencil. Yontef's heart was racing while Flom jotted down three or four words. Then came his moment as Flom finally decided to ask a question and turned to him, inquiring what his best guess would be for the amount of Canadian tax payable were Texaco to sell Texaco Canada. As Yontef was stuttering and mumbling, he remembers thinking that he had sent the wrong guy, and where was Robert Couzin when you needed him most.

It was an extraordinary transaction. The first stage involved paying a dividend of some $900 million out of Texaco Canada. There was not much point in leaving the cash there since any buyer would simply have had to add to the purchase price to get the cash inside the company. In addition, some exploration rights off the coast of Brazil were rolled into a new subsidiary, Texaco Canada Petroleum Inc., along with some cash flow producing properties to fund the exploration. As the team went off to Brazil to work on the transfers, in a most unusual development to enable a deadline to be met and notwithstanding the skepticism of Texaco Canada's Canadian lawyers, the Ontario Securities Commission permitted the firm to effect a transfer of 100 per cent of the TCPI shares to a trustee, pending the preparation and filing of a disclosure document that would be sent to all shareholders of record of Texaco Canada some weeks down the road, together with their share certificates. In effect, the shares were transferred on the basis of an IOU for compliance. The first day after the transfer, the OSC called to explain its concerns that a "grey market" had developed in the stock to be distributed and that feverish trading was going on, without the benefit of any disclosure. The regulatory hysteria was calmed down with the provision of assurances that the firm would work diligently and quickly to get a disclosure document filed. The best was yet to come and began when the auction for Texaco Canada proceeded.

Ultimately, the auction was a two-horse race. There were a number of problems, such as moving the head office to Alberta, having the purchaser buy the Texaco Canada holding company instead of the actual shares, and many more. Imperial Oil was the frontrunner, but there was significant competition risk because of the resulting increased market share in retail gasoline distribution. The dark horse was Allan Bond from Australia, and fortunately, it did not prove necessary to test his ability to get to the finish line nor to predict the ignominy that would befall him in later years. Texaco's position was that if Imperial were to prevail, it would have to hit the ball out of the park with plenty to spare – namely, to pay a very high price because of the completion risk (that the transaction might have to be undone as a result of the regulatory process). In an interesting example of reversal of the normal burden in such transactions, Imperial would be required to take on all regulatory risks. In the end, they did what was necessary.

The transaction, which was huge at the time, had a number of interesting postscripts. In what may have been the best piece of competition work ever done before the tribunal, Gordon, a novice and never to repeat the feat as a competition lawyer, negotiated a deal with the Canadian competition authorities and Imperial Oil pursuant to which all risk was borne by Imperial Oil. It was so successful that over a year later, while Texaco was still reminiscing about the wonderful deal, and in this self-congratulatory glow ignoring Robert Couzin's suggestion that they pursue a tax refund, the firm finally got their attention and Couzin got them a tax refund of some $163 million. The amount was so large that the team spent a couple of days trying to choose appropriate wording for the press release announcing that quarter's earnings to avoid embarrassing the Canadian government. We sent Texaco a very significant account, perhaps the largest ever sent by the firm, which the client determined to be extraordinarily reasonable and paid by return mail – in US dollars. When Yontef called to ask how we should deal with the more than one million dollars of excess payment without embarrassing whoever had overpaid, the answer was that the firm should hold on to it and work it off in trade. To some extent, this was the genesis of the firm's current relationship with Skadden Arps because Joe Flom, ever shrewd, made the suggestion to one of his colleagues that he stick close to the firm because the firm was close to Texaco and they had lots of cash that one day would need to be spent.

In addition to Texaco/Getty, the firm had been retained to act for Chevron, which at about the same time was acquiring Gulf. In an effort to maintain some commercial separation between the transactions, a Chinese wall was established within the firm, whereby Stanley Hartt would be the corporate lawyer, with Jim Arnett the FIRA specialist on the Chevron deal, while Gordon and Yontef would work in parallel on Texaco/Getty. The arrangement seemed to be working tolerably well until Yontef got a call from Texaco, announcing that they were flying people up to Toronto to visit with Gordon and him. When they arrived, Yontef excused himself from a Dome meeting in the main boardroom and went to another board-room to meet with Gordon and the Texaco people. The reason they had wanted to meet, they said, was that they had learned that the firm was acting for Chevron, which made them very uncomfortable and more than a bit suspicious that the firm might be tempted to sell one out so that the other would get a better deal. This meeting had followed an all-nighter for Yontef, and whether it was because he was tired and impatient or merely full of himself as the big shot responsible for Dome, he did not hesitate in answering. He told the Texaco people that virtually anyone needing im-portant work of this nature done in Canada would turn to our firm first. Both Chevron and Texaco had been long-standing clients of the firm, so it was not going to choose between them. Canada was a small country when you got down to it, and he assured them the firm would do its best to make sure each got a fair deal. He remembers noticing that Gordon, not one to become easily perturbed with heavy "marketing," of which he was himself a dedicated practitioner, had developed a bit of a tremor while they waited for Texaco to say something along the lines of, if that was our attitude, then here were the consequences. Instead, they agreed with the assessment and as they were leaving, said that they had just wanted us to know that they were a little sensitive about it. In one of life's ironies, Chevron and Texaco later merged.

Arnett remembers the tension that surrounded the closing of the Chev-ron transaction. FIRA acknowledged in its letter approving the deal that this was the largest transaction that it had ever handled and stated that its approval had been given on the basis that Chevron would seek a buyer for Gulf Canada. In any event, it was something that Chevron wanted to help pay down its debt, and Chevron negotiated a deal with Olympia & York through Paul Reichmann. When the closing was organized, there were two stages. In the first, Olympia & York was to transfer by wire transfer $1.2 billion to Chevron's account in Pittsburg to pay for the Gulf Canada shares. When everything was ready, instructions were given to "push the button." Chevron was standing by in Pittsburg to receive the funds. An hour later, the funds had not arrived. Arnett and Chevron asked Olympia & York what had happened. Olympia & York did not know; they had sent the funds. Late in the afternoon, the funds still not in hand, Arnett said to the Chevron counsel, Ken Dure, that they would have to contemplate the position Chevron would take if the funds did not arrive by the end of the day. They waited and waited for four or five hours, and the funds finally arrived just before the close of business. They speculated that Olympia & York had transferred "federal" funds, which would take effect at the end of the day instead of immediate funds, probably trying to squeeze an extra day's worth of interest out of the transaction.

In October 1986, Nova Corporation, which owned approximately 57 per cent of Husky Oil Limited, a public oil and gas corporation, entered into discussions with the Li Group concerning its purchase of an interest in Husky. One of the goals of Nova was to secure arrangements that would provide Husky with more effective access to medium and long-term capital markets. Yontef was preparing to go to Bermuda for a board meeting at the time that the Li Group was going to Calgary to start negotiating what turned out to be the first part of the Husky transaction. He asked Stransman to go to Calgary while he went to Bermuda on the basis that he would get to Calgary as soon as he could. After a couple of days in the islands, he received a message from Stransman, who told him that he had been cooling his heels in his hotel room for two days, that the firm was not going to be participating until Yontef got there, and that he was returning to Toronto. The last plane of the day had already left Bermuda for Toronto, so he chartered a jet for him and his wife to go back to Toronto, where he went to an adjacent terminal to catch the flight to Calgary while his wife went home.

They negotiated in Calgary for several days, making little progress. Nova, the majority holder of Husky, was pressing to receive a premium for its voting control position. This position was completely at variance with the then prevailing securities law rule that all shareholders had to be treated equally. The Nova team had come up with what they thought was an innovative way to do indirectly what was prohibited directly – namely, to do this by way of an amalgamation. Arguments on the issue were acrimonious in the extreme. Nova and its subsidiary, Husky, were adamant that the statute did not prohibit such a premium. As a self-styled expert in the legacy of Henry Knowles, Yontef was equally adamant that it did. The client was about to throw in the towel and pay the premium in order to make the deal since the risk rested largely with Nova, when over dinner on Sunday night, Simon Murray, Li Ka-shing's lieutenant on the transaction, came to the table of lawyers with a Cheshire cat smile. Apparently, the Ontario Securities Commission had just called to say that it had finally taken a closer look at the papers that were to be filed the following day. The OSC had concluded that if Nova were to proceed, the OSC would bring an action to block the transaction because it would not be in the public interest to permit shareholders to be treated unequally in such a transaction. Murray allowed that he had been quite sanguine about the position and had responded to Nova that we had been saying this all along.

Another day of negotiations was going poorly when the Li team decided that the site of negotiations should switch to Hong Kong. This created a new problem since Yontef did not have his passport with him in Calgary. He reasoned, however, that anyone who could charter a jet from Bermuda to Toronto could also figure out what to do in such circumstances. He got on the phone and corralled a student, who was despatched to take a cab to his house, pick up the passport from his wife, and take a first-class flight out to Calgary to deliver the passport. Yontef had agreed to meet the student in the first-class lounge at the Calgary airport, and as he looked toward the door at the appointed time, in staggered a young man who exuded every evidence of having partaken, to the fullest extent possible in the allotted time, in all the liquid sustenance that first-class flights then offered. Yontef suggested that perhaps he would like to sit down to have a drink and a chat. The student responded, carefully framing each word, that he would take a rain check because he just wanted to get back on the plane. Yontef's parting words were to warn him not to even think about driving home when he got back to Toronto.

The several days in Hong Kong were an eye-opener. The travelling entourage from Calgary made its way through Hong Kong's airport in record time because with Li Ka-shing himself and his people forming the greeting party, only royalty might have had a better welcome. Yontef checked in with the Hong Kong office and had a brief chat with Frank Sixt, the junior of the firm's two representatives there, who asked if he could help on the matter. Any help would have been welcome, and Sixt's was not just any help. That marked the beginning of Sixt's relationship with the Li family and their personal friendship over so many years. Gordon remained back home, refining the Investment Canada strategy. Just as negotiations were getting bogged down in a welter of frustrating minutiae, George Magnus of the Li Group came in to pull Yontef away for an important caucus. As they left the room, Magnus confided that they should leave "those idiots" alone while they went antique hunting. Several weeks later, when the late Andy Sarlos threatened to sabotage the transaction unless more consideration were offered by the Li Group, Li Ka-shing was persuaded to stare Sarlos down, and this bold strategy worked.

Gordon, operating at his best to the almost universal disbelief of observers, got the Investment Canada approval after many middle-of-the-night calls. Bob Blair, the chairman of Nova, spent endless hours off in the corner of the room where negotiations were taking place, working on the press release. It is difficult enough to write a press release even when you know what it is meant to describe. It is all the more difficult, if not impossible, when the deal has not yet been made. Yontef remains convinced, from what he learned through subsequent events, that although they corrected Blair's press release, Blair may never have understood the deal that he made until several years later.

On December 7, 1986, the Li Group and Nova entered into a memorandum of agreement in which it was agreed that the shares of Husky would be reorganized, with the effect that Nova, through a single-purpose holding corporation, would own 43 per cent; Hutchison Whampoa, a Hong Kong public company in which Li Ka-shing held indirectly a major equity interest, would own 43 per cent; Li's son, Victor, would own 9 per cent; and CIBC would own 5 per cent of the Husky shares. To carry out such steps, it would be necessary to purchase the existing shares held by the public in Husky. The purchase structure was carefully worked out to accommodate corporate, tax, and foreign investment considerations. The arrangements among the parties included a detailed Husky shareholders agreement containing a carefully structured Husky board, the latter provisions including the ability of Li Ka-shing to become a Husky director if in his judgment the ownership arrangements of Husky were no longer satisfactory – the so-called golden vote.

Compliance with Investment Canada regulations was a key factor in the proposed transaction, and Gordon obtained an opinion from Investment Canada confirming that on the completion of the Husky reorganization, Husky would not be foreign controlled and would remain Canadian within the meaning of the act. The public meeting of Husky shareholders to approve the reorganization was held on March 24, 1987 in Calgary. The proposed reorganization was approved, and the purchase and related transactions closed on April 30, 1987. The Li Group team included Li Ka-shing, George Magnus, Victor Li, Canning Fok, and John E. Burns. The firm's team included Gordon, Shaw, Yontef, Durand, Sixt, Braithwaite, David Weekes,[30] and Alison Youngman.[31] On completion of the original acquisition, Yontef and Shaw joined the Husky board as Hutchison Whampoa nominees. Yontef later stepped down because the position might have jeopardized relations with clients such as Texaco, but Shaw has been on that board ever since.

The parties carried on with their Husky investment over the next few years, with the firm advising on the usual operational and shareholder issues. In 1991, Nova commenced a major corporate reorganization that essentially divided its business into a pipeline company (Nova) and a chemical company (Novacor Chemicals). Nova's Husky investment stayed with Nova, but as it was not a pipeline asset, Nova announced that efforts were under way to sell its interest in the company. This, of course, brought into play the terms and conditions of the Husky shareholders agreement. That agreement contained specific buy-sell provisions that allowed certain of the non-Nova parties the opportunity to purchase Nova's shares in Husky on a proposed sale by Nova or if Nova's entity holding the Husky shares ceased to be a Nova affiliate. The firm assisted Hutchison Whampoa in a full analysis of the terms of the Husky shareholders agreement in light of Nova's proposed actions, and Kathryn Chalmers was added to the team to advise on those issues.

One key element of the purchase was that they needed Investment Canada's approval. With Husky in financial difficulty (in part due to the collapse of key commodity prices, particularly natural gas and heavy crude oil) and the Li family's commitment to seeing Husky through, Investment Canada found that this acquisition would meet the statutory test of constituting a net benefit to Canada. After several months of negotiations, Hutchison Whampoa, the Li family and CIBC, and Nova agreed on purchase and sale terms for Nova's 43 per cent interest in Husky. The transaction closed December 31, 1991. Not only did Hutchison Whampoa and the Li family, with the co-operation of the CIBC, purchase Nova's interest, they also provided much-needed financing to Husky. The post-acquisition structure saw Hutchison Whampoa increase its holdings in Husky from 43 to 49 per cent and the Li family increase its holdings in Husky from 9 to 46 per cent. The CIBC continued its Husky interest at 5 per cent. At the same time, the continuing shareholders rearranged their ownership structure in Husky. The 1991 Husky transaction was particularly intense, including the initial litigation review of the Husky shareholders agreement, advising as to documentation of purchase and sale terms on the related financing as to regulatory approvals, and shareholder restructuring and assisting with closing and post-closing matters. By this time, the Li family had a new but familiar face at the table in the person of Frank Sixt.

During this period, the firm established cutting-edge techniques that became the norm for a number of years to come. Specifically, in the mid-1980s, after the adoption of the *Investment Canada Act,* a number of structures were developed that permitted foreign controlled companies to acquire Canadian book publishing companies notwithstanding a policy prohibition that existed at the time. These enabled non-Canadians to acquire equity and factual control of Canadian companies while keeping the majority of voting interests in the hands of Canadians. The firm, headed by John Leopold in the Montreal office, a rapidly emerging leader in the M&A field, was the first to develop these structures in the Bertlesmann acquisition of Doubleday Canada and the acquisition by Harcourt Brace Jovanovich of the CBS book publishing operations, which consisted of Holt Rinehart and WB Saunders. In almost all subsequent transactions involving a Canadian book publishing company, the structure that the firm had developed became the norm. The firm also acted for Pearson PLC when it acquired the educational book publishing operations of Simon and Schuster, which included Prentice Hall Canada. This was a transaction that had a very high profile in the press. Most notable from a Canadian perspective were the regulatory implications of this transaction and more specifically, the required approval under the *Investment Canada Act*. After negotiating for almost a year with Investment Canada, the jurisdiction for cultural matters, which included books, was shifted from Industry Canada to Canadian Heritage, resulting in having to start the process essentially all over again with a new governmental agency. This was the first cultural case that fell within the purview of Canadian Heritage after this decision had been made, and the approval was eventually obtained. The whole process took more than a year and established a very important precedent for Canadian cultural foreign investment cases.

In 1983, the Montreal office handled the IPO for Guardian Trust Company, then run by Howard Kelly and Edward Cleather, in which André Roy was involved. The following year, Roy began a long association with Radiomutuel Inc., which commenced with a management buyout and IPO and led a fifteen-year period of acquisitions of radio stations and in December 1992, his most difficult mandate – the acquisition of certain billboard assets of Gallop & Gallop. A scheduled meeting to conclude the transaction was postponed from a Friday due to a major snowstorm that affected Montreal and Toronto. He and the client left for a one-day meeting in Toronto on Sunday morning, both fully expecting to return the same day, neither with a change of clothing. They finally signed the purchase agreement the following Friday, having thought each day that they would be going home. Radiomutuel was acquired by Astral in 1999.

The Montreal office, acting for the underwriters, handled the public issues of the CMP Funds, which involved in excess of twenty offerings of mining and oil and gas flow-through shares for proceeds in excess of a billion dollars. It was also involved in the privatization of SOQUEM, a mining company set up by the Quebec government. When the Quebec Liberals came back to power in 1985 under the reinvented Robert Bourassa, they followed the fashionable trend of privatizing Crown corporations. The transaction, which occurred in mid-1986, would not by today's standards be particularly exciting at $150 million, but it was nevertheless a very big deal at the time and was highly political. The technique adopted was to create Cambior, for which the firm acted, which bought the assets from SOQUEM and then proceeded with an IPO. The political aspect of it was that many people in the company did not like the idea of privatization, and it was like pulling teeth to get everything done in good order. Considerable business was later directed to the firm from the new board, the chairman of which was Gilles Mercure, former chief executive officer of the National Bank, who knew Jean-Pierre Ouellet from work in the political campaigns. He had directed the initial work to the firm, and the firm became co-counsel with Lafleur Brown; its point man on the deal was John Claxton, a very able lawyer and father of current partner Ted Claxton.[32] There was naturally a fair amount of friction as the new boys elbowed their way to the table.

Grant was involved in a Western transaction – a purchase of an Alberta company, Kerr Construction, owned by Dave Keen, a former bulldozer operator who wore cowboy boots, jeans, a pearl-button shirt, and a Stetson at all times. The purchaser was NSU, a Dutch tugboat company servicing North Sea offshore rigs, and Keen Construction had barges on the MacKenzie River servicing Prudhoe Bay. The negotiations were protracted but finally finished late in the day in Edmonton after the banks had closed. NSU delivered a $28-million cheque to Keen, who put it in his shirt pocket and snapped the pearl button shut. Everyone then trooped over to the Hotel Macdonald for the night, where the clerk asked Keen for his credit card. He did not have one, so he reached into his pocket, pulled out the $28-million cheque, handed it to the clerk, and said, "Just take it out of this." The clerk fainted dead away.

In the fall of 1987, the Government of British Columbia, through British Columbia Enterprise Corporation (BCEC), a provincial Crown corporation, called for expressions of interest from parties interested in developing the former Expo 86 site in Vancouver. This major waterfront property, some 200 acres on the north shore of False Creek adjacent to downtown Vancouver, would be a long-term multi-billion-dollar project, which would be a major focus of commercial and residential activity in Vancouver for the next decade. With its impeccable real estate development reputation in Hong Kong, the Li Group had the experience, capability, and financial resources to carry out such a development. This was a natural for them.

Formal expressions of interest had to be submitted by October 15, 1987. The Li Group (through the newly created Concord Pacific Developments Ltd.) was included in the short list of developers who were asked to submit detailed purchase and development proposals by February 15, 1988. Prior to the submission of the proposal in February 1988, the Li Group added the CIBC and two major Hong Kong developers, Cheng Yu Tung and Lee Shou Kee, as minority shareholders in Concord Pacific. The Li Group asked the firm to assist in the project. It was a very successful and exciting mandate. Starting in November 1987, Hess and Shaw spent considerable time in Vancouver, ably assisted by John Dow and others in Toronto, as well as David Dalik and a team from Russell & DuMoulin, the local Vancouver agents. The Li group team consisted of George Magnus and Victor Li, the primary contacts from Hong Kong, with Li Ka-shing staying closely involved. In Vancouver, the Concord Pacific team included Stanley Kwok and Jon Markolis. Of note, the BCEC team included lawyers Nicholas Paczkowski and Bruce Woolley, both of whom, after the Expo Lands transaction was completed, joined the firm's Vancouver office.

The Concord Pacific proposal for the Expo lands contemplated a coordinated and imaginative development of commercial, residential, and office space (15 million square feet), framed by more than forty acres of parks, pedestrian paths, and open space, including more than three miles of waterfront, walkways, and three major park areas. The proposal provided for upwards of $12 billion in capital investment and was projected to generate $6 billion in spinoff spending and up to 28,000 person-years of employment over the development period. The whole development was to be phased in over fifteen to twenty years. The proposal was exciting, first-class, and in the end, successful. Once Concord Pacific had been chosen as the successful developer, the various transaction documentation had to be negotiated and finalized. The transaction was controversial and very high profile in Vancouver, and some of the issues included whether the BC government should be selling the Expo Lands at all, at what price, and whether the lands should be sold to a non-resident group. While the province, through BCEC, was the vendor, the City of Vancouver was responsible for and controlled all development approvals. Since the land bordered False Creek, various Canadian government approvals were required through the federal Ministry of Fisheries. Apart from needing to deal with and satisfy various levels of government, the transaction had numerous other problems and challenges: did Aboriginal claims extend to the lands; had all littoral rights (i.e., a right of unimpeded access to and from every point along the foreshore adjacent to a waterfront) been extinguished; would certain legislative amendments be needed to ensure that title to the lands passed as all parties expected; how were those portions of the site that contained contaminated soil to be dealt with; and countless others. In addition, various civic projects and amenities had to be accommodated, and numerous related and support agreements had to be negotiated.

On April 25, 1988, after lengthy negotiations and with the specific approval of the British Columbia cabinet, a purchase agreement was signed between BCEC and Concord Pacific, which set a closing date of May 11, 1988. But even with an all-out effort by all parties (including various members of the firm), it was clear that by that date, several key matters requiring final agreement would remain open. However, a trust and respect had developed between the parties, and it was determined to close the transaction on May

11, 1988 and to have the remaining open issues resolved on a best-efforts basis after closing. With the purchase transaction substantially complete, the Concord Pacific Place (the project name) development began.

Nearing the end of the Expo Lands purchase transaction, George Magnus and Victor Li met with Stikeman and Shaw to ask that the firm consider opening a Vancouver office to service the ongoing Expo Lands development. It was clear from these discussions that they did not want just a representative office but a full working office to service all their needs. Their request was both a compliment to the firm and a testimony to the close relationship we had with the Li Group. It was, of course, also an excellent opportunity and one that other firms would die for. With no hesitation, they assured them that a full working office would be opening soon. This undertaking was made formal by direct confirmation, made personally by Stikeman to Li Ka-shing. The ties with the Li Group, which had been strong before, became even stronger with the firm's performance in the Expo Lands purchase transaction. Also, a solid base had been established and was available for the new Vancouver office to grow and flourish.

Another busy year was 1987. The firm in Montreal acted for BioChem Pharma on its IPO. That small enterprise would grow spectacularly and become a landmark Canadian biotechnology company, eventually to be sold in 2001 for $6 billion to Shire Pharmaceuticals Group Inc. Rovinescu and Guy Masson worked on the IPO, which was relatively small, amounting to some $12 million. The principal shareholder of the company was the Institut Armand Frappier, and the shareholders thought it would be helpful to have some English-speaking directors. Rovinescu and Masson suggested Jim Grant for the purpose, which was acceptable to the shareholders, and they tracked him down during a cycling holiday in France. Clearly annoyed to have been disturbed, Grant asked in response to the request whether this would be good for the firm. They assured him it would. "Put my name in," he said and hung up the phone, not realizing at the time what a fortunate decision that would prove to be.

The firm also represented BCE Inc. in its public acquisition of Montreal Trust Company, once the flagship trust company associated with the Royal Bank of Canada, comparable to the Bank of Montreal's former relationship with The Royal Trust Company. The Westburne International acquisition in early 1987 by Dumez SA, one of Maurice Riel's French clients, was a huge transaction for Dumez. The company was listed on the Toronto Stock Exchange as well as the American Stock Exchange, which naturally led to the extensive involvement of Ed Waitzer. It was a cross-border acquisition that had many FIRA as well as securities law issues. The takeover had started out as friendly, but it eventually became competitive when the sellers tried to get other bidders and then to get out of the arrangement, which finally led to an increase in the offer. The ongoing work for Westbourne became significant enough that Michel Vennat from the Montreal office was eventually lured away and remained with the company until it was later acquired by another, at which time he returned to the firm for a few years before returning to quasi-public service as president of the Industrial Development Bank.

In June 1987, Simon Romano represented Pegasus Gold, which was considering a $60-million cross-border offering. It was a well-established US company, which wanted to raise funds in Canada. Where new mining companies were involved in public issues, there were escrow requirements applicable to the selling shareholders, which lasted for three years. US-based companies were, however, treated as new public companies, and the Ontario Securities Commission refused to exercise its discretion to regard Pegasus Gold as anything other than a new mining company. The result was that the financing did not happen in Canada. The rules have since been changed.

In the latter part of the 1980s, a group was put together to buy the venerable Ritz Carlton Hotel, a Montreal landmark. The real owners were the heirs of a Paris hotelier by the name of Dupré, who bought the hotel in the late 1940s. He had owned two hotels in Paris (one of which was La Tremouille) and had apparently collaborated with the Nazis, became a bit panicky about the possible fallout, and came to Montreal to buy the Ritz Carlton. He took the company public in order to get money, well before the 1955 *Securities Act* was enacted, and the controlling interest, some 62 per cent, was held by seven Panamanian companies. This was to get around the requirement making it necessary to disclose the identity of all shareholders having an interest of more than 10 per cent. The seven Panamanian companies each held about 9 per cent and so were able to avoid any such disclosure. The shares of the Panamanian companies were owned by Liechtenstein trusts following the death of Dupré. The half-sister of his widow contested her will and claimed that she was the sole heir. The significance of this in the context of any purchase of the Ritz Carlton was to be sure that if one got the shares of the Panamanian companies, one was getting full title to the hotel. This led to all sorts of arrangements with the trustees and the lawyers of the Dupré family, all of whom had inflated views of the value of the property.

The negotiations were a nightmare. One day in the office, Jim Grant announced to Ouellet, who was acting in the negotiations, that Ouellet had just joined a long list of lawyers (including Stikeman on more than one occasion) acting on behalf of clients who had tried to buy the Ritz. The group for which Ouellet was acting included Dan Fournier, the McConnell interests, Galen Weston, and Les Coopérants, which later went bankrupt. There had been a plan to add two or three floors on the top and build deluxe apartments for sale as condominiums, together with a fifteen-storey office complex at the west end of the property, which was to become the headquarters of BCE and Bombardier. The real estate market suffered a severe decline, and the project failed. The consortium fell apart. The owners later found a Saudi prince willing to buy the property, and the Ritz later became part of the Kempinski chain of hotels.

In 1988, the firm was engaged by Air Canada in connection with the first stage of a privatization of the company, then wholly owned by the federal government. The firm had done some corporate and financing work for Air Canada, including its arrangements for the lease of several of its fleet of aircraft, but this was the first high-profile mandate, and it led to much more ongoing work after the government sold approximately 45 per cent of its Air Canada holdings for $246 million. The firm also acted in 1999 when the government sold the rest of its interest in the airline. This transaction provided the firm with additional expertise in privatization matters and was particularly helpful in generating similar mandates, both in Canada and the foreign offices.

In the spring of 1998, Ticketmaster was looking to change its counsel in Canada. The company interviewed several firms in Toronto, and with the help of the marketing group, the firm put together a brochure of its capabilities and personnel directed specifically at the Ticketmaster business. The firm was added to Ticketmaster's list of potential firms because it had assisted one of the first automated ticketing groups in Canada (BASS – Bay Area Seat Services) with their start-up operations in the late 1970s and early 1980s. One of the principals of BASS, Ronald D. Bavré, is now an executive with Ticketmaster Canada, and he remembered the firm's involvement with BASS. After the interviews, the firm was selected. Since starting to represent Ticketmaster in June 1998, the firm has assisted it with various ticketing agreements, including with Maple Leaf Sports and Entertainment Limited/ Air Canada Centre, SkyDome, Corel Centre, as well as with the acquisition of Admission Tickets in Montreal, including required regulatory approvals by Lawson Hunter and Jason Gudofsky, and with all corporate acquisition matters by Shaw, France-Margaret Belanger, and Adam Atlas.

In 1989, Stone Corporation began a string of acquisitions in the pulp and paper industry with its takeover of Consolidated Bathurst. This was a mandate obtained by the persistent work of Sonny Gordon and the relationship he established with Roger Stone. The first connection had been through Maurice Sauvé, for whom Gordon had worked in Ottawa, in which Gordon was the middleman between the Desmarais interests, represented by Yves Pratte, and Roger Stone, then represented by Davies Ward & Beck in Toronto. Gordon was asked for ideas to persuade Paul Desmarais to sell and undertook to have some by the following week. After lunch, he told Robert Hogan, a junior tax lawyer who had joined the firm in 1985, that he needed a memorandum with ideas right away. Stone was impressed by Gordon's enthusiasm. The second time around, Stone asked Gordon to represent him. Roger Stone told his legal representative, Gar Emerson of Davies Ward, in a most direct way, "I want you to meet my new lawyer, Sonny Gordon."

If you gave Gordon even a crack, says Hogan, he would burst through the line. The file was going very well. Elinore Richardson was in charge of the bank financing, which was in the order of $1.2 billion, but she had missed many of the preparatory meetings. The night before the documents were to be signed, Gordon said to Hogan, "You go in there and control her," an impossible brief for a partner let alone a junior lawyer. A conference call began at 9:30 on a Sunday evening. Richardson was on page one of the lengthy document, and she said they would have to redraft all of page one. And so it went, page by page. Gordon came in somewhat later, found that she was not in her office on the call, and asked Hogan what was going on. "Dougie (her son) is in the next room, and she keeps putting them on hold while she goes to work on his science project." To keep her on the call, Hogan had to take over the supervision of Dougie's school project.

Two of the major reorganizations for which the firm was retained through the latter part of the 1980s involved the LaFarge reorganization, which reversed the existing Canada-US structure and turned the former company (of which Elliott was a director) inside out over a three-year process. The complex tax issues were dealt with by Tamaki and Finkelstein, an enormous responsibility since the reorganization proceeded without the comfort of advance income tax rulings, while the corporate and securities aspects were handled by Davis and Waitzer in Toronto and Rovinescu in Montreal. A similar transaction that flipped the organizational structure and operating arms of Alcan required detailed tax rulings obtained by Tamaki and Finkelstein.

The 1990s were times of harvesting. When a strategic interest in Four Seasons Hotels was put up for sale (before the Law Society rules had changed), Yontef in Toronto was working with an Asian group that was bidding for the stake while Gordon in Montreal was acting for the competing Saudi Arabian prince. Gordon's prince came in and was successful. Counsel for Four Seasons Hotels said to him, "Is there anybody you folks don't act for?" It seemed that every major file presented the firm with multiple opportunities. Jim Riley took on and did a wonderful job acting for Citibank in the Olympia & York insolvency and restructuring. This meant turning down the steering committee for the Canadian bank position, a number of potential buyers, and other possible clients. John Stransman was working on a major mandate with lenders and investment bankers for MacMillan Bloedel, while at the same time, Yontef was working with another group unwinding several of MacMillan Bloedel's joint ventures. When the possibility of the Weyerhaueser transaction came up, Yontef received a call from a partner at Skadden Arps. He said that there had been a heated argument taking place in New York that morning because the chief financial officer of MacMillan Bloedel was pressing to hire someone named John Stransman, while the Skadden partner said that Yontef was the only man for the job. The discussion progressed, he was told, for quite a while before those sitting at the table realized that Stransman and Yontef were from the same firm.

Silcorp, like Asamera, had a special place in the hearts of the Toronto office. Silcorp had come to Ed Waitzer to help the company through its restructuring, and for several years, this became a prime example of how to restructure a company so that it could return to prosperity. When Silcorp was just hitting its stride, a Quebec convenience store company, Alimentation Couche-Tard, which wanted to buy Silcorp, launched a hostile takeover bid. When Yontef was introduced as a speaker at a mergers and acquisitions conference, the program's chairman began by saying it was sad that Silcorp was such a small company because its defence should be "must" reading for people studying mergers and acquisitions at law and business schools. Although Silcorp was very happy with Rob Nicholls[33] for its regular work, its chairman asked if Yontef would get involved to help in dealing with its board. As the matter progressed, they sparred with Couche-Tard for weeks over a confidentiality agreement and whether the company would permit them into the data room made available to potential bidders. During that time, Silcorp made an acquisition of rival Beckers, completing a transaction it had been working on over the course of several months. While the bid was outstanding, this fact served to accelerate what needed to be done with Silcorp's US operations, and these were sold. Also during the period that the bid was outstanding, Silcorp organized a recapitalization, which provided that part of the US sale proceeds, and additional credit lines would be used to make a self-tender by way of Dutch auction for some of its stock. This followed an auction of the whole company, which did not yield a successful result and a counter-offer to Couche-Tard, which rejected it out of hand. All of these activities led to dramatic rises in Silcorp's stock price, so much so that the rarest occurrence in hostile takeovers happened – Couche-Tard abandoned its bid. Two years later, obviously chastened, Couche-Tard returned. Offering more than double where it had been with its first folly and after extensive private negotiations to substantiate the best price, Silcorp was taken over by Couche-Tard.

In Montreal in 1990, the firm acted for Schneider SA in its public acquisition of Federal Pioneer Limited. That client had been brought in by Jacques Courtois, who had left his former firm, Courtois Clarkson (now McCarthy Tétrault), to join us in March 1982. The following year, Alcatel Cable SA acquired the cable division of Noranda in a private transaction, on which the Montreal office acted for Alcatel. In 1992, Stone Corporation, for whom the firm now acted, spun off all its newsprint assets into Stone Consolidated and organized an IPO of Stone-Consolidated in 1993. This was the first of, and the blueprint for, a number of spinoffs in the pulp and paper business. Stone-Consolidated later acquired Rainy River in 1996 and merged with Abitibi Price in May 1997 to create the largest newsprint producer in the world.

In 1992, Westcoast Energy made a bid for Union Gas. Rob Nicholls and Simon Romano were acting for Westcoast, the bid of which was to be financed in part by bank loans. The company felt it might be beyond its banking experience and went to Riley, who was too busy to take on the matter. He told Westcoast to go ahead on its own and merely ask him if there were any questions. On the other side of the transaction was Blake Cassels, which was working off a standard form. Romano remembers asking a series of innocent questions, which led to the deletion of a great deal of boilerplate. In the result, an eighty-page, unintelligible agreement was reduced to a simple twenty-two-page document. It was the largest bank loan in Canada that year.

Michel Vennat's involvement with the Toronto airport matter between 1995 and 1997 was extremely important in resolving a major legal and political crisis. In the final days of the Mulroney government, in fact after the issuance of the electoral writ, the government had granted a licence to a group to build and operate the Toronto airport. The Liberals vowed to cancel this deal if they won, which they did, and they introduced a bill to remove any right to sue for damages on the ground that the arrangement to grant a licence after the issuance of the electoral writ had been unconstitutional or at the very least, contrary to a general custom. Legal proceedings by the group involving the Greater Toronto Airport Authority (GTAA) had already commenced in the Ontario courts. Vennat was retained by the operators, led by the Claridge group, to find a commercial solution. GTAA was also the owner of Terminal 3. The solution, instead of suing the government, was to conclude that it was in the best interest of the group to buy Terminal 3 and to operate the whole thing as an integrated unit. There would be savings and operational efficiency involved. Vennat got a settlement on this basis with the Department of Transport and the Department of Justice, and after a year and a half of negotiations, it appeared that everyone came out as winner. The players involved included Claridge, the Bitove interests, Donald Matthews (a Toronto entrepreneur), and Brackwell (a construction firm). The GTAA renegotiated its lease with the Department of Transport and bought Terminal 3. The sole tenant in the terminal at the time was Canadian Airlines International Limited, which was later acquired by Air Canada, so the combination of the two operations was a good outcome.

November 1995 marked the extraordinarily successful privatization of Canadian National in a transaction that produced in excess of $2 billion for the federal government and gave tangible recognition in the international marketplace that Paul Tellier and Michael Sabia had changed the Canadian railway industry beyond anything that could possibly have been imagined ten years earlier. CN had for years been hamstrung by political considerations, unprofitable routes from which it was not permitted to withdraw, and an impossible administrative overburden. Although the two executives had no railway experience and were regarded with the usual business contempt within the private sector reserved for former public servants, they set about making the company lean, responsive to customers, and profitable, the latter a concept almost unknown to CN since its formation in 1919. They wanted to get the company into the position of being able to stand on its own and to be ready some day to become private and to command the respect that similar railways in the United States had among the investing community. This was a task that seemed Herculean at the outset, but they persisted, and the prospect of becoming private began to obtain some degree of resonance both within and outside government.

The final push toward privatization occurred in 1994, and the firm, primarily though Lawson Hunter and Ouellet, became involved from the outset. CN had begun discussions in the latter part of 1993 with Canadian Pacific to consider the possibility of merging their Eastern businesses. There was enormous overcapacity in the market, and both railways were losing money. CN first consulted Hunter, whom Tellier had known from their respective days in Ottawa, in order to obtain some competition expertise and to steer any successful arrangement through the Competition Bureau since any successful merger would, in effect, have created a monopoly east of Winnipeg. As matters progressed, they needed some mergers and acquisitions expertise, which led to Ouellet's involvement. The talks failed over the value of the assets during the summer of 1994 when it appeared that the two railways could not agree on anything. That fall, Canadian Pacific made the mistake of putting forward an unsolicited offer to the government for CN's Eastern assets at a ridiculously low price. In addition to the assets that were the object of the proposed acquisition, Canadian Pacific also wanted the CN tax losses. This drove CN into high gear to get something done. The board of directors was convened and authorized management to seek approval to privatize CN in late 1994. Not many people thought that this would be possible, but in February 1995, the minister of Finance approved the idea. His officials told the company that it might be in the next federal budget.

Ouellet got the privatization mandate because Tellier and Sabia had been satisfied with his earlier services during the negotiation phase with Canadian Pacific. There was resistance in Ottawa to the appointment of the firm; the politicians wanted to give the work to friends in Toronto at Fraser & Beatty, who later ended up acting for the underwriters. The underwriters wanted Ogilvy Renault, but former Prime Minister Brian Mulroney was there, and there was well-publicized bad blood between him and the Liberal government. Marc Lalonde was very helpful in calming the waters. Over the course of the summer and fall of 1995, the ambitious public offering was put together, and the closing occurred in late November. The saga is well described in the book entitled, *The Pig that Flew*.[34]

Prior to October 1992, ConAgra, Inc.'s Canadian operations had been handled by one of the other major Bay Street firms in Toronto. ConAgra, headquartered in Omaha, Nebraska, is one of the world's largest diversified food companies. A conflict arose with its existing Canadian law firm, and ConAgra looked around for other counsel. Working closely with ConAgra's US external counsel, McGrath, North, Mullin & Kratz, the firm has provided a variety of legal services for ConAgra over the past ten years, including several major acquisitions. In 1995, ConAgra purchased Canada Malting Co. Ltd. from John Labatt Limited, the Molson Companies, and the public. This acquisition was part of ConAgra's commitment to build and expand its global malt business, Canada Malting being one of the world's largest producers of malted barley used by brewers, distillers, and food manufacturers. It also assisted with various Canadian aspects of ConAgra's formation of a worldwide malt joint venture with Tiger Oats Limited, of South Africa, including Canadian regulatory approvals and Canadian financing. The various joint venture agreements were signed, and the transaction closed on May 23, 1996.

In May 1992, Maple Leaf Mills Inc. was incorporated with the shares owned equally between ConAgra Limited and Maple Leaf Foods Inc. The latter contributed its flour and bakery mix facilities to Maple Leaf Mills, and ConAgra's US milling operations in Buffalo, New York were contributed to a similar fifty-fifty US joint venture company, ConAgra/Maple Leaf Milling Inc. In November 1995, Maple Leaf Mills, supported by its two shareholders – Maple Leaf Foods and ConAgra Limited – agreed to sell the Maple Leaf Mills business and assets to agrifood giant Archer Daniels Midland Company. One of the key conditions of the sale was obtaining all required regulatory approvals. MLM and ADM were the two largest wheat flour millers in Canada. The Competition Bureau had previously undertaken an extensive review of the Canadian flour milling industry in 1990–91 and had rejected certain transactions, which meant that the current situation was also likely to be disapproved unless it could be distinguished from the earlier ones. On February 28, 1997, after lengthy negotiations, a definitive asset purchase was signed by the parties. On the same day, the parties closed the transaction even though regulatory approval had not been obtained. However, they did so only after ADM had agreed to dispose of the MLM Oak Street Mill.

In the spring of 2000, the firm assisted ConAgra in its $2.9-billion acquisition of International Home Foods (IHF), the makers of Chef Boyardee pasta products, PAM cooking spray, and Golden's Mustard. The Canadian portion of this acquisition was relatively small. We assisted with the due diligence and secured all necessary Canadian regulatory approvals. Paul Collins and Sandra Walker assisted ConAgra with those. After the acquisition, the firm assisted ConAgra in reorganizing the IHF Canada structure, including the transfer of the various ConAgra Grocery Products divisions of ConAgra Limited to ConAgra Grocery Products Limited, and advising on various employee matters (Bruce Pollock). On October 8, 2000, ConAgra entered into a letter of intent with the shareholder of Artel Inc. of Montreal to purchase all the shares of that company and its various subsidiaries. Again, it was necessary to obtain regulatory approvals, and once more, Paul Collins (assisted by Eric Dufour) secured such approvals. The firm assisted in the drafting and negotiation (with McGrath, North) of the Artel share purchase agreement. The latter document was signed January 26, 2001, with the transaction closing on the same day. Artel became part of the ConAgra Frozen Prepared Foods Group. Artel and one of its subsidiaries amalgamated post-closing and changed its name to ConAgra Frozen Foods Inc.

ConAgra has been a valuable client over the past ten years. The firm has assisted it, in most cases in conjunction with McGarth, North, with not only those matters noted above but numerous other mandates. ConAgra is a particularly valuable client for the firm as so many of the offices are involved with providing service: Montreal advising on the Artel acquisition and ongoing post-acquisition matters (Peter O'Brien and Arden Furlotte), Ottawa advising on intellectual property and trademark matters (Stuart McCormack and Mirko Bibic), and Calgary advising the Lamb Weston division in Alberta (Barry Emes and Duane Gillis). Also, Brian Hansen has advised ConAgra and Donald da Parma (one of the McGrath, North attorneys) on potential investments in China and Australia.

In the fall of 1998, the Montreal office handled the private acquisition of Stella Foods by the Saputo Group, which tripled the latter in size with this landmark acquisition in the United States. During the same period, it acted for Quebecor in its public acquisition of Sun Media.

Without doubt, the most significant deal of Rovinescu's career with the firm and one of the major exercises for it as a whole was the hostile takeover bid of Air Canada, commenced by Onex Corporation in August 1999. It was also the first in a series of fascinating steps that ultimately led to

Rovinescu's leaving to join Air Canada. Robert Milton had been appointed CEO of Air Canada just eighteen days before Onex launched its raid. He was thirty-nine years old and by all accounts, a brilliant chief operating officer, seen as the mastermind behind Air Canada winning out in the transborder open skies battle, revamping schedules, innovating marketing, and driving performance from maintenance to airports. Onex Corporation and Gerry Schwartz are generally seen as the most successful LBO (leveraged buyout) firm in Canada, with some $14 billion in annual revenues. Onex had lined up some big guns to force Air Canada into submission – AMR, the parent of American Airlines, Canadian Airlines International, and, some would say, the Government of Canada itself, which had suspended Canada's competition laws to permit Onex to kick off the initiative. Onex thought that it had done such a good job of locking Air Canada into the box that they code named their takeover plan "Peacock."

When the bid was launched on August 24, 1999, Robert Milton, some key executives, and several advisors including Rovinescu sat around the board-room table listening to the live feed from CBC Newsworld that this takeover bid was being made despite the ownership restrictions and at least in part, as a result of the Government of Canada's suspension of competition laws the previous August 13. On that date, the federal government agreed to take the extraordinary step of suspending competition rules under never-before-used section 47 of the *Canada Transportation Act*. The Onex bid had the effect of shutting off any possible auction or competing deal since as part of their agreements with Onex, American Airlines and Canadian had irrevocably agreed to lock up their support. Onex was convinced that Air Canada would have no option but to negotiate. Instead, Air Canada was quietly preparing for war. Instead of accepting the offer, which had been made at a 30 per cent premium over the market value of the shares, Air Canada wanted to use it to gain other advantages, including a $500-million payment from United Airlines for the code-share agreement between Air Canada and UAL. Milton assembled a team of takeover strategists, including Stikeman Elliott, and a comprehensive plan was cobbled together to win the legal, public affairs, and ultimately, shareholder value fights. It was the most hostile and most public of bids in Canadian history and had the added dramatic sideline of involving organized labour (CAW had Buzz Hargrove embracing the Schwartz bid, to the chagrin of Air Canada employees), pitting airline titans American Airlines and United Airlines against each other (which managed to assist in keeping Air Canada within the Star Alliance), and bringing to the surface fundamental conflicts between government policies on the competitive airline industry, guaranteed employment, and airline stability.

The file was quarterbacked by Rovinescu in Montreal but involved several lawyers from the other offices, including Lawson Hunter from Ottawa to deal with the competition issues, Simon Romano in Toronto for the securities side, and Sean Dunphy from Toronto also to handle the litigation aspects. It was politically charged and became a media event, with almost daily front-page coverage. There was litigation on three fronts: negotiations with, and advocacy before, the competition authorities and

securities regulators; generation of some of the most creative legal documents ever seen in Canadian takeover bid struggles; and an unparalleled
level of commitment among the lawyers involved.

The objective was to throw as many roadblocks in the way of the takeover
bid as possible. The strategy sessions went on for four months and often
involved discussions with Rovinescu at 2:00 in the morning. Three separate
suits were launched (Ontario, the Federal Court of Canada, and Quebec),
and it required success in only one of them to thwart the offer. In the end,
it was the Quebec action, handled by Louis P. Bélanger and Marc-André
Coulombe, described in chapter 10, that put the final nail in the Onex coffin.
Sean Dunphy was responsible for the Ontario portion of the attacks on the
offer through the courts, but with the Quebec victory, it was not necessary
to push the actions to a conclusion.

In addition, it was the precursor to the troubled times Air Canada would
face through a difficult integration process with Canadian Airlines and the
horrific events of September 11, 2001 and their aftermath. By the fall of 1999,
Air Canada also finally cleared the confusing situation with its acquisition of
Canadian Airlines Corporation, an adventure that also involved most of the
principal areas of the firm, not the least of which was Lawson Hunter's competition group. The transaction was handled by Sean Dunphy, operating out of the
Calgary office, who stickhandled the complicated acquisition in bankruptcy
protection under the *Companies and Creditors Arrangement Act* (CCAA).

In 2000, the firm handled the demutualization and IPO of Industrielle
Alliance Compagnie d'Assurance sur la Vie on behalf of the underwriters
and the sale of Ernst & Young's consulting business in Canada to Cap
Gemini. The firm acted for Best Buy in connection with its acquisition of
Future Shop, a transaction completed in November 2001 for a purchase
price of $580 million. Best Buy Co., Inc. is the largest US retailer of technol-
ogy and entertainment products, and Future Shop is the largest Canadian
retailer of consumer electronics. This was a significant transaction with a
high profile in the press, much of the attention of which centred around the
regulatory process, particularly in relation to the *Competition Act,* where
the Competition Bureau had decided to review the proposed transaction even
though Best Buy did not have any existing Canadian operations. This was a
precedent-setting case from a regulatory perspective based on the somewhat
extraterritorial position taken by the bureau.

Wolseley PLC acquired from Rexel Canada Inc. its plumbing, HVAC, and
industrial products distribution operations for an aggregate cash purchase
price of $550 million. Rexel Canada Inc. (formerly Westburne Inc.) is a
subsidiary of Rexel SA, the world's largest distributor of electrical products
and supplies. The target employed approximately 3,000 employees in 300
sales outlets. Wolseley is the world leader in the distribution of plumbing
material, with a strong presence in the United States through its subsidiary
Ferguson Enterprises. The transaction closed in July 2001 after an agreement was signed in May of that year.

The firm acted for BAE Systems PLC in connection with the sale of its
controlling interest in BAE Systems Canada Inc. to Oncap LP, a $400-million

investment partnership established in December 1999 by Onex Corporation and several of Canada's largest pension funds and financial institutions. BAE Systems Canada Inc. was a publicly listed company and formerly operated under the name of Canadian Marconi. The total value of the transaction was approximately $594 million. The transaction was completed in 2001 by way of a statutory plan of arrangement.

The firm brought the first oppression action under the recently revised *Ontario Business Corporations Act*. Waitzer, with the help of Stransman and Howard, both as regulator and offended investor, had been pursuing Bruce McLaughlin, the real estate entrepreneur behind Mascan Corporation, which had developed much of Mississauga. Over time, he had assumed responsibility for representing most of the minority shareholders, including the Thomson family holding company, Standard Life Assurance, John Templeton, and Doan Development Corporation. The efforts had come to little avail other than to generate a good deal of publicity until they were able to find a "smoking gun" in the form of a series of transactions entered into by McLaughlin by which he had effectively misappropriated corporate assets for his own purposes. The evidence was sufficiently compelling to enable them to obtain interlocutory relief, replacing McLaughlin and the entire board of directors, appointing a receiver, and forbidding McLaughlin from entering into any transactions with the company. The assets were ultimately sold, and the minority shareholders realized a significant gain. The oppression action directed against McLaughlin personally continues to this day, and a trial is expected within the next year or so, some twenty years after the matter began.

One of the largest and most complicated transactions on which the Toronto office ever acted as lead counsel was the $10-billion acquisition by British American Tobacco PLC (BAT) of Imasco Limited. While the Imasco board was a reluctant seller, in the end, BAT was able to smoke out Imasco, or at least that is how some saw it. Imasco was Canada's largest conglomerate, owning Imperial Tobacco, Canada Trust, Shoppers Drug Mart, and Genstar Developments. BAT owned 40 per cent of Imasco and was interested in acquiring 100 per cent of Imperial Tobacco, but to do that, it first needed to acquire 100 per cent of Imasco and then dispose of the other businesses on a tax-effective basis. The first step saw BAT reach an agreement to sell Canada Trust to Toronto-Dominion Bank for over $8 billion. With that agreement in place, BAT made an offer to the Imasco board to buy the remaining Imasco shares, and the process with Imasco began. Stikeman Elliott and Imasco's counsel, Oslers, developed a unique transaction structure to implement the deal, which included the creation of something called "callable shares" (since used in a number of other transactions including the recent acquisition of Clarica by Sun Life). The firm also had to apply for and ultimately obtained a crucial advance income tax ruling. An auction procedure was developed and implemented to sell off Shoppers Drug Mart and Genstar. At the end of that process, BAT and KKR (Kohberg Kravis Roberts) reached an agreement on the sale of Shoppers Drug Mart, and BAT, using the Shoppers and Canada Trust purchase prices, was able to put forward its final price for the Imasco shares. The board of Imasco ultimately recommended the transaction to the shareholders, and the deal closed a couple of months later.

Throughout this six-month process, all of the negotiations between Imasco and BAT teams took place in the Paris boardroom in the firm's Toronto office. With a blind eye turned to Toronto's bylaws, members of the BAT team were allowed to smoke. No one on either side objected. When the deal was announced, the *Globe and Mail* coverage of the transaction included a report on the front page describing the smoked-filled negotiation sessions in the Paris boardroom. Apparently, the Toronto police also read the financial press because the firm received a visit from Toronto's finest. Although the firm got off with a warning, the Brits found this all quite amusing, and even the London *Financial Times* ran a piece – not on BAT's great success in acquiring Imperial Tobacco – but in dodging the "Smoke Police" in the far away colony.

BUSINESS TRAVEL

The hectic pace of business was not for the faint of heart. In one transaction, the Bank of Montreal was selling some Brazilian assets to a French bank, in a transaction that had opted for Canadian alternative dispute resolution. Yontef was to do the corporate work and had to go to São Paulo for the purpose. He flew down overnight with Sid Lederman, and the meeting was held the following morning. After spending an hour in a museum, Yontef got back on the plane for Toronto. This had followed a similar lightning trip to Italy on another deal with Stransman. Lederman stayed a day longer and vowed never again to go on trips with the corporate lawyers.

Another example was Simon Romano,[35] who was a summer student working on a transaction with Bill Braithwaite. During his first week, Braithwaite asked him to go to London that same evening with some $200 million in bonds, which were needed for a closing the next day at the Royal Trust Company. He could, however, stay for the weekend since he would be arriving on a Friday. He had no time to get a cash advance but was told he could fly business class and that a ticket would be waiting for him at the airport. He went home, packed, and took a car to the airport. There was no ticket when he arrived, so he had to buy one. Unfortunately, the limit on his Visa card ($800) was not enough to permit him to buy a business class ticket, so he flew economy for $780, leaving him only $20 on his credit limit. He took the tube from Heathrow into the city, delivered the bonds, and asked for tea, to be told that they only served coffee. He thought about his credit limit, looked at the £4 in his pocket, got back on the tube, went to the airport, and took the next flight home.

Romano is also famous for his wedding. It was meant to be a low-key affair at City Hall, to be attended by a few friends, following which they would have a dinner with eight or ten people; then they planned to tell their parents after this was all over. It was only three weeks after his call to the Bar. Rod Barrett had given him a related public party reverse takeover transaction to handle. Romano found himself opposite a senior lawyer who was third on the letterhead of another major Toronto firm, but he had control of the agreements, further evidence of the responsibility given by Stikeman Elliott to its junior lawyers. The difficulty arose when he discovered that the wedding (Justices of the Peace have their own scheduling problems) and the closing had been fixed for the same time. Neither could be moved. He put a completely green student in charge, told him that he had to leave for a couple of hours, and told the student to review each document very carefully but to agree to no changes. Romano leaped into a limo, whisked off to City Hall, got married, and returned to the closing. Once that was over, he ran to the restaurant and joined the wedding dinner, only about half an hour late.

Romano also recalls working with Yontef in the days of the Dome Petroleum reorganization when the firm was acting for the banks. At one of the first meetings of creditors in New York, Ken Ottenbreit showed up with two large legal document cases. Someone observed that the firm must be very well prepared to require two bags of documents at the first meeting. No, they replied, the bags were empty. They were to be filled with wine, which was not easy to get in Toronto, and delivered to Yontef.

Colson was involved in a "beauty contest" to land the British Gas privatization and called Yontef and Stransman to come over to London to be ready to go first thing on a Monday morning, assuring them that he would handle the hotel reservations. They found a flight, having to go through New York, but arrived on Sunday and went to the Goring Hotel in Mayfair, where they were each checked into the smallest hotel rooms they had ever seen. Yontef's television set had an eleven-inch screen, suspended by a string at the foot of the single bed that barely fit in the room. On the other hand, damning with faint praise, it was the first hotel in London to have central heating.

IT AIN'T OVER TILL THE FAT LADY SINGS

Corporate closings seem to many to be entirely routine, involving mainly the shuffling around and signing of documents, which have all been fully negotiated and drafted, attended by bored lawyers and impatient clients. In fact, however, they are the real moments of truth and are often attended by high drama when something that is supposed to happen does not happen or something that should not happen and has never been contemplated occurs at the last moment.

Jim Arnett remembers a tense closing in the transaction by which the CDC sold its Kid Creek mine to Falconbridge. CDC insisted that all closings in which it was involved were to be held at its offices in Toronto. There were two stages to the closing of the deal. The first was to obtain a release from the CDC bankers to allow the second, main closing, to occur. Arnett was running back and forth between boardrooms to see how each was proceeding. The divestiture was all set, and in the other room, things were pronounced to be under control: all the necessary releases had been obtained. Arnett announced that they were ready to close. They received a cheque for almost $1 billion. The CDC went to the bank to deposit the cheque. Half an hour later, Nigel Grey, the general counsel of CDC, said that there seemed to be a problem; the banks were taking the position that they had not yet closed. The difficulty was that the cheque had already been deposited. It took a very tense hour and a half to settle the difficulty, which was potentially enormous since everything contemplated in the closings had already in fact occurred.

Arnett was also one of the lawyers acting on the privatization of Teleglobe, which had been owned by the federal government and was being sold to Memotech, the successful bidder. The chief executive officer of Teleglobe was Jean-Claude Delorme, who was in effect a public servant. Our client, the federal government, the Crown in Right of Canada in the person of Barbara McDougall, the responsible minister, was required to give a certificate as to the representations and warranties of the seller. All of the background information had been provided by the Teleglobe staff, and Delorme was going to remain in place as the CEO of the privatized company. We believed that to protect the minister, we should get some backup to the representations and warranties since she had no personal knowledge of the underlying facts. This backup was to take the form of a certificate from Delorme addressed to the minister. It was not intended to fix him with any particular liability but to give comfort to the minister. He was a bit worried about the idea. The closing was at the offices of Heenan Blaikie, where Peter Blaikie was acting for Memotech and Richard Clark was present there for the same purpose for Teleglobe. There was a rush to get the closing completed by March 31, the fiscal year-end of the government, and the amount was significant – some $850 million. As they were going round the table at the closing, all the documents were signed except for Delorme's certificate. Everyone was waiting, including the media, when the word came back that Delorme was not prepared to sign. Arnett said that if he did not sign, there would be no closing and that Delorme would have to take full responsibility for the failure to close. There was a standoff for about an hour, until Delorme finally capitulated and signed the certificate.

&

At the end of the first fifty years of its existence, the firm has developed the capacity and the talent to handle the most complex commercial transactions and to attract the major corporations in Canada and elsewhere. This path to the top echelon of practice began initially by picking up the crumbs from Stikeman's tax work, but it soon blossomed into a full commercial capability, which has now grown to such an extent that the commercial transactions are far greater in importance than the original tax specialty, but which integrate the firm's tax expertise into a full-service capability that is second to none.

CHAPTER 10

Stikeman Elliott Before the Courts

It is in the nature of litigation that it is episodic and dependent on cases arising that call for legal assistance to enforce or defend rights. In consequence, it is difficult to provide a seamless review of the development of a law firm in this sector of practice. This chapter is, therefore, a series of snapshots, not unlike a family photograph album, that can be studied or skimmed, as the interests of the viewer dictates. These snapshots are depictions of some of those who have stood on their feet in court, the real crucible in which the law is formed and decided, extended, or cut back; of the clients willing to take their chances for whatever reason before the courts, armed with their convictions and served by the robed samurai who defend their interests; and of their war stories.

Rights may be rights, and agreements may provide whatever the parties might have thought they meant, but when things go wrong, in the final analysis, it is the courts that decide. And to assist the courts in reaching the proper conclusions, the parties need capable, competent, and cocky litigators who are not afraid to get on their feet to argue, to examine and cross-examine witnesses, and to build a compelling case. The litigious objective is to win the crucial points that will determine the outcome but that are often not readily apparent to those with no experience before the courts. They then apply the full force of their efforts to those portions of the case that will lead the courts to the desired conclusion. They regard themselves as the "real" lawyers and enjoy the pressures on the cutting edge of emerging law. Stikeman Elliott has had the good fortune to have attracted more than its share of intelligent, aggressive, and talented lawyers who have broken new ground as advocates for both popular and unpopular causes.

At the end of its first half-century, driven by the expanding corporate practice of the firm, there is now in place one of the best commercial litigation teams in the country, which specializes in the law surrounding business transactions and the enforcement of contractual and other rights of clients. This achievement was attained only after many years of careful building of litigation departments in the main offices of Montreal and Toronto, together with local expertise in the other offices of the firm. High-level commercial litigation is not an easy field in which to establish a significant foothold, requiring as it does both size and experience. In addition to the business law component, there is a group of civil, administrative, and regulatory lawyers who have had experience before virtually every court and administrative tribunal in the country. In the beginning, however, the firm's litigators took almost any mandates that came their way, often for the sole purpose of creating a reputation and profile that would lead to major cases. Clients approach litigation like patients approach the selection of a surgeon – they look for a good reputation. So without a good reputation, clients with good cases tend to look elsewhere. Earning a litigation reputation requires finding cases of legal and public interest since that is where the reputation is born; therefore, many of the early cases were unrelated to the business law centre of gravity of the firm. Indeed, they might easily be seen as being counterproductive to the business law concentration. Underdog clients make for better press and enhance the status of the litigators without necessarily bringing concomitant remuneration. But without the status derived from such cases, clients who might otherwise be inclined to stay with the firm for their litigation matters will go elsewhere.

There were two pivotal events that heralded the deliberate entry of the firm into the litigation field. The first was the call from Fraser Elliott to François Mercier in mid-1963 that led to Mercier's arrival with André Brossard. The second was the search for senior counsel in Toronto that presaged the entry of John Sopinka and Sidney Lederman fourteen years later. Despite his personal conviction that the main engine to drive the firm would be the combination of corporate and tax law for business clients, Elliott nevertheless understood that without the ability to handle important litigation matters, the firm would be condemned to remain a boutique operation, and its growth would be limited accordingly. To his credit, he decided that the firm must be one that could offer the best services in all fields, and with typical dispatch, he acted to complete the roster.

LITIGATION IN MONTREAL

When Mercier and Brossard first arrived, they brought with them some 200 active insurance files, their then specialty, driven in part by the fact that Mercier had lectured on non-marine and marine insurance at the Université de Montréal from 1951 to 1964. But they soon became resolved to expand into more complex and more remunerative areas of general litigation. The new reality was prompted by the talent and ambition of George Tamaki, James Grant, David Angus, James Robb, Gerald McCarthy, Donald Johnston, Jean Monet, and a few others who were in the firm before they joined. To achieve the broader objective, recruiting new talent became a principal focus of activity. They consulted the Gagnon Register of litigation lawyers to select the best possible candidates and located among others Mortimer Freiheit, Gérald Tremblay, Marc Prévost, Louis P. Bélanger, Marc Laurin, Denis Lachance, Michel Décary, and Richard Rusk.

In *Domglas Inc. v. Jarislowsky, Fraser & Co. Ltd. and Paul Heller Ltd.*, Mercier and Denis Lachance represented thirty-one respondents in a petition addressed to the Quebec Superior Court pursuant to section 184(15) of the *Canada Business Corporations Act* to fix the fair value of the common shares of certain dissenting shareholders who opposed a takeover bid for the company. In a lengthy decision covering 165 pages, Judge Benjamin Greenberg of the Quebec Superior Court (who is now a senior consultant with the firm) postulated four approaches to the valuation of corporate shares: market price, assets, earnings, and finally, a combined approach using the first three. This judgment, the first to provide an in-depth consideration of the several possible approaches to the valuation of shares in the context of dissentient shareholders, became a judicial authority and had a coast-to-coast impact within the legal world; copies were sought by corporate attorneys from Halifax to Vancouver.

With Marc Laurin, Mercier pleaded the case of *Canadian Pacific Ltd. v. Quebec North Shore Paper Company* before the Superior Court in Baie Comeau and subsequently in the Quebec Court of Appeal. The issue dealt with a navigation contract between the parties, which granted Canadian Pacific the exclusive right to ferry bulk newsprint manufactured by Quebec North Shore Paper Company across the St Lawrence River from Baie Comeau to Matane on the South Shore. From Matane, the newsprint was then shipped by rail to New York and Chicago, to be used in printing the *New York Daily News* and the *Chicago Tribune*. Unbeknownst to Canadian Pacific, a senior executive of Quebec North Shore had negotiated a new agreement with Canadian National Railways, which also owned a ferry, at a much more beneficial rate. Judge Kenneth McKay ruled in favour of Canadian Pacific and rescinded the agreement that Quebec North Shore had negotiated illegally to the prejudice of Canadian Pacific. As Quebec North Shore was one of the leading producers of newsprint in the province of Quebec, the trial enjoyed tremendous publicity in and around Baie Comeau.

One of the highest profile cases that Mercier argued, this time assisted by Jean-Judes Chabot, who is now a judge of the Quebec Superior Court, was *Roger Taillibert v. La Régie des Installations Olympiques*. Taillibert was the well-known French architect who designed the now-famous Olympic Stadium at the request of Jean Drapeau, then mayor of Montreal. Taillibert was suing the Olympic Installations Board, established in 1975 by the Quebec government, as the costs of the 1976 Olympic Games began to spiral out of control. The board refused to pay the fees, arguing, *inter alia*, that the architect had committed major errors in architectural drawings, which quadrupled the length and cost of construction in view of its complexity and particular spatial geometry. Quebec Superior Court Justice Charles Doherty Gonthier, who now sits as a highly respected judge on the Supreme Court of Canada, ruled that there were no such errors but instead, a plethora of defects that occurred during the erection of the structure. The action was spectacular in its presentation because of the personality of the French architect, who was almost uniformly disliked by his local confreres in Quebec; moreover, they were furious that Drapeau had gone outside Quebec to find his Olympic architect. The dislike was less personal than the result of ruffled professional feathers. The changes suggest that it may have been his personality, but then all architects think of themselves as gods. The case was also of special interest because of the fact that Taillibert had no written contract with either the City of Montreal or its successor, the Olympic Installations Board. Mayor Drapeau had referred the matter to Mercier only a week before the prescription period of the claim was due to expire, with the result that an action *de in rem verso*, based on the unjustified enrichment of the board to the prejudice of the plaintiff, had to be initiated with little time to prepare the proceedings. Apart from the general notoriety of the case, it was important because there are very few reported cases dealing with this type of recourse of Roman law origin.

In *La Cité de Pont Viau v. Gauthier Manufacturing Limited,* Mercier acted as counsel to a young lawyer from another firm on a matter of great importance in civil procedure. The relevant article in the *Code of Civil Procedure* provided that an inscription in appeal (in effect, the notice of appeal from the judgment of the lower court) had to be filed within thirty days from the date of judgment, failing which it would become null and void. In this particular case, the bailiff (an officer of the court) had erroneously served the inscription upon the wrong firm of attorneys representing the respondent, with the result that the lawyer had to repair this gross negligence by issuing a new inscription in appeal seven months after the lower court decision had been rendered. Matters of procedure are very seldom heard by the Supreme Court of Canada, but Mercier succeeded in obtaining leave to appeal, and their position was maintained by the five judges of the court who recognized the validity of the late notice. Justice Pigeon stating that henceforth, civil procedure *"serait la servante du droit, et non pas sa maîtresse."* His colleague, Justice Yves Pratte, added that no litigant should suffer any prejudice as the result of an error committed by a justice officer.

In the mid-1980s, the federal government had encouraged citizens of Canada to insulate their homes with urea-formaldehyde in order to save the costs of fuel, which had been subject to considerable inflation due in part to conflicts in the Middle East and the emergence of the OPEC cartel. It turned out that the product, once installed behind the walls of the structure, would rot after a certain time to such an extent that in many cases, supporting walls of residences and other buildings had to be torn down and rebuilt. This situation generated some 8,000 actions in Quebec alone, and the firm appeared in more than 800 of them on behalf of a client who insured one of the companies manufacturing the insulating material. *Isolation Val Royal Inc. v. Antoniata Trunzo* was a test case. There were twenty-three different lawyers at the trial, and the political aspects of the issue attracted extensive coverage by the media as the trial went on for a period of three and a half years. Judge Hurtubise, who presided at the hearing, dismissed the six test cases that were before him, and his decision was unanimously confirmed by the Court of Appeal. Although the judgment was not as a matter of law *res judicata* vis-à-vis the other plaintiffs, it provoked desistments in almost 90 per cent of the pending actions.

Asbestos Corporation, which quarried asbestos from two huge mining deposits that it owned in Thetford Mines in the province of Quebec, was a wholly owned subsidiary of General Dynamics of Saint Louis, Missouri. The Quebec government expropriated the subsidiary, and General Dynamics objected. Mercier recalls with some amusement that he advised the Saint Louis corporate board and its chairman that they had no case and would ultimately lose in court. This is exactly what happened in *General Dynamics and Asbestos Corporation v. Attorney General of Quebec* as the court, presided by the then Chief Justice Jules Deschênes, sanctioned without restriction the right of a provincial government to expropriate a private corporation provided that the order-in-council ordering the takeover was enacted in the general interest of the citizens.

François Mercier had a very synthetic mind and could reduce a problem to three or four major issues and not waste time separating the wheat from the chaff. In cross-examination, he was brilliant yet polite and respectful. Once, he was acting in a winding-up case in which the issue was the appointment of a receiver, a matter that was hotly contested. He had the president of the company in the witness box and slowly worked him to the point where he was able to ask, quite reasonably, "So you really do not care if a receiver is appointed?" The president replied, "no" – and that was the end of the case. He always had a copy of the *Civil Code* and the *Code of Civil Procedure* side by side on his otherwise pristine desk.

Jim Robb, whose arrival antedates all active lawyers in the firm except Fraser Elliott, has had a varied litigation practice, which is part of his self-description as the firm's "generalist." This may be a partial legacy of having been the only student and gofer for the seven lawyers who comprised the firm when he began. His duties included the court run and research in anything that needed to be done. Throughout his career, he has worked in the fields of tax, insurance, trust and estates, maritime, labour, corporate, real estate, environmental, intellectual property, international trade, civil responsibility, product liability, regulatory, engineering, and construction, all of which include some elements of litigation. His litigation repertoire reflects the general nature of his practice, including a case that involved responsibility for inaccurate taxi meters. As it turned out, the reason for the incorrect fares was a missing ball in the workings of the meter, which led John Turner to suggest that Robb consider writing a legal text, entitled *Robb on Balls*. He had an insurance case in a collision matter in which the only defence that could be offered was that the driver's wife had told him that there was no car coming at the intersection. The matter was settled. He argued the first case of consumer responsibility under the 1969 *Civil Code*, which dealt with a split roller in a paper machine. He succeeded, before the Court of Appeal, in overturning a will that left an estate to the operator of a nursing home, which began a new line of jurisprudence and led to amendments to the *Civil Code*. Acting for the CIBC, he was successful in defending the bank on the grounds of forgery and in the process, created jurisprudence on the use of expert evidence in such cases. He also defended the bank in injunction proceedings that sought to prevent the bank from exercising its security in the case of Gourd and St Lawrence Mining, and he represented the CIBC in the aborted negotiations for the financing of Lockheed Patrol aircraft by the Canadian government, which eventually decided that such financing was inappropriate.

Typical of the range of cases handled before the development of litigation specialties, Robb appeared in a variety of regulatory and administrative cases. In one such case, he appeared on behalf of the Taxi Owners Association of Montreal in their effort to remain exempt from liability for unemployment insurance premiums in respect of drivers of the taxis, which took him to the Supreme Court of Canada on two separate occasions. He participated in the Restrictive Trade Practices Commission investigation of shipping conferences and later became involved in writing and negotiating the *Shipping Conferences Exemption Act* and its various renewals. He had numerous appearances before transportation and energy boards provincially and federally and in particular, the CRTC and predecessor bodies.

In product liability proceedings, he was unsuccessful in a collection action against the Canadian Post Office, defended largely on the basis of poor programming of the automated equipment installed in the Montreal facility. He was more successful in a collection action against the Autoroutes de Québec on behalf of Automatic Toll, owners of toll collection equipment on the Eastern Townships Autoroute (tolls on the autoroute were subsequently removed), upon unilateral cancellation of the contract by the government. The claim for payment had been challenged on the basis that the automated equipment did not supply appropriate checks on monies deposited. He successfully defended John Deere against a claim by numerous insurance companies in respect of a fire north of Baie Comeau, which lasted for three months and burned the forest and everything else in sight, where the claim was that the fire had been started by defective John Deere equipment. Moving from there to competition law, he acted for Standard Paper Box in the late 1950s and early 1960s paperboard case and obtained a minimal fine for the infractions. On behalf of Solomon, he successfully defended a claim for retail price maintenance of ski boots, establishing jurisprudence in one of the few litigated cases in this area. He represented Clairol in *Clairol v. Small Pharmacies Association,* an attempt to restrain retail price maintenance, where he was unsuccessful in the Supreme Court of Canada. During the Clairol appeal before the Supreme Court of Canada, Robb cited William Lyon Mackenzie during the course of his argument, only to have Douglas Abbott on the bench ostentatiously turn his chair around and face away from him with the mention of such a political activist.

Mortimer Freiheit[1] has become one of the toughest and most imaginative litigators in Quebec, handling a broad range of cases with remarkable success. He would be the first to admit that when he first came to the firm, he was entirely raw and had no experience whatsoever, but he learned remarkably quickly. When he joined, there were four lawyers in the litigation group. His mandate was to develop, along with the lawyers in the corporate section, a corporate and commercial litigation practice, an area into which Mercier and Brossard, with their more classic civil law practice, were unlikely to make major inroads. The Montreal office has now developed the largest commercial and corporate litigation department of any law firm in the province. Despite the desired focus on the corporate and commercial practice, the firm nevertheless allowed him and others to take on mandates from a variety of non-conventional clients. This was particularly beneficial in allowing litigation lawyers to develop, without restraint, various areas of expertise as well as a social conscience. An early example of this occurred very shortly after Freiheit joined the firm. He remembers thinking then that the first name on the letterhead was the person he should consult when faced with a file issue. After a few months, he received a call from the Jamaican government asking if he would represent a student caught up in the Sir George Williams University dispute in which the university computer centre was occupied and severely damaged by radical students. The request was to represent a female student who had brought food for the protesters into the building and had promptly been arrested. He went to Stikeman and explained the situation. He was concerned that considering the publicity and political issues involved, it might not be something he should accept. Stikeman looked up at him from his desk and asked, "Do you think she has a good defence?" "I think so," replied Freiheit. "Then, what's the issue?" asked Stikeman. There was absolutely no question raised about anything other than the role that a lawyer would be expected to fill when asked to act for a client.

In a similar vein, on a second occasion, Freiheit had been working late one evening when a member of the building cleaning staff told him that his sister had just delivered a baby, but she woke up blind. Could he help her? Freiheit said he knew nothing about such matters but referred her to an eminent obstetrician, Peter Gillett, his wife's doctor, and again went to Stikeman to ask whether he should accept the mandate since he was almost certain that he would not get paid for his services. Stikeman explained that from time to time, at the end of a year, he would have to write off an account that he had originally expected to be paid. He thought that it would have been better, on some occasions, to choose in advance what accounts he would write off; at least then, Freiheit would have the luxury of choosing where not to be paid. Freiheit took on the file and won. Mr Justice Bisson (subsequently a judge on the Court of Appeal), who heard the case at trial, would always tell him when they met thereafter that it was the most interesting case of his career. It turned out to be a leading medical malpractice case, with great witness cross-examinations.

The Canadian Imperial Bank of Commerce has been one of the firm's main clients from the beginning. At the outset, the firm handled substantially all of the bank's corporate security work but did very little of its litigation or insolvency work, which was then handled by a variety of boutique firms. The litigation section proceeded to develop that practice area to the point that it is now involved in almost all of the bank's major insolvency work. Among the interesting files generated was the case of Wallcrete Construction Ltd., one of the principal contractors in the 1976 Olympic Games. Other projects that generated work included what is now the Sheraton Hotel at the corner of René-Lévesque Boulevard and Stanley Street, which was at the time intended to be one of the largest Holiday Inns in the country. The contractor, Bruce McLaughlin, got into serious financial difficulties during the course of construction, including those described in chapter 9 in which Ed Waitzer has been acting. Liquidation of the assets of the company on behalf of the bank was extremely complex due to the fact that there were numerous construction projects under way and equipment located in many different jurisdictions. So complex was the liquidation process that one of the firm's corporate partners, Martin Claude Lepage, decided to assist by himself acting as auctioneer, auctioning off, in front of a live audience, substantial quantities of construction equipment. He still keeps one of the hats given to him by the auctioneer in recognition of his fine auctioning skills in his office.

A major case generated from the CIBC relationship was the insolvency of Maislin Transport, which had decided to expand into the United States by acquiring numerous transport companies. Unfortunately, it was just at the time when the United States began deregulation of the transportation industries. The resulting insolvency of the company entailed taking control of hundreds of vehicles while some were still in transit, with many terminals located in different states, and the liquidation of these assets under US insolvency legislation. In addition, they were still subject to state legislation in many areas. In particular, upon the insolvency of the American transport companies, many of the drivers developed immediate cases of shoulder and elbow disabilities and filed claims in the various states under various worker protection statutes. That, combined with the complexity of pension claims, triggered a seemingly endless series of transborder insolvency and civil liability issues.

On a portion of the transactions that related to Canada, the opposing party was represented by Peter Mackell of Martineau Walker, with whom Freiheit was negotiating the terms of an agreement that would have to be approved by the court the following morning. Freiheit says he started off strong but that by 3:00 or 4:00 in the morning, he was getting blurry. Mackell, a very able and persistent lawyer, was getting the better of him, and he realized that he needed help. So, at 4:00 AM, he called Jim Grant and asked him if he could get down there "real soon." Grant showed up within an hour and finished the negotiations before the court session scheduled for 9:30 that morning.

Another of the interesting cases was the one in which Peter O'Brien represented Birks and Freiheit represented the CIBC in connection with the reorganization required as a result of Birks's acquisition of a number of jewellery retailers in the United States. The operations in the United States proved to be a significant drain on the Canadian company's financial resources, and the existence of various corporate guarantees posed a significant threat not only to the US operations, but also to those in Canada. In order to protect the Canadian operations of the venerable Montreal-based company from the unfortunate consequences of having expanded in the United States, quite sophisticated reorganization plans were required, all of which were subject to the bankruptcy legislation of the United States and the laws of individual states where the retail stores were located. In the end, they were successful in resolving all of the US problems through a filing under chapter 11 of the US bankruptcy legislation and resolving all the other contractual issues, insulating the Canadian operations from the liquidation of the US operation.

In another case, the CIBC had taken as security millions of dollars of product of a large grocery wholesaler, located in warehouses in various locations, which the bank officer would visit from time to time. When the company defaulted on its loans and the bank came to take possession of the inventory, the warehouses were found to be empty. More accurately, there was a visible wall of product, from floor to ceiling, giving the illusion of a full warehouse, but in fact, nothing remained behind that first wall of product. The CIBC experienced, in a different context, the effects of a Potemkin village. The owner protested that there must have been a theft, and at this point, cloak-and-dagger rather than legal work was required. After some detective work, a middle-of-the-night seizure took place in several different locations, and the bank was successful in recovering its debt. Had it not been for a disgruntled employee who did not get his share of the missing inventory, it is unlikely that anything would have been recovered.

In connection with the insolvency practice, the firm had significant involvement in many real estate projects, resulting from foreclosures by creditors, corporate reorganizations, or simply dealing with real estate development in difficult times. Montreal landmarks such as Le Faubourg de Sainte-Catherine, Simpson's, the Dominion Square Building, and a good part of the real estate in Old Montreal, as well as the portfolio of Belcourt Properties, were all significant real estate projects in which Freiheit was involved.

In one case, a client had a great idea – namely, converting a not-for-profit development into a for-profit one. The plan was to divide a development containing hundreds of duplex and quadruplex buildings into single units and to sell them as extremely low-cost condominiums to persons who might not otherwise be able to own their own homes. This was a wonderful idea, except that it coincided with a change of government when the Parti Québécois came into power in 1976. That government did not look favourably upon real estate developers. In addition, a family member of one of the important ministers was a tenant in the project, and she was extremely vocal in her opposition to the land development, fearful that she might be required to leave what was then very favourably low-cost housing. A noisy battle developed in the media, and the government announced that it would prevent our client, whom it labelled a "speculator," from profiting in what was a perfectly legal and a socially beneficial development plan. The government then commenced to enact various forms of legislation, including penal legislation, with the declared objective of preventing division of duplex and quadruplex buildings. The real focus of the legislation, however, was solely the client's activities.

The firm was successful in defeating attempts to apply the legislation to the point that the government, frustrated in its attempts to block the project, indicated that it intended to enact new legislation, purportedly of a general nature, but that would specifically identify the lot numbers that the firm's client was planning to develop so that he could no longer proceed with the development. Freiheit travelled to Quebec city on Christmas Eve and sat in a small room located behind the seat of the Speaker of the legislative assembly, an extremely impressive chamber of great national historical significance. The negotiations with the government were unsuccessful as the client refused to cease the development, although he agreed to protect fully the rights of any tenants who might not wish to purchase a unit. Nevertheless, determined to prevent the "speculator" from making a profit, the government insisted on passing legislation that referred to the specific lot numbers of the client to prevent further development. The client then instituted legal proceedings, claiming significant damages. At the same time, to up the ante, the client hired buses filled with prospective purchasers, who followed then Premier René Lévesque in his various travels to the United States, where he was seeking to reassure the capital markets of the stability of the Parti Québécois government. The battle was fought in the media and in the courts. A very significant settlement in damages was obtained, and in the end, the client proceeded with the successful development.

Among the various real estate developers that the firm has represented was one involved with the Dominion Square Building. The owner of the property contacted Freiheit in order to set aside what a would-be purchaser contended was an agreement on the part of Freiheit's client to sell the building to him. Lengthy court proceedings began, and a bitter battle ensued. Even though the client would have benefitted enormously from the transaction, the prospects of an ever-increasing market for real estate had convinced him that he should not proceed with the sale. The litigation was extremely successful; the client obtained exactly what he wanted, and the agreement was set aside. Unfortunately, after winning the pitched battle, he lost the war. The real estate market turned against him. Instead of ultimately ending up making a significant profit, he sustained enormous losses and had to give up the building to the mortgage lenders. Whenever they meet, the client always remarks that he wished that Freiheit had been less successful in having set aside what in retrospect would have been a great deal.

Freiheit acted in the case of a German real estate mogul who suffered the largest-ever real estate bankruptcy in Germany. He had many buildings in Montreal, including the YMCA on Stanley Street. The values in Canada alone were in the range of $70 million, and he owned even more in the US and, of course, still more in Germany. The mogul detested lawyers, so he never incorporated. Over his desk was the Shakespearean admonition, "Kill all the lawyers." When the economy deteriorated in Germany, the banks started to descend. He could not handle the pressure and hanged himself. His widow came to see Freiheit in Montreal, and his involvement in the complicated affair began. While cross-border insolvencies are always complex, this worldwide one was unique. There was, in the midst of the proceedings, an amusing story of how a student flew from Montreal on a Friday night to Paris to research a point at the Sorbonne on Saturday and returned Sunday morning. On the Friday, Freiheit was apologetic, thinking that perhaps he would unfairly burden the student by sending him to Paris for such a short period and offered to let him off the hook. He said, "But look, you will barely sleep, and when you get there, you will be locked up in the library the entire day and will fly back almost immediately. Are you sure you want to go and that I am not being unfair?" "Mr. Freiheit," the student said, "It is enough for me just to be able to breathe the Paris air."

Freiheit and many of the litigation lawyers have been involved as well in the largest insolvency in Canada (about $2 billion, also real estate related), which gave rise to the largest auditors liability law suit in Canada. That is the *Castor* case, with the highly secretive Wolfgang Stolzenberg as the main actor. The firm initiated lawsuits on behalf of probably every known Swiss and German bank against the accounting firm of Coopers & Lybrand, and the matter will likely take years to resolve.

The firm acted on several constitutional law cases on behalf of Cargill Grain Company. One of particular interest arose from the desire of Cargill to develop a facility in the Port of Quebec, which was to be the most modern facility in the world, allowing the unloading, from Great Lakes' ships, of grain from the Midwest into storage facilities (transfer elevators), which would then be loaded onto ocean-going vessels for shipment to other parts of the world. In addition, local grain would be delivered into trucks for use by local farmers. All of the loading and unloading of ships and trucks was to be done by a small number of employees in a control booth, operating through vacuum tubes, conveyor systems, and computerized storage and testing facilities, ensuring the delivery and storage of the proper type and grade of grain in each of the various elevators. The problem was that the Port of Quebec had been organized by a particular union, and its officials were fearful of a new operation entering the port, either non-union or (perhaps worse) another labour organization entirely. Cargill responded to this development by purchasing a small local firm – Gagnon and Boucher.

Proceedings began by determining whether federal or provincial legislative authority governed for labour law purposes. To represent the employees, Freiheit enlisted the support of Gérald Tremblay, a former partner of the firm, and he himself acted for the company. They entered the courtroom, accompanied by their respective *stagiaires*, and spent the entire morning arguing that the case should be referred to a court of different jurisdiction, from which they emerged with a judgment in their favour. They then repaired to a nearby restaurant to celebrate the victory in the customary litigation lawyer fashion, one developed almost to an art form by Tremblay. By 4:00 in the afternoon, however, after many toasts to the postponement, one of the young *stagiaires* asked earnestly and seriously, if they celebrated a mere postponement this way, what type of celebration would take place if they were to win at the end. It was far too late in the day to generate a sensible response, but eventually the two of them won the case on the merits as well.

Freiheit argued a case that was somewhat out of the ordinary since it involved a bank that was insolvent while his client was not. Mont Tremblant, the mountain and the hotel complex, was financed by the Canadian Commercial Bank. For no apparent reason, the bank called its loan, and Freiheit had little time to react. He found an old and seldom-used law, called the *Companies and Creditors Arrangement Act*, a twelve-page statute dating from the 1930s. Reading it, Freiheit noted many similarities to chapter 11 reorganizations in the United States. He brushed the dust off it and considered the possibilities it created. It had never been used in Quebec and had languished long in the deep-freeze in the rest of Canada. He based his argument on the old statute, and somewhat to everyone's surprise, he succeeded. After the success he had and the publicity given to certain of the court orders he obtained, it became one of the most popular tools to restructure companies in difficulty both in Quebec and Canada.

One of the orders was that the bank be required to comply with its own lending agreements. Freiheit had argued that in the circumstances, the statute must be interpreted to mean that the bank be ordered to advance monies in accordance with its agreements. Such an order had never been issued before. Whenever he meets Judge Denis Lévesque who issued the order, they still wonder exactly what was intended. In the event, acting under the possibility that it might be held in contempt of court if it did not continue to do so, the bank made the advances. Freiheit's submissions were that it was not the debtor that was insolvent but rather the bank, which drew some skeptical looks from the court. Although the injunction remained in effect, Freiheit lost on the merits in first instance and then proceeded to appeal. The day before the appeal was to be heard in the Court of Appeal, the press headlines were "CCB Bank Files for Bankruptcy," so he was spared from having to argue too forcefully in appeal. Ultimately, the client refinanced, recovered damages from the CCB, and later sold the property to Intrawest. Freiheit used this statute on many occasions thereafter, and playing off his precedent, others also started using it, with the result that it has now become the virtual mainstay of Canadian bankruptcy practice.

Another case involved a dispute over the ownership of a company that was selling in North America a health product that originated in Germany many years ago. Freiheit represented the shareholder whose father originally developed the product in 1920. The client had agreed to a passive role in the company, only to find out that over time, the sales of the product had declined by some $100 million from a peak that exceeded $300 million a year at the time of his departure. The judge who commenced hearing the case wanted to know what it was exactly that the company was selling since when one examined the bottle, it was a disturbingly unpleasantly coloured product with, when the bottle was opened, an absolutely revolting taste and smell. Freiheit was obliged to tell the very attractive female judge that the product was an *elixir d'amour.* The case ended in a unique fashion, never seen before or since. In the interim, another judge, Mr Justice Gomery, had been assigned to the case, and he ordered an auction of the shares of the company to take place in open court. Each party had five minutes to consider the offer of the other and to decide whether he would better it by a minimum of $100,000. The bidding proceeded. The firm's client had previously agreed with Freiheit about the maximum value of the company, but as the bidding levels approached that value, the client became emotionally involved and continued bidding well above a realistic level. The *elixir d'amour* apparently extended into the corporate world. Freiheit tried to physically restrain the client, but he insisted on keeping the bidding going. Finally, Freiheit remembered the apocryphal words of the famous Montreal grocery magnate, Sam Steinberg, and told the client, "Don't fall in love with the merchandise." The client thought about it, and stopped bidding.

More directly connected with Sam Steinberg, Freiheit acted for his daughter, Mitzy Steinberg Dobrin, in forcing the sale of the family company, which was built by her father, one of the icon grocery chains in Quebec. She wanted to sell, but her two sisters did not. A battle ensued, with bitter allegations and motions. A sale was finally forced, and a premium was obtained over the already handsome sale price that the valuators thought reasonable. About two years later, with a change in the market, Steinberg's filed for bankruptcy. The client's decision to sell and the firm's ability to force it resulted in getting the client out just in time.

From time to time, cases involve dealings with unusual adversaries. In one of these, it was necessary to travel to Venezuela to examine a plaintiff who was involved in a very heated shareholder dispute with Alcan. So heated was the dispute that among other matters, he claimed to have suffered a serious heart attack as the result of the protracted litigation. The individual also happened to be a very long-established cattle rancher with significant influence on a national scale in Venezuela. The lawyers landed in Caracas, went to the hotel, and organized the documents to be ready for the examination that was to take place the following day. They had arranged to be picked up by a local attorney who was acting as the Venezuelan agent and primary contact. At 9:00 AM, as arranged, the attorney was at the door. His assistant took the bags, and as they entered the vehicle, the attorney who was driving reached into the glove compartment and placed a .44 magnum revolver on the passenger's seat. He proceeded to explain to the lawyers in the back seat that the adversary was a very "influential" man and that he felt somewhat ill at ease in taking them to the place where the examination was to occur. They made it safely to the examination and proceeded to complete the procedure in a very polite, expeditious, and efficient manner. They also made it safely back to the aircraft and home. The examination proved to have been sufficiently thorough to lead to a very favourable settlement.

A somewhat different situation arose with a client who was a former Mossad agent. The lawyers had spent many a day hearing of his numerous exploits, including examining photographs of him in the desert at the signing of the 1967 armistice agreement with Moishe Dayan and Gamal Abdul Nasser. They became aware of his many other activities that involved the bringing to justice of various Nazi war criminals and how in some instances, this involved surreptitiously placing individuals in the trunk of a vehicle. In one of the cases in which the firm was involved, on their way to court, they opened the trunk of the vehicle to place their briefcases inside. To their surprise, in a corner of the trunk was an object that resembled a shotgun. The client explained that in view of his past, he had the legal right to retain arms in his vehicle and had placed them in the trunk since based on his previous experiences, he feared being kidnapped. If he were thrown in the trunk, he felt that he would be protected. They never felt the need to travel with him in future.

There have been other shareholder disputes although not as heated as the Venezuelan matter. One involved Consolidated Textiles Ltd., one of the largest manufacturers of textiles in Canada at the time, which had devised a method of converting very ordinary looms, which were based on eighteenth-century technology, to twentieth-century water jet looms. The latter shot the thread across the loom with a jet of water at extraordinarily high speeds, and these were the most advanced looms in the marketplace. Our client had thousands of old-fashioned looms, and through this conversion process, he would be able to adapt the manufacturing process to state-of-the-art technology at a fraction of the normal cost. The company proceeded to develop the conversion kit in secret.

As there was no invention capable of being the subject matter of a patent, it was necessary to treat it as a trade secret and maintain both the finished product and the kit in complete secrecy. Access was limited to people who needed to know of it, and they had to sign secrecy agreements. All persons gaining access to the premises had to sign in and sign out, not carrying any papers, using special codes. Everything was kept under lock and key. All the operations of the converted machines were in a separate warehouse, subject to high security. Unfortunately, one of the subcontractors had an employee who recognized the market value of this idea. There were literally millions of looms in many different countries that could be converted. This entrepreneurial employee proceeded to develop on his own a conversion kit based upon the plans of Consolidated Textiles. The firm obtained a countrywide injunction preventing the individual from proceeding with the development of the conversion kit and in the process, succeeded in pushing him permanently out of business.

A similar result was obtained in another case involving attempted piracy. Home Box Office, as well as other special event broadcasters, scrambled television signals in the United States and utilized particular companies who sold the descramblers to ensure that only subscribers to their services would receive the broadcasts in question. An underground movement, which claimed that signals in the air ought to be free and available to all, developed a very sophisticated piracy scheme. As this could constitute criminal behaviour under us law as well, Canada in general and Vancouver Island in particular became very specialized areas for the piracy of signals emanating from the United States. To complicate the matter further, the us signals could not be the subject matter of a sale in Canada so that the theft of the signals could not constitute a theft in Canada under then existing law.

Accordingly, piracy of the us signals flourished in Canada. A very clever engineer in Vancouver had devised a method of extracting a numeric key contained in the client's descrambler and was able to design a machine that would descramble the signals emanating from the United States. His machines were sold in Canada and exported secretly to the United States. At one point, Freiheit had to defend Stuart McCormack of the Ottawa office, who was assisting in the action, in a contempt of court citation in Federal

Court because of an enthusiastic execution of a *Mareva* injunction order that he was executing on Vancouver Island. In order to succeed on the merits of the case, one of the hurdles to overcome was to convince a court that a number can be the subject matter of copyright. One of the novel arguments that was argued successfully, at least at the interlocutory stage, was that a series of numbers could be subject to copyright even if a single number were not. The firm obtained a nationwide injunction that effectively put the defendant out of business.

An unusual passing-off case came to Freiheit's attention as he was driving home one evening. Listening to the news on the radio, an interview was being conducted with an individual who was leaving a McDonald's restaurant. He was asked what he thought of McCondoms. He then proceeded to describe to the listening audience the Golden Arches, which were modified to resemble a new product called McCondoms. It did not take long for Freiheit to receive a phone call at home from the senior officer of McDonald's, requesting that he immediately stop the sale of this new product. He obtained an injunction, including a seizure of all of the offending material, and had a number of television interviews in which he explained that McDonald's was not opposed to the use of condoms but was merely seeking to protect its intellectual property.

At a cocktail party recently, Freiheit met Mr Justice Daniel Tingley who reminded him of a case in which the firm was acting on behalf of a mother seeking authorization to proceed with a religious confirmation to which her former husband, the father of the child, had objected. During the course of the negotiation process, the character of the father began to show through, and he became more and more adamant in refusing to allow the child to undergo the confirmation. He became abusive toward all concerned, and there was no alternative but to go to court. In court, the other children, by then in their teens, testified on behalf of the mother and child. The testimony of the nineteen-year-old daughter, a law student, was quite touching and dramatic as she related how everything with him was a "control" issue and how abusive and threatening the father could be. She explained in great detail how difficult it was to live with her father. For example, when living on their 150-foot yacht, he came charging out of the washroom in his stateroom, screaming, "Which asshole was squeezing my toothpaste from the middle of the tube!" At this point, Mr Justice Tingley, attempting to alleviate the tension in the courtroom said good naturedly, "I believe I, too, have squeezed the tube from time to time in the middle." Without missing a beat, the daughter replied, "I guess that makes you an asshole as well." Judge Tingley then turned to the father, and the child was authorized to proceed with the confirmation.

Stephen Hamilton's[2] first file at the firm, while he was still getting used to the place, was with Freiheit. The firm's client was the plaintiff, and Nat Salomon, prior to his disbarment and criminal conviction, was acting for the defendant. They went with their client to Salomon's office to examine Salomon's client, and although Hamilton was nominally in charge of the documents, by the time the examination was a few minutes old, Freiheit had the documents spread all over the table. At one point, Salomon objected to a question. Freiheit asked whether Salomon would allow his client to answer the question under reserve of the objection, but Salomon refused. Freiheit wanted to use the phone to call the sitting judge in chambers in order to get an immediate ruling on the objection, but Salomon refused to even allow him to use the phone. Much yelling and pounding on the table followed. Hamilton was in shock. Finally, Freiheit announced that if Salomon would not allow the witness to answer, then the examination was over. He grabbed the client and stormed out of the room. Hamilton was left sitting there in shock, with documents all over the table. Gathering everything up as quickly as he could, he joined them in the lobby only to find Freiheit and the client laughing loudly about the whole thing. He knew then that Freiheit loved his work, that theatre – even if it were theatre of the absurd – was still alive and well at the firm. It promised to be a fun place to work.

Without doubt, the greatest loss in the Montreal litigation group came from Gérald Tremblay's[3] decision to move to what is now McCarthy Tétrault. He had become a partner of the firm and was obviously on his way to the top of the profession as senior counsel, but he did not feel that the firm was fully committed to litigation as a central part of its ongoing strategy and did not see any prospect of becoming the recognized leader of the litigation section as long as Mercier was there. The other firm persuaded him that litigation was central to its plans and that he would become its leader, which was enough to tip the scales. He has continued to develop and in fact became the chairman of that firm within a few years. His many friendships within the firm have nevertheless continued, and we often refer work to him when we encounter conflict situations.

Tremblay recalls, with amusement, an incident during his early days with the firm. Apparently he had a really subpar secretary who used to make such gaffes as typing that an action should be allowed, "the hole with costs," but for some reason, he could not bring himself to fire her until one day, he was late with something for Elliott and said that he had problems with his secretary. Elliott said, "If you don't have the moral fortitude to do it, I'll do it for you." Thus motivated, Tremblay axed her without delay.

Peter O'Brien joined the firm as a student in 1970, when there were nineteen lawyers in Montreal and one in London. The firm had three general areas of specialization – tax, corporate and commercial law, and litigation – but everyone, and in particular everyone below partner level, had some experience in litigation. O'Brien started off as a corporate commercial lawyer with some real estate and some court work. The court work on which the juniors cut their teeth was a combination of legal aid cases (which were distributed to all lawyers in the firm by the Bar and then trickled down to the most recent arrivals) as well as automobile accident or bumper cases for one of the insurance companies that François Mercier represented.

A disproportionate number of O'Brien's early cases actually got reported although not in the traditional law reports of decided cases. Two of the legal aid matrimonial cases that trickled down from more senior lawyers found their conclusions reported on page one of the tabloid *Le Journal de Montréal* – one, a murder and the other, a suicide – thankfully of the opposite party in both cases. His practice in matrimonial law seemed to dry up soon after that. His first serious pleading, in terms of the law, was a procedural issue relating to the Quebec *Code of Civil Procedure,* but which was pleaded before the Federal Court Trial Division. The judge was Louis Pratte, who had been his obligations professor at the Université Laval. O'Brien believes Pratte saw more of him in the forty-five minutes during which he pleaded that motion than in the two semesters of the course at Laval. Terrified as he was to get up and argue law for the first time in front of the person who had previously judged him (somewhat severely, he thought, in terms of marks), he nevertheless considered himself to be more than adequately prepared. Initially, he was dry-mouthed and needed prompting from the bench to get on with it, but once his arguments started, they evolved into (this is his clear and unbiased recollection) an eloquent, coherent, and convincing exposé of the law on the point and why it should be interpreted in favour of the estate of the late individual he was representing. It must have been good, he thought, because Mr Justice Pratte rendered a judgment in his favour supported by reasons that were coherent and important enough to be reported in the *Federal Court Reports,* the *Dominion Law Reports,* and elsewhere. Of absolutely no importance to him and his pride at having won and being reported was the fact that not one of the several reasons he cited in favour of O'Brien's interpretation had actually been raised by O'Brien or even alluded to by either side in the pleadings.

Looked at from the context of the first years of the twenty-first century, O'Brien's early experience pleading before the Supreme Court of Canada is nothing short of remarkable for no other reason than that it happened at all, much less that it all happened within his first six or seven years of practice. Within his first two or three years, he was there on three different appeals as the junior on the file – twice with Jim Robb and once with David Angus. In all cases, he got his name mentioned in the reported judgments on the basis of the typical shuffling of papers that young lawyers do and responding in each case to the presiding judge's ritual question that he had "nothing further to add, My Lord." In any event, these Supreme Court appearances clearly were not hurting his reputation and were no doubt the springboard to his first (and last) solo appearance before the top court.

As a second-year lawyer, he was working on a litigation case, *Consolidated Textiles Ltd. v. Leesona Corp.,* which was being handled by Freiheit, who at the time had the lofty advantage (in addition to his acknowledged extraordinary pleading skills) of being a four- or five-year lawyer. The firm was representing a company that was defending a patent infringement claim before the Federal Court of Canada. Lacking any clear case on the merits, they sought judicial satisfaction elsewhere and landed on the following facts: (a) the parent company of the client group rather than the operating company had been, incorrectly, sued (their names were identical but for one additional word in the parent's name); (b) while the suit was taken within the relevant Quebec prescription period (which applies by reference to Federal Court cases of this type), the prescription period subsequently expired prior to the firm having pleaded that the wrong company had been sued; and (c) that since the matters of prescription are substantive law rather procedural law in Quebec, the case against the company that had not been sued could not be taken, and a motion to amend by changing the name of the defendant should not succeed.

Some may see a certain potential for injustice in this fact and law pattern, which may have had something to do with the decision that the junior lawyer should be sent to plead the case before the Federal Court Trial Division. Notwithstanding the impassioned pleading of a lawyer from Gowling & Henderson in Ottawa, who was somewhat his senior (by fifteen years), O'Brien's arguments prevailed, and the court dismissed the motion for leave to amend by substituting defendants. Not surprisingly, as there were serious dollars in royalties hinging on the outcome, Gowlings appealed to the Federal Court of Appeal, where the same two combatants duked it out with the same result. In a 3–0 decision, O'Brien was once again victorious.

The next step was a motion from the other side for leave to appeal to the Supreme Court. Fresh from his earlier victories, O'Brien was once more dispatched to Ottawa to tell the Supreme Court why there was nothing special about this case that would justify wasting their precious time hearing it. However, he knew he was in trouble when Mr Justice Martland turned to him, the respondent, first and said that he thought that this was just the sort of case the Supreme Court should hear and did O'Brien not agree. It did not seem to bother the court that he did not, arguing that the highest court in the land should not be troubling itself with minor procedural issues. Leave was granted. Afterwards, Mr Justice Martland, whom O'Brien had known previously through his college friendship with Martland's son and daughter, sent his clerk to invite him up to his chambers, at which time he told him how impressed he was with his pleading. O'Brien told him that on that particular day, he would have preferred to have been a lousy pleader if it could have achieved another outcome.

On to the hearing on the merits. By now it was 1977, and O'Brien had been at the Bar for six years, and for the preparation of the Supreme Court case, he had his own junior, Louis P. Bélanger, who was called to the Bar that year.[4] On the other side, as they entered the courtroom, they found themselves being opposed by the same senior lawyer from Gowling & Henderson, but this time he was a mere spear carrier for Gordon Henderson, Q.C., a leader of the Bar and Supreme Court advocacy at the time. The court had apparently determined that there were sufficient issues of a quasi-constitutional nature involved in the case that they decided to sit as a full bench of nine. Although that decision had been made, Martland, the only one of the nine that O'Brien knew, had been called away to Edmonton to the funeral of one of his former partners. So the court actually sat as a bench of eight, which suggested that it was not expecting a close decision. (Were the judges to have been evenly split, the judgment of the lower court would have stood.) The inevitable happened. The Supreme Court decided, at least for that day, that it was an equity court, and notwithstanding the strongest legal arguments to the contrary, O'Brien and Bélanger lost, eight to zero.

While this was O'Brien's last case pleaded before the Supreme Court (he left litigation behind in the early 1980s), it was not strictly speaking his last appearance in that august chamber. When a couple of years later Ronald Martland was retiring from the bench, he asked O'Brien if he would like to attend the retirement ceremonies in the Supreme Court chamber. He gladly accepted. In those days, all the judges of that and other courts and certain political luminaries, including in particular the minister of Justice, showed up for such official retirement ceremonies. This was followed by a coffee and cookies reception in the Supreme Court library. The bad news was that when the judge asked that O'Brien's name be added to his personal ticket list for the event, he was told that due to space limitations, it was "family only" in terms of his personal invitees. Family to him at that time consisted of his wife, Iris, his three children (Patricia, John, and Brigid), and their various children, his grandchildren. The judge consulted with O'Brien, and it was concluded that it would be important to maintain the solemnity of the occasion and that these grandchildren be accompanied by their "nanny," for whom a ticket was quickly obtained. And so it was that as the "nanny" to Ronald Martland's grandchildren, he got to sit in on the official retirement ceremonies and afterwards meet for the first time the minister of Justice, Jean Chrétien.

O'Brien's junior on the case, Louis P. Bélanger, has developed into a prodigious litigator, with sharp elbows, a sharp tongue, legendary energy, and boundless self-confidence. In the process, he has developed a major reputation across a wide variety of cases and has pioneered the use of court proceedings as pre-emptive strikes to achieve spectacular results for clients of the firm, whether in the form of final decisions or tactics that have forced opposing clients to settle in favour of his own. It took almost no time for the firm to recognize that he could handle matters far beyond what might be expected from a junior lawyer, and in his early years, he was allowed to flourish with only minimal supervision. He proved to be particularly adept at using seizures before judgment as a tactical weapon for turning the tables against opponents, and a few of these occasions are described among many of the other fascinating cases.

Vallée et al. v. Hotel Hyatt Regency was an action in damages that arose in 1978 when a convention of dieticians contracted salmonella food poisoning (the Lord works in mysterious ways) at the Hyatt Regency in Montreal. Although the matter was eventually settled out of court, it was and still remains one of the most important cases in Quebec that dealt with food poisoning. That same year, the case of *B.G. Checo Inc. v. Iranian Power Generation and Transmission Company (Tavanir)*[5] was one of the first Canadian cases that arose following the Iranian revolution. It was an action successfully taken by the firm's client, a turnkey project engineering firm, against Tavanir, the Iranian equivalent of Hydro-Québec. The objective was to stop, by way of injunction, the payment of performance and standby letters of credit to Iranian Bank as well as to obtain judgment for the amounts, in excess of $20 million, which were owed to the client in respect of its contract.

In 1981, the firm had an unusual mandate for the CIBC. As had happened to other financial institutions, the bank fell victim to a racket masterminded by a prominent organized crime group, which consisted of kidnapping bank managers and their families, and while holding the family members hostage, forcing the bank manager to hand over the contents of the bank vault at the daily opening of the branch. The then vice-president of the CIBC, Marcel Casavant, decided that he wanted to take a stand and authorized the firm to institute legal proceedings to "retaliate." Co-operating closely with the police and using the information supplied by Donald Lavoie, the notorious police informant who was himself associated with as many as forty murders, Bélanger initiated a seizure before judgment of the properties – residences and all their contents, as well as automobiles – of several suspects, even though in some cases, the individuals were holding these assets through nominees such as girlfriends. Bélanger had lunch on two occasions with the infamous Lavoie, who had been placed under "protective" custody, and six plainclothes detectives, to prepare the case, which was pleaded under heavy security. He got the seizure orders.

This was a precedent, and it was particularly disturbing to the under-world, which was not accustomed to having its own property seized (except where it constituted evidence) since there were no laws at the time that permitted general seizure of property obtained from the fruits of crimes, much less to be forced to testify in civil court. In this particular case, one of the suspects refused to answer questions and was convicted for contempt of court and sent to jail as a result. The outcome was that although other financial institutions continued to fall victim to similar crimes, the CIBC was left alone and was never similarly victimized. Marcel Casavant won his gamble, and the firm provided him with exceptional and successful services in a recourse never before attempted. Others were also prepared to try to use seizures as part of their litigious tactics. *Nelson Matthew Skalbania v. Montreal Alouette Football Club*[6] dealt with an unusual purported seizure before judgment of the Montreal Alouette franchise, which the firm, having acquired considerable expertise in such matters, contested successfully on behalf of Skalbania.

"Divorce – Italian Style" was the description applied to a matter that came to the firm through Stanley Hartt, who enlisted the services of Bélanger. It involved an Italian contessa who had discovered that her husband was having an affair. She had decided to come to Canada for the purpose of cleaning out the joint bank deposits they had here. Across the Atlantic, the husband, having been made aware of what she had done, went to Switzerland, where he in turn emptied their Swiss joint bank account. The particular irony of this case was that neither party could risk debating the division of assets in their divorce proceedings before the Italian courts since at the time, it was a crime to have taken such assets out of Italy. Proceedings in Quebec were instituted by the ex-husband to claim his alleged share of the some $15 million located there. Bélanger had to go to Milan to investigate the evidence available as to the source of the funds, which might have had an impact upon the determination of ownership.

Although some co-operation was proffered, it fell well short of allowing him to take copies of any documents. In effect, he could look but not touch. He had to memorize all the information gathered in Milan, and each day he was driven by the client's chauffeur to Lugano, Switzerland, where he would "download" onto paper all the information he had memorized and then send it to Hartt in Montreal. The back-and-forth shuttle to and from Milan continued for several days. Back in Montreal, he and Hartt proceeded to move some of the assets from the Bank of Montreal branch at 630 René-Lévesque Boulevard to another bank in Ontario out of concern that there might be some effort to seize them before judgment. The assets included several million dollars of gold bullion in a safe deposit box, which he and Hartt physically carried out in suitcases under heavy escort to a Brinks truck that they had hired for the mission. In addition, there was a couple of million dollars worth of troy ounces of silver, fortunately for their backs, in the form of a paper certificate.

Last but not least, while examining the husband in court as to the source of the assets, Bélanger had noticed that while the witness had a very selective if not failing memory when he asked him the questions during his examination, each time after they returned from a break, the husband all of a sudden would have fairly complete answers for him. Suspicious about these remarkable recoveries of memory, Bélanger followed him during one of the breaks. He noticed that he was going to another floor in the courthouse to use a public pay phone. Since the witness was dialing a local number, Bélanger deduced that he was phoning somebody locally to get the answers to the questions. He knew that the husband had dealt with a Swiss banker as a financial advisor, whom he had met briefly in Lugano, so Bélanger asked his assistant to call all the major hotels in Montreal to see if the banker had checked in. As luck would have it, they found out that the banker had indeed checked in to the Ritz Carleton Hotel. Shortly prior to lunch recess on that day, Bélanger called the office to have a subpoena prepared for the Swiss banker, and at lunchtime, proceeded to the Ritz to help the bailiff, Abraham Selinger, identify the individual since Bélanger was the only one who had actually met the banker face to face and knew what he looked like.

Proceeding to the banker's floor, the elevator doors opened to reveal him standing there, suitcases packed, having obviously been alerted to the possibility that they may have caught on to his presence in Montreal. Before service of the subpoena could be effected (Selinger was late), the witness fled down the fire escape of the Ritz and jumped into a taxi, which Bélanger followed in another taxi to Dorval airport, where he contacted the RCMP. They alerted the US immigration authorities, who stopped the banker attempting to board a flight for Boston en route to Switzerland. The bailiff was finally able to catch up and serve him with the subpoena. When the banker inquired what he should do, he was advised to go back to his hotel, and when he asked what would happen if he did not, he was told that a warrant would be issued for his arrest. That was true, but it might have been difficult to have had it issued fast enough to stop him from boarding a plane and fleeing the jurisdiction. However, the banker did not know that. As a result, the banker came back to his hotel but was never examined. The other party, who had been adamant in firmly contesting the wife's position in the proceedings up until then, decided to settle upon terms acceptable to her.[7]

Leonard Rosen was a specialist in tracing individuals who had forgotten they had money in a bank and charging a commission to retrieve these funds after they had been turned over by the banks to the Bank of Canada, a routine process after an account has been inactive for ten years. Rosen's modus operandi was to have the individuals sign a power of attorney for him to retrieve the funds, pay himself his commission, and then hand over the balance. Had he told the people where the funds were, it was likely they would have retrieved them directly and he would not have been paid his commission. However, the CIBC had a problem with the powers of attorney since the signature, in most cases, could not be authenticated without the bank contacting its client directly, which Rosen resisted for fear of losing his commission.

Rosen therefore decided to sue the CIBC for damages in each case in which the bank refused to honour the power of attorney and turn over the funds to him. What was particular about this case is that he sued the bank in small claims court where at the time, lawyers were not authorized to appear on behalf of clients. The law was then amended to provide that where an important or complex question of law was raised before that court, permission could be sought to be represented by a lawyer, which required the chief justice's approval. The Rosen case, *Investors Research Service (Leonard Rosen) v. CIBC*, became the first case in Quebec history in which lawyers actually appeared for their clients before the small claims court, and it is the first time Stikeman Elliott, together with Phillips & Vineberg for the Bank of Canada, represented a client before the court. The firm won the case, and Rosen stopped harassing the CIBC.

The CIBC faced a major loss in 1986 with respect to a "cheque-kiting" operation, which was possible when manual processing of cheques between banks allowed enough time for such type of fraud. The perpetrators were a group that engaged in selling extended warranties associated with consumers' purchases and then without any intention to honour the warranties, factored postdated cheques obtained from the consumers. Bélanger initiated the bank's claim in *CIBC re: Extension Guaranty Services Corp.* by way of a seizure before judgment of all the furniture in the offices and residence of the two major suspects. In the course of one such seizure, a machine gun was found on the premises, which led to calling in the police. An ex-partner of one of the two suspects and his girlfriend had been found murdered some time before in Laurentian Park, and the police suspected the gun might be the murder weapon. While the seizure was still in progress, a provincial police officer flew by helicopter to Montreal to pick up the weapon for ballistic examination, but it did not prove to be the murder weapon. Having later realized that the two principal suspects were back in business after buying new furniture for their offices, Bélanger proceeded to a second seizure of all their office contents, which included a suitcase full of several thousand postdated cheques from consumers. As a result of both seizures before judgment, the defendants decided to settle. They came to the firm's offices one evening with a suitcase full of cash to reimburse the bank for all its losses, including interest and legal costs. The effect of the seizures before judgment was that the case was settled within two to three weeks, whereas without this tactic, protracted litigation and uncertainty would likely have lasted for several years.

In this, as well as in numerous other cases, Stikeman Elliott was a pioneer in the proactive use of seizures before judgment to bring about a speedy resolution of cases against otherwise resilient defendants who could have dragged things along in court indefinitely with little, if any, prospect of finding assets in the end. *Aur Resources v. Louvem and St Genevieve*[8] was a major piece of litigation during the mid-1980s in which the firm exercised a seizure before judgment of the shares held by a majority shareholder in a public company in an attempt to enforce an agreement to buy the shares. This was countered by an injunction sought against the client, alleging that he had breached his fiduciary duty in not revealing information obtained in the course of the joint venture, which resulted in a depreciation of their value and a would-be purchase of the shares at a cheap price. The most interesting feature of the case is that it established the precedent of actually seizing the majority shareholding of a public company, and the judgment dismissing the interim injunction was the first of its kind. On the strength of the firm's seizure and the loss of the injunction by the other side, a settlement was effected that made it possible for the client to achieve his objective.

In *CIBC v. Chayer,* the bank had discovered that one of its employees, with an otherwise impeccable record, had been living with her boyfriend who was an armed robber and had targeted its branches other than the one at which the employee was working. The employee was fired, but she contested her dismissal with a labour arbitrator under the *Canada Labour Code.* The bank lost before the arbitrator, who decided that since there was no evidence that she was aware of her boyfriend's activities, the bank could not find her guilty by association. The matter then went to the Federal Court of Appeal under section 28 of the *Federal Court Act,* and by unanimous judgment of the court, the decision of the arbitrator was quashed, with the court deciding that this was a flagrant situation of conflict of interests and that the bank was justified in terminating its employer-employee relationship. The employee then tried without success to obtain leave to appeal to the Supreme Court of Canada despite raising *Charter* provisions in her application for leave.[9]

In *Columbus Intec Enterprises Inc. v. Empresa Navigacion Mambisa,* the plaintiff client had a claim against a Cuban navigation company, and using the alter ego theory since the navigation company was beneficially owned by the Cuban government (all such companies had been "nationalized" by the Castro government), the firm was initially successful in seizing the assets of another Cuban navigation company. The plaintiff argued that the company of which the assets were seized was also owned by the Cuban government, the ultimate effective defendant, so that the plaintiff was entitled to seize any assets belonging to the Cuban government. On this basis, it proceeded to the arrest of a cargo ship that was then the flag ship of the Cuban merchant marine. As it departed the Montreal harbour, the firm caused it to be stopped by the harbour authority, and while it was being anchored in the St Lawrence River between Montreal and Sorel, Peter Cullen and Bélanger boarded the ship with bailiffs in the middle of the night, only to be greeted not by the captain, who was not really in charge, but by the political officer on board who had an Uzi automatic weapon hanging ostentatiously on his belt. After protesting that the ship was Cuban territory, the political officer finally ended up realizing that he would not get very far with his argument (or his Uzi), and the ship was duly arrested. The case was later settled.

The CIBC continued as the source of interesting litigation. The firm represented one of its subsidiaries, CIBC Mortgage Corporation, against one of its former senior employees, Murray Bockus, who had been involved in what was then (and most likely is still today) the biggest real estate fraud in Quebec history. Various individuals were buying and selling the same real estate several times, each time boosting the sale value with the complicity of evaluators and notaries, and ultimately mortgaging such properties up to 75 per cent of this inflated and artificial value. The firm's role was to resist (successfully) the employee's complaint of unjust dismissal.

In 1988, a class action was initiated against most, if not all, major chartered banks, including the CIBC on the heels of the Senate finance committee's findings that banks had been increasing bank charges over time without following the provisions of the *Bank Act* to notify clients in advance. The class action sought reimbursement of all such increases for the benefit of all the banks' clients, which would have amounted to several hundred million dollars and perhaps more. Each bank was represented by a separate and prestigious firm, but Stikeman Elliott, in the person of Bélanger, was designated as lead counsel to spearhead the common defensive strategy, which was successful in having the case dismissed following preliminary proceedings, all under considerable media scrutiny.

❧

The firm even tried its hand at neighbourhood relations when it represented George Petty, the founder of Repap Enterprises, in a suit against his neighbour, the owner of Future Electronics, who had installed a huge satellite dish behind his house next to Petty's property. It was a good case, and Bélanger was successful before the Quebec Court of Appeal[10] in establishing a precedent that Petty, as a resident, not just the city, had the capacity to intervene in court to enforce municipal regulations prohibiting such satellite dishes. The substance of this victory was thwarted when the neighbour erected a building enclosing his satellite dish in what would then qualify as an accessory building, which was permitted by the bylaws. As a result, Petty lost the case despite the argument that the new structure was nothing short of a scam.

During the mid-1980s, the Doucet family had been in control of, and/or working for, a Canadian company that manufactured mining equipment, *inter alia,* under licence from Litton Systems in the United States. In the aftermath of an acquisition of this company, the firm's client discovered that the family had gone into business for itself and was manufacturing the same type of equipment without a licence. Bélanger hired the services of a private investigation firm to follow the suspected individuals and discovered that they were subcontracting the work and taking possession of it only upon completion, for immediate sale thereafter. Having determined where the subcontractors were located, Bélanger prepared a writ of seizure before judgment based on intellectual property ownership of the equipment and any documents associated therewith. The seizure was effected simultaneously at the defendants' places of business and personal residences as well as at the subcontractors' places of business on a Friday evening in the winter in the middle of a snowstorm. Using four teams – each consisting of a lawyer, bailiff, and movers – to ensure that the seizures were well coordinated (starting all at the same time), heavy cranes and forty-foot flatbed trucks were moved into position to remove the seized equipment that was manufactured without a licence; all went smoothly.

One very interesting feature of this huge seizure before judgment was that upon proceeding to an arena operated by one of the defendants and searching the offices in the building next to the arena, Bélanger became intrigued by the building's architecture, which seemed to suggest that the initial use of a part of the building was not for offices. Instructing the bailiff to check for floor safes where documents could be kept, he discovered that the floor of the office beneath the carpet had a different structure from that of the rest of the structure. He instructed the bailiff to remove as much of the carpet in the office as he could, and this exposed a trap door in the false floor, covering what used to be a swimming pool next to the main structure. He climbed down into the swimming pool area and found thousands of pages of blueprints, which had been illegally copied or taken by the former employees of the client and were now being used to manufacture the equipment. Although the defendants were represented by Ogilvy Renault in the person of their most senior intellectual property partner, Nelson Landry, faced with this indisputable evidence, the case was quickly settled for the client's benefit. As in this case, there are countless instances in which by using a seizure before judgment or an injunction, the firm has been able to avoid protracted litigation and impress upon the opponent the necessity of resolving the problem immediately.

Three class actions were taken in 1991 against Solvac, now Signature Vacations, one of Canada's largest travel wholesalers, as a result of flight delays for the members of groups going on or coming back from holidays in the ill-fated days of Nationair, the bankrupt charter airline. While there is nothing extraordinary about the cases, the nature of the settlements that the firm was successful in implementing was a precedent. Historically, settlements in class actions involved the payment of a sum of money for each member of the group multiplied by the number of individuals in the group; while one could expect that not all members of the group would actually claim their damages, it was of little comfort to the defendants who settled since the unclaimed amounts were not returned to them but rather, at the direction of the court, forfeited for the benefit of a consumer protection group or other public interest group that were usually interested in the area that was the subject of the claim. In this particular case, the firm devised a settlement *in specie* – namely, granting one or two weeks free holiday at the same hotel, providing the plane tickets at no cost to all members of the group who exercised their right to such settlement, and adding a sunset provision for such right to be exercised within a period of two years. The practical result was that Solvac would have to "pay" for only those members of the group who actually claimed the benefit of the settlement. As a result, while the settlement appeared initially quite satisfactory and in fact, more generous than what could be expected by judgment, it ended up costing the client next to nothing since only a relatively low percentage of the members included in the class action actually took the offer. It was the first time that this type of class action settlement was negotiated, and it showed how creative or innovative counsel can be in search of new avenues to help clients.

In *Trottier v. Fortin et al.*, Bélanger acted in a case involving a young teenager who drowned while enrolled in a scuba diving course. His family, represented by a bâtonnier, was suing for damages. The principal point of interest was that Bélanger was recruited not for his legal skills, which were unknown to the client at the time, but because of the fact that in addition to being a litigation lawyer (albeit having never specialized in personal injury cases), he was also a scuba diver instructor and therefore had personal knowledge of the professional standards of conduct, which when applied to this case, would result in the defendant being found liable or not. In the end, following a rather difficult but successful public coroner's inquest, he was able to achieve a satisfactory settlement.

In 1993, possibly the worst propane gas tank explosion in Canadian history occurred in Warwick, Quebec in which four volunteer firemen were instantly killed and others injured. Representing Inter-City Gas (ICG, now part of Superior Propane), the gas distributor that owned the tank, Bélanger participated actively at the coroner's inquest and through expert witnesses (*inter alia* in metallurgy), he was able to show that fault rested not with the tank but primarily with the fire fighting methods that had been used, thus avoiding a major liability claim. In the normal course, ICG would not have participated at the coroner's inquest except to the extent required by subpoena, but Bélanger was able to convince them that the investment was worth it if it could result in avoiding civil suits, which would have led to much longer and more costly proceedings.

Following the introduction by Ultramar of its Valeur Plus program, which promised to match the lowest price for gas including those of independent gas retailers, which had an edge in advertising lower prices than the majors, several complaints were levied against Ultramar under the *Competition Act*. As a result, the firm represented Ultramar successfully before the Competition Bureau, which concluded that this program was perfectly legitimate. However, in the wake of this, because of the unprecedented price war that had erupted as a result of its implementation, the Quebec government, under pressure from the independent gas retailers, amended the provisions of the *Quebec Energy Board Act* to extend its jurisdiction to the price of gasoline and diesel fuels, allowing the provincial board to determine the operation's costs on a per-litre basis for gasoline retailers and to decide whether such costs would be included in a minimum floor price structure. The firm acted as lead counsel in 1996 for the first major inquiry into gasoline price control in Quebec, first representing Ultramar and then the CPPI (Canadian Petroleum Product Institute) of which most major petroleum refiners, distributors, and retailers are members. In the course of this inquiry, the firm was initially successful in avoiding a minimum price structure, which would include the operation's cost of retailing throughout Quebec.

In 1989, the firm was retained by the Paris office of Shearman & Sterling to represent their client, the Algerian government, through the Algerian Development Bank, which was being sued by CEGIR, a Quebec-based company, for amounts allegedly owing as a result of a turnkey project that had been cancelled in Algeria. While the case is still ongoing after more than ten years, one of its noteworthy features was the service by a bailiff of the initial proceedings upon the Algerian Embassy in Ottawa. The plaintiff then proceeded to obtain judgment by default for several million dollars, the purported validity of which the firm contested successfully. This may have been the first time that the Vienna Convention and the diplomatic immunity of an embassy, personnel, and grounds were ever pleaded and upheld by the Quebec Superior Court, much to the satisfaction of the Algerian Ambassador of the time.[11]

The firm represented the largest limousine company in Montreal (formerly Murray Hill Limousine Service) in its fight for survival, which included putting itself under creditor protection provisions. That in itself was fairly standard practice in such circumstances. What was exceptional in this case, however, was the fact that the protection order remained in force for some eight years without holding a single meeting and vote of the creditors. This extended period was used to pursue negotiations with creditors and to try to find a formula for restructuring, which were unsuccessful. As a result of the failure, one of the shareholders, having bought the secured debt of the CIBC for a limited amount, took over all the assets, and the company slipped into bankruptcy. In those proceedings, the firm's client, the shareholder, was able to get the assets debt-free. In the process, the firm also pleaded a constitutional case against the federally certified union, successfully arguing that the company was now under provincial jurisdiction.

In 1998, Sommer-Allibert (SA), a French conglomerate having a floor products division that was at the crossroads in terms of market efficiency, decided either to sell or make a new acquisition. It entered into negotiations to purchase the major US company in the field, Armstrong, while pursuing a parallel option consisting of selling its floor products division (which included, among other worldwide assets, a majority interest in Domco, a Quebec public company) to a German company (Tarkett) and in turn, taking a majority interest in the German company. The latter arrangement proved successful, and Armstrong, having lost the deal, decided to make a strategic challenge before the Quebec Securities Commission, alleging that the part of the selling price of this floor products division that should be allocated to the Domco shares (included in the assets sold by sa to Tarkett) resulted in a Domco share value substantially higher than the allowed percentage above market value within which there was no obligation to buy out the minority shareholders. Armstrong, which had purchased a nominal position in Domco, wanted to force sa to buy the minority shares at a substantial price, creating economic hardship for sa and thereby weakening its newly created competitor.

However, even if such were the case, which Bélanger and Pierre Raymond contested on the basis of complex business valuation evidence, they also contended that as a result of the reverse takeover effected concurrently, sa had retained "control" of such assets, and the takeover provisions of the *Securities Act* did not apply. Armstrong countered that the structure of the transaction was a scheme (or a sham) to avoid the takeover provisions. This was one of the longest and most complex cases to be heard before the Quebec Securities Commission, but it resulted in a resounding victory for sa in one of the longest decisions rendered by the commission.[12] Bélanger and Raymond acted as lead counsel on the defending side, and although the matter was taken to appeal, it was eventually dropped. This was the quintessence of pure business litigation and a prime example of close co-operation between the firm's corporate and litigation groups.

In 1998, a dispute arose between the firm's client, Impregilo-Atlas, and the Société Québécoise d'Assainissement des Eeaux (sqae) with respect to a major construction project on the south shore of the St Lawrence River, consisting mainly of digging a water interceptor with a tunnel digging machine. As a result of what it claimed was faulty geophysical data, the client encountered serious problems and experienced major cost overruns. While the matter was before the Quebec Superior Court, the firm was able to convince the court that although each party had its own experts, it might be a good thing to have a court-appointed expert who could look at the evidence and render a neutral report (which would not bind the judge but might have more persuasive influence). The court agreed, and from a short list of world-renowned experts, chose one from France. Having a court-appointed expert is relatively rare, but what made the case even more particular is that the court's expert availed himself of the very rarely used provisions of the law, allowing him to require witnesses to appear before him to question them and to review the evidence in order to prepare his report. As a result of this, after having been provided with the basic material in the file, the court-appointed expert proceeded to meet with the parties and examine witnesses from both sides in an inquiry that was held in the firm's large boardroom on the fortieth floor of the cibc building in Montreal. He produced a report sufficiently supportive of the client's position that it was possible to achieve a satisfactory settlement. It was another example of the ability to find unconventional or rare ways of dealing successfully with clients' needs.

A, B, and C v. Her Majesty the Queen is a case in which A, an rcmp informant working as an undercover agent in an operation against a high-ranking member of the Medellin cartel (having been in direct contact with the famed but ill-fated Pablo Escobar), was to testify in criminal proceedings related to drug trafficking in Montreal in respect of which he was promised protection and financial compensation by the RCMP. The issue arose when the informant also sought protection for members of his family, B and C, which the RCMP did not think was necessary. A's recourse was initiated under section 24 of the *Charter* as regards the right of A, B, and C, all Canadian citizens, to the protection of their lives, which they alleged were at risk as a result of A testifying. The matter was initially heard by the Superior Court, the Court of Appeal, and the Supreme Court of Canada on a procedural or jurisdictional issue. The Superior Court, confirmed by the Court of Appeal, dismissed the application, and the Supreme Court, by a majority decision of seven to two, allowed the appeal and remanded the matter back to the Superior Court to hear the application on the merits. What was exceptional about this case is that it was the first time a section 24 recourse was initiated to force the government to protect a witness's family and to compensate those affected for financial losses as a result of relocation, the whole incidental to criminal prosecution.

Even more exceptional was the fact that the matter was heard in camera, and by order of the Supreme Court of Canada, all the proceedings, including the judgment and the reasons for judgment, were kept sealed, with the exception of the reasons for judgment and the factums before the Supreme Court of Canada, which were released to the presiding Superior Court judge who was rehearing it. The matter was then heard by the Quebec Superior Court on a Saturday (when the courthouse was otherwise closed), thus affording the highest level of security for the witnesses appearing before the court in an in camera hearing, with the Superior Court file also sealed and the issuance of a non-disclosure order. This matter was so secret that there is no Superior Court file number. The firm was successful on the merits, the court finding that there was a risk to B and C, ordering full and adequate protection within two hours of handing down the judgment, and ordering compensation for all losses sustained as a result of coming under police protection, including the difference between the fair market value of their business and all assets disposed of or lost and any proceeds obtained from disposition of the said assets, the government having to pay the respondent's costs on a solicitor-client basis.

Bélanger was the litigation partner who, with Marc-André Coulombe, handled the Quebec litigation in the case involving the biggest hostile take-over battle in Canadian history. The firm represented Air Canada, while Davies Ward & Beck advised Onex. The latter firm was at a distinct disadvantage because its team did not understand French, the language in which the proceedings were conducted and had to retain McCarthy Tétrault, one of its competitors in Montreal, to argue its case. (This was prior to the Davies Ward merger with Phillips & Vineberg.) This had been a major effort by all segments of the firm, but the decision of the Quebec Superior Court on November 5, 1999 in *Air Canada, Claude Taylor, Christiane Brisson, and Jean-Pierre Masse v. Airline Industry Revitalization Co. Inc.*[13] put the final nail in the coffin of the takeover bid. Simon Romano from the Toronto office also assisted in the Quebec court proceedings and admired the way in which Bélanger could, in mid-argument, receive a note that raised a technical point of importance in the complex case and include it seamlessly in his submissions. The court concluded that the tender offer made by Onex was illegal under the 10 per cent restriction contained in the *Air Canada Public Participation Act,* and that brought an end to the whole matter as Onex was enjoined from proceeding any further with its bid. It was a measure of the professionalism demonstrated by counsel[14] that Mr Justice André Wery, who heard the case, went out of his way to mention the assistance he had received: "In closing, the undersigned wishes to acknowledge the work of both teams of attorneys which appeared before the Court. They took on an almost insurmountable task plagued with daunting delays. Despite the far-reaching implications of the case and the pressures of time and of media scrutiny, they were able nonetheless to present detailed and compelling submissions with consummate professionalism, in a manner which should make the legal profession proud."

Michel Décary,[15] until then the youngest person ever to hold the position of associate deputy minister of Justice of Quebec, joined the firm in 1982 as a partner to co-head the litigation department. He was recruited by Mercier, with whom he had crossed swords all the way to the Supreme Court of Canada in the nationalization of the asbestos industry case. Décary had represented the government of Quebec, and Mercier, General Dymanics. Mercier had won a major battle, convincing the Superior Court of Quebec to issue for the first time in its history an injunction against the Government of Quebec despite the Crown's immunity from the application of this prerogative remedy, which had until then been considered to be absolute. Décary, however, won the war, convincing the court that the law was valid.

Décary had also met John Sopinka in 1980 during the *Reference* case, which was initiated by the Province of Newfoundland concerning the validity of its legislation to terminate, *inter alia,* an agreement to supply Quebec with electricity from Churchill Falls at an extremely low rate. Décary represented the Government of Quebec (together with Lucien Bouchard, the future premier, and Paul-Arthur Gendreau, now a judge on the Court of Appeal of Quebec), and he remembers jogging "behind" Sopinka every morning to the top of Signal Hill in St John's and playing a few tennis matches against him during the week when the case was heard before the Court of Appeal of Newfoundland. Sopinka emerged successful, but the decision was eventually reversed by the Supreme Court of Canada, and the Newfoundland law was declared null and void.

Soon after joining the firm, Décary and Diane Marcelin-Laurin, a counsel and vice-president at Steinberg's (and today, a judge of the Quebec Superior Court), began a long battle against the Quebec Food Retailers Association and the major food retail chains at the time to cause the *Régie des permis d'alcools, loteries et courses* of Quebec to acknowledge that Steinberg's had found a loophole in the prohibition against the sale of wine and beer by food retail chains. Steinberg's had acquired and merged with the Jean-Marie Jean convenience store, which had held a licence to sell beer and wine before the prohibition affecting food retail chains came into force. Quebec consumers were happy: Steinberg's won the case, and the other major food retail chains followed suit and themselves acquired the right to sell beer and wine. Shortly thereafter, Décary, who had convinced a judge not to issue an injunction against Club Price to force the company to close its stores on Sundays at the request of the Attorney General of Quebec, was – together with Pierre Migneault, Pierre Michaud (later chief justice of Quebec), Yves Archambault, and other officers of the major Quebec retail chains – involved in a long process resulting in the revocation of the provisions prohibiting retail sales on Sundays, as set forth in the *Business Hours Act*.

In 1984, Décary and Réal Forest challenged the constitutionality of the new federal *Competition Act* on behalf of Alex Couture Ltée, a squaring business that had just acquired two of its competitors and thus had increased its share of the Quebec market to more than 75 per cent. The Court of Appeal of Quebec reversed the decision rendered by the trial judge and determined that the new law was valid. However, the stay of the merger dissolution proceedings issued by the trial judge, which was followed shortly after the Court of Appeal rendered its final decision by a settlement with the director of competition, allowed Alex Couture to continue with the merger and retain its market share.

Morris Rosenberg, who became deputy minister of Justice of Canada in 1998, was counsel for Howard Wetston, the director of Competition at the time of the *Alex Couture* case, and was in charge of selecting the lawyers responsible for possibly defending the Canada/United States Free Trade Agreement. Rosenberg asked Ian Binnie – who is now a judge at the Supreme Court of Canada but was then associate deputy minister of Justice of Canada – and Décary to head the legal team in charge of defending the first Free Trade Agreement. The case did not last long, however, as no one had thought it wise to mount a challenge to the agreement despite all the political and media fuss at the time regarding its validity and its adverse effects on the Canadian economy.

Décary was also involved in almost all of the major public inquiry boards in Quebec: the Cliche inquiry, with regard to the construction industry, where he represented the *Fédération des travailleurs du Québec*; the Keable inquiry, concerning police force actions, where he represented Commissioner Keable all the way up to the Supreme Court of Canada; Justice Albert Malouf's inquiry on the cost of the Olympic Games in Montreal, where he represented the Secretary-General of the *conseil exécutif* and the premier of Quebec; the Doyon inquiry, where he represented several parties; the Poitras inquiry on *Sûreté du Québec* officers' actions, where he represented some of the officers involved. He was also part of inquiries by coroners, the *Commission municipale de Québec,* and other governmental inquiries. In addition to these cases, Décary has acted in countless corporate, commercial, securities, and competition disputes before the courts of Quebec, the Federal Court of Canada, the Quebec Securities Commission, and various arbitrators and boards of arbitration. He has acted as a special negotiator for the Government of Quebec with regard to workforce mobility between Quebec and Ontario in the construction industry and as a special mediator in the Montreal Place des Arts conflict. He has been a Fellow of the American College of Trial Lawyers since 1993.

Richard Rusk[16] has acted on behalf of the Government of Canada in negotiations with the Quebec Cree, Inuit, and Naskapi; and the Government of Quebec and Hydro-Québec on implementation of the James Bay and Northern Quebec Agreement. He has developed a considerable expertise in environmental matters and has represented Laidlaw Inc. and certain of its officers and directors in significant environmental prosecutions, as well as Laidlaw Inc. subsidiaries and Safety-Kleen in various civil lawsuits over responsibility for one of the most significant cases of regional soil and groundwater contamination. He also represented Philip Services and certain of its officers and directors in a civil lawsuit over responsibility for soil and groundwater contamination at facilities in the Port of Quebec. He has acted on behalf of CP Hotels, seeking to block construction of a waste disposal site near its Château Montebello property. He has also acted generally as counsel on environmental matters on various projects involving environmental impact assessment studies and public hearings, including dredging of contaminated sediments and enlargement of port facilities for Cargill, remediation of contaminated sites for Laidlaw, and a wind-power electricity generation site for Kennetech. In addition, he has acted as counsel for the Government of Canada on the application of federal impact assessment procedures to James Bay hydroelectric projects.

In general litigation matters, he has represented Maruslex before the Supreme Court of Canada in litigation over the exercise of first refusal rights by a minority shareholder in a target company and Imperial Windsor Group in contesting the authority of a CEGEP to acquire certain lands. He represented Aur Resources in a dispute with Louvem Mining over control of a joint venture mining property containing substantial base metal deposits. He has also been part of the ongoing Castor Holdings litigation with Mortimer Freiheit.

Suzanne Côté[17] has earned a reputation as a tough and capable litigator and has become the head of the Montreal litigation section. Her experience has been earned across a broad range of files, many of which have been complex and hotly contested. In *QIT Fer & Titane Inc. et al. v. Commission d'Accès à l'Information et le Grand Conseil des Cris*, she was successful in preventing access to confidential electricity supply contracts between QIT and Hydro-Québec. In the case of *Jardins Lachenaie Inc. v. Mitcobell Development Limited et al.*, she shepherded a major lawsuit for our client who had been defrauded when his agents, supposedly acting on his behalf, had acquired for their own purported benefit extensive vacant real estate at the intersection of Autoroutes 40 and 640, north of Montreal. These lands had been earmarked for major development, which included expropriation by the Quebec government for a regional hospital, a Home Depot centre, and other commercial and residential development; they were, therefore, extremely valuable. The key was to get the title of the lands for our client and not to permit the defendants to limit the claim to one of damages in which the quantification of loss would have to be established. She succeeded. Acting on behalf of the former hockey star Larry Robinson, she was successful in establishing a breach of contract on the part of Restaurants Sportscene Inc., which had backed out of an agreement to build and operate a restaurant, La Cage aux Sports, and obtained damages for his share of the profits that would have accrued if the other party had honoured its word. On occasion, as a lawyer, it is necessary to draw a line in the sand, and she personally sued the union representing the employees of the City of Gaspé for defamation during the negotiations for a collective labour agreement on behalf of the city, winning both moral and exemplary damages. The case was later cited in the Supreme Court of Canada in the highly publicized (and successful) action for libel taken by Montrealer Gerald Snyder against the *Gazette* and several other papers, which had published stories claiming he was part of a "Jewish mafia." She obtained judgment confirming a $4-million finder's fee in *MNC Multinational Consultants Inc. v. Dover Corporation*, which was upheld by the Quebec Court of Appeal.

Stephen Raicek[18] has learned the better part of discretion on a number of occasions. In one file during the latter part of the 1980s, he was representing an insurance broker from the Beauce, who had been working at a brockerage agency, which he left to set up shop on his own. The brokerage agency was suing for loss of clientele that had followed our client. Raicek, who had met his client a few times in Montreal, went to Beauce, where the client came to pick him up at the airport in a truck – with a German shepherd beside him and more disturbing, five rifles in the back of the car. He explained, but did not convince Raicek, that he had just come from hunting. They proceeded to prepare for trial. Upon arrival at court, he realized as soon as things started that something was turning very wrong. As the judge walked into the courtroom, he greeted the president of the plaintiff company and his lawyer effusively. Initially, he thought it was just that they were old chums, and he did not know that the three of them played golf together only days before the trial. As his client testified, the judge sat there looking at different times either bored, disinterested, or totally disbelieving of what Raicek's client had to say. He decided to settle and did not have much to do to convince his client that that was the best strategy.

In 1985, he represented Chrysler in what seemed like a pretty obvious case. The client had noticed that a substantial number of Chrysler-stamped parts were missing from one of its depots. Eventually, after inquiry, Chrysler focused its attention on one employee, and a criminal seizure was conducted at that employee's house. There was a technical error on the seizure documents carried out by the Crown, and the seizure was declared invalid. However, the goods had been fully identified for purposes of the criminal seizure, and there was a confession from the employee, who said, *"C'est avec amertume que je dois admettre avoir volé de mon employeur Chrysler."* (It is with bitterness that I must admit having stolen from my employer Chrysler.)

Armed with these facts, Raicek proceeded to seize the parts in a civil seizure before judgment in the hands of the employee on the basis that they belonged to Chrysler. To his surprise, the employee contested the seizure and contended that the parts were his. He pleaded the seizure before Mr Justice Yvon Macerola and in the reported judgment, the judge accepted the argument that in fact, Chrysler was prima facie owner of the parts, successful proof having been made of its clear right of ownership. The judge did not accept the argument by the employee that the confession was somehow improperly extracted or that Chrysler could not establish its ownership right.

The seizure remained in force, and because the employee did not give up his claim, Chrysler was forced after a delay of eighteen months to have it made final along with a judicial declaration that Chrysler was the legal owner of the parts and for damages. The judge on this occasion was Mr Justice Philip Cutler, who heard essentially the same proof as had Mr Justice Macerola at the preliminary stage – namely, Chrysler's right of ownership and the seizure of the goods in the garage of the employee. At trial, the employee's wife stood up and said that the confession had been (somehow) extracted from her husband and that her children were crying as a result of the presence of the police officers. The employee stood up and said that he had never taken the parts from Chrysler, but that he had in fact bought each one of the thousands of parts from friends.

Much to his surprise and shock, Mr Justice Cutler started giving Raicek a most difficult time, talking about how huge companies attempt to force their will over "the little guy." Much discouraged after one of many difficult days in court, Raicek encountered Jim Robb on the elevator, who asked why he looked so dejected. Raicek explained that he was representing Chrysler and the bizarre circumstances he was facing in court. Robb told him that the judge had been a well-known labour lawyer prior to his appointment and had often represented unions against large companies. Not only had he a predilection for the little guy, but Robb, who had also represented Chrysler over the years, remembered that Justice Cutler had been involved in some personal litigation against Chrysler. Upon verification, Raicek discovered that the judge had indeed sued Chrysler for a defective car but had never indicated to the parties in the case before him that he had acted against Chrysler. Clearly, this required some action – namely, a motion to recuse the judge but since this was an extremely serious step, he consulted not only the client but all the senior partners in the litigation section. They agreed that he should make the motion but that he should as a matter of professional courtesy first inform the judge that he was going to make it and only then present it. As a lawyer with three years' experience, Raicek was understandably nervous but proceeded nevertheless. As is the custom with motions for recusation, the proceedings stopped immediately, and the motion was referred to the chief justice for adjudication.

The trial had adjourned in the spring, and the motion was put off until November. During the summer, Mr Justice Cutler died of a heart attack. In the circumstances, all the proceedings that had gone on in front of him were rendered moot, and the trial would have to be continued before another judge. Because the motion was still outstanding, Raicek did appear that November in front of Chief Justice Alan Gold, who after fifteen minutes of praising the deceased judge, referred the matter to another judge. The defendant must have decided that his luck had run out and settled the claim, with Chrysler getting its parts back and the employee becoming an unlamented ex-employee.

Marc-André Coulombe,[19] one of the younger litigation partners, recalls a case in which he was involved with Freiheit. In this case, the firm had been engaged by a businessman in the context of a fight between two brothers. They both owned 50 per cent of a large real estate company but had stopped speaking to each other some ten years previously. As the only feasible solution to the standoff, the company had been ordered to be liquidated, and one of the major accounting firms was appointed as liquidator. The process was very slow, which did not stop the liquidator from collecting healthy monthly payments. The brother had decided that this leisurely and costly process should come to an end. Freiheit and Coulombe appeared in court before Mr Justice Pierre Michaud (who was sitting at the time in the Superior Court of Quebec) to announce that there was a change of attorneys, and the gloves then came off in the liquidation process. After a few months of fighting, the brothers finally agreed on a division of the properties, which terminated the liquidator's role and the blank cheque on which it had come to rely. On a human perspective, the two brothers spoke for the first time in ten years. Our client said to his brother, "You're drunk, again!" It would require asbestos pages to print the brother's reply.

Coulombe was involved in a case that proved that size was not everything. The firm had been retained by an individual who had built a very successful business in the telecommunications industry. The client had been a Holocaust survivor who had fought for the creation of the state of Israel and had done some work for the Israeli secret service. To say he was tough is to understate the situation. He was being sued by a former partner who had left the business before it became profitable and sold his share to our client, although the paperwork evidencing the sale was somewhat deficient. The former partner, now that there was a successful business, was much more interested and sued to be declared owner of one-half of the business. As part of the pretrial process, we asked to examine the plaintiff on discovery at the courthouse at which our client also attended. The client was about five feet one inch tall, while the plaintiff was six foot two. For some reason, the plaintiff was terrified of our client and was shaking throughout the discovery. The examination was interrupted by a bomb threat, which was phoned in, and the courthouse was evacuated. Our client did not leave, explaining that from his personal experience, people who place real bombs do not generally call to warn the intended victims. The plaintiff, however, left as soon as the warning was given and refused to come back in. Not only that, he abandoned the entire proceedings shortly thereafter.

The firm learned the advantage of keeping things simple when we were retained by Unvala Limited, a UK company operated by a Cambridge engineer, Dr Bhikhu Unvala. He had developed a sophisticated device to monitor the existence and growth of microscopic cracks on the wings of combat aircraft. He had sold a prototype of the device to a Canadian company and then continued to develop even more sophisticated versions. The Canadian company had sued to obtain the intellectual property rights to the more advanced prototypes. The matter was referred to an arbitrator, and more than a month was spent fighting over the differences between each prototype, using very sophisticated experts for the purpose including Unvala himself and one of his students (who had himself obtained a doctorate from MIT and was in charge of surveying metal fatigue in the propellers of nuclear submarines). After three weeks, it was clear that the arbitrator was having a difficult time (not without reason) grasping all the scientific details. However, Unvala gathered from something the arbitrator said that he had some interest in stereos, and he switched his approach by comparing the difference between the prototypes to two different kinds of home stereos. The case was won on the basis of that analogy.

Rounding out the team of senior litigators in the Montreal office are Marc Laurin,[20] Monique Lussier,[21] Jean Fontaine,[22] and Yves Martineau,[23] who are assisted by a young group of lawyers already carving out their own reputations in the field. One of the reasons the litigation group has grown to be so capable is that the firm has always given a lot of leeway to the young, up-and-coming litigators to allow them to push themselves to their limits and then beyond. As such, it has regularly sent young lawyers against much more experienced counsel, very often successfully. When the firm's young litigators were already pleading before the Superior Court, the Court of Appeal, and occasionally the Supreme Court of Canada, lawyers from other firms with the same seniority were merely acting as second chair (often silent) to a more experienced lead counsel. The litigation group has been very active before judicial courts, administrative tribunals, and arbitration boards, both at the provincial and federal levels. In so doing, some specialized and others did not, instead becoming trial lawyers willing and able to take cases to court in various fields of law, all of which has led to developing a wide range of expertise.

LITIGATION IN TORONTO

Significant litigation in the Toronto office began with the arrival of John Sopinka. Prior to this event, not even the most ardent booster of the firm could make any case for the Toronto office as a centre of meaningful civil litigation, notwithstanding the occasional forays of Don Bowman outside his specialty of tax litigation. Until 1978, Stikeman Elliott had virtually no presence let alone profile for litigation in the Toronto legal community. It was simply seen as a tax firm. In the mid-1970s, a law student applied to the firm for an articling position, and when asked about his area of interest, he indicated litigation. He was then advised that Stikeman Elliott did not do litigation in Toronto, and the balance of the interview was devoted to a lively discussion of sailing. Sopinka came as a known quantity, already recognized as one of the leading counsel before the Ontario courts, and set out to establish himself as the head of a major litigation group, with a great start by bringing Sid Lederman with him.

Sopinka left Fasken & Calvin in 1977 to join the firm – then still known as Stikeman, Elliott, Robarts & Bowman – and start a litigation department in Toronto. His defection took the Toronto legal community by surprise because Faskens had a reputation as one of the leading litigation firms in the city. There, Walter Williston was at the pinnacle of his career and had developed a number of proteges, including Sopinka and Ronald Rolls, who were breaking into the top ranks of senior counsel. Sopinka had become one of the top counsel in the city and had been attracting appellate briefs from other counsel across Ontario. He left Faskens to be able to control the development of his own litigation department and to escape the infighting that had been apparent at Faskens, even to the articling students. Wanting to start afresh, Sopinka did not bring any Fasken juniors with him, although he was able to entice one of his former juniors, Sidney Lederman, to join him. Lederman had been at Faskens for a couple of years before leaving the rigours of practice to become a professor at the Osgoode Hall law school at York University, having always had an interest in academic matters. Lederman was a natural choice for Sopinka to call on since in 1974, they had co-authored and published a textbook on the law of evidence in civil cases, and Sopinka had also taught at Osgoode Hall from 1974 to 1982, so they were in regular contact. This text had become a bestseller within the Canadian legal community, and it also helped propel Sopinka's career to even greater heights. Sopinka called him and said he was going to go to Stikeman Elliott, of which Lederman knew nothing, but he did not relish the thought of running a practice entirely on his own. Lederman was by then ready to give up full-time teaching, and the idea of working with Sopinka was very appealing. He asked whether the Stikeman Elliott people wanted to meet him. Sopinka said he was not sure, but that it should be no problem.

It remained only to consolidate his reputation, to attract as many cases as he could in the process, and to recruit young litigators who could assist him and grow into senior counsel in their own right. John Judge[24] had articled at Fasken & Calvin, where he had worked with Sopinka on a wide range of files. After his call to the Bar in 1977, he worked for a small firm, Carson Poultney, since Faskens had decided not to hire back anyone in litigation at that time. John Carson was the son of the renown counsel Cyril Carson, but he had broken away from Tilley Carson to establish the small boutique litigation firm. Shortly after his start at Carson Poultney, Judge learned of the strategic decision at Stikeman Elliott to start practising "real law," as Stikeman would later put it, by bringing in a serious litigator.

By the spring of 1978, Sopinka was busy on a number of high-profile briefs. He and Lederman recognized that they had more work than the two of them could handle, and that summer, they decided to expand the Toronto litigation department. In June 1978, Judge received a message that Sopinka was trying to reach him, and they traded calls over the next few weeks but never made contact. He then learned that Robert Reuter, a classmate at the University of Toronto who had clerked at the Ontario Court of Appeal, had been hired at Stikeman Elliott, and it appeared that his opportunity to join Sopinka had slipped by. To his surprise, in August, Sopinka again contacted

him for a game of tennis, which turned out to be an interview. Sopinka loved
to arrange meetings over a tennis or squash match. Just as he loved to win
his cases in court, he also loved to win on the tennis court, and that day,
Sopinka won the game of tennis; Judge also appeared to pass the interview.[25]
After Lederman met Judge, it was determined that he would become the
next member of the Stikeman Elliott litigation department, and he joined
on November 1, 1978, immediately after returning from his honeymoon.
Judge was the fourth member of the Toronto litigation department and only
the twenty-first member of the Toronto office.

Following Judge's arrival in late 1978, Sopinka brought in one last lateral
hire, Jan Weir. He was hired to develop the Toronto litigation group more
fully, but specifically, to work with Sopinka on a major criminal trial. This
trial started the same fall that Sopinka was also working with François
Mercier from the Montreal office. Weir had been called to the Ontario Bar
in 1974 and was somewhat more senior than either Reuter or Judge, so he
was able to add more depth to the department. Following Weir's arrival, the
litigation department grew slowly but steadily and followed the practice of
growing internally by hiring the articling students. These included Kathryn
Chalmers and Bruce Pollock[26] in 1980, Don Houston in 1981, Peter Howard
in 1982, David Brown[27] in 1983, Patrick O'Kelly[28] in 1984, Sean Dunphy[29]
in 1985, and Doug Harrison[30] in 1988. Sopinka arranged for two lateral
hires shortly before his elevation to the Supreme Court of Canada. David
Byers,[31] the present head of the litigation department, and Katherine Kay[32]
joined that year. Of the current Toronto litigation partners, all but two were
at the firm while Sopinka was the head of the Toronto litigation department.
Liz Pillon,[33] who was made a partner in 2000, and Eliot Kolers,[34] who made
it the following year, are the only partners in the department who did not
have an opportunity to work with Sopinka.

Lederman recalls an amusing incident with Jan Weir, who came into his
office on a Monday morning to ask if he could speak with him. Lederman
said he could. Weir closed the door and said, "Sid, I got married over the
weekend." Lederman told him not to worry and proceeded to give him all the
legal arguments that could be developed in order to get out of the situation.
"No," said Weir. "I wanted to get married." "You did?" asked Lederman.
"Yes." "Well, then, congratulations."

David Brown's most vivid litigation memory of his articling rotation was
assisting the two senior litigators, Sopinka and Lederman, on the contested
takeover of Turbo Resources when the firm acted for Genstar. As the takeover bid proceeded, an injunction was brought to restrain the bid. He recalls
the two leaders working furiously on the matter because Mr Justice Walsh,
a judge with family law experience, was going to hear the motion for an
interlocutory injunction on a Friday evening. When they appeared before
Justice Walsh, Sopinka stood up even before the argument got under way
to propose some interim terms that would effectively allow our client to do
what it wanted to do but would avoid the prospect of a full-blown injunction.
Sopinka's submission of the terms completely took the wind out of the other
side's sails and disposed Walsh toward his position from the start.

Following his call to the Bar, Brown began working as an associate in the litigation department in April 1983. He became involved in fascinating cases from the beginning. One involved acting for the Bank of Montreal. Bryce Mackassey, the former Liberal cabinet minister, was the subject of a parliamentary investigation into whether or not he had abused his position to obtain favourable treatment. The matter involved a suggestion that he was somehow able to obtain a reduction or an elimination of a debt that he owed to the Bank of Montreal. The Bank of Montreal senior officials were horrified by the publicity and any suggestion that they were engaged in wrongdoing. The firm had to prepare them for a hearing before a committee of the House of Commons, which involved extensive research into some of the finer points of parliamentary privilege and procedure. In the result, the bank did not suffer any damage from the parliamentary inquiry nor the subsequent criminal charges that were brought against Mackassey. Sopinka, who had a taste for "statement" cars including a pink Cadillac of his own, which he drove with great flourish enjoyed driving around with one of the Bank of Montreal's senior vice-presidents in the banker's flashy sports car. Brown also remembers embarrassing Sopinka at a dinner with the client at the old Four Seasons Hotel in Ottawa when he dared to order a glass of milk during dinner – a cub wet-behind-the-ears offence.

The Hamilton dredging affair involving Marine Industries, for whom Sopinka acted with François Mercier of the Montreal office, was a criminal conspiracy bid rigging trial. It was marked as one of the longest criminal trials of its day and eventually found its way to the Supreme Court of Canada on issues relating to corporate liability for criminal conduct.[35] One of the Crown attorneys who has since been appointed to the bench still recalls the incredible talents of Sopinka arguing in the Ontario Court of Appeal and then the Supreme Court of Canada to develop new law on the issues of corporate responsibility for criminal conduct.

The *Hydro-Québec-Churchill Falls* case was a matter of Newfoundland trying to get more electrical power from the Churchill Falls installation, which it could then sell to Hydro-Québec, whereas Hydro-Québec said that it could not take any more power than had been originally contracted for. There were several collateral issues in the complicated matter, including the tail race tunnel. The trial took ninety-nine days, and the Newfoundland government lost. Its response was to enact a *Water Rights Reversion Act* to in effect take back the falls. Sopinka and Chalmers represented Churchill Falls, in which the government was a major shareholder, but they had to be careful that they only argued on the basis of the interests of the client that was party to the proceedings. We argued that the provision was unconstitutional. The Newfoundland government then instituted a reference case to the Newfoundland Court of Appeal, which perhaps, not unsurprisingly, found the enactment to be constitutional. This led to the inevitable appeal to the Supreme Court of Canada, where it was held to be unconstitutional.

Sopinka's national reputation was established as a result of his actions on behalf of Susan Nelles, a registered nurse at the Hospital for Sick Children, who in 1981 had been charged with four counts of murder on the basis that she was alleged to have poisoned four young patients in the cardiac ward with the drug digoxin. Nelles's preliminary inquiry on the criminal charge was coming to an end just as Brown was beginning to work at the firm as an associate. Jan Weir was contacted by Austin Cooper, Nelles's counsel in the criminal proceedings, who was forming the view that Justice Vanek was going to discharge his client at the end of the preliminary inquiry. Weir got Sopinka involved because Cooper thought some consideration should be given to a civil malicious prosecution action against the police and the Crown because her reputation had been severely damaged and her family harmed as a result of the charges and related publicity. Cooper proved to be correct in his assessment, and after she was discharged, Nelles came up to the firm's office. It was cloak-and-dagger stuff. By then, her face was known throughout the country, and to avoid publicity, she came up through the freight elevator. She had a brief meeting with Sopinka and Brown, following which Brown was sent to do research to prepare a statement of claim in the malicious prosecution action.[36]

From the purely legal point of view, the case set a precedent. Once the firm had filed the action, the Attorney General of Ontario brought a motion to strike out the statement of claim, arguing that an action for malicious prosecution could not be brought against a Crown attorney prosecuting a criminal case. The Attorney General asserted a principle of absolute immunity from suit. The court ruled in favour of this argument in the first instance and also in the Ontario Court of Appeal. They were, however, granted leave to appeal to the Supreme Court of Canada, and there they succeeded.[37] Although Brown had been with Sopinka at the Supreme Court on two previous occasions, this was the first time he had a piece of the argument, and it served to develop a lifelong love for standing at that podium. The case established an important principle of Crown liability.

A few weeks after the claim for malicious prosecution had been filed, Sopinka said to Brown in a taxi on the way to the MacKassey committee hearing in Ottawa that he had a case in which he thought Brown might be interested. Sopinka had learned that the Ontario government was appointing Mr Justice Grange to conduct a public inquiry into the deaths that had taken place at the Hospital for Sick Children and into the circumstances surrounding the prosecution of Susan Nelles. Brown spent the next year and a half as a junior for Sopinka at the Grange inquiry, which had several interesting features – some personal, some professional. On a personal note, it was the first opportunity for Brown to work extensively with Sopinka, who was a fabulous mentor and gave Brown as much responsibility as he was prepared to assume. As a result, Brown attended all of the 180-odd days of hearing before Justice Grange, while Sopinka was there for only about eight or ten. Naturally, those were the most important dates, but he was extraordinarily supportive in allowing Brown to conduct most of the examinations and cross-examinations, notwithstanding that he was fresh out of law school. Brown will never forget one day when he was engaged in a heated argument before Justice Grange with the arch-enemy, counsel for the Metropolitan Toronto Police. After the lawyers had said their piece, Brown sat down at the counsel table, and Justice Grange made his ruling. Thirty seconds later, Sopinka slipped into the seat beside him and said, "good argument." Brown asked him how he would know since he thought he had just come from the airport from a trip out West. Sopinka said that in fact, for the last thirty minutes, he had been in the TV room watching him conduct the argument on the television monitors. With support like that from one's senior, it was easy to see how Sopinka not only instilled great confidence in his juniors, but great loyalty as well.

On the professional front, there were several highlights during the inquiry, most involving Sopinka, but one including Brown. Certainly, the climax of the whole inquiry was Nelles's first attendance to testify in the phase dealing with the death of the children at the hospital. Sopinka had negotiated a deal with commission counsel in which they would step down to allow Sopinka, as her counsel, to conduct the first examination-in-chief of Nelles. The day of her testimony was memorable, with Sopinka bustling around the tribunal room acting like a protective father toward Nelles, complete with affectionate hugs around the shoulder and other demonstrations of support. When his examination-in-chief began, you could cut the air with a knife. He spent the first twenty minutes of it going through her background, painting her for what she was – a young woman who had grown up in a small town in Ontario and had only recently moved to the big city. With that by way of background, he then immediately proceeded to ask her three questions. They were all variations on the same theme: "Did you kill the children?" She answered "no" to each, and by the time she had uttered the third "no," they could feel the tension leaving the room. From then on, it was a virtual love-in between Mr Justice Grange and Nelles.[38]

The second highlight involving Sopinka was his cross-examination of Tony Warr, one of the two homicide detectives who arrested Nelles. Sopinka questioned Warr for an hour before a luncheon break, and it was obvious from the signals that Justice Grange was giving that he wanted Sopinka to show Warr some mercy, but Sopinka was relentless. At lunch, he commented that cross-examining Warr was like shooting fish in a barrel, and after the break, Grange brought an end to Warr's misery and politely but firmly moved Sopinka on to a conclusion of his cross-examination.

The third highlight, the one involving Brown, was memorialized in Sarah Spink's book about the Grange inquiry, called *Cardiac Arrest*.[39] Simply put, Brown came to the defence of a fellow lawyer when no one else would. Fran Kiteley, now Madam Justice Kiteley of the Superior Court of Justice, was among the lawyers acting for the Registered Nurses Association, one of the parties at the hearing. Grange had asked counsel, at an in camera portion of the proceedings, not to discuss a certain matter publicly. A day or two after he made that request, Kiteley gave a speech at a convention of her client, the Registered Nurses Association of Ontario. The speech made the press the following day, and Doug Hunt, counsel for the Attorney General who appeared to have had no love for the Registered Nurses Association or Kiteley, immediately brought the matter to Grange's attention. Grange decided that he would hold a mini "show-cause" hearing into Kiteley's conduct. As the hearing proceeded, every male lawyer in the room stood up and condemned Kiteley's conduct. Every male lawyer, that was, except Brown. Being a great lover of freedom of expression, Brown went to bat for Kiteley, and he likes to think that he was able to mollify Grange to the point that he just gave Kitely a gentle rap on the knuckles instead of a potentially more serious sanction.

In his final report, Grange concluded that there were a number of suspicious deaths at the hospital, some of which were probably murders, but he effectively exonerated Nelles and recommended that the Attorney General make an *ex gratia* payment to her. There were meetings with both Robert Welch and Ian Scott, the Attorneys General over the period. It took a while, but they ultimately negotiated compensation for Nelles, which was one of the first such payments for wrongful prosecution in Canadian history.

During the *Nelles* case, Brown also learned the hard way about the perils of dealing with the media. Nelles's action for malicious prosecution had not been the first such action brought in Ontario. Quite by coincidence, there were two others that had been commenced around the same time. One of them, *Richmond*, had also attracted a motion by the Attorney General to strike out the statement of claim. On the day the *Richmond* decision came out, Brown happened to be at the court on some other matter. As he was walking down the hall, he heard two people talking about the *Richmond* decision, which had just been rendered. Curiosity got the better of him, so he walked over and asked them what the result had been. It turned out that the two of them were reporters. Being the naive first-year lawyer that he was, he started to chat away to the reporters about the implications of the *Richmond* decision and how it might affect Nelles's case.

The next day, Sopinka was up in Ottawa. The headline story on the front page of the *Globe and Mail* dealt with the *Richmond* decision and its implications on the *Nelles* case, and Brown was liberally quoted. By 9:15 AM, Vivian Prus, Sopinka's secretary, had walked into Brown's office and handed him a three-sentence memo from Sopinka, dictated from Ottawa. The memo essentially said: "Who the hell are you to talk to the press? Our client must be thrilled to learn about our strategy from the press. Do not speak to the press." Brown spent the rest of the day in absolute terror waiting for Sopinka's return around 4:30 PM. As he made the walk down the hall to Sopinka's office, Lederman fell in behind him with a big grin on his face. Sopinka duly chastised Brown, told him never to trust reporters, and to learn from the lesson. Typical Sopinka.

The Nelles file generated a host of requests for Sopinka to act in other matters. There were dozens of telephone messages every day, and he would assign juniors in the litigation department to follow up and to decide whether the firm should take on the cases – to add to the reputation of the firm in the litigation field.

The Sinclair Stevens inquiry arose out of political swirling around the House of Commons regarding involvement of Stevens's wife, Noreen, with Frank Stronach and others. Deputy Prime Minister Eric Neilsen, who dealt with possible situations of conflict, probably could have nipped the entire thing in the bud, but he was resolutely not saying anything (he was nicknamed Velcro Mouth), and the media and the opposition leaped all over the issue and were making a big deal about it. The involvements included those of Noreen Stevens (who had separate counsel) with Magna and other companies such as Hyundai. Kathryn Chalmers is convinced that if Eric Neilsen had simply mentioned Noreen's involvement with Stronach, there would have been no problem. There were also what they came to refer to as "Sinc's warts," a whole bunch of offbeat projects such as the proposal for a Christ coin development with some New York bank. Sopinka's only advice to Stevens was that whatever he did, he must not let the matter turn into a Royal Commission. Faint hope. The commissioner was Mr Justice William Parker, who was armed with a full battery of lawyers, accountants, and other experts. The commission counsel were David Scott, Marlys Edwardh (a criminal lawyer), and Ed Belobaba. There was ongoing tension as to their role. If the purpose of commission counsel was to present all facts fairly to the commissioner, that was one thing, but if it was a prosecution, then Parker should not have been in consultation with counsel. He seemed to be in betwixt and between. The matter lasted for months.

Near the beginning of the whole process, they learned that Sinclair had a long-time loyal secretary who unbeknownst to pretty well everyone, had kept detailed diaries of everything that had occurred. She had them in Boots (the British drugstore chain that was then operating in Canada) plastic bags, which they ended up referring to as "BB1, BB2," etc. (which stood for Boots bag number one, number two, etc.). Chalmers and a student got into some locked closets where these bags were stored and tried to read the documents by flashlight since there was, they suspected, a search warrant out for the documents, and they wanted to see what was in them before they were seized. It was these diaries that gave everybody full notice of all of "Sinc's warts." Chalmers remembers an occasion, while preparing to deal with either evidence or argument on the warts, on which Stevens wanted to go to the Royal Winter Fair with Noreen and asked her if she could look after the matter of the warts while they went to the event, only to have Chalmers say that they were his warts, and he should stay with them and work on the problem. Also, Sinclair apparently asked Chalmers, who was putting in sixteen-hour days representing him before his inquiry, to bake some better muffins for him as he did not like the ones served in the office boardroom. It seems he genuinely expected that being a woman, she would be delighted to ensure that his tummy was content. However, he still continued to ingest the boardroom muffins when she refused.

In and around the Stevens matter, there arose the only serious issue that strained the relationship between Sopinka and Elliott. Sopinka had a view that counsel should be completely independent, even to some extent from the firm of which he was a partner. He had separate letterhead prepared for himself that simply described him as "counsel" to the firm, almost as if he were a sole practitioner attached to the firm. In May 1986, he issued an opinion on this letterhead, advising Sinclair and Noreen Stevens that their acts did not constitute a breach of the conflict of interest and post-employment code for public office holders or predecessor guidelines. Stevens produced this letter in public, and it came to the attention of Elliott, who was furious, saying in essence that either Sopinka was a partner of the firm, as all the other partners, or he was not, and he could decide where else he might like to practise. Sopinka did not use the letterhead after that, but he had sharp elbows and a determination to run the litigation department his own way, with no interference from the other sections of the firm.

Reflecting on Sopinka and his style, Lederman says that the loyalty he engendered from his juniors was absolute. They could relate to him but without the slightest diminution in their respect for him and his abilities, and he could squeeze more production out of himself and the juniors by asking for identification of the issues and what it would take to win on each one before a court. He was always ready to delegate work, and the fact that it came from Sopinka made them do their best to live up to his expectations. The process was one of extraordinary mentoring from which he never remained the slightest bit aloof. In every case, the juniors got a witness and part of the argument. The courts liked him because of his ability to simplify the issues and get right to the crucial point. Lederman remembers a securities case in which the other side had produced enormous binders of documentation that all but overwhelmed the presiding judge. The judge turned to Sopinka and said, "Mr Sopinka, I do not seem to have anything from you." Sopinka replied, "My Lord, all you really have to look at is this document." He could pare down every case to the barest of essentials. Working with Sopinka was almost enough in itself. He knew exactly where he was in his profession.

Jim Grant remembers the occasion when the firm's management committee had decided that more resources were required for the Toronto litigation department. He went to Toronto and invited Sopinka for dinner to discuss the situation. He spent some time discussing the idea that as the department head, he should adopt the principle that Stikeman and Elliott had long espoused – namely, that he should attempt to surround himself with people who were as bright as or brighter than he was. Sopinka's response was, "That may be easy for you, Jim, but it certainly won't be easy for me."

Lederman had his share of media exposure as well. In January 1987, he was retained by Ivan Fleischmann, an Ontario Liberal Party fundraiser and lobbyist who believed he had been defamed by Phil Gillies, a sitting Tory MPP. Brown and Harrison worked with him on the file and duly drafted a statement of claim. Harrison recalls having to spend time scouring Hansard to determine whether the statements at issue, which had appeared in the *Toronto Sun,* had been made inside (where he would be protected by parliamentary privilege) or outside the House. When it was ready, they then put the statement of claim in the hands of a process server, with instructions to serve Gillies at his legislative office.

The process server spoke to Gillies's executive assistant, who said he was in a committee meeting, to which the process server replied that he would wait until the end of the meeting. Later, the executive assistant informed the process server that the committee members were on a break and that he could give it to him at that time. Unfortunately, the process server agreed. He went to the committee room as directed and let Gillies know that he was there. Gillies went to the back of the committee room and was duly served with the statement of claim. As soon as he got the document in his hands, Gillies proceeded to the front of the committee room, called the session to order, and immediately launched into a diatribe to the effect that his parliamentary privilege had just been violated because he had been served within the inner sanctum of the legislature, possibly the greatest assault on parliamentary democracy in history.

A great brouhaha ensued. The legislature's privileges committee called an inquiry, and Lederman was summoned to testify to explain his conduct and the incipient fall of the nation as a result of this extraordinary breach of parliamentary immunity. Sopinka acted for Lederman and was able to turn the inquiry into a complete non-event. Nevertheless, as a result of that inquiry, the Ontario Legislature passed an amendment to the *Legislative Assembly Act,* which specified where service could and could not be made on a member of the provincial parliament. Within the firm, this is still referred to as the "Lederman amendment."

In the days leading up to Desert Storm in 1989, Lederman got a call from someone who said he had information that an Iraqi minister wanted to defect. The caller wanted to know who he should call. Lederman said he had no idea, but that Allan Gotlieb might know based on his extensive government experience. They decided they should call Raymond Chrétien in Ottawa for advice and gave him the name of the official. Chrétien replied that the government was already aware of the case and had been in touch with the Canadian embassy in Vienna on the matter. He thanked them for the call, and that was the end of the conversation. The following week, the media were filled with stories that Lederman, Sopinka, and Stikeman Elliott were responsible for using influence to get the individual (Marshat) to the head of the immigration queue.

In May 1986, Sopinka was counsel to the Ukrainian Canadian Committee, appearing before the Commission of Inquiry on War Criminals, presided over by Jules Deschênes. His specific role was to cast doubt on the Soviet propaganda directed at Ukrainians generally by exposing the political bias that made any evidence obtained from Soviet sources unreliable as to what role, if any, the Ukrainians might have played in war crimes. It was important to the Ukrainian community that Sopinka, one of their own, be their counsel. He was assisted by Sean Dunphy and Kathryn Chalmers, although Chalmers acknowledges that she did not have too much to do with the commission other than to deal with a person who was convinced that the Soviets had put a transmitter in his head and was forever breaking into places to try and find out where the main transmitter was located.

Sopinka acted for the Ontario Human Rights Commission, which was expanding its mandate and becoming very active in promoting human rights. As a result, the firm acted on a wide array of challenging high-profile cases, frequently involving government as a respondent. The human rights cases included *Jamie Bone v. The Canadian Football League and the Hamilton Tiger Cats; Simpsons-Sears v. O'Mally; Baseo and the Ontario Human Rights Commission v. The Ontario Rural Softball Association; Karumanchiri and Ontario Human Rights Commission v. The Liquor Control Board of Ontario;* and a host of other Human Rights Commission cases.

The Ontario Human Rights Commission and Jamie Bone v. The Hamilton Tiger Cats[40] was a human rights case that attracted national attention in 1979. Sopinka, with Judge as his junior, was acting on a complaint by a Canadian college quarterback from the University of Western Ontario, Jamie Bone, who complained that the designated import rule in the Canadian Football League (CFL) operated to discriminate against Canadian quarterbacks. This case illustrated Sopinka's method of operating – giving tremendous responsibility to the junior on the case. While Sopinka focused on the legal argument regarding the designated import rule, Judge had the task of organizing the evidence of witnesses from a host of Canadian quarterbacks who played in the CFL, including the likes of Gerry Datilio of the Montreal Alouettes. These Canadian quarterbacks all had evidence as to how their Canadian citizenship was a handicap in light of this rule. One Canadian quarterback who refused to participate was Russ Jackson, one of the greatest of all time. His view was very simple: Canadian quarterbacks were not good enough.

Judge called a number of quarterbacks to prove that the bias was simply wrong. In any event, the week-long hearing attracted national media attention. They eventually had difficulty overturning the designated import rule, which the board of inquiry upheld as not inherently discriminatory. However, they succeeded in proving actual discrimination in the circumstances by reason of the fact that Jamie Bone was not given a fair tryout. They proved that the coaching staff of the Hamilton Tiger Cats had actively discriminated against Canadians and operated on assumed biases in favour of American quarterbacks. This evidence came out when Sopinka, himself a former CFL football player, cross-examined Coach Tom Demitrioff. Demitrioff never recovered from the first question on cross-examination when John Sopinka asked him "Who do you think is faster: an American or a Canadian?" Demitrioff danced around that question, changing his mind three or four times, all of which went on to prove the client's case.

Another interesting and landmark human rights case the firm had in the 1980s was *Karumanchiri v. The Liquor Control Board of Ontario.*[41] In this case, Sopinka and John Judge established a novel proposition within the Commonwealth on human rights issues whereby if someone had been discriminated against in being refused a promotion, a board of inquiry could remove the successful candidate and order that the party discriminated against be given the position. Karumanchiri was a scientist who analysed wines and spirits sold in Ontario to ensure that there were no toxins in the products. He became world-famous when he discovered the presence of glycol in certain French wines, a substance that had been improperly used by certain vintners. On the retirement of the head of the Ontario LCBO laboratory, he applied for that position and was eminently qualified. However, he was passed over by an old boys' network within the LCBO, which promoted a lesser-qualified but white technician. After a lengthy battle, the board of inquiry agreed with the firm's position, finding that there was a subtle but insidious discrimination, giving Karumanchiri the promotion and one of the largest human rights awards ever granted – approximately $150,000.

The Supreme Court of Canada's decision in *Simpsons-Sears v. O'Malley*[42] stands as one of Sopinka's most significant contributions to the development of human rights. In this case, the Supreme Court of Canada decided that a respondent may be found responsible for discrimination even though there is no intention to discriminate if its conduct had the effect of causing discrimination. The concept was known as "constructive discrimination."

The Pope and CPR case was very well known. It was one of the largest cases that went to trial on the rights of dissenting minority shareholders and the peculiarities of rights of the defunct Ontario & Quebec Railway (O&Q) in relation to CPR, and it made its way to the Supreme Court of Canada. The issue was the legal effect of certain leases granted by O&Q to the CPR in connection with some of its lines during the previous century. O&Q took the view that they were only leases and that since CPR was merely a lessee, it was not entitled to sell the properties. Pope had bought stock in O&Q, which still existed as a public company, although the market had shown minimal interest in it and the stock had little value. Pope believed that if it could be established that O&Q owned the properties that the CPR had sold or that were still governed by the O&Q leases, the value of the stock would be considerably greater. One of the Montreal office clients, investment counsellor Richard Lafferty, espoused the case and went so far as to support the costs of the litigation. The question was what exactly had been given under the terms of the leases. The stakes were enormous, and the implications for the CPR were potentially disastrous. The trial before Mr Justice Hughes took almost a year, and under Sopinka's leadership, the Pope interests were successful. The O&Q shares increased in value from approximately $100 to $35,000 per share. The judgment was appealed, and Chalmers's involvement occurred at that level. The hearings took some five weeks in the Court of Appeal, and there, Pope was unsuccessful.

Pope was a very unusual character and always wanted the originals of all documents. The firm was allowed to make copies of them, but he had to have the originals . He once sent back a message that he did not want any of the firm's "ink-stained clerks" to have any of the original documents. When it was announced that the decision would be issued by the Court of Appeal, Sopinka was in Florida on holidays. The decision was to be released by the court after the close of the stock market that day. Chalmers was instructed by the court that she was not to tell the client, and that she was to appear at 4:30 to receive the judgment. She called Sopinka in Florida to find out what should be done because she had a responsibility to the client, but as an officer of the court, she was faced with a particular order. They agreed that she would go to court and that she would dial all but the last digit of Pope's phone number, and the moment the judgment had been issued, she would dial the last digit. When this happened, Pope did not say anything but simply dropped the phone. Moments later, when Chalmers went downstairs, she saw him running to court through the streets to get the original judgment. He burst into Osgoode Hall and ran past her, and because it was clear that he was on his way into the court and would have caused, as she says, "heaven knows what fuss" by trying to get the original document, she said, "Mr Pope, you get right back here." Surprisingly, he did.

In the Supreme Court of Canada, the late Justice Estey wrote the decision.[43] There had been four days of extended hours of hearing before the court, an unusual occurrence, and then it took some two years to deliver a judgment. Estey's decision was not, so far as they were aware, rendered on the basis of any point argued during the course of the appeal. The case had dragged on long enough that some of the senior people involved, such as Pierre Genest, died before it was concluded. In the early heady days of having won at trial, Pope had said that when the case was all over, he would invite everyone to a celebratory dinner. Even though he lost, Pope nevertheless had a big dinner for everyone at the National Club, and it provided the therapeutic opportunity to relive a long and stressful trial.

ʒ▲

The collapse of the Canadian Commercial Bank and the Northland Bank sent shock waves through the financial community in Canada, and a commission was set up by the Canadian government in September 1985 to investigate. Willard Z. Estey, then a judge on the Supreme Court of Canada after being chief justice of Ontario, was appointed head of the commission that was directed to investigate the failures of the two Western Canadian-based chartered banks, to report upon the causes of these failures and the regulatory response to them, and to recommend any changes in the regulation of the banking industry that these experiences may have shown to be necessary and advisable. This was not a major economic issue since the two banks represented only about 1 per cent of the Canadian banking system measured by assets, earnings, or any other reasonable standard, but Canadian banks were not supposed to fail. Sopinka was appointed commission counsel.

The commissioner's report was issued in August 1986. In the foreword, Estey stated:

The investigation and organization of the hearings fell entirely upon our Commission counsel, John Sopinka, Q.C., of Stikeman Elliott, Toronto. A leading counsel in Canada and with particular experience in Commission of Inquiry work from both sides of that process, John Sopinka's contribution to the Inquiry was invaluable. He laid out the investigative program, examined almost all the witnesses, and presented in a series of submissions over the life of the Inquiry both sides of all the issues seen to be relevant to the Commission's mandate. With an already full schedule of counsel work around the country, all this was accomplished at the expense of weekends and holidays.

In all this, Mr Sopinka was assisted by a brilliant young lawyer from Stikeman Elliott, Mr Peter Howard. On him fell the burden of taking possession of the extensive documentation of the federal agencies and departments, of the two banks, and of related organizations; and of analyzing, organizing, and presenting the relevant portions of this material as exhibits for the Inquiry. In all, he culled out and processed some thousands of pages of documents. While other counsel participating may sometimes have thought they should have received their bound books of exhibits with more lead time, no one challenged the fairness and efficiency with which Mr Howard approached this monumental task. He also supervised the expurgation of this vast record of documents in order to protect the private information of persons who dealt with these banks in the ordinary course of business. Mr Howard examined witnesses during the hearings and prepared submissions from various points of view on the issues raised in the evidence. All these studies were made available to all counsel before presentation at public hearing to the Commission. This great volume of work taxed to the limit even a young counsel of the vigour and training of Mr Howard.

Re The Ombudsman of Ontario and the Minister of Housing of Ontario[44] was a case related to a broad investigation into allegations of wrongdoing by Ontario government land agents in the acquisition of large tracts of land in the Pickering area, to be used for construction of a second international airport in Ontario. Sopinka and Judge acted on behalf of various land agents accused of wrongdoing. At that time, in the late 1970s and early 1980s, the Ontario ombudsman was the renowned criminal lawyer Arthur Maloney, and he was conducting the investigation.[45] Ian Scott represented a number of individual landowners who had claimed that they were misled as to the value of the properties. In his recent book, Ian Scott, who later became a leading Liberal politician and Attorney General of Ontario, commented that this case helped convince him to run for Ontario politics to displace the Ontario Conservatives. He also noted that his clients' search for justice was frustrated by the effective advocacy of Sopinka on behalf of the land agents. In the reported cases, Sopinka and Judge had attempted to limit the scope of an ombudsman investigation. Again, this case showed the extent of Sopinka's delegation to, and reliance on, juniors. Although the other senior counsel had juniors working on the file, Judge was the only one given a part of the argument. It is an extraordinary learning experience to argue against top counsel such as Ian Scott.

The firm was also involved in a number of prominent Supreme Court of Canada cases. Sopinka worked with Brown in the *Pitt Steel* case, which related to the powers of the competition commission to conduct inquiries.[46] He acted, again with Brown in the *Bill 30* case, which dealt with the extension of funding to the senior grades of Roman Catholic separate schools in Ontario.[47] Lederman argued and won the *Pettkus v. Becker* constructive trust case in the late 1970s.[48]

In the *Barrie Annexation Municipal Board* case and related litigation, Sopinka acted for the Innisfil Township and resisted the annexation of large tracts of land by the City of Barrie, in the course of which he raised novel issues of law regarding ministerial responsibility for internal memoranda written with a view to influencing Ontario Municipal Board proceedings. In order to frustrate the annexation, Sopinka raised the prospect of bringing the government minister into a hearing, to be cross-examined on this memorandum. This issue got sidetracked into the courts and significantly delayed the entire annexation process. Other senior counsel coined a phrase to describe what happened in that case: it had been "Sopinkafied." Sopinka would frequently say that in every case, there was a unique legal issue that could be raised to one's advantage. The creative challenge was to find that interesting and unique issue.

In *Seaway Trust, Greymac Trust, and Crown Trust Company v. Ontario Government*,[49] the firm became involved in one of the largest commercial frauds in Canadian experience, in which more than $400 million had been siphoned out of trust companies by William Player and his company, Kilderkin Investments Limited. The firm acted on behalf of The Clarkson Company, the court-appointed receiver of Kilderkin Investments Limited, to track down assets. The case made headline news for weeks on end, and fresh evidence was frequently garnered from the newspapers. One of the more interesting aspects of this mandate for Judge was his responsibility in handling the litigation out of the Cayman Islands to trace $109 million purportedly paid by wealthy Saudis, to be held on account of the "flip" of a wide variety of apartment buildings in Toronto and Southern Ontario. This $109 million represented the profit made by Player on the resale of these buildings, which he had acquired from Cadillac Fairview.

The name Stikeman, Elliott was well known to senior Cayman lawyers not just because of transactions that had occurred through that island, but also because Fraser Elliott had drafted the first Cayman corporations law statute in the early 1960s. Judge helped to develop a legal manoeuvre to circumvent the Cayman secrecy laws through the use of a court order recognizing the Ontario interim receivership. Through that mechanism, they were able to obtain all of the relevant bank documents, which confirmed that the $109 million were not there. This revelation proved the huge fraud, which was reported to the Ontario court with widespread attention in the media that turned the case against Player and company. Unfortunately, the Cayman court was not impressed by the manoeuvring, which undermined a pillar of the Cayman industry – the secrecy laws – and the court promptly threatened to hold The Clarkson Company, acting as the interim receiver, and its counsel in contempt after discharging the recognition order. Judge attended in the Cayman Court of Appeal with London counsel, Leonard Hoffman (now Lord Hoffman of the House of Lords), to vindicate the accounting firm and to restore the recognition order.

Lederman acted in a libel trial on behalf of CTV, which had broadcast a television program in which Imre Finta, a Hungarian, was identified as someone taking part in the Holocaust. Finta sued for libel, and it became necessary to obtain evidence in Europe and in Israel from Holocaust survivors. During cross-examination of one of the CTV witnesses, an old woman, her ability to identify Finta some forty or fifty years after the fact was challenged by Finta's counsel. The old woman, a survivor of Auschwitz, had positively identified Finta and was sticking to her story, while his counsel kept at it by asking how it could be possible for her to remember a face that long afterwards. She replied, "Mr (x), there are only two faces in the world that I will never forget." The lawyer did not have enough sense to stop, but asked the fatal question, "Who are they?" "Imre Finta and Adolf Eichmann," she replied.

A commission of inquiry into the Air Ontario crash at Dryden, Ontario, which occurred on March 10, 1989, was established later the same month, with Mr Justice V.P. Moshansky as commissioner, to inquire into the contributing factors and causes of the crash of Air Ontario's Flight 363, a Fokker F-28, and to report thereon including such recommendations as the commissioner might deem appropriate in the interests of aviation safety. Fred Von Veh was appointed commission counsel. In his final report, Mr Justice Moshansky stated:

No Commission can function effectively without the assistance of a highly competent, dedicated, and motivated Commission counsel. I was most fortunate to have such a counsel in the person of Mr Frederick Von Veh, Q.C., of Toronto. A veteran of several Commissions of Inquiry, Mr Von Veh's previous Commission experience and his background in administrative and transportation law proved invaluable to me ... Mr Von Veh had the heavy responsibility of organizing and overseeing the work of my entire Commission staff throughout the life of this Commission ... Mr Von Veh has discharged his multiple and weighty responsibilities as Commission counsel in a most professional manner. I am greatly indebted to him.

Peter Howard worked with Earl Cherniak, one of Toronto's best-known counsel, on a matter that pertained to a letter of comfort between the Toronto-Dominion Bank, represented by John Campion at Faskens, and GE Capital, represented by Howard and Cherniak. The bank was attempting to sue on the basis of that letter that consisted of 145 words and stated that there was not a legally binding commitment. There were one hundred separate causes of action in the claim brought by the bank, including fraud, and the trial took up 140 days of court time. Howard was successful on all counts and obtained solicitor-client costs because of the fraud allegation. The Ontario Court of Appeal dismissed the bank's appeal, and the Supreme Court of Canada refused the bank's application for leave to appeal. The matter took ten years from start to finish, and the total costs were in the neighbourhood of $7 million, generating nine or ten reported cases in the process.

Doug Harrison acted for a Greek landlord who was suing his tenant, a Greek restaurant. On the eve of trial, the client asked him, "Mr Harrison, what happens if the judge believes their lies and not ours?" Harrison settled the case before trial. He also acted for Ludovit Katona, a hockey agent who specialized in smuggling Czechs out of the Eastern Europe in the 1970s and 1980s before there was free movement in the Soviet-controlled Central Europe. Katona wanted to strike a deal with Bob Pulford, the general manager of the Chicago Blackhawks, to bring Dominik Hasek to Canada, which would involve the Blackhawks paying Katona a "finder's fee." When the Blackhawks were in town, Katona and Harrison paid Pulford a visit at Maple Leaf Gardens. The timing was not good because they approached him after the game, which the Leafs had won. Harrison spoke to Pulford, who confirmed he was still interested in Hasek, whose rights were actually owned by the Quebec Nordiques at the time, and then he said that Katona wanted to discuss the finder's fee. Pulford stuck his face in Harrison's and said, "Finder's fee? What finder's fee? There's no fucking finder's fee!" Harrison thought he was about to get a severe bodycheck, or worse. He looked around for Katona, who was now twenty-five feet away. Fortunately, Pulford then moved over to talk to Katona, and Harrison got out of there without any bruises. Some agreement must have been reached since Hasek was drafted by Chicago in the tenth round of the 1983 NHL draft.

There are good reasons why lawyers unfamiliar with court work should be cautious about getting to their feet. In Peter Hamilton's[50] very early days with the firm, he worked extensively with Jim Riley. He recalls Riley being very exercised about a speeding ticket and decided to fight the ticket in court. Hamilton never knew exactly what happened between the police officer and Riley, but it must have been at least somewhat unpleasant because he received a ticket for more than 15 kilometres over the limit, which would result in demerit points. (Ordinary practice in Riley's circumstances would have been to write the ticket for less than 15 kilometres over the limit.) For some reason, thinking that this trial would be amusing, Hamilton went along. The trial was held in the night traffic court at Old City Hall. The courtroom seemed to be mostly filled with bikers. They were certainly the only two people there wearing suits. When Riley's case was heard, the police prosecutor called evidence from the officer in charge of the speed trap. The evidence was that the speed gun had been pointed, a reading was taken, and a ticket given. However, the prosecutor was clearly having some difficulty with his evidence because he kept asking the same or a slightly different question in the hope, apparently, of getting more information. He eventually gave up and rested his case.

When Riley rose to cross-examine, he began to put his first question, but the judge interrupted him, looked directly at him, and said, "Mr Riley, sometimes silence is golden." Riley paused and then began to put his question again. The judge again interrupted him, somewhat more forcefully, and again said, "Mr Riley, sometimes silence is golden." At this point, the police prosecutor tapped Riley on the shoulder and whispered in his ear, after which Riley said, "I move for a non-suit," which was granted, and the case dismissed. What the judge was trying to tell Riley and what the prosecutor obviously knew was that the prosecutor had missed an essential element of his case, namely identifying Riley's car as the one at which the speed gun had been pointed. Riley's question was about to establish the prosecution's case. Both Riley and Hamilton had entirely missed this point.

Sometimes, even when silence may be golden, you do not always get away with it. Dave Byers and Hamilton were once involved in seeking court approval for a plan of arrangement, which was intended principally to rectify significant deficiencies in the corporate records of a client. The case was being heard by Mr Justice Farley. On the application for the final order, the motion was presented by an associate, John Hunt, with Byers and Hamilton in attendance to monitor the performance. Hunt did very well, but eventually, a number of questions arose for which he did not have the answer. Justice Farley then decided that he wanted to hear from the horse's mouth (being then rather aggravated, he probably would have described Hamilton somewhat differently) and asked Hamilton to rise from the back benches, as it were, and respond to his questions. It seemed to Hamilton that he was grilled for at least half an hour. Somewhat mollified by his answers, Justice Farley then turned to Byers and asked him whether he had anything to add. Byers, in a masterful replication of Pontius Pilate, responded that he had nothing to add, that his presence in court was entirely ceremonial, and that Hamilton had refused to attend unless he went. Justice Farley granted the order.

The last case argued by Sopinka, assisted by Chalmers, in the Supreme Court of Canada was *City National Leasing v. General Motors*.[51] This was a case under the *Competition Act*, which had been amended to allow for a civil cause of action where a plaintiff had been injured by actions that were inappropriate under the statute. General Motors, represented by Edgar Sexton, moved to strike the claim on the basis that the legislation was not constitutional. When it was heard in the Ontario Court of Justice by Mr Justice Alvin Rosenberg, who was to rule on the motion, he said that having heard the argument in favour of the motion, he did not have to hear from Sopinka. He then decided the case on precisely the basis that had been argued, observing in passing that it was true he had told Sopinka that he did not want to hear from him, but that he had thought about it a little more, and that was what he had decided. The Court of Appeal obviously heard the case on that point, and Sopinka was successful and was successful again in the Supreme Court of Canada, although by the time the decision was rendered, Sopinka had already been appointed to the court.

By 1988, Stikeman Elliott in Toronto was clearly on the radar screen of persons looking for top counsel to represent them in litigation. During his tenure, Sopinka had turned down appointments to the Trial Division of the Supreme Court of Ontario as well as to the Ontario Court of Appeal. However, he could not resist the Supreme Court of Canada. When the call came in May 1988, he accepted, going straight from the Bar to the highest court without paying dues as a judge in the provincial superior courts. Such direct appointments to the highest court were not common. At the time, Sopinka recognized that his appointment came at least five years too early for his maturing of his department. Indeed, after his appointment, the Toronto litigation department struggled to redefine itself.

At the time of Sopinka's appointment to the Supreme Court of Canada, Lederman was already a highly respected counsel in his own right, but he was only just breaking into the ranks of top senior counsel. No one could fill Sopinka's shoes, and Lederman did not pretend to try. Sopinka had very strong views as to how his department and the firm should be run, and he generally stuck to them, operating the department as a largely enlightened despot. Lederman was more flexible in trying to build consensus within the department, which for the most part consisted of lawyers in their twenties and early thirties. After losing its big star, the department saw a significant drop in the amount of pure counsel work that came to it. It was also then starting to experience considerable change in the practice of litigation.

In the late 1980s, the economy fell into a deep recession, which took well into the mid-1990s to abate. There was significant growth in corporate commercial litigation, particularly in the area of insolvency, which appeared to be pervasive. This became a new speciality within the department. The hard economic times were a mixed blessing for litigation as clients were increasingly avoiding litigation and finding other ways to resolve differences in order to avoid the attendant costs. However, the failure of many companies led to lengthy disputes, particularly for various real estate projects and companies, land developers, shopping centre owners, and retail companies. Under Lederman's guidance, the Toronto litigation department recovered from the loss of Sopinka and of a number of lawyers who left the firm following his departure. Within five years, the department was, under the leadership of Lederman, significantly larger than it had been under the tutelage of Sopinka.

In 1994, the Toronto department faced yet another setback. Just as it was hitting a groove, Lederman was offered an appointment to the bench with the Ontario Court of Justice (General Division), now the Superior Court of Justice for Ontario, which he accepted. Again, the Toronto litigation department was thrown into some turmoil as it was challenged once more to redefine itself. Dave Byers emerged as the next head of the department. He was also a consensus builder who was respected by every member of the department, and he was able to utilize his refreshing sense of humour not only as a means to manage the department, but also as an effective tool in his advocacy. The groupings within the department are around Byers, Howard, and Dunphy, who do bankruptcy and restructuring, and Chalmers, who acts for numerous large corporations (American Home Products, Siemens, Hyundai, Wyeth-Ayerst), together with life, health, and disability insurance work for Industrial Alliance and Lloyd's, also negotiating the terms of insurance policies with carriers against environmental and other risks. David Brown became interested in energy and has published a service on the subject, but he also does a lot of the administrative constitutional and human rights litigation.

In one of the largest and highest-profile disputes handled by the department, Byers acted for the Pepsi Cola Company in a franchise dispute with Scotts Hospitality (our client wanted to terminate the franchise agreement), which in turn affected a high public profile takeover of Scotts. He had taken this case on after a number of other Toronto law firms had given negative opinions to Pepsi Cola. Welcoming a challenge, Byers and Katherine Kay embarked upon a fast track and lengthy trial, developing the facts in a sympathetic manner for their client to overcome the legal obstacles in this case. To the surprise of the Toronto legal community, Byers was successful at trial, obtaining declarations that one of the larger franchise agreements in the fast food industry be terminated as a result of improper conduct by Scotts. One of the highlights of this trial was Byers's cross-examination of a lawyer who had sworn an affidavit that was not altogether truthful. Since this witness was also an officer of the court, Byers pressed him ultimately into "seeking forgiveness" from the trial judge for his indiscretion. Before the appeal from the trial judgment was heard, Byers and his client had the good sense to arrive at a settlement that resulted in a restructuring of the corporations and the further protection of the interests of Pepsi Cola as a franchisor. When the appeal did proceed, the Court of Appeal saw through the successful trial tactics and restored the legal principles that Byers had persuaded the trial judge to minimize. While Pepsi Cola's appeal was successful, it was rendered academic by Byers's negotiations on behalf of the client to restructure their affairs. This case typifies many of those that now dominate the workload of the Toronto litigation department – high profile public disputes involving large corporations.

Other examples are the downfall of Livent Inc. and the bitter litigation against its founder, Garth Drabinsky, and likely others as the facts continue to emerge. Peter Howard is acting on this matter as well as on the high profile YBM Magnex dispute, which is still before the courts and involves allegations of impropriety against directors of that company, including the former premier of Ontario David Peterson. Other high-profile cases involving both insolvency and securities issues include the downfall of Philip Services Inc., a large North American waste disposal company that ran into a combination of environmental and employee fraud problems in the mid-1990s, for which Byers was lead counsel and led the workout team.

Sean Dunphy's most prominent recent case has been the merger of Air Canada and Canadian Airlines International, the former Canadian Pacific Airlines, and all of the resulting fallout. He was the main litigation partner on the Ontario aspects of the Onex bid to take over Air Canada. Kathy Kay has emerged as one of the lead competition litigators in the office, currently defending Air Canada against the allegations launched by West Jet. Kathryn Chalmers has developed a fairly broad corporate litigation and insurance-based practice, and Doug Harrison does much of the same. John Judge has a more general civil litigation practice, but he has a particularly good focus on the information technology industry. Part of the wages of this particular sin was that he was designated as the partner mainly responsible for the infamous Y2K preparations for the anticipated "end of the world" (at least technologically) as of January 1, 2000. David Brown has developed two streams of practice. Since 1994, he has been involved in a number of well-known constitutional cases before the Supreme Court of Canada on a variety of issues: *Adler*,[52] funding for private religious schools; *Robert Latimer*[53]; *Winnipeg Child and Family Services*[54] and *Dobson v. Dobson*,[55] a series of cases involving the legal status of the unborn; current same-sex marriage cases and some of the same-sex benefits cases, including *M. v. H.*[56] and *Rosenberg*[57]; as well as some religious liberty cases, including *Trinity Western.*[58] The other stream has been the development of an extensive regulatory practice in both the natural gas and electricity sectors.

The litigation department occasionally gets strange mandates from the corporate section of the firm. Anne Ristic,[59] who joined the firm as a student in 1984 (and first worked on the Grange inquiry), had become responsible for the recruitment efforts of the Toronto office. She was on maternity leave during the February 1994 summer student interview week, having "thoughtlessly" given birth on February 12. At the request of Brian Rose, Harrison drafted a prank statement of claim against Davies Ward & Beck and Anne's husband, Michael Creery, a partner of that firm, claiming damages of $1,000,000 for conspiracy and interference with economic interests (caused by his getting her pregnant) as the firm was unable to do a proper job of recruiting without her. Rose sent the claim to Derek Watchorn at Davies Ward, who responded, in like manner, by saying, among other things, that he could not see why the fact that Stikeman Elliott had a maternity leave policy of more than nine days, which, he observed, seemed unusually generous for Stikeman Elliott, should be Davies's problem. Copies of the claim and the exchange of correspondence have been carefully preserved.

The balance of the 1990s was marked by the economic recovery and the explosion of corporate activity, particularly in the mergers and acquisitions field. The growth of business also had its impact on the nature of the firm's litigation practice. It became more and more business focused, dealing with shareholder disputes, corporate restructurings, and large commercial disputes. The core of the Toronto litigation practice is now geared almost exclusively toward business issues, including some of the new technology disputes that have emerged with the growth of the Internet. The Toronto litigation department has become one of the most respected departments for large complex business disputes in Toronto.

CHAPTER 11

Tax – Rendering unto Caesar …

Stikeman, with the backup of the superb George Tamaki, continued to drive the tax practice of the firm as it grew larger. But he had also attracted a number of extremely talented lawyers as part of the group, and the tax section operated as a cohesive and collegial unit over the years with the exception of the last year or so of Bruce Verchere's involvement.

Two stellar additions to the tax section had arrived as summer students in 1971, in the persons of Robert Couzin[1] and David Finkelstein.[2] Couzin had come from Chicago to study law at McGill University and was a fringe benefit derived by the firm from the unsuccessful adventure of the United States in Vietnam. Finklestein studied at McGill University for his undergraduate and master's degrees and then went to the Université de Montréal for his law degree. It was clear, even from the time they were students, that they would become first-class tax lawyers. When the tax reform emanating from the Carter Commission of the mid-1960s was introduced in 1971 by Finance Minister Edgar Benson, to become effective the following year, the new *Income Tax Act* was radically different from the old statute and complicated enough that the Canadian Bar Association organized a series of courses on variouts aspects of the new law, made available to practitioners. Since the firm was the acknowledged leader in the tax field, several of the tax lawyers were asked to teach portions of the course (each of which was accompanied by an explanatory booklet prepared by the Canadian Bar Association) and to give regular courses at the end of the working day, which practitioners would attend in the Montreal office boardroom.

Both Couzin and Finkelstein were pressed into service for this purpose, and Couzin, in particular, was assigned the partnership area, one of the most complex parts in the new act. He may well have been the only one among the group who understood the provisions. At one stage during the course of the various sessions, an older lawyer from another firm asked me who was the bright young lawyer who knew absolutely everything about partnerships and how long had he been in practice. I was delighted to astound him with the revelation that not only had Couzin not been in practice very long, he was not even a lawyer.

It was reminiscent of a discussion I once had with Colin Irving, a Montreal practitioner who was teaching a course in civil procedure at the McGill law faculty. I had asked him, around exam time, how his class had fared that term, and he said that he had the normal bell curve of students, with some who clearly knew the subject matter very well. Others were in the middle, and there were a few at the bottom of the class who he thought did not know enough to pass. But then he described another student whom the faculty did not require to sit in the same room with the other students writing exams, but who typed his exam papers rather than writing them by hand. Irving said that it was obvious that his course had practically been an insult to this student's intelligence and that the student knew far more about civil procedure than the instructor would ever know. I immediately identified his star student as Couzin and informed him that he was a student at our firm.

Both Couzin and Finkelstein became, as expected, superstars in the tax section. Couzin was a lightning-fast, immensely creative, humorous, and edgy practitioner who was filled with countless original ideas. Finkelstein was of a different style – just as knowledgeable but more cautious and ready to work in agonizing detail. If Couzin was a junior Stikeman, then Finkelstein was a junior Tamaki, and he indeed worked with Tamaki on many complex files in which every detail was carefully considered and analysed from every possible perspective. Couzin, more often than not, flew on his own.

When Peter Cumyn returned from London, the new legislation directed at international tax was already enacted, but the transitional provisions had the effect of postponing their effects until 1976, which gave him four years to get ready for the new system. Cumyn became the firm's acknowledged expert in international taxation and worked primarily in this field until he left the firm at the beginning of 1993. He pioneered a number of complicated international arrangements before changing rules made this practice more difficult. But his pièce de résistance was the "double-dip" structures, which used a Dutch company with a branch in some compliant jurisdiction – such as Switzerland, Barbados, or Cyprus – and which allowed for deduction of the same interest in two jurisdictions. These were designed to take advantage of the different laws (and sometimes disparate legal characterizations of the same entities) in separate jurisdictions and were used by a wide variety of clients, including many public corporations. No double-dip plan created by Cumyn was successfully challenged by the taxation authorities. Instead, the authorities have preferred to change the legislation and have begun in some of the negotiated tax treaties to try to limit the benefits that are available to taxpayers and to cut down on what is referred to as "treaty-shopping."

He worked for many years with Stikeman on a complex transfer pricing dispute with Revenue Canada, Taxation, on behalf of Hoffman-La Roche, headed by René de Grafenreid, in respect of the proper transfer price for the wonder drugs of the day: Valium and Librium. He remembers being driven with Stikeman from Basel, the headquarters of Hoffman-La Roche, to the Zurich airport in the chairman's Mercedes. Stikeman looked at the speedometer and commented to the chauffeur, "Gee, I don't even land my plane this fast." The dispute was never satisfactorily resolved, as a result of which

Hoffman-La Roche simply abandoned its Canadian operations, leaving its huge building in Vaudreuil, Quebec vacant for several years.

A client from Calgary, Fred Mannix of the famous oil and construction family and one of two sons of the legendary F.P. Mannix, organized a dinner party in a private room at the Château Champlain and invited Stikeman, Cumyn, and Jacques Courtois (then still at his old firm) and their wives, among others. After the main course, Mannix stated that he did not know much about wines and asked what was the best wine to accompany dessert. They agreed that Château d'Yquem would be the best, but Stikeman interjected that they would not have any in the Château Champlain wine cellar. Courtois, a renown master of one-upmanship, quickly said that he bet Stikeman was wrong and offered the wager that if Stikeman was wrong, he (Stikeman) should pay for the wine. This was a one-sided wager, but Stikeman rose to the bait. Courtois then called the wine steward and asked him whether they had any Château d'Yquem. The answer was, "Of course, sir." Courtois responded at once, "We'll have two bottles, and Mr Stikeman is paying."

Tax reform meant that a major rewrite of the *Canada Tax Service* was required, and all the lawyers in the tax section were pressed into the effort. The ordinary demands of the practice were such that progress was sporadic, so Stikeman hit on the very popular ploy of arranging for the entire team to spend a week in Bermuda in the early spring of 1973 on the understanding that no other work would be done during that period other than the writing of the service. It was a much-appreciated tonic, at least within the tax section, which produced a burst of material for the publication.

Elinore Richardson[3] came to the firm in 1975 from Borden Elliot in Toronto. Stikeman had encountered her on a case on which he was working, and when he learned that she would be coming to Montreal, following her husband-to-be, he was very enthusiastic about trying to get her to join the firm. I was dispatched to the November 1974 Canadian Tax Foundation Annual Conference in Quebec City to try to see whether it would be possible to reach an agreement, which would involve her working at the office while studying for her Quebec Bar exams. An agreement was reached, and she joined the firm, got called to the Bar in 1977, and remained almost twenty-five years before leaving late in 2001 to rejoin the now-expanded firm of Ladner Borden Gervais in Toronto. In the interim, she was a prodigious worker who developed an extremely high level of practice in the financing area, and she was the principal innovator in the creation of a number of financial derivatives, currency swaps, and hedging transactions, working with many of the merchant banks as they sought to bring new financial products to the market, many of which were tax-driven strategies. She was a somewhat unusual addition to the tax section, practising for the most part more or less on her own; in the process, she established, among others, the firm record for the number of different secretaries who worked for her.

Claude Désaulniers joined the firm from the Quebec Department of Justice, where he had been a solid litigator and one of the principal draftsmen of the Quebec *Taxation Act* and related legislation that became necessary as a result of the federal reforms. He developed a specialty in litigating virtually all provincial matters together with the provision of general taxation advice during his twenty years with the firm prior to leaving in 1993 to join McCarthy Tétrault. Martin Scheim[4] began his career in the firm in the corporate section, but he spent a few years in the tax section working on a variety of public issues during the time of the Quebec Stock Savings Plan legislation and in some of the early film financings handled by the firm. He eventually returned to the corporate section and more latterly has been involved in the international services group, the activities of which are described in chapter 5.

Pierre Archambault[5] joined the tax section in 1978, having been identified by his classmate at McGill, Glenn Cranker, after a couple of years in Bruce Verchere's firm, where his talents had gone largely unrecognized. He became a careful practitioner in the tax section, acquiring special expertise in the field of mining and oil and gas exploration during the period when the federal government was encouraging such activities. The program allowed junior research companies to raise from the public the funds necessary for exploration and development activities, to apply the funds for those purposes, and to transfer the tax deductions to the taxpayers who had provided the funds even though the taxpayers themselves had not carried on the exploration and development activities. He accepted an appointment to the Tax Court of Canada and was sworn in at Montreal on May 13, 1993, the day following a well-lubricated dinner at the University Club, hosted by the firm, to celebrate his ascension to the bench.

Guy Masson[6] joined the firm in 1979 following graduation from the Université de Montréal and a decade with Bell Canada. He has now become chairman of the tax section in the Montreal office, with a varied practice on behalf of public and private corporations. Masson acted in the final cleanup of a long-standing case for Avram Goldstein on a real estate case that had been started by Jim Robb in the 1960s and argued by me, without success, in the mid-1970s in the Federal Court of Appeal. Goldstein had bought large tracts of raw land on Laurentien Boulevard during the 1950s, which would now be extremely valuable but which had also appreciated considerably when he sold them in 1956. Others were mortgaged to the hilt, and the funds were used to build a Volkswagen plant in Brazil, where he made a fortune. There were no assets left in Canada by the time the litigation was finally completed. Nevertheless, Goldstein wrote to the firm when he was ninety-two years old and said he did not want to leave the world with any debts, and in a humorous postscript, inquired about the possibility of Revenue Canada having an office in hell. Masson settled the case, which started with an initial liability of some $8 million, for about $400,000 on the basis of the documents in the firm's litigation files since Revenue Canada had not kept the forty-year-old records.

Once the amount was agreed upon and Goldstein obtained bank drafts, Masson, who was concerned with the possibility of a garnishment until the new reassessments were issued, arranged for him to send it to Elizabeth Skelton in the New York office. Once he got a written acknowledgment that there were no further taxes outstanding, the bank drafts were transferred to the account of Revenue Canada. A couple of weeks later, Revenue Canada called to say that the drafts had been returned, indicating NSF. The drafts had been sent to the Taxation Centre at Shawinigan, which tendered them to the CIBC. The CIBC had asked for forty-eight hours to clear them and had told Revenue Canada to hold on to them for that period. For some reason, which has never been made clear, the Revenue Canada official instead sent the drafts to the last known address of Goldstein, and they disappeared. Goldstein was advised of the error and could have simply ignored the matter, but he sent a replacement draft, and the emergency came to a happy end. As a footnote to his good judgment regarding real estate, in the early 1950s, long before it was developed, Goldstein had someone row him across to Nun's Island (the Champlain Bridge was not even planned at the time) and concluded, with remarkable prescience, that the island would in the not-too-distant future become prime real estate.

Masson had collateral involvement on the *Olympic Stadium* case in which Mercier had acted for Roger Taillibert, taking on a complete underdog case and won some $15 million for him. Because the fees constituted professional income for the French architect, there was an issue of whether he should be taxed in Canada or only in France, where he worked and had, for treaty purposes, his permanent establishment. Masson settled the tax case for Taillibert, who was a difficult client and refused to sign a Canadian income tax return even though it was a "nil" return. Unfortunately, the government would pay interest on a tax refund only from the date the return was filed. For Taillibert, the question was a matter of principle; he had no fixed base in Canada, was not therefore subject to Canadian tax, and would not submit to the jurisdiction of another government. *"Je suis citoyen français,"* he insisted. As part of the settlement in this dialogue of the deaf, a negotiated amount of interest was paid on the refund of taxes.

Probably the most serious incident affecting the tax section occurred in 1987, and Masson was delegated to handle it. One of the tax lawyers, Robert Langlois, together with an associate in the corporate section, Ralph Faraggi, had concocted an artificial scheme to generate tax-free surpluses under the *Income Tax Act,* which were designated as capital dividend accounts (CDA) and which could be distributed tax-free to corporate shareholders of private corporations. This was part of the tax policy whereby the non-taxable portion of capital gains realized by private corporations would not be subject to double tax when eventually distributed to the shareholders. Langlois had developed a highly technical plan that had the effect of creating artificial CDA as a result of the interaction of the statutory provisions even when there had in fact been no underlying capital gain. Without disclosing that he had in mind an extensive plan to market such CDA, he got Maurice Régnier to sign a generic form of opinion that he proposed to show to prospective "purchasers" of the CDA since he knew that his own reputation would not be sufficient and that Régnier was known in the community as a careful and reliable lawyer. Régnier was completely unaware of the plan, and Langlois had simply asked him to provide an opinion on a single facet of the plan, which as such was clearly without any negative effect since if CDA actually existed, there was no untoward benefit to shareholders were it to be distributed.

With this in hand, they proceeded to arrange for the creation of dozens of different companies and marketed the scheme to hundreds of taxpayers. They generated millions of dollars worth of purported CDA and charged a commission to the purchasers. This was discovered only after the fact. It was radically different from the surplus strips done a couple of decades earlier in a much more benign tax administration climate, and the prospect of attacks on the new scheme was beyond doubt. Apart from that, the earlier surplus strips were not clandestine within the firm. The concern with the CDA scheme was that despite the fact that the firm as such knew nothing about it and Régnier had no idea how his opinion was to be used by the two perpetrators, anyone who might be assessed would probably try to look to the firm for recovery of losses. Langlois and Faraggi were asked to leave the firm forthwith, and a firm-wide effort was made with the taxation authorities to ensure that CDA purchasers would be given a chance to receive the normal treatment of surpluses and to the extent necessary, "undo" the purchases of the notional CDA. It was a trying situation that was time-consuming (especially for Masson), embarrassing, and potentially costly to the firm, but the very favourable settlements arranged for those who had been misled showed the capability of the firm when challenged by unusual circumstances.

While teaching at the Université de Sherbrooke in international tax, Peter Cumyn identified Paul Setlakwe[7] as a prospect for the tax section. Setlakwe was notable not only for his ability in the course and excellent results, but principally for his practice of ostentatiously reading a newspaper at the back of the room during lectures. Setlakwe had a varied tax practice as a member of the group before being recruited to the Hong Kong office in 1989, where he soon became highly expert in advising high net worth individuals in Hong Kong on how to take advantage of Canadian tax legislation to protect their assets and to ensure effective intergenerational transfers of wealth. After returning to Montreal in 1992, his relationships with many of the Hong Kong clients continued, so much so that in 2000, the Ho family persuaded him to become their private advisor, and he accepted the offer while still retaining a connection with the firm.

Setlakwe once flew to Ottawa with Stikeman for a meeting with Revenue Canada on behalf of a client who had turned over all his money to an individual in Bermuda who was to explore business ventures on his behalf. These came to naught and the funds were lost, so the client sought to deduct the losses as business expenses. Revenue Canada took the position that they were non-deductible and that there was no reasonable expectation of profit from the ventures. The expenses included an item of $400 for a suit for the Bermuda individual. How could the client justify an expense of that nature, they asked. "Well," said Stikeman, blithely ignoring the Bermuda climate, "a man has to keep warm."

Robert Raizenne[8] had already accepted an offer from Phillips & Vineberg when Julian Cools-Lartigue, a paralegal in the firm who had decided to become a lawyer, approached him at lunch one day at the McGill law faculty and took a copy of his curriculum vitae to Michael Richards. This led to an interview with Richards, Yvon Martineau, and Claudette Picard; Raizenne came on board as a student in the summer of 1980. He knew me from McGill, where I was the "colour commentator" in John Durnford's tax course, and he started working right away in tax, although not initially exclusively so, with me and later with Elinore Richardson. He became a very capable and careful lawyer, willing to spend whatever time might be required to understand the nature of each problem and the entire statutory scheme that governed it as well as the administrative framework. That meant that representations to the tax authorities were complete and persuasive and that opinions he gave to clients were as reliable as possible, even in circumstances where the law might not be clear. This was an extremely valuable quality, both for transaction work and in the support of the more complicated litigious matters in which the firm became involved.

From his early years, Raizenne remembers Stikeman – who was retained to advise on the winding up of the Ludmer offshore funds when they were attacked by Revenue Canada, Taxation – setting the bar very high as to the professional standards that were to govern, and he left him and Richardson to find the path through the technical minefields that dotted the tax landscape. In the "small world department," he assisted in the appeal before the Supreme Court of Canada at his new firm, where an important decision on the deductibility of interest on borrowed money used for investment purposes was handed down in 2001, arising out of the same offshore fund.[9] His favourite non-tax story involves an elevator ride with Fraser Elliott and Patricia McDowell, at the time Harold Gordon's secretary. The elevators in the CIBC building have never been one of the building's stellar qualities. One day, the three of them got on and the elevator dropped from the thirty-ninth floor all the way to the basement in something barely short of a free fall. It stopped with a bounce, and Elliott broke the silence with the comment "Quite a ride, wasn't it?"

Robert Hogan[10] was hired after graduation from Sherbrooke and has now emerged as one of the leaders of the tax section, with a fertile and productive mind combined with a sense of the commercial priorities of clients. He has become the new ideas man and coordinates, with the assistance of Frédéric Harvey,[11] a talented group of lawyers and accountants who provide the structuring and support of the most complicated business transactions and reorganizations, including cross-border transactions, handled by the firm. This group includes Luc Bernier and Marie-Andrée Beaudry; Michel Legendre in the pension and compensation area; our newest tax partner, Roanne Bratz[12]; a US tax specialist; and several juniors. Several others spent some time in the Montreal tax section before moving on to different careers or firms, including Monique Mercier, Yvon Bolduc, Hugh Berwick, Hillel Frankel, André Dorais, Mathieu Krepec, Hélène de Kovachich, Lucie Lamarre, François Picard, François Vincent, and Jonathan Leopardi.

Pierre Martel[13] has become a very capable tax litigator, now able to handle major cases in his own right, having appeared before the Tax Court of Canada, the Federal Court of Appeal, and the provincial courts in a broad range of appeals, including one we argued together before the Quebec Court of Appeal on behalf of The Royal Trust Company on the complex issue of computation of capital for purposes of the Quebec capital tax. One of his many strengths, apart from understanding what has to be established as a matter of fact, is his ability to work his way through the statutory provisions to shape an effective argument. He is also skilled at convincing his opponents that they should settle on satisfactory terms, thus taking out of play the risks inherent with litigation. He succeeded in doing this for several clients, including Superior Propane of Calgary and Hasbro Canada Inc.

As the firm increased in size and began to handle larger commercial and financial transactions, there was a definite shift in the nature of the work performed within the tax section. When the firm began, it had been Stikeman's tax expertise that attracted clients to the firm from across the entire country and abroad, many of which were then recruited by Elliott for ongoing corporate matters. This arrangement was effective while the firm was still at the level of a boutique, but over time, its corporate section expanded far beyond the tax group and was able to leverage the tax expertise of the firm to attract more and bigger clients for larger and larger transactions. Unlike many firms, it could provide sophisticated tax expertise to the structuring of arrangements, which provided the firm with a competitive edge in the marketplace. In addition, with the firm's growing presence in the bigger and more active Toronto marketplace, clients and law firms in that city were less likely to refer tax mandates to the Montreal office as they had in the past. They had a justifiable concern that the clients they referred might be all too satisfied with the service they received and stay with the firm.

Although the section became more and more an adjunct of the corporate law practice over time, there were still many pure tax-driven mandates that themselves generated corporate work for financing and other arrangements – many of which were developed by Cumyn, Couzin, Hogan, and Richardson – as well as ongoing litigious matters in both Montreal and Toronto. An economic historian could undoubtedly trace the first appearance of a bearer bond with interest coupons attached, but such instruments were certainly in existence throughout the twentieth century. In the early 1980s, Ken Matheson, at what was then McLeod, Young, Weir & Co., contacted the firm to determine the tax consequences of interest that would be accruing and for that matter, compounding on a bond. One thing led to another as people began to imagine all of the tax-free buyers, such as pension funds and registered retirement savings plans, of the appropriate instrument. Fortunately, the investment banker musings were directed to Robert Couzin. By the time Couzin had finished thinking about it, the issue was clearly framed. If you detached the interest coupons from a bearer bond, were the individual coupons a free-standing obligation? The importance of this is illustrated by considering an interest coupon payable nine years from today. If that coupon were a free-standing obligation, its present value, applying the appropriate compound interest rate assumptions, would be very small by comparison with the face value of the coupons. What a perfect instrument for a registered retirement savings plan where, for example, one might buy coupons with a face value of $100,000 for $10,000 and lock in a current long-term yield. After reviewing a number of examples, the firm concluded that most of the coupons examined were free-standing obligations – an executed promise to pay that was in essence a promissory note – and this was the beginning of the "strip coupon" market in Canada. The firm gave the first legal opinion on this device.

McLeod Young & Weir was clever enough to stay close to Couzin, apparently recognizing that there was more to come. Acknowledging that Canada had to invest in scientific research if it were to remain competitive in a rapidly developing world, the federal government developed a tax-based scheme that allowed research funds to be provided by taxpayers who did not themselves conduct scientific research but who could benefit from a new scientific research tax credit (SRTC) under prescribed conditions if they funded such research. Couzin mapped out how to package scientific research tax credits for the securities market, and for the fifteen to eighteen months that this was allowed, an amazing number of transactions were concluded. They ranged from large institutional placements by the likes of Northern Telecom (at that time) to small, homemade ones for an engineering company in suburban Toronto. Couzin mentioned how to do this to someone who was between jobs, and the latter made a tidy sum putting together a transaction. Couzin got a case of champagne, and the man went on to a successful career in investment banking. The firm did a great deal of work with flow-through shares, much of which was handled in Montreal by Martin Scheim. Unfortunately, however, a large number of scoundrels got into the SRTC business, and many abusive schemes were developed, some of which were deliberate tax evasion, which has led to several criminal prosecutions and punitive assessments. These became so pervasive that the government withdrew the program.

The tax section of the firm has provided advice in connection with countless corporate reorganizations that have had significant tax implications. In 1970, Hunter Douglas Limited changed its residence from Canada to the Netherlands as part of a reorganization of the business of Hunter Douglas NV in Europe. The firm represented the company; the corporate aspects were handled by Stanley Hartt, and the tax section, primarily under the leadership of Tamaki, developed the tax structures that made it possible. Proof of the validity of the tax advice was provided when the company was successful in its appeal against assessments of Canadian withholding tax sought to be imposed as a result of the reorganization in *Hunter Douglas Ltd. v. The Queen*.[14] In 1976, the firm acted for Atlantic Richfield Corporation (ARCO) on the sale of its Canadian subsidiary, Atlantic Richfield Canada (ARCAN), to the Government of Canada. This subsidiary was a significant element in the formation of Petro-Canada.

Canadian International Power Company Limited (CI Power) was a Canadian public corporation that was in the business of the generation and sale of electricity, directly and through its subsidiaries, mostly in South America and Barbados. In 1977, the corporation was liquidated. This was probably the first time after the tax reform was introduced in 1971 that a significant

Canadian public company was liquidated. The firm acted on the liquidation, and Tamaki and Finkelstein obtained an advance income tax ruling. Cash and shares of foreign subsidiaries were distributed, and eventually, a second ruling was obtained in connection with the use of a liquidating trust to complete the liquidation. In 1983, Tamaki and Finkelstein did the extremely complicated tax planning in connection with a major reorganization of the Lafarge North American Interests. This involved one of the first, if not the first, use of exchangeable shares of a Canadian corporation, which could be exchanged for shares of the US parent. The firm has acted for the Lafarge group of companies in both planning and compliance issues for many years, more recently in connection with the acquisition by Lafarge SA of Blue Circle Industries PLC.

In 1986, Tamaki and Finkelstein coordinated a major restructuring of Alcan Aluminium Ltd., now Alcan Inc., which was one of the early so-called somersault transactions in which the Canadian operating subsidiary became the parent, public corporation for all of the Alcan interests. An advance income tax ruling was obtained in connection with this transaction. In 1992, the Nabisco Group sold its cereal business to Kraft Canada Inc. The firm obtained an advance income tax ruling to facilitate a cross-border purchase "butterfly" on the sale. This was one of the last purchase butterflies that was carried out with an advance ruling prior to the changes in the *Income Tax Act*, which eliminated cross-border purchase butterflies and ultimately all purchase butterflies. In 2000, British American Tobacco PLC (BAT) acquired all of the publicly held shares of Imasco Limited. Following this, Imasco sold Canada Trust to the Toronto-Dominion Bank and Shoppers Drug Mart to a Canadian corporation controlled by KKR (Kohberg Kravis Roberts) of New York. BAT disposed of the Genstar real estate business, and it retained the tobacco business, now Imperial Tobacco Canada Limited. The firm's tax section, headed by Finkelstein, acted on all aspects of this transaction, including obtaining an advance income tax ruling from CCRA and the Quebec taxation authorities.

Much of the restructuring work on the many transactions during the late 1980s and throughout the 1990s to which Stone and Stone Consolidated were parties was built around the tax aspects, on which Raizenne was particularly active with several other members of the tax section of the firm given the huge amounts involved and the complexities of the deals. Managing the tax aspects occupied a substantial part of his practice. He was active with Hogan on the tax aspects of the first portion of the privatization of Air Canada and also on the privatization of Canadian National Railways, where Rovinescu and Ouellet were the lead corporate lawyers. Hogan did most of the tax work on the subsequent second portion of the Air Canada privatization.

The relocation of Couzin, then Tamaki and Finkelstein, to Toronto in the late 1970s was a major loss for the Montreal office, although systemic loss to the firm was avoided by the significant addition to the taxation bench strength of the Toronto office. It took several years to regain the ground that was lost in Montreal, and it was not until the mid-1990s that it recouped sufficient technical capacity to handle major commercial transactions in stride. Others from the Montreal tax section who turned to the Toronto office over the years included Tom Vowinckel,[15] Gary Nachshen,[16] and Angelo Nikolakakis.[17]

Retirements of partners are often sad occasions, representing as they do a recognition by the individual that he or she no longer has the energy or desire to continue at the pace required of a lawyer in today's dynamic and often hectic world. No retirement of a partner in the firm was accepted with such regret as that of George Tamaki, effective January 31, 1990. His elegant letter of March 2, 1990 to Stikeman is so typical of his generosity of spirit that will always be a guide to partners of the firm.

It seems hard to believe that it was 45 years ago when we first met. It was in the middle of the War, and I am forever grateful to Dick De Boo and you for having given me the first real opportunity to work in the field of law. We have had many good years together, of course some better than others.

I never cease to admire you for your energy and enthusiasm and your deep appreciation of the law and the workings of government. I was also amazed and still continue to be amazed at the way you can deal with clients and the infinite patience exhibited by you in the process. Some of the lawyers in the firm have missed a lot in not having seen you in action dealing with the tremendously difficult matters such as the dividend strips in the sixties. I also recall with immense admiration how you were able to convince George Nowlan that Johns-Manville should be able to deduct the cost of removing a cathedral! There are so many other victories, such as Royal Trust and Hollinger Mines, just to mention two. I think some of our young people these days give up too easily and are inclined to feel that because the black letter of the law seems to say something, there is no hope.

I thought long and hard before finally telling Jim Grant that I wanted to give up the formal status as a partner. This will give Yuki and me much more freedom of movement and, as you know, I did not feel completely comfortable about continuing to draw from the partnership when I was not contributing to it on an active basis. You are different because you continue to be active on client matters and to draw people to the firm ...

Sad as his retirement from the firm was to everyone, it was nothing compared to the shock and grief we experienced upon learning of his sudden death less than three years later, on February 19, 1993, in Vancouver while dining at the home of Pat Thorsteinsson, one of the firm's distinguished alumni. The firm established the George Tamaki Memorial Research Assistantship in his memory at Dalhousie University, his alma mater.

There was a further setback to the Montreal tax section in 1993 when Régnier and Désaulniers left the firm to go to McCarthy Tétrault and Guy Fortin left for Ogilvy Renault. Shortly thereafter, Robert Hogan and Frédéric Harvey decided they would become movie impresarios with Malo Films. Fortunately, Régnier, Hogan, and Harvey all returned to the firm, rejuvenated by their sabbatical endeavours, which added much welcomed enthusiasm and creative expertise to the group. The only losses of note through the balance of the 1990s were Peter Cumyn, who left to pursue interests in the international investment community, where his structuring of tax efficient arrangements for high net worth individuals could be pursued at the same time, and Robert Raizenne in 1996 for a complicated variety of reasons, which saw him move to Toronto with Davies Ward & Beck, then back to Phillips & Vineberg in Montreal, only to see that firm merge with Davies Ward & Beck a few years later.

Toronto, too, had its share of tax partners who for various reasons moved on to other firms. By far the most serious loss was Robert Couzin, one of the most talented lawyers the firm has had the good fortune to attract. Losses also included William Innes – a talented litigator very closely allied with Don Bowman – who moved on to Genest Murray and later to Thorsteinssons. Scott Wilkie, master of the endless sentence and interminable paragraph, left for Ogilvy Renault, and Hemant Tillak went on to pursue a more actuarially oriented career, which had been his first love. Fortunately for Toronto, it was able to attract John Lorito,[18] Joanne Swystun,[19] and David Glicksman,[20] the latter two providing a tax litigation capacity that had all but disappeared with the departures of Bowman, Innes, and Couzin. In the meantime, however, Durand and Finkelstein have continued to add to the section with Lianne Miller,[21] Kevin Kelly, Dean Kraus, Julie Muirhead, Tim Hughes, and Alan Kenigsberg.

TAX LITIGATION

Although many of the tax lawyers, not to mention the corporate ones, in the firm probably have only the vaguest idea of where the courts are located, the tax section continued to have an effective presence before the courts and maintained Stikeman's early example of appearing in major tax cases, many of which were or became leading cases and several of which led to changes in the tax legislation. Others were more mainstream in nature, simply involving efforts to make sure that clients were properly treated by the taxation authorities. From time to time, it is necessary to litigate, if only to show that the firm is not willing to allow its clients to be mistreated as a result of the overwhelming administrative power exercised by the tax authorities. The majority of cases in tax matters are settled well before getting to court, as they should be, but good settlements are often the result of making it clear, through court appearances, that if sensible settlements are not reached, there will be a formidable opponent to be overcome in court. There are new generations of income tax assessors and justice lawyers who have to learn the hard way that even with the onus of proof that rests on taxpayers to discharge the burden of demonstrating that an assessment was wrong, this burden can and will be discharged.

Don Bowman was one of the best tax litigators in the business prior to his appointment to the Tax Court of Canada, where he is now associate chief judge, and he has become one of the finest tax judges to have appeared on the Canadian bench.[22] While at the firm, he had splendid victories in the *Asamera* case,[23] the trial of which lasted several weeks arising from the

Indonesian activities of that company, and before the Supreme Court of Canada in *Canadian Johns-Manville*.[24] He also had a wonderful real estate trading case on behalf of a German taxpayer, where the issue, not exciting as such, was whether the profit on disposition of a piece of land was a capital gain or whether it should be treated as income. One of the tests applied by the courts in such matters is whether there have been some other similar transactions in the past, which might indicate a pattern of behaviour that could point to a business rather than realization of an investment. Bowman's client was a member of a family with many land holdings both in Canada and in Europe, and the young tax lawyer representing the Department of Justice jumped on the usual bandwagon during his examination of the client. Had the family ever disposed of real estate in the past? he demanded. The client responded affirmatively, that there had been dispositions in the past. Sensing victory as a result of this admission, the young lawyer persisted, asking when this had occurred. The answer that stopped him in his tracks and proved to be decisive in the win was that once, sometime in the seventeenth or eighteenth century, the family had disposed of a castle in Germany under pressure from one of the ruling barons, but that there had been no dispositions of any land since that time. Bowman and Shaw handled a lengthy tax evasion case involving Robert W. Larson, a legend in the woodlands industry from Thunder Bay. Even though Larson was unable to pay much for the legal services, Shaw and Bowman saw him through two separate criminal trials, which resulted in his being acquitted of the charges. The civil assessments were also contested, but eventually because of his age and the lack of financial resources, Larson was compelled to make a declaration in bankruptcy, and the matter ended.

Stikeman continued his own litigation with a number of cases. In one case, *Elgin Cooper Realties Ltd.*,[25] on a variation of Bowman's real estate trading case, he managed to convince the Exchequer Court that someone who was an acknowledged real estate trader could nevertheless have investment properties, the disposition of which did not give rise to ordinary income. I appeared with him in the case of *Bendix Automotive Ltd. v. M.N.R.*,[26] which had to be argued all the way up to the Federal Court of Appeal before we were successful. In the Tax Review Board, the appeal had been heard by its chairman, Keith Flanagan, generally a very capable and practical judge. Some time after the Federal Court of Appeal had eventually accepted the taxpayer's argument, I encountered Flanagan at a Canadian Tax Foundation Annual Conference, where he mentioned that he had seen that we had eventually prevailed in the matter. I said that we had been somewhat surprised that he had not "seen the light" when we were in front of him. He laughed and said he really had not been sure which way the case should go, but when he had seen Heward Stikeman in front of him in his morning coat and stripped trousers, he had figured that the taxpayer must be in real trouble if it needed to have Stikeman appear for it in the Tax Review Board and decided against. Stikeman and I appeared in *Quasar Investments*[27] on behalf of his long-time friend, Francis Winspear, on a relatively simple matter, which should have been resolved as a result of negotiations with the tax authorities, and we won the case in front of the Tax Review Board.

One of the biggest cases, and one of the last in which Stikeman took an active part, was on behalf of Irving Oil Limited in a transfer pricing case involving the sale of Middle East crude oil to a Bermuda company at essentially wellhead prices and the subsequent sale into Canada at market value. Several of the lawyers in the firm were involved at various times, including Bowman, Régnier, Couzin, Masson, and myself. The tax authorities had taken the view that this amounted to tax avoidance and had assessed on the basis that the Bermuda company was a sham and that the "real" price of the crude oil to Irving was the wellhead price. At the time, the company was jointly owned by the Irvings and San Francisco-based Chevron, essentially on a fifty-fifty basis. Stikeman had had a long relationship with both K.C. Irving and Chevron, and we were engaged to argue the case. The relationship between the Irvings and Chevron was always fractious, with the family constantly suspicious that they were being taken advantage of by the larger company.

The case was equally fractious, having been raised as the result of assessments made by the tax avoidance section of Revenue Canada, Taxation. The company documents were not particularly helpful, and there was a memorandum in the Chevron files that made it clear that the purpose of a particular arrangement was to make sure that the entire profit represented by the difference between the Middle East wellhead prices and the fair market value of the crude oil in Canada (essentially the profit on the transportation of the crude oil by supertanker) was to be captured in the Bermuda company and not in Canada. No one from the company saw any reason why Canada should tax profits that had been earned outside the country. When shown the memorandum and asked what he thought, Stikeman said, "It's a killer," and we went on with the preparation of the case. Much of the groundwork for the eventual successful litigation was laid during the process of examinations for discovery. They were led for the Crown by Al Sarchuk, who had done criminal prosecutions for the Department of Justice and who approached the civil tax avoidance case almost as if it were a criminal matter. It was such a disagreeable examination, with many disputes between us and many questions posed to the Chevron witness, its vice-president, Thorne Savage, that I instructed him not to answer. Fortunately, Sarchuk was appointed to the bench of the Tax Court of Canada part way through the process, and the case was handled thereafter by John Power.

We examined Lyall Mulligan of the tax avoidance section after we had insisted on having access to the files of Revenue Canada, Taxation. The examination lasted several days, during which Power often gave long rambling answers to many of the questions posed to Mulligan, adding many pages to an already bulky transcript. To our agreeable litigious surprise, in the Revenue Canada files located in Saint John, New Brunswick, we found that there were several working papers in which were recorded the evident dislike of the local authorities for the Irvings. Stikeman had let me handle the discoveries, and I had particular satisfaction in identifying some of those documents, proffering them to Mulligan, and on the transparent pretext that I could not read my copy, forced him to read into the record of the discovery all of the damaging material that the documents contained so that this evidence could be used if necessary at trial to demonstrate an overall negative attitude toward the taxpayer, including recorded observations to the general effect that Revenue Canada, Taxation simply did not think that the Irvings paid enough tax.

We ended up not acting in the matter at trial because of the suspicions on the part of the Irvings that we might be favouring the interests of Chevron over theirs. At the suggestion of Stikeman, Arthur Irving had engaged Edgar Sexton of Oslers (now a judge on the Federal Court of Appeal) to act for him in connection with his divorce, and over a period of a couple of years, Irving began to rely more and more on Sexton. At one stage, he insisted that Oslers become involved in the tax appeal as well. Stikeman was prepared to accept this on the basis that two heads were better than one as long as it was clear that we continued to have the final responsibility for the appeal. This uneasy truce lasted for a while, but Arthur Irving eventually insisted that Oslers become joint counsel with us on the appeal. After considering the implications of this (that there would be no one with ultimate responsibility for the matter), we decided that this was not possible, and following consultation with Chevron, we said that we would withdraw from the appeal. Chevron, which was looking for a way to get out of its unsatisfactory relationship with the Irvings, had not wanted any further bone of contention between them. Therefore, now that we had laid the groundwork for what we thought should be a winnable case, Chevron agreed that we should withdraw, and the company made it clear to the Irvings that the Irvings would assume the responsibility in the event of a loss. The case was ultimately successful before the Federal Court of Appeal, and Stikeman took particular delight in sending Arthur Irving a letter of congratulations on the successful outcome, pointing out how pleased he was that the evidentiary foundations and main lines of argument that had led to the success had been those developed by us in the early stages.

Régnier was an excellent litigator and acted on a number of important cases, including *D'Auteuil Lumber*,[28] *La Cie. Immobilière BCN*,[29] and *Teleglobe*,[30] and although he seldom goes to court any more, he provides extraordinarily good counsel on any cases that are in progress. Over the years, he has built a huge database of useful references derived from Canadian, British, and American cases from which he is able to extract at will important principles, references, and arguments that often prove decisive in developing the approach to new cases. He remains a fount of knowledge for the younger members of the tax section of the firm.

In my early days with the firm, I argued several cases with Bruce Verchere, including *Elias Rogers*[31] in the Federal Court of Appeal, where I first encountered Wilbur Jackett, whose published biography I would write a quarter of a century later.[32] We were the appellants in the case and had divided the argument into two sections, of which Verchere took the first and I, the second. While I was arguing (my first case in front of the Federal Court of

Appeal), Verchere passed me a note that stated in effect to hurry up and sit down since he had been observing Jackett and thought that Jackett had not only seized the point, but was anxious to have a go at the Crown. I finished as quickly as I could, sat down, and watched Jackett take apart the argument by the Crown, represented by one of his former juniors when he was deputy minister of Justice, the very capable George W. Ainslie. They had known each other for many years, so the dialogue was quite animated, punctuated by the occasional, "Mr Ainslie, you can't be serious," from Jackett. We won easily, and it was a great start to my years before the court.

We were unsuccessful in the appeal on behalf of *Longueuil Meat Exporting Co. Ltd. v. M.N.R.,*[33] which went all the way to the Supreme Court of Canada. Longueuil Meat was a rendering company that had purchased the assets of a competitor leaving the business, and it sought to deduct the costs. The president of the company, despite our urgings not to do so, announced during his testimony to the trial judge, Louis Pratte, that "rendering was the second oldest profession," to which Pratte exclaimed, with some alarm, that it was not necessary for the witness to tell him which was the oldest. Between the Federal Court of Appeal decision and the Supreme Court of Canada, Verchere had left the firm and was trying to get the client to retain him for the Supreme Court appeal, but we persuaded the client that Don Bowman was a much more experienced litigator, and he and I went to the Supreme Court, where we were, alas, demolished. My initial appearance as a junior before the Supreme Court of Canada involved my meek acknowledgment, "I have nothing to add, my Lord." Bowman and I had developed a series of terrible puns about the case as we prepared for the Supreme Court hearing, such as, "This is an 'offal' case, my Lord." As it turned out, the case did stink.

Verchere had earlier won two excellent cases in *Algoma Central Railway*[34] and *Canada Starch,*[35] which dealt with an expansion of the deductibility of business expenses and the cost of protecting a trademark. He and I lost *John McAdam v. M.N.R.*[36] in which the taxpayer had sought to get the advantage of special tax rules relating to mining claims, obtained a complete capitulation by the Crown on a capital gains issue in *Nouvelle Isle v. M.N.R.,* and won a capital gains appeal on behalf of *E.R. Squibb & Sons Ltd. v. M.N.R.*[37] before the unpredictable and occasionally unnerving Mr Justice Alex Cattanach. Stikeman and I lost the *Lois Hollinger*[38] appeal, which involved a Canadian branch of a us partnership and a mismatch between the Canadian and us taxation systems, which led to a potential result of tax liability in excess of the profits of the partnership. We had a very unsympathetic hearing before the Federal Court of Appeal, and during the course of argument, Chief Justice Jackett, sparring with Stikeman, acknowledged the potential excessive level of tax but offered the consolation that the taxpayer's husband was a doctor, and he could afford to pay the extra tax. Stikeman and Bowman lost the *Dominion Bridge*[39] appeal, an offshore tax planning arrangement developed by Charles Gavsie, former deputy minister of National Revenue. In this appeal, Jackett was railing against "these Americans," who were obviously trying to circumvent the Canadian tax system. Our client, Kenneth Barclay, was practically cowering behind Stikeman in the courtroom, especially when Stikeman advised the court that this loathsome American was in fact not American but a Canadian, and furthermore, he was present in the courtroom.

Robert Couzin and I took on the fascinating case of *GTE Sylvania Canada Ltd. v. M.N.R.*,[40] which involved the question of whether a reduction in provincial taxes pursuant to a provincial incentive program amounted to a "grant, subsidy, or other assistance" for the purpose of establishing the cost of particular assets for federal capital cost allowance purposes, and we won in the Federal Court of Appeal. This win led to a legislative amendment that has itself given rise to dozens of subsequent tax appeals. Another case, *QNS Paper Company Limited v. M.N.R.*,[41] involved the question of whether adjustments should be made to inventories in respect of depreciation (not deductible for tax purposes) that had been included in the value of the closing inventories. The case was argued before Dubé, J. in the Federal Court Trial Division against George Ainslie and Wilfrid Lefebvre. It was such a complicated case that even with careful preparation, it was hard to hold all of the elements together in a cohesive whole for more than an hour or two at a time. Early in the afternoon of the second day of hearing, Ainslie suddenly abandoned one of the grounds that he had been prepared to argue and sat down. I could tell from the look on the face of the trial judge that he had not yet got his mind around the issues. It was just after 3:00, and I stood up to say that I was of course ready to argue but that I had been taken somewhat by surprise when Ainslie dropped his second ground for support of the assessment, and if it would be of any help to the court, we could prepare some written notes of argument to assist and be ready to start first thing the following day. The trial judge was so relieved at this that he did not even ask Ainslie for comment but announced that we would resume in the morning, after which he stood up and left. We were successful on the appeal, and an eventual appeal by the Crown to the Federal Court of Appeal was held in abeyance until the legislation could be changed to achieve the result, going forward, that the Crown considered to be appropriate.

We argued several cases on behalf of various companies in the grain industry. In *Saskatchewan Wheat Pool v. The Queen*,[42] we were never able to convince the courts that the taxpayer was entitled to claim the inventory allowance introduced during the height of inflation to try to reduce the effects of inflation on taxation in respect of grain that had been held for sale to the Canadian Wheat Board. The case involved some interesting questions of law, but it was ultimately unsuccessful, and we were unable to obtain leave to appeal the matter to the Supreme Court of Canada. On the day leave application was presented, Peter Cumyn and I were before the court (in the days when leave applications were presented to a panel of three judges), and while in the lawyers' robing room after the application had been heard, a clerk came down to say that the late Bud Estey, then on the Supreme Court of Canada, had heard I was in the building and wearing his hat as chairman of Hockey Canada, wanted to talk about some Olympic matters. I went up to his chambers, and he asked what I was doing before the court. I told him I was there on a leave application. He asked what kind of a case it was. I said it was a tax case. He said I was out of luck (expressed considerably more earthily than that) since he was the only one willing to grant leave to appeal in tax cases. He was right. We had no better luck in the Cargill[43] appeal, also an inventory allowance issue, this time in respect of grain owned by the company at hundreds of locations in the areas where it carried on business; again, the Supreme Court of Canada refused to hear us.

I was finally successful on behalf of Cargill[44] in a case that probably ought to have been settled but on which Revenue Canada, Taxation, had dug in, persuading the tax court that the large pieces of machinery attached to tractors and used to fertilize soil were indeed "wagons" for purposes of categorization for capital cost allowance purposes. The highlight of the argument was my submission to the court, as one of my authorities, of an extract from a Dr Seuss book, where the letter "w" was used to illustrate that "w is for wagon." In *Bunge of Canada Ltd. v. The Queen*,[45] we had to go as far as the Federal Court of Appeal in order to demonstrate that for purposes of capital cost allowance and investment tax credits, the equipment used to unload lake freighters and to move the grain they carried into transfer elevators and then to move grain from the elevators into holds of ocean-going ships was equipment used for the purpose of storing grain. The argument was that it was an integral part of the process of "storing" grain that the grain be placed in the elevators and removed from them at the end of the storage period.

In Toronto, Couzin and Durand had a good initial win in *Marsh & McLennan Ltd.* on the issue of whether interest on short-term investments should be considered active business income, but they lost in the Federal Court of Appeal.[46] Kathryn Chalmers won an important tax case, which she argued before the Tax Court of Canada and later the Federal Court of Appeal, on behalf of Manufacturer's Life Insurance,[47] dealing with the proper computation of capital taxes. It was a very important case for the insurance and financial industry, and after some vacillation, the tax authorities decided not to apply for leave to appeal to the Supreme Court of Canada.

Robert Murray of General Motors of Canada Limited (GMCL), Pierre Martel, and I argued a case on behalf of Sandra Gernhart, an employee of General Motors Corporation (GMC), who had been assigned to work at one of the GMCL Canadian plants on a temporary assignment.[48] GMC had a policy that was designed to ensure that employees transferred within the organization at the request of GMC were not penalized financially as a result of such transfers. In this case, the policy involved paying the difference between the net take-home pay she would have received had she stayed in the United States and what she got in Canada, where the tax rates were higher. Although the computations were complex, the policy was clear. The question for Canadian tax purposes was whether the tax equalization payment was a "benefit" she enjoyed, which should in turn be taxable as employment income in Canada. It was an important issue for many multinational companies operating in Canada, and this was a test case. Judge Bonner in the Tax Court of Canada thought it was employment income. Knowing the importance of the issue, Roger Leclaire (the Justice lawyer) and I agreed that we should ask the Federal Court of Appeal to assign five instead of the usual three judges to hear the case. Chief Justice Isaac decided that a panel of three experienced judges would be sufficient. On the day of the appeal, I got to the court early and saw the three experienced judges in the corridor on the way to the courtroom. I went to the main lobby area of the Supreme Court building (where the Federal Court of Appeal sits in Ottawa) and saw Leclaire coming in. I stuck out my hand and said, "Congratulations." He asked what I was talking about. I said, "We have Isaac, Pratte, and Marceau." He thought for a second and then said he thought I was right. I argued all morning, to little avail. During the lunch break with Gernhart and the two General Motors people, Murray and David Penney, the tax manager, I said I thought this panel was adamant against us and that if the appeal were to be dismissed, I thought we should apply for leave to appeal to the Supreme Court of Canada.

When we got back, the court said that it did not even have to hear from Leclaire and proceeded to render judgment off the bench. The reasons for judgment started off with, "in spite of the very able presentation of Mr Pound ..." and proceeded to reject everything we had argued. When the chief justice finished, I stood up and asked if the judgment was now complete. It was. Was it a final judgment of the court? Yes, it was. In that case, I said, I hereby applied to this court for leave to appeal to the Supreme Court of Canada and gave the reasons, which included the extreme importance of the case, the disregard of established jurisprudence, and the disregard of important evidence that had been before the court. The chief justice replied that he was not sure that the court should entertain the motion. "Excuse me, my Lord," I said, "but I have made the motion, which I am entitled to make pursuant to the rules of the court, and I insist that you entertain it." The other two judges were signalling to him that indeed the motion must be dealt with it. They conferred, all too briefly for my liking, and then said that although the court had the power to grant leave in such circumstances, it was not its practice to do so and that the Supreme Court of Canada had a better view of the cases that it considered worth hearing. My motion was dismissed. When the printed version of the reasons for judgment were issued, the initial portion mentioning my "very able presentation" had been deleted. The Supreme Court of Canada also refused leave to appeal.[49]

An interesting tax-related issue arose from the same case. Roger Leclaire and I had discussed from time to time the requirement in section 176 of the *Income Tax Act* that whenever a taxpayer appealed from an assessment, the minister of National Revenue was required to send to the court a copy of the taxpayer's income tax return along with the notice of objection, the assessment, and other documents, which were to be placed in the court file for the appeal. As such, they would become public documents available for inspection by the public, any member of which could also get copies of them for a few cents per page. We thought this might well be unconstitutional under the *Charter* as an unreasonable seizure, and apart from this, it was a frightful nuisance and cost for the minister. We spoke one day of trying a case, which I said I was ready to do on a pro bono basis, but we first needed a real taxpayer so that the case would not be entirely academic. I asked Sandra Gernhart if she would mind being the subject of the case. She had no objection. I triggered the matter before Judge Bonner in the tax court. He was unwilling to consider the motion, which he preferred to have heard by the Federal Court of Canada, but he did agree to have her income tax return sealed in the court record pending the outcome.

Pierre Martel and I proceeded before Mr Justice Dubé of the Federal Court Trial Division, and he seemed to agree that the seizure was unreasonable but was not willing to find that it was an infringement of the *Charter*.[50] We fared better in the Federal Court of Appeal,[51] which seized on the fact that the mere filing of a tax appeal might force public disclosure of very personal matters of taxpayers, such as the amount and nature of their income, the extent of medical and other expenses, their investments, and a whole range of matters that had nothing to do with the matter in the appeal. In addition, because the material was in the court file, the court might have recourse to evidence that had not been put in by counsel and that had had no chance to be discussed as to relevance. The court agreed unanimously that this amounted to a violation of the *Charter* protection afforded to taxpayers and declared the provision to be unconstitutional. It was my first outright *Charter* case and reconfirmed my belief that specialty litigation, such as tax litigation, should be handled by tax lawyers. The "shorthand" used before expert courts by specialists is such that without familiarity with the field, one cannot be a successful advocate. I had nowhere near the same familiarity with the "usual suspects" in *Charter* litigation as I did with tax matters.

Gary Nachshen and I inherited a case from Ogilvy Renault that had two unusual issues. One was whether an insurance broker, J.H. Minet, should be taxable on insurance commissions earned by related companies in the United States. The circumstances were such that the risks were insured in the United States by local insurers, and only brokers licensed in that country could legally receive a commission. In fact, the US insurers were prohibited by law from paying commissions to unlicensed brokers, and Minet had no licence. In those cases, even though Minet had done most but not all of the work in Canada, it remitted the premiums to the US affiliate, which then placed the insurance as brokers of record and received the commissions from the insurers. Revenue Canada, Taxation, assessed the commissions in the hands of Minet even though it never received them and even though it would have been illegal for it to have done so.

The second issue was whether Minet had conferred a taxable benefit on the US brokers. Revenue Canada, Taxation, thought there had been such a benefit, and because no withholding tax had been collected, it assessed Minet for such taxes as the Canadian payor. I concentrated on the first issue, and Nachshen, on the second. Before Judge O'Connor in the tax court,[52] we won on the argument dealing with Nachshen's issue but lost on mine. Each party appealed, but the Crown decided not to proceed and withdrew its appeal. In the Federal Court of Appeal, we eventually succeeded with a nail-biting split decision.[53] On the other hand, we struck out before the same court in *First City Financial (Harrowston) v. The Queen*,[54] where the client had failed to deduct withholding taxes on an interest payment, was unable to collect the taxes from the non-resident, and had to "eat" the expense. It then sought to deduct this expense as part of the costs of doing business as an unusual but nevertheless an ordinary risk of doing business such as damaging someone else's property and having to pay damages. We knew we were in trouble when I stood up to argue and the chair of the panel, Mr Justice Hugessen, said, "Mr Pound, I must say that you have had better cases in the past."

In *Hasbro Canada Inc. v. The Queen*,[55] Glenn Cranker and I won an important victory in the Tax Court of Canada, dealing with the issue of withholding taxes on buying commissions paid to non-residents for services performed in connection with the procurement of goods, which the taxation authorities thought should be taxed in Canada. On behalf of Avon of Canada, we obtained a settlement with the Quebec authorities in connection with the deductibility of the costs of sample goods provided to sales personnel for purposes of demonstrating the qualities of the products. And, with Randall Hofley of the Ottawa office, we managed a successful intervention before the Supreme Court of Canada on behalf of Reebok Canada on the issue of whether commissions on certain imported goods should be included in the value for duty of the related goods.[56]

There will always be opportunities to provide assistance for clients who need capable representation before the courts. The biggest danger in the tax practice today, which is dominated by the large accounting firms, is that most accountants have a tendency to settle their cases too soon, before the weaknesses of the positions of the taxation authorities have been exposed. Up to the time assessments are issued and even through the administrative review that follows the filing of notices of objection, the taxpayer operates at a disadvantage. The taxpayer has no knowledge of what the authorities have in their possession and no idea of how certain they may be of their position. It is only once an appeal has been filed that the opportunity arises to examine an officer of the taxation authorities under oath on discovery and to see the materials in the departmental files – the first time in the entire process when the playing field becomes level.

A good discovery can be vital in determining whether a case is good or bad as well as to show that the taxpayer can provide evidence that will be credible to a court. I have used this process on many occasions to obtain far better settlements than would otherwise have been possible, even in cases that challenge major policy positions adopted by the authorities. It is often the first time that a lawyer from the Department of Justice has an opportunity to study the matter from the perspective of a lawyer who will have to get up in court to support the assessments. In *Algoma Steel Inc. v. The Queen*, following the discovery of the Crown, there was a complete capitulation on a case that involved more than $200 million of tax losses, which had been denied to the taxpayer. And recently, the discoveries in *Priori v. The Queen* demonstrated such complete bias on the part of the taxation authorities that they agreed to settle on a sensible basis, far removed from the position reflected in the assessments.

Tax law is one of the few remaining "great games" played between individuals and the state. The moves and countermoves have led to one of the most complex statutes in Canadian experience, and it is a matter of some speculation as to which of the players has the upper hand at any time. The machinery of the state is powerful, but the ingenuity of the taxpayer, which seeks to limit the size and extent of the shovel placed by the state into its stores, is almost equally unbounded. If there are two certainties that prevail in the human condition – death and taxes – one is certainly inevitable (if deferrable to some degree), while the other can occasionally be avoided altogether, and hope springs eternal especially if combined with the best professional advice available.

CHAPTER 12

Shipping and Insurance

The early work by John Turner in marine law was picked up by David Angus once he became a lawyer in 1964, and he became determined to elevate it into a full practice area within the firm despite the long head start of other established firms in the area. He had some connections with the industry through his father's activity in the shipping business, some contact with the actors in the area coming through Stikeman and Elliott, and a personal drive to make his name in the field. The Port of Montreal was among the most important in North America, especially once the St Lawrence Seaway officially opened in 1959, although the combination of labour strife, containerization, seaway fees, increasing ship sizes, and an American concern over the future of Canada that focused attention on the Mississippi system have, to some extent, eroded that position. These factors notwithstanding, the firm's original maritime work evolved into a broader shipping, insurance, and transportation section within the firm.

Even before he was established as a marine lawyer, Angus experienced the acceleration of responsibility always available within the firm. This is not ideally suited to all lawyers, but it has been very much part of the firm's tradition and has meant that the Stikeman Elliott lawyers who can stand the pressure have always been among the youngest on big transactions. A good example was an occasion when Angus, as a very junior lawyer, was in London with Stikeman on a Furness, Withy matter. The issues revolved around the operation of ships and the access to relieving provisions of the Canada-United Kingdom Income Tax Agreement. Furness, Withy, which was resident for tax purposes in the United Kingdom, acted as ship agents and stevedores, both for its own ships and for other shipowners while ships were in port, handling the provision of the ships and other related activities. If these activities were to be considered as "operating" the ships, then it qualified for the tax exemption; if not, the treaty protection would be unavailable. It was a question of fact and custom of the business; the tax question was quite straightforward.

Stikeman blithely announced to the client that Angus knew "everything" about shipping and would "report" on the operational questions. Stikeman was clearly bored with these non-tax issues and said he had some calls to make, whereupon he departed for three days, leaving Angus all alone with the directing minds of this major client. When Stikeman eventually returned, he discovered that the client had been completely satisfied with everything Angus had said and the meeting was successfully concluded, although the income tax point was eventually lost before the Supreme Court of Canada. The client may never have known how junior Angus was as a lawyer, but as a result of general knowledge picked up through his father and having spent a couple of years in the merchant marine before going to university, he was able to deal effectively with all of the issues.[1]

Angus has led the group with distinction and energy, appearing in many cases up to and including the Supreme Court of Canada. He says the worst experience in his professional life was in a case argued in the Federal Court of Appeal before Chief Justice Jackett, Louis Pratte, and the late Miller Hyde, who sat as a deputy judge upon his retirement from the Quebec Court of Appeal. The case was *Resolute Shipping v. Jasmin Construction,*[2] which he had argued for the former and won before Walsh, J. in the Trial Division on the basis of facts and the application of civil law. Jasmin filed an appeal, and Angus got an order for full security to be provided pending the appeal. The money was in the Canadian Imperial Bank of Commerce, and the appeal was, in Angus's opinion, without merit. When the case began, Jackett said to Angus, as counsel for the respondent, "What do you have to say before I maintain this appeal?" Clearly taken aback, Angus started to argue, but he claims he was continually abused by Jackett along the lines that there was "no room for the civil law in this court," that "you lawyers from Westmount think you can do anything you want," and so forth. After several minutes of this, Angus asked for an adjournment until after lunch so that he could consult with other lawyers in the firm as to what steps he should take, such as getting a stenographer into court or to take some other extraordinary action. It seemed to him that he was almost to be held in contempt of court for making his argument. The court allowed Jasmin's appeal. The company got the security money back and disappeared since it was going out of business. The Supreme Court of Canada gave judgment in the subsequent appeal in favour of Angus's client, but by then, it was too late and the money was gone. Angus says that Miller Hyde later called his father to apologize for Jackett's behaviour.

Angus once acted for an Italian client who operated a wine business involving importing grapes and wine concentrate into Canada and then processing and bottling it for sale here. It was well short of vintage quality, but the business was successful for several years. There was obviously some tension connected with the business, of which Angus was unaware, to the point that the client appeared to consider himself in some physical danger, and Angus was startled one day in the office to find that his client was carrying a firearm. He said that in the future, the client could not come to the office armed. The client discontinued this practice, at least to Angus's knowledge.

One of the first to join Angus in this practice was Vincent Prager,[3] who had come to the firm in 1967 during his third year of law after already agreeing to article at Cate Ogilvy. Stephen Scott was an articling student that year before returning to McGill as a professor of constitutional law. The firm also offered a position to Juanita Westmoreland, a radical black student who eventually became dean of law at the University of Windsor and is now a municipal court judge in Montreal. She was recently given an honorary doctorate of laws by Concordia University. Scott knew Prager through his family and advised him that Angus needed some help, so he arranged for them to meet, and Prager was taken on as a student for three days a week. He felt obliged to honour his commitment to article at Cate Ogilvy, but during the course of the process, he decided he would rather work at Stikeman Elliott and joined the firm immediately upon being called to the Bar in 1968. Shortly thereafter, the group was joined by Marc De Man,[4] Peter Cullen,[5] and Laurent Fortier.[6] Apart from De Man, who left following an enormous professional blunder that exposed the firm to legal action, they make up the bulk of the section, now part of the litigation group today.

There is probably no one in the firm who has travelled as much as Prager, although when he arrived at the firm, he had never been on an airplane and was terrified of the whole idea. His first big case was handed to him by Angus. On the ship *Montcalm*, a large Caterpillar tractor, lashed on board by our client, Eastern Canada Stevedoring, had come loose and made a large hole in the side of the ship. The ship, which almost sank, was able to limp back to port in Halifax, and Angus sent Prager to Halifax to be there for the arrival to inspect the damage and to interview everyone he could find. Prager booked himself on the night train from Windsor station to Saint John, NB, from where he was to take the ferry to Digby, NS and then carry on by train to Halifax. As soon as he arrived in Saint John, he was met by the manager of the client who advised him that the ship would be getting in early and that they were leaving by plane from Saint John to Halifax within the hour. In front of the client, he had to be brave, and his first flight, on a TCA Viscount, was a smooth one. Thus began a career that has since measured many millions of miles in the air. He was sufficiently impressed with himself that he flew all the way back to Montreal from Halifax on a TCA Vanguard. The experience thrilled him so much that he has kept ever since the boarding passes for the first two flights – as well as for most of his other flights!

In a case for the Vardinoyannis family, founders of Motor Oil Hellas, these Greek shipowners had ordered three 80,000-ton tankers to be built at the Davie Shipyard. Persons claiming to be their agents sued the shipowners for commissions to which they alleged entitlement. In a particularly acrimonious dispute, Robb and Prager defended the claims all the way to the Supreme Court of Canada (unsuccessfully), argued for the plaintiffs by Emile Colas, Andrew Pytel, and Philippe Casgrain. Prager had to meet the clients in Athens, and having little confidence in Olympic Airways, he chose to fly KLM to Amsterdam and connect there to Athens. On his first trip, he spent the evenings in the King George Hotel in Athens, going through his materials and, as he did on numerous trips thereafter, trying to learn the Greek alphabet by comparing the English and Greek versions of the menu. It was the time of the colonels junta, and one had to be careful. When the time came to return to Montreal, Theo Vardinoyannis asked for his tickets in order to reconfirm his reservations. Prager handed them over, but two minutes later, the client returned, furious. Prager asked what was wrong. "I hired a first-class lawyer. A first-class lawyer should always travel first class. Why did you book tourist?" The ticket was exchanged, and Prager learned the valuable lesson that in a service business, appearances are important.

The clients lost faith in the Canadian judicial system despite the fact that one of them had actually applied for landed immigrant status. They refused to come to Canada either for the preparation of the evidence or for the trial, which made preparation particularly difficult and meant many trips to Athens. During the trial, for five weeks in a row, Prager was in Montreal Monday through Thursday, flew to Athens Thursday evening, worked there Friday afternoon, Saturday, and part of Sunday, and then flew back to Montreal. The client, Vardinoyannis, was darkly referred to by Casgrain, one of the opposing counsel, as the "Godfather." One of the plaintiffs, William Roloff, was asked a question at trial by Colas, to the general effect of whether he thought that he had been of value to the Vardinoyannis interests, to which he answered "yes." However, the trial transcript indicated that "(witness pats himself on the back)." The week following the trial, Prager was invited to the gala opening of a new refinery in Corinth, outside Athens. Since Robb and his wife could not go, their place was taken by Angus and his wife, this time on a chartered Olympic Airways plane from New York, which stopped in London to pick up some other guests. They had the exciting but occasionally unnerving experience of being met on arrival as VIPs by the senior of the ruling junta's colonels and being ferried to all events in motorcades.

Like almost all of the early lawyers, Prager has a couple of Fraser Elliott stories. A year or two after joining the firm, he decided that he would try something different and wore a pair of grey flannel trousers and a Harris tweed jacket to the office. By ten o'clock, Elliott came into his office, sat down, stated that the office dress code was a suit, got up, and left. It was Prager's longest conversation with him during his first few years as a lawyer. He was also present at a party given by the Elliotts for the lawyers at their home on Aberdeen Avenue and witnessed Elliott talking at some length with the husband of Claudette Picard, the first female lawyer to join the firm and eventually the first female partner. Toward the end of the conversation, Elliott asked him the name of his wife, and Picard, no shrinking violet, told him that she, not he, was the lawyer.

As the practice of maritime law developed within the firm, it evolved from one of representing local stevedores, agents, and cargo underwriters to international shipowners and operators, protection and indemnity associations, hull and machinery insurers, liability insurers, the Lloyd's market, the Institute of London Underwriters, the London Insurance and Re-insurance Market Association, the International Underwriting Association, as well as European, American, and Japanese-based insurers. Along the way, the group expanded the practice to include non-marine insurance as well, with expertise in comprehensive general liability, directors and officers insurance, errors and omissions, product liability, property and special risks, as well as energy risks involving offshore activities (such as the Hibernia, Sable Island, and Terra Nova oil and gas fields). It also established a network of relationships with a considerable number of commercial firms in Europe, Asia, and the United States.

The practice was particularly interesting because it was "international" long before the globalization of commerce and legal services. Being at the mouth of the St Lawrence Seaway, the deep-sea waterway for foreign vessels trading into the United States and Canadian Great Lakes, Montreal was well situated for such a practice. The group had its share of groundings, collisions, sinkings, pollution incidents and fires, arrest of ships, cargo, and freight, bills of lading, contracts of affreightment, charter party, shipbuilding contracts, purchase and sale, salvage, arbitrations, mediations, litigation, international sale of goods, letters of credit disputes, and seizure-forfeiture cases. Over the years, it has represented major deep-sea ship operators as well as the major owners and operators of the Canadian Lakes Fleet. It has been on a regular retainer by both the Shipping Federation of Canada and the Canadian Shipowners Association; it is currently counsel to the St Lawrence Seaway Management Corporation.

One seizure-forfeiture case handled by the firm in the early 1990s was particularly memorable for Peter Cullen. It involved the confiscation at Sept-Îsles, Quebec by Canada Customs and Revenue officials of a tug and semi-submersible ocean-going barge worth $US14 million.[7] The offence was the smuggling into Canada of 44 tonnes of hashish worth $US750 million! In 1991, Angus received a call from the London-based hull insurers of a large, reputable Dutch salvage company. It required the firm's services to obtain the release of the barge so that she could be redelivered to her owners in order to move an oil rig in the North Sea. As time was of the essence, Cullen, who had Dutch connections, went to Rotterdam and London to meet the owners and insurers and to run the file.

The barge had been on a bare-boat charter to a Dutch tug company, which had operated it on a tramp container delivery basis around the east and west coasts of Africa. The tug company had taken delivery of the barge in Singapore and had agreed to operate it for one year, with redelivery in the North Sea. The owners of the barge, the Dutch salvage company, which had chartered her out without any crew, received noon position reports from the tug company every few days confirming the barge's location.

Unbeknownst to her owners, the barge had picked up a substantial load of hashish off Pakistan on her way to the African coast. As Interpol would later advise us, the charter arrangement and the container delivery business were a complete subterfuge, and our innocent clients had been unknowingly duped into participating in a large, well-organized international drug smuggling ring, the purpose of which was to deliver the hashish to the New England market via the quiet north shore of the St Lawrence River below Sept-Îsles. It was an elaborate procedure that involved submerging the barge, off-loading the sealed barrels of hashish (as a flotilla), towing them to shore for burial in a trench the smugglers had bulldozed in advance, and then keeping the barrels under water until they were ready to be taken out and dealt with. The hashish was to have been packed with boxes of frozen seafood and trucked to dealers in Boston and New York.

The landing craft proved to be underpowered and could not manage the job, so as daylight was approaching, the barrels were cut loose. A number were found by native fishermen. Fearing a vessel had been lost, they advised the authorities, who descended in strength and later seized and confiscated the barge. To obtain the release of the barge, our clients would be required to establish that they had taken reasonable steps when chartering the barge to the tug company to ensure that the latter would not contravene Canada's customs laws. As the barge was never to go to Canada as far as the clients were concerned, this was a considerable hill to climb!

However, a number of factors were working in the clients' favour. When they had chartered the barge to the tug company, they had had the presence of mind to run the operation by a reputable Dutch shipping broker who had vouched for the tug operator. (The broker also had been taken in unwittingly.) We could therefore establish to the court that our clients had not acted recklessly or simply turned a blind eye. Our clients also testified at the criminal trial in Montreal against the tug crew and operators who had brought the barge into Canada. Once our clients' innocence had been established to the satisfaction of Interpol and the Montreal police authorities, we applied to the court and successfully argued for the release of the barge; she was able to make her North Sea connection. In the interim, to protect the barge from early winter weather, she was largely submerged in the bay at Sept-Îsles. As for the hashish, the story on the river was that it was incinerated at Baie Comeau, upwind of the local penitentiary!

Other memorable shipping mandates for Cullen include working with Angus to protect the St Lawrence Seaway Authority's interests in the Welland Canal collapse and the striking of the St Louis Bridge (by an Indian flag vessel) in the mid-1980s. Both these events caused considerable backup and delay to international shipping, and he successfully defended the Canadian Coast Guard[8] when the domestic and international shipping community brought suits for delays to some 100 vessels caused by a questionable strike in 1989 at the height of one of the harshest and earliest onslaughts of river ice seen in recent history.

River ice had been a factor in an earlier "safe berth" case in *Duteous*,[9] where Angus and Laurent Fortier successfully defended the liability insurers of the vessel's charterers and agents. In 1981, below Montreal, the river had frozen to such an extent that the water level in the harbour had risen several feet, and the *Duteous* was encased in ice. When the ice jam was broken, "a force of awesome proportion" was unleashed, causing the vessel to be swept away from her moorings, leaving her to drift helplessly in the packed ice, where she collided with a neighbouring vessel and two shore cranes. One of the shore cranes ended up on the stern of the *Duteous*, and the other was pushed off the wharf and into the river. Adding to the unreality of the whole situation, the harbour master (in a helicopter overhead) ordered the *Duteous* to proceed to the "south shore." This is a common enough expression for Montrealers, but in fact, the "south" shore is actually east not south of the port, and the bewildered foreign master of the *Duteous* could be heard shouting over the radio, "There is no south shore" since, of course, there was none on his charts!

On October 14, 1978, the day before Fortier finished his articling period and became a lawyer, the vessels *Cielo Bianco* and *Algobay* collided in the Bay of Sept-Îles, crushing and sinking the tug *Pointe Marguerite*. Two crew members died in the accident. Angus and Fortier were retained by the insurers and owners of the tug. They left Montreal for what they expected to be the day and ended up in Sept-Îles for four days, hitching a ride back to Montreal on one of the Iron Ore Company's planes, a company then headed by Brian Mulroney. The mandate extended to six weeks of commission hearings conducted under the chairmanship of Mr Justice François Chevalier in Quebec City, where Fortier marvelled at the staying power of Angus, who needed only four hours of sleep a day. A grisly aspect of the case was attending the salvage operations in Sept-Îsles for the raising of the tug and the recovery of the bodies of the two victims.

Two years later, there was a fire on board the *Cartiercliff Hall* while she was traversing the Great Lakes and seaway system, which resulted in the loss of some eighteen lives. This led to another commission of inquiry headed by Mr Justice Kenneth McKay, to which Transport Canada appointed Angus as commission counsel and Fortier the secretary. In the course of this, Fortier learned "everything" about fires on board ship, and the commission made recommendations that led to amendments to the safety regulations incorporated in the *Canada Shipping Act*. Fire remains one of the principal dangers aboard ship, and the following year, there was a fire on the *Hudson Transport,* which led to loss of life during the abandonment of the ship when a life raft filled with water. Ironically, among those lost was the former second mate of the *Cartiercliff Hall,* who had survived that first disaster. The firm was retained by the insurers and the manufacturers of the life rafts, RFD (Rescue from Disaster) Ltd. in the United Kingdom, which led to Fortier learning the history of life rafts and their manufacture in the United Kingdom, Holland, and Norway. The case was settled a week before the scheduled trial.

Expertise in the matter of fires led to another mandate for Prager and Fortier, which ended up in the Supreme Court of Canada. There had been a fire aboard a bulk grain vessel, and they were retained by the Belgian shipowners, Bocimar, to recover general average expenses that were challenged on the basis of the unseaworthiness of the crew due to lack of firefighting experience. After losing before the Federal Court Trial Division, they won at the Federal Court of Appeal but eventually lost before the Supreme Court of Canada.[10]

Fortier had an initially unpleasant but ultimately satisfying experience confronting the Irving Group in 1993. The firm had for many years acted for Irving on a variety of tax and domestic matters, but the relationship had cooled with the retirement of K.C. Irving and the passing of operational control. As Irving no longer used the firm, we were free to act in the case of the *Trio Trader,* a barge under tow by an Irving company, Atlantic Towing

Ltd., which sank off the east coast. The firm was acting for the owners and insurers of the barge and its cargo against the Irving Group, the insurers of which had become insolvent. A week before the trial, the vice-president, legal, of the Irving Group came to Montreal from Saint John, NB, Irving's headquarters, on a mission to settle the action. He was contemptuous of the claim and offered to settle for $400,000. Fortier countered with $900,000, much less than the full claim, but the offer was rejected and the six-week trial proceeded. The firm was successful for the full claim of $2.5 million, and the award was confirmed by the Federal Court of Appeal, with interest plus costs totalling $300,000.[11]

CHAPTER 13

Employment Law

Apart from some early cases argued by Robb that dealt with the legal issues of whether reasonable notice was a requirement of Quebec law[1] and the effect of non-competition clauses in employment agreements,[2] as well as the occasional case taken on by Freiheit (arguing for CAE that professional engineers could not unionize because they were management), the firm's activities in the employment field were started in earnest by Stanley Hartt. His initial mandates were pedestrian enough, but he was not, and over time, matters of increasing importance were directed his way, including some of national importance such as the air traffic controllers' strike.

Air traffic controllers are a different breed. They have enormous responsibility for safety in the air, and they work at busy airports and in crowded air corridors under conditions of high stress. They all consider themselves to be the CEOs of the skies and constantly resent the fact that they are not paid as much nor treated with the same awe and respect as the pilots, who merely fly where and when they are told by them. Stanley Hartt was called in to deal with a threatened strike in 1976.[3] The final issues after lengthy negotiations were reduced to two. They wanted a cost-of-living increase of $500 and a settlement of the other monetary issues on a regional basis, in which the amounts would vary according to the circumstances in each area, as had been negotiated by another bargaining unit in the federal public service. On the first issue, Hartt arranged to call Bud Drury, the responsible federal minister, who agreed that he could support a one-time adjustment in the amount requested for all public servants, including the air traffic controllers, and he agreed to make the announcement that very day in the House of Commons. As to the remaining financial issues, he agreed with the aggregate amount involved and sent the confirmation to Hartt. The meetings with the leaders of the air traffic controllers' union were being held in Quebec City. Hartt took everyone to the Continental Restaurant, one of the finest of the many excellent Quebec City establishments, and treated them all to a good dinner. Cognacs were called for and consumed in generous quantities. When the requisite degree of mellowness had been achieved, Hartt said, "Let me tell you what I have done. I have taken the financial package and have asked the Treasury Board to spread it on a regional basis." He then passed the paper to the bargaining group, and each person studied it one by one. When the paper had been scrutinized by each member, the chairman returned it to Hartt and said, "Now, put it back in your fucking pocket and let's never mention it again." The matter was thereupon settled, without the previously non-negotiable regional allocation.

More problematic was the Toronto teachers' strike in November 1975. This was a dispute that had its origins in certain test negotiations in the smaller areas of Ottawa and Windsor. It had simmered for several years, with resignations and legislation imposing working conditions, a desire to establish bargaining units between teachers and the school boards, demands for major salary increases, and other benefits. The Windsor strike had oc-curred in November 1974, and others followed in Thunder Bay and Ottawa. When the Ottawa strike was settled, the stakes escalated to the major Metro Toronto area. The salary demands alone were in the order of 45 per cent increases, but Hartt had negotiated these down to some 39 per cent over a three-year period. He knew that something was going to happen in the area of wage and price controls, and he used that leverage to get the matter settled. The unions were agreeable, and they were in the process of signing the many agreements "like mad" when Trudeau made the wage and price control announcement on October 14, 1975. The signing stopped. Every-one felt that they now had to re-examine the political ramifications. The negotiations stopped as well, and a strike ensued on November 12, 1975. Hartt remembers being on the CBC radio program *Cross-Country Checkup* during which Donald MacDonald, then minister of Finance, accused him of the historical precedent of having caused a major strike. Unions, said Hartt, did not cause inflation (the ostensible reason for wage and price controls). The only party that could prevent inflation, through control of the money supply, was the government. The matter was eventually referred by the Ontario government to Justice Charles Dubin, who gave the unions the same 39 per cent increase that Hartt had negotiated. It was a bad strike, which resulted in the biggest defeat for the union and in the union leader taking his own life.

Hartt also represented the Air Canada pilots and attendants and the Que-bec truckers in labour matters. In the spring of 1985, he was handling the National Economic Conference. Prime Minister Brian Mulroney wanted to be seen as consulting a broad spectrum of the community and had convened the event to bring together labour, the volunteer sector, and the business community, represented by Rowland Frazee, then chairman of the Royal Bank of Canada. Just as this was about to unfold at the Congress Centre in Ottawa, a strike by post office employees loomed. Mulroney said that the only way to hold the conference was to get the strike settled. Hartt prepared a report that both sides of the dispute were ready to accept – it contained a balance between what the union could have obtained on a voluntary basis from management and what management had been disposed to concede. Strikes, observed Hartt, are settled when people want to settle.

Despite the high-profile work of Hartt, the firm had no specialized em-ployment group as such until the late 1980s. Hartt had interested Edward

Aust[4] in the field, and he became increasingly active in the mid-1980s, but there was no sense of urgency within the firm's management to expand the area. Traditional labour work tended to be divided between those lawyers who were perceived as "union" lawyers and those who were "management" lawyers, and there was little, if any, crossover between them. Despite the occasional headline case in which Hartt had acted for the unions, the firm was generally on the management side of labour negotiations. The practice, particularly in highly unionized Quebec, was generally routine, dealing with negotiations and grievances under collective labour agreements, occasionally with certification of bargaining units thrown in and even more rarely, a strike. It was a high-volume, low-return practice, which required the ability to put lawyers in the field for days or weeks at a time for bargaining sessions and a plethora of unimportant but time-consuming proceedings. The time demands of the traditional practice had been the prime reason that Hartt decided to give up the activity and to start doing arbitration work.

Aust was equally conscious that the firm had no appetite for a high-volume practice in the labour field, and while still handling the usual work, he began to think about a variation on the theme – about the kind of services that might be attractive to clients of the firm, which would act as a drawing card in a niche that was largely unoccupied. He and Pierre Jauvin, who had been called to the Quebec Bar in 1985, began to explore the nature of the employment contract as it related to business executives. Aust also attracted the attention of Patrick Benaroche,[5] who was then doing mainly commercial and banking litigation, and because of his background in industrial psychology, he thought he might be a good fit within the practice he was developing. Benaroche had joined the firm in 1985 after having done most of his *stage* (the Quebec articling period) with McCarthy Tétrault (Clarkson Tétrault at the time). The qualifier "most" is the result of Freiheit's insistence that Benaroche start immediately, so he completed the stage with the firm. He joined the litigation department, which at that time was unofficially divided into two subgroups: Michel Décary, headed up a group with Marc Prévost, Marc Laurin, Denis Lachance, Julie-Martine Loranger, and others, doing general civil litigation; and Freiheit, Stephen Raicek, and Isabelle Paquet concentrated on commercial litigation. Benaroche was the fourth person to work directly with Freiheit and his team. There was no formal labour department, and a number of the litigation lawyers responded to labour and employment work on an as-needed basis. Aust began to mentor Benaroche and to feed him a few labour files, which Benaroche found that he enjoyed. In 1987, while on holidays in the Caribbean, Aust contracted a virulent strain of food poisoning, which left him unable to work for almost six months. During his absence, Benaroche handled some of his files, finding that he received much more satisfaction from them than from the other work he was doing at the time.

Upon his return to good health and to the office, Aust arranged to hire Danielle Grenier, who had been employed in the public sector for some time but who had a very good reputation as a lawyer and was working on Lyse Charette,[6] a *stagiaire* who was showing interest in the labour and employment field. By 1989, it had been agreed between Aust and Freiheit that Benaroche would transfer from the litigation group to the labour group. There was excellent chemistry at the time largely as a result of Aust's personal involvement with all of the younger lawyers, and Jauvin and Benaroche complemented each other quite well. They made jurisprudence in the file of *Patrick Kealty v. SITA*,[7] having the Quebec *Charter of Human Rights and Freedoms* declared constitutionally inapplicable to federally regulated undertakings. Kealty, who was fired from SITA for refusing to take a urine test for drug use, claimed the dismissal was in violation of his Quebec *Charter* rights. The case was settled on appeal.

Aust lectured for ten years at Concordia and Queen's universities, did a great deal of professional writing, and was chairman of the labour department within the firm. The firm supported him in his efforts to break into a league that would otherwise have been virtually inaccessible despite the fact that it was not considered to be a mainstream area for the firm. Aust nurtured the group as it developed expertise, and he turned to the promotional and pedagogical tool of writing. He wrote, with Lyse Charette, *The Employment Contract (le contract d'emploi)*, which was published in 1988 by Les Editions Yvon Blais Inc. He produced and coordinated *Executive Employment Law*, which he started writing in 1991; the first edition was published in 1993 by Butterworths. His book *Les Dirigants: Leurs Droits et Leurs Obligations*, published by Yvon Blais in 1995, was the first French language publication on the subject. The final publication was *Executives and Managers: Their Rights and Duties*, published by Butterworths in 1997. Publication of the books had the desired promotional effect, leading to several international invitations to speak and advise on labour matters. Aust was invited as a state guest by the Ministry of Labour of the People's Republic of China and by two of that country's largest provinces for a series of lectures at all major universities with governments and labour departments. He recalls speaking virtually non-stop for a month until midnight every night. The labour book was published in a Chinese edition as well. He was also invited to Russia for a two-week stint by the faculty of law at St Petersburg University, where he lectured on North American law as it pertains to executives.

One of two books used in the course of the reform of the Quebec Civil Code in the field of labour law was Aust's employment law book, and it has been cited in the Quebec Court of Appeal many times. Aust himself has appeared before every labour tribunal, the Quebec Superior Court, the Quebec Court of Appeal, and the Supreme Court of Canada on labour matters. He spent a year representing the board of governors of Concordia University and its chairman, Reginald Groome, dealing with charges of abuse of power by the rector, Patrick Kenniff, and the vice-rector, which led to their dismissal by the board of governors.

One of Benaroche's first experiences in the litigation group involved a family law matter that Jean-Judes Chabot was handling at the time: the Peter McConnell divorce, which bounced around the courts for about ten years. The firm represented Peter McConnell; his wife was represented by a series of constantly changing attorneys. Chabot was leaving on vacation and asked Benaroche to cover for him. A couple of days later, Benaroche received a call from Micheline Parizeau – then known as the infamous attorney Mimi Popovici, with the best hairdo in the courthouse and tough as nails when it came to beating up on wealthy husbands. In the call, Popovici told him that she was the new attorney of record for McConnell's wife and asked if he would mind if she sent a messenger over to the office to sign a consent to substitution of attorney form so that she could start working on the file. Although he had heard enough about her to be cautious in dealing with her, Benaroche assumed that little harm could be done by signing the consent, which he thought was simply showing good form vis-à-vis a confrere. The messenger arrived at approximately noon, and he signed the document. At 12:30 that same day, he received a motion requiring him to be in court that afternoon at 2:30 for a revision of alimony and other provisional measures that had previously been awarded. He tried to explain to Popovici that he was not the attorney of record for Peter McConnell and suggested that she put off the motion for a week until Chabot returned, but she rewarded his earlier co-operation by adamantly refusing any postponement and insisted that the motion proceed.

Benaroche went to court and made his representations before the judge to the effect that a postponement would better serve the interests of justice and of his client. At that point, Popovici, perhaps wanting to make an impression on her client, began her pleadings by referring to Benaroche as "this young lawyer" and repeated this reference quite arrogantly two or three times. At one point, Mr Justice Maurice Mercure looked up at her and said angrily, "Would you stop referring to him as 'this young lawyer.' I am sure that if he got up and started referring to you as 'this old lawyer,' you would not like it very much." He then proceeded to grant the request for a postponement of the motion. In another of life's ironies, she later became a client of the firm when she had her *démêlé* with the Bar regarding allegations of unethical conduct against her.

In 1988–89, Benaroche inherited the publicly sensitive file of *E.J. Gordon v. The Gazette*. Elsie Jean (known to everyone in Montreal as "E.J.") Gordon had been the social columnist at the *Gazette* for forty-two years and was a close personal friend of Stikeman. There was a musical event scheduled as a fundraiser at Place des Arts, and an organizer had called E.J. Gordon to attend the event. She mentioned to the organizer, "I hope you aren't going to sit me at that terrible Jewish table that I sat at last year." She went on to explain that at the previous year's function, the people at the table were smoking obnoxious cigars and refused to put them out when she and her escort had asked them to do so. The Place des Arts organizer responded by saying, "You will be sitting at Senator (Leo) Kolber's table," to which she responded, "Oh well, he is okay."

Bad news travels quickly, so naturally, word got back to the *Gazette* about Gordon's conversation, and she was summoned into the editor's office. Within fifteen minutes, she was told that "she had insulted the Jews" and she was fired. Gordon explained that perhaps her remarks were thoughtless, but they were certainly not intentional, and she offered to apologize or do anything else to make amends, but the *Gazette* would not hear of it and simply asked her to leave. She then called Stikeman to seek advice, who handed the file over to Aust. E.J.'s case was discussed quite thoroughly by the members in the employment group, who all found it to be a difficult case. Even Stanley Hartt called it a "loser," feeling that there was just cause for her dismissal. Benaroche was not initially involved, but because of his litigation background, his practice leaned strongly toward employment litigation. After the file had been tossed around a while within the group, it eventually ended up on his desk. He would like to think that it was mere coincidence that he was the only Jewish member of the group.

Gordon was seventy-seven years old at the time, had never married, and her entire life was her work. She was writing two or three columns a week for the *Gazette* on a so-called freelance basis and was earning no more than $15,000 to $20,000 a year. There were a number of obstacles, including the fact that because of E.J.'s limited income, she did not have the means to afford legal fees for a lawsuit against the *Gazette*. Benaroche went to see Stikeman and delicately raised this point with him to see what he wanted him to do. After a brief moment of reflection, Stikeman looked up at him and said, "Well, after all, we are lawyers first, aren't we?" Benaroche then did whatever was needed to defend Gordon, not knowing whether the firm would ever get paid. He took the case because he felt that E.J. Gordon had been wronged. Although her remarks were inappropriate, he did not believe they warranted dismissal and thought the *Gazette* was simply using her conversation as a pretext for getting rid of an elderly columnist whom they otherwise could not fire because of Quebec's labour laws that prohibit mandatory retirement based on age. He also felt that the Jewish community would be indirectly blamed for her dismissal, which he thought would also be unfair.

The other obstacles were that E.J. was working under a so-called freelance structure, so there was a whole debate as to whether she was even an employee of the *Gazette*. If she was not, her recourses were seriously curtailed. Benaroche decided to file a complaint with the Labour Standards Commission alleging that E.J. Gordon was an employee of the *Gazette* and having accumulated more than three years of uninterrupted service, she had the right not to be dismissed without just and sufficient cause. Of course, by now her pride was severely wounded, and she had no interest in returning to the *Gazette*, so she was left with a claim for damages. However, given her low salary, even an award of one year's wages would not cover her legal fees. Benaroche looked for a way to put some pressure on the *Gazette* to obtain a higher award and came up with the idea of asking the arbitrator hearing the case to order the *Gazette* to publish an apology to E.J. Gordon on the front page of the paper.

The case was heard before arbitrator Pierre Laporte. Benaroche's closing arguments lasted approximately one and a half hours, immediately following which E.J. turned to him and said, loud enough for the entire room to hear, "Oh Patrick, that was terrific. You were just like Gregory Peck in *To Kill a Mockingbird!*" The decision was rendered approximately one month later.

Benaroche won the case, and in addition, the arbitrator granted his request that the *Gazette* publish an apology to E.J. on the front page of the paper. Richard Beaulieu at McCarthy Tétrault, who acted for the *Gazette*, called Benaroche immediately thereafter, in quite a fit, to say that, "No one would ever tell the *Gazette* what to publish," and that this case was going all the way to the Supreme Court of Canada, which clearly meant to Benaroche that he was now going to get a decent settlement. He did in fact settle out of court, the legal fees were covered, and there was enough money left over to make E.J. happy. Aust organized a victory party with Stikeman and a bunch of other socialites and E.J.'s closest friends in the firm's boardroom. Benaroche was a hero for a day, and Aust took a very comical photograph of Stikeman and Benaroche, reproducing the classic Karsh portrait of Stikeman and Elliott that hangs in all the firm's offices, in which Benaroche is seated in a chair, posing in the place of Elliott, with Stikeman behind him.

He continued to work in the labour and employment group and to develop a very close working relationship with Aust. Jean-Pierre Belhumeur[8] has maintained his own niche within the section, in which his practice follows the more traditional labour law model across a variety of employment-related issues. Danielle Grenier was appointed to the bench of the Quebec Superior Court and has become a well-respected judge of that court. Lyse Charette departed to have a family and pursue an MBA, and Pierre Jauvin left the firm to work in-house at Yellow Shoes. By 1994, the group consisted of Aust, Belhumeur, Benaroche, and Hélène Bussières. They hired Eveline Poirier and Lily Germain and following them, Julie Patry. Aust left the firm in 1998 to pursue other ventures, and approximately one year after that, Benaroche assumed the leadership of the section.

Bruce Pollock in Toronto heads up the small practice group that consists of himself and Lorna Cuthbert[9] as partners and (as at the end of the first half-century of the firm) Julie Thibault and Jennifer Hirlehey. When Fred Von Veh had been with the firm, the practice had been very much labour-oriented, acting on behalf of companies that had unionized work forces, dealing with certification of bargaining units, collective bargaining, unfair labour practice complaints, and the usual range of issues arising from such relationships. It has now evolved into a supportive practice for clients of the firm who are involved in M&A transactions, providing the related employment and labour advice, and it has much less stand-alone labour work. In many M&A situations, there can be wrongful dismissal issues that arise, whether by accident or deliberately, and several important other aspects such as pension and deferred compensation on which they work closely with Gary Nachshen, who has made a specialty of this field. The Toronto practice has not focused to the same extent as the Montreal one has on the executive employment area, although it has a significant volume of such work for executives who are transferring in or out of corporations in the course of reorganizations. Pollock's practice includes the barrister portion of the group's activity, and he appears before the courts, boards, and tribunals dealing with employment matters, while Cuthbert plays a more traditional solicitor's role on the transactional side of the practice.

As is often the case, the litigators have a view that they see real life quite removed from the multimillion- or multibillion-dollar transactions. Pollock had such an exposure when one of his clients had suspended a unionized worker for two months after he had become inebriated at a company golf outing and threatened his supervisor. The matter proceeded to arbitration, where the position advanced on behalf of the employee was that the company had it in for him and the suspension was part of the overall attitude. The plant manager was being cross-examined by the union lawyer who was representing the employee. He was asked whether he was upset with the employee because he had refused to work overtime a few months earlier. The manager allowed that he was disappointed because the employee had come to him earlier to say that he wanted to buy a new car and would like to get some additional income. The first time that he was asked to put in some overtime, he refused to do so. He said that under the circumstances, this had been disappointing. The lawyer persisted and asked the manager whether he had in fact said to the employee that he was going to "fuck him into the ground?" No, the plant manager said, that was not an expression he would ever have used. What would he have used, asked the lawyer? "I told him I was going to fuck him from here to eternity," replied the manager. When he got off the witness stand, he came over to Pollock and said, "I guess I left that part out, didn't I?" Pollock allowed that this was true, but they managed to sustain the suspension nevertheless.

The principal legacy has been the development of a very important niche practice with executive employment contracts at the centre. The firm, particularly in Montreal, was the first to concentrate in this area and by doing so, got into an emerging area of high-end law. It did not try to compete with the thirty-man traditional labour law firms but adopted a multidisciplinary approach to the employment contract, providing one-stop shopping as a boutique capable of putting out contracts at this level while still retaining a reputation before the courts. An example of this was Bussières's successful defence of an employee who had been dismissed for having made non-business use of the Internet during working hours. It also provided tremendous exposure to Canada's corporate elite, where employment contracts have become increasingly important in the face of mergers and acquisitions and activist boards that have no reservations in exercising their power to terminate CEOs and other officers. The Toronto office has generally followed the same trend away from pure labour matters, although it still maintains the capacity to serve clients whose work forces are unionized.

CHAPTER 14

Trade, Competition, Intellectual Property, Real Estate, and Alternative Dispute Resolution (ADR)

TRADE

In the early 1950s, international trade was a description generally applied to overseas commerce. Trade with Canada's closest partner, the United States, was referred to as cross-border trade and was regarded as a normal commercial or civil law matter, one without any special considerations. International trade was generally considered in the same way, other than regarding issues such as financing contracts, letters of credit, bank guarantees and so forth, which were somewhat exotic essentially because they posed collection problems.

With the arrival in the 1950s of Japanese trading companies in Canada, international trade, aside from selling to and buying from the United States, gained importance for Canada and more particularly, for the firm. Most of the major trading companies at that time were heavily involved in textiles and ready-made goods. Quebec, especially Montreal, was not only a major textile centre but also a North American fashion leader, with the result that by the end of the decade, most of the major Japanese trading companies had established branches in the province.

When it came to legal advice for many of these companies, George Tamaki was the natural choice because of his Japanese ancestry. At this time, Jim Robb was a junior, theoretically doing tax and other litigation, but as the low man on the totem pole, he got anything that came along. As a result, a number of problems encountered by the Japanese as they sought to establish themselves in Canada ended up on Robb's desk. While none of these early mandates could properly be characterized as international trade, they nevertheless evolved from international trade and began to develop into the more extensive trading relationships that now exist as the Japanese began acquiring Canadian products, beginning with asbestos and expanding into other minerals, pulp, food, and other products.

Tamaki had a rapidly developing tax practice. Because the tax problems of international trade were minimal (halcyon days!), he suggested that Robb take direct responsibility for handling a number of the Japanese companies for two reasons. First, the Japanese clients expected Tamaki to speak Japanese, and when they discovered that he did not, there was an embarrassing loss of face for both counsel and client. Tamaki pointed out with his usual admirable grasp of the situation that there was no such built-in expectations with Robb. Second, dealing with the rag trade was a source of immense frustration to someone of Tamaki's legal sensibility. It seemed to him that if people in that industry could avoid or void a contract, whether legally or otherwise, they simply did so. On one occasion, Tamaki had drafted a perfectly adequate guarantee for payment of goods, which was duly signed by a Montreal individual. When the time came for performance of the obligation, it was refused on the flimsiest of legal arguments. The case went to court and was appealed all the way to the Supreme Court of Canada. By the time of final judgment, which entirely supported the validity of Tamaki's carefully worded guarantee, the individual who had signed it had fled the jurisdiction and disappeared. Tamaki decided in disgust to give up any pretense of practising civil law.

With the expansion of trade between Canada and Japan as well as other countries, providing legal advice in a variety of ways began to define international trade. The advice covered what is now known as FDI (foreign direct investment) – sales and purchase contracts for delivery from or to other countries and the obligation to pay for such products, the most compelling element of which was to ensure that payment be made only upon satisfactory delivery. Work in this field on behalf of the Japanese trading companies also involved structuring their Canadian as well as US marketing activities through agents, distributors, consignees, or subsidiaries.

By the end of the 1960s, the firm was representing eight of the ten major Japanese trading companies. In the early 1970s, during a visit to Japan with a Quebec trade delegation, Robb was treated to a magnificent lunch by one of the companies that the firm did not then represent. This company wanted him to act for it but also to give up all other Japanese clients. Robb suggested to a representative from the company that Canada was too small to allow him to enter into an exclusive arrangement. Since the Japanese had the cultural habit of introducing only deals that were in progress and had already been negotiated, there were minimum business or legal conflicts. Several major mandates were later received even from the company that had wanted Robb to act exclusively for it.

Two other areas of international trade also developed in the 1960s. One of Tamaki's clients was a small engineering company that developed expertise in making paper from exotic fibres, which began to carry out large international contracts particularly in the Middle East. The company was structured to develop its international expertise as a corporation rather than a partnership and entered into a number of contracts and developments in various parts of the world. The company was sold to American interests in the early 1970s in order to obtain financing for a major contract in Iran.

In the 1960s, the firm also began acting for several Shipping Conferences. Even when the marine law section of the firm emerged as a separate specialty, the shipping conference work remained in international trade since it involved issues of competition law. Indeed, at that point, there was a restrictive trade practices investigation under way regarding shipping conferences. The firm was very closely involved in this matter, working with a shipping agent, Montreal Shipping, then headed by James Tom. The eventual but not unexpected negative recommendation of the inquiry was deflected into the *Shipping Conferences Exemption Act,* which exempted shipping conferences from application of the *Combines Investigations Act* under certain conditions – specifically, registration and reporting. The firm continues to act for various shipping conferences in connection with their registration, internal contracts, and international shipping contracts. This activity has always provided a technique for monitoring international trade and its flow.

In the late 1960s, acting in general concert with a number of other countries, Canada refined its practices with regard to anti-dumping, which had previously been negotiated on an ad hoc basis with government departments. It enacted legislation to establish the Anti-Dumping Tribunal, now the Canadian International Trade Tribunal, which also deals with countervailing duties. The first case before the newly constituted Anti-Dumping Tribunal, then chaired by Judge Buchanan, was a complaint lodged against Hitachi Ltd. (as manufacturer) and ITOCHU (as importer) concerning hydro turbines manufactured for the British Columbia and Saskatchewan power authorities. The firm represented the two Japanese companies, and James K. Hugessen, formerly associate chief justice of the Quebec Superior Court and now a judge of the Federal Court of Canada, represented an association of electrical machinery manufacturers, chief among which was Canadian General Electric. The strength of the Japanese yen at that time made proof of dumping particularly difficult. The matter was effectively resolved, as were possible future complaints, by the establishment of an assembly plant for turbines in Saskatchewan. Other major early cases in which we were involved included a complaint on footwear, which the firm was engaged to follow by Consolidated Footwear, a subsidiary of ITOCHU, of which its own imports from South America had not been subject to complaint. A complaint by the Canadian Zipper Manufacturers Association against YKK Corporation turned into a valuation battle in which a minimum valuation, upon which the anti-dumping award was based, resulted in a victory in name only for the complainants, most of which quickly ceased manufacturing in Canada. YKK went on to establish an extensive manufacturing operation in Ville St Laurent.

Activity in the customs and anti-dumping area as well as a potential for a federal sales or consumption tax led to attempts to convince lawyers in the firm's tax section to take an interest in this area of law. After several false starts, Glenn Cranker[1] took up the challenge and has been involved in most major anti-dumping cases in Canada for over twenty years, with support and referrals from both the Toronto and Ottawa offices. Toward the beginning of his association in the tax group, it became evident to him and, he thinks, probably to others in the group (including at that time Robert Couzin, David Finkelstein, and George Tamaki, who were still in Montreal) that he would never be a wizard in income tax reorganizations and the like. That left him with all sorts of tax-related cases that no one else in the group was particularly interested in handling. Finkelstein started him off on his first customs case involving imported snowmobiles that the customs authorities alleged had illegally entered Canada. Cumyn gave him a file that sent him to Ottawa for the first time, having moved to Canada in 1973 to attend McGill for much the same reasons that had brought Couzin. The subject was the tariff classification of imported diagnostic kits. Somewhat to his surprise, he enjoyed such customs and sales tax cases, and at the same time, he learned the ins and outs of administrative appeals and litigating before tribunals and the Federal Court of Canada.

Harold Gordon got him involved in his first anti-dumping case involving steel imported from West Germany. Using the "sink or swim" theory, which has so characterized the development of the firm, he learned how to spend weeks before the Anti-Dumping Tribunal arguing about imported slow cookers, microwave ovens, televisions, and more varieties of steel than he could ever imagine. He attended verifications at steel mills in France, Belgium, and all over the USA with Canadian customs officers who were determined to prevent unfair dumping of steel into Canada. Another anti-dumping case involved the dumping of cat litter in Canada, which took him to the ghettos of Chicago and to South Bend, Indiana.

Jim Robb took Cranker under his wing and introduced him to his Japanese clients, which he had inherited from George Tamaki. He learned how to eat sushi, hit a golf ball (rather pathetically, he admits), and how important friendship and trust are in an attorney-client relationship with Japanese clients. One of his most exciting cases involved the dumping of hydraulic turbines from Japan and China. He spent three weeks at verifications in Japan, both in Tokyo and Hitachi City, working exceedingly long hours, followed by fine meals lubricated by industrial quantities of sake and Japanese beer. He was fortunate enough to be in Tokyo, joined by his wife, Maria, when the cherry blossoms were just beginning to bloom. A portion of the turbines had been manufactured in China, and it was up to the firm to convince the Canadian government not to assess an arbitrary margin of dumping on these components because they had been manufactured in a "state-controlled economy." The firm's contacts with the China Council for the Promotion of International Trade and the China Global Law Office were at that time excellent. Jacques Courtois had started an exchange program, and two of their senior lawyers, Yang Peiyun and Xioa Zhiming, had spent six months working at the Montreal office. They were met at the airport by friends from the China Global Law Office and with their help, were able to get information related to the costs of the components manufactured in Harbin and to lessen the margins of dumping significantly.

The relationship with the China Global Law Office thrived, and the firm had a series of lawyers coming to Canada to work in the Toronto and Montreal offices. Mrs Liu Yuehua worked closely with Fraser Elliott in the Toronto office and became best of friends with his long-time secretary, Claire Fisher. During her stay in Montreal, Mrs Lui Yuehua lived with both Marc Lalonde's and Cranker's families, undoubtedly learning more about the Canadian way of life than how to practise law in Canada. She returned to China to work for Baker & Mackenzie and later as general counsel with IBM. One of the more exciting events in the relationship with the China Global Law Office occurred during the Tiananmen Square crisis. Both of the lawyers working for the firm at the time defected to Canada rather than returning to China. Heward Stikeman was instrumental in getting a job for Dong Li, a maritime lawyer who was working in the Montreal office at the time. Stikeman's long-time friend, Ladi Pathy, owner of Fednav, was kind enough to offer Dong Li a job, where he has worked ever since.

Upheavals in Iran in the late 1970s, which led to the expulsion of the shah, and the establishment of a fundamentalist regime made doing ordinary commercial business in or with that country all but impossible. The unsettled and hostile conditions led to the necessity of bringing to an end all contracting activities. The firm had a client, Stadler Hurter, that was faced with termination of almost a billion dollars' worth of existing contracts. The resulting legal issue was how to enforce the contracts and to obtain recovery of the amounts due under them. This involved, with the assistance of the Canadian government, the evacuation of some 300 personnel and their families from two sites in Iran, seizing assets in Canada belonging to the Iranian entity with which the company had contracted and taking actions in Montreal despite a contractual arbitration clause that called for all disputes to be resolved in Iran. The firm obtained a court ruling that held that the arbitration clause was impossible to enforce due to the circumstances in Iran. The judgment was obtained in part on the basis of evidence given by the deputy director of the US Central Intelligence Agency. It was well known that the CIA had supported the shah of Iran against the Ayatollah Khomeini. One of Robb's great courtroom experiences was watching the two Iranian government representatives practically levitate from their seats whenever the CIA was mentioned. Eventually, twelve years later, the sum seized, along with the related interest, produced enough cash to pay all creditors of the company. All the company's assets other than the Iranian contracts were sold to the German company Klöckner in order to raise money to finance the protracted litigation, and Stadler Hurter Limited's corporate name was then changed to the president's name spelled backwards. His laconic comment on this to Robb was, "Lucky my name was not Tihs."

Over the years, the firm has provided a broad range of services for Louis Dreyfus, one of the famous Seven Sisters of the international grain trade. In the international trade sphere, it enforced an export sales contract against Rexfor, an arm of the Quebec government, when that company could not perform its obligations due to flooding, for which Hydro-Québec was responsible. Witnesses in the action included many Quebec cabinet ministers, including René Lévesque.

The addition of Marc Lalonde to the firm following his retirement from partisan politics produced international trade arbitration and policy capability. This led to a significant number of government-mandated international trade arbitrations and mediations in which Lalonde has been involved and the obtaining of additional arbitration work for other members of the firm.

In more recent times, the firm has developed the capacity to deal with appeals under the North American Free Trade Agreement and interpretation of that agreement, resulting in involvement in legal disputes, representing many clients in what used to be called "cross-border trading" – in particular, the problems of defining the country of origin of goods imported and the scope of the NAFTA.

The firm continues to represent Klöckner Stadler Hurter Ltd. on international contracting and financing issues, including an $800 -million contract for a pulp plant in Musi, Indonesia. The plant was successfully completed although unfortunately not without legal action, having suffered a period during which the former president's daughter acted as the original president of the local company, economic collapse in Indonesia during the building period, and the burning of the plant's first wood pile in Sumatra, probably by Aceh separatists.

An important often unmentionable but ever-present aspect of international trade is the matter of foreign corrupt practices. This became relevant in the 1970s when Stadler Hurter became a subsidiary of a US company. Although the firm was never aware of any infringement of the *Foreign Corrupt Practices Act* and related SEC regulations, problems nevertheless arose. Since 1992 in Canada, with the enactment of tax legislation prohibiting the deduction of bribes and similar types of payments, it became necessary to ensure that all payments made were not criminal and hence deductible. As is the case in many other industries, all arrangements entered into by salespersons had to be carefully scrutinized.

The international trade group is now in the process of moving into the area of World Trade Organization arbitrations, mediations, and reviews, maintaining its presence in major anti-dumping and countervailing duty cases in Canada and advising on complaints under these headings while continuing to participate in international contracts and financings, dealing with the legal consequences and enforcement of those contracts.

Peter Cumyn had been approached by one of his best clients, Johnson & Johnson, which had filed an appeal claiming that feminine hygiene products should not be subject to federal sales tax on the grounds that they were articles of clothing. He subsequently learned that the genesis of the appeal was the idea of Norman Guerin of Samson Belair, who was a pioneer of commodity taxation in Canada. Guerin was lying on a nude beach at a Club Med in Jamaica when a naked woman walked by wearing only a sanitary napkin. For whatever reason, Cumyn thought Cranker was the best suited to take the appeal. After receiving regular encouragement from his wife and other women when he was brave enough to ask, Cranker convinced himself that feminine hygiene products were in fact worn like articles of clothing, and as such, there was no reason why they should be taxed. His job was then to convince the Tariff Board, the administrative tribunal in Ottawa that decided such appeals, that this was a reasonable interpretation of the law.

Johnson & Johnson enlisted the support of Laura Sabia, the former head of the Advisory Council on the Status of Women (and the mother of Michael Sabia, now heading up BCE Inc.), who invited Cranker to her house in Toronto for dinner where he, not she as he had anticipated, was interviewed. Eventually, she agreed to be a witness and told the court quite directly that it was discriminatory to tax feminine hygiene products when other articles of clothing were not being taxed. Monique Charlebois, an associate in the Montreal office, helped immensely with the case. She examined a professor from the Université de Montréal, who gave testimony on the meaning of *vêtement* (clothing), and with the help of a number of other experts, they won the case. Even the Federal Court of Appeal agreed that the meaning of clothing was broad enough to include feminine hygiene products.

Johnson & Johnson received a very significant refund of federal sales tax, which it had paid in earlier years. The next question was whether the refund was taxable. Robert Hogan, Pierre Martel, and I came up with the idea that since the refund was a prior period adjustment, it should (if it were taxable at all) be taken into account in the calculation of the company's income in the years the duties had been imposed and not included in the income of the year in which the refund was received. The Federal Court of Appeal agreed with the submissions of Cranker and me, who argued the case, and by then, those earlier years were statute barred, producing a windfall for Johnson & Johnson. The result was an amendment to the *Income Tax Act,* but applicable only for future years.

In 2001, members of the international trade group and I joined forces in a successful intervention before the Supreme Court of Canada on behalf of Reebok. The court agreed with Reebok's position that royalties paid for the use of trademark rights in Canada are not generally dutiable. The members of the international trade group who worked on the case included, besides Cranker, Randall Hofley and Nick McHaffie, both former Supreme Court clerks.

Some of the key provisions of the FTA were negotiated by Stanley Hartt during his time in the Prime Minister's Office under Brian Mulroney. Allan Gotlieb was Canada's ambassador to the United States when the Free Trade Agreement was being negotiated. He was at the time, and continues to be, a strong proponent of the agreement. One of the roadblocks to finalizing the FTA related to an agreement on anti-dumping and countervailing duties. Canada's position was that neither country should be able to initiate such proceedings. The United States, buttressed by protectionist lobbies including softwood lumber and steel, insisted on retaining these remedies against imports from Canada that were dumped or subsidized. The binational dispute settlement provisions in the FTA constitute a compromise for both countries. Under these provisions, domestic decisions (of the International Trade Commission and the Department of Commerce in the United States and of the Canadian International Trade Tribunal and Revenue Canada, [now CCRA] in Canada) could be appealed to a binational dispute settlement panel. Each panel consisted of five members selected from a roster of trade experts and retired judges. Two members were appointed from one country and three from the other, rotating with each appeal.

The decision of a panel is final except for the limited right of appeal to an extraordinary challenge committee. The same binational dispute settlement system was reproduced in NAFTA when Mexico joined with the United States and Canada. The roster includes Cranker, Lawson Hunter, and Brad Smith. Cranker was appointed to the first case involving a decision of the Department of Commerce with respect to red raspberries imported from Canada – clearly a great threat to the US economy. The panel unanimously decided that the US Department of Commerce had erred in its determination of the applicable margin of dumping. Hunter was appointed to the controversial softwood lumber case, which ultimately was appealed to the extraordinary challenge committee. The three Canadians on the panel decided in favour of Canada and set aside an injury finding of the International Trade Commission. The two Americans on the panel were in favour of the US position. The United States appealed to the extraordinary challenge committee claiming that two of the members, Hunter and Rick Dearden of Gowlings, were biased since their law firms represented Canadian lumber interests. The extraordinary challenge committee, consisting of three retired judges, upheld the majority decision, with one American judge in dissent. After that incident, the Stikeman Elliott roster members were generally not called upon until Smith was appointed to an appeal. The stipend for hearing a case is only $400 a day, so not being appointed has its benefits.

COMPETITION

An aspect of trade and commercial law generally that has become increasingly important, especially with transactions involving large clients, is the consideration of competition and antitrust law. Lawson Hunter heads the firm's practice group in this field. Although technically attached to the Ottawa office, a great percentage of his business is derived out of the Toronto office, and he spends a lot of his professional time managing the competition group as it has become bigger. Prior to his joining the firm, the only lawyer who concentrated in the field was Donna Kaufman in Montreal. From the time Hunter arrived at the beginning of 1993 with Susan Hutton, the group has grown to more than twenty lawyers, which may be the largest group of such specialists in Canada. In an area previously dominated by the firms Davies and Oslers, the firm has become a leader through Hunter's leadership.

The proposed bank merger between CIBC and the Toronto-Dominion Bank in 1998 was very important to the competition group, and the fact that the firm had a strong competition group was a major factor in getting the mandate. The firm ran that case, and the view on the street was that it was much better than the firm acting on behalf of the Royal Bank of Canada and the Bank of Montreal. It was known that a key point of the merger would be the regulatory side, and everyone thought that Hunter and his group did an excellent job on this, which lead to an even greater reputation in the field. The matter was somewhat traumatic for Blake Cassels, especially in its relationship with the CIBC, where our firm's was solidified, and it now acts on more of the CIBC work in this area. On a strategic basis on the bank merger proposals, Hunter made a point of making certain that the competition regulators got all of the documents on a voluntary basis, whereas on the Royal-Montreal proposal, subpoenas were served by the regulators on all senior officers down to the level of vice-president of which banks tend to have dozens.

In the Lafarge SA acquisition of Blue Circle Industries PLC, although Lafarge eventually acquired control of Blue Circle on July 11, 2001, the saga actually started in January 2000 with a hostile takeover bid launched on the London Stock Exchange. The firm's competition team was led by Hunter and Hutton of the Ottawa office, but at various times, it included at least eight members of the competition law group in both Ottawa and Toronto. From the beginning, it was clear that there were significant competition law issues in Canada since Lafarge and Blue Circle were the number one and two cement, concrete, and aggregates producers in Ontario. Moreover, the cement production in particular was aimed both at Canadian and at US customers. Given that both the Canadian Competition Bureau and the US Federal Trade Commission claimed jurisdiction over the deal but conducted separate investigations, all remedies and discussions had to be carefully coordinated between the firm and Lafarge's US counsel. Although the hostile bid was ultimately unsuccessful (by a narrow margin), competition advice provided by the firm was crucial in enabling Lafarge to take a sufficient minority position during the hostile bid so that a friendly outcome was all but inevitable.

The friendly stage of the affair led to many firsts in Canadian competition law, including the first time that orders were issued by both the Competition Tribunal in Canada and the FTC, requiring the divestiture of the same assets and the obvious need to coordinate timing and to stickhandle diverse administrative procedures and requirements to ensure that the orders did not conflict. The businesses required to be divested in Canada, valued at over $1 billion, also constituted the largest divestiture ever ordered by the tribunal. As is increasingly the case, the competition and Investment Canada mandates led to the corporate mandate to handle the divestitures – a mandate that kept approximately twenty-five people busy in the Toronto office at one time or another during much of 2001.

Another large mandate coming from the Ottawa office was CN/Cast in 1994, wherein CN challenged the acquisition of Cast, a North Atlantic shipping line, by Canada Maritime, another shipping line that was a subsidiary of CP. In challenging, the firm commenced formal public interest proceedings before the National Transportation Agency (as it was then called) and filed significant submissions with the Competition Bureau in an attempt to convince it to take formal action to block the merger. The transaction involved the close coordination of efforts in Ottawa (Hunter and Bibic), Toronto (Paul Collins[2]), and Montreal (Rusk). In keeping with the firm's philosophy of "throwing them into the deep end," the mandate represented the first involvement of Bibic and Collins, first-year associates at the time, in formal contentious competition law matters, and they were given the responsibility to prepare submissions, retain consultants, prepare them as witnesses, and plead before the NTA.

Other significant mergers handled principally by the Ottawa office include the 1999 acquisition by Alcoa Inc. of Reynolds Metals Company;

the takeover of Newbridge Networks by Alcatel in 2000; the acquisition of Hoechst AG by Rhone-Poulenc SA in 1999; the merger of the French, German, and Spanish defence aviation and aerospace industries to form the European Aerospace and Defence Company (EADS); the merger of AOL and Netscape in 1999; and the merger of AOL and Time Warner in 2000. The competition group often works seamlessly across several offices, and many members of the group based in Toronto also worked on these mandates, just as several members of the Ottawa contingent were key team members for the defence of the hostile takeover bid for Air Canada in 2000 followed by the acquisition of Canadian Airlines by Air Canada in 2001 and various competition and transportation regulatory matters that ensued.

The Ottawa office team of Hunter, Hofley, Hutton, and Tamra Alexander was responsible for the successful claim by the H.J. Heinz Company of Canada Ltd. of injurious dumping against the sole US exporter, Gerber. The litigation was vigorously defended by both Gerber and in an unusual administrative law twist, by the commissioner of competition, who essentially acted as a full party litigant on behalf of (and during the appeal phase to the NAFTA Binational Panel, instead of) Gerber. The success in the baby food litigation was preceded, for example, by successful representation in antidumping matters of Exeltherm (Polyiso Insulation Board), Domtar (NAFTA panel challenge of Gypsum Wallboard decision), Johnson & Johnson (refined sugar), and Collins & Aikman (floor coverings). It was followed by a recent success in defending against a claim of dumping and subsidization of US grain corn on behalf of Maple Leaf Foods.

International trade law mandates, however, have not been limited to the realms of domestic law such as customs or anti-dumping/countervail laws. The Ottawa office has developed expertise in both North American Free Trade Agreement (NAFTA) and World Trade Organization (WTO) issues, representing both the private sector and the European Commission in respect of disputes in these forums. It has also advised the Canadian government on compliance of its policies and laws with these agreements as well as foreign governments such as Chile in respect of the negotiation of free trade agreements with Canada, which followed upon the NAFTA and WTO.

INTELLECTUAL PROPERTY

The firm has always been active in the intellectual property area, with Jim Robb and Peter O'Brien in the Montreal office having pursued matters on behalf of clients for a number of years. However, in 1987, a decision was made to create a focused intellectual property group, and with that in mind, Harold Gordon in Montreal in conjunction with Greg Kane in Ottawa recruited Stuart McCormack, who had recently returned to Canada after three years in the intellectual property department of Sony Corporation of Japan. McCormack joined the firm in the Ottawa office in 1987 and was promptly thrust into the acquisition by the National Archives of Canada of the archives of Yousuf Karsh, a national figure in Canada for his world-famous portrait photography. From the outset, in what has turned out to be a common feature of the way the firm has evolved, lawyers from Montreal, Ottawa, and Toronto were involved in various facets of the transaction. In addition to ensuring the security of the Karsh collection, the lawyers who worked on the file had the pleasure of working with Yousuf Karsh and with his wife, Estralita.

Shortly thereafter, McCormack received a phone call from Brian Rose in Toronto who asked him to attend in Toronto "immediately" to deal with the spinoff of the Northern Stores' division of Hudson's Bay. This was one of Canada's national retailing icons, basically the continuation of the old Hudson's Bay fur trading posts. The trip was scheduled to last four hours, but due to the complexity of the transaction and the unavailability of any hotel rooms in Toronto, he spent several days in a row sleeping at Brian Rose's apartment and working with him on a daily basis.

One of the cornerstones of the intellectual property practice has been its integral involvement in the intellectual property aspects of mergers and acquisitions. This has involved dealing with complicated intellectual property issues relating to restructuring of those rights for such companies as British American Tobacco, the divestiture of assets by CAE in its military simulator business in the United States, and the acquisition and sale of businesses by Nortel.

In addition to transactional work, the intellectual property group has been actively involved in a variety of litigation matters in the intellectual property area in both the federal and provincial courts of Canada. It has pursued several infringers of intellectual property in cases of counterfeit goods as well as situations involving passing off, trademark infringement, and patent infringement. It has also been deeply involved in defending a leading US manufacturer that acquired the assets of a major Canadian retailer and was then sued by a trademark holder in Canada, alleging that the client's name infringed the registered trademark of the Canadian company. The matter was heard by way of interlocutory injunction motion in the Federal Court of Canada, and after several days of argument, the firm prevailed on behalf of its client, saving it millions of dollars in possible transition costs. The matter involved the coordinated efforts of Kathryn Chalmers, who led the litigation aspects in Toronto, as well as Mirko Bibic and Stuart McCormack in Ottawa, who supported from the intellectual property side.

The group acted on behalf of Motorola and Showtime Inc. (a division of Viacom Inc.) in connection with a suit that was brought by WIC Communications Inc. WIC alleged that Motorola's distribution of satellite cable systems and Showtime's transmission of programs in the United States that spill over to Canada infringed the rights of WIC Communications Inc., which claimed exclusivity in Western Canada to distribute certain programming. This litigation was multi-faceted, involving claims of copyright infringement, breaches of the *Broadcasting Act,* the tort of conspiracy, and unlawful interference with economic relations. The litigation, coordinated by lawyers from Toronto and Ottawa, was brought in the Federal Court of Canada as well as in the Court of Queen's Bench of Alberta. The firm was successful in having the Federal Court action stayed (where the jurisdiction might have been too narrow to deal with all the issues raised but was an avenue that could not be completely precluded), and the matter proceeded solely in the Alberta courts. After several years of litigation and successfully defending another injunction motion, the matter was brought to a conclusion satisfactory to the clients, Motorola and Showtime.

The group has assisted the federal government in reviewing and providing alternate guidelines with respect to its revision of Treasury Board guidelines relating to ownership of intellectual property in government contracts. It has acted before the Patent Medicine Prices Review Board and dealt with fundamental issues relating to the jurisdiction of the board to regulate the prices of patent medicines in Canada. The group also handles the standard intellectual property filings for patents, trademarks, and industrial designs on behalf of several major companies including Sony Corporation, NEC Corp, ConAgra Inc., Sony Computer Entertainment Inc., Air Canada, Telesat Canada Inc., EDS Inc., and the Hockey Hall of Fame.

The firm has obtained a considerable amount of expertise and is considered a leading practitioner before some of the more important intellectual property tribunals in Canada. In particular, the firm is considered preeminent in its practice before the Copyright Board of Canada and acts for the Border Broadcasters Collective in conjunction with the allocation of retransmission royalties relating to the use of signals by cable companies in Canada. Further, it has been instrumental in the formation of the Canadian Storage Media Alliance and has appeared on its behalf before the Copyright Board on numerous occasions relating to setting the levy for blank audio recording media, the proceeds of which are to be distributed to artists and producers, in theory to compensate them for home-taping of their works. Hofley, McCormack, and Kane have all appeared before the Copyright Board in conjunction with these matters.

Over time, the nature of the group has changed and gone from a one-person practice to multiple lawyers in several offices practising in the area. Moreover, the nature of intellectual property practice has undergone a metamorphosis to include a much greater diversity of matters, including such issues as agreements and arrangements for outsourcing, Internet, development, and system supply and integration. The practice has remained diverse enough to require negotiating with Alan Eagleson, the players' group representing the 1972 Team Canada, and a film production company on behalf of Hockey Canada in conjunction with the celebration and making of a documentary of the twenty-fifth anniversary of the famous 1972 Canada-Soviet Union ice hockey series.

Olympic Rings

My position as a member of the International Olympic Committee (IOC) led to considerable exposure to the intellectual property field after I became responsible for the negotiation of television contracts for the Olympic Games in 1983. Although until the early 1980s the television contracts were not huge, beginning with the one for the 1988 Calgary Olympic Winter Games, which was negotiated in early 1984, the amounts became astronomical, and the IOC began to pay much more attention to such contracts rather than leaving the local Olympic organizing committees to handle the negotiations. Initially, I did the negotiations on a volunteer basis, but the demands on my time and the increasing sophistication of the agreements led to a request in 1985 by the then IOC president, Juan Antonio Samaranch, that the firm be reimbursed for the loss of my time. I agreed to such an arrangement, provided that no portion of any profit from firm billings to the IOC would accrue to me since I did not want to be perceived as earning money from my Olympic association.

As a matter of intellectual property law, the television rights to the Olympic Games belong to the IOC, as do the rights to the five-ring symbol, which has become the most recognized trademark in the world. As the value of the television rights escalated, the television broadcasters became much more demanding in the legal assurances that the IOC would have to provide, including complete exclusivity in their broadcast territories. The IOC dealt with the rights on a territory-by-territory basis, and the broadcasters insisted that no other broadcaster be given any rights in their territories. Over and above that, they wanted the IOC to take whatever action might be necessary to stop any unauthorized broadcasts of Olympic material. They insisted on the legal right to use the Olympic rings during their broadcasts. They insisted on security arrangements to ensure that any payments on account of the rights prior to the Olympic Games could be recovered if the Games did not take place, if they were less than the full seventeen days, if they were moved from the agreed-upon dates, if certain key sports were not on the program, and even if certain major countries did not participate. These and other important matters, such as the facilities that would be provided by the host countries, led to some of the most complex legal agreements in the history of television broadcasting. To give some idea of the amounts involved, the worldwide rights for the 1976 Olympic Games in Montreal were $US35 million. For the 2008 Olympic Games in Beijing, they will approach $US2 billion.

Beginning in 2000, with the Sydney Olympics, the issue of the Internet became important. There was much pressure from the web-casting industry to permit dissemination of the Olympic Games on the Internet, although the industry was unwilling to pay anything for the related rights. The problem for the IOC was that it had exclusive contracts with broadcasters around the world on a territorial basis, a concept that was antithetical to the Internet, which knows no borders. We solved the problem by granting the interactive rights to our Olympic broadcasters, but we stipulated that they could exercise them only if they could establish to our satisfaction that whatever they put on their web sites could be accessed only from their own broadcast territories. The technology did not exist to ensure this, so it was agreed that no one would have any full-motion video or audio of the Olympic Games on their sites. We agreed to assist the broadcasters by monitoring all known web sites that had any significant Olympic material and to help them close down any unauthorized web-casts. We prepared affidavits to be used for obtaining speedy injunctions against any infringers and engaged sophisticated monitoring software to identify any such web-casts. Fortunately, there was insufficient available bandwidth to support any commercially driven web-casts in 2000, but in the future, the IOC may well have to use such legal measures, and where the offenders may be in jurisdictions that are unable or unwilling to stop them, it may consider engaging its own hackers to attack and disable the servers used by those who are in effect attacking the IOC's rights.

Much the same issues arise with Olympic marketing sponsors, which must be ensured that the rights granted to them by the IOC can be protected against ambush or parasite marketers that pretend that they have rights but who do nothing to support the Olympic Games. In addition, the IOC must be certain that it has the legal right to approve advertising messages so that its own brand is not diminished by sponsors, which by acting in their own interests, may damage the Olympic brand.

All this proved to be an exciting and high stakes immersion into the emerging fields of intellectual and intangible property rights. When people would ask me how I managed not to panic with contracts running to billions of dollars (the NBC contracts for the 2004, 2006, and 2008 Olympic Games alone came to more than $US3 billion), I used to say that I dealt with them as if we were discussing Italian lira.

REAL ESTATE

One of the first major projects Michael Richards dealt with after he joined Stikeman Elliott in 1967 was the assembly of land in Montreal at what is now the northeast corner of McGill College Avenue and de Maisonneuve Boulevard, where the office tower, 1981 McGill College, is erected. Louis Dreyfus Canada decided to invest some of its grain profits in real estate, and the company established a real estate division known as Louis Dreyfus Properties. The work involved closing lanes and the street between Sherbrooke Street and de Maisonneuve Boulevard, known as Victoria Street. The land for Victoria Street, part of the original Burnside Estate of James McGill, had been ceded to the city of Montreal in 1857 by McGill University. The issues related to the closing of that street and all of its lanes in the area were significant. It had once been a residential area, part of Montreal's legendary Square Mile, and each of the lots had a right of passage on the street and the lanes. Cancelling all of those rights was a major project.

While this was going on, the Rouse Company, a big shopping centre development company from the United States, was in the process of acquiring the property at the southeast corner of McGill College Avenue and de Maisonneuve Boulevard from the T. Eaton Realty Co. Ltd. It planned on building an enclosed shopping complex that would be connected to the Eaton's store. It determined that the cost of the land was significant enough that having only a shopping mall on the property was not economical. It wanted, therefore, to build an office building on top of its shopping mall, and it came into contact with Louis Dreyfus Properties. Trying to integrate an office building with one owner and a shopping mall with another owner on the same property was not an easy task. Rouse looked initially at leasing air rights, something that is possible in the United States, but Richards advised that such a lease would not be financeable as it was not possible under Quebec law to mortgage or hypothecate a lease or a building built on leased rights.

Quebec had recently introduced legislation for condominium ownership, a then growing form of residential property ownership in the United States. Richards worked out a plan with Clarkson Tétrault, which was acting for Rouse, and with Martineau Walker, which was acting for Rouse's lenders, Mercantile Bank. As Rouse insisted on retaining ownership of the land, the plan developed was to create a condominium with two exclusive units – one being the shopping unit and the other, the office tower. The only condominium work in Quebec done up to that time involved residential properties, so this was a first. Again, because of Rouse's insistence on controlling the land, it would not sell Dreyfus the rights to the office unit, which at this point was merely a cube of air designated by a subdivision lot number. The solution we used was an emphyteutic lease whereby Rouse would lease to Dreyfus an area on the roof of the shopping unit, which would be the base or pad for the cube of air constituting the office unit in the condominium. Under this lease, Dreyfus then built a 350,000 -square-foot office building in the cube as an emphyteutic lessee. Mercantile Bank provided the construction financing and had a hypothec on the condominium unit. As a matter of caution, they arranged for an amendment passed by the Quebec legislature to make it very clear that it was possible to have emphyteusis as part of a condominium, all of which was concluded in 1975.

Two considerable complications were involved in the declaration of co-ownership in integrating and providing services to two distinctly different types of units – one being a shopping component with a multitude of tenants on several levels, and the other being an office unit of ten floors of 35,000 square feet each. Shortly after, the parties involved negotiated an expansion of the metro station at University Street to extend it westward so that it was accessible from the complex. The complex was known as Les Terrasses since Rouse built a multi-terraced entrance from St Catherine Street adjacent to Eaton's. The interior also had several levels, each one of which provided access into the Eaton's store. It was a novel situation for Eaton's to allow competing shops to be in a building with direct and open access into its own store. This complex later became more complicated after Rouse sold the shopping unit to a company called York-Hannover, which did a complete remake of the shopping unit. In the process, York-Hannover needed the consent of Dreyfus, as owners of the office unit, to a number of physical changes they wanted to make. These included the connection of a pedestrian tunnel under McGill College Avenue to Place Montreal Trust, the acquisition of a couple of properties on St Catherine Street next to the Laurentian Bank building into which they wanted to expand the centre, and the construction of a pedestrian connection under St Catherine Street through to Place Ville Marie. As part of that process, they wanted to build another office tower on top of this expanded shopping unit, so a further declaration of co-ownership was put together involving the expanded space in the shopping unit and a pad above it on which another office building would be built. In this instance, there was not an emphyteutic lease, and Dreyfus had a contract to acquire the pad for $20 million, with York-Hannover having the obligation to construct it and provide the integration of services and other features that were needed.

York-Hannover got into financial difficulties with cost overruns and delays, and it eventually told Dreyfus that it would not deliver the pad for $20 million; instead, it wanted $30 million. The connecting tunnel that York-Hannover was planning to Place Montreal Trust required Dreyfus's consent because it would penetrate the outer wall of the Les Terrasses condominium. This connecting tunnel was seen as being very important for shopping traffic in Les Terrasses shopping unit as it would provide access for the office workers in Place Montreal Trust to and from the metro station. The need for that consent from Dreyfus gave it the leverage to negotiate with York-Hannover, and ultimately, in return for a significant payment from York-Hannover, Dreyfus gave up its rights to the pad and consented to the connection under McGill College Avenue to Place Montreal Trust. York-Hannover subsequently sold the pad to Polaris Realty, which built what is now called Tour McGill College. The entire complex – which is bounded by de Maisonneuve Boulevard to the north, McGill College Avenue to the west, St Catherine Street to the south, and the old Eaton's store to the east – consists of two condominium projects, with the lower part of each condominium project being the retail unit, which is really from a practical point of view all one unit, and on top of the retail unit are two separately owned office towers.

As to the property at the northeast corner of de Maisonneuve Boulevard and McGill College Avenue, Dreyfus leased it to a parking lot operator for several years before it determined that the market might be right for another office building. In 1976, when the separatist Parti Québécois government was elected, all investment in Montreal ground to a halt, including any plans that Dreyfus had for this property. Eventually, as time went on and investors got more comfortable with the political situation, and it seemed likely that the Liberals might win the next election, Dreyfus decided to build its office building on the property. However, not being sure how quickly it could lease it up, the building was designed to be built in two phases. One-half of the building (the south half) was designed, and construction started in 1980. The second half (to the north) was to be added later after the south-half was leased. The two would then be fully integrated to make it one building. Leasing went better than expected, and Dreyfus moved into the second phase in 1981 before it had even finished building the first phase, so it ended up looking like just one construction project. This explains the v-shaped entrance off McGill College Avenue. William Louis Dreyfus then filled the space with Raymond Mason's sculpture, *The Crowd*. As one enters the entrance lobby, it is possible to see how the south half of the building could have been a stand-alone office complex. Eventually, the complex was sold to SITQ and Caisse de Dépot, and that brought an end to the firm's involvement with 1981 McGill College.

One of the most exciting real estate matters with which the firm dealt during the 1980s was a development known as Les Vergers LaFontaine Inc. to the clients and the developers, but which was known to the public, through the media, as Overdale. The firm represented companies controlled by Robert Landau and Douglas Cohen as joint venture developers of a proposed residential condominium development in downtown Montreal. It all started off innocently enough in the mid-1980s when our clients asked for assistance in putting together a land assembly that involved the entire city block surrounded by Dorchester Boulevard (now René-Lévesque Boulevard) to the north, Mackay Street to the west, Lucien L'Allier to the east and south – a mainly overlooked and somewhat droopy residential/industrial/rooming house street called Overdale Avenue.

At the start of the process, the city block contained a parking garage, a gas station, an abandoned ice factory, three old red brick apartment buildings of about four stories each, and half a dozen greystone row houses. The block also included a rooming house/apartment complex with an interesting facade and a footnote in Canadian history. In 1849, a rioting crowd of marchers set out from the Canadian Parliament, which was then further downtown, and wended its way to the residence of Louis-Hippolyte LaFontaine, the French-Canadian Reform leader of Canada East. The crowd tried to break into the house, and it is said that a couple of shots were fired, which ricocheted off the stone facade.[3] The building behind that facade evolved into the rooming house/apartment building on Overdale Avenue.

The city block was divided into five private ownership interests, in addition to the City of Montreal, which owned a couple of lanes and a very short dead-end street. The firm met with the clients, and an acquisition strategy evolved regarding who should be approached first, the prices they were prepared to pay, as well as the usual aspects of intrigue and secrecy that developers associate with land assemblies. As it turned out, though, the land assembly was the easy part. The clients envisaged the construction on the site of twin thirty-nine-storey residential condominium towers. In the 1980s, things were booming, and the construction industry was doing well, so plans were prepared, drawings were drawn, designs were designed, and the public approval process was embarked upon.

First, some background. In 1986, Jean Doré and the Montreal Citizens Movement came into power as mayor of Montreal and its governing party, taking over from Jean Drapeau who had been mayor for most of the three decades from the mid-1950s. In the last dozen years of his mayoralty, there had been a growing grassroots opposition to his style of governance and the levels of debt incurred by his administration, particularly in the construction of the facilities for the 1976 Olympics. Drapeau's tenure finally came to an end in 1986 (Drapeau did not run) with the election of Doré and his party, with its platform of power to the people, promises of local consultation, and the like.

One of the features of municipal zoning that was introduced in that era was an overall freeze on any downtown construction over a certain basic minimum level, with a regime of spot-zoning that required municipal approval. The Vergers LaFontaine condominium development needed this type of zoning approval. The project also obviously required that the existing residential buildings be vacated so that they could be demolished to make way for the new construction. The occupants, all tenants, immediately protested that they were losing their homes and beat a path to the door of Jean Doré and of his executive committee chairman, John Gardner. The rules relating to the emptying of buildings were mainly provincial from a landlord/tenant perspective, but also municipal from a public safety aspect. Whatever the jurisdiction, the matter landed firmly in the lap of the mayor in terms of the blurring of the lines between approval to remove the tenants and the overall approvals required from a zoning perspective to build the new buildings. There followed, as a result of this, a dizzying sequence of protests, police interventions, fire department inspections and condemnations, injunctions, evictions, more protests, arrests, forced evictions, negotiations, delays, expenditures, and so on, and so on. In the end, the greatest difficulty was not in making deals with the politicians; it was in getting the arrangements to stick in the face of public pressure.

Back to the house in which LaFontaine had lived. In Quebec, there are provisions for the preservation of cultural properties, which are divided between the provincial government and the municipalities. The province can designate entire buildings, place restrictions on work carried on in them, and limit what can be built around them. Such a designation, however, carries with it automatic access to the public purse to subsidize the maintenance and restoration of the public monuments. The municipalities are entitled to protect the external facade of a property considered of a historical/cultural importance, but this does not impact on the neighbourhood or on the public purse. In the case of the LaFontaine house, the province declined to intervene, but the city put its classification on the facade of the building. It is said that on (very) close inspection of the stonework, the bullet marks from 1849 can still be seen. This may be the case, but if it is, the marks have been joined over the intervening century and a half by many similar ones of considerably lesser historical importance.

The ultimate result of the politics, court appearances, negotiations, exchanges in the media, and the like was that the firm's clients, in an enlightened gesture, agreed to construct a building containing replacement housing for the LaFontaine house tenants. The building, which they did in fact build for this specific purpose, was situated down the street on Lucien L'Allier Avenue; it is still in operation to this day. The occupants of the buildings moved or were moved as a result of private agreement or eviction, but all with the full sanction of the law. The residential buildings were demolished, all but one: the LaFontaine house. With its protected facade, it was given a new shell on the other three sides, a new roof, and substantial improvements on the inside, with a view that it be integrated into the condominium project. The approval process for the construction of the twin towers followed its course at City Hall toward completion, but the developers still found themselves a couple of years behind their originally envisaged schedule for the commencement of construction.

Then the 1989 recession hit. When it hit, it hit, at least in Montreal, real estate first; within the real estate market, it hit residential first, and within the residential sector, it hit condominiums the hardest. This resulted in the clients being faced with the clear prospect of having no one to purchase their condominium units once they were built. So, no construction occurred, then or later. The irony of the politics of the late 1980s on Overdale Avenue is that the delays incurred by the process no doubt saved the developers from having a project that would have been looking for purchasers of luxury condominium units at the exact time that the market for this product disappeared.

The action of the lawyers of the firm during this period covered all areas described above: pleading, negotiating, politicking, being spokesperson, and developing strategy. In addition, the Overdale property fronts on what is now René-Lévesque Boulevard, as do the firm's offices, which are three or four blocks to the east and forty floors up. This resulted in the lawyers not only being active in all legal aspects, but also being able to watch the street action from their office windows. Today, as they look out office windows toward the Overdale project, they see lots of outdoor parking together with a gas station, the original indoor parking building, and the LaFontaine house, which sits empty and faces its neighbours across the street on Overdale Avenue. A few months earlier, during the summer of 2001, it found itself, in somewhat of a repetition of history, the destination of a march protesting for or against a number of issues, including more low-rent housing from the city. The protestors took over the empty building and lived there for a couple of weeks. Doré's successor, Mayor Pierre Bourque, found himself having to deal with the occupants of the LaFontaine house in a city block that had been largely forgotten since 1989.

The firm was also involved in many other interesting real estate deals. Doug Burdon was someone who attended McGill for a time in the early 1970s. His family had a house in Morin Heights, and being something of a ski enthusiast, he decided to build a new ski hill in the area. Ralph Hood, a retired inventor in NDG, seemed disposed to invest in various projects. Burton went to see Hood, who said that he should come back with plans, and then he would decide whether or not to invest in the project. Burton borrowed about $25,000 from family and friends, came back with a proposal, and Hood gave him two cheques of $500,000 each for the project. Burton's accountant, James King, came to Peter O'Brien[4] for advice as to what the tax implications of the two cheques might be. About this time, Hood's family intervened, apparently not wishing their presumptive inheritance to be frittered away, and a settlement was reached whereby Burton kept $600,000 for the project. Thus was Ski Morin Heights, a long-time client of the firm, created. It was a difficult venture, which went through a series of hard times and failures since without a real estate play, possibly including a golf course development for year-round usage, the economics of a bare ski operation are fragile at best. One of my clients, the Van Ginhoven family, tried to run the development for several years, but sufficient financing was never forthcoming to see the project over the financial hump.

O'Brien, who had been much involved in the Overdale project, had some real estate experience that was partly personal and partly professional. He became part owner of a string of Chinese restaurants, Buffet Oriental, which boasted four outlets. The introduction had come in 1979 from Doug Burdon, who approached him saying that there were nine people who had each put $10,000 into this restaurant (then called Le Pot au Riz, in Ville LaSalle), and they needed a lawyer to round it out, with his $10,000, of course. Two weeks after O'Brien had written his cheque, the others got nervous, and there was a meeting in the firm's boardroom on the thirty-ninth floor of the Montreal office. Six of the partners thought that because the three Chinese partners were the only ones who knew anything about running a Chinese restaurant, they should have the unlimited liability portion and the non-Chinese should have limited liability. The Chinese, unsurprisingly, did not agree, and the partnership was terminated. They had already made arrangements to rent space on Sources Boulevard in Dorval. O'Brien called the three Chinese partners, and they decided to go ahead together. They started in 1979, expanded to four restaurants, and sold the last one in 1988–89. Most were successes, with the exception of number four, a disaster in Le Faubourg on St Catherine Street, on the third floor, where there was no traffic at all. Salvation came with the opening of Hot and Spicy on the ground floor. O'Brien got out their lease and to his great relief, he found that they had been granted exclusivity in their category, so he was able to go to the owners of the building and get them to buy out the lease.

An unusual Montreal project was the Christ Church Cathedral development. Westcliffe Developments (Irwin Adelson and others) approached the church to make use of the land at the north end of the property bordering on de Maisonneuve Boulevard. The project evolved into an office tower at the north end, which was leased to Les Coopérants, and a shopping complex underneath the church known as Les Promenades de la Cathedrale. The firm acted for Citibank, which did the construction financing for the shopping centre portion of the complex. The developers excavated under the cathedral and stood it on stilts while they were doing so. It was a remarkable engineering feat since the cathedral stood there literally in the air while all the excavation and construction took place under it. There is now an underground multi-level shopping complex, which is connected to the lower portion of the office building built on the north side of the church. In turn, the church received a new foundation and some much-need funding. Citibank was quite aggressive, and the construction financing was non-recourse. The shopping centre had difficulties and never achieved its targets, so it was taken over.

Michael Richards was involved with the building known as Place Mercantile on Sherbrooke Street opposite McGill College Avenue. Its novelty was that the greystone residences along Sherbrooke Street were all taken down and then rebuilt in their identical positions as a facade behind which the multi-storey office building was built. It was a joint venture between Louis Donolo Inc., a significant construction company in Montreal in those days, and Mercantile Bank. Both have since disappeared, and the building is now owned by SITQ. The firm acted for Mercantile Bank in the joint venture arrangements with Louis Donolo, dealing with the acquisition of the properties, the co-ownership arrangements, the construction contract, and the leasing. Richards had a smaller involvement with the Alcan Centre. Alcan was assembling all the property in the proposed construction area – including the old Berkeley Hotel (the old mansion at the corner of Stanley and Sherbrooke streets owned at one stage by the Hallward family) and the Salvation Army building (situated between Stanley and Drummond streets) – in order to build its big complex. Walter Klinkhoff, of Walter Klinkhoff Gallery Inc. on Sherbrooke Street, who helped Elliott with many of his art acquisitions, was a target, and he did not want to sell. He engaged the firm to represent his interests. He was the last piece of Alcan's puzzle, but he refused to sell in spite of the handsome price the company was offering him. The firm finally came up with a solution that allowed Alcan to get on with its project and for Klinkhoff to keep his building: it created servitudes that permitted Alcan to build its complex and integrate Klinkhoff's property. The company acquired the land behind his building (which is now part of the atrium of the Alcan complex), and under that land, it built him a garage and access to his building from Drummond Street. They were allowed to build around his property and connect the atrium to the top of his building. Everybody was happy. Alcan got its complex, and Klinkhoff was able to keep his gallery, which to this day is probably the most significant gallery in Montreal. Klinkhoff has since died, but his two sons, Eric and Alan, manage the gallery; it retains its location on Sherbrooke Street, and Alcan has its striking complex behind it.

Richards acted for the CIBC when it bought out the Webster family interests in the CIBC building in which the Montreal office is located. He also acted for the CIBC when it took first mortgage security on the entire Place Ville Marie complex in the late 1980s at a time when real estate was getting somewhat overheated. The mortgage was in the amount of $400 million, based on a valuation of $600 million of the building. When the real estate meltdown struck in the early 1990s, the building's value had dropped to some $400 million, but the bank did get fully repaid.

On the corporate side, one of the more interesting mandates Richards had was the unfriendly takeover of Drummond-McCall by Marshall Steel, another distributor of steel products. The firm acted for Marshall Steel. With the quiet and behind-the-scenes encouragement of a couple of significant shareholders of Drummond-McCall, a bid was launched for 51 per cent of the shares. The target was a Montreal institution, having been founded in the latter part of the nineteenth century as a steel distribution company, and the Drummond and McCall families still held seats on the board. The Marshalls, on the other hand, were "upstarts with a lot of nerve" in taking on the establishment. It was a bitter fight with court challenges, joint hearings of the QSC and the OSC, amended offers, and many other manoeuvres. It went on for months, and there were many evening meetings in the Westmount homes of significant shareholders. Eventually, the Marshalls prevailed, and more than 70 per cent of the shares were tendered. As their financing was limited, they took up only 51 per cent. This need for financing later proved to be their undoing as the economy took a downturn, the steel business declined, and they were unable to pay off their acquisition loan from the bank. Nor were they able to get the loan into an operating company in which the interest on the loan would have been deductible. The bank eventually took over the control block, and the Marshalls lost everything.

Milton Hess[5] has led the Toronto office real estate group since his arrival at the firm in 1978 and even from the firm's boardroom window, there are many Toronto landmarks with which the group has been involved, including the Air Canada Centre, the SkyDome, the Redpath Sugar factory, a number of lakefront condominium buildings (including some developed by the Li family and some by David Wex, a former associate of the Toronto office), the Olympia & York buildings, a project concerning Regent Park that has been put on hold, and many others. He, together with Brenda Hebert,[6] who was very much involved in the Air Canada Tower adjacent to the Air Canada Centre, and Jim Harbell[7] have built a solid real estate group, which has weathered severe recessions and crises in a market that proved to be more volatile and often less buoyant than the developers and their institutional backers had ever anticipated. When the recession struck the Toronto real estate market in the late 1980s, it was far more unexpected, severe, and traumatic than in Montreal, which had become more accustomed to volatility beginning in the mid-1970s.

John Dow[8] arrived at the firm as a student and returned as a lawyer following his call to the Bar in 1981 when the real estate section at the time consisted essentially of Hess, Hebert, and Harbell. It had never been his intention to become a real estate lawyer, but at the end of his articling period, Hess took him to lunch and twisted his arm, with the result that two hours later, he emerged as a real estate lawyer. Given the firm's involvement with the Li family, he was involved, with Shaw and Hess, in both the Harbour Castle acquisition and the Expo lands in Vancouver. He was often on the other side of deals with Olympia & York, finding that the projects were high quality but that it was extremely difficult to negotiate with the organization. Their deals were quite inflexible, and it seemed a matter of pride that the Olympia & York template would be applied to them. He recalls writing a lengthy letter on a transaction with Cadillac Fairview on twenty-one separate points, to which he received a "no" to every single point. There was a high level of market power and arrogance that went through all of the deals. He was involved in the purchase and sale of the Shepherd Centre in which eighty-two separate units were bought and held for five years and sold at a profit of approximately $100 million. He has acquired a special expertise in hotel matters, buying, selling, and financing, often with Lehman Brothers in New York. He was involved in Metropolitan Hotels transactions in both Toronto and Vancouver on behalf of the Wu family. These were boutique hotels, the one in Toronto being known as the Soho Metropolitan near the

SkyDome, which had approximately eighty rooms. He acted in connection with the Intercontinental Hotel on Bloor Street and the Wyndham Bristol Place Hotels.

Although he is formally part of the real estate section, Dow has become more of a corporate lawyer over the years. He is counsel for the Hockey Hall of Fame, having started with the leasing and construction contracts when the Hall of Fame moved from its former location to BCE Place. The early days of the Hall of Fame arose out of a call by John Ziegler, then commissioner of the NHL, who asked him to come to New York to discuss a confidential project. It was hardly a state secret that the Hockey Hall of Fame was moving to BCE Place. The firm got the work, and this evolved into Dow being the only lawyer for the Hall of Fame. In the mid-1990s, after Alan Eagleson had been indicted for fraud, there had been a great deal of pressure to expel him from the Hall of Fame. Dow was saddled with the task of managing that very difficult relationship within the media spotlight. In the end, it did not prove necessary to deal with the issue since Eagleson resigned.

In the field of sports stadiums, Dow was involved in the permanent financing on the old Palladium, now the Corel Centre in Ottawa, and in the financing for GM Place in Vancouver. In the Montreal Canadiens ownership change from Molson to George Gillette, Ron Durand worked on the financing aspects, while Viateur Chénard of the Montreal office handled the real estate aspects of the transactions relating to the Molson Centre since the arrangement was as much a real estate play as a sports franchise.

On the subject of hockey, the intense interoffice rivalry mirrored the Toronto-Montreal competition in the NHL. All of the games were in Montreal. There was no interest in alternating the sites, and it was quite clear that the Montreal lawyers had no interest in the cultural wasteland of Toronto. Dow remembers with great satisfaction that the Toronto office won the encounters about six years in a row, which was particularly satisfying because the Montreal Canadiens were then riding high, and the Toronto Maple Leafs were enduring one of their many slumps. (I used to love starting speeches I gave in Toronto by saying that "it was nice to be here in Toronto, home of the 1942 Stanley Cup champions.") Dow recalls boisterous weekends involving occasional fights on the ice. He was responsible for hiring a large bus to take everyone to the game. By the time they got checked in to one of the hotels, the police were already there because of the noise level. All this may have been just interoffice rivalry or possibly the innate competitive attitudes of lawyers.

Dow, too, has his favourite Fraser Elliott story. Dow had his eye on a painting by a Quebec artist and wanted to get Elliott's expert view on whether or not he should buy it. Elliott's gruff questions was, "Who is the artist?" Dow told him. "Never heard of him," said Elliott seeming, to Dow, anxious to get rid of him. "How much is this painting worth anyway?" $1,700. This was followed by the Archie Bunker look and the question, "How can you go wrong?" This left Dow terrified of Elliott for the next ten years.

In 1990, during the deep recession of the real estate industry, Canada found itself following the US experience whereby financial institutions were brought low after being caught overextended in their real estate loans and investments. As the Resolution Trust Company started selling off distressed real estate assets in the United States, liquidators were appointed for one Canadian financial institution after another. As the Toronto office saw its lending and development practices shrink as the recession continued, its lawyers in that group turned their hands to dealing with distressed real estate assets, including loan portfolios and real property. Beginning with acting for the liquidator of the bankrupt Dominion Trust Company, the firm moved on to act for the purchasers (many of them US vulture funds) of distressed real estate assets from Standard Trust Company, North American Trust Company, Confederation Trust, Confederation Life, and others. Transactions involving millions and even billions of dollars of real estate assets traded hands as the financial institutions were wound up or reorganized. This included the old Massey-Ferguson plant in Brantford, Ontario, which marked the end of a distinguished era in Canadian industrial history. This led the firm to represent the servicing companies that were retained to manage these assets for the purchasers as they restructured and realized on loans, sold the real property assets, and did whatever they had to do to try to survive.

While other Toronto law firms with formerly significant real estate practices dissolved or separated or released associates and partners, the firm's Toronto real estate practice grew each year during the recession, adding associates and partners – including Dana Porter,[9] Larry Cobb,[10] and Mario Paura[11] – and hiring many lawyers on a contract basis because there was more due diligence and processing work than there were students and associates available to perform the services. When the economy moved into another recession in the first years of the new millennium, the real estate lawyers did not see a repeat of this activity mainly because the financial institutions took such a beating in the early 1990s that they have changed their lending practices and attitudes to real property investments.

ALTERNATIVE DISPUTE RESOLUTION (ADR)

The popularity of alternative dispute resolution (ADR) methods is a result of the slowness of the court process, the need for expertise in the matters to be resolved, and a desire to be certain of both the substantive law to be applied and the forum in which any resolution will be achieved. It is a technique that was steadfastly resisted in many jurisdictions until fairly recently, but as international trade has continued to expand and with it the need for relatively quick certainty when disputes arise, this resistance has crumbled. Although there are still ways to get such matters before the ordinary courts when there is an agreement in place to arbitrate, most courts will now require the parties to exhaust that recourse before they will consider hearing any complaint by a party. Canada has been no stranger to the ADR phenomenon, with the result that the lawyers in the firm have been exposed to the process both as advocates and as arbitrators.

By far the most prominent of the firm's partners in ADR to date has been Marc Lalonde,[12] who was ranked by the European Legal Media Group in its 2001 expert guide, *The Best of the Best 2001,* as one of the top twenty arbitrators in the world in commercial matters. Lalonde observes, with amusement, that he got into the field of international arbitration essentially by default. It began with a phone call from Christian Salbaing, then in the Hong Kong office, who had received a call about a difficult and politically charged matter between an agency of the French government and the new Islamic fundamentalist regime in Iran. The French wanted someone with prestige and political weight to act in the arbitration proceedings and was considering Pierre Elliott Trudeau. Salbaing called Lalonde to get in touch with Trudeau. The former prime minister was not interested, but he agreed to receive them. The meeting was short, and as predicted, Trudeau said that he was not interested and suggested that they approach Lalonde. So, they went to lunch and asked Lalonde if he would be interested? Lalonde replied that he was, which led to his first case of international arbitration, which was followed a year later by a similar appointment in a somewhat parallel case. He was off and running in an esoteric series of important international arbitrations, all because the French could not get Pierre Elliott Trudeau.

Unfortunately for the readers of this work, the requirement that the names of the parties and even the issues before an arbitral panel, other than those that have been made public in some official manner, remain confidential prevents disclosure of most of the fascinating mandates with which members of the firm have dealt. One high-profile matter that made its way to the Swiss courts and is therefore in the public domain was the dispute between the French atomic energy agency and the government of Iran, Lalonde's first case as an arbitrator. The matter had begun as a private arbitration, arising from a contract awarded by the shah of Iran before he was deposed in 1979, which engaged the French agency to build a number of nuclear power stations in Iran, a contract worth several billions of dollars. When the Ayatollah Khomeini came to power, he was not interested in nuclear power and simply cancelled the contract. The French had some leverage in the circumstances since they had insisted during the negotiations on getting a loan from Iran to build a facility in France for the production of enriched uranium. When the Iranian government announced the cancellation of the contract, the French announced that they did not intend to repay the loan. Arbitration ensued. The contract had provided that no arbitrator could be a citizen of either of the countries that was a party to the dispute. There was the usual difficulty in selecting a presiding member of the panel, which was somewhat amusingly resolved when the Iranians suggested a retired judge from *La Cour de cassation* (court of appeal) of France. The judge was as surprised as anyone since he had previously resigned in protest from an arbitral panel when one of the participating Iranians had physically attacked a US arbitrator. He asked how they could possibly consider him after he had resigned in such circumstances, to which the Iranians replied that they liked a man of strong views!

The portion of the case that made its way to the Swiss Federal Tribunal arose from the application of the Swiss *concordat* that was applicable to the contract, which had been executed in Geneva. The Swiss law provided that if one of the parties invoked the concept of compensation (offsetting obligations), the arbitration proceedings should cease until the matter of compensation was resolved. The French had raised the issue as part of a strategy that had an impact on a third matter, which was not before the arbitral panel. The panel, faced with what they thought was a rather silly rule, nevertheless decided that it was bound to apply the law, which led to the recourse to the Swiss courts. The Swiss Federal Tribunal held, overruling the majority of the panel, that the arbitration should have continued to the extent that it could determine at least that portion of the claim that was not covered by compensation. This court decision eventually led to a political solution that ought to have occurred in the first place.

In addition to arbitrations, Lalonde has served as an ad hoc judge of the International Court of Justice concerning a dispute between Canada and Spain and another involving the use of force in *Yugoslavia v. Canada et al.* during the NATO actions during the civil war, which is still ongoing. The dispute with Spain, in what the media labelled the "Turbot War," had arisen from the seizure by Canadian authorities, acting on instructions from Brian Tobin, then minister of Fisheries, of a Spanish trawler that had been fishing within the 200-mile zone, which was brought to the International Court of Justice in 1995, where Canada was successful. Because Canada had no member on the court, it was entitled to appoint an ad hoc judge in respect of the case against it, as did Spain. The court appears to expect that the ad hoc judges will be partisan, but it also expects that they will not be domineering in their advocacy. Lalonde played his part perfectly, taking only ten minutes, a welcome contrast to the hour and a half presentation by the Spanish judge.

The Yugoslavian matter had been commenced in 1999 when the Yugoslav government of Slobodan Milosevic sued the governments of ten NATO countries for genocide and the illegal use of force, contrary to the charter of the United Nations, there having been no resolution regarding the use of force before military action had been launched against Yugoslavia. In accordance with the usual practice, all countries not represented on the court appointed ad hoc judges, and Canada appointed Lalonde. Only the matter of jurisdiction has been argued thus far, and most countries have so far been successful in their arguments that there is no jurisdiction for the court to exercise in the circumstances, with the result that the only cases outstanding are those involving Canada, Portugal, Belgium, and the Netherlands. The United States, following the outcome of the *Nicaragua* case, adopted a policy of accepting the jurisdiction of the court on a selective basis, and it refused to do so in this matter. All of the ad hoc judges agreed that even though the arguments on behalf of all ten countries were essentially the same, they would participate in the decisions affecting only their own countries.

In *Amco v. Indonesia*, Lalonde was appointed by a Hong Kong Chinese living in Vancouver in connection with a dispute over a hotel that was a joint venture between him and the Indonesian army. The hotel had a somewhat salacious reputation, but the army officers appeared to enjoy the creature (and other) comforts it afforded them until they decided that their co-venturer was cheating them. The short-term problem was solved at machine gunpoint, and the Chinese was taken under heavy guard to the airport and expelled from the country. The arbitration that followed this brief and one-sided discussion of expropriation by the government was held under the rules applied by the International Centre for Settlement of Investment Disputes, a subsidiary of the World Bank. The panel determined that mistreatment had indeed occurred, and an amount, albeit less than had been claimed, was eventually awarded to the disgruntled and dispossessed former joint venturer. Lalonde was also a special envoy in the Canada-Brazil regional aircraft dispute involving Bombardier and Embraer, which has soured relations between the two countries for several years.

After a judicial career of twenty-two years, Hon. Benjamin J. Greenberg[13] retired from the bench of the Quebec Superior Court in May 1999 and immediately joined the firm, adding considerably to its capacity and reputation in ADR. Greenberg was one of the most experienced judges of the court in commercial matters and was a natural recruit for purposes of expanding this area of practice. As senior counsel, he worked primarily with the litigation group in the Montreal office, providing advice in strategy and in the fields of negotiation, mediation, and arbitration. He is active in international arbitration and has played an important role in establishing and developing a domestic commercial arbitration practice to complement the firm's existing international arbitration activities. In February 2000, not long after Greenberg's arrival, the Right Honourable Antonio Lamer, PC, CC, formerly the chief justice of the Supreme Court of Canada, joined the firm's Ottawa office as senior advisor following a thirty-year career on the bench of various courts.

During the fall of 2000, the firm established its first identifiable group, co-chaired by Lalonde and Greenberg, concentrating on alternative dispute resolution, formerly carried on as an ad hoc activity within the litigation group. In addition to Lalonde, Greenberg, Lamer, Gotlieb, myself, and others, the firm recruited Babak Barin,[14] formerly a senior legal advisor to the Claims Resolution Tribunal for Dormant Accounts in Switzerland (CRT). The CRT, which in the fall of 2001 fulfilled its mandate after three and a half years, was an independent institution under the supervision of the Independent Committee of Eminent Persons (ICEP), chaired by Paul A. Volcker, former chairman of the board of governors of the US Federal Reserve System and the Swiss Federal Banking Commission. The CRT was established to resolve all claims to dormant accounts opened by non-Swiss customers, which were published by the Swiss Bankers Association in July and October 1997. During its mandate, the CRT processed approximately 10,000 claims submitted in more than fifteen languages by individuals from over seventy countries. The cost of the procedure, which amounted to thirty-two million Swiss francs, was fully borne by the Swiss banks, and the CRT awarded a total of sixty-five million Swiss francs to successful claimants.

According to Barin, during its mandate, the CRT struggled for truth and fairness in very difficult, complicated, and occasionally tragic circumstances. The application of negotiated[15] rather than specifically drafted rules of procedure for the resolution of historic disputes such as the ones before the CRT was not easy. It was a unique experience, which included receiving numerous telephone calls from anxious elderly claimants,[16] often late in the evening because of different time zones, who often simply wanted to find out the status of their applications and when they could expect to receive the decisions relating to their claims. This, along with involvement in the early stages of the creation of the International Commission on Holocaust Era Insurance Claims, has been a particularly rewarding aspect of Barin's professional practice.

In addition to lecturing and teaching in the field, Barin has edited a very useful handbook on international dispute resolution,[17] which is frequently resorted to by practitioners around the world. He has also been involved in a number of very interesting state-to-state arbitrations, which for reasons of confidentiality, unfortunately cannot be discussed here. On the international conciliation front, Barin has represented the Government of Canada as a delegate to the United Nations Commission on International Trade Law (UNCITRAL) in Vienna, where the Working Group on Arbitration is currently drafting a model law on international commercial conciliation. In the very near future, this document will remind people in the ADR field of the early days of the 1958 New York Convention,[18] now adhered to by more than 120 jurisdictions, including, as recently as January 2002, Iran.

Thereafter, the increase in international business transactions and the firm's interest in this area led to the creation of a team focusing on international commercial arbitration as a key component of a larger ADR practice group, the members of which give advice to clients on the drafting and negotiation of arbitration agreements and other types of ADR clauses, act for clients as counsel in such matters, and sit as arbitrators in a variety of cases. From June 1999, Greenberg served as a member of the NAFTA Chapter Eleven Arbitral Tribunal concerning the softwood lumber dispute between an American investor (Pope & Talbot, Inc.) and the Government of Canada.

CHAPTER 15

Taking Stock

Anniversaries such as the fiftieth provide a useful occasion to look back on what the firm has accomplished and to consider how and why that occurred. A law firm is essentially a pool of intellectual capital, gathered around a shared vision of what the members hope to accomplish, led by those among them with the most talent, ambition, and ability to mobilize the collective effort. That effort combines the commitment to attracting the best talent, permitting it to develop, and a willingness to insist that there is no substitute for the mastery of the professional skills. It involves a recognition that different types of lawyers, with different backgrounds, experience, and perspectives are just as essential to a vibrant firm. However, the pool of talent, no matter how deep or how broad, means little without the ability to attract, serve, and build enduring relationships with clients. Nor can a firm prosper without the background work of a dedicated support staff that shares the excitement of building a firm. And the additional factor of luck, of being in the right place at the right time, is a reminder that no matter how smart any group of people may think it is, there are mysteries that can make or break any enterprise.

Stikeman and Elliott, in addition to being talented themselves, knew from the beginning that it was important to get the best people associated with them, and they were disciplined in their insistence on the best talent. They were not perfect in all their choices – no one is – but on the whole, they did get the best they could. Those who did not meet the firm's high standards realized that fact as quickly as did Stikeman and Elliott and moved on to other pastures. There were different phases or stages of the firm's growth, and the nature of the talents required changed from time to time. Those who started with the small Toronto office in the early 1970s were not necessarily the same lawyers who could push the envelope of the 1980s and 1990s as that office began its assault on the mega-transactions arising in the Toronto market. The pace of action did not remain the same as the firm developed, and although no one ever coasted, the acceleration of the demands of the legal marketplace was not suited to everyone who may have been comfortable in earlier times.

Law firms are not the only organizations that recognize talent. Many of the firm's clients liked what they saw in the firm's lawyers, enough so that they made sufficiently attractive offers to lure them away. From a domestic perspective, as the US legal market expanded, the search for talent brought those firms north of the border to recruit at the Canadian law faculties and from among Canadian law firms. The combination of the powerful US dollar (as one recruiter was wont to say, "We're talkin' dead presidents here, son, not yer Northern peso...") and the possibility of a bigger brass ring at the end of a period of associateship (even if the odds against that would make a Las Vegas bookie blush) proved irresistible to many of the young Canadians and created a retention problem for the best Canadian law firms.

Over the years, it has always been the practice of the firm when recruiting to look carefully at the academic results of candidates. This is far from the only measure, but it was always a fairly reliable indicator of whether the candidate had the wherewithal to become a good lawyer. Good marks did not necessarily produce good lawyers, but bad marks highlighted an issue that would have to be dealt with before going forward. If a candidate did not seem to be able to handle the conceptual study of law at the university level, it suggested the possibility that the professional practice of law might pose a greater challenge. The search for talent did not confine itself to a single model or a shared background, and this was one of the fundamentals that was established by the founding partners. They did not care where a person came from or from what background. They were the first to have a partner of Japanese descent after World War II and the first to break down the barrier that separated Jewish and non-Jewish firms. Although not the first to hire women lawyers, they were not far behind, and there was never any suggestion once women were part of the firm that they be treated differently from the male lawyers. The founders seemed to recognize instinctively that the broader the legal gene pool, the stronger the resulting firm. They knew that they were in the process of developing a new approach to the emerging fields of tax and business law and that the best people to go across the new frontiers with them were not ones who were comfortable and established. They wanted fellow explorers who were hungry and who wanted to build something new. It was a new legal paradigm they were creating, not just a variation of the old.

So their lawyers came from Quebec and Ontario and across Canada, from the United States, from the Commonwealth, from Western Europe, from Central and Eastern Europe, from Africa, from the Middle East, and from Asia. And together, they built the firm. It was a firm that first understood the potential of post-war Canada in the specialty fields and that made specialties out of them. Precocious as it may have been, the new firm forced others to respond and to change themselves in order to compete, to try to gain entry into fields that were now already occupied. Many of the competitors were themselves quite successful in adapting to the new circumstances, but many others, even some that had been household names in their day, were not and have disappeared from sight. It was an eclectic collection of scholars, athletes, meteorologists, Rhodes Scholars, rock singers, newspaper reporters, accountants, songwriters, ecologists, pharmacists, foresters, musicians, engineers, and others, each with a different story and a different slant on the world. They came, attracted by others who had the same vision of building something new and of which they would be an integral part. And they built.

As the horizons expanded, first across the Atlantic and then to Toronto and other locations, it is important to recall just how unusual it was at that time for a small Montreal-based firm to have the audacity to consider such initiatives. Canadian firms, especially small new ones, did not do things like that. It required a combination of bravado, foresight, and chutzpah, plus the willingness to assume the financial risks of new ventures, not to mention the risk of derision on the part of those who may have waited, hoping for a failure of the two upstarts who had deliberately differentiated themselves from the legal establishment. The gambles paid off. Who was to guess that there would be so many road warriors willing to take the firm colours abroad and to build a name recognition that is unmatched for Canadian firms?

The diversity of background and culture was augmented by a range of interests among the members of the firm. These included passions for business, politics, the arts, and cultural pursuits. It reflected the sense that one could not be "just" a lawyer – it was necessary to be plugged into the community as a whole. This feature attracted those with different backgrounds, which enabled development of a shared vision that could contemplate a national and a global firm, and those who were willing to take the necessary risks.

The firm was willing to play a role in the politics of the country. During one of the Liberal leadership campaigns, there were three separate initiatives being managed from the office. Michel Vennat was supporting Jean Chrétien (along with John Rae, David Collinette, and Eddie Goldenberg); Jim Grant was supporting Don Johnston; and Jim Robb was standing by John Turner. David Angus was a vociferous Progressive Conservative. The firm also took positions in the Quebec situation, and on the referendum questions of 1980 and 1995, it had partners on both sides of the issue. Robb was a long-time Quebec Liberal backroomer, and he remembers Stikeman coming into the office early on the morning of November 16, 1976, the day after the Parti Québécois had won the provincial election, saying, "Don't worry, Jim, we thrive on confusion." After that same election win, Vennat went back to Ottawa as special counsel to Prime Minister Pierre Elliott Trudeau on a ten-month assignment, where he worked on the initial strategy of how to deal with a separatist government and to prepare for the referendum that would inevitably occur.

Several members of the firm maintained university teaching roles over the years at McGill, Concordia, Ottawa, Sherbrooke, and Montréal and, from the Toronto office, University of Toronto, Osgoode Hall law school, and Queen's. Others were active in university affairs, including alumni associations, fundraising, university governance, and athletics. I was active in the Canadian Olympic Association as secretary and then president and in the International Olympic Committee, reaching the level of vice-president. At McGill, I was president of the alumni association (as was Jim Robb and as Kip Cobbett has become in this anniversary year), chair of the board of governors, and chancellor. Mike Richards has been very active at McGill and is presently a member of the board of governors. Jim Grant is a member of the important finance and administration committee. Many others, including Elliott, Mercier, Grant, Hartt, O'Brien, Yontef, and Hess have also been active in a broad range of community affairs.

The commitment to build a single firm consisting of several offices remained paramount even when provincial and other legislation required separate legal entities. The firm simply managed itself around these impediments and treated itself as a single economic unit. This sounds easy in retrospect, but there were times of tension and dissension as economic changes occurred and personalities emerged or flared, all of which had to be absorbed. There always remained sufficient mutual goodwill that the bumps in the road were smoothed over and the firm continued to grow and prosper. In due course as well, the issue of the firm name loomed on the horizon, and there was the potential for a degree of tension as law firm names generally were gradually shortened, largely for branding purposes, and consideration was given to a single name for the legally separate firms in Montreal and Toronto. Three of the Montreal partners – Tamaki, Mercier, and Robb – had become used to seeing their names on the letterhead, and although Robarts had died, Bowman's name was still on the Toronto letterhead. In 1983, with remarkably little bitterness, the name appearing on all firm letterhead changed to Stikeman, Elliott, and the firm moved one step closer to actualizing the dream of a single firm in law as well as in fact. Several years later, when the legal constraints preventing interjurisdictional firms were resolved, consultants were hired to design a uniform look for the firm, and in the process, the comma was removed (along with several thousands of dollars to the branding consultants for the purpose), and the firm became a single partnership under the name of Stikeman Elliott.

RELATIONSHIPS

One of the most important relationships responsible for the development of the firm has been that between the firm and the CIBC, led by the involvement of Elliott and later Grant as members of its board. We had incorporated the Mercantile Bank of Canada, and Elliott was a director there for a while before he got the chance to go on the CIBC board, and Stikeman took his place for several years. In any case, although we got a good deal of work from the association, it was never a major bank.[1] The key to any successful commercial law firm is a close relationship with a major bank, which provides not only a source of work on the many transactions between the bank and its clients, but also introductions to businesses that have relationships with the banks. Particularly in a small country such as Canada, without such a relationship, a law firm is necessarily condemned to a niche role. The firm began as one of several providing regional services to the CIBC in Quebec, but it never approached the level of becoming one of its principal counsel in the Toronto area and had no chance of becoming so without first establishing a foothold in that financial capital. It even took several years to develop to the point where the firm was on a list for several banks of possible counsel

Marjorie Cornell, Mary Stikeman, and portrait of Heward Stikeman.

Fraser Elliott and portrait.

Ken Ottenbreit and Prime Minister
Jean Chrétien following "Canada
Loves New York" rally,
December 1, 2001.

William Braithwaite and
Fraser Elliott.

Pierre Raymond and Fraser Elliott.

Robert Hart and Joanne Gravel.

Tonie Lepore as Marilyn Monroe,
Christmas party 2001, singing
"Happy Birthday, Stikeman Elliott."

Brian Rose and Mary Stikeman.

Fraser Elliott's 80th birthday dinner, 2001. Left to right: Ron Durand, Michael Richards, Lawson Hunter, Peter Howard, David Finkelstein, Brian Rose, Gregory Kane, William Braithwaite, Pierre Raymond, Jamie Davis, James Robb, Fraser Elliott, Stuart Cobbett, Mortimer Freiheit, Peter O'Brien, Claire Fisher, Michel Vennat, Richard Pound, David Angus, Rod Barrett, Marvin Yontef, Richard Taylor.

Toronto litigation group at summer retreat, 1988. Left to right: Robert Reuter, John Sopinka, Kathryn Chalmers, John Judge, Donald Houston, John Field, Peter Jervis, James Orr, Andra Pollak, Katherine Kay, Bruce Pollock, Sean Dunphy, Douglas Harrison, David Brown, Patrick O'Kelly, David Byers.

Ottawa lawyers, Whistler retreat, 2002. Left to right: Jonathan Blakey, Kim Alexander-Cook, Jeffrey Brown, Mirko Bibic, Gregory Kane, Susan Hutton, Nick McHaffie, Justine Whitehead, Roula Eatrides, Eugene Derenyi, Stuart McCormick, Nicole Brousseau, David Fewer.

Vancouver lawyers, Whistler retreat, 2002. Left to right: Michael Allen, Argiro Kotsalis, C. Inge Poulus, Richard Jackson, Phil Griffin, Susan Lloyd, John Anderson, Rachel Hutton, David Gillanders, Gordon Turriff.

Calgary lawyers, Whistler retreat, 2002. Front: Leland Corbett, Alyson Goldman. Standing, left to right: Tyler Robinson, David Brett, Stephanie Uhlich, Michael Dyck, Keith Chatwin, Michael Witt, Brad Grant, Barry Emes, Scott Whitby, Glenn Cameron, Fred Erickson, Mary Henderson, Gordon Chmilar, Mike Styczen, Christine Wright, Duane Gillis, Dean Burns.

in cases of conflict of interest, actual or perceived, between the banks and their regular counsel. It was this position as stand-in that led to the Dome Petroleum restructuring mandates in the early 1980s, which put the firm fully on the map as one that could handle the largest and most complex financing transactions.

A defining relationship that contributed enormously to the success of the firm over the years has been that with Li Ka-shing and his family. This relationship, resulting from the firm's connection with the CIBC, came as a result of an introduction by Russell Harrison of the CIBC at the time that Li became a member of the bank's international advisory board, and this led to the growth of trust and friendship between Li and both Stikeman and Elliott. Not only did the friendship with Li give the Hong Kong office instant credibility, but the subsequent business ventures of Li in Canada also provided the firm with a very high profile in the business community, starting with the acquisition of the Harbour Castle Hotel in Toronto, followed by the successive interests acquired in Canadian Husky. The Vancouver office became a reality far sooner than would otherwise have been possible because of Stikeman's promise to Li that if he acquired the Expo Lands in Vancouver, the firm would open an office in that city to help with the project. In turn, the opening of the Vancouver office led to far greater credibility among the Hong Kong Chinese as they looked for refuge in North America during the period when its status as a colony of Great Britain came to an end. Both the London and Sydney offices have also become involved in helping the Li family. The relationships spread downward through the firm, and over the years, three immensely talented younger lawyers have become part of the Li family operations – beginning with Frank Sixt and followed by Christian Salbaing and Eugene Kwan. Relationships are established between the next generation of the Li family and that of the firm itself with Marvin Yontef, Wayne Shaw, Ron Durand, Brian Hansen, and others as senior and trusted advisors in respect of much of the Canadian activities.

In more recent years, the relationship with Air Canada has grown considerably. The relationship started with a few isolated mandates, but it has expanded, with the position of David Angus on its board, to handling the two segments of its privatization, the acquisition of Canadian Airlines International, and the desperate fight against the hostile takeover bid by Onex. It was close enough that Calin Rovinescu was identified, following the trauma of the challenge and the success in defending the takeover bid, as someone who could handle all of the complex aspects of running an international airline other than that portion of the business that keeps the planes in the air, in which the CEO, Robert Milton, is an acknowledged star. The liaison with Canadian National is not quite as close, but it was strong enough to lead to the firm obtaining the enormously complicated privatization work, at the end of which Jean-Pierre Ouellet was also lured away as its vice-president and general counsel.

Stikeman and Elliott had many other personal relationships that led to work for the firm, and the example these provided to the lawyers who followed them has never been lost. It was important to be good lawyers because informed clients would always demand the best, but it was equally important to generate a "top of mind" relationship so that when potential clients were determining where legal work should be assigned, the firm would be among the first they considered. This is a particular challenge as the firm has evolved into a transactional one with an appetite for the large deals that emerge, often with little advance warning, and the choice of counsel may mean that twenty, thirty, or forty lawyers may become active in a transaction lasting several months – or not.

WOMEN IN THE FIRM

The world, including the professions, has struggled with the difficult issues affecting women in the workplace. The firm can claim no particular breakthrough on these matters that would put it in the vanguard of social progress. It has had female partners and associates for many years and has wrestled with the evident social dilemma that has women assuming a disproportionate share of the responsibility for bringing up families, but the firm has not found a panacea to that dilemma. In the end, there is no doubt that such responsibility has slowed the progress of women in the firm to the highest levels of remuneration since time taken off to raise a family has interfered with the acquisition of experience and progression to the top of the firm.

It is, however, safe to say that there has been no discrimination against women as such (especially with women beginning to form the majority of many law schools and to dominate the academic rankings), and several have been among the top practitioners in the firm. Kathryn Chalmers and Katherine Kay in Toronto are seasoned litigators who take no back seat to anyone; Lianne Miller is a recognized tax expert, especially in the oil and gas fields; and Kathleen Ward is a recognized player in the corporate field. Claudette Picard served as bâtonnier of the Quebec Bar; Louise Pelly was an expert in the legislation governing financial institutions; and Elinore Richardson was a creative designer of financial products and an implacable negotiator whether with the taxation authorities or opposing parties in commercial transactions.

I remember a case in Vancouver in which Revenue Canada (now CCRA) was balking at resolution of several issues affecting the client for which Richardson and I were working. We had proposed the terms of a settlement that the client would accept, but Revenue Canada could not appear to make up its mind. I finally suggested that they should agree to the points because otherwise, I was going to sic Elinore on them. I said, "She will come into your office; she will take off her shoes and tuck her feet under her in your visitor's chair; she will have her cans of Coca-Cola and her package of cigarettes, and she will talk to you. And talk to you. And talk to you. I will go back to the hotel to sleep, and when I come back in the morning, she will still be talking to you. Now, do you want to settle, or should I call her?" They settled.

When Margaret Grottenthaler started as an articling student, she had notions of coming to a staid corporate environment, where she would work on legal problems of the highest academic standards with pillars of the Bay Street financial community. Instead she was thrown into litigation and a family law divorce and property hearing involving a well-known client in which her grounds for divorce were his adultery and his grounds for divorce were her adultery with another younger woman. For a girl from Guelph, this was all a bit eye-popping. Sopinka and Chalmers handed her many tasks that law school education had not prepared her for. Grottenthaler went on an examination of the client's wife's tacky nouveau riche household furnishing, including the gaudy silverware and the faux medieval lamps. She had to interview the alcoholic ex-household help about whether they had ever found the wife and her girlfriend in compromising situations. And worst of all, she had to transcribe "the most godawful book of poems" that the wife had written to said girlfriend. One good thing did come out of this trial and that was meeting and later recruiting, through John Sopinka, David Byers (the present head of the Toronto litigation department), who was acting for the wife. The case, notwithstanding the seriousness for the parties, provided many occasions for hilarity despite the sordid subject matter. The judge was quite disgusted with everyone by the end, but the firm got a very good result for the client.

It appeared to be no better when she returned as an associate to the litigation department. The Sinclair Stevens inquiry into whether he was in breach of his conflict of interest obligations as a cabinet minister had begun, and she was again the junior for Sopinka and Chalmers. They rented their own set of not very elegant rooms in the inquiry building and hung out there most of the time. Moments of levity were important in this file because some days, the hearings were so boring that everyone, including counsel, had trouble staying awake. She and Chalmers had an arrangement to pinch each other every couple of minutes, and if they both fell asleep, the court commissionaire would surreptitiously throw little wads of paper at them or give them gum to chew. Some days were interesting, however, and several leading lights of the Toronto business community were called as witnesses, including Frank Stronach.

After these thrilling exposures to litigation practice, Grottenthaler had had pretty much enough of litigation and became a research lawyer instead. This was a new phenomenon within the firm, and she was given the opportunity to forge her own path, notwithstanding some initial skepticism about whether a research lawyer was something the firm needed. But there was also some senior support for the initiative and help in shaping the role into something valuable, challenging, and rewarding. The idea was a reflection of the entrepreneurial spirit of the firm and in a way, its eccentricity. Gunfighters know that they need someone who can make the bullets they shoot. Grottenthaler doubts that she would still be a lawyer had she started out anywhere other than with the firm.

Anne Ristic was the first of the women partners to make her career in the firm in something other than law when she took on the vital role of student recruitment. This is a model that was subsequently adopted in Montreal, with specific lawyers assigned to the task of recruitment in the persons of Lyse Charette and more recently, Jill Hugessen. When Ristic started working on recruitment full-time in the early 1990s, she had the opportunity to see Stikeman in action. He always made a huge impression. He regularly attended the career fair at McGill and would stand at the booth with her and a Montreal lawyer. She was as impressed by this as were the students. He would stand beaming at our booth, introducing himself with great enthusiasm to all the students who came their way, showing great interest in them and their questions, while they stood somewhat in awe. This was compared to all the other firms, which had third- and fourth-year associates stationed in their booths. One student commented on how impressive it was that we had our founding partner coming out to visit the law schools, and Heward said, "I wouldn't miss it – I come whenever I can! It is just wonderful for me to meet and talk to all of you just starting out on such a rewarding career! And," turning to Ristic and the Montreal lawyer, Katharine McDougall, "I have such lovely young ladies as Katharine and Anne to come with me. What could be better?" Not very many people could pull that off sounding sincere, but he certainly did. They did not really object to being called "lovely young ladies," although in this case, that was also not the norm, and they stood beside him, also beaming.

In the early 1990s, late one night on a recruiting trip to Dalhousie with Ristic, Peter Howard committed the firm to pay for a new, safety-compliant staircase to the cellar of the Domus Legis Society, which is essentially a law students' bar housed in a very old house that was about to be closed down as a fire trap. Howard made this promise while they were actually drinking in the cellar/fire trap, and the student representative suggested that Howard might want to take the idea back to the firm since it was about a $10,000 outlay. Perhaps he also thought that by the cold light of day, the bar-induced undertaking might be displaced by a severe headache. Howard replied grandiosely that this would not be necessary; they could rely on his word. The students got their staircase, the recruiters got the understandable flak upon their return to sobriety, and Toronto and the committee recruited thereafter within an approved budget. Ristic is the first woman lawyer elected to the firm's partnership board.

Alison Youngman has evolved from a paralegal in Montreal to a senior partner in the corporate section of the firm in Toronto. The firm encouraged her to enrol in law school, hired her back as an articling student and then as an associate, and provided an environment that allowed her to develop into a fine lawyer. Christine Desaulniers in Montreal has been a road warrior with difficult assignments and has emerged as a very capable corporate lawyer dealing with many complex transactions. Shawna Miller has had varied experience within and outside the firm and has become the first female managing principal of the London office. Danielle Grenier would certainly have risen to the top of the employment group had she not accepted an appointment to the bench, where she has emerged as a very fine jurist. Suzanne Côté is the first female head of the Montreal litigation section. Susan Hutton is a leading member of the firm's competition team and brings international experience with her.

All the female lawyers who have decided to make the law a full-time career have demonstrated abilities that make them leaders in their field, fulfilling the potential that was identified when they began. Others have made the decision not to make the full-time commitment for family or other reasons, and their careers have not been as spectacular. There is no apparent solution to this problem, especially in a demanding profession in which experience is the key to assuming full responsibility and in which other lawyers, who do not face the same social and family demands, can acquire the necessary experience faster than those who cannot devote the same time and single-minded focus to their professional careers. That said, within the firm, the playing field is level and decidedly gender-neutral.

STAFF

A successful law firm requires superb lawyers, but that is not enough. It also requires excellent support staff, and the firm has been fortunate in being able to attract and, perhaps even more importantly, to retain a dedicated and loyal staff. The needs have evolved and expanded as the firm has grown, and technology has dramatically changed the way the practice of law is now carried on. However, the nature of the commitment to the firm has not changed as the staff have embraced the challenge of building something new and special and have absorbed the inherent difficulties of working on a daily basis with a collection of what must have seemed to be nothing but Type A personalities. The ability to turn out first-class work under pressure is by no means limited to lawyers, and the output that forms the product of advice and negotiation depends on a capable secretarial and technological support personnel who can read the illegible, interpret the unintelligible, and guess at the rest, all on the basis that whatever comes out must be perfect and that it had to be ready yesterday. The stakes are high, and the consequences of getting it wrong are dire. It is not an environment suited to everyone, and those who can handle the pressure are worth their weight in gold although the lawyers try not to let that go to their heads.

In addition to their regular workload, the staff, especially the secretaries, spend time organizing the lives of lawyers, many of whom have only the most rudimentary idea of filing and personal organization. Most of the examples given are derived from Montreal, which has the longest existence of the firm's history, but there are doubtless similar examples in each of the offices. The staff pioneers included Margaret Dawson, Joanne Gravel, and Marjorie Maud Cornell in the original office, but there are several others who have been with the firm for well over half of its existence. Four Larivière sisters have worked for the firm over the years – Darlene, Sandra, June, and Donna – all of whom have been unfailingly cheerful and supportive. Iona Carrington carried on assisting Stikeman after Marjorie Cornell retired. Claire Fisher followed Elliott to Toronto, where she remains as his secretary to this day, and Valerie Higgins followed George Tamaki, remaining with him until he retired. Many other lawyers had secretaries who stayed with them for decades. It is impossible to name everyone, but it is worth noting that many of the staff have stayed with the firm until their retirement. In the Montreal and Toronto offices, there have been many who have gone well past the quarter-century mark; in the other offices that have a more abbreviated history, a remarkable number have been with the firm since the offices opened.

If one ever wants to know what is really happening in the firm or in one of the offices, it is generally a complete waste of time to ask a partner; the real source of knowledge are the secretaries and staff, who know everything before it actually happens. My daughter worked at the firm for a summer, and I learned far more from her than from anything we discussed at the management committee meetings. Cornell was for many years the source of all knowledge, especially as Stikeman's secretary and the person responsible for the delivery of mail, including cheques for the payment of fees. She also took over from Margot Farrell as official house mother and saw to it that nothing was out of place. Margot Bissonette and Betty Richer have greeted clients at the Montreal reception for many years with competence and good cheer and have helped set a similar tone for each of the other offices.

Some, but far from all, of the production burden has been lifted from the secretaries as a result of technology and the growing familiarity of the younger lawyers with computers, which enables them to do more work on their own. But the paper burden, instead of decreasing as experts predicted, has actually increased since everyone wants hard copies of electronic documents for their files. My secretary, Donna Brown, has had to cope with the paper produced from three separate sources – the office, McGill, and the Olympics – enough paper to drive anyone to distraction, not to mention all the related telephone calls. The volume of memoranda has increased as a result of e-mail and interoffice networks as well as the size of the firm, but much of this can be done by the lawyers themselves. Accounting and personnel administration have become far more complex as the firm has grown and the need for standard procedures has replaced the ad hoc approach that could support a smaller firm. Success does have its price.

We have gradually moved in the direction of more professional management techniques, a far cry from the days when there was nothing more than an office manager who followed Elliott's instructions. Now, the staff includes accountants, paralegals, as well as technical service and support staff for the computerized practice that dominates modern law firms. Bob Hart managed the financial affairs of the firm along with supervising personnel and other functions well into the 1990s, but he retired in 1998. Richard Taylor in Toronto was officially appointed the chief financial officer of the firm effective January 1, 1998, and Scott Morgan manages the Montreal office as the second largest concentration of lawyers. The organization now more closely resembles a corporate structure than the loose arrangements that prevailed when the total number of lawyers was less than the current 400. Staff complement is scaled accordingly. Much more attention is focused on good operating and reporting practices, standardizing operations, keeping track of billable time, ensuring timely billings, and following up on outstanding accounts.

The firm governance has evolved in a similar fashion. It is now too big to allow full collegiality in all matters or to allow decisions to be made by one or two individuals, and we have moved to a structure that is more corporate. On a regular basis, a partnership board is formally elected by the partners and given a general mandate to run the business of the firm. Most lawyers are lawyers because they do not want to be business managers. They want to practise law and are for the most part delighted that there are others willing to assume the administrative burden of running the firm so that they can do what they like best. Firm-wide partners meetings are difficult to arrange even when using video conferencing techniques, and one annual meeting is about enough for most partners. The key to a successful arrangement with a partnership board is confidence in its members to be responsible custodians of the values of the firm and to have the ability to have access to them for purposes of bringing forward any issues that may be important to partners. The partners look for the leaders of the firm to be willing to take on these extra duties and to map out the directions and strategies for the future.

Elliott gradually withdrew from active management of the firm, including the Toronto office, and in 1990, David Finkelstein was selected as managing partner of that office. He shepherded that office for ten years until Rod Barrett assumed the mantle at the turn of the century. They have had to manage the many changes that come from growth that occasionally seemed exponential, while at the same time, the Toronto market went through two recessions during a period of generally unparalleled expansion. Over and above this, they have done a good job in handling the shift of economic power from Montreal to Toronto without damaging the morale of the firm as a whole but especially that of Montreal, which has always regarded itself as the senior office from which all else has flowed. Finkelstein's roots in Montreal were helpful in promoting the osmosis of the recognition of the changing circumstances. But as the stockbrokers say, "one cannot fight the tape," and there can be little residual doubt that for a business law firm, the economic concentration in Toronto far surpasses that in Montreal. Today, Montreal has become to Toronto what Boston is to New York.

All law firms must deal not only with the challenge of recruiting legal talent but also with its retention. There is a considerable investment in the development of the raw talent that comes through the door into superior, seasoned lawyers, and it is important to keep them motivated to keep them in the firm. For the most part, although money is important (and lawyers are well paid), it is the excitement of the work and the intellectual stimulation that remain the biggest magnets, and it is the task of the management of any successful firm to maximize each of those elements. From the very beginnings of the firm, there has been an extraordinary collection of lawyers who have shared in the excitement of building something special. On the other hand, the type of person who is attracted to such an enterprise is one who may be too restless to spend his or her entire career with the firm. It is a measure of the firm's success that it has produced a prime minister, a judge of the Supreme Court of Canada, several other distinguished judges, many chief executive officers, senior corporate executives, academics, and others. Their common trait is that of seeking and welcoming challenges. They tend to be so performance-oriented that they are continually looking for new and stimulating tasks and problems to solve and can only repeat themselves so often before tedium sets in and they go looking for new challenges. Even those who have remained with the firm have developed outside interests to supplement their professional careers.

The loss felt when some of these stars move on, which is a tragedy in some firms, is in the case of Stikeman Elliott not really a loss at all. Viewed in one way, it is particularly healthy since it generally reflects new horizons built upon positive experience often made possible by the training and exposure they have received at the firm. In a manner of speaking, the leaving of the aggressive and driven individuals for new pastures actually expands the firm's diaspora and extends its influence even more widely within the greater community. The ex-Stikians remain ambassadors of the firm and more often than not, its clients.

It is worth reflecting on the vision of the firm that was developed during the 1970s, which was the first comprehensive statement drafted by an in-house committee, of what we thought we were trying to accomplish: "We are building the first and best national law firm in Canada; a national law firm with international offices and a significant international presence; a national institution that will contribute to, and have a meaningful impact upon, the legal, business, political, and social life of Canada." By the time both Elliott and Grant had completed their stewardship of the firm, it had accomplished those objectives. They delivered a firm that practised high-level law on a national and international scale, the members of which also made major additional contributions to the communities in which the firm was active.

I confess to being occasionally amused when I hear that other law firms recruit against us by saying that the firm is a "sweatshop," where lawyers are overworked and that there is great pressure. In the first place, it is not true. We all work hard, but we enjoy it, and there is, after all, some fundamental reason why it is referred to as the "practice" of law. The stock in trade of lawyers is their experience, and the only way to get that is to work. In the second place, we have little interest in those who might shy away from hard work, so if they look elsewhere on that basis, they are welcome to do so. If, however, they are labouring under the delusion that they can become good lawyers without hard work, they will soon be disabused of that notion, wherever they may end up. In the process, they will have shut the door on a unique opportunity to practise with a firm in which their talents could have flourished. My experience has been that the best of our junior lawyers are constantly looking for more, not less, work. That is one reason they become so good so quickly and find themselves across the table from much more senior lawyers. In fact, rather than the traditional phrase of throwing young lawyers into the deep end, I suggest that most of them dive in themselves.

৯

Almost everyone in the firm who knows I am producing this work has begged me to include something about the firm's annual Christmas parties. They started in Montreal and have spread to each of the other offices, and they are by far the most important social events of the year. They do not involve spouses or significant others, initially from disinclination and lately from a combination of that and because of the large number of people who would be involved, half of whom in any event would not know the other half. Besides, it provides an out-of-office occasion for the lawyers and the support staff to share war stories, gossip, recollections, and usually some incredibly corny entertainment put on by those in the firm who delude themselves into imagining they have talent that surpasses their evident legal abilities. These self-professed scriptwriters, musicians, and singers inevitably believe that they are so good that they do not need to rehearse. It is bad enough that their peers must witness their theatrics, but there is no earthly reason to inflict such painful performances on outsiders. The recent scourge of political correctness is such that sadly, many events that were riotous and amusing for all concerned at the time might well be perceived today as politically incorrect, and the purpose of this work is not to invite censure from those (not in the firm) who might be sitting around waiting to be offended. Suffice it to say that the Christmas parties continue be the social highlight of the year. Stikeman and Elliott both made it a point to attend every party and to dance with as many of the distaff members of the firm as possible. At the Montreal Christmas party in 2001, on the eve of the firm's fiftieth birthday, Tonie Lepore, who works with Glenn Cranker, did a marvellous takeoff on the famous "Happy Birthday, Mr President" performed by Marilyn Monroe for John F. Kennedy, including the strapless gown, platinum hairdo (she had a wig), and husky voice. All sorts of lawyers, who clearly had no idea how to dance, could be seen valiantly trying to look at ease on the dance floor. The parties never finished early, but the firm has always made sure that everyone took a taxi home at its expense.

THE SUMMER OF OUR DISCONTENT

The myth that Elliott discriminated against the francophone lawyers on the basis of their language was kept alive and actively encouraged by one of the firm's francophone lawyers, Yvon Martineau, who exploited the perception and positioned himself as the protector of his fellow francophones. He told them they could rely on him personally to ensure that a balance was kept between the anglophone and francophone lawyers in the firm, and he nurtured a bloc of supporters in his quest to hold the line against this old WASP (itself a mischaracterization) firm. Over time, a poisonous atmosphere developed. Stanley Hartt concluded that the problem was approaching a crisis level when he invited a group of the younger francophone lawyers for an evening at his home in the Town of Mount Royal and a Pavarotti concert at Place des Arts. He was on the board of the Montreal Symphony Orchestra at the time and had obtained a few tickets for the concert. The following day, Martineau circulated a memorandum accusing Hartt of entertaining the juniors in an effort to upset the political balance in the firm. This kind of troublemaking persisted for years, and even a two-year stretch in London, which was intended to help Martineau broaden his vision, did not have any beneficial effect.

Matters reached a head in 1993 over the admission to partnership of Stuart Cobbett. The firm had been wooing Cobbett, who had started his professional career at what is now Heenan Blaikie but had left them to run Astral Bellevue for a few years. Cobbett was looking to get back into the practice of law, and after a series of discussions with him, Grant made a verbal arrangement with Cobbett that he would be admitted as a partner in the firm if he agreed to come. Martineau looked upon this as the metaphorical Rubicon and told Grant that he and his bloc would vote against such an admission. This led to Martineau's departure from the firm and created a deep schism, which also caused the departure of several of the francophone lawyers in a diversified gesture of solidarity.

For some time, there had been discontent brewing within the firm. Many of the partners, particularly among the francophone partners, were not satisfied with the manner in which the firm was being managed. As the Toronto firm grew in importance and its economic results surpassed those in Montreal due to the economic doldrums brought about by the political uncertainties in Quebec, the Montreal partners grew increasingly apprehensive about the future of the Montreal office. They, and not just their francophone colleagues, were concerned that Montreal would become a second-class operation notwithstanding that it was the founding office and that Stikeman was still there and still active. There was much tension and a desire to have management be seen as transparent and supportive of a strong role for Montreal. Many of the Toronto partners were aggressive in promoting their desire to have a more active role in determining the future direction of the firm. Access to the Quebec Inc. business establishment, which was asserting itself as a dynamic class of business entrepreneurs, probably unequalled at the time in Canada, appeared to require that the Montreal office adopt a more "Quebec" profile and be seen to be far more francophone in nature rather than an English firm with some francophone members.

The principal lightning rod in this issue was Yvon Martineau, who was aggressive and ambitious in his efforts to woo the Quebec business community and to preserve and promote the role of the francophone partners. He was not happy with the management style of Grant and the manner in which he and a few others ran the firm as well as the level of compensation of some of the francophone partners. There were constant meetings behind closed doors, a practice that had been until then almost non-existent. Grant took a long time to recognize the extent of the problem and hoped that he could manage his way out of it without confrontation, but he was unable to do so to the general satisfaction of Martineau and his followers. Matters came to a head in the spring of 1993 when there was a direct challenge to Grant's leadership.

The firm rapidly polarized into two factions, and in the ensuing fallout, Martineau withdrew from the partnership. Unfortunately, his departure led to the exodus of several others, some of whom followed him to Martineau Walker, including Michel Décary, the leading francophone litigator of the firm, Réal Forest, a brilliant constitutional lawyer, and Denis Lachance, one of the workhorses in the litigation section. The discontent had become so profound that in a sort of solidarity reaction, other lawyers also left for different firms. Marc Prévost, another partner in the litigation section, joined Ogilvy Renault, as did Guy Fortin, an intelligent but almost obsessively secretive lawyer from the tax section. More importantly, Maurice Régnier and Claude Désaulniers, both from the tax section, left to join McCarthy Tétrault, located next door in the old Windsor Hotel building. Despite the best efforts of those who remained, it proved impossible to dissuade them from departing.

Not only were these for the most part serious losses to the firm from the perspective of service to the firm's clients, but also the optics for a Quebec-based firm that suddenly appeared to be anathema for francophone lawyers were disastrous. This made access to the Quebec business community, now the driving force in Montreal, much more problematic and was devastating to the ability to recruit new francophone lawyers from among the law faculties in the province – notably Montréal, Laval, and Sherbrooke – as well as students from Ottawa. This was probably the biggest crisis that we have ever faced.

There was, however, one ray of hope from among those who decided to leave. Michel Décary, albeit not pleased with the management of the firm, was not happy to be part of anything that might lead to damaging it. In the heat of the matter, he had told Martineau that he would leave the firm and go with him to Martineau Walker. As a leader among the francophones, this was our most serious loss, and great effort was made to dissuade him from leaving, including pleas from Edward Aust and Stikeman himself. Many meetings were held with him, but the ethical problem for Décary was that he felt that he had given his word to Martineau Walker and that he could not resile from that position as a matter of professional ethics.

I remember participating in a meeting with him, which Aust had organized as part of our efforts to keep him with us. Aust was trying to persuade Décary that there was nothing to prevent him from changing his mind, and Décary was struggling with the dilemma. I could see at once what his problem was and that no matter how badly he may have felt about having agreed to go, he simply could not reconcile that commitment with the principal asset of any lawyer – that his word was his bond. Trying to get him to renege on a personal commitment, even verbal, went against everything for which he stood. I intervened with Aust and said that the issue seemed to me to be quite clear: Décary had given his word, and he could not go back on that promise no matter how he now felt about remaining. We should not be trying to persuade him to do something that none of us would do, for the very same reason. I said to Décary, "You have given your word, and that is the end of the matter. If you have changed your mind, you must ask Martineau Walker to release you from that promise. Their answer to that request will indicate at once whether it is the kind of firm of which you would like to be a member. If they say, 'yes,' you will have an answer; if they say, 'no, we insist that you come,' that will be a different indication, and you will then have another decision to make." Martineau Walker did not give Décary back his "word," so to honour the promise he had made, he went at the end of 1993, but within a year, he left them to return to our firm, to the great pleasure of all partners.

Three years later, the firm was also delighted to be able to persuade Maurice Régnier to return. He had never really been happy at McCarthy Tétrault, but he was a man of high principle and had nevertheless done his best in an environment to which he did not feel himself particularly suited. He had approached one of our tax lawyers, Pierre Martel – with whom he had done a lot of work while at the firm and whose mind and ability to concentrate on a problem until he had solved it he greatly admired – to see if Martel might be willing to come over to McCarthy Tétrault to beef up a desultory tax section. Martel discussed the matter with me since I was at the time the head of our tax section, and he said that he thought we should try a reverse gambit. Instead of Régnier recruiting Martel, maybe we might consider trying to persuade him to come back. We agreed to try, and Martel invited him to lunch for the purpose. We chose a restaurant he liked, La Rapière, in the Sun Life Building. He was cautiously receptive to the idea, and over the next couple of months, I cleared the idea with the management of the firm, principally Calin Rovinescu, then the managing partner of the Montreal office. Régnier rejoined the tax section in June 1997 as our resident guru.

Régnier's return coincided with that of Robert Hogan and Frédéric Harvey, both of whom had left the tax section a couple of years earlier to try their hand in the film business with Malo Films. This had left a gaping hole in the firm's ability to deal with the tax ramifications of major corporate deals. After a short period of "tycooning," however, they were ready to come back to what they really enjoyed and to what they were best suited for – namely, the developing of complex business and tax structures as lawyers rather than as principals. Having this triumvirate back in place meant that the firm was again at full strength in its tax section, and it has been remarkably effective as a section ever since. The inventiveness of Hogan and Harvey has been instrumental in the structuring of dozens of complex reorganizations including Air Canada, Canadian National, and Stone Consolidated; moreover, the wise counsel of Régnier on any question makes the team a unique collection of lawyers who can provide the corporate lawyers with the ammunition to attract and serve the largest and most complicated clients.

The summer of our discontent, despite the particular circumstances that gave rise to it, had nevertheless shown that changes had to be made within the firm to prevent similar occurrences in the future. With this in mind, the firm went through a period of self-examination to see how best to get back to the kind of atmosphere that was, as Mortimer Freiheit described it during one of the sessions, "light and loose, with magic in the air." There was a need to get at some of the basic elements including new focus on the manner of governance, an appropriate mission statement, a variety of problems faced by women in high-pressure firms, teamwork and coordination of efforts in the service and attraction of clients, elections to management positions, and creating an atmosphere that ensured francophone lawyers that they were fully part of the firm.

The year was not a total disaster by any means. We had occasion to celebrate Stikeman's eightieth birthday. Obviously the world's youngest octogenarian, he continued to ski in the annual firm races and to be part of the Air Canada Cup sailing races. Claudette Picard was elected vice-president of the Quebec Bar, which meant that she was now the *bâtonnière*-in-waiting, only the second member of the firm to achieve this position. She served her term as *bâtonnière* in 1994–95 and shortly thereafter, accepted an appointment to the bench of the Quebec Superior Court, joining Jean-Judes Chabot and Danielle Grenier, two partners who had preceded her to such office. David Angus finally decided, after refusing previous offers from Prime Minister Brian Mulroney, to accept the appointment as a member of the Senate of Canada, where he has become an active and effective member.

FIRM LEADERSHIP: A GENERATIONAL CHANGE

Early in 1996, it became clear that the time had come for the next generation of leaders to take more space and leave its mark on the firm. In the late 1980s, Elliott had become chairman emeritus of the firm, his place taken over by Jim Grant, and had no wish to remain involved other than in a senatorial capacity. Grant had suffered a heart attack and as he was recuperating, he no longer wished to continue as managing partner in Montreal in addition to his other responsibilities as chairman of the firm. The previous generation of leaders was now approaching the age of sixty, and many of the expected leaders who would have been in the range of fifty had either left, had no interest in managing the firm, or were not seen as sufficiently energetic to assume the leadership roles. There appeared to be a willingness at all levels of the partnership, both senior and junior, to have the leadership devolve on those who were just turning forty, a sentiment shared in both Toronto and Montreal. This group included, in Toronto, John Stransman, Bill Braithwaite, Ed Waitzer, Rod Barrett, Ron Durrand, Sean Dunphy, and Jim Riley (who was to depart in early 1997); in Montreal, it included Pierre Raymond, John Leopold, Guy Masson, and Calin Rovinescu.

Grant started working on Rovinescu early in 1996 to come back to Montreal in order to succeed him as managing partner, but by then, Rovinescu had fallen madly in love with London and after much soul-searching, decided that he would turn Grant down and stay in London even if it meant having to find some other career. As one might imagine, delivering this news to

Grant resulted in a very short telephone conversation and elicited a series of grunts and a closing dial tone even before Rovinescu could finish his explanation of why he had made that decision. In his inimitable style, Grant put no further direct pressure on him, but Rovinescu noticed that he seemed to be getting calls almost daily from two of his closest office friends – Pierre Raymond and John Leopold. The ultimate effect was to wear Rovinescu down until he agreed to return to Montreal. It would be wrong to say that the feeling toward moving to a much younger generation was universal, but the tendency of the great majority was quite clear. In Montreal, as a matter of principle, Edward Aust put the matter to a vote, running unsuccessfully against Rovinescu for the position of managing partner in Montreal.

The new group saw this as an opportunity to couple the generational change with a fundamental modification to the way the firm carried on its business. Members of the firm's executive committee embarked on a major revamp of the governance of the law firm – from the method of electing partners to the executive to the combining of the executive and remuneration functions (previously deliberately kept separate) to the further entrenchment of the notion of a single profit pool within the firm. They championed a greater focus on the "business" of law as opposed to the "practice" of law and instituted greater business "drivers," which included the firm's first strategic plan, policies intended to discourage certain types of work or dealing with certain types of clients, and attaching greater rigour to financial reporting and controls.

This group proposed changes in the partnership agreement to enable the firm to deal with underperforming partners. The new vision was presented at the 1997 annual partners meeting, and perhaps marking the nature of the change, the presentations were made with the assistance of a high-tech PowerPoint backdrop, which put the new strategy in writing rather than leaving it to the vagaries of assorted memories. It was decided that the firm would no longer practise family law, and that some sectors such as labour law would be relegated to slower growth, reflecting different priorities for the "core" sections of the firm. The focus thereafter would be to promote the firm as a leading business law firm, with the emphasis on business. While personal initiative would continue to be encouraged, it would nevertheless have to be exercised within the approved general framework. The proposals were adopted by the partners.

As part of the business focus, much closer analysis was given to the contribution of the foreign offices. Although recognizing their enormous contribution to the firm's franchise, the new executive considered that the cost of the foreign operations was becoming a drain despite the "halo" effect of business generated for the Canadian offices and that significant paring and cost-cutting was in order. The executive committee determined to reduce significantly the operations in Singapore and Hong Kong, to cut costs dramatically in Sydney, and to shut the Budapest office. Rovinescu was charged with this aspect of the changes and had the not-so-pleasurable task of visiting Hong Kong, Singapore, and Sydney and making concrete recommendations for the various cuts, as well as negotiating the shutdown of Budapest and the spinoff of operations into the association with Robert Hayhurst and his new firm. For the new leadership, these were defining moments since it had the delicate task of not destroying an extraordinary international franchise that the firm's predecessors had built and financed, while at the same time focusing on the business realities of cost-cutting and profitability, where the firm had to compete on the ground with domestic firms that carried no international operations in lean times.

The mission statement of the firm underwent some alteration as well, with the 1998 version reflecting a somewhat lesser commitment to the building of a national institution, replacing it with a more nuanced approach, which was not as overtly ambitious as the spirit that governed the firm in its younger days. The brash sense of adventure was no longer part of the mission statement: "Stikeman Elliott is a firm of individuals who desire to practise law together to serve our clients at the highest professional level in Canada and throughout the world, with the primary objective of consolidating and building upon our reputation as Canada's national and international law firm." The choice of language is revealing and reflects an acknowledgement by the succeeding generation of partners that the former mission statement had been accomplished. Use of the word "consolidating" would not have been appropriate had the earlier objective not been accomplished, and the reference to a national and international "reputation" already earned gives further evidence of that accomplishment. International "presence" as part of the earlier mission statement was muted to serving clients throughout the world.

However, leaving everything but the primary objective unstated carries with it some risk that the values exemplified by those who brought the firm to the stage where the concept of consolidation could even be entertained might be forgotten or ignored. That would be a fundamental change indeed, and one that should be given the most careful attention in a world that is moving considerably faster and with more volatility than at any time in history. It is true that the partners have come together (as they have from the beginning) to practise law, and to identify that as a primary objective is well worth remembering as is the commitment to the highest standards of practice and service to clients. In earlier times, these were unstated since they were self-evident to everyone in the firm. This reminder for new lawyers may be useful. But perhaps an even more important element could be that in the process of accomplishing the primary objective, there is an additional context that must be part of the fabric of the firm, one that sets it apart from the mere utilitarian practice of law, albeit at high levels and for comfortable financial reward. Only good can come from being willing to embrace the full community in which we practise. The best law is practised as part of a fully integrated life in that community.

The sense of building something special has probably been the principal reason why the firm has never merged. This is not to say that the question was never considered; it was, on many occasions. It would have been reckless not to have done so particularly once the accounting firms began the trend and the law firms followed several years later. The degree of consolidation within the accounting profession has been astounding as hundreds of small firms became medium-sized or regional and were in turn swallowed up by the Big Eight, then the Big Five, and now, with the fallout from the Enron Inc. collapse of 2001, perhaps the Big Four. The question became whether law firms, traditionally much smaller than accounting firms, could obtain the same benefits, actual or anticipated, by following a similar course. The possibility of doing so has been assessed in principle and against actual possibilities, but it has always been rejected.

The firm's shorthand for such rejection has always been that we would inevitably end up having to deal with significant cultural differences were a merger to occur. The client conflicts were occasionally an issue, but they were relatively minor and could have been managed with minimal difficulty. It was the people in the other firms, who would not have shared our culture, who presented the greatest problem. We never encountered a firm that had the same sense of adventure, the huge ambition, and the willingness to take risks that our firm personified. As we moved forward, we may have been guilty from time to time of a "ready ... fire ... aim" syndrome, but the direction was always forward, and the constant urge was to push the envelope. We could never have accommodated or even tolerated the "ready ... aim ... aim ... aim ... aim ..." approach, and we knew ourselves well enough to step back from the edge whenever it looked as if there might be a deal to be made. Most of the firms that approached us did so because of our obvious sense of adventure, one that they could not seem to generate on their own. They wanted us in effect to get them jump-started. We knew that it was precisely their inability to act that would create conflict if we were to take on the burden of reinventing them, a conflict that we neither needed nor wanted. We would not be building anything new. We were already or were in the process of becoming a national and international firm based in Canada, and we knew what we wanted – to be ourselves and masters, for better or for worse, of our own vision for the future, with colleagues of similar commitment whom we knew and trusted. And so, each time after a genuine ready, aim, fire exercise, we said thank you, but no thank you.

The third generation of firm leadership, under Ed Waitzer, is now dealing with the present challenges.

As this work was going to press, the firm suffered a devastating loss of one of its best and brightest lawyers with the death on April 21, 2002 of John Stransman, who succumbed with great courage and an unbelievably positive attitude to a particularly virulent brain tumour that struck him a few months earlier. He had become a remarkably capable lawyer and was a recognized leader among the corporate lawyers in Canada and a much-admired leader within the firm. The shock of his death was even greater than that caused by the passing of Stikeman, less than three years earlier on June 12, 1999, our only other death of an active partner, after a full and immensely active life.

CHAPTER 16

Conclusions

The conclusion of a work of this nature should be short. Although fifty years may seem like a long time to many, in fact it is not. It is but a beginning – a promising one and in some respects, spectacular, but a beginning nonetheless.

It could not have happened but for the juxtaposition of Stikeman and Elliott and the extraordinary complementarity of their skills and personalities. The effervescent and voluble Stikeman, for whom nothing was impossible and whose enthusiasm for life and the practice of law rubbed off on everyone around him, was the inventor of modern tax practice. It was around his expertise that the firm became possible. The younger Elliott did not have the initial following of Stikeman, but he extended the concept of business law, building off Stikeman's clients, and became the epitome of the "can do" lawyer whom clients had always wanted. He acquired his own business experience, which gave him additional credibility in both the corporate and legal communities. Within the firm, this solidified his role as responsible for building the business and guiding it through the many stages of a rapidly growing professional organization. This was not an area in which Stikeman was interested, and much of what had to be done to organize the many different people involved (accounting, personnel, premises, and financial planning) to move from five to more than 400 lawyers fell to Elliott. Stikeman did the business of law superbly, but he did not establish the framework that built the firm.

Many law firms begin; in fact, hundreds start and then disappear. Some get to be about half a dozen lawyers but never go on to the big leagues. It is hard to get the big mandates, to dislodge established counsels of major corporations from their positions, and it is not enough to be good. When they started, Stikeman and Elliott wondered how they would be able to get major work and found the secret to be the combination of Stikeman's tax work and the follow-up business work of Elliott. And they travelled, wherever they could, to meet prospective clients, to speak to anyone or any group who would listen to them. And they published. And they worked hard. The essence of the firm was that it began with a concept of how to add value for clients, not just to make fees for the firm. Clients related well to a law firm that provided them with the opportunity to end up with more money than they started out with. This involved looking at the entire situation affecting the business affairs of the client and not just a particular slice of the problem. This approach was originated by people who played outside the normal analysis and led to a desire to surround themselves with other such people. Key periods in the field are often associated with cultural changes. These include being associated with emerging fields of law, as was the case with tax law at the beginning of the firm, and of having somebody there who had been directly associated with those changes. By combining this feature, in the case of Stikeman, with Elliott – a businessman lawyer who was probably one of the first practitioners to approach legal problems with the parallel perspective of a Harvard MBA – the basis of the cultural change was in place.

The quality of the relationship between the two original partners had just the right synergy to create sparks and to combine this with the ability to learn from their experience. They certainly learned from the exodus in 1967, but the approach of being willing and able to adapt to new situations, including crises, has enabled them to handle everything that came along. Their adaptability led to, among other things, the creation of a firm that made partners of its young lawyers and allowed them to take responsibility as soon as they could. Most firms do not embrace lateral thinkers but instead prefer those who fit within the current mainstream of the firm. It was clear that Stikeman Elliott valued different cultures and approaches and was rigorous in recruiting them. The result has been a firm that is a combination of ambitious people and the so-called lawyer's lawyers. This combination has been quite effective in a profession in which most firms have tended to go one way or the other.

From his position as chairman emeritus, Grant reflects that in the 1970s, he wrote a vision statement for the firm that was quite different from the one that existed at the time. When he stepped down as chairman, he turned over to his successor (Ed Waitzer) a firm that had accomplished everything in that vision statement. Grant sees the principal challenge to the firm to be to continually attract special people and persuade them to stay because without them, the firm may risk becoming utilitarian over time. Such a diminished firm would be quite different from the one that has been instrumental in making a significant contribution to Canada as well as generating a good living for its members.

Grant underlines that the firm started with some special people who attracted other special people, and that they were positioned to ride a wave of great expansion and prosperity in the legal profession. They hired the most energetic and self-reliant people they could find, and the firm has generally stayed out of their way, giving them the maximum freedom within the environment of an ambitious group that shared the common values of a desire to accomplish something. The environment has become, of necessity, more bureaucratic as the firm has grown, but the basic freedoms remain to a far greater extent than in any comparable organization. Other firms have also grown exponentially, but none so quickly and so pervasively within this country and with the same initiative of looking beyond our borders. Moreover, no other firm has produced so many people who have done so many things outside the legal profession while still remaining pre-eminent in the practice of law.

David Angus believes the success of the firm stemmed from the fact that Stikeman and Elliott complemented each other so well. Whatever quality one may have lacked, the other filled completely. They understood that a law firm should not be a democratic organization; it operated best as an enlightened form of autocracy. Neither founder was afraid of being challenged, which is reflected in the "sink or swim" approach and the demand for intellectual excellence, which in turn developed the confidence needed to provide first-class advice to clients, often in situations of great pressure. The founders had the courage to resist any mergers and had the requisite egocentricity regarding the Stikeman Elliott brand and the desirability to institutionalize that brand. This was the glue that held the firm together during a remarkable growth period. The people they hired were smart, sparky, impatient, and obsessed with moving forward. They drove each other and the firm. The danger often lies in overdemocratization, when the risk of descending to the lowest common denominator is an operating factor. The only times that Angus has had any misgivings have been when vacuums in leadership have occurred.

The principal disappointment for everyone in the firm is that Heward Stikeman was not able to share the pride with everyone of reaching the milestone of the fiftieth anniversary. Right up until his death on June 12, 1999, he was still as enthusiastic as ever about life and all its facets, although he was impatient about how long it was taking him to recover from yet another throat operation made necessary by years of polyps on his larynx. Only weeks before his death, he reapplied for his driver's licence, fully expecting to use it for the full five-year extension. The memorial service was held on June 21, and it was the natural result of his legacy. For Stikeman, that very date was the most meaningful one of the year. On the longest day of the year, there was more time to do more things than on any other day. It was a warm, reflective, and reassuring celebration of a remarkable life that left everyone feeling more energized, not sadder. As Elliott noted: "Besides a deep friendship, my attraction to Heward always centred on his intellectual capacity. It was incomparable and stretched everyone else. On the other hand, he could move from those heights because he had something in common with everyone he met. It did not matter where that person was from or what his academic standing was or, for that matter, what it was not. Heward's interest, combined with his enthusiasm and friendliness, conquered all."

Ladi Pathy, Stikeman's long-time friend and client, spoke of his guidance as a mentor to him at the head of Fednav, his down-to-earth common sense, his consistently optimistic and upbeat personality, his insatiable interest in people and in events big and small, and his participation in so many diverse activities. "He was a doer, whose appetite for challenge, both intellectual and physical, seemed endless. He was a historian, writer, philanthropist, computer buff, wine connoisseur, beekeeper, skier, tennis player, fisherman, sailor, and chief pilot of StikeAir (one of the few activities, by the way, that some of us were hesitant to join him in)." At the 1996 annual firm retreat, Stikeman instructed the young lawyers to be sure to introduce themselves to him, saying, "Maybe I won't remember you the next time I see you, but that's fine because then we can get to know each other all over again."

Elliott, too, has passed down the mantle of control. In the late 1980s, he stepped down as chairman of the firm and shortly thereafter, resigned from all management positions. The willingness of the builders of the firm to step aside at the right time is an example to all firms that need to manage transition. Timing and confidence in such matters are everything. Jim Grant took over the position until he, too, participated in the next handover after more than a decade at the helm – to Ed Waitzer.

Each generation has its stars, and the current one is no exception. Waitzer, Stransman (until his death in 2002), Barrett, Braithwaite, Byers, Howard, Dunphy, Durand, and several others have emerged in Toronto, having been identified and given responsibility beyond their years right from their beginnings with the firm. Yontef, Rose, Hunter, Chalmers, Kay, Ristic, and Youngman are at the head of the profession. In Montreal, Raymond, Leopold, Huot, Côté, Raicek, Hogan, Fortier, Benaroche, and others have enjoyed the same opportunities to get to the top of their game early in their professional lives. Miller and Ottenbreit are running foreign offices as young managing principals. The other Canadian offices have identified their next generations. These new leaders now face the challenge of identifying their own successors and taking the responsibility for accelerating their development so that they will be ready when their time comes.

The current leaders know how they got to where they are in this demanding profession, which moves at speeds unlike ever before. They will have to nurture the highest professional standards in a world that is increasingly insistent on results and sometimes uncaring of some of the considerations that must govern the conduct of a profession. The law is a learned profession, and what they have learned, now they must teach. Some of the aspects of the business of carrying on the practice of law must adapt to modern management techniques, but the law itself is a profession and not a business. It is far more important than a business. Far more.

Elliott, sanguine about the ambition and ability of the new leadership, had only one piece of laconic advice (reminiscent of his traffic directions years earlier, "and then you stop."), which grew out of a conversation that he had with Waitzer several years earlier regarding growing on the one hand and keeping careful control of the costs on the other. At the time, he had mentioned to Waitzer that attention must be paid to the smallest detail, including the cookies, because in the final analysis, controlling costs was a matter of attitude. After Waitzer had been unanimously elected as the new chairman of the firm, Elliott deadpanned, "Ed, don't forget the cookies."

Appendices

Stikeman Elliott Fiftieth Anniversary Retreat Keynote Address by Richard W. Pound Whistler, BC, April 19, 2002

WHO ARE WE, HOW DID WE GET HERE, AND WHAT ARE WE DOING?

We are all members of a young but unique firm. Fifty years may seem like a long time to some of you, and I am sure that some of you cannot imagine getting to be as old as I am. It is not, however, a long time, and all you can really deduce with certainty from the fact that I am drooling from both sides of my mouth is that the floor is level. I want you to take note of this occasion, fix it in your minds, and remember it when you may be wheeled up to speak at the seventy-fifth or one hundredth anniversary of the firm.

My purpose this morning is to help you appreciate what kind of law firm you have joined. There are a few among you who will understand what it was like when the firm consisted of only ten or twenty or thirty lawyers. Some will know what it was like to have had only a single office. Some will know what it was like to start an office. Some will know the misgivings about foreign adventures. Some will know the excitement of having been part of those adventures. Others will know only the association with an established firm with hundreds of lawyers, playing bit (or larger) parts in huge transactions that have shaped the business landscape of this country. Whatever the experience, it has been interesting and challenging.

My role is to act as something of a guide – to help you understand what has made the firm you decided to join and what it is that attracted all of you, as the best and the brightest of the lawyers of your generation, to get into this particular canoe. I have chosen the analogy of a canoe with some deliberation. I suppose I could have used other analogies. I could have used the Wright brothers and their Kitty Hawk experience. That was certainly a seminal moment since between Kitty Hawk and 118 feet of flight, only sixty-two years elapsed before man set foot on the moon. I could have used *Sputnik*, the first suborbital flight into space, which occurred in 1957 when the firm was only five years old. Or maybe Alexander Graham Bell, who made history with, "Come here Watson, I want you." Or Neil Armstrong, with "one small step for man, one giant leap for mankind." Or Pierre Elliott

Trudeau, when he said, under enormous pressure in October 1970, "Just watch me."

But the canoe is the most appropriate analogy because it exemplifies the pioneers of former times – the sense of discovery moving into the unknown, the exploration of a new continent under the power of those who paddled the canoe, having some idea of opening up a vast new land even though they did not know for certain where each stroke of the paddle might lead. It is also uniquely Canadian. The territory was uncharted and the maps were made as they explored. The rapids, the shoals, the falls had yet to be experienced; the rewards were anticipated, but what forms they might take were completely unknown. What was important was the common desire of the voyageurs and their confidence in the courage and desire of their compatriots to go where others had not yet dared to venture. They provided their own power; they were the young adventurers, not like the old Ulysses and his companions, setting out "to strive, to seek, to find, and not to yield."

Most of us have lived with two Ulysseses at our helm, and all of us with one. Some of the crew are a bit slower, a bit stouter, certainly greyer, and perhaps less erect than when their personal voyages began, but the fire that brought them to the voyage and put them into the canoe still burns and the eyes still gleam. It has been an extraordinary odyssey, and it deserves to be put in perspective, not only to understand from whence we have come, but also to understand where we must go in order to maintain the momentum they have created.

It is no accident or whimsical gesture that unites us under the banner of Stikeman Elliott, nor that this banner is not Stikeman & Associates nor Elliott & Associates. Our firm name is Stikeman Elliott – without an ampersand or even a comma between. It is instead an affirmation of the remarkable chemistry that two very different, yet wholly complementary, individuals generated as they set off on a legal exploration that has reached the peak of its first fifty years and has just embarked on its second.

I invite you to cast your minds back to some of the times through which you have lived, or perhaps studied, to February 1, 1952, when the voyage began. Louis St Laurent was prime minister of Canada; Winston Churchill was prime minister of Britain; George VI would still be king of England for a few days; Maurice Duplessis was the iron premier of Quebec; Harry Truman was president of the United States; Stalin still ruled the Soviet Union; television would arrive in Montreal and Toronto only seven months later; the Korean War was in progress; and the Cold War was near its zenith. Canada had emerged from World War II after an unprecedented national effort, which had nevertheless generated considerable domestic tension. Montreal was still the undisputed business capital of Canada and had a dominating establishment that decided most of the directions in which business, economics, and politics would move.

In the midst of this were two young lawyers, who were products of the Great Depression that had affected the previous generation and their own to an extent that we can barely imagine. When Stikeman was at McGill, the conditions were so bad that several of his university friends committed

suicide in the face of the bleak prospect of no work after graduation. Stikeman could not get a job after four years of undergraduate study and three
years of law despite being reasonably well connected through family and
friends. There simply was no work. He resorted to trying to sell life insurance
to people who could barely feed themselves let alone protect their families
with life insurance. He finally got a job with the federal government in the
Department of National Revenue.

Throughout the war, he worked in Ottawa under the indomitable Colin
Fraser Elliott, who was the deputy minister of National Revenue, and at
Elliott's home, he met a young Queen's University commerce student – the
Fraser Elliott we know. They struck up a friendship, and in the way young
people plan, they decided that they would one day practise law together.
Stikeman finished the war in Ottawa, learning everything there was to
know about a new field of law – income tax. Upon returning to Montreal,
he joined a small firm, where his reputation and ability soon made him its
most important partner while still in his thirties. Elliott went on to Osgoode
Hall, got his call to the Ontario Bar, and immediately enrolled at Harvard
for an MBA. He then came to Montreal, qualified for the Quebec Bar, and
joined the firm in which Stikeman was practising. They were far and away the
most productive lawyers in the firm, and within a few short years, it became
obvious that the two had such different ideas from the other partners of how
the future of the practice of law should develop that they conceived the idea
of setting out on their own. Stikeman was forty, and Elliott, thirty-three.

The new firm was to be a boutique built upon Stikeman's pre-eminence in
the new field of taxation and Elliott's grasp of the needs of businessmen by
understanding what they wanted to do and having the ability to find ways
to help them do it. The complementarity between the two was remarkable;
they shared many characteristics, but whatever the one may have lacked, the
other filled. While they may have hoped for this and intuitively recognized
it, they could not have imagined how successful the chemistry would be or
how it would lead to what the firm has now become.

Because what they dared to do challenged the existing models of legal
firms, the establishment hoped they would fail. The law firms of the day
operated – to use an expression that is more current – very much inside the
box; lawyers willing to think outside the box made the old-timers nervous.
Imagine the concept of clients leaving a meeting with their lawyers with
more money in their pockets than when they arrived! The practice of law
became the art of using the law to help clients accomplish what they wanted
to do rather than telling them why the law made something impossible. It
was little short of a revolution.

But it was a revolution that had an astonishingly magnetic core. It attracted clients who finally saw what first-class, reoriented professionals could
do *for* them instead of *to* them. And it attracted talented young lawyers
who saw the chance to accomplish something new, not just to sink into a
conservative profession of staid respectability, plodding on until a genteel
retirement (possibly, if they were persistent enough), with their names on
a lengthy letterhead. Stikeman and Elliott did not sit as do doctors in their

offices, waiting for sick patients to come for the occasional cure but mostly
for palliative relief for some of the symptoms of their conditions. They went
out and beat the bushes. They wrote and they spoke to anyone who would
listen. They travelled across the country, initially by train and later on Trans-
Canada Air Lines, to meet prospective clients. They went to Asia. Stikeman
took the north Atlantic liners, speaking to everyone he met. They published.
They taught. They entertained. And they practised with imagination, with
daring, with consummate skill, setting new standards in areas of the law
that were beginning to emerge and flourish as the post-war era in Canada
began to take shape.

As the core grew, they were faced with a number of decisions. The first
was whether they should remain as a niche firm, even if it was an extremely
profitable one. Fraser Elliott was convinced that they could probably have
made more money had they done so, but by the early 1960s, the horizons
for the firm had begun to expand, and the shape of what might be possible
for a firm that extended to other areas was becoming clearer. They had
already attracted the delightful and talented George Tamaki, becoming the
first firm to break the mould and have a partner of Japanese descent. They
recruited François Mercier, one of the finest of the Quebec counsel, and
began to challenge in the field of litigation. They expanded into shipping
law and explored the rich potential of commercial litigation. They allowed
their younger lawyers to grow into the fields of employment and intellectual
property. They recognized, long before anyone else, the need for Canada to
look beyond its borders for new business. At a time when there were only
about fifteen lawyers in the firm, they opened an office in London, then
possibly the leading financial centre of the world.

They recognized the trend that was beginning to make Toronto the financial capital of Canada as Montreal began the transition of becoming the
Boston to Toronto's New York. And they did something about it – something
that no other firm had dared to contemplate. While the other Montreal
firms wrung their hands, they started their own firm in order to capture
the business that was leaving Quebec and to get their share of the existing
Toronto market. And they did this when there were perhaps twenty-five
lawyers in the entire firm. From there, it seemed inevitable that they would
go to Hong Kong, New York, and more exotic outposts such as Budapest,
Kiev, Sophia, Bucharest, Prague, Singapore, Sydney, Taipei, Paris, and even
Washington. For a variety of reasons, not all of these ventures were equally
successful, and some have been discontinued or cut back. But think of the
audacity that each of these initiatives demonstrated. They pursued the idea
of a truly Canadian firm, and they made it a reality, opening offices in Ottawa, Vancouver, and Calgary.

Each of you here today has been a part of that adventure or have joined
the firm because of that sense of adventure. You have seen your firm grow
and become part of the national fabric of this country, not just within the
profession but in the country at large. This achievement did not just happen.
It was made to happen by a company of adventurers who share a common
vision of what practice at the leading edge of a profession like the law can

contribute to our society as a whole. Business and the improvement of economic conditions are the principal engines of the community. The protection and defence of the rights of individuals, before the courts if necessary, are hallmarks of an enlightened society. We are in the forefront of these pursuits. We have broken down the silos within which law used to be practised and have brought forth the interdisciplinary, firm-wide approach and capability needed in a complex world.

This has led us to work together as an integrated team in the service of our clients. We are a single team that can bring to bear the best professional advice that our clients need to succeed in their own endeavours – whether here in Canada or around the world – since Canadians are part of a larger society that is increasingly interconnected and interdependent. As the world both grows and shrinks, that team needs to be integrated and focused even as it grows in size. What may have begun as a doubles team, grew into a hockey team and then into a football team. It became a cohort and then a legion, but always playing and working together, each member relying on every other one to do his or her part. That is the spirit that has made this firm great, and it is the single most important element, over and above our professional skills, that we bring to the table. Never, ever, forget this. If you do, there will not be a Whistler for you in twenty-five or fifty years.

We are here this weekend as part of a team-building exercise, not because we need to build a team – we are already a team – but to reinforce something we know and live with on a daily basis. The danger with intangibles is that they risk becoming mundane and blurred, no longer constantly top of mind. Because they are so precious to the firm, from time to time, it is worth taking a step back, to examine what our values really mean, and to recommit ourselves to those precepts that have made it possible to get to where we are today and that will make it possible for us to get to where we want to be tomorrow. They are the mortar that holds the building blocks together, that enables us to build on a solid foundation, that provides the base from which we can be flexible, ambitious, creative, effective, and successful together.

As I look around this room today, I see a unique collection of individuals from across the country and beyond, with many fascinating backgrounds. It is a collection that fills me with a combination of pride and optimism. Some of you are already at the peak of your powers; others are well on your way, and still others are just beginning to taste what this exciting profession can offer. There are too many of you to identify individually, and I would risk leaving out some of you were I to give examples. Indeed, if I omitted anyone in the room today, I would be doing an injustice since every one of you fits within one of those categories. On a personal level, I admire each and every one of you for what you have already done or for the drive to succeed that you represent, and I see a continuum that reflects the spirit that has resulted in this remarkable collective effort in which I have been privileged to have played a small part.

Having been part of the adventure one way or another since 1964, I also see in my mind's eye many of the earlier members of the firm who have gone on to become alumni but who are nevertheless part of what we have become today. John Turner went on to become a prime minister of Canada. John Sopinka went to the highest court of this land, where a distinguished career that was just developing was unfortunately cut short by his untimely death in 1997. Sid Lederman, Don Bowman, André Brossard, Jean-Judes Chabot, Mike Bonner, Claudette Picard, Danielle Grenier, and Pierre Archambault have gone to different benches to render vital public service in the law. Others have gone to teach future generations. Some have gone to senior positions in the business community and other endeavours, including with governments or governmental agencies.

It is sometimes tempting to see these as losses to the firm, and in some respects, this is certainly true. But, in a larger sense, they are not losses at all because they have spread the Stikeman Elliott brand even more widely in our community and brought with them the values and disciplines that they learned and honed while they were with us. If you think about it, it is not surprising that the type of people we attract to the firm and who are attracted by it will be exactly the same people who will be valuable contributors in other areas of our society; moreover, other elements in society will seek them out precisely because they are the type of people who would gravitate to Stikeman Elliott. To name but a few – and in doing so, to acknowledge that I will inevitably fail to give full honour to all those who deserve it – I mention Stanley Hartt, Danny Colson, Sonny Gordon, Frank Sixt, Robert Couzin, Monique Mercier, Rowland Harrison, and Calin Rovinescu. I rejoice, and we should all rejoice, in the fact that they were with us, even for a time, and that we are parts of each other's diaspora. Whether still with us or around us, they are part of what makes us great and the envy of every other law firm in this country.

Our weekend is not meant to be a series of magisterial speeches from the "old guys," but a celebration of where we intend to go in the future and a collective commitment to how we are going to get there. As part of that dynamic process, let me leave you with a few thoughts that may help you appreciate where you will be going and how best to get there. I have in mind ten. They are not commandments, but they may be useful guidelines for you.

1 Never lose sight of the need for diversity among us. We will need the broadest range of talents and backgrounds as we face a national and international future. Embrace and seek out differences; do not reject them.
2 Anticipate and be ready for change, not as a passive condition that will inevitably occur, but as an agent that will enable us to remain in the forefront as leaders, not unwilling followers.
3 Be ambitious, both in the perfection of your talents and in the application of those talents as part of your team. You can be sole practitioners in the desire to become the best you can be, but you practise law as members of a team.
4 You are in a service profession. Render the best, the most useful, and the most timely service for the benefit of your clients. If they succeed, you succeed.

5 Work hard and play hard. You cannot work effectively and to the best of your potential without the release valve of play. What you play at is up to you, but be sure you leave enough space in your lives for it.

6 You practise within the context of a community and a society that is bigger than the profession. The law in the public practice in which we engage is not abstract. Our job is to understand both the law and its social context. One without the other cannot succeed.

7 Think outside the box. Anyone can stay inside the box, but the way you add value to our clients is to be creative. Lots of lawyers know the law, but only the best know it well enough to use it, not just parrot it. Know the law better than all the others in the profession, and then you will be able to use it.

8 Remember how we got here. It is fashionable in this age of instant sound bites and no sense of history to forget that there are roots. This firm has the greatest of roots, and it will be a mark of your own sense of who you are and where you are going that you give daily honour to those roots.

9 Stay young. You cannot fight the calendar, but you can stay young in outlook and attitude. There is no better example than Heward Stikeman, who was never old. He died young. He renewed his driver's licence just weeks before he died, fully intending to renew it five years later. He embraced computers at the age of eighty, and not long after that, he participated as part of the firm's crew in a dangerous and demanding boat race around the Isle of Wight. In his eighties, he also raced in the firm's ski races, wearing out ski guides in the Alps, and in Montreal, we would see him at seven in the morning returning from his tennis sessions. He never got old. Don't you get old.

10 Never, ever, forget that above all else, you are professionals within a profession that is unique and that has a particular responsibility within society. You must have the courage to recognize the responsibilities implicit in being a professional and to act in accordance with the highest standards that the profession exacts from its members.

Thank you for the chance to speak with you this morning. I am sure we will emerge from the weekend with an even greater commitment to our common enterprise.

Remember the words of Rudyard Kipling: "For the strength of the wolf is the pack, and the strength of the pack is the wolf."

Ladies and gentlemen, colleagues, that *is* Stikeman Elliott.

Partners of the Firm at the Fiftieth Anniversary (as of January 31, 2002)

TORONTO

Roderick F. Barrett
Richard Brait
William J. Braithwaite
David M. Brown
David R. Byers
Michael R. Carman
Stuart S. Carruthers
Kathryn I. Chalmers
Richard E. Clark
Larry Cobb
Paul Collins
Curtis A. Cusinato
Lorna A. Cuthbert
James C. Davis
Rocco M. Delfino
John R. Dow
Sean F. Dunphy
Ronald K. Durand
R. Fraser Elliott, CM, Q.C.
Ron Ferguson
David N. Finkelstein
David W. Glicksman
Margaret E. Grottenthaler
Peter E. Hamilton
James W. Harbell
Douglas F. Harrison
Brenda Hebert
Philip J. Henderson
L. Milton Hess, Q.C.
Samantha G. Horn

Peter F.C. Howard
Karen E. Jackson
John A.M. Judge
Katherine L. Kay
Jay C. Kellerman
Kevin B. Kelly
Eliot N. Kolers
Dean A. Kraus
Martin Langlois
Jennifer G. Legge
John G. Lorito
Daphne J. MacKenzie
David R. McCarthy
Nathalie L. Mercure
E. Lianne Miller
Gary F. Nachshen
Shawn C.D. Neylan
Robert W.A. Nicholls
Angelo Nikolakakis
Jennifer Northcote
Kieran P. O'Donnell
Patrick J. O'Kelly
Mario C. Paura
Elizabeth Pillon
Sharon C. Polan
Bruce R. Pollock
Dana S. Porter
Brian M. Pukier
Dee Rajpal
Darin R. Renton

Anne L. Ristic
Simon A. Romano
W. Brian Rose
Michael D. Rumball
William A. Scott
Wayne E. Shaw
John M. Stransman

Joanne E. Swystun
Mihkel E. Voore
Thomas Vowinckel
Edward J. Waitzer
Kathleen G. Ward
Marvin Yontef
Alison J. Youngman

MONTREAL

Hon. W. David Angus, Q.C.
Bruno M. Arnould
Marc B. Barbeau
Louis P. Bélanger
Jean-Pierre Belhumeur
Patrick L. Benaroche
Luc Bernier
Roanne C. Bratz
Hélène Bussières
Jean Carrier
Peter Castiel
Viateur Chénard
Edward B. Claxton
Stuart H. Cobbett
Suzanne Côté
Marc-André Coulombe
Glenn A. Cranker
Peter J. Cullen
Alix d'Anglejan-Chatillon
Michel Décary, Q.C.
Christine Desaulniers
Sterling H. Dietze
Jean Farley
Jean Fontaine
Laurent G. Fortier
Donald Francoeur
Mortimer G. Freiheit
Michel Gélinas
Hon. James A. Grant, P.C., Q.C.
Josée G. Gravel
Stephen W. Hamilton
Frédéric Harvey
Robert J. Hogan
Sidney M. Horn
Jean Marc Huot

Kevin Kyte
Hon. Marc Lalonde, P.C., O.C., Q.C.
Jean G. Lamothe
Marc J. Laurin
John W. Leopold
Monique Lussier
Pierre Martel
Yves Martineau
Alain Massicotte
Étienne Massicotte
R. Guy Masson
Bertrand P. Ménard
Éric Mongeau
Peter O'Brien
François H. Ouimet
J. Anthony Penhale
Frédéric Pierrestiger
Richard W. Pound,
    O.C., O.Q., Q.C., FCA
Vincent M. Prager
Stephen M. Raicek
Pierre A. Raymond
Maurice A. Régnier, Q.C.
Michael L. Richards
Erik Richer La Fleche
James A. Robb, Q.C.
Steeve Robitaille
William B. Rosenberg
Howard J. Rosenoff
André J. Roy
Franziska Ruf
Richard J. Rusk
Martin H. Scheim
Anik Trudel

OTTAWA

Mirko Bibic
Mark E. Burton
Randall J. Hofley
Lawson A.W. Hunter, Q.C.

Susan M. Hutton
T. Gregory Kane, Q.C.
Donald A. Kubesh
Stuart C. McCormack

CALGARY

James T. Bruvall
Glenn N. Cameron
Leland P. Corbett
Barry E. Emes
G. Frederick Erickson
Duane K. Gillis

David A. Holgate
Christopher W. Nixon
Stuart M. Olley
L. Greg Plater
David G. Weekes
C. Kemm Yates, Q.C.

VANCOUVER

Michael S. Allen
John F. Anderson
David R. Brown
Jonathan S. Drance
David E. Gillanders

Richard J. Jackson
Ross A. MacDonald
John N. Paton
Hein Poulus, Q.C.

LONDON

Richard J. Hay
Shawna M. Miller

Marianne C. Sussex

NEW YORK

Kenneth G. Ottenbreit

HONG KONG

Clifford Louie
Clifford S.M. Ng

Douglas G. Smith

SYDNEY

Brian Hansen

Associates with the Firm at the Fiftieth Anniversary (as of January 31, 2002)

TORONTO

Susan Allen
Drew K. Allen
Andrea L. Alliston
Aaron Atcheson
Anjali Banka
Timothy Banks
Christopher C. Bean
Donald G. Belovich
Michael Burkett
Roberta Carano
Gwen Cheung
Timothy Chubb
Christopher J. Cosgriffe
  (director, student & associate
  programs)
Chantelle Courtney
Pina D'Agostino
Bradley Davis
Matthew Dooley
Eric Dufour
Andrés Duran
Jeffrey Elliott
Manizeh Fancy
Richard Farris
Lana Finney
Roger Flaim
Christopher Flood
Brian Freeman
Mark Gannage
Marie Garneau

Patrick Gay
Lynn Gluckman
Allan Gotlieb, CC (consultant)
Loreto Grimaldi
Andrew Grossman
Jason L. Gudofsky
Christopher Hanson
Jennifer Hirlehey
Gregory Hogan
Stacey Hoisak
Ruth A.C. Horn
Matthew Howorth
Timothy R. Hughes
Adam L. Kalbfleisch
Abas Kanu
Mark Katz
Alan Kenigsberg
Marianne Kennedy-Beaulne
Michael Klinck
Dean P. Koumanakos
Jason Kroft
Adrian C. Lang
Samantha Levy
Jonathan Linden
Darren Littlejohn
Eric Lowy
Zahir Manek
Quentin Markin
Craig Martin
Robert K. Mason

Raymond A. McDougall
Lisa McDowell
Mark E. McElheran
Justin McKellar
Kara McLaren
Trent Mell
Kate Menear
Craig Mitchell
Dean Moroz
Julie J. Muirhead
Wesley Ng
Kelly Niebergall
D'Arcy Nordick
Ermanno Pascutto (consultant)
Catherine Phillips
Steven Portelli
Melissa L. Ross
Danielle Royal
Debbie Salzberger

Orysia Semotiuk
Lewis T. Smith
Sam Sniderman
Leslie Sole
Jay Sung
Stewart Sutcliffe
Maurice J. Swan
Maureen S.W. Tai
Gary Tamura
April Tate
Ashley Taylor
Julie Thibault
Daniel H. Thomson
Sean Vanderpol
Sandra Walker
Edward Weidberg
Jason Wilson
Glenn Zacher

MONTREAL

Adam N. Atlas
Éric Azran
Christian Azzam
Dominique Babin
David Banon
Babak Barin
Selin Bastin
Marie-Andrée Beaudry
France Margaret Bélanger
Donna Benedek
Fabrice Benoît
Mireille Bergeron
Nicolas J. Beugnot
Valérie Biron
Caroline Boutin
Suzanne Bréard
Robert Carelli
Derek Gardner Chiasson
Catherine Cloutier
France Comeau
Judith Dagenais
Marc Daigneault
Philippe Décary
Philippe DeMontigny
Michèle Denis

Hélène Deschamps-Marquis
Benoît C. Dubord
Caroline Émond
Patrick Essiminy
Arden R. Furlotte
Charles C. Gagnon
Michel Généreux
Patrick Girard
Natalie Gosselin
Hon. Benjamin J. Greenberg, Q.C.
    (senior counsel)
Jill K. Hugessen
Catherine Jenner
Nadia Jubinville
Annie Lagacé
Hon. Marc Lalonde, P.C., O.C., Q.C.
    (consultant)
Geneviève Lavertu
Sara Leclerc
Pierre-Yves Leduc
Michel Legendre
Thomas Lellouche
Jonathan Leopardi
Martin Claude Lepage (consultant)
Daniel J. Levinson

Howard Liebman
Valérie Mac-Seing
Christian Meighen
Dominique Ménard
Louis Morisset
Charles Nadeau
Nicole Nobert
Gayle Noble
Julie Patry
Michèle Patry
Ronald Peck
Éveline Poirier
Frédéric Poirier
Éric Préfontaine
Michel M. Ranger
Simon Richard
Hon. Maurice Riel, PC, Q.C.
   (consultant)

Anna C. Romano
Paul J. Setlakwe (consultant)
Jean-Guillaume Shooner
Marie-Pierre Simard
Jason Streicher
John Swan
Mireille Tabib
Marc Tanguay
Johanne Tanguay
Louise Touchette
Serge Tousignant
Marie-Hélène Toussaint
Maxime Turcotte
Marie Vanasse
Nicolas Vanasse
Kathleen Wong
Claire Zikovsky

OTTAWA

Tamra A. Alexander
Kim D.G. Alexander-Cook
Jonathan A. Blakey
Nicole Brousseau
Jeffrey Brown
Eugene F. Derenyi
Roula Eatrides
Vicky Eatrides

David Fewer
Rt. Hon. Antonio Lamer, C.C.
   (consultant)
Nicholas P. McHaffie
T. Bradbrooke Smith, Q.C.
Justine M. Whitehead

CALGARY

Harold K. Andersen
P. Dean Burns
Keith R. Chatwin
Michael L. Dyck
Alyson F. Goldman
Stephen R.W. Goltz
Brad B. Grant
Jessica L. Green

Mary L. Henderson
Wendy M. Moreland
Tyler W. Robinson
Michael J. Styczen
Stephanie L. Uhlich
Scott D. Whitby
Michael B. Witt

VANCOUVER

Warren G. Brazier
Deborah A. Fahy
Jason B. Gratl
Philip G. Griffin

Argiro M. Kotsalis
Michael J. Libby
David A. Martin
Neville J. McClure

Greg T. Palm
Margaret R. Payne
Gordon D. Phillips

Inge C. Poulus
Gordon N. Turriff
Thomas S. Wachowski

LONDON

Jeffrey Keey
Erin Needra
Robert L. Reymond

Heather Tibbo
Liza Zucconi

NEW YORK

Terence W. Doherty
Marie-Josée Henri
Ralph Hipsher

Christine Jurusik
Isabelle Laflèche
Donna Saleh

SYDNEY

Roy M. Randall (consultant)

HONG KONG

Stephanie Cheung
Bridget Chi
Hayden Hui

Cynthia Lee
Katy Suen

Staff Members at the Fiftieth Anniversary (as of January 31, 2002)

TORONTO

Nancy Adler
Bev Albert
Sabrina Allen
Lorena Almeida
Dawn Anderson
Karen Anderson
Sandra Andrade
Antonette Arthur
Susan Baird
Paul Bakowski
Sharda Balram
Sofia Barradas
Donna Barrett
Vicki Bassett
Diana Batcheler
Terri Baxter
Cordell Beals
Michael Bedo
Constantine Belegris
Marivic Bernal
Kasey Besson
Irene Bewski
Lynn Blake
Andrea Blazenko
Cathy Bleakley
Fe Bolneo
Marco Bossio
Mark Bouckaert
Marian Bournas
Gemma Boyd

Bernadette Brannigan
Barb Brickus
Michael Bridges
Mary Brock
April Brousseau
Donna Brown
Lizanne Brown
Sarah Brown
Scott Bull
Kerry Burke
Kim Burns
Karen Burridge
Nancy Byer
Edith Cameron
Brenda Cannon
Judy Carbonaro
Janice Carr
Joan Carr
Sofia Casinha
Helen Cek
Lydia Chandra
Denise Chin
Vince Cina
Tanya Cleary-DeSantis
Gabriele Clynes
Lori Colasanti
Gary Collins
Lillian Cooper
Caroline Cosentino
Michelle Coutinho

Lynda Crago
Teresa Cravinho
Rosey Crean
Tanya Cunliffe
Andrew Cunningham
Andrew P. Cunningham
Bev Cyr
Mary Dagg
    (director, finance)
Sandra Daher
Joanne Davies
Anne Dawiczewski
Ben De Los Santos
Marlene DePeuter
Leslie Deschamp
Amanda Dewinter
Sue Di Luca
Kimberley Diamond
Yvonne Dias
Sandra DiFalco
Demetra
    Dimitrakopoulos
Enzo Distefano
Pat Donaldson
Haig Douglas
Richard Dube
Madeline Duke
Norma Earley-
    Kulczyski
Anna Edwards

Helen Edwards
Linda Eisner
Mylene Farand
Cheryl Fath
Theresa Fergusson
Claire Fisher
Sallia Fitzpatrick
Jackie Flanaghan
Fergus Flattery
Margaret Flynn
Margaret Foley
Shauna Forcht
Jennifer Forestell
Ciceley Fortune
Katherine Foteeva
Susie Freeman
Vera Fritz
Bonnie Fu
Sabina Furfaro
Rosalie Galang
Christine Gascoyne
Donnette Gayle
Babak Ghiravanian
Michele Gillette
Linda Gleaves
Heather Gordon
Josephine Gordon
Judith Graetsch
Laima Gravelson
Elena Greco
Franca Greco
Michele Grespan
Caroline Grieve
Connie Grillo
Lucy Grivicic
Christine Gruszka
Wei Gu
Margaret Gunraj
Lyle Halcro
Shanna Hanas
Jocelyn Hannah
Patti Harrison
Lenna Hartford
Violet Hatzes
Kayon Hay
Dianne Haye
Angela Heale

Ingrid Hebel
Shalene Hill
Jo-Anne Ho
Charlotte Holmes
Micaela Howell
Rose-Ann Hrenczuk
Kim Hulme
Stephanie Hunter
Mohamed Hussain
Pauline Hussain
Shelly Ilgner
Diane Iliadis
Shannon Inglis
Helene Jackman
Mariann Jagnjic
Jennifer James
Erin Jennings
Gloria Jewett
Farzana Jiwani
Roshan Jiwani
Michelle Joslyn
Tanya Karafilis
Suganthi Kathiravelu
Leanne Kennedy
Kristin Kightley
Maria Kolliopoulos
Eliana Koosau
Teresa Koren
Sylvia Krzymowska
Sandra Lad
Denise LaFleur
Francis Lam
Robin Lamb
Sally Lamorte
Jennifer Lanteigne
Joan LaPointe
Darlene Lariviere
Cristina Larosa
Angela Lau
Diana Lawrence
    (director, marketing)
Valda Lemonius
Rosa Leonardelli
Barbara Leung
Jo-Ann Levesque
Jean Lew-Lum
Karen Linfield

Jessica Liu
Esther Loh
Michael Loreto
Karen Lowe (director,
    human resources)
Wojciech Luba
Edmund Ma
Patricia MacCormack
Suzanne MacPherson
Dionne Malcolm
Tom Mantziaris
Beth Marlin
Ophelia Mars
Christine Marshall-
    Smith
Mary Masucci
Zaida Mavroukas
Beverley McAndrew
Keith McCalmont
Karen McCullam
Kate McDerby
Nancy McDougall
Dale McGill
Lorraine McIntosh
Marlene McIvor
Jeff McKay
Samantha McLaughlin
Leslie McLelland
Jean McLeod
    (general manager)
Margaret McLeod
James McMartin
Robin Medeiros
Doreen Mendes
Mary Misevski
Eleanor Monteith
Heather Moorhead
Diane Moreira
Cathy Moss
Shirley Muir
Yasmin Murji
Erin Murphy
Raj Namachandran
Dean Nazir
Marilyn Nelson
Agnes Nemes
Gurpreet Nijjor

Melinda Noordman
Linda Nourse
Loree O'Brien
Wendy O'Connor
Heidi Oehlschlager
Barbara O'Kane
Cheryl Osborne
Cathy Pamli
Naseem Pariag
Vina Patel
Savita Patil
Lisa Peers
Elizabeth Pegas-
  Ferreira
Mary Perikleous
Beverley Peterson
Joanne Pierucci
Nicole Plotkin
Kali Porikos
Daphne Ramdial
Barbara Raposo
Belinda Raposo
Linda Roberts
Valerie Robertson
Denise Robins
Natasha Robinson
Paula Rodgers
Andrew Rodomar
Kimberly Rosenback
Paige Royal
Rowena Rubio
Greg Russell
Angie Sapalovski
Priya Sasenarayan
Sharon Saunders
Donna Schirle

Connie Scott
Natalia Seepersaud
Michelle Senack
  (director, facilities
  & office services)
Yolanda Serradilla
Edna Servos
Lillian Shany
Amita Sharma
Colleen Shaughnessy
Donna Shepherd
Anita Shiels
Donna Sholdra
Mary Sibenik
Dolores Sideris
Christine Simon
Vicky Simon
Ophia Smith
Indira Sookdeo
Steven Sousa
Linda Spina
Venky Srinivasan
  (director,
  technology)
Gina Stamatopoulos
Christine Starret
Linda Sterling
Stuart Stoby
Rose Strazzeri
Charmaine Stuart
Donna Sukman
Jill Sutherland
Katrina Svihran
Cathy Sweeney
Mike Sylvester

Richard Taylor (chief
  financial officer)
Rob Taylor
Tharma Thambyrajah
Normand Theriault
Shan Thirunathan
Colleen Thompson
Heather Tobin
Trina Torrance
Lori Trudel
Doris Tsiakalakis
Marianne Turner
Mariana Tzvetkova
Sheila Van Spronsen
Cindy Varcoe
Marta Vaskevych
Genevieve Vel
Sandee Vincent
Catherine Vinzenz
Fernando Waisfeld
Grace Walker
Stacey Walker
Sheri Walter
Darcie Anne Warren
Nancy Watts
Kim Webber
Maureen Wiber
Evelyn Williams
Rhonda Williams
Caroline Wong
Melissa Wood
Laura Woodworth
Kent Woollam
Valerie Wright
Ann Zappi

MONTREAL

Teresa Abbott
Daphnée Abraham
Sylvie Adam
Patrick Addison
May Aina
Suzanne Alepin
Evelyne Alloul
Jocelyne April

Nicole Arcand
Michèle Baillargeon
Chris Barnett
Estelle Barrette
Marie-Gérard
  Barthélemy
Clémence Beauchemin
Diane Beauclair

Josée Beauclair
Josée Beaudry
Annie Beaulieu
Diane Beaupré
Jeannine Beausoleil
Suzanne Bédard
Suzanne Benlolo
Céline Bergeron

Louise Berman
Germaine Bertin
Kathy Bidwell
Margot Bissonnette
Patrick Blanchet
Diane Bois
Marie-Laure Boisselle
Carmen Bossé
Michel Bossé
Marie-Lise Bouchard
Lorraine Boulais
Isabelle Breunig
Monique Brisson
Natalie Brouillard
Josée Brousseau
Donna Brown
Brigitte Brunet
Daniel Brunet
Pierre Caporicci
Gabrielle Carignan
Louise L. Carignan
Maria Carreira
Michèle Carrier
Rolande Carrière
Ana Cristina Carvalho
Nancy Chabot
Pierrette Champagne
Jackie Chan
Hélène Chantal
Louise Chaput
Lyse Charbonneau
Colette Charest
Rosemonde Chiasson
    (manager, facilities
    services)
Sylvie Choquette
Ghislaine Comtois
Sylvain Cordeau
Francine Côté
Louise Côté
Pierrette Coulombe
Lise Craig
Monique Crevier
Louise Cunningham
Francine Daigle
Marc Daigneault
Lorraine Daneau

Rae Davies
Susan Davidson
Denise De Paola
Louise De Sève
Adele Del Torto
Francine Dépôt
Danielle Desharnais
Thomas Deslauriers
Diane Desormeaux
Giovanni Di Meglio
Linda Di Tomasso
Nataly Domingo
Mireille Doodnath
Denise Doss
Louise Doyon
Lyne S. Drolet
Diane Du Sablon
Nathalie Duceppe
Jean Duchesneau
Nicole Duplantie
Francis Dupuis
Nicole Dussault
Caroline Emond
Raymond Espley
Marie-France Éthier
Nicole Ethier
Tony Figueiredo
Renée Filion
Josée Forest
Roger Forget
Chantal Fortin
    (controller)
Jean-Yves Fournier
Huguette Fournier
Elizabeth Fraser
Lorraine Frost
Denyse Gagné
Johanne Gagnon
Jocelyne Galipeau
Mark Gandey
Annette Gauthier
Martine Gauthier
Robert Gauthier
    (manager,
    information
    systems)
Suzanne Gauthier

Sylvie Gauthier
Suzanne Gavard
Edith Giguère
Maryse Giroux
Nathalie Giroux
Sylvana Giulione
Tina Glassman
Lucie Godin
Kathleen Gore
Alain Goudreau
Paulette Goudreau
Mélissa Gravel
Joan Grenon
Suzanne Grenon
Michelle Grimard
Jean Guénette
Nathalie Guertin
Pierrette Guérin
Monique Guilbault
Naya Hachem
Mary-Ann Hanley
Gail Harris
Louise Hébert
Jocelyne Heffernan
Alain Hétu
Danka Hryn
Andrée Isabelle
Josée Jodoin
Marlene Kempthorne
Angela Kussey
Gabrielle Labbé
Suzanne Lachapelle
Sylvie Lacoursière
Carole Lafrance
Jean Lalonde
Jo-Anne Lamoureux
Véronique Langelier
Josée Lanni
Gisèle Lanoie
Donna Lariviere
June Larivière
Michèle Larocque
France Laviolette
Huguette Lebeau
Hélène Lebel
Leonora Lee
Andrée Lefebvre

Diane Legris
Robert Lemieux
Yves Lemieux
Tonie Lepore
Arlette Lesage
Rita Levig
Jennifer Li
Marie-Claude Li-Fun
Sylvie Locas
Charlotte Lortie-
  Thibaudeau
Roméo Ludford
Aline Lussier
Marco Magini
Frédérique Malka
Yolande Marandola
Lyne Maurice
Ginny McDonough
Heidi McFall
Ann Medeiros
Louise Melançon
Jean-Pierre Mercé
Aline Mercier
Marie-Josée Méthot
Lynda Mill
Caroline Mintas
Lise Miron
Louise Mondoloni
Frédéric Monette
Denise Monjot
Nicole Moreau
Scott Morgan
  (director, finance &
  administration)
Sonya Mourand
Lili Nadon
Dudley Nelson
Tien Hung Nguyen
Madeleine Noiseux
Sébastien Noiseux
Madeleine Oakes

Kristy O'Brien
Lesly Octave
Louise Ortmann
Denise Ouellette
  (manager, human
  resources)
Faye Papazian
Andrée Paquette
Jocelyne Paquette
Mirabel Paquette
  (director, marketing)
Sylvie Parent
Linda Passero
Hélène Paulhus
Ronald Peck
Francine Pelletier
Yvon Péloquin
Josée Peters
Renata Petruccelli
Dolores Phillips
Christina Piccione
Lise Piché
Marjorie Pierre
Nelson Pires
Sylvie Pitre
Barbara Popowich
Céline Proulx
Johanne Proulx
Louise Renaud
Linda Ricci
Elizabeth Richer
Patricia Rivers
France Roberge
Nicole Robert
Sylvie Robitaille
Corinne Rognon
Josée Rondeau
Christine Roy
Suzanne Roy
Rose Sabourin
Marie Saint-Gelais

Ginette Saintus
Claudette Sauvageau
Paula Sauveur
Line Savard
Sylvie-Anne Scarinci
Franca Sechi
Louise Sexton
Denise Soucie
Lyne St Pierre
Ginette Stakou
Sylvie St-Arnaud
Shaunagh Stikeman
Gordon Stojanov
Susan Sztrolovics
Camille Texidor
Diane Therriault
Lucille Thibaudeau
Judy Tilton
Pamela Tornsgard
Martine Touré
Claire Tousignant
Isabelle Tremblay
Jacky Tremblay
Jocelyne Tremblay
Sylvie Trépanier
Lorraine-Claire
  Trudeau
Madeleine Trudeau
Odette Trudel
Catherine Tsikalas
Susan Turchetto
Julie Veniez
Micheline Viau
Josée Viel
Claudia Vigneault
Michèle Volanis
Mary Voutselas
Marie White
Grant Whitham
Irene Wlodarczyk

OTTAWA

Carmelina Barresi
Lori Barron

David Brown (office
  administrator)
Janis Brown

Tina Campagna
Sonja Capustinsky
Kathy Facer

Renata Falcone
Nancy Hopkins
Suzan Hum
Barbara Hunter
Sheila James
Richard D. Kargus

Kerrianne Knudsen
Joelle Laflamme
Brenda Maahs
Catherine Markadonis
Holly McCormick
Avril Milne

Kim Poulin
Marg Regensburger
Pamela Sauve
Tammy Smith
Trudy St John
Valerie Woodward

CALGARY

Tara Ablonczy
Beth Anderson
Eliza Arentewicz
Lisa Bailey
Norma Beaton
Toni Bennett
Patricia Brandrick
Jennifer Brietzke
Marilyn Brown
Barbara L. Castle
   (director,
   administration)
Irene Chan
Karen Churches
Mirella Doherty
Robin Dorie

Jodi Forster
Wendy Fraser
Lee Ann Gelfand
Robyn Grantham
Linda Greer
Anne-Lise Haney
Hali Hellevang
Anne Heynen
Hugo Huynh
Jered James
Jennifer Jones
Karen Kaczkowski
Judy Klincker
Lisa Lorenzo
Monique Malo
Terri Markey

Paula Marko
Andrea Martin
Jennifer Martison
Heather McDonald
Wendy Morel
Lac-Thu Nguyen
Cindy Paget
Wilma Quan-Forsyth
Liana Reschke
Christina Reti
Delores Sangwais
Nicole Stafiniak
Cindy Sterling
Marian Talaga
Jin Wu

VANCOUVER

Louisa K. Cheng
Rosanna P. Cheung
Heidi L. Cooke
Stephanie C. Cornell
Dee Doromal
Jennefer L. Dricos
Jim S. Foo (director,
   administration)
Delaine S. Foster
Kim R. Frezell
Lisa D. Geosits
Michele M. Gould
Giovanna Irving

Karen A. Johnson
Jeanne E. Kennon
Louisa T. Kwok
Diana M. Lee
Esther Y. Lee
Karen L. MacMillan
Gayle C. Mann
Kim J. McDonald
Lorraine C. McFarlane
Wendy E. Ng
Lynore K. McLeod
Jennifer Y. Okuchi
A. Maria Pellizzari

Lynn A. Pratt
Angelina E. Rodrigues
Susan E. Rotzien
Tamera S. Scheer
Jodi M. Shragge
P. Louise Smith
Augustina W. Tang
Cheryl D. Thomson
Jennifer A. Tipper
Jocelan K. Tracey
Sheryl Walker
Cynda K. Yeasting
Eliza K. Yuen

LONDON

Selina Baxter
Wendy Carter
Yvonne Chandler

Louise Deeks
Susanne Dure
Francesca Forde

Barbara Francis
Debra Last-Sutton
   (office manager)

Carole Ann Manning   Sarah Smith
Leigh Nicoll   Gillian Spindler

NEW YORK

Gaell Blackman   Dawn France-Somersel   Sandra Petrisor
Tenaz Dubash   Veronica Ottley   Louise Siudy

SYDNEY

Fleur LeBas   Ian Foster
(office manager)

HONG KONG

Jane Choi   Ciria Li   Louis Tang
Ruby Kwok   Rachel Lim   Ruby Tsang
Amy Lam   Tracy Lo   (office manager)
Rony Lam   Jodie Lok   Clara Yip
Ivy Lee   Lillian Moh

Notes

1 This had arisen out of Mackenzie King's first, cautious, efforts to begin a rearma-
ment program, as it seemed increasingly clear that war in Europe was inevitable
and the British, also realizing this, were concentrating on their own needs. Since
they were the traditional source of Canadian military supplies, the alternative was
to begin manufacturing arms in Canada. The "scandal" was that a contract was
entered into, in March 1938, with a cost-plus clause, for the manufacture of Bren
machine guns. This became a *cause-célèbre* in the media, especially in *Maclean's*
magazine, and led to a Royal Commission, that found no evidence of wrongdoing. Matters became largely academic when war was declared in September 1939,
and the Liberals won the general election in March 1940. The contract was eventually replaced by two new ones in 1941, and the production was at a set price
thereafter. Some 186,000 Bren guns were manufactured by the end of the war.

2 *Canada's Taxfalers, A History of Administration at Revenue Canada – Taxation,*
1916–1981, by Ralph C. Armorer and Ron Lemieux (unpublished), at page 140.

3 Colin Fraser Elliott was born in Toronto on October 7, 1888. He obtained a
B.Eng. from the University of Toronto and studied law at Osgoode Hall prior to
his call to the Ontario Bar. He died on December 15, 1969.

4 S.C. 1926–27, c.34, assented to March 31, 1927.

5 [1942] C.T.C. 65.

6 These included some criminal prosecutions with Paul Boivin in *R. v. Maloney
et al.* [1942] C.T.C. 77 and *R. v. Donat Paquin et al.* [1942] C.T.C. 153 and
[1942] C.T.C. 164; *Samson v. M.N.R.* [1943] C.T.C. 47; and civil appeals in
Kenneth B. S. Robertson, Limited v. M.N.R. [1944] C.T.C. 75, a very important case dealing with the timing of income recognition; *Wrights' Canadian
Ropes Limited v. M.N.R.* [1945] C.T.C. 177 (Ex. Ct.), [1946] C.T.C. 73 (SCC)
[1947] C.T.C. 1 (PC); *Nicholson Limited v. M.N.R.* [1945] C.T.C. 263; and
Siscoe Gold Mines, Limited v. M.N.R. [1945] C.T.C. 397; *Trapp v. M.N.R.*
[1946] C.T.C. 30; *Pure Spring Company Limited v. M.N.R.* [1946] C.T.C. 169;
and *The M. Company Limited v. M.N.R.* [1948] C.T.C. 213.

7 (1942) 20 *Canadian Bar Review,* 77.

8 To give some measure in the increase in the level of taxation, the total collections of the Department of National Revenue in 1932 were $61,257,400 and, in 1942, were $1,453,373,300. In 1932, it cost $3.48 to collect $100 of tax; in 1942, it cost $.81. The cost of auditing a return in 1932 was $15.27, and in 1942, was $4.95.

9 This was as the result of an accident that occurred while wrestling competitively at university. From that time, the eye deteriorated until it had to be removed.

10 Senate Proceedings of the Special Committee on Taxation, April 3, 1946, p. 93.

11 Ibid, May 7, 1946, p. 31.

12 Ibid, p. 313.

13 Armorer and Lemieux, op. cit, p. 166.

14 "Taxes and Related Matters," *The Canadian Chartered Accountant,* April 1947, pp. 237–8.

15 In 2001 dollars, this would be $101,460.55.

16 Sherbourne eventually retired as chairman of the British Oil Corporation after a stellar career in finance and law, for which he was knighted in 1983. He was at the time of the appeal and remained, in Stikeman's estimation, the most brilliant man he has ever known. Besides intellectual pre-eminence, he brought to his practice a wide practical knowledge of business, accounting, law, and a sixth sense of how to deal with the Inland Revenue authorities.

17 Elliott's immediate successor was Frank Herbert Brown, who served in the position from 1946 to February 1948, when he was followed by Vincent William Thomas Scully, who served until August 1951. Gavsie was appointed in August 1951 and remained until July 1954, when he left to join the Montgomery firm in Montreal. Gavsie was an excellent deputy minister, who did not believe in protracted litigation of tax disputes and was generally prepared to settle cases that did not involve questions of principle. He became affectionately known in the tax trade as "fifty-fifty" Gavsie.

18 William John Hulbig was born in Toronto on July 23, 1915. He attended West Hill High School in the NDG district of Montreal, the Université de Montréal, and McGill University, obtaining a BA in 1935 and a BCL in 1938. He was called to the Quebec Bar in 1938. He practised as associated general counsel to the Sun Life Assurance Company of Canada in Montreal during 1940 and 1941, before leaving to join the armed forces from 1941 to 1945. Following the war, he worked in the legal branch of the taxation division of the Department of National Revenue in Ottawa, recruited to the position by Stikeman. After Stikeman had moved to Foster, Watt, Hannen & Stikeman in 1946, he then re-recruited Hulbig to the firm in 1947.

19 Albert L. Bissonnette was born in Weyburn, Saskatchewan on August 24, 1918. Upon completion of a "bac" at the Collège St Boniface in Winnipeg in 1939, and after enrolling in both Sir George Williams University and McGill University, he joined the Canadian armed forces and had the misfortune to be part of the disastrous raid at Dunkirk, where he was taken prisoner and spent the entire war in captivity. He studied in prisoner-of-war camp and wrote the BCL exams for McGill from that unenviable location. He was admitted to the Quebec Bar in July 1950 and joined Foster, Watt, Hannen & Stikeman that fall. Bissonnette was the author of *Canadian Estate Tax Service,* another Richard De Boo

Limited publication. Bissonnette left the new firm of Stikeman & Elliott in 1963 to become a partner in the firm of Riel, LeDain, Bissonnette, Vermette & Ryan. Maurice Riel of that firm would eventually join Stikeman, Elliott, and Gerald LeDain became, successively, dean of Osgoode Hall, a judge on the Federal Court of Appeal, and a judge on the Supreme Court of Canada. Bissonnette was later appointed by John Turner to the Anti-Dumping Tribunal and finished his career as a member of the Canadian International Trade Tribunal.

20 In 2001 dollars, this would have been in excess of $654,000.

CHAPTER TWO

1 Later, it became known as the Canadian Imperial Bank of Commerce, following the amalgamation on June 1, 1961 with the Imperial Bank of Canada. The main branch at the time was at 265 St James Street West, opposite the Insurance Exchange Building at 268 St James Street, and a bit farther west, the old Molson's Bank building. When the Bank of Commerce building had been rebuilt from 1907 to 1909, after the demolition of the Temple Building on the same spot, it was discovered to be on the site of an Indian burial ground, evidence of which is still on display at the branch.

2 The CIBC eventually disposed of its real estate holdings in 2000, including the Montreal and Toronto buildings, to British Columbia Investment Management, an arm of a teachers' pension fund, but the firm has remained in both premises and has significantly expanded the space occupied in each building.

3 In 2001 dollars, $959,000 and $374,000 respectively.

4 In 2001 dollars, this would be $7,871,653 each.

5 The splits were as follows: 1963, three-for-one; 1965, three-for-two; 1979, three-for-one; 1981, three-for-one; 1984, two-for-one; 1986, two-for-one; and 2001, two-for-one. Doug Reekie recalls that when Patrick was offering all his shares of CAE for sale at $4 per share in 1957, his total investment portfolio was $1,845 in Canada Savings Bonds, all of which he sold to buy 462 CAE shares, the expanded total of which he still holds today.

6 It was then Montgomery, MacMichael, Forsyth, Common, Howard, Ker & Cate.

7 John Napier Wyndham Turner was born on June 7, 1929 in Richmond, Surrey, not far from London. Coming to Canada in his early years, he attended the Normal Model School, Ashbury College, and St Patrick's College, all in Ottawa. Entering the University of British Columbia in 1945, he was graduated with honours in political science in 1949 and was awarded a Rhodes Scholarship in the fall of that year, proceeding to Magdalen College, Oxford, obtaining the degrees of BA (in jurisprudence), BCL, and the customary MA. He was admitted to the English Bar in 1953, after the requisite dinners at Grey's Inn. He then went to Paris to get a doctorate in private international law, studying under the famous professor, Henri Battifol, but the family wanted him back in Canada, so he did not complete the degree. The next year, his step-father, Frank Mackenzie Ross, at the time lieutenant-governor of British Columbia, encouraged him to join Stikeman & Elliott, which he did, turning down offers from both the Scott, Hugessen (now McCarthy, Tétrault) and Duquet, MacKay firms to do so. Turner was also a gifted athlete and would, undoubtedly, have been a

member of the 1952 Olympic track team, but he could not afford to return to Canada for the Olympic trials. The selectors, somewhat pigheadedly, refused to recognize the results of his events in the United Kingdom for the purpose.

8 Turner was an effective and productive minister in all portfolios, but none more so than as minister of Justice, where he engineered many significant reforms, including the replacement of the former Exchequer Court of Canada with the Federal Court of Canada. His role is described in more detail in Pound, *Chief Justice W.R. Jackett, By the Law of the Land*. Montreal: McGill-Queen's University Press, 1999.

9 The Progressive Conservatives got the largest majority in Canadian history, with 211 seats. The Liberals got forty, and the NDP, thirty.

10 James Alexander Robb was born in Huntingdon, Quebec on May 3, 1930 and received his early education there at the Huntingdon Academy, from which he was graduated in 1947. He obtained a BA in 1951 and a BCL in 1954, both from McGill University. Called to the Quebec Bar in 1955, he was recruited by Bill Hulbig the same year. Robb was managing editor of the *McGill Daily* in 1950, president of the McGill Students' Union in 1952, and president of the McGill Students' Society (the undergraduate student body) from 1953 to 1954.

11 Gerald McCarthy was born on November 3, 1929 and studied at Loyola College, the Université de Dijon, and McGill University, obtaining the degrees of BA and BCL. He was admitted to the Quebec Bar in 1954. He joined the firm in 1955 and became assistant editor of the *Quebec Corporations Manual*. He was appointed to the Quebec Superior Court on November 10, 1976 and sworn in on January 2, 1977. He remembers having to explain to his friends, during the intervening period, that he had not accepted the appointment out of concern for the forthcoming Quebec elections, which brought the Parti Québécois to power for the first time less than a week later, on November 15, 1976. He was later appointed to the Quebec Court of Appeal on October 16, 1980 and retired at age sixty-five.

12 Thomas McKenna was born in Montreal on October 22, 1921, attending Loyola High School, Loyola College, and McGill University. He was called to the Quebec Bar in 1947, after serving with the Royal Canadian Navy Volunteer Reserve from 1943 to 1945, and practised with Hackett, Mulvena from 1947 to 1949. He died in Montreal on August 6, 2001. McKenna's parents ran the well-known McKenna florist business in Montreal.

13 Jean Monet was born in St Jean, Quebec on March 31, 1932, studying at Loyola and St Patrick's College before attending University of Ottawa for his LLL and being called to the Quebec Bar in 1957, joining Stikeman & Elliott the same year. He was an assistant editor of the *Estate Tax Service*.

14 Paterson Neil Thorsteinsson was born in Vancouver on February 19, 1930. He was matriculated in Vernon, BC, and under the Veterans Accelerated Program, he was able to do two years of arts at UBC before going directly into the faculty of law, where he obtained an LLB in 1951 at the age of twenty-one. He was admitted to the BC Bar in 1952, the Ontario Bar in 1955, and the Quebec Bar in 1958, joining the firm in 1958. He left in August 1964 to return to Vancouver, where he started the firm, now known as Thorsteinssons, which practises exclusively in tax law. It was at his home in February 1993 that George Tamaki died while having dinner, during a visit to Vancouver.

15 The cases included *Curran v. M.N.R.* [1959] C.T.C. 416; *Ontario Paper v. M.N.R.* [1959] D.T.C. 1327; *Sterling Paper Mills* [1960] C.T.C. 215; *Western Leaseholds v. M.N.R.* [1961] C.T.C. 490; *Woodward's Pension Society v. M.N.R.* [1962] C.T.C. 11; *Parsons Steiner v. M.N.R.* [1962] C.T.C. 231; *Adilman Estate v. M.N.R.* [1962] C.T.C. 245; *Colford v. M.N.R.* [1962] C.T.C. 546; *Hollinger v. M.N.R.* [1963] C.T.C. 51; *Dobieco v. M.N.R.* [1963] C.T.C. 143; *R.K. Fraser v. M.N.R.* [1963] 130; *Robwaral v. M.N.R.* [1964] D.T.C. 5266; *Johnston Testers v. M.N.R.* [1965] C.T.C. 116; *George Steer v. M.N.R.* [1965] C.T.C. 161; *Dobieco v. M.N.R.* [1965] C.T.C. 507; *BC Power v. M.N.R.* [1966] 454; and *George Steer v. M.N.R.* [1966] C.T.C. 731.

16 Donald James Johnston, born in Ottawa on June 26, 1936, studied at McGill University, the Université de Grenoble, and the Université de Montréal, and was admitted to the Quebec Bar in 1961, pursuant to a private bill passed on February 22, 1961, joining Stikeman & Elliott the same year. He practised corporate law and left the firm in 1967. He became a Member of Parliament and cabinet minister, and is currently serving his second five-year term as a very capable Secretary-General of the OECD in Paris.

17 James Andrews Grant was born in Montreal on May 31, 1937, studied law at McGill University, became a *stagiare* with the firm in 1961, was called to the Quebec Bar in 1962, and joined the firm that year.

18 Maurice Duplessis died in office as premier of Quebec on September 7, 1959. He was succeeded by Joseph-Mignault-Paul Sauvé, who died in 1960 and was replaced by Antonio Barrette on January 7, 1960. On June 22, 1960, Jean Lesage led the Quebec Liberals to victory in the Quebec general election, giving rise to the so-called Quiet Revolution. Less than two years later, at the McGill University spring convocation, his minister of Education, Paul Gérin-Lajoie, made the statement that the (Roman Catholic) Church had no place in the educational system of Quebec, a declaration that he might not have been so comfortable making on the other side of Mount Royal, at the Université de Montréal.

19 Dominion Square had become a Roman Catholic cemetery in 1799. Nearby was St Antoine cemetery, which had been used to bury many of those who succumbed to the cholera epidemic of 1832, extending as far west as Stanley Street and south to the present location of the cathedral. The population of the city began to surround the burial place, which led to a decision to create a larger cemetery on the mountain in 1855. The city continued to spread, and the English portion began to build houses in the area to the northwest of the old city, which led to subdivision of the old cemetery and the relocation of the coffins and tombstones to the new cemetery, off Côte-des-Neiges Road. A controversy arose during the clearing of the land and the exhumations. Some were concerned that a new outbreak of cholera might occur as a result of digging up the graves, while others were outraged at the sacrilegious manner in which the remains were removed. A recommendation was made by the Sanitary Association of Montreal to turn the area into a park, which was followed by a petition in 1869 addressed to the municipal authorities to the same effect. Dominion Square became a park shortly thereafter. The graves that remained were left undisturbed, and some were discovered later, near the main entrance of the Windsor Hotel during the construction of the CIBC building.

CHAPTER THREE

1 In 2001 dollars, these figures would be $3.2 million and $1.3 million respectively.

2 Professional firms regularly adopted January fiscal year-ends to defer tax on professional income until the following year since taxation of partners' incomes was based on receipts of income during the calendar year. It the case of Stikeman & Elliott, this was not an artificial deferral since the firm had commenced business on February 1, 1952, and the normal twelve-month fiscal period ended on January 31 of each subsequent year.

3 In 2001 dollars, this total remuneration would be $262,000. The "bonus" represented his de facto position as an economic, but not legal, partner of the firm.

4 Now McCarthy Tétrault.

5 William David Angus was born in Toronto on July 21, 1937, and after completing secondary school at Lower Canada College in Montreal, he went to Princeton University, graduating cum laude in 1959, and attended McGill University, earning his BCL with first-class honours. Admitted to the Quebec Bar in 1963, he joined the firm the same year.

6 Maurice Régnier was born on August 18, 1931 in Rockland, Ontario. He studied arts (BA, 1952), pharmacy (LPH, 1953), and law at the University of Ottawa (LLL, 1956), and in 1957, he was called to the Quebec Bar. He joined the legal branch of the Department of National Revenue that year, remaining until 1960, when he joined a small Montreal firm. He left soon after, with Stikeman's help, to join the firm of Duquet, MacKay & Weldon. He was called to the Ontario Bar in 1978.

7 Now McCarthy Tétrault.

8 Angus was there as the firm's maritime "expert" and had been actively involved in the development of the evidence of the maritime practices involved. His immersion into the substantive aspects of the file is described in chapter 12.

9 *Interpretation Bulletin* was issued on April 8, 1976. It remained in force until September 19, 1985, when a special release effected changes in paragraphs 2, 4, 28, 35, and 36; otherwise, it remains as originally drafted.

10 Reported at [1969] C.T.C. 558.

11 Born in Paris on April 13, 1923, François Mercier completed studies at Loyola College with a BA magna cum laude in 1942 and went on to obtain his LLL at the Université de Montréal, also magna cum laude, following which he was called to the Quebec Bar in 1945. He became a member of the firm of Patenaude, Patenaude, Hébert, Trahan, Hodge & Mercier from 1945 to 1950, leaving in 1950 to go to the Brais, Campbell firm. After only five years of practice, Mercier was elected secretary of le Barreau de Montréal and became *professeur agréé* in the faculty of law at his alma mater.

12 André Brossard was born on January 10, 1937 in Montreal. He obtained a BA (cum laude) from Collège Ste-Marie in 1956 and his LLL from the Université de Montréal in 1959. He was admitted to the Quebec Bar in 1960, winning the gold medal of the Barreau de Paris for the highest marks in civil law. He practised with Tremblay, Deschênes & Forget, then with Brais, Campbell, Mercier, Leduc & Pepper for two years before coming to Stikeman Elliott with Mercier in 1964, where he remained until 1978. He was bâtonnier of the Province of Quebec in

1976–77 and left the firm to join Desjardins, Ducharme. He remained there until his appointment to the Quebec Superior Court in 1983, where he sat until his elevation to the Quebec Court of Appeal in June 1989.

13 Stanley Herbert Hartt was born in Montreal on November 11, 1937 and attended the High School of Montreal and McGill University, from which he was graduated with a BA with honours in economics and political science, specializing in labour economics and industrial relations. Upon graduation, he received a Guy Drummond Fellowship to study economics at the Faculté de Droit at the Université de Paris and at the Institut d'Études Politiques. In Montreal, he re-entered McGill to obtain a MA in 1961; at the same time, he was enrolled in the faculty of law, from which he obtained a BCL in 1963. Returning to Paris the same year on a Macdonald Travelling Scholarship, he studied law at the Université de Paris.

14 The only quasi-exception to this had been the hiring of Charles C. Gavsie, former deputy minister of National Revenue (August 1951 to July 1954), as counsel to what is now Ogilvy Renault. Phillips & Vineberg waited until Robert and Michael Vineberg were hired before they broke the barrier. Casper Bloom was hired at Ogilvy after Hartt was at Stikeman Elliott, which was responsible for opening it up.

15 She stayed at the new firm until 1971, when she resigned. She then made a few calls to see about new employment, one of which was with Stikeman, Elliott, which responded very quickly, saying that George Tamaki needed a secretary. So she started at once and remained with him for twenty-three years until he retired.

16 Michael L. Richards was born in Estevan, Saskatchewan on April 2, 1939. He received a BA and BCL in 1963 from McGill University. He wrote the notarial board examinations and practised as a notary from 1964 to 1967. He was called to the Quebec Bar in 1967 and to the Ontario Bar in 1980.

17 Now Ogilvy Renault.

18 Harold P. Gordon, Q.C. was born in Montreal on April 19, 1937. He obtained a B.Com. from McGill University in 1958 and proceeded from there to the graduate division of the Wharton School of Business and Finance of the University of Pennsylvania for a year before getting a BA from Sir George Williams University in 1961. (This academic detour was the result of a rather archaic rule in Quebec that required, as a condition of admission to the Bar, that the candidate have, in addition to a law degree, a BA and have studied Latin and philosophy, and that the BA had been acquired four years prior to admission to the Bar. This rule has, happily, been repealed.) He attended McGill for his BCL, which he obtained in 1964, articled with the Mendolsohn Rosenzweig firm, and was called to the Quebec Bar in 1965. He then went to Ottawa for two years as special assistant to Maurice Sauvé, at the time, minister of Forestry and Rural Development. In 1988, he became a director of Hasbro Inc. and joined the company in 1994 as vice-chairman.

19 John Nolan was appointed to the Quebec Superior Court on April 3, 1969 and later to the Quebec Court of Appeal on February 22, 1979. He became a supernumerary judge in 1983 and retired on March 23, 1986.

20 Adam Peter Francis Cumyn was born in Ottawa on July 17, 1941. He attended Selwyn House School in Montreal, Bishop's College School in Lennoxville, and

Neuchatel Junior College in Switzerland before obtaining a BA from McGill University in 1962. He studied law at the Université Laval and got his LLL in 1965. He was admitted to the Quebec Bar in 1966. He was then recruited to the firm in 1967 by Stikeman, who had known the Cumyn family from Senneville. He was called to the Ontario Bar in 1977. He taught the international tax course at McGill University from 1981 to 1991, which was taken over by Paul Setlakwe, whom Cumyn had found as a student while teaching tax at the Cours de Maîtrise en Fiscalité at the Université de Sherbrooke and hired for the firm.

21 A partially complete and only partially accurate description of Verchere's career is contained in Stevie Cameron, *Blue Trust: The Author, the Lawyer, His Wife and Her Money.* Toronto: MacFarlane Walter & Ross, 1998.

22 Michel Vennat was born in Montreal on September 17, 1941 and graduated magna cum laude from Collège Jean-de-Brébeuf in 1960 before obtaining the degree of LLL from the Université de Montréal in 1963, winning the Prix du Barreau in the process. He was selected as a Rhodes Scholar for Quebec and attended Merton College at Oxford University, earning an MA in the Honour School of PPE in 1965 and Double Blue in lacrosse and (ice) hockey.

23 This was with the Fusiliers Mont-Royal, of which regiment Vennat is now honourary lieutenant colonel.

24 Brossard was appointed to the Quebec Court of Appeal on June 30, 1989. His father, Roger, had been a judge before him, having been appointed to the Quebec Superior Court on September 8, 1950 and to the Quebec Court of Appeal on November 19, 1964. Roger Brossard retired on October 1, 1976.

25 In 2001 dollars, this would have been $7,743,000 and $2,600,000 respectively.

CHAPTER FOUR

1 The final disposition of the case is reported as *Black v. Law Society (Alberta)* [1989] S.C.R. 591. The Law Society of Alberta had enacted rules prohibiting, *inter alia,* a member of the Law Society of Alberta from practising as a partner or associate in more than one firm and a member from entering into a partnership or association with anyone not an active member of the society ordinarily residing in Alberta. Although upheld at trial, on appeal, the rules were held by the Supreme Court of Canada to infringe upon or deny the mobility rights under section 6(2)(b) of the *Charter* and were not otherwise justified by section 1. British Columbia tried, unsuccessfully, to exclude non-Canadian citizens. See *Andrews v. Law Society (British Columbia)* [1989] S.C.R. 143.

2 Donald G.H. Bowman was born in Guelph, Ontario on July 14, 1933. He attended Guelph Collegiate Vocational Institute before enrolling in the University of Toronto, Victoria College. There he completed an Honours BA in languages (French and German). He obtained his law degree from the University of Toronto. Bowman taught high school at the Ontario College of Education before going to law school. Later, he became director of tax litigation at the Department of Justice before joining Stikeman Elliott in 1971, where he stayed until 1992, when he accepted an appointment to the Tax Court of Canada, where he is now associate chief judge.

3 This was the basis for the massive tax reform that would come into effect (generally) as of January 1, 1972. The White Paper was based in large measure on the Carter Commission Report of 1966 and led to the introduction of the legislation contained in Bill C-259, introduced on June 18, 1971. The "Lindsay" referred to was Robert Lindsay, who went to Osler, Hoskin & Harcourt.

4 Frederick R. Von Veh was born in Lodz, Poland on July 31, 1943. He completed his undergraduate studies at Sir George Williams University in Montreal in 1963 with a BA (economics and political science) and received his LLB from Queen's in 1967. Von Veh was called to the Ontario Bar in 1969 and began his legal career with the firm on March 1, 1971. He became a partner on February 1, 1972 and left the firm in 1998 to go to Weir & Foulds. Then he went to Bennett Jones, where he is currently the senior member of the employment and labour law department in the firm's Toronto office.

5 Thomas C.H. Baldwin was born in Windsor, Ontario on July 19, 1940. He graduated from Birmingham High School, Birmingham, Michigan. He then obtained a B.Sc. (industrial engineering) from Michigan State University in 1961, following which he worked for a few years before enrolling in Osgoode Hall and receiving an LLB in 1968. He was called to the Bar of Ontario in 1970 and left for Thomson, Brans, Lehun and Champagne on July 15, 1993, which is now Brans, Lehun, Baldwin LLP.

6 James C. Davis was born in Toronto on June 20, 1946. He attended UCC (Upper Canada College) and received a B.Sc. from McGill in 1968 and an LLB from Osgoode Hall in 1971. He was called to the Ontario Bar in 1974, qualified in the UK in 1992, and became a partner in 1979.

7 John R. Dingle was born in Toronto on September 30, 1942. He obtained a BA in philosophy from York University in 1968 and an LLB from Osgoode Hall in 1971, prior to articling with Don Bowman and a call to the Ontario Bar in 1973.

8 Wayne E. Shaw was born in Lacombe, Alberta on April 2, 1944. He received his BA from the University of Calgary in 1966 and his LLB from the University of Alberta in 1967. Shaw was called to the Bar of Alberta in 1968 and the Ontario Bar in 1972. He worked for Howard, Mackie from 1967 to 1971 before moving to Stikeman Elliott in 1972, following a year's study for a master's degree at the University of Toronto. He became a partner in 1977. While Shaw was doing his master's degree, his wife, Marilyn Pilkington, enrolled in the LLB program, from which she was graduated and went on to a career in academe, including an appointment as dean of the Osgoode Hall law school.

9 E. James Arnett was born in Winnipeg, Manitoba on September 29, 1938. He received a BA from the University of Manitoba in 1959, his LLB from the same institution in 1963, and an LLM from Harvard in 1964. He articled with Brian Dickson prior to the latter's appointment to the Supreme Court of Canada and joined the federal Department of Justice for a brief period before turning to private practice with Davies Ward & Beck. Arnett is featured in Jack Batten, *Lawyers*. Toronto: Macmillan, 1980.

10 W. Brian Rose was born in Toronto on September 20, 1945. He attended Chapleau and John Rennie High Schools before studying at McGill University, where he received a B.Com. and an LIA in 1967. Rose worked at MacDonald Currie

(now PricewaterhouseCoopers) from 1967 to 1969, and at Space Research Corporation from 1969 to 1971. Rose was called to the Ontario Bar in 1976 and to the Bar of England and Wales in 1983. From 1978 to 1986, Rose was out of Canada; thus, he attained formal partnership at Stikeman Elliott only in 1987, when he was again a Canadian resident.

11 Marvin Yontef was born in Lodz, Poland on February 12, 1946 but has lived in Toronto since 1949. He graduated from W.L. Mackenzie Collegiate Institute and attended the University of Toronto for two years. He received his LLB from Osgoode Hall in 1969 and an LLM from Harvard in 1971. Yontef was called to the Ontario Bar in 1972 and articled at Goodman & Carr from 1969 to 1970. He then worked for Blake Cassels & Graydon (1972–75) and was consultant to the federal government on securities law (1974–79) before joining Stikeman Elliott in 1975. He became a partner in 1978.

12 Sam Wakim joined the firm in September 1975, but soon became involved in Brian Mulroney's leadership campaign and withdrew in the spring of 1977. Wakim and Mulroney were schoolmates when they both attended St Francis Xavier University, Wakim graduating with a B.Sc. in 1959, and Mulroney graduating with a BA in the same year. He subsequently joined the law firm of Weir & Foulds as an associate in 1985 and is now a partner there.

13 Richard G. Pyne was born in Toronto on July 10, 1945. He graduated from Richview Collegiate as an Ontario Scholar and enrolled in the University of Toronto, where he received an Honours BA (1968) and his LLB (1971). Pyne graduated with honours from the Bar course and was called to the Ontario Bar in 1973. He worked at the Department of Justice from 1971 to 1975 and at Stikeman Elliott from 1975 to 1978. He began at the Montreal office but moved to the Toronto office in 1976. At that time, the tax group in Toronto was headed by Don Bowman, who was Pyne's direct superior. Two other lawyers left the firm at the same time as he did: Ernie Rovet, with whom Pyne practised briefly in partnership; and John Dingle, whose departure was unconnected to Pyne's and Rovet's.

14 Richard Clark was born in Toronto on August 10, 1948. He has a BA.SC. (chemical engineering), B.Com., LLB, and MBA, all from the University of Toronto. Clark received the J.P. Bickell Scholarship for engineering. He was called to the Ontario Bar in 1976 and became a partner in 1982.

15 Roderick F. Barrett was born on July 12, 1950 in Toronto. He obtained a B.Sc. in chemistry from the University of Western Ontario in 1972, having entered without a high school diploma, and thereafter enrolled at Osgoode Hall, graduating with his LLB in 1975. He was called to the Ontario Bar in 1977.

16 Michael J. Bonner accepted an appointment to the Tax Court of Canada in 1978 and became a supernumerary judge of that court in 2001.

17 Elliott had been a director of Mercantile prior to Stikeman, who had gone on the board after Elliott had resigned to become a director of the much larger CIBC. In due course, the Mercantile Bank got into financial difficulties during the 1982 real estate crash when its loan portfolio was badly affected and was acquired by the National Bank of Canada.

18 Sidney Lederman was born in Toronto on January 11, 1943. Following his call to the Bar in 1968, he joined Fasken & Calvin for a brief period between 1968 and 1971. He then became a professor of law at the Osgoode Hall law school at

York University. He taught until 1977, at which time he joined Stikeman Elliott, where he became a senior partner and the head of the litigation department.

19 John Sopinka and Sidney N. Lederman, *The Law of Evidence in Civil Cases.* Toronto, Butterworth's, 1974. The current edition is John Sopinka, Sidney N. Lederman, and Alan W. Bryant, *The Law of Evidence in Canada.* 1999.

20 Robert Reuter was born in Toronto on May 22, 1949. He obtained an Honours BA from York University in 1972 and an LLB from University of Toronto in 1975. He articled with the Honourable Justice Charles Dubin of the Ontario Court of Appeal, who then arranged an introduction to John Sopinka.

21 John A.M. Judge was born in Toronto on March 2, 1951. After attending R.H. King Collegiate Institute in Scarborough (and obtaining the highest average in the graduating class), he obtained a BA from the University of Toronto in 1992 and an LLB from the same institution in 1975. He was called to the Ontario Bar in 1977 and became a partner of the firm in 1983.

22 Jan D. Weir was born in Windsor, Ontario on December 3, 1945. He graduated from Assumption High School and received a BA from University of Windsor in 1967 and his LLB from the University of Toronto in 1972. Weir was called to the Bar of Ontario in 1974 and practised on his own for a number of years before being asked by John Sopinka in 1979 to join Stikeman Elliott. He became a partner at Stikeman Elliott in 1982 and left to pursue private practice in 1989. Weir taught business law at Humber and Seneca Colleges, authored *Critical Concepts of Canadian Business Law,* and writes a commercial litigation column for *Lawyer's Weekly.*

23 Couzin and Finkelstein are described in chapter 11.

24 We were close to Durnford, a former dean of the law faculty at McGill, who spent his sabbatic year at the Montreal firm, as he shifted from a specialist in civil law to a careful and thorough tax professor.

25 James A. Riley was born on April 18, 1952 in Winnipeg, attended Queen's University for two years, and obtained his LLB, winning the gold medal in the process from the University of Toronto in 1977. He was called to the Ontario Bar in 1979 and received his LLM from Harvard University in 1980. Riley became a partner at Stikeman Elliott on February 1, 1986, leaving the firm in August 1996 for Ogilvy Renault, where he currently heads the business law practice of the Toronto office and serves as a member of the executive committee.

26 Ron Durand was born in London, Ontario on January 30, 1950. He graduated from South Huron District High School (1969) and attended the University of Western Ontario for a bachelor of business administration (1973) and his LLB (1976). He received an LLM from Harvard University in 1978. Durand was called to the Ontario Bar in 1979 and became a partner at Stikeman Elliott in 1983.

27 William Innes was born in Moncton, New Brunswick on November 28, 1950. He graduated from Moncton High, then attended Mount Allison University, where he received a B.Sc. in 1971. Innes received his LLB from the University of New Brunswick in 1975 and an LLM from Osgoode Hall in 1984. He was called to the Bar of New Brunswick in 1975 and the Bar of Ontario in 1978. He worked at a small law firm in New Brunswick before joining Stikeman Elliott on November 20, 1978. Innes became partner in 1983 and left on October 7, 1994 to join Genest Murray and later, Thorsteinssons.

28 Kathryn Chalmers was born in Oakville, Ontario on December 29, 1952. She attended Thomas A. Blakelock High School before enrolling at McMaster University, where she earned an Honours BA and an MA in philosophy. She received her LLB from the Osgoode Hall law school. Chalmers received the following awards during her studies: high school: Ontario Scholar. BA: dean's honour list, Moulton Hall Scholarship, Brian Scholarship in philosophy. MA: Ontario Graduate Scholarship. LLB: bronze medallist, Citizenship Scholarship (three years), York Scholarship, the Ivan Cleveland Rand Scholarship, Income Tax Award, Senate Scholarship, Wilson Memorial Scholarship. She was called to the Ontario Bar in 1980 and became a partner at Stikeman Elliott in 1985.

29 Peter F.C. Howard obtained a BA from York University in 1975, an LLB from Osgoode Hall in 1979, where he was the bronze medallist, and a first in his BCL from Oxford University in 1989. He was admitted to the Ontario Bar in 1982. From 1975 to 1980, he was a member of the Canadian Equestrian Team and participated in the 1975 Pan American Games, where he won a silver medal. He became a partner of the firm in 1987.

CHAPTER FIVE

1 Cumyn seems to have "danced" with the idea of some form of association with one or two accountants in London: J.P. Smith of Cooper Bros. and someone by the name of Wheatcroft, who had offices in the West End. Nothing ever developed from this. He also considered an arrangement for a joint office with a Washington law firm, but he decided not to proceed.

2 Paul Baatz, one of the firm's juniors of the period, coordinated invitations to the event. There was a blue ribbon list of invitees that included Viscount Weir; Lord Thomson of Fleet; Guy Roberge of Quebec House; Julien Fayet, formerly of Riddell, Stead, Graham & Hutchison; Hobart Moore; C.E.M. Hardie, chairman of BOAC; Sir Roy Matthews; Sir Harold Gillett; Lord Sainsbury; Donald Warburg; E.P. Taylor, the Earl of Airlie; Marcel Odier of Lombard Odier; and many of the leading legal and accounting firms in London.

3 Lalonde joined the firm after concluding a distinguished career in politics and public service. The Honourable Marc Lalonde was born in Île Perot, Quebec on July 26, 1929. He received his MA (droit), LLL (1954); MA (Oxon) (1957), Montreal (1956); and DES Ottawa (1959). Lalonde went on to have a remarkable career in both the public service and in government. He began as a researcher in the combines branch of the Department of Justice and taught law thereafter for two years at the Université de Montréal. In 1965, Prime Minister Lester B. Pearson asked him if he would like to be president of the Canadian Broadcasting Corporation or to come to Ottawa as a policy adviser in the Prime Minister's Office. He took on the latter position in 1966. He later headed a task force on securities regulation and corporate disclosure at the federal level, bringing his report within the six-month deadline contemplated and on budget, a matter that he still remembers with some satisfaction. In 1968, he became Pierre Elliott Trudeau's chief of staff, was appointed Queen's Counsel in 1971, and remained as chief of staff until the general election in 1972, when he ran for office and was elected in the Montreal riding of Outremont. Once elected, he soon became one of the

leading ministers of the day, holding several important portfolios: minister of
National Health and Welfare (1972–78); minister of State for Federal-Provincial
Relations (1975–78); minister responsible for the Status of Women (1975–78);
minister of Justice (1978–79); minister of Energy, Mines, and Resources (1980–
82); and minister of Finance (1983–84). He retired from partisan politics and
went into private practice with the firm in Montreal in 1985.

4 The *International Financial Law Review* of February 1988 showed the firm as
number six in the ranking of "Euro-Bond Lawyers of the Year," only seven issues from being number four. Those ahead of us were the legal giants: Linklaters
& Paines; Allen and Overy; Slaughter & May; Davis, Polk & Wardwell; and
Cleary, Gottlieb, Steen & Hamilton.

5 Colleen Ryan and Glenn Burge, *Corporate Cannibals: The Taking of Fairfax*.
Port Melbourne, Australia: Heinemann, 1992.

6 Peter Wright, *Spycatcher: The Candid Autobiography of a Senior Intelligence
Officer*. New York: Viking, 1987.

7 Richard James Hay was born in Ottawa in 1954 and raised in Toronto. He attended University of Toronto, Victoria College, getting a BA in 1972. He then
went to Osgoode Hall for his LLB in 1977, articled with McCarthy & McCarthy,
lectured at the School of Continuing Studies in Commercial Law, clerked for
Chief Justice Evans of the Supreme Court of Ontario, and obtained an LLM in
corporate finance and taxation at the Columbia University school of law before
teaching law at the University of Ottawa (1981–84) and later at the National
University of Singapore (1984–87). He is admitted to practice in Ontario, New
York, and England.

8 The Canada Club is one of the oldest dinner clubs in London, dating back to
1806, started by the fur traders. Sir John A. Macdonald attended several times
while in London during the preparations for Confederation. Scott of the Antarc-
tic spoke there the night before his departure for the South Pole. By tradition, the
Canadian High Commissioner chairs the occasions, and the club has met in the
Savoy Ballroom for the past fifty years. The club holds several black-tie dinners a
year, addressed by leading figures in the world of business and politics. This provided the firm with a unique opportunity to spend time with political, business,
and academic leaders and be at the leading edge of current thinking. Stikeman
Elliott has run the Canada Club for twenty years, an association commenced by
Colson, who has been closely involved throughout that period. Hay was honourary secretary (chief executive) from 1995 to 1998. The speakers addressing the
club during this period included Matthew Barrett, chairman and chief executive
of the Bank of Montreal and later the chairman of Barclays Bank; Jaques de
Larosiere, president of the European Bank for Reconstruction and Development;
and the Rt. Hon. Jean Chrétien, prime minister of Canada.

9 Stuart H. Cobbett was born in Montreal on June 3, 1948. He attended Selwyn
House School and Bishop's College School, finishing his secondary education
in 1966. He obtained a BA from McGill University in 1969 and a BCL from
the same institution in 1972. Following his call to the Quebec Bar in 1974, he
practised with Heenan Blaikie until 1985, when he left to work with Astral
Communications. He joined the firm in August 1992 and became a partner in
1994.

10 Philip J. Henderson was born in Toronto, Ontario on November 3, 1959. He received a BA from Trinity College, University of Toronto, in 1981 and an LLB from the Osgoode Hall law school of York University in 1984. He was called to the Ontario Bar in 1986 and was admitted as a solicitor in England and Wales in 1996. He joined the Stikeman Elliott partnership in 1992.

11 In fact, Colson was fully aware of her previous employment. That was precisely why he had hired her.

12 On November 20, 1979, Prime Minister Pierre Elliott Trudeau had announced that he was stepping down as Liberal leader and had called a leadership convention for the following March. Some three weeks later, the Clark government was defeated on a motion of non-confidence, and Trudeau would later reverse his decision and lead the Liberals to an election victory in February 1980.

13 Brian Hansen was born in Wellington, New Zealand on September 10, 1950. He was awarded an LLB (first-class honours) in 1972 and an LLM (distinction) in 1973 from Victoria University. He then obtained an LLM from Dalhousie University in 1973. Subsequently, he taught for six years in Canada before commencing private practice. He has played key roles in Stikeman Elliott's offices in London, Vancouver, Hong Kong, and Sydney. He was called to the Alberta Bar in 1980 and the British Columbia Bar in 1989.

14 Ralph Lutes was born on September 13, 1955 in Bathurst, New Brunswick. He obtained a B.Com. from Queen's University in 1977 and an LLB from the University of New Brunswick in 1980. He was called to the Ontario Bar in 1982 and the BC Bar in 1991. After beginning in the Toronto office, he worked in the Hong Kong office from 1987 to 1990 and in the Vancouver office from 1990 to 1995, before joining CIBC World Markets. Thereafter, he engaged in private entrepreneurial activities until 2002, when he rejoined the firm in Vancouver.

15 Ching-wo Ng was born on September 4, 1950 in Fukien, China.

16 Tsun remembers that when Gordon recruited him to go to Hong Kong, he said that the greediest people all went to Hong Kong and that Tsun was the third-greediest person he knew.

17 See, for example, Christopher Patton, *East and West*. Toronto, McLelland & Stewart, 1988. Christopher Patton was the last British governor of Hong Kong.

18 Elizabeth A. Skelton was born in Brisbane, Australia on June 2, 1946. After receiving a Diplôme Supérieur d'Études Françaises at the Université de Paris (the Sorbonne) in 1966, she obtained her BCL in 1978 and her LLB in 1979 from McGill University. She received the William Jacob Prize for most improved student in 1978. Following her call to the Quebec Bar in 1980, she joined Stikeman Elliott, where she practised for sixteen years. She became a partner in 1986. Elizabeth played a key role in developing Stikeman Elliott's New York office. In 1996, she retired from Stikeman Elliott and continued her education at Northeastern University in Boston.

19 Ken Ottenbreit was born in Regina, Saskatchewan on September 24, 1958. He received a B.Admin. with great distinction from the University of Regina in 1980. He then obtained a LLB from the University of Toronto in 1983. He was called to Ontario Bar in 1985 and the New York Bar in 1991. He joined the Stikeman Elliott partnership in 1991.

20 John E. Walker was born in Toronto on November 19, 1955. After graduating with a BBA from Wilfrid Laurier University in 1979, he then worked for Campbell Valuation Services and Arthur Anderson Consulting before attending law school. He attended Osgoode Hall where he obtained an LLB in 1993. His call to the Ontario Bar came in 1994. He joined the partnership on January 1, 2000.

21 William Rosenberg was born in Montreal, Quebec on November 19, 1963. He received a BA in 1984 in political science from McGill University. He was a Faculty Scholar in 1982–83, and graduated as a University Scholar in 1983–84. He then obtained a BCL (1988) and a LLB (1988) from McGill University, graduating with second-class honours. He was called to the Quebec Bar in 1989.

22 The Stikeman Elliott personnel at the office at this time included Robert Hayhurst (M), Alain Massicotte (M), Robert Hyndman (T), Susan Hutton (O), Caroline Musselman (T), Bertrand Ménard (M), David Farrell (L), Duane Gillis (C), William Scott (L), David and Karen Skinner (M), Martine Band (O), Kathleen Ward (T), Lawrence Wilde (T), Andrea Villani, David Ross (T), Valerie Helbronner (T), Pierre-Georges Roy (T), Heather McMaster (T), Neil Berlad (T), and Jean Philippe Ewart (M). We also had occasional visits by Calin Rovinescu from London and various other Canadian lawyers hired off the street. The project even led to romances and eventual marriages (i.e., Pierre-Georges Roy and Heather McMaster). We also had several key support staff on hand: Louise Guérin from Montreal, Colleen Thompson and Franca Greco from Toronto, and Karen Clifford from London.

23 The firm learned that care had to be taken in interpreting the reports from all the foreign offices to be sure that elements of the Graham Greene novel, *Our Man in Havana,* did not creep in to the appreciation of the situation in each country.

24 Roy M. Randall was born in South Africa on September 25, 1936. He obtained a B.Com. in 1958 and an LLB in 1976 from the University of Witwatersrand. He was called to the Bars in England and Wales in 1964, New South Wales in 1980, Australian Capital Territory in 1984, and Hong Kong in 1987.

25 Erik Richer La Fleche was born in Montreal on February 22, 1956. After attending Collège Stanislas, he obtained a BCL in 1977 and an LLB from McGill in 1978. In 1985, he attended the Kyoto Japanese Language School in Japan. His call to the Quebec Bar came in 1979, and to the Ontario Bar in 1986. From 1981 to 1984, he was a foreign legal apprentice with Anderson Mori, a well-known Tokyo-based Japanese law firm.

26 Martin H. Scheim was born in Montreal on February 21, 1950. He obtained a B.Sc. from McGill University in 1971, followed by a BCL in 1974 and an LLB in 1975. He was called to the Quebec Bar in 1976, worked for a year at Phillips & Vineberg, then for a year at Consolidated Textiles, before joining the firm in January 1979. He was called to the Alberta Bar in 1980 and became a partner of the firm in 1984.

27 Jean Carrier was born in Hauterive, Quebec on May 4, 1961. He studied at UBC and Mount Royal College in Calgary prior to obtaining an LLL from the University of Ottawa in 1990, following which he studied at the University of London, Queen Mary and Westfield College, and the London School of Economics and Political Science. He was called to the Quebec Bar in 1993, worked for a year with the Quebec Ministère de l'environment, joined the firm in 1994, and became a partner in 2000.

28 Viateur Chénard was born in Shawinigan, Quebec on December 8, 1953. He completed a degree in political science in 1973 and an LLL in 1976 from the Université de Montréal. He became a partner at Stikeman Elliott in 1992.

29 Christine Desaulniers was born in Montreal on September 12, 1961. After attending the Collège Jean-de-Brébeuf, she graduated from the École des Hautes Études Commerciales in 1983. She obtained her BCL in 1986 from the Université de Montréal. Her call to the Quebec Bar came in 1987. In 1995, she became a partner at Stikeman Elliott.

30 Sterling Dietze was born on October 19, 1960 in Toronto. In 1985, he received a BA in economics from the Université Laval. In 1983, while at Laval, he received the Bourse d'echanges bilingues en études canadiennes, and in 1985, the Bourse spéciale maîtrise du conseil de recherches en sciences humaines du Canada. In 1986, he obtained an MA in economics from Queen's University. He then proceeded to graduate with honours from the University of Toronto with an LLB in 1989 and the Université de Montréal with an LLB in 1990. He was called to the Quebec Bar in 1991 and the Ontario Bar in 1996.

31 Sydney John Isaacs was born in Montreal, Quebec on July 6, 1956. He received his BA in 1978, BCL and LLB, all from McGill University, in 1982, and was called to the Quebec Bar came in 1983.

32 Simon Romano in Toronto handled the Ontario aspects of the transactions.

33 Michèle Baillargeon is a paralegal, who studied at the Université de Montréal, obtaining her LLL in 1978. She became a notary in 1979.

34 Roger Forget is also a paralegal, who obtained his LLL from the Université de Montréal in 1978.

CHAPTER SIX

1 Eugene H. Kwan was born in Shanghai, China in 1946. He obtained his LLB from the University of British Columbia in 1970 and was called to the BC Bar in 1971.

2 John N. Paton was born in Vancouver on December 10, 1949. He received a B.Sc. in 1971 and an LLB in 1975 from the University of British Columbia. He was called to the British Columbia Bar in 1976 and the England and Wales Bar in 1995. He became a partner in 1999.

3 Ross A. MacDonald was born in New Westminster, BC on July 20, 1957. He graduated from the University of British Columbia with an LLB in 1982 and was called to the British Columbia Bar the following year. He joined the Stikeman Elliott partnership in 1991 and has been the managing partner of the Vancouver office since 1999.

4 David E. Gillanders was born in Vancouver on June 19, 1938. He received a B.Com. in 1964 and an LLB in 1965 from the University of British Columbia. He was called to the British Columbia Bar in 1966 and the England and Wales Bar in 1994. He was the former coach of the Canadian Olympic pairs in rowing, which won the Olympic gold medal in 1964.

5 Jonathon Drance was born in Edinburgh, Scotland on January 27, 1954. He is a graduate of Harvard, where he received his BA magna cum laude. He then graduated with an LLB from the University of Toronto in 1978, where he was

the gold medallist. Between 1978 and 1983, he worked for McMillan Binch, and from 1983 to 1989, he was at Lawson Lundell in British Columbia. He joined Stikeman Elliott as a partner in 1989. He was called to the Ontario Bar in 1980 and the British Columbia Bar in 1984.

6 Richard Jackson was born in Peitnmotitchs, England on June 28, 1963. After receiving a BA from Harvard University in 1985, he attended the University of Victoria, were he obtained an LLB in 1988. While at Harvard, he was a three-time All-American/All Ivy League squash player. He joined the partnership in 1997.

7 David P. Farrell was born in Windsor, Ontario in 1968. He graduated from the University of British Columbia in 1991 with a B.Com. with honours in finance and an LLB in 1994. He was called to the BC Bar in 1995.

8 Hein Poulus, Q.C. was born in Jakarta, Indonesia on February 24, 1947. He graduated from the University of British Columbia with a BA in 1969 and an LLB in 1972. After obtaining his law degree, he attended the London School of Economics on a Commonwealth Scholarship, where he received an LLM. He was called to the British Columbia Bar in 1974 and joined the partnership in 1996.

9 Clifford S.M. Ng was born in Hong Kong in 1996. He obtained a BA from the University of British Columbia in 1988 and an LLB from Dalhousie University in 1991 before being called to the BC Bar in 1992.

10 John F. Anderson was born in Toronto on January 9, 1962. After graduating from Carleton University with a B.Com. (high honours) in 1987, he attended the University of British Columbia, where he received an LLB in 1990. He was a Wesbrook Scholar and the recipient of the Raymond Hebert Award. Following his studies, he spent three years as a naval officer. His call to the British Columbia Bar came in 1991, and he joined the partnership on January 1, 1999.

CHAPTER SEVEN

1 Thomas Gregory Kane, Q.C. was born on August 24, 1942 in Kingston, Ontario. After two years in arts at Queen's University, he was graduated from the University of Ottawa with an LLB in 1969. He worked in Ghana, West Africa under the auspices of CUSO before he was called to the Ontario Bar in 1973. In 1983, he joined the Stikeman Elliott partnership.

2 Donald Kubesh was born in Winnipeg on October 30, 1939. In 1961, he received a BA from the University of Manitoba, then an MA from the same institution in 1964. Between the years of 1964 and 1967, he attended the University of Toronto for his doctoral studies on a Canada Council Scholarship. He then attended McGill University, where he received a BCL in 1975 and an LLB in 1976. His call to the Ontario Bar was in 1978. He worked at the federal Department of Justice from 1978 to 1984, joined the firm in 1984, and became a partner in 1987.

3 McCormack had been successful in obtaining the first *Anton Pillar* order in Canada on behalf of his client, Sony Corporation, in the unreported decision of *Sony v. Makers International et al.* During the course of the proceedings, he had the rare privilege of explaining to some twenty irate lawyers and their clients what such an order meant.

4 Stuart C. McCormack was born on July 23, 1952 in Alderidge, England. In 1976, he received an Honours BA from York University. In 1977, he then attended the University of Windsor, where he obtained an LLB in 1980. He was called to the Ontario Bar in 1981, joined the firm in March 1987, and became a partner in 1991.

5 The names of the firms are their original names, and some have merged or have been disbanded.

6 Metal Bulletin Books Ltd., Surrey, England (1991).

7 Sir Adam Ridley was the leader of the banking group, and Michael Metcalfe and Kestenbaum were leaders of the brokers group involved in the disputes.

8 Mark E. Burton was born on November 4, 1963 in London, Ontario. He obtained an Honours B.Sc. in life sciences in 1986 and was graduated, with distinction, from the University of Western Ontario with an LLB in 1990. He was called to the New York Bar in 1990, where he practised with a major US law firm, and to the Ontario Bar in 1993. He practised with the Toronto office from 1991 until 1998, when he left to become president and CEO of Digital Processing Systems Inc., which was sold to one of its competitors. He then returned to the Toronto office, from which he transferred to Ottawa to start the corporate section of the office in the summer of 2001.

9 Lawson A.W. Hunter, Q.C. was born in Florenceville, New Brunswick on January 11, 1945. He received a B.Sc. in 1967 and an LLB in 1970 from the University of New Brunswick. He then attended Harvard in 1971, where he obtained an LLM. In 1971–72, he received a post-doctoral fellowship in marine policy and ocean management from Woods Hole Oceanographic Institution. He was called to the New Brunswick Bar in 1971 and the Ontario Bar in 1986. He became a partner at Stikeman Elliott in 1993.

10 He is the Hunter of the well-known case of *Hunter v. Southam* [1984] 2 S.C.R. 145.

11 Susan M. Hutton was born in Halifax, Nova Scotia on February 8, 1963. In 1985, she was graduated from McGill University with an Honours BA in economics and the gold medal for the faculty of arts, following which she worked in the research department of the Bank of Canada in Ottawa. She obtained her LLB (bronze medal) from the University of Toronto in 1991 after working for a year at Baker & McKenzie in Bangkok from 1989 to 1990. She was called to the Ontario Bar in 1993 and became a partner in 2001.

12 Randall Hofley was born on May 27, 1964 in Chapel Hill, North Carolina. After obtaining a BA in 1985 at the University of Winnipeg, he attended McGill University, where he received a BCL and a LLB in 1989. In 1991, he was called to the Ontario Bar and the following year, to the Quebec Bar. During 1991–92, he was a clerk at the Supreme Court of Canada for Madame Justice Beverly McLachlin. He joined the firm in 1995 and became a partner in 1998.

13 Mirko Bibic was born on July 19, 1967 in Montreal. In 1989, he graduated from McGill University with a B.Com. At McGill, he was the recipient of the Sir Edward Beatty gold medal in economics. In 1992, he obtained an LLB from the University of Toronto. He was called to Ontario Bar in 1994 and joined the Stikeman Elliott partnership on January 1, 2000.

14 Decision CRTC 2000–747 (December 7, 2000).

15 When the office opened in 1981, it had a telex address to "STIKEOTT." Kane recalls numerous notes in response to announcement cards wishing the firm well and hoping we would not "strikeout." It is reported that the Stikeouts lived up to their name in their first season.

CHAPTER EIGHT

1 Barry E. Emes was born in Sydney, Nova Scotia on September 12, 1945. He graduated from the University of Calgary with a BA in 1967. He then attended the University of British Columbia, where he graduated with an LLB as the gold medallist in 1973. His call to the Alberta Bar came in 1974, and he became a partner at Stikeman Elliott in 1992.

2 Glenn Cameron was born on September 24, 1948 in Brandon, Manitoba. In 1970, he graduated from the University of Calgary with a BA. He attended law school at the University of Alberta, where he received an LLB in 1971. He was called to the Alberta Bar in 1973 and became a partner at Stikeman Elliott in 1992.

3 *Black et al. v. Law Society of Alberta,* 27 D.L.R. 4th (Alberta Court of Appeal) March 2, 1986. Appeal to Supreme Court of Canada dismissed [1989] 4 W.W.R. 1, April 20, 1989.

4 G. Frederick Erickson was born in Calgary on March 25, 1960. In 1982, he received a B.Com. from the University of Calgary. He then travelled north to the University of Alberta in Edmonton, where he earned an MBA in 1986 and an LLB in 1987, graduating with distinction and as gold medallist. In 1988, he was called to the Alberta Bar and became a partner at Stikeman Elliott in 1995.

5 Duane Gillis was born in Drayton Valley, Alberta on May 18, 1963. He received a B.Com. in 1985 and an LLB in 1990 from the University of Alberta. In addition to winning numerous awards at the University of Alberta law school, he was awarded the George Bligh O'Conner silver medal in law. Duane spent two years in Stikeman Elliott's Budapest office and joined the partnership in 1998. He was called to the Alberta Bar in 1991.

6 James T. Bruvall was born in Thunder Bay, Ontario on November 28, 1961. He received a B.Sc. and then an LLB from the University of Alberta in 1988. He was called to the Alberta Bar in 1989 and became a partner at Stikeman Elliott in 1996.

7 David A. Holgate was born in Ottawa on August 8, 1952. After receiving a BA from St Mary's University in 1974, he attended Dalhousie University, from which he graduated with an LLB in 1977. He was called to Alberta Bar in 1978. He joined Stikeman Elliott in 1996 as a partner.

8 L. Greg Plater was born in Nanaimo, British Columbia on August 5, 1963. In 1985, he graduated from the University of British Columbia with a BA in economics. In 1988, he received an LLB from the University of Victoria. He was called to the British Columbia Bar in 1989 and the Alberta Bar in 1997. He joined the Stikeman Elliott partnership on January 1, 1998.

9 Stuart M. Olley was born on July 1, 1965 in Leeds, England. In 1987, he received a BA from the University of Toronto. In 1991, he obtained an MBA from the University of Alberta, followed by an LLB in 1992. He was called to the Alberta Bar in 1993. He joined the partnership on January 1, 1999.

10 David G. Weekes was born on December 17, 1955 in Toronto. He graduated from the University of Toronto in 1977 with a B.Sc., then obtained an LLB from the University of Western Ontario in 1982. While studying at Western, he received awards for the highest grades in income tax and estates and trusts. He was called to the Ontario Bar in 1984, the British Columbia Bar in 1990, and the Alberta Bar in 1998. He became a partner in 1990.

11 Kemm Yates, Q.C. was born in Edmonton, Alberta on February 19, 1950. In 1969, he completed a BA at McGill University. He then entered the University of Toronto law school and graduated with honours in 1973. Subsequently, he was called to the Alberta Bar in 1974 and began practising with the firm of Milner Fenerty. He joined Stikeman Elliott as a partner in March 1998.

12 Chris Nixon was born on July 14, 1956 in Kimberly, British Columbia. He received his LLB from the University of Alberta in 1979. He joined Stikeman Elliott as a partner in November 2000, and before that, he was a former partner at Osler, Hoskin & Harcourt.

13 Leland Corbett was born on September 5, 1968 in Calgary, Alberta. He received a B.SC. in mechanical engineering (with distinction) in 1990, an MBA in 1993, and an LLB in 1994, all from the University of Alberta. He articled with the firm in Calgary and was called to the Alberta Bar in 1995.

14 Other successful alumni of Pincher Creek are Chief Justice Beverley McLachlin of the Supreme Court of Canada (who has a painting by Robert McInnis of the Pitcher Creek area in her chambers) and Mr Justice Warren Winkler of the Ontario Superior Court of Justice, who used to "Tom Sawyer" Emes into helping him deliver his newspapers.

CHAPTER NINE

1 Jean-Pierre Ouellet was born in Montreal on January 17, 1948. He attended the Université de Montréal, where he received a BA in 1967 and an LLL in 1970. He then attended Oxford in 1971 on a Rhodes Scholarship, graduating in 1973. His call to the Quebec Bar came in 1971.

2 Martin Claude Lepage was born in Rimouski, Quebec on January 26, 1942. He attended the Collège Jean-de-Brébeuf and then the Université de Montréal, from which he obtained a BA in 1961 and an LLL in 1964. He was called to the Quebec Bar in 1965, joined the firm in that year, and became a partner in 1976. From 1969 to 1971, he took a sabbatical to attend the University of Western Ontario to get an MBA.

3 Peter R. O'Brien was born in Montreal on October 1, 1945. He attended Loyola High School, followed by Bishop's University, where he obtained a BA in 1967. Then he attended the Université Laval, where he earned an LLL in 1970. He was called to the Quebec Bar in 1971 and became a partner of the firm in 1980.

4 My contribution to our adoption of the new technology came from my background as a CA and some familiarity with cost accounting. I thought it might be helpful for the firm to have some ongoing idea of the approximate value of its work in progress. I suggested the idea of establishing minimum billing rates for the lawyers, which could be inserted in the program so that an approximate value could be estimated from time to time while recognizing that depending

on the circumstances of each case, the amount actually billed might vary. This has proved to be a useful management tool for the firm and is widely used by almost every sophisticated firm today. In some respects, it has become a bit of a Frankenstein, used by some clients to turn professional legal services into a commodity for comparison "shopping" among firms, with little critical assessment of special expertise.

5 Jill K. Hugessen was born in Montreal on October 27, 1960 and graduated from McGill University with a BA in 1981. She then continued at McGill, receiving her BCL and LLB in 1985. She was called to Quebec Bar in 1986.

6 François H. Ouimet was born in Montreal on January 5, 1955. He graduated with an LLL in 1976 from the Université Laval and an LLM from the University of Toronto in 1977. He was named a Canada Council Scholar in 1976. His call to the Quebec Bar was in 1978, and he became a partner in 1985.

7 Donald Francoeur was born in Montreal on December 29, 1950. After attending Glendale College, he obtained an AB from the University of California, Berkeley in 1975. He received his BCL from McGill University in 1978. His call to the Quebec Bar was in 1979, and he became a partner in 1990.

8 The 1993 revisions to the *Civil Code* were so extensive that in order to maintain their professional standing, all Quebec lawyers (excluding lawyers who were members of the Assemblée Nationale, who declared themselves sufficiently knowledgeable of its provisions since they had enacted the legislation!) were required to attend compulsory courses at which attendance was taken. Most lawyers attended with relatively good humour, but they paid little attention to the lectures. One of the more amusing sidebars was to see McGill professor Paul-André Crépeau – who had designed the revised code as a comprehensive, internally consistent code – attending the lectures after the legislators had got through tinkering with it. I remarked to him that he must feel somewhat like Janis Joplin's song "Look What They've Done to My Song, Ma." I used the time to complete a paper that I had promised to deliver at a Canadian Tax Foundation conference, and others had similar materials on which they worked. The firm was astute enough to note that this was probably the case and took the initiative of hiring experts to give courses in the principal areas of the new law, which were better attended and provided considerable added value to the formal Bar courses.

9 The Honourable Maurice Riel, P.C., Q.C. was born on April 3, 1922 in St Constant, Quebec. He attended the Collège de St-Jean, Collège Ste-Croix, and the Université de Montréal. There, he received a BA in 1940 and an LLB in 1944. He was called to the Quebec Bar in 1945. Before joining Stikeman Elliott in 1975, he practised with the firms of Riel LeDain Bissonnette & Vermette and Riel Bissonnette Vermette & Ryan. In 1973, Pierre Trudeau appointed him to the Senate of Canada. Riel was later named Speaker of the Senate, a role that he liked to describe as the Number One Member of Parliament. In 1997, he retired from both the Senate and the partnership.

10 This expression had been made famous in Voltaire's *Candide*, published in 1759.

11 Calin Rovinescu was born in Bucharest, Romania on September 15, 1955. He attended Sir Winston Churchill High School and then West Hill High School

and finished at McGill University in the last year before the CEGEP system became fully operational in Quebec. He got an undergraduate degree at McGill University in political science and started law there, but transferred to the Université de Montréal, from which he was graduated in 1978. He got a call to the Quebec Bar in 1979 and immediately went to the University of Ottawa for a common law degree, obtained in 1980. He wrote the Ontario transfer exams in 1983.

12 Frank J. Sixt was born in Montreal on November 29, 1951. He attended West Hill High School before obtaining a BA from McGill in 1972. He enrolled in law at the Université de Montréal, where he obtained an LLL in 1978, the same year that he earned an MA (in Middle English literature) from McGill. He was called to the Quebec Bar in 1979 and the Ontario Bar in 1980.

13 Pierre A. Raymond was born in Ottawa, Ontario on August 27, 1954. After receiving his LLL from the Université de Montréal in 1977, he attended the London School of Economics in 1979. He was called to the Quebec Bar in 1978.

14 R. Guy Masson was working at Bell Canada while going to law school, so he did not mix as much as the regular students.

15 Sixt had the distinction of going to Gordon to ask for more money, not something that was as important to the others as it was to him. He was of modest means, and his wife insisted that he do so because his work for the firm was costing the band some paying work that it would otherwise have earned.

16 Jimmy N. Wyatt had come to the firm from his native Texas and worked in the Montreal office until 1984, when he moved to Toronto, where he stayed until 1994 before moving on to private practice.

17 John W. Leopold was born in Montreal, Quebec on April 2, 1954. He obtained a BA from McGill University in 1976 and an LLL from the Université de Montréal in 1979. He was called to the Quebec Bar in 1980.

18 Elizabeth A. Skelton was born in Brisbane, Australia on June 2, 1946. After receiving a Diplome Supérieur d'Études Françaises at the Université de Paris (the Sorbonne) in 1966, she obtained her BCL in 1978 and her LLB in 1979 from McGill University. She received the William Jacob Prize for most improved student in 1978. Following her call to the Quebec Bar in 1980, she joined Stikeman Elliott, where she practised for sixteen years. She became a partner in 1986 and retired from practice in 1996.

19 Étienne Massicotte was born in Port-Cartier, Quebec on November 14, 1964. In 1987, he received an LLL from the Université de Montréal. He was called to the Quebec Bar in 1988 and became a partner at Stikeman Elliott in 1997.

20 William Braithwaite was born in Windsor, Ontario on June 11, 1952. He attended Vincent Massey Secondary School. He received a BA from the University of Windsor in 1972, where he won the Board of Governors Medal, then went on to the University of Western Ontario, earning an LLB in 1975 and the gold medal in law. He also obtained an LLM from the London School of Economics in 1976. He received various prizes, awards, and scholarships during his studies, including a Canada Council Grant. Braithwaite was clerk to Chief Justice Bora Laskin 1977–78, was called to the Ontario Bar in 1980, and became assistant, then associate, professor and assistant dean at the Osgoode Hall law school (1978–83). Having tenure there, he took a leave of absence to work at the firm

in 1983, extended it for a second year, and then cut his academic ties. He became a partner at Stikeman Elliott in 1985.

21 Jean-Marc Huot was born in Quebec City, Quebec on October 21, 1961. At Université Laval, he obtained a BA in 1983 and an LLB in 1986. His call to the Quebec Bar came in 1987.

22 Edward J. Waitzer was born in Norfolk, Virginia on January 24, 1954. He attended University of Toronto Schools (UTS) and SEED, then received both his LLB (1976) and his LLM in law and economics (1981) from the University of Toronto. Waitzer was called to the Ontario Bar in 1978 and to the New York Bar in 1985. He served as vice-president of the Toronto Stock Exchange from 1978 to 1981 before joining Stikeman Elliott. He became a partner in 1983. He left Stikeman Elliott in 1993 to become chairman of the Ontario Securities Commission and returned to the firm from that post in 1996. Waitzer was also an adjunct professor at Osgoode Hall 1990–93 and 1998–99.

23 John N. Stransman was born on June 5, 1952 in Toronto. He obtained a B.Com. from the University of Toronto in 1974, followed by his LLB from the same institution in 1977. He then attended Harvard University, earning an LLM in 1978. He was called to the Ontario Bar in 1980 and the Bar of New York in 1981. After joining the firm as an associate in October 1981, he became a partner in 1984.

24 Michael Allen was born in Toronto on October 4, 1951. He attended Burnhamthorpe Collegiate before attending Victoria College at the University of Toronto, where he studied commerce and finance for two years and then law, where he earned his LLB in 1974. Allen was called to the Ontario Bar in 1976 and worked for Borden Elliot until 1979. He joined the firm in 1979, becoming a partner in 1982. He remained with the firm in Vancouver until 1999, then joined Fasken, Martineau DuMoulin. He returned to the firm in 2001.

25 Life insurance companies, the largest of the institutional investors, were permitted to invest only in the fully paid common shares of a company that paid, or had earnings available to pay, a dividend over a specified period of years.

26 André Roy was born in Sherbrooke, Quebec on January 19, 1955. Before being called to the Quebec Bar in 1981, he obtained a management degree from McGill University in 1977 and a BCL from the Université de Montréal in 1980. He became a partner in 1988.

27 Donna Kaufman was born in Toronto on November 23, 1943. After graduating from Westdale Secondary School in Hamilton, Ontario, she attended McGill University in Montreal, where she obtained a BCL in 1984. In 1985, she completed her LLM from the Université de Montréal. Called to the Quebec Bar in 1985, she was admitted to the partnership in 1989. Subsequently, she was called to the Ontario Bar in 1997.

28 Jim Grant recalls a similar tactic used by Baillie in the Air Canada-Onex matter years later.

29 James M. Farley was appointed to the Ontario bench on October 4, 1989, and he has developed a considerable reputation in very complicated corporate restructurings and related litigation.

30 David Weekes was born in Toronto on December 17, 1955. He received a B.Sc. from the University of Toronto in 1977 and his LLB from the University of Western

Ontario in 1982. Weekes began his legal career at Stikeman Elliott as an articling student in 1982. He was called to the Bar of Ontario in 1984, the BC Bar in 1990, and the Alberta Bar in 1998. From 1982 to 1989, Weekes practised in the Toronto office. Between 1989 and 1994, he was in the Vancouver office, and 1994–97, he was back in Toronto. From 1997 to the present, he has been in the Calgary office. Weekes became a partner at Stikeman Elliott in 1990.

31 Alison J. Youngman was born on May 23, 1948 in London, England. She attended Sir George Williams (now Concordia) University and the University of Toronto for arts. She began working at Stikeman Elliott in 1972 as a law clerk and left this post to attend Osgoode Hall, attaining her LLB in 1984. Youngman was called to the Ontario Bar in 1986 and became a member of the Bar of England and Wales in 1994. She became a partner at Stikeman Elliott in 1992 and received her LLM from Osgoode in 1999.

32 Edward B. Claxton was born in Montreal on September 2, 1956. He received a BA from McGill University in 1979 and a BCL in 1982. He completed his university studies at Dalhousie in 1983, when he obtained an LLB. He was called to the Quebec and Ontario Bars in 1985 and became a partner in 1992.

33 Rob Nicholls was born in Toronto on November 29, 1961. He graduated from the University of Toronto with a BA in 1983 and an LLB in 1986. He achieved the highest standing in a three-year arts program during his undergraduate studies, won the Toronto Stock Exchange Prize for corporate finance, and was on the dean's list at law school for his first and third years. Nicholls was called to the Ontario Bar in 1988 and became a partner of the firm in 1994.

34 Harry Bruce, *The Pig that Flew: The Battle to Privatize Canadian National.* Vancouver: Douglas & McIntyre, 1997.

35 Simon Romano was born on December 4, 1959 in Sutton Coldfield, England. He attended Pierrefonds Comprehensive High School and Marianopolis College (CEGEP) in Montreal. He received an Honours B.Sc. in physics from McGill University (1981), working thereafter in Halifax as a weather forecaster prior to enrolling in law school, where he obtained an LLB from the University of Toronto (1987). Romano received the following awards during his studies: Fasken & Calvin Prize (corporate income iax); dean's list (U of T) 1986–87, J.S.D. Tory Legal Writing Fellowship; Natural Sciences and Engineering Research Council of Canada (NSERC) post-graduate award ($12,000); Faculty and University Scholar (McGill), 1978–81; and J.W. McConnell Entrance Award (McGill). He was called to the Bar of Ontario in 1989. He worked for the Ontario Securities Commission – special counsel (secondment) from January 1995 to July 1996, and at the Supreme Court of Canada as a law clerk. He was the first of the third clerks now assigned to the judges of the court to Mr Justice John Sopinka (October 1988 to April 1989). Romano became a partner at Stikeman Elliott in 1994.

CHAPTER TEN

1 Mortimer G. Freiheit was born in Montreal on December 23, 1942. Following his graduation from McGill University in 1963 with an Honours BA in philosophy and an LLL from the Université de Montréal faculty of law in 1966, he was called to the Quebec Bar in 1967 and the Ontario Bar in 1978.

2 Stephen W. Hamilton was born on April 5, 1961 in Montreal. In 1985, he graduated as a gold medallist from McGill University with a BCL and an LLB. The following year, he attended the University of Oxford to complete an LLM. In 1986–87, he completed a Supreme Court clerkship. He was called to the Quebec Bar in 1986 and the Ontario Bar in 1988.

3 Gérald R. Tremblay was born in Jonquière, Quebec on February 5, 1944. He obtained a BA from the Université Laval in 1964 and an LLL in 1967 from Ottawa University and was called to the Quebec Bar in 1968. Tremblay and Yves Bériault, another former litigation lawyer in the firm, were the first two law clerks assigned to the judges of the Supreme Court of Canada, and each of them worked for several judges during their period with the court, although not all of the judges were even willing to use clerks, especially Justice Louis-Philippe Pigeon, who held firmly to the view that judges should do their own work.

4 Louis P. Bélanger was born on February 19, 1953 in Montreal. He was educated at the Collège Jean-de-Brébeuf, obtained his LLL from the Université de Montréal in 1976, graduating magna cum laude, and was called to the Quebec Bar in 1977.

5 Quebec Superior Court, District of Montreal, No. 500-05-008556-803 (September 15, 1981).

6 Quebec Superior Court, District of Montreal, No. 500-05-003814-827 (May 20, 1982).

7 *Pizzoli v. Pizzoli,* Quebec Superior Court, District of Montreal, No. 500-05-020760-821.

8 *Aur Resources Inc. v. La Société Minière Louvem Inc.* [1990] R.J.Q. 767.

9 *CIBC v. Chayer* [1984] T.A. 300; [1986] 2 F.C. 431 (FCA); application for leave to appeal to the Supreme Court of Canada denied October 1, 1986.

10 *George S. Petty v. Robert C. Miller and The City of Westmount,* Quebec Superior Court, District of Montreal, No. 500-05-012580-880 (May 16, 1989); Court of Appeal, District of Montreal, No. 500-09-000677-890 (August 4, 1999).

11 *CEGIR Inc. v. Banque Algérienne de Développement et al.,* Quebec Superior Court, District of Montreal, No. 500-05-002950-895 (May 19, 1989).

12 Reported as *Armstrong Acquisition Canada Inc. (Armstrong World Industries) v. Domco Inc.,* Quebec Securities Commission Decision No. 1998-C-0448, in *Bulletin Hebdomadaire:* 1998-12-25, Vol. XXIX, No. 50, p. 4.

13 Quebec Superior Court, District of Montreal, No. 500-05-052906-995.

14 Gérald Tremblay, a former partner of the firm, was on the other side.

15 Michel Décary was born in Montreal on January 10, 1945. He obtained a BA in 1964 and an LLL in 1967 from the Université de Montréal and was called to the Quebec Bar in 1968. He became a partner of the firm in 1981.

16 Richard J. Rusk was born in Ottawa on October 4, 1952. He obtained his BA from the Universities of Waterloo and Guelph in 1979 and in 1982, an LLB from McGill University, followed by a BCL in 1983. He did further studies at the London School of Economics. He was called to the Ontario and Quebec Bars in 1985.

17 Suzanne Côté was born in Gaspé, Quebec on September 21, 1958. She received her LLB in 1980 from the Université Laval. After being called to the Quebec Bar in 1981, she worked in private practice in Gaspé until 1988, when she joined Stikeman Elliott. She became a partner in 1991.

18 Stephen M. Raicek was born in Montreal on July 5, 1956. He received a BCL and LLB from McGill University in 1980. In 1981, he obtained a master of law degree from Columbia University. His call for the Quebec and New York Bars came in 1982.

19 Marc-André Coulombe was born in Montreal on September 8, 1969. He attended the Université de Montréal and the Osgoode Hall law school, obtaining an LLL in 1991. He was called to the Quebec Bar in 1993.

20 Marc Laurin was born in Montreal on February 23, 1953. He received an LLL from the Université de Sherbrooke in 1978. After his call to the Quebec Bar in 1979, he worked as in-house counsel for Canadian Pacific until 1983, when he joined Stikeman Elliott and became a partner in 1988.

21 Monique Lussier was born on May 4, 1957 in Montreal. In 1981, she received an LLL from the Université de Montréal. She was called to the Quebec Bar in 1982 and joined the firm the same year. She became a partner in November 1990.

22 Jean Fontaine was born on June 4, 1966 in Montreal. He obtained an LLL from the Université de Montréal in 1988 and was called to the Quebec Bar in 1989.

23 Yves Martineau was born in Quebec City on September 1, 1965. He obtained a BA in psychology from the Université Laval in 1987 and an LLL from the same institution in 1990. He was called to the Quebec Bar in 1992.

24 John A.M. Judge was born in Toronto on March 26, 1952. He was educated at R.H. King Collegiate Institute in Scarborough, then obtained a BA from University College, University of Toronto in 1972 and an LLB, also from the University of Toronto, in 1975 prior to a call to the Ontario Bar in 1977. He articled with Fasken & Calvin and worked at Carson Poultney before coming to the firm on November 1, 1978. He became a partner in 1983.

25 I enjoyed a period of popularity with the Toronto juniors when it became known that I had played a great deal of tournament squash and was able to handle the extremely competitive Sopinka with relative ease. When we had partners meetings in Toronto, I would bring my equipment, and we would retire as soon as decently possible (sometimes sooner) to the University Club, where Sopinka was a member, to have our regular game. I would tell the Toronto juniors that I would "bagel" (beat him 9–0) Sopinka in one of our games just to let him know that there was one court in which he was not king. It used to drive Sopinka crazy when I would tell him that he could pick the bagel game because there would certainly be one, and he could get it over with whenever he wanted.

26 Bruce Pollock was born in Toronto on May 7, 1953. He attended Lawrence Park Collegiate Institute and graduated from Queen's University in 1975 with a B.Com. with honours. He received the D.I. McLeod Scholarship at Queen's School of Business in 1971 and 1973, and he obtained his LLB from the University of Toronto in 1978. Pollock was called to the Ontario Bar in 1980 and began his career with Stikeman Elliott shortly thereafter. He became a partner in 1985.

27 David Brown was born on July 8, 1954, obtained a BA (laws) from the University of Toronto in 1976, followed by certificates from the Beijing Languages Institute (1977) and Nanking University (1978). He then returned to the University of Toronto to earn a JD in 1981 and was called to the Ontario Bar in 1983.

28 Patrick O'Kelly was born on May 23, 1959 in Toronto. After two years of undergraduate study at St Michael's College, University of Toronto, he enrolled in

law and obtained his LLB in 1982. He was called to the Ontario Bar in 1984 and became a partner of the firm in 1990.

29 Sean Dunphy was born on June 28, 1959 in New York and was raised in Toronto. He did his first year of law at the University of Paris from 1979 to 1980, then attended University of Toronto for his BA (1982) and LLB (1983), where he was on the dean's list that year. Dunphy was called to the Ontario Bar in 1985 and the BC Bar in 1992. He became a partner at Stikeman Elliott in 1991.

30 Douglas Harrison was born in Hamilton, Ontario on August 17, 1960. He attended Hillfield-Strathallan College in Hamilton, Queen's University (BA, political science, 1982), and the University of Toronto (LLB, 1985). He worked for the *Globe and Mail* from 1982 to 1985 and was called to the Ontario Bar in 1988. He became a partner of the firm in 1995.

31 David R. Byers was born in Sarnia, Ontario on May 17, 1955. He obtained an Honours BA in psychology from the University of Western Ontario in 1978 and an LLB from the Osgoode Hall law school in 1981. He was called to the Ontario Bar in 1983 and joined the firm in late 1987. He is often referred to as "Billy" Byers, which stems from his introduction, as the newest member of the department, to the other members of the department by John Sopinka, toward the end of a lengthy cocktail party and dinner, "my good friend Billy Byers."

32 Katherine Kay was born in Weyburn, Saskatchewan on February 25, 1963. She attended West Island College High School in Montreal, graduating in 1979, and then went to Carleton University, where she obtained a BA with distinction in 1983. She obtained an LLB from the Osgoode Hall law school in 1986. She was called to the Ontario Bar in 1988, joined the firm that year, and became a partner in 1994.

33 Liz Pillon was born in Toronto on February 9, 1969. After two years of undergraduate study in accounting at the University of Waterloo, she went to the University of Western Ontario to obtain her LLB in 1992. She was called to the Ontario Bar in 1994. She joined the firm as a summer student in 1991, became an associate upon her call to the Bar, and became a partner in 2001.

34 Eliot Kolers was born in Red Bank, New Jersey on July 4, 1970. He obtained a BA in 1991 and an LLB in 1994 from the University of Toronto. He was called to the Ontario Bar in 1996 and became a partner in 2002.

35 Cited as *Canadian Dredge & Dock Company, Limited et al. v. The Queen* [1985] 1 S.C.R. 662. The companies had been charged with conspiracy to defraud, where bids to certain public authorities had allegedly been tendered on a collusive basis such that the low bidders for the contracts included compensation in their bids for the high bidders and non-bidders. The companies had sought to escape criminal liability for the actions of the employees involved, generally on the basis that they were not acting on behalf of the companies (but themselves) and also on the basis that there could be no corporate liability for offence that involved *mens rea*. Their defences were unsuccessful.

36 Brown had actually had some personal contact with Nelles prior to his professional involvement in her cases. While at law school, one of his friends, Alison Woodbury, had roomed with Nelles. He remembers going with his wife to a party one fall evening at Woodbury's home, where they had a long conversation with Nelles about the goings-on on the cardiac ward. There had been some

deaths of patients that troubled the staff, and Nelles thought the coroner might become involved. Several months later, as Brown was walking along Bloor Street on his way to class at law school, he was stunned to see the front page of the *Toronto Sun* bearing a graduation picture of Nelles under the headline of "Baby Killer." She had been arrested the day before. One of the suspicious elements that had prompted the police to formally arrest her was that when they went to her house to question her, she had in her pocket the name of a lawyer who specialized in coroner matters. Woodbury had given her the name of the lawyer. As later testimony before the Grange inquiry would reveal, the fact that she had a name of a lawyer in her pocket solidified her guilt in the minds of the two police officers.

37 *Susan Nelles v. The Queen in Right of Ontario et al.* [1989] 2 S.C.R. 170.

38 The transcript of the examination, including the questions posed to Nelles, are included in appendix 4 of the second edition of Sopinka and Lederman's text, *The Trial of an Action.* Toronto and Vancouver: Butterworths, 1988.

39 Sarah Spinks, *Cardiac Arrest.* Toronto: Doubleday, 1985.

40 See also *Canadian Football League v. Canadian Human Rights Commission* [1980] 2 F.C.R. 329 (FCTD).

41 *Ontario Human Rights Commission v. Liquor Control Board of Ontario* [1988] 19 C.C.E.L. 172.

42 Cited as *Ontario Human Rights Commission v. Simpsons-Sears* [1985] 2 S.C.R. 356.

43 *Joseph Pope et al. v. Canadian Pacific Limited et al.* [1987] 1 S.C.R. 952.

44 [1979] 26 O.R. (2d) 434; [1980] 30 O.R. (2d) 768 (CA).

45 For another account of the matter, see: Charles Pullen, *The Life and Times of Arthur Maloney: The Last of the Tribunes.* Toronto: Dundurn Press, 1994, chapter 13.

46 *Irvine v. Canada (Restrictive Trade Practices Commission)* [1987] 1 S.C.R. 181.

47 *Re An Act to Amend the Education Act* [1987] 1 S.C.R. 1148.

48 *Pettkus v. Becker* [1980] 2 S.C.R. 834.

49 *Seaway Trust Company and Greymac Trust Company v. Kilderkin Investments Limited, William Player, Leonard Rosenberg and Andrew Markle,* Superior Court of Ontario, Action No. 2004/83. The civil proceedings, including the Kilderkin receivership on which the firm acted, were focused on fraud investigations and tracing of assets in sophisticated real estate transactions. Before any civil trial and after years of fighting, the defendants were charged criminally and pleaded guilty. For a more thorough description, see Terence Corcoran and Laura Reid, *Public Money, Private Greed: The Greymac, Seaway and Crown Trust Affair.* Toronto: Collins, 1984.

50 Peter Hamilton was born in Montreal (St Lambert) on March 6, 1958. He attended Loyola High School and Champlain CEGEP (St Lambert). He was enrolled in the McGill faculty of law from 1976 to 1980 and in Wadham College, Oxford from 1980 to 1982. He attained the Elizabeth Torrance gold medal at McGill and first-class honours at Oxford, as well as numerous course prizes and awards. Hamilton was called to the Ontario Bar in 1984, worked for Fasken & Calvin (articling 1982–83), and Tilley, Carson & Findlay (1984–87). He joined Stikeman Elliott in 1987 and became a partner in 1990.

51 *General Motors of Canada Limited v. City National Leasing* [1989] 1 S.C.R. 641.

52 *Adler v. Attorney General for Ontario* [1996] 3 S.C.R. 609.

53 *R. v. Latimer* [2001] s.c.r. 3.

54 *Winnipeg Child and Family Services v. G. (D.F.)* [1997] 3 s.c.r. 925.

55 *Dobson v. Dobson* [1999] 2 s.c.r. 753.

56 *M. v. H.* [1999] 2 s.c.r. 3.

57 *Rosenberg v. Attorney General for Canada* [1998] 38 o.r. (3rd) 577 (ca).

58 *Trinity Western University v. British Columbia College of Teachers* [2001] 1 s.c.r. 772.

59 Anne Ristic was born in Toronto on November 25, 1961. She attended the University of British Columbia for two years, then the University of Toronto, where she received her llb in 1984, winning a prize for real estate law. Ristic began as a summer student in 1984, was called to the Ontario Bar in 1986, joined the firm, and became partner in 1995.

CHAPTER ELEVEN

1 Robert Couzin was born in Chicago on November 24, 1945. He obtained an ab in philosophy from the University of Chicago in 1967, an am in philosophy from the same institution the following year, and a bcl from McGill University in 1972 (winning the gold medal). He was called to the Quebec Bar in 1974, followed by the Ontario Bar in 1977. He left the firm in 1997 to join Ernst & Young.

2 David N. Finkelstein was born in Montreal on December 15, 1946. He attended Mount Royal High School, then McGill for a ba in 1967 and an ma in 1969. He received his lll from the Université de Montréal. He is the current editor-in-chief of the *Canada Tax Service* and has been a lecturer at the McGill faculty of law and a member of the Joint Committee on Taxation of the Canadian Bar Association and Canadian Institute of Chartered Accountants. He began with Stikeman Elliott in August 1971 as a summer student, became a partner on February 1, 1978, and transferred to the Toronto office in March 1979.

3 Elinore Jean Richardson was born in Hamilton, Ontario on November 27, 1945. She obtained an Honours ba from McMaster University in 1967 and an llb from the University of Toronto in 1970. She was called to the Ontario Bar in 1972, the Quebec Bar in 1977, the Bar of England and Wales in 1990, and to the New York Bar in 1992.

4 Martin H. Scheim was born in Montreal on February 21, 1950. Following early education, he obtained a B.Sc. (with distinction) from McGill University in 1971, a bcl in 1974, and an llb in 1975, winning several academic prizes in the process. He was called to the Quebec Bar in 1976.

5 Pierre Archambault was born in Drummondville, Quebec on May 22, 1949. He graduated with a ba from the Université de Sherbrooke in 1969. He continued his studies at uqam and finished in 1972. He was the recipient of the William Jacob Prize in 1975. After being called to the Quebec Bar in 1976, he joined Stikeman Elliott in 1978. He joined the partnership in 1983.

6 R. Guy Masson was born in Montreal on March 20, 1949. He attended the Collège Militaire Royal in St Jean, Quebec for studies in engineering, then studied philosophy and administration at the Collège du Vieux Montréal, the Collège Edouard Montpetit, and Concordia University between 1969 and 1975. He then

enrolled in law at the Université de Ottawa for two years and finished at the Université de Montréal in 1978 before being called to the Quebec Bar in 1979. During the period 1969–79, he was employed in various functions by Bell Canada. He joined the partnership in 1985 and is a former president of the Association de planification fiscale et financière.

7 Paul J. Setlakwe was born on July 2, 1953 in Sherbrooke, Quebec. He obtained a BCL from the Université Laval in Quebec City and a master's degree in tax from the Université de Sherbrooke. He is a member of the Quebec Bar (1981) and Ontario Bar (1985).

8 J. Robert Raizenne was born in Montreal on January 6, 1955. He obtained a BA in economics from Concordia University in 1976, an MA in economics from the University of Toronto in 1977, and a BCL from McGill University in 1980. He was called to the Quebec Bar in 1981 and the Ontario Bar in 1997.

9 *Ludco Enterprises v. The Queen* [2001] 3 C.T.C. 95.

10 Robert J. Hogan was born in Montreal, Quebec on July 7, 1958. He attended the Université de Sherbrooke, where he obtained an LLL in 1982 and an LLM in 1985. He was called to the Quebec Bar in 1985.

11 Frédéric Harvey was born in Alma, Quebec on May 5, 1964. After completing his studies at the CEGEP in Alma, he obtained his LLL from the Université de Montréal in 1986, was called to the Quebec Bar in 1989, and became a partner of the firm in 1998.

12 Roanne Bratz was born in Montreal on April 22, 1953. She obtained a BA in political science from McGill University and a BCL in 1978, followed by a JD from Nova University in Ft Lauderdale, Florida in 1979. She was called to the Florida Bar in 1980 and the Quebec Bar in 1982. Bratz joined the firm in November 2000 after several years with accounting firms and the Royal Bank of Canada.

13 Pierre Martel was born in Quebec City on May 1, 1958. In 1983, he graduated from the Université Laval, where he received a B.Sc. in geological engineering. He then pursued graduate studies in geological engineering at the University of Manitoba, graduating in 1985. He then entered the University of Ottawa, where he finished second in his class and was on the dean's list. In 1989, he completed his legal studies and joined Stikeman Elliott in the same year. He joined the partnership on January 1, 1998.

14 [1979] C.T.C. 424.

15 Thomas Vowinckel was born in Abensberg, Germany on October 2, 1947. He graduated from McGill University with a B.Sc. in 1970, a Ph.D. in 1976, and an LLB in 1980. He was called to the Ontario Bar in 1981, and he has worked in the income tax area at Stikeman Elliott since that time. He became partner in 1986. He is co-author of *Canadian Tax Reform* and contributor to the *Canada Tax Service*.

16 Gary Nachshen was born in Montreal on December 8, 1959. He attended Wagar High School (1977); Marianopolis College, DEC (1979); Princeton University, BA (1982); and McGill University, BCL, LLB (1987). Nachshen was on the dean's list and honour roll at Marianopolis, graduated magna cum laude from Princeton, and received the Wainwright Scholarship, James McGill Entrance Award at McGill, where he graduated with second-class honours. He was called to the Quebec Bar in 1988 and the Ontario Bar in 1997. He worked for Lee and Li

in Taipei, Taiwan from 1982 to 1983 as an English proofreader. He joined the partnership at Stikeman Elliott in 1996.

17 Angelo Nikolakakis was born in Montreal on April 6, 1967. He attended three high schools (Outremont, Western Laval, and Chomedey) before attending Dawson College. He received a BA from McGill in political science in 1989, where he was awarded the Students' Society of McGill University Public Eye Award for political action that same year. He began the study of law at the University of Manitoba, completing his first year with a number of awards: dean's honour list; Lieutenant M.M. Soronow Prize (highest standing in LLB I); Carswell Book Prize (highest standing); Oscar Wilder Memorial Prize (constitutional law); and H.I. Corne Prize (contract law). Nikolakakis then attended McGill to complete the national program of LLB/BCL in 1993 and was awarded the following; upper second-class honours; Phillip F. Vineberg Award (taxation and corporate law); dean's honour list; H. Heward Stikeman Scholarship in taxation; Bereskin & Parr Prize in intellectual and industrial property; faculty scholar; James McGill Award; Robins, Appleby, and Taub Prize (highest standing in LLB II); Stikeman, Elliott Prize (taxation and corporate law); and Allan Neil Assh Memorial Award (business associations). He was called to the Quebec Bar in 1994, the New York Bar in 1997, and the Ontario Bar in 1998. He became a partner in 2001 but left to join Davies Ward Phillips Vineberg in February 2002.

18 John Lorito was born in St Catharines, Ontario on August 14, 1961. He graduated from Denis Morris High School, UWO (economics: 1980–82), and University of Toronto (LLB 1985). He received the Fasken & Calvin Prize in corporate taxation and the Russell Baker Prize in international taxation. Lorito was called to the Ontario Bar in 1987. He worked at Fasken Campbell Godfrey from 1985 to 1998 and joined the firm as a partner in 1998.

19 Joanne Swystun was born in Winnipeg, Manitoba on February 24, 1954. She graduated from Silver Heights Collegiate Institute (1971) and attended the University of Manitoba (BA, 1974) and the Royal Conservatory of Toronto, where she received the ARCT in 1974. She received her LLB from Osgoode (1977) and her chartered financial planner designation in 1985. She was on the dean's honour list at the University of Manitoba and won a prize for biology. Swystun was called to the Bar of Ontario in 1979. She was with the Department of Justice for her articling year and as a first-year associate (1979–80), and with Goodman & Carr in Toronto (1980–97). She became a partner at Goodman & Carr in 1986 and joined Stikeman Elliott in January 1998 as a partner.

20 David W. Glicksman was born in Toronto on August 13, 1955. He graduated from Vaughn Road Collegiate Institute and received a B.Com. from the University of Toronto in 1977 and his LLB from the Queen's law school in 1980. Glicksman received the McCarthy Income Tax Prize in the Bar admissions course (1981–82). He was called to the Bar of Ontario in 1982 and worked for Goodman & Carr and Touche Ross (now Deloitte & Touche) before joining Stikeman Elliott as a partner in 1998.

21 Lianne Miller was born in Winnipeg on February 19, 1954. She attended the University of Manitoba for a B.Sc. (1975) as well as for her LLB (1979). During her studies, Miller attained the gold medal in science for highest standing in her graduating class (1975), the Law Society of Manitoba Prize for fourth-highest

standing in her graduating class (1979), and the Canada Law Book Prize in taxation (1979). Miller was called to the Bar of Manitoba in 1980, the Alberta Bar in 1981, and the Ontario Bar in 1987. She worked with Bennett Jones in Calgary as well as with the rulings division, Revenue Canada, under the executive exchange program, before joining Stikeman Elliott in June 1987. Miller became a partner in 1989.

22 The firm is unique in Canada for its contribution to the specialized tax judiciary of the Tax Court of Canada. In addition to Bowman, Bonner, and Archambault, both Lucie Lamarre and Pierre Dussault worked at the firm. Lamarre was a lawyer in the tax section, and Dussault articled with the firm before going into the academic world at the Université de Sherbrooke.

23 *Asamera Oil (Indonesia) Ltd. v. The Queen* [1973] C.T.C. 305 (FCTD).

24 *Johns-Manville Canada Inc. v. The Queen* [1985] 2 C.T.C. III (SCC).

25 *Elgin Cooper Realties Ltd. v. M.N.R.* [1969] C.T.C. 426 (Ex. Ct.).

26 *Bendix Automotive of Canada Ltd. v. The Queen* [1974] C.T.C. 2080 (TRB); [1975] C.T.C. 464 (FCTD).

27 *Quasar Investments Ltd. v. M.N.R.* [1972] C.T.C. 2666 (TRB).

28 *The D'Auteuil Lumber Co. Ltd. v. M.N.R.* [1970] C.T.C. 122 (Ex. Ct.).

29 *La Cie. Immobilière BCN Ltée v. The Queen* [1975] C.T.C. 316 (FCTD); [1976] C.T.C. 282 (FCA).

30 *Teleglobe Canada Inc. v. The Queen,* [2000] 4 C.T.C. 2448 (TCC).

31 *The Elias Rogers Co. Ltd. v. M.N.R.* [1972] C.T.C. 253 (FCTD); [1972] C.T.C. 601 (FCA).

32 Richard W. Pound, *Chief Justice W.R. Jackett: By the Law of the Land.* Montreal: McGill-Queen's University Press, 1999.

33 *Longueuil Meat Exporting Co. Ltd. v. The Queen* [1973] C.T.C. 386 (FCTD); [1974] C.T.C. 486 (FCA); [1976] C.T.C. 193 (SCC).

34 *Algoma Central Railway v. M.N.R.* [1968] C.T.C. 161.

35 *Canada Starch Co. Ltd. v. M.N.R.* [1968] C.T.C. 466.

36 *John McAdam v. M.N.R.* [1973] C.T.C. 215 (FCTD).

37 *E.R. Squibb & Sons Ltd. v. M.N.R.* [1973] C.T.C. 120 (FCTD).

38 *Lois Hollinger v. M.N.R.* [1972] C.T.C. 592 (FCTD).

39 *Dominion Bridge Company Limited v. The Queen* [1975] C.T.C. 263 (FCTD).

40 *GTE Sylvania Canada Ltd. v. The Queen* [1974] C.T.C. 408 (FCTD); [1974] C.T.C. 751 (FCA).

41 *Quebec North Shore Paper Co. v. The Queen* [1978] C.T.C. 628 (FCTD).

42 *Saskatchewan Wheat Pool v. The Queen* [1983] C.T.C. 248 (FCTD); [1985] 1 C.T.C. 31 (FCA).

43 *Cargill Limited v. The Queen* [1996] 2 C.T.C. 2102 (TCC); [1998] 2 C.T.C. 192 (FCA).

44 *Cargill Limited v. The Queen* [1996] 3 C.T.C. 2023 (TCC).

45 *Bunge of Canada Ltd. v. The Queen* [1982] C.T.C. 313 (FCTD); [1984] C.T.C. 284 (FCA).

46 *Marsh & McLennan Ltd. v. The Queen* [1981] C.T.C. 410 (FCTD); [1983] C.T.C. 231 (FCA).

47 *Manufacturer's Life Insurance Co. v. The Queen* [2001] C.T.C. 2481 (TCC).

48 *Sandra Gernhart v. The Queen* [1996] 3 C.T.C. 2369 (TCC); [1998] 2 C.T.C. 102 (FCA).

49 Leave to appeal to the Supreme Court of Canada refused, [1998] 2 S.C.R. viii, July 2, 1998.

50 *Sandra Gernhart v. The Queen* [1997] 2 C.T.C. 23 (FCTD).

51 *Sandra Gernhart v. The Queen* [2000] 1 C.T.C. 192 (FCA).

52 *Minet Inc. v. The Queen* [1996] 3 C.T.C. 2018 (TCC).

53 *Minet Inc. v. The Queen* [1998] 3 C.T.C. 352 (FCA).

54 *Harrowston Corp. v. The Queen* [1993] 2 C.T.C. 2247 (TCC); [1997] 1 C.T.C. 101 (FCA).

55 *Hasbro Canada Inc. v. The Queen* [1999] 1 C.T.C. 2512 (TCC).

56 *The Queen v. Mattel Canada Inc., Reebok Canada Inc., Intervena,* [2001] 199 DLR (4th) 598.

CHAPTER TWELVE

1 The initial contact with Furness, Withy, which goes back to the very beginnings of the firm, has continued to the present day. It has survived the metamorphosis of the original UK company into part of the Hong Kong-based OOCL Group, of which the former chairman, C.Y. Tung, is now Hong Kong's chief executive. Vincent Prager has been the sole director of the Canadian portion of the OOCL empire for more than a decade.

2 [1974], 6 NR 578; see also [1978] 1 S.C.R. 907.

3 Vincent Mark Prager was born on May 4, 1944 at Gerrards Cross, Buckinghamshire, England. Following the war, he accompanied his parents to Canada and was educated at St George's School, Selwyn House School, and Trinity College School before going to McGill University for a BA with honours in history and political science in 1964 and a BCL in 1967. He worked part-time at the firm in early 1967 before articling at Cate Ogilvy (now Ogilvy Renault), and he later joined the firm in 1968 after his call to the Quebec Bar in 1968.

4 Marc De Man was born in Antwerp, Belgium on November 4, 1946, and received early schooling at Belgrano Day School in Buenos Aires. Following his family to Montreal in 1958, he went to St Leo's Academy, then studied music at the Congrégation de Notre Dame and philosophy at McGill University, where he obtained a BA in 1968. He obtained a licence in diplomatic and political science from Brussels Free University in 1969 and a BCL from McGill in 1972, and he was called to the Quebec Bar the following year.

5 Peter J. Cullen was born in Montreal on August 2, 1953. He attended Upper Canada College and Lower Canada College. After receiving a BA (psychology) from the University of New Brunswick in 1975, he obtained law degrees (BCL and LLB) from McGill University in 1979 and 1980. His interest in maritime law stemmed from his shipping background, his experiences as a teenage supernumerary cadet on merchant cargo ships, and sailing to the United Kingdom, Europe, and North Africa. He also had summer jobs as a stevedore in the ports of Quebec and Saint John, NB and with a tug company in the Port of Montreal. He joined the firm in 1975 and was called to the Quebec Bar in 1981 and the Ontario Bar in 1990.

6 Laurent Fortier was born in Montreal on June 26, 1954, did his secondary schooling at the CEGEP St-Laurent, and obtained a BAA at the École des Hautes

Études Commerciales in 1974, followed by an LLL in 1977 from the Université de Montréal and a call to the Quebec Bar in 1978.

7 The firm had first been retained on the matter by the insurers of the tug, but there turned out to be no coverage under the P&I policy, so it could not take steps on behalf of the insurers to release the tug. However, the firm was able to gather information from the captain and crew of the tug that ultimately led to obtaining the mandate for the barge's owners and insurers.

8 *CSL Group Inc. et al. v. Canada* [1997] 124 F.T.R. 1.

9 *A/S Ornen v. Ship Duteous et al.* [1986] 4 F.T.R. 122.

10 *Century Insurance v. Hasselt* [1987] 1 S.C.R. 1247.

11 *Engine and Leasing Co. v. Atlantic Towing Ltd.* [1993] F.C.J. No. 741.

CHAPTER THIRTEEN

1 *Bartlett v. Columbia Builders Supplies* [1967] C.C.S. 244; [1967] B.R. 111 (CA).

2 *Deghenghi v. Ayerst, McKenna & Harrison Ltd.* [1998] A.Q. No. 1252. Superior Court, District of Montreal No. 500-05-008720-805.

3 Hartt was called in to help with a threatened strike, which later developed into an actual walkout. The strike ended on June 28, 1976 when an agreement was signed between the air traffic controllers and the federal government.

4 A. Edward Aust was born in Montreal on July 14, 1947 and attended Mount Royal Catholic School in Montreal and St Michael's College School in Toronto before obtaining an Honours BA in political science from Sir George Williams University in 1972. He was graduated from McGill University with a BCL in 1975 and was called to the Quebec Bar in 1977, the year he joined the firm. He joined the Law Society of the Northwest Territories in 1978.

5 Patrick L. Benaroche was born in Casablanca, Morocco on January 1, 1959. He received a BA in industrial psychology from McGill University in 1980 and was a university scholar. He also obtained a BCL and an LLB from McGill University in 1984. He was called to the Quebec Bar in 1985 and became a partner of the firm in 1993.

6 Lyse Charette was born in Toronto on July 1, 1964. She received a BCL and an LLB from McGill University in 1987, followed by a call to the Quebec Bar in 1988. In 1999, she obtained an MBA from the École des Hautes Études Commerciales, which was affiliated with the Université de Montréal. After having her family, she returned to the firm on a part-time basis for several years, managing the recruitment process for students, but she left in 2001 for a new career in government relations with Air Canada.

7 *Patrick Kealty v. SITA Inc.* [1991] R.J.Q. 397 (Quebec Superior Court).

8 Jean-Pierre Belhumeur was born in Montreal on February 10, 1949. Following a BA (with distinction) in 1969 from the Collège Sainte-Croix, he obtained an LLL (also with distinction) from the Université de Montréal in 1972 and was called to the Quebec Bar in 1974. He worked for the federal Department of Justice from 1972 to 1976 before joining the firm on November 1, 1976.

9 Lorna Cuthbert was born in Bridlington, England on January 21, 1966. She received a BA (magna cum laude) from the University of South Florida in 1987 and her LLB from UWO in 1990. She received a Canadian Golf Foundation Scholarship, the Jack Nicklaus Award for Academic Excellence, Blake Cassels &

Graydon Entrance Scholarship (UWO), and the Dean Ivan C. Rand Award (for academic and extracurricular during law school). She was called to the Ontario Bar in 1992, worked for Davies, Ward & Beck (January 1995 to June 1996), and became a partner of the firm in 1999.

CHAPTER FOURTEEN

1 Glenn A. Cranker was born on July 18, 1947 in Stamford, Connecticut. He obtained an AB from Dartmouth College in 1968 and a JD from New York University in 1972. He was called to the New Jersey Bar the same year. He moved to Canada in 1973, obtained a BCL from McGill University in 1975, and was called to the Quebec Bar in 1977 upon becoming a Canadian citizen (then a requirement for admission to the Bar). He joined the firm the same year and became a partner in 1983.

2 Paul Collins was born in Toronto on May 12, 1966. He attended Applewood Heights Secondary and received his Ontario secondary school honours graduate diploma in 1985. He was an Ontario Scholar and won a prize for Canadian literature while in high school. Collins completed an Honours BA in economics at the University of Toronto, where he was awarded several partial scholarships. He received his LLB from the University of Toronto faculty of law, where he won the prize in corporate tax. Collins was called to the Ontario Bar in 1994 and became a partner of the firm in 2000.

3 This had followed Lord Elgin's giving of royal assent, as Governor General of the Province of Canada, to the Rebellion Losses Bill to provide compensation for losses suffered during the rebellions in 1837 and 1838. It was in the summer of 1849 that prominent Montreal citizens, including a future prime minister, John Abbott, signed the Annexation Manifesto, advocating that Canada join the United States.

4 Peter O'Brien was born on October 1, 1945 in Montreal. He attended Loyola High School and Bishop's University, obtaining a BA in 1967. He studied law at the Université Laval and graduated in 1970 with the degree of LLL. He was called to the Quebec Bar in 1971.

5 Milton Hess was born in Montreal on June 15, 1942. He attended Viscount Alexander Collegiate Institute in Fort Garry, Manitoba and Port Arthur Collegiate Institute in Thunder Bay, Ontario. He received an Honours B.Com. at Queen's (1964) and his LLB from the University of Toronto in 1968. He was called to the Ontario Bar in 1970. He articled and practised with Holden Murdoch Walton Finlay & Robinson from 1968 to 1973 and then with Morris Bright Rose Hess from 1973 to 1978. He joined Stikeman Elliott in 1978 as a partner and was made Queen's Counsel in 1984.

6 Brenda Hebert was born in Belleville, Ontario on March 26, 1946. She graduated from Rockland High School, attended Bishop's University for an Honours BA (English and history, 1965), the Ontario College of Education (Secondary School Teacher's Class A Certificate), and York University for an MA (English, 1975). She received her LLB from Osgoode in 1976. Hebert was on the dean's list at Osgoode. She was called to the Bar of Ontario in 1978 and worked at Osler Hoskin & Harcourt (articles) and Weir & Foulds before joining Stikeman Elliott, where she became a partner in 1985.

7 James Harbell was born in Hamilton, Ontario on May 13, 1958. He attended the University of Toronto (Trinity College) from 1977 to 1979 and was graduated from Osgoode with his LLB in 1982. He was called to the Ontario Bar in 1984 and worked with Borden Elliot from 1984 to 1989. He became a partner at Stikeman when he joined in 1990.

8 John Dow was born in Toronto on July 11, 1953. He attended Northern Secondary School in Toronto, the University of Toronto for a BA and an LLB (1978), and the London School of Economics for an LLM (1979). He received various awards during his studies. He was called to the Ontario Bar in 1981 and became a partner at Stikeman Elliott in 1985.

9 Dana Porter was born on November 8, 1959 in Chatham, Ontario. He completed Regina Mundi College in London, Ontario in 1979, obtained a BA (honours history) from the University of Western Ontario in 1982, and then got an LLB from the University of Ottawa in 1989. He was called to the Ontario Bar in 1990 after articling with the firm and became a partner in 1997.

10 Larry Cobb was born in Montreal on June 25, 1960. He attended École Secondaire St Luc (1972–75), Maymount High School (1975–77), CEGEP Vanier (1977–79), CEGEP Dawson (1981-82), Concordia University (BA Honours, 1982-85), and Queen's University (LLB, 1985–88). He won the William McCallum Memorial Scholarship in 1985, 1986, and 1987. He was called to the Ontario Bar in 1990, worked at Campbell, Godfrey & Lewtas (1988–89), Fasken Campbell Godfrey (1990–93), Torys (1993–96), and became a partner at Stikeman Elliott in 1999.

11 Mario Paura was born in Toronto on December 16, 1968. He attended St Basil-the-Great College School, York University (two years in the bachelor of science program), and University of Western Ontario (LLB conferred in 1992). Paura received a York University entrance scholarship (1987); First Ranking Chemistry Freshman Award (1988); UWO Law Association entrance scholarship (1989); dean's honour list (1988–91); and the Inter-Provincial PipeLine Bursary. He was called to the Bar of Ontario in 1994 and worked for the Government of Ontario, Ministry of the Attorney General, before joining Stikeman Elliott. He became a partner in 2000.

12 Lalonde has been recognized as a certified arbitrator of the Arbitration and Mediation Institute of Canada (AMIC). In 1989, he was appointed an officer of the Order of Canada.

13 The Honourable Benjamin J. Greenberg, Q.C. was born in Montreal on December 2, 1933. He attended Baron Byng High School, finishing in 1950. Then he attended McGill University, obtaining a BA in 1954 and a BCL in 1957, winning the Torrance gold medal. He also won the Macdonald Travelling Fellowship for study at the Sorbonne in Paris and was called to the Quebec Bar in 1959. He was appointed Queen's Counsel in 1976, the same year as being named to the Quebec Superior Court, where he served for more than twenty-two years prior to joining the firm as senior counsel on May 1, 1999.

14 Babak Barin was born in Iran on February 22, 1966 and was educated in Switzerland at Aiglon College in Villars. He obtained a baccalauréat international at the École Active Bilingue J.M., a BA from Northwestern University in Chicago in 1986, then studied law at McGill University and the University of Moncton, from which he received an LLB in 1992.

15 The rules of procedure for the resolution of claims submitted to the CRT were negotiated by the Swiss banks.

16 In the information guide sent to all claimants, in response to the question, "Do I need to hire a lawyer?," the answer was, "No. It is not necessary to hire a lawyer. The arbitrators are responsible to determine the facts and the law that apply to your claim and to assist you in submitting relevant information …"

17 Babak Barin, *Carswell's Handbook of International Dispute Resolution Rules*. Scarborough, ON: Carswell, 1999.

18 Formally known as the Convention on the Recognition and Enforcement of Foreign Arbitral Awards.

CHAPTER FIFTEEN

1 The government had allowed the Mercantile Bank of Canada to be incorporated as a wholly owned subsidiary of the Dutch Handelsbank, which was absorbed into Rotterdamsche Bank (now Amsterdam Rotterdam Bank). Not long after this, the Royal Commission on Canada's Economic Prospects was created under the chairmanship of Walter Gordon, and it reported in November 1957. This commission expressed concern about the level of foreign ownership of Canadian businesses. The Mercantile Bank had not prospered between 1953 and 1963, and in the latter year, Rotterdamsche Bank agreed to sell its shares to First National City Bank of New York. There was an incident that led to a change in the *Bank Act* as a result of a courtesy visit to the minister of Finance (by then the same Walter Gordon) by Stillman Rockefeller, chairman of First National, who was reported in the media to have said he was a clerk coming to see a bookkeeper (Gordon was a chartered accountant). This was not taken in the jocular spirit in which it had clearly been made. The *Bank Act* was amended to restrict the growth of Mercantile until Canadians owned 75 per cent of its shares, and at the same time, foreign ownership of banks generally was limited to 25 per cent, with a maximum of 10 per cent for any single shareholder.

Index